TOWARD A PENTECOSTAL THEOLOGY OF GLOSSOLALIA

Toward a Pentecostal Theology of
Glossolalia

Randal H. Ackland

CPT Press
Cleveland, Tennessee

Toward A Pentecostal Theology of Glossolalia

Published by CPT Press
900 Walker ST NE
Cleveland, TN 37311
USA
email: cptpress@pentecostaltheology.org
website: www.cptpress.com

ISBN-13: 978-1-935931-96-6

Copyright © 2020 CPT Press

All rights reserved. No part of this book may be reproduced or translated in any form, by print, photoprint, microfilm, microfiche, electronic database, internet database, or any other means without written permission from the publisher.

Dedication

To Connie, Annie, and Joylnn for your love and support

Contents

Acknowledgement ix
Abbreviations x
Charts of Early Pentecostal Periodicals xii

Chapter 1
Introduction and Methodology 1
   Definition of Pentecostalism 4
   Time Frame 5
   Methodology and Primary Sources 6

Chapter 2
Bibliographic Review of Literature on Glossolalia 17
   I. Early Literature, 1888 to 1929 18
   II. Mid-Century Literature, 1930 to 1969 35
   III. Contemporary Scholarship, 1970 to 2019 50
   IV. Dialog Partners with an Eastern Perspective 97
   V. Literature Utilizing the Early Periodicals 104

Chapter 3
The Wesleyan-Holiness Pentecostal Periodicals 111
   I. *The Apostolic Faith* 111
   II. *The Bridegroom's Messenger* 147
   III. *The Whole Truth* 179
   IV. *The Church of God Evangel* 183
   V. *The Pentecostal Holiness Advocate* 212

Chapter 4
The Finished Work Pentecostal Periodicals 239
   I. *Triumphs of Faith* 240
   II. *The Pentecost* 263
   III. *The Pentecostal Testimony* 272
   IV. *Word and Witness* 280
   V. *The Pentecostal Evangel* 291

Chapter 5
Oneness Pentecostal Periodicals..330
   I. *The Good Report*... 330
   II. *Meat in Due Season* and the *Blessed Truth*............................ 336

Charts of Theological Categories... 347

Chapter 6
Revisioning a Pentecostal Theology of Glossolalia 349
   I. Metaphor as a Means of Revisioning................................. 349
   II. Encounter Metaphors... 353
   III. Public Metaphors.. 377
   IV. Personal Metaphors.. 387
   V. Two Final Metaphors 394

Chapter 7
Conclusion 400

Appendix 1
Walter J. Hollenweger's Black-Oral-Inclusive Root 405

Appendix 2
Glossolalic Outpourings in Church History......................... 410
   I. Introduction.. 410
   II. The Didache through Augustine 411
   III. The Middle Ages through the Reformation 431
   IV. The Eastern Church 440
   V. Post-Reformation to 1900 444
   VI. Conclusion to Appendix 2 462

Bibliography 463
Index of Biblical (and Other Ancient) References..................... 488
Index of Authors 492

ACKNOWLEDGMENTS

This monograph is an updated version of a PhD thesis completed at Bangor University under the supervision of Dr. John Christopher Thomas. Dr. David Hymes and several Yale Divinity students were used by the Holy Spirit to inspire this project. The dear fellowship of Cornerstone Assembly of God, Oxford, CT was there when God created a hunger in my heart. A research project like this is not done without collaboration and sacrifice.

Dr. John Christopher Thomas' supervision was remarkable from conception to completion. There were many hours of supervision, friendship, mentoring, and prayer. The other doctoral supervisors have their fingerprints on this work as well: Drs. Chris Green, Frank Macchia, Lee Roy Martin, and Robby Waddell.

My fellow PhD students provided valuable feedback: Jonathan Alvarado, Melissa Archer, Becky Basdeo-Hill, Odell Bryant, Justin Dennis, Clayton Endecott, Edward George, Stetson Glass, Chris Green, Edwin Gungor, Jeff and Karen Holley, Daniel Isgrigg, David Johnson, David Kentie, Tom Kurt, Michelle Marshall, Philip W. Jacobs, Larry McQueen, Ray Robles, Chris Rouse, Jared Runck, Steffen Schumacher, Rick Waldholm, Lisa Ward, Ben Wiles, and Andrew Williams.

I cannot imagine many churches having staffs capable of such great theological insight: Dr. Joseph Lear, Ed Lambright, Andrew Colón, and Dr. Andrew Sargent.

I have deep love and gratitude for Connie, Annie, and Jolynn who sacrificed a husband and dad over these ten years. John and Linda Baldino's friendship constantly encouraged us. John Baldino edited every version of every page of this work before passing it onto Dr. John Christopher Thomas. Crossroads International Church, South Attleboro, MA, deserves a hearty thank you for encouraging their pastor.

ABBREVIATIONS

Early Pentecostal Periodicals

AF	*The Apostolic Faith, Los Angeles*
CE	*Christian Evangel*
COGE	*The Church of God Evangel*
MDS	*Meat in Due Season*
PE	*The Pentecostal Evangel*
PT	*The Pentecostal Testimony*
PHA	*The Pentecostal Holiness Advocate*
TBM	*The Bridegroom's Messenger*
TBT	*The Blessed Truth*
TGR	*The Good Report*
THA	*The Holiness Advocate*
TP	*The Pentecost*
TWT	*The Whole Truth*
TOF	*Triumphs of Faith*
WE	*Weekly Evangel*
WW	*Word and Witness*

Other Works

AASS	*Acta Sanctorum*
AG	Assemblies of God
AJPS	*Asian Journal of Pentecostal Studies*
ANF	Ante-Nicene Fathers
ASM	Azusa Street Mission
BibSac	*Bibliotheca Sacra*
CG	The Church of God (Cleveland, TN)
CI	Conversion-initiation
COGIC	The Church of God in Christ
CU	Christian Union
ExpT	*The Expository Times*
FW	Finished Work
HA	Heavenly Anthem / singing in the Spirit
HCCC	The Holiness Church at Camp Creek
IE	Initial Evidence
IPCC	International Pentecostal Church of Christ
LXX	Septuagint
JBL	*Journal of Biblical Literature*

JEPTA	*Journal of the European Pentecostal Theological Association*
JETS	*Journal of Evangelical Theological Society*
JPT	*Journal of Pentecostal Theology*
JPTSup	*Journal of Pentecostal Theology*, Supplement Series
JTS	*Journal Theological Studies*
MT	Missionary Tongues
NIDPCM	*New International Dictionary of Pentecostal and Charismatic Movements (revised)*
NPF	*Nicene and Post-Nicene Fathers*
NT	New Testament
OT	Old Testament
RCC	Roman Catholic Church
RQ	*Restoration Quarterly*
SB	Spirit Baptism
WH	Wesleyan-holiness

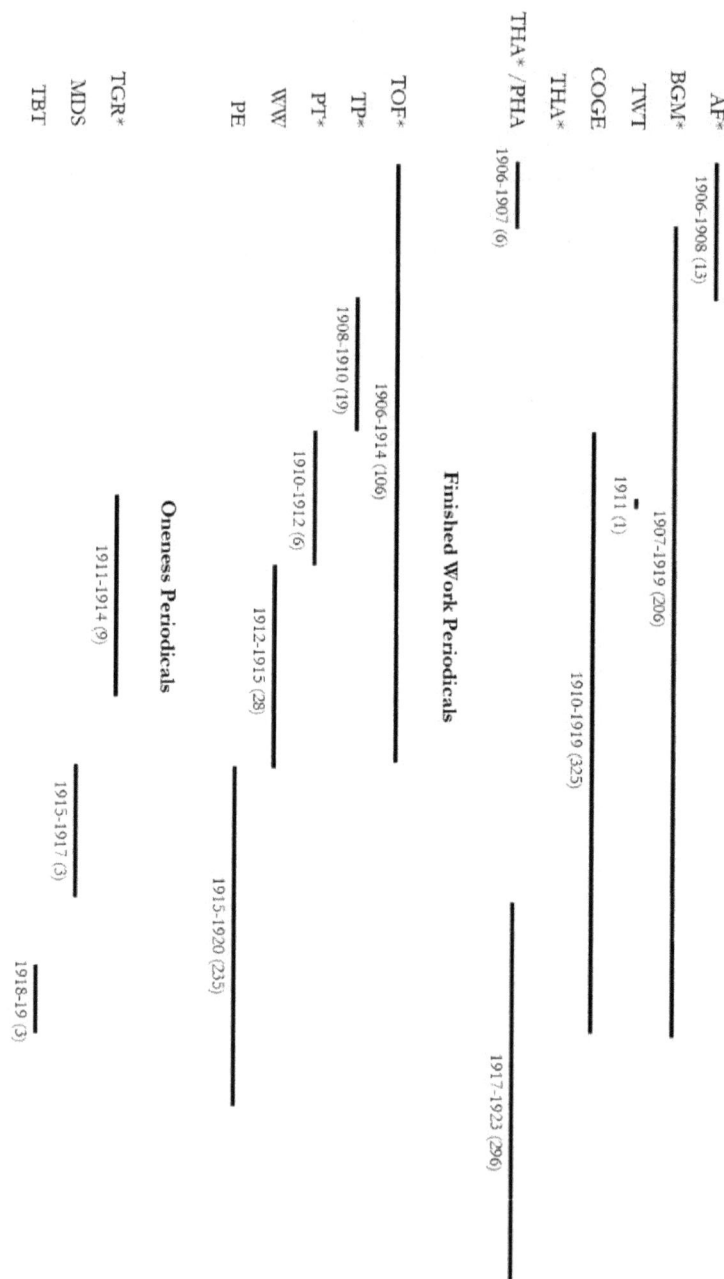

Relevant Information on the Wesleyan-Holiness Periodicals

Pub.	Editor	Denomination	Context	Time Frame?	Other
AF	Clara Lum & Florence Crawford	Independent	Los Angeles, CA.	1906-1908 (13), all extant.	The most prominent paper and considered to be the start of the Pentecostal movement.
BGM	Gaston Cashwell & Elizabeth Sexton	Independent	Atlanta, GA.	1907-1919 (206), though the IE crisis of 1918.	Though independent, it was the informal voice of what would become the PHC.
TWT	Justus Bowe	COGIC	Argenta, AR.	Oct, 1911 (1), all extant.	Regrettably, there is the only one extant issue of this important and influential, largely African American denomination.
COGE	Ambrose Tomlinson	COG	Cleveland, TN.	1910-1919 (325), through the IE crisis of 1918.	With pre-ASM glossolalic experiences in its history, the COG was the largest, predominantly white WH denomination.
THA	Ambrose Crumpler	Independent	Clinton, NC.	1906-1907 (6), all extant.	These 6 issues coincide with the ASM revival and reveal the introduction of the revival to their WH readers.
PHA	George Taylor	PHC	Falcon, NC.	1917-1923 (296), 5 years after the IE crisis of were read to ensure no major theological issues were overlooked.	Formed later than other Pentecostal denominations, their people read the BGM & the HA before the formation of the PHC in 1917.

Relevant Information on the Finished Work Periodicals

Pub.	Editor	Denomination	Context	Time Frame?	Other
TOF	Carrie Montgomery	Independent	Oakland, CA.	1906-1914 (106), to the formation of the AG.	Montgomery's ministry bridged the WH & FW traditions with a large network of friends. She was a founding member of the AG.
TP	Joseph Flower	Independent	Indianapolis, IN.	1908-1910 (19), all extant.	The stated mission of *TP* was to promote the Pentecostal message.
PT	William Durham	Independent	Chicago, IL & Los Angeles, CA.	1910-1912 (6), all extant.	Durham originated the FW doctrine and was very influential on Oneness Pentecostalism.
WW	Eudorus Bell	Independent / AG	Malvern, AR, St. Louis, MO.	1912-1915 (28), All extant.	This paper originated with Parham's group in TX. It became the official voice of the AG after its formation. It was succeeded by the more popular weekly *PE*.
PE	Eudorus Bell / Joseph Flower	AG	Findlay, OH, St. Louis, MO, Springfield, MO.	1915-1920 (235), all extant through the window of this study.	The official voice of the AG, the largest FW group. It had several names before settling on the *PE*.

Charts of Early Pentecostal Periodicals xv

Relevant Information on the Oneness Periodicals

Pub.	Editor	Denomination	Context	Time Frame?	Other
TGR	Robert McAllister	Independent	Ottawa, Canada / Los Angeles, CA.	1911-1914 (9), all extant.	This paper reveals the emergence of Oneness theology from FW theology.
MDS	Frank Ewart	Independent / Oneness.	Los Angeles, CA.	1915-1917 (3), all extant.	The earliest Oneness periodical.
TBT	Daniel Opperman	Independent / Oneness.	Eureka Springs, AR.	1918-1919 (3), all extant.	Another early Oneness periodical. It would take some time before the Oneness denominations stabilized.

1

INTRODUCTION

'Pentecost has surely come and with it the Bible evidences are following, many being converted and sanctified and filled with the Holy Ghost, speaking in tongues as they did on the day of Pentecost', states the opening lines of the *Apostolic Faith* (*AF*), the periodical of the Azusa Street mission (ASM) revival.[1] Though much has been written about speaking in tongues, few have taken the time to research what these pioneers of Pentecostalism meant by those words. There are many excellent histories by scholars[2] and

---

[1] 'Pentecost Has Come', *AF* 1.1 (Sep 1906), p. 1.
[2] Walter J. Hollenweger, *The Pentecostals* (Peabody, MA: Hendrickson Publishing, 1972); Robert Mapes Anderson, *Vision of the Disinherited: The Making of American Pentecostalism* (New York, NY: Oxford University Press, 1979); Donald W. Dayton, *Theological Roots of Pentecostalism* (Peabody, MA: Hendrickson Publishing, 1987); James R Goff, *Fields White unto Harvest: Charles F. Parham and the Missionary Origins of Pentecostalism* (Fayetteville: University of Arkansas Press, 1988); Harvey Cox, *Fire From Heaven* (Reading, MA: Addison-Wesley Publishing Co., 1995); Walter J. Hollenweger, *Pentecostalism: Origins and Development Worldwide* (Peabody, MA: Hendrickson Publishing, 1997); Vinson Synan, *The Holiness-Pentecostal Tradition: Charismatic Movements in the Twentieth Century* (Grand Rapids, MI: Eerdmans, 2nd edn, 1997); Vinson Synan, *The Century of the Holy Spirit: 100 Years of Pentecostal and Charismatic Renewal* (Nashville, TN: Thomas Nelson Publishers, 2001); Grant Wacker, *Heaven Below: Early Pentecostals and American Culture* (Cambridge, MA: Harvard University Press, 2001); Alan Anderson, *An Introduction to Pentecostalism* (Cambridge, UK: Cambridge University Press, 2004); Cecil M. Robeck Jr., *The Azusa Street Mission and Revival: The Birth of the Global Pentecostal Movement* (Nashville, TN: Thomas Nelson, 2006); Randall J. Stephens, *The Fire Spreads: Holiness and Pentecostalism in the American South* (Cambridge, MA; London: Harvard University Press, 2008); Estrelda Y. Alexander, *Black Fire: One Hundred Years of African American Pentecostalism* (Downers Grove, IL: IVP Academic, 2011).

eye-witness accounts.³ Most Pentecostal denominations have official or semi-official histories that include a carefully parsed examination of tongues.⁴ However, there has not been a careful and comprehensive analysis of the preferred method of communication for these early Pentecostals – their periodicals. This monograph fills that gap.

Chapter 1 lays out the methodology for this study. Chapter 2 surveys the theological literature of glossolalia. Then, following the *Wirkungsgeschichte*⁵ methodology of Kimberly Alexander,⁶ fourteen periodicals are examined. These periodicals fall generally into three groups: first, those from Wesleyan-Holiness (WH) roots (Chapter 3); second, those with Reformed or independent roots (Chapter 4), the latter identifying with William H. Durham's Finished work (FW) theology. The third group,

---

³ Ethel E. Goss, *The Winds of God: The Story of the Early Pentecostal Movement (1901-1914) in the Life of Howard A. Goss* (Hazelwood, MO: Word Aflame Press, 1977); Frank Bartleman, *Azusa Street: An Eyewitness Account*, The Centennial Edition, 1906-2006 (Gainesville, FL: Bridge-Logos, 2006); Tom Welchel, *Azusa Street: They Told Me Their Stories* (Mustang, OK: Dare2Dream Books, 2008).

⁴ Stanley H. Frodsham, *With Signs Following* (Springfield, MO: Gospel Publishing House, 1946); Carl Brumback, *Suddenly … From Heaven: A History of the Assemblies of God* (Springfield, MO: Gospel Publishing House, 1961); Carl Brumback, *A Sound from Heaven: The Dramatic Beginning of the 20ᵗʰ Century Pentecostal Revival* (Springfield, MO: Gospel Publishing House, 1961); Charles W. Conn, *Like a Mighty Army* (Cleveland, TN: Pathway Press, 1977); Gary B. McGee, *People of the Spirit: The Assemblies of God* (Springfield, MO: Gospel Publishing House, 2004); H. Vinson Synan, *Old Time Power: A Centennial History of the International Pentecostal Holiness Church* (Franklin Springs, GA: LifeSpring Resources, 1998); David A. Reed, *'In Jesus Name': The History and Beliefs of Oneness Pentecostals* (JPTSup 31; Dorset, UK: Deo Publishing).

⁵ Also called, reception history or history of effects. In 1888, Hermann Gunkel wrote, 'we find in our (biblical) sources absolutely *no doctrinal statements* regarding the Spirit, though we find a host of *descriptions of the Spirit's activities*', Hermann Gunkel, *The Influence of the Holy Spirit: The Popular View of the Apostolic Age and the Teaching of the Apostle Paul* (Roy A. Harrisville and Philip A Quanbeck II [trans.]; Philadelphia, PA: Fortress Press, 1979), p. 14. He is likely the first to highlight that the Spirit is known by 'effects', 'symptoms', or signs, pp. 31, 39.

⁶ Kimberly Ervin Alexander, *Pentecostal Healing: Models in Theology and Practice* (JPTSup 29; Dorset, UK: Deo Publishing, 2006). Others who used the same methodology include, Chris E.W. Green, *Toward a Pentecostal Theology of the Lord's Supper: Foretasting the Kingdom* (Cleveland, TN: CPT Press, 2012); Larry R. McQueen, *Toward a Pentecostal Eschatology: Discerning the Way Forward* (JPTSup 39; Dorset, UK: Deo Publishing, 2012); Melissa L. Archer, *'I Was in the Spirit on the Lord's Day': A Pentecostal Engagement with Worship in the Apocalypse* (Cleveland, TN: CPT Press, 2015); David R. Johnson, *Pneumatic Discernment in the Apocalypse: An Intertextual and Pentecostal Exploration* (Cleveland, TN: CPT Press, 2018).

Oneness Pentecostalism, emerges out of the FW tradition (chapter 5). Together, these periodicals represent the development of an oral tradition that arises largely from the people rather than a doctrine hammered out in ecclesiastical conference.[7] Harvey G. Cox writes that,

> while the beliefs of the fundamentalists, and of many other religious groups, are enshrined in formal theological systems, those of Pentecostalism are embedded in testimonies, ecstatic speech, and bodily movement. But it *is* a theology … (only) Pentecostals have felt more at home singing their theology, or putting it in pamphlets.[8]

This *voca populi* converged with a respect for the printed word, a move towards common sense reading of the Bible, an economical means of printing, and an established literature distribution network through the WH movement.[9] Finished Work (FW) leader E.N. Bell considers these Pentecostal periodicals to be a 'mighty factor' in spreading the revival.[10] Therefore, the periodicals of the early Pentecostals are considered representative of their theology and practices surrounding glossolalia.

The review of literature reveals that contemporary definitions of Pentecostal glossolalia have been constrained by modernistic categories of theology. The dogmatic statements that arose after the advent of Pentecostalism utilized what was at

---

[7] 'Authority flowed not from the learned elite but from those stalwart leaders whose personality and rhetoric grab the attention of the common folk', Stephens, *The Fire Spreads*, p. 102.

[8] Cox, *Fire From Heaven*, p. 15.

[9] Stephens believes that most converts heard of tongues through 'a substantial print culture' initially created by the WH movement, Stephens, *The Fire Spreads*, p. 198. Cf. Malcolm John Taylor, 'Publish and Be Blessed: A Case Study in Early Pentecostal Publishing History' (PhD Thesis, Birmingham, UK: University of Birmingham, 1994); W.E. Warner, 'Periodicals', in Stanley Burgess (ed.), *NIDPCM* (Grand Rapids, MI: Zondervan, rev. and expanded edn, 2002), pp. 974-82; Alexander, *Pentecostal Healing*, pp. 70-72; Stephens, *The Fire Spreads*, pp. 100-102, 110-27, 191-93, 199-200.

[10] 'Early in this modern outpouring of the Holy Ghost the printed page began at once to be a mighty factor. When the outpouring reached Los Angeles, it was spread over the earth from that place by the printed page. In hundreds of places were men filled with the Spirit through this outpouring had not yet gone, the fire was kindled through these papers', E.N. Bell, 'Removal To St. Louis', *WE* 83 (Mar 27, 1915), p. 2.

hand theologically, but ultimately these Modernistic categories were ill-fitting. Chapter 6 seeks to revision a contemporary theology of glossolalia that is truer to both the theology and experience of yesterday's pioneers and today's Pentecostals. In other words, this investigation's goal is to arrive at a thoroughly Pentecostal theology of glossolalia.

Definition of Pentecostalism

Because Pentecostalism is a movement that can 'embrace and transform almost anything it meets',[11] any thorough definition of North American Pentecostalism one hundred years after its beginning would be imperfect. However, Donald W. Dayton's definition of Pentecostalism by its doctrinal distinctives;[12] Steven J. Land's definition of a vibrant 'five-fold' spiritually,[13] and Walter J. Hollenweger's black-oral-inclusive spirituality[14] come as close as possible.[15] Though Pentecostalism 'cannot be simply defined in terms of glossolalia',[16] it is a large part of any definition. If one were to remove glossolalia from either the practice or doctrinal statements, it would cease to be Pentecostal.[17] Tongues are called the 'root and

---

[11] Cox, *Fire From Heaven*, p. 147.

[12] Dayton highlights the doctrinal statement from the Pentecostal Fellowship of North America, Dayton, *Theological Roots*, pp. 17-18.

[13] The five-fold gospel is: '1. Justification by faith in Christ. 2. Sanctification by faith a second definite work of grace. 3. Healing of body as provided for in the atonement. 4. Pre-millennial return of Christ. 5. The baptism in the Holy Spirit evidenced by speaking in tongues', Steven Jack Land, *Pentecostal Spirituality: A Passion for the Kingdom* (JPTSup 1; Sheffield: Sheffield Academic Press, 1993), p. 18. Land would include those of the 'four-fold' gospel as Pentecostals as well, pp. 185-88.

[14] For a fuller treatment of Hollenweger's black, oral, and inclusive root, see Appendix 1.

[15] Two works offer single faceted definitions and do not fully encapsulate the dynamic of Pentecostalism: 1) Pentecostalism first arose as 'a protest against "man-made creeds" and the "coldness" of traditional worship', Cox, *Fire From Heaven*, p. 14. 2) 'Pentecostalism may be viewed as … long-term protest against the whole thrust of modern urban-industrial capitalist society', Anderson, *Vision of the Disinherited*, p. 223; cf. pp. 223-40.

[16] Alexander, *Pentecostal Healing*, p. 65; cf. Dayton, *Theological Roots*, p. 15.

[17] 'The present movement, which is called by some the "Pentecostal movement," and is called by others by way of ridicule, the "Tongues" movement', 'Manifestations of the Spirit', *COGE* 1.17 (Nov 1, 1910), p. 4; cf. Vinson Synan,

stem' of Pentecostalism's *gestalt*.[18] Therefore, for the purposes of this study, Pentecostalism will first and broadly constitute all people who claim an encounter with the Holy Spirit, an experience not expressible in any other way than glossolalia.[19] Second, and more narrowly, it will constitute those who hold to either the five-fold or four-fold doctrinal beliefs as outlined by Dayton, practice a spirituality as outlined by Land, and have their roots in a Black-oral-inclusive spirituality as noted by Hollenweger.[20]

Time Frame

The ideal time-frame for this study would be April, 1906 to April, 1916, based on Hollenweger's thesis that the first 'five to ten years of its history ... (was) the heart of pentecostal spirituality'.[21] He notes that the further one moves from this time-frame, the characteristics of Pentecostal spirituality become restrained by bureaucracy, diminished by segregation,[22] and harder to define.[23] However, due to the availability of these early issues, along with the consideration of world events and significant events within the Pentecostal denominations, the years of issues read will vary from periodical to periodical. Please note the periodical timeline chart above. The rationale for each periodical's timeframe is explained below.

'The Role of Tongues as Initial Evidence', in Mark Wilson (ed.), *Spirit and Renewal* (JPTSup 5; Sheffield: Sheffield Academic Press, 1994), p. 68; Hollenweger, *Pentecostalism*, p. 23.

[18] 'Edward Irving, said in 1832 that tongues 'is the root and stem of them all [the gifts] out of which they all grow, and by which they are all nourished', Synan, 'The Role of Tongues', p. 75; cf. Frank D. Macchia, 'Tongues as a Sign: Towards a Sacramental Understanding of Pentecostal Experience', *Pneuma* 15.1 (1993), pp. 61-76 (69).

[19] Cecil M. Robeck, Jr, 'Azusa Street Revival', in Stanley Burgess (ed.), *NIDPCM* (Grand Rapids, MI: Zondervan, rev. and expanded edn, 2002), pp. 344-50 (349).

[20] See Appendix 1.

[21] Walter J. Hollenweger, 'Pentecostals and the Charismatic Movement', in Cheslyn Jones, Geoffrey Wainwright, and Edward Yarnold (eds.), *The Study of Spirituality* (London: SPCK, 1986), pp. 549-54 (551).

[22] Hollenweger, 'Pentecostals and the Charismatic Movement', p. 551.

[23] 'It will become harder and harder to make a clear-cut distinction between American Pentecostals and American non-Pentecostals in the future, now that the experience and message of the baptism of the Spirit have found a way into all the American denominations', Hollenweger, *The Pentecostals*, p. 15.

Methodology and Primary Sources

The methodology of this investigation is to allow these early primary texts to speak for themselves, to permit the *voca populi* to speak their beliefs and practices clearly without the noise of theological structures being imposed upon them.[24] Alexander writes that 'rather than imposing a scheme or grid on the texts, an attempt has been made to allow the beliefs and practices of each group to emerge'.[25] Called the 'grounded theory', this method reviews the collected data and then 'repeated ideas, concepts or elements become apparent ... (finally, they) are grouped into concepts, and then into categories'.[26]

In this case, the periodicals were carefully read and relevant texts about glossolalia were orally read into a working document using speech recognition software. This, in a limited way, allowed the researcher to hear the voice of the people. Then, this working document was read and re-read looking for themes to emerge. Some ideas were overt and had support from numerous voices; for example, the emphasis on evidential tongues. Others were subtle and had fewer references, such as the liminal worldview or sacramental nature of glossolalia. Then, the data in this working document was rearranged into theological themes and categories. Finally, theologies of glossolalia were extracted from this working document, summaries were written, and conclusions were drawn for this monograph. This was done for each periodical.

There are limitations with this method. First, these periodicals are all from North America. However, the voices of global Pentecostalism are occasionally heard through the testimonies and articles of missionaries and others who submitted letters, reports, and articles. Second, and regrettably, there is just a single extant issue of *The Whole Truth* available, the official periodical of the Church of God in Christ. Given Hollenweger's observation that Pentecostalism has a decidedly black-oral-inclusive root, the absence of the largest African American Pentecostal denomination's voice is

---

[24] In contrast to works that trace the theology of Pentecostal leaders, such as Douglas Jacobsen, *Thinking in the Spirit: Theologies of the Early Pentecostal Movement* (Indianapolis, IN: Indiana University Press, 2003).

[25] Alexander, *Pentecostal Healing*, p. 73.

[26] https://en.wikipedia.org/wiki/Grounded_theory (14-11-2019).

huge. Nevertheless, the methodology of this study attempted to hear all voices equally and there are a significant number of contributions from African American Pentecostals in the form of testimonies, articles, and even songs. Third, the same is true for women's voices: no attempt was made to distinguish gender; however, the female perspective is exceedingly well represented in the periodicals. Finally, this research was limited by the periodicals that survived.

Nearly all of the periodicals listed below were accessed online from the Consortium of Pentecostal Archives.[27]

In the Wesleyan-Pentecostal stream, the *AF* will be the first to be reviewed. It was published by the Apostolic Faith Movement of Los Angeles, California[28] and was the 'most prominent paper in the early months of the Azusa Street outpouring'.[29] Thirteen issues published between September, 1906 and May, 1908 claimed a press run of 40,000 copies by the end of 1907.[30] Its four pages were published sporadically as funds were available.[31] It was comprised of testimonies and articles, most of which were unsigned, with a good number probably written by the editorial staff.[32] William J. Seymour, the leader of the mission, signed 20 articles.[33] Clara Lum carried most of the editorial responsibility, though it was a labor of love and mission for a larger volunteer staff.[34] A statement of faith appears in six issues.[35] To maintain the integrity

---

[27] https://pentecostalarchives.org/index.cfm? (9-21-2014).

[28] For issues 1.3, 1.4, and 1.5 the title of the mission in the subscription was changed to *The Pacific Apostolic Faith Mission*.

[29] Warner, 'Periodicals', p. 978.

[30] Warner, 'Periodicals', p. 976.

[31] One eight page issue contains both February & March 1907. Cf. 'The Apostolic Faith Movement', *AF* 1.1 (Sep 1906), p. 2; 'To Our Correspondents', *AF* 1.2 (Oct 1906), p. 4; 'Published Free by Faith', *AF* 1.4 (Dec 1906), p. 2.

[32] 'We wish no human writer to receive any honor but that it might be all to the glory of God', 'The Lord Leads', *AF* 1.1 (Sep 1906), p. 4. 'Most of these messages have been taken down in shorthand in meetings of great power, messages that are inspired by the Holy Ghost', 'To Our Correspondents', p. 4.

[33] This includes one transcribed sermon and meeting notes that was published in the 7th number of the 1st issue, *AF* 1.7 (Apr 1907), p. 2.

[34] Robeck, *Azusa Street*, p. 99. 'The power of God comes down on the workers as they fold the paper', *AF* 1.8 (May 1907), p. 2.

[35] The standard statement of faith appears on p. 2 in issues 1.1; 1.3; 1.9 and 1.13; an abbreviated statement appears on p. 4 of issue 1.2; and a question and answer statement of faith appears on p. 2 of issue 1.11; cf. 'Questions Answered', *AF* 1.11 (Oct 1907), p. 2; Robeck, *Azusa Street*, p. 119; Renea

of the newspaper, the editors printed three official corrections and generally allowed people's testimonies to be printed even if their theology was not precise.[36] After these 13 issues, the periodical came under Florence Crawford's leadership in Portland, Oregon.[37] How this transfer came about remains a question, but it was a severe blow to Seymour and the mission.[38] All thirteen extant issues published of *AF* at Azusa Street were read.

Second, Gaston B. Cashwell's inaugural issue of *The Bridegroom's Messenger* (*TBM*) appeared on October 1st, 1907, and was intended to promote the Pentecostal message and edify believers in the southern portion of the United States.[39] In addition to articles and testimonies similar to the *AF*, it contained reports from missionaries, ads for camp meetings and conferences, Bible schools, and publications. Cashwell vetted these to exclude 'any tricks or schemes of any backslidden preacher'.[40] Many prominent former WH preachers served as corresponding editors.[41] The paper received encouragement from Seymour and the revival in Los Angeles after just two issues.[42] Cashwell elevated Mrs. Elizabeth A. Sexton to 'Editor and Proprietor' with the 15th number of the 1st issue (June 1, 1908) so that he would have time to promote Pentecostal interests.[43] Though generally bimonthly, during WWI the

---

Brathwaite, 'Tongues and Ethics: William J. Seymour and the "Bible Evidence": A Response to Cecil M. Robeck, Jr', *Pneuma* 32.2 (2010), pp. 203-22 (213).

[36] The first correction is that the prophesied earthquake in Los Angeles would not occur on a Sunday, *AF* 1.3 (Nov 1906), p. 1. The second corrects a confusion between hades and gehenna, *AF* 1.5 (Jan 1907), p. 4. The final confesses that a revival report at a CMA meeting in Portland was exaggerated and that the CMA did not officially come under the ASM organization, *AF* 1.12 (Jan 1908), p. 1.

[37] There is one indication of trouble in what became the final ASM issue: 'for the next issues of this paper address The Apostolic Faith Campmeeting, Portland, Ore.', *AF* 2.13 (May 1908), p. 2.

[38] Cf. Robeck, *Azusa Street*, pp. 284-87, 301-10; Warner, 'Periodicals', p. 976.

[39] G.B. Cashwell, 'Editorials, An Explanation', *TBM* 1.1 (Oct 1, 1907), p. 1.

[40] Cashwell, 'Editorials, An Explanation', p. 1.

[41] The list includes N.J. Holmes of the Holmes Bible and Missionary Institute; H.H. Goff and G.F. Taylor of the Pentecostal Holiness Church; A.J. Tomlinson of the Church of God (Cleveland, TN); and others like M.M. Pinson, J.A. Culbreth, R.B. Hayes, T.J. McIntosh, and A.H. Butler.

[42] 'So we praise God for the new paper and ask God's blessing on you', Clara Lum, 'From Los Angeles', *TBM* 1.3 (Dec 1, 1907), p. 1; cf. William Seymour, 'Letter From Bro. Seymour', *TBM* 1.5 (Jan 1, 1908), p. 2.

[43] 'Notice of Change', *TBM* 1.15 (June 1, 1908), p. 2.

publication nearly ran out of money and became irregular, regular printing resumed after the war.[44] *TBM* was published under the same name until 1942,[45] and served the International Pentecostal Church of Christ denomination (IPCC)[46] under various other monikers.[47] Between October 1, 1907 and September, 1919, a twelve year window of all extant issues[48] were read (206 issues). September, 1919 was chosen as an end date to the readings primarily to see if there was any significant theology in response to the initial evidence (IE) discussion of 1918.

Third, *The Whole Truth* (*TWT*) began publication 'in the late 1890's'[49] as the official mouthpiece of the predominantly African-American[50] WH denomination Church of God in Christ (COGIC). When the founders of COGIC, C.P. Jones and Charles H. Mason, split in 1907 over Mason's Spirit Baptism (SB) at the ASM, *TWT* and the denomination's name came with Mason into

---

[44] *TBM* 10.202 signals its troubles: 'in the event that the Messenger is no longer published' they wanted to meet their 'obligation to subscribers', 'Our Obligation To Subscribers', *TBM* 10.202 (Sep 1, 1917), p. 1. They offered to reimburse the subscriber with extra copies of back issues or extra gospel tracts they had on hand. Regular publishing returned with issue 11.206 (Oct 1, 1918).

[45] https://ifphc.org/index.cfm?fuseaction=publicationsguide.thebridegroomsmessenger (9-19-2014).

[46] The IPCC's history is best seen through a series of mergers among smaller Wesleyan Pentecostal organizations. It began with the early Pentecostal churches who organized because of the influence of Paul and Hattie Barth and was called the Association of Pentecostal Assemblies (APA) in 1921. Then in 1936, the International Pentecostal Church merged with the APA and it was renamed the International Pentecostal Assembly. Finally, the Pentecostal Church of Christ officially joined in 1976, resulting in its current name – IPCC, W.E. Warner, 'International Pentecostal Church of Christ', in Stanley Burgess (ed.), *NIDPCM* (Grand Rapids, MI: Zondervan, rev. and expanded edn, 2002), pp. 797-98.

[47] It was named *I.P.A. Messenger* (1942-46), *Bridegroom's Messenger* (1946-74), *Bridegroom's Messenger and Pentecostal Witness* (1974-76), *Bridegroom's Messenger* (1976-96), https://ifphc.org/index.cfm?fuseaction=publicationsguide.thebridegroomsmessenger (9-20-14).

[48] The missing issues are: 1.10; 1.20; 1.21; 2.24; 11.203; 12.208 through 12.211; 12.213; cf. Warner, 'Periodicals', p. 976.

[49] 'Its first publication is not really known', http://www.cogic.org/thewholetruth/twt-history/ (Sep 18, 2014).

[50] Despite the racial environment of the day, Stevens notes that 'periodicals edited by African-Americans, including *The Whole Truth* and *Voice in the Wilderness*, showed remarkable inattention to matters of racial justice', Stephens, *The Fire Spreads*, p. 210.

a reformulated Pentecostal COGIC.[51] D.J. Young, Mason's lifelong friend and 'constant companion', became the editor after the split.[52] There is only one extant edition of *TWT* during the early years and it was edited by Justus Bowe.[53] The single extant issue, October, 1911, of *TWT* was read.

Fourth, the *Church of God Evangel* (*COGE*) began in 1910 and has been the official publication of the Church of God (Cleveland, TN) ever since.[54] Similar to other Pentecostal periodicals of the day, it provided teachings, testimonies, and kept the church's constituents up to date on church business. It was 'a great contributor to the success of the Church',[55] where,

> in its columns the poorest and most illiterate may tell their joys and sorrows and ask prayers of the Evangel Family ... it stands for Pentecost and all that Pentecost includes, the baptism of the Holy Ghost, speaking in other tongues and the spiritual gifts and signs following.[56]

More noticeable than in other periodicals was a strong push for new subscribers.[57] A.J. Tomlinson was the publisher and editor until December 1922, when J.S. Llewellyn assumed the post.[58] All extant copies[59] between March 1, 1910 and December 27, 1919 were read (325 issues). Again, 1919 was chosen as an end to the reading due to the IE controversy of 1918.

---

[51] J.C. Clemmons, 'Charles Harrison Mason', in Stanley Burgess (ed.), *NIDPCM* (Grand Rapids, MI: Zondervan, rev. and expanded edn, 2002), pp. 865-67 (866).

[52] Clemmons, 'Charles Harrison Mason', p. 866.

[53] *TWT* 4.4 (Oct 1911), p. 2.

[54] Originally titled, *The Evening Light and Church of God Evangel*, it was shortened to *COGE* in 1911, Conn, *Like a Mighty Army*, p. 117.

[55] Conn, *Like a Mighty Army*, p. 117.

[56] 'The Evangel's Mission', *COGE* 5.37 (Sep 12, 1914), p. 3.

[57] For example, 'let every subscriber secure at least one more yearly subscription and send it in at once', A.J. Tomlinson, 'To Our Subscribers and Friends', *COGE* 1.8 (Jun 15, 1910), p. 1.

[58] Llewellyn's first issue is 13.47 (Dec 9, 1922); cf. Conn, *Like a Mighty Army*, p. 173.

[59] There are only 22 extant issues between 1910 – 1913 (21 from 1910 and 1 from 1912). During this period it was published bi-monthly. A full collection of weekly publications begin with the January 3, 1914 issue. There were 51 issues a year as the *COGE* was not published the week of the annual General Assembly in November.

Fifth, and final in the Wesleyan-Pentecostal stream, the *Pentecostal Holiness Advocate* (*PHA*), began in May 1917 as the official voice of the Pentecostal Holiness Church. However, many of its readers were familiar with its forerunner, *The Holiness Advocate* (*THA*) which was the 'sine qua non of instantaneous sanctification as a second work of grace', but went out of business due to a lack of funds.[60] Many of the regular features of the *PHA* continued those in the *THA*.[61] The *PHA*'s rather late start[62] was due to the fact the *Apostolic Evangel* and the *Bridegroom's Messenger* were informal voices of the church.[63] George F. Taylor, a former general superintendent, was chosen as the editor.[64] There are six extant issues of the *THA* that were published after the start of the ASM revival, these six were examined.[65] Between May 3, 1917 and April 26, 1923, a six year window, all extant issues of *PHA* were read (296).[66] This periodical was read beyond the 1920 window of this

---

[60] Synan, *Old Time Power*, p. 82. From Lumberton, NC, Ambrose B. Crumpler started the paper in April 1901, and bi-monthly published articles relevant to the WH movement. After many of his subscribers experienced SB and tongues, they pulled their subscriptions due to Crumpler's 'bitter anti-Pentecostal attacks', p. 107; cf. Stephens, *The Fire Spreads*, p. 125. The once popular paper ceased publication in 1908. Synan notes that this periodical added to the holiness conflict with the Methodist church and may have facilitated the 'come-outism' of the day, Synan, *Holiness-Pentecostal Tradition*, p. 63. For a thoughtful look at the impact of periodicals and publishing on the WH movement, see Stephens, *The Fire Spreads*, pp. 99-135.

[61] These include a sermon, testimonies, reports from the mission field, a 'Children's Corner', and 'Our Dead'.

[62] After publication began in 1917, it was said that '*The Advocate* was a part of the church that had "long been lacking"', as it would help with the centralization and growing activities of the denomination, Synan, *Old Time Power*, p. 154.

[63] Synan notes that 'the privately-printed *Apostolic Evangel* of Falcon, North Carolina, had served as the informal, but officially approved, voice of the church', Synan, *Old Time Power*, p. 152. Also, 'Cashwell's paper, *The Bridegroom's Messenger*, was adopted as the "organ of this church until further arrangements"', Synan, *Holiness-Pentecostal Tradition*, p. 119; cf. pp. 118-19.

[64] Synan, *Old Time Power*, p. 153.

[65] They are: *HA* 6.3 (May 15, 1906); *HA* (Jun 1, 1906 [?]), pp. 3-8; *HA* 6.5 (Jun 15, 1906); *HA* 6.6 (Jul 1, 1906); *HA* 7.3 (May 15, 1907); *HA* 7.4 (Jun 1, 1907).

[66] Volume-wise, this equalled 312 volumes because 16 volumes were considered double issues [2.28 & 29 (Nov 7 & 14, 1918); 2.30 & 31 (Nov 21 & 28, 1918); 2.33 & 34 (Dec 19 & 25, 1918); 2.36 & 37 (Jan 2 & 9, 1919); 2.44 & 45 (Mar 6 & 13, 1919); 3.1 & 2 (May 1 & 8, 1919); 3.4 & 5 (May 22 & 29, 1919); 3.7 & 8 Jun 12 & 19, 1919); 3.12 & 13 (Jul 17 & 24, 1919); 3.16 & 17 (Aug 14 & 21, 1919); 3.19 & 20 (Sep 4 & 11, 1919); 3.23 & 24 (Oct 2 & 9, 1919); 3.25 &

study because 1) the late start of the *PHA* and 2) because it was chosen as representative of all the Pentecostal periodicals to see if any significant theology of glossolalia emerged or changed after 1920.

In the FW stream, the significance of *Triumphs of Faith* (*TOF*) is that it 'bridged the Holiness and Pentecostal movements, and ... provided a non-sectarian forum for a variety of denominations' and independent people who connected with the founder and publisher, Carrie Judd Montgomery.[67] It was 24 pages of devotional writings, biblical and theological articles, along with personal testimonies and revival reports. Though Montgomery published *TOF* for 65 years, only a nine year window between January, 1906 and December 1914, was read (106 issues).[68] This reading of the independent *TOF* ceases in 1914 because that is when Montgomery joins the AG.

The second FW periodical, *The Pentecost* (TP), was begun by J. Roswell Flower in August, 1908 in Indianapolis, IN.[69] He served as the founder / editor and then passed the publication onto his assistant editor, A.S. Copley in 1910.[70] At first the publication charged fifty cents annually, but soon made it 'free to all who desire it' by means of 'free-will offerings'.[71] It was usually twelve pages of revival reports, articles, testimonies, and the last page listed an 'Apostolic Faith Directory' to promote the Pentecostal

---

26 (Oct 16 & 23, 1919); 3.31 & 32 (Nov 27 & Dec 4, 1919); 4.44 & 45 (Mar 3 & 10, 1921); 4.50 & 51 (Apr 14 & 21, 1921)].

[67] W.E. Warner, 'Carrie Judd Montgomery', in Stanley Burgess (ed.), *NIDPCM* (Grand Rapids, MI: Zondervan, rev. and expanded edn, 2002), pp. 904-906 (905).

[68] Two issues are not extant, 26.5 (May 1906) and 30.8 (Aug 1910). This window was chosen because it covers the material prior to the ASM revival and goes through the founding of the AG.

[69] The publication moved to Kansas City, MO in March 1909, *TP* 1.6 (Apr/May 1909), p. 6.

[70] Of the extant copies, Flower was listed as the 'Foreign and City Editor', 1.1 (Aug 1908) and 1.2 (Sep 1908); 'Foreign Editor', 1.3 (Nov 1908); 'Editor', 1.4 (Dec 1908) to 1.12 (Nov 1909); and then, 'Associate Editor', 2.2 (Feb 1910) to 2. 9 & 10 (Sep/Oct 1910). Copley was listed as 'Associate Editor' between 1.4 (Dec 1908) to 2.9 & 10 (Sep/Oct 1910) and is listed as 'Editor' 2.2 (Jan 1910) and 2.11-12 (Nov/Dec 1910). They had a good working relationship: 'it is about two years since I first met Brother Copley and since that time our hearts have slowly been joined together in a peculiar and wonderful manner', *TP* 1.6 (Apr/May 1909), p. 6.

[71] *TP* 1.8 (Jul 1909), p. 6.

message.⁷² Little is known of its circulation or print-runs. All nineteen extant issues between 1908 and 1910 were read.

The third FW periodical, *Pentecostal Testimony* (PT), was published between 1910-1912 'as the Lord leads, and gives time and strength to prepare the materials'.⁷³ *PT's* purpose was to 'stand for the real truths of Pentecost'.⁷⁴ Its significance is that its editor and primary contributor, William Durham, defined the FW stream. There are six extant issues that had print runs between 25,000 and 51,900.⁷⁵ However, due to Durham's untimely death, the final issue was a memorial issue that largely reprinted articles from other editions.⁷⁶ All six extant issues were read.

The fourth FW publication is *Word and Witness* (WW). Editor E.N. Bell traced *WW's* root to be 'the earliest Pentecostal paper'.⁷⁷ Under Bell, it was primarily a clearing house for revival announcements, missionary reports, testimonies, devotional writings, and

---

⁷² Warner, 'Periodicals', pp. 975-76.

⁷³ William Durham, 'Editorial', *PT* 1.5 (Jul 1910), p. 1. He noted that God 'will provide the funds for printing and mailing' the paper as well. At times *PT* was 'under great disadvantages and difficulties ... we have been in the midst of a real revival which took practically all our strength', William Durham, 'Editorial Note', *PT* 2.2 (May 1912), p. 1.

⁷⁴ Durham, 'Editorial', p. 1.

⁷⁵ *PT* 1.1 (Mar 27, 1909) had a press run of 25,000 copies, William Durham, 'Criticisms Answered', *PT* 1.5 (Jul 1910), p. 11. Non-extant issues (1.2; 1.3; 1.4) had a press run either of 25,000 or 51,900. The most controversial issues, 1.6 and 1.7 (Jan 1911), are not extant. Durham wrote that 1.6 'stirred up considerable opposition' but with 1.7 'the intensity of the heat of battle increased', William Durham, 'The Great Battle of Nineteen Eleven', *PT* 2.1 (Jan 1912), pp. 6-8 (7). Other extant issues are: 1.8 (Aug 1911); 2.1 (Jan 1912); 2.2 (May 1912); and 2.3 (Jul or Aug 1912).

⁷⁶ The memorial edition is *PT* 2.3 (Jul or Aug 1912).

⁷⁷ Others predated *WW* but morphed into Pentecostal periodicals. Bell's claim is that Parham's paper was the first periodical birthed of Pentecostalism. Bell wrote, 'the earliest Pentecostal paper to be issued was the "Apostolic Faith" of Texas ... after seven or eight years ... (it) began to come forth monthly from Malvern, Ark. ... the same became Word and Witness', E.N. Bell, 'Great Enterprise For God', *CE* 78 (Feb 20, 1915), p. 1. Brumback wrote, 'the Apostolic Faith contingent which in 1909 rejected the leadership of Charles Parham had maintained fairly close fellowship among themselves ... (and) selected (Bell) to edit the publication *Apostolic Faith*', Brumback, *Suddenly From Heaven*, p. 152; cf. p. 155. William W. Menzies notes the editorial change in 1910, William W. Menzies, *Anointed To Serve* (Springfield, MO: Gospel Publishing House, 1971), p. 89. Parham continued to publish his own *Apostolic Faith* at 'Baxter Springs, KS 1910-17, 1925-29', James R. Goff, 'Charles Fox Parham', in Stanley Burgess (ed.), *NIDPCM* (Grand Rapids, MI: Zondervan, rev. and expanded edn, 2002), pp. 955-57 (956).

updates on the new AG fellowship after the Dec. 20, 1913 issue. This periodical became the monthly 'official organ' of the newly formed AG, while 'those who desire a weekly paper (could) avail themselves of *The Christian Evangel*'.[78] Bell noted that the circulation of the *WW* 'reached nearly 25,000 monthly' with one edition reaching 60,000.[79] However, soon Bell wrote that 'the Weekly paper has grown ... (and) our good old monthly, the Word and Witness ... has been crowded into the background. **A whole month is now too long.**'[80] The final issue of *WW* was December, 1915 when all subscriptions were 'transferred to the Weekly Evangel'.[81] All twenty-eight extant issues from 1912 through 1915 were examined.

The fifth FW periodical was the official publication of the AG and went through several names – *Christian Evangel* (CE),[82] the *Weekly Evangel* (WE),[83] and back again to the *Christian Evangel*[84] – before settling on the *Pentecostal Evangel* (PE).[85] PE was chosen because of the 'initial evidence controversy' and the desire to 'speak

---

[78] Joseph R. Flower, 'The Evangel's Roots', *PE* 4132 (Jul 18, 1993), pp. 7, 22 (22); cf. Edith L. Blumhofer, *The Assemblies of God: A Chapter in the Story of American Pentecostalism* (Springfield, MO: Gospel Publishing House, 1989), p. 204.

[79] Bell, 'Great Enterprise For God', p. 1. The Oct. 1912 issue noted that 12,000 copies were printed, Editor, 'Blessings In Bundles', *WW* 8.8 (Oct 1912), p. 2. Menzies believed that there was a combined circulation of 25,000 between the two periodicals at the time of the AG's formation, Menzies, *Anointed To Serve*, p. 132.

[80] Advertisement, *WW* 12.11 (Nov 1915), p. 3 (emphasis original). Cf. Flower, 'The Evangel's Roots', p. 22. Further, *WW* was running many of the same articles and testimonies in both the *WW* and *CE*.

[81] Advertisement, *WW* 12.11 (Nov 1915), p. 3.

[82] The *Christian Evangel* was published at Plainfield, IN from Jul 19, 1913 to Jul 4, 1914, at Findlay, OH from Jul 11, 1914 to Jan 30, 1915, and at St. Louis, MO from Feb 13, 1915 to Mar 6, 1915.

[83] The *Weekly Evangel* was published at St. Louis from Mar 13, 1915 to May 18, 1918. This name change was at the request of the Post Office which had another publication with a similar name being published from St. Louis, Flower, 'The Evangel's Roots', p. 22.

[84] The *Christian Evangel* was published at Springfield, MO from Jun 1, 1918 to Oct 4, 1919, and on Jul 1, 1918 it became bi-weekly for the duration of this study's window. 'Due to paper shortage and high production cost brought on by World War I, the *Weekly Evangel* went bi-weekly' and returned to weekly in March 1923, Flower, 'The Evangel's Roots', p. 22.

[85] The *Pentecostal Evangel* was published at Springfield, MO from Oct 18, 1919 to Jun 9, 2002.

out with conviction for the distinctiveness of the Pentecostal positon'.[86] For a brief period Bell was the managing editor of both periodicals.[87] All 235 extant copies from Jan 9, 1915 through Dec 25, 1920 were read. 1920 was chosen as the ideal end of the readings due to the finalization of the major controversies about glossolalia.

The third major stream is Oneness Pentecostalism which emerges out of the FW stream. The independent periodical, *The Good Report* (TGR), was published between May 1911 and at least March 1914 and reveals two streams in the same periodical. Significantly, one can see an emerging Oneness theology in the final seven extant issues.[88] Two earlier extant issues were published by Robert E. McAlister in Canada to further the Pentecostal message.[89] Probably in June or July, 1913 McAlister amalgamated *TGR* with 'The Apostolic Faith' of Los Angeles, CA for unknown reasons.[90] At that time, Frank J. Ewart, Durham's assistant pastor in Los Angeles, became co-editor with McAlister. Print-runs were more successful in Canada.[91] All nine extant issues were read and incorporated into this study.

The final material to be reviewed represents the official Oneness branch of Pentecostalism. Its significance is a unique theology of glossolalia that differs from both WH and FW Pentecostalism.[92]

---

[86] Flower, 'The Evangel's Roots', p. 22.

[87] This was 'during the interval from July 1914 to March 1915 when the national headquarters was located in Findlay, Ohio', Flower, 'The Evangel's Roots', p. 22.

[88] *TGR* 2.1 (Jun 1, 1913); *TGR* 2.3 (Aug 1, 1913); *TGR* 2.4 (Sep 1, 1913); *TGR* 1.6 (Nov 1, 1913); *TGR* 1.7 (Dec 1, 1913); *TGR* 1.8 (Jan 1914); *TGR* 1.10 (Mar 1, 1914).

[89] *TGR* 1 (May 1911); *TGR* 1.3 (1912).

[90] 'It is now six months since the "Good Report and The Apostolic Faith" were amalgamated and sent forth under the first name', Ewart & McAlister, 'Letter To Our Readers and Correspondents' (1), *TGR* 1.7 (Dec 1, 1913), p. 1.

[91] In Canada: 'so we are enlarging this issue ... from 8 to 16 pages, and publishing 50,000 copies', Editor, 'Our Publication', *TGR* 1.3 (1912), p. 16. In Los Angeles: 'we are dropping the subscription price for the time being ... we expect to print 20,000 copies of this issue', *TGR* 1.3 (1912), p. 2. 'We have on our subscription list about 1000 names ... but we will need 5000 regular subscribers to make the paper pay for itself', Ewart & McAlister, 'Letter To Our Readers and Correspondents' (2), *TGR* 2.3 (Aug 1, 1913), p. 2.

[92] Specifically, initial tongues are a sign of a completed or 'full salvation', 'Fundamental Doctrine', *Articles of Faith of the United Pentecostal Church International* (UPCI Manual, 2018 edition), p. 31.

There are two extant early Oneness periodicals.[93] First, the *TGR*'s name was changed to *Meat in Due Season* (MDS) and became fully Oneness in belief.[94] Two of the three issues of *MDS* were published between the 3rd and 4th General Councils of the AG and provide a fascinating snapshot of theology just prior to the formal schism.[95] Second, three copies of *The Blessed Truth* (*TBT*),[96] published by Daniel C.O. Opperman are extant.[97] Finally, seven tracts by three prominent preachers[98] as well as a songbook by Mattie Crawford, *The Pentecostal Flame*, were reviewed.[99]

---

[93] Many thanks to the *Flower Pentecostal Heritage Center*, Cecil M. Robeck, Jr and John Christopher Thomas for their help in locating these largely heretofore unexamined periodicals. Even the editor of *MDS*, F.J. Ewart, commented 'that we cannot hang on too many back numbers. We find ourselves with only a few of No. 18, and we don't expect to have these on hand long', 'Editorial Note', *MDS* 1.21 (Aug 1917), p. 2.

[94] *MDS* was published in Los Angeles, CA, by Ewart. Extant issues are: 1.9 (December 1915); 1.13 (June 1916); 1.21 (Aug 1917). Talmadge L. French, *Our God Is One* (Indianapolis, IN: Voice & Vision Publications, 1999), p. 63.

[95] For example, Oneness' evolving Christology can be seen in, Ewart, 'The Record of the Son', *MDS* 1.13 (June 1916), p. 1. Or consider the developing Oneness view of the godhead: 'we saw from this premise (baptism in Jesus' name) that the old trinity theory was unscriptural. That there was not three Gods in the sense of individual embodiment ... so we had to abandon the old essential tenet of all Orthodox theology as absolutely unscriptural, and we denounced the so-called trinity as such ... *The very fact that universal Christendom had accepted this tenet of Christian theology constitutes a strong proof that it is incorrect*', F.J. Ewart, 'The Unity of God', *MDS* 1.13 (June 1916), p. 1 (emphasis added). Cf. F.J. Ewart, 'Editorial', *MDS* 1.13 (June 1916), p. 2. Emotions among friends were raw because of the conflict. Cf. Homer Faulkner, 'From Brother Faulkner', *MDS* 1.9 (Dec 1915), p. 2; Ewart, 'Editorial', p. 2; F.J. Ewart, 'To Our Friends', *MDS* 1.13 (June 1916), p. 4.

[96] *The Blessed Truth* was published semi-monthly in Eureka Springs, AR, by Daniel C.O. Opperman. Extant issues are: 3.11 (Aug 15, 1918); 4.2 (Jan 15, 1919); and 4.11 (Jun 1, 1919).

[97] Daniel Charles Owen Opperman studied at several colleges and was recognized as an educator. He was a founding member of the AG but 'withdrew in 1916 to become chairman of a fledgling Oneness association', Edith L. Blumhofer, 'Daniel Charles Owen Opperman', in Stanley Burgess (ed.), *NIDPCM* (Grand Rapids, MI: Zondervan, rev. and expanded edn, 2002), pp. 946-47.

[98] Donald W. Dayton, *Seven 'Jesus Only' Tracts* (New York: Garland Publishing, 1985). The preachers are F.J. Ewart, G.T. Haywood, and A.D. Urshan.

[99] Mattie Crawford (ed.), *The Pentecostal Flame* (Los Angles, CA, 1923).

2

BIBLIOGRAPHIC REVIEW OF LITERATURE ON GLOSSOLALIA

Introduction

The purpose of this chapter is to review the scholarly literature concerning Pentecostal glossolalia. Because 'the literature on glossolalia ... is immense', this survey will limit itself to significant or pioneering monographs from 1888 to the present.[1] Overall, approaches to the topic could be categorized broadly as having an historical, psychological, sociological, linguistic, exegetical, or an interdisciplinary approach.[2] Many pieces of literature about glossolalia were read but could not fit within the word limitations of this work. For example, the entire method of looking at tongues through psychology is not included due to space, except where it is deemed essential as background to subsequent readings. The first section, 1888 to 1929, looks at the earliest works among non-Pentecostals and Pentecostals. The second period, between 1930 and 1969, reveals these two streams of literature largely flowing independently of the other. The third section, 1970 to present, marks an engagement between these two streams of literature and

---

[1] Wacker, *Heaven Below*, p. 283 n. 1.
[2] See for example, Mark J. Cartledge (ed.), *Speaking in Tongues: Multi-Disciplinary Perspectives* (Studies in Pentecostal and Charismatic Issues; Bletchley, Milton Keynes, England: Paternoster Press, 2006), pp. xiv-xxiv, his introduction cites even a 'health' approach; for an excellent summary of the wide variety of approaches within the exegetical category, see, Mark J. Cartledge, 'The Nature and Function of New Testament Glossolalia', *Evangelical Quarterly* 72.2 (2000), pp. 135-50.

a veritable flood of publications. This third period suffered the greatest omission of many fine pieces due to space. The fourth section examines works on glossolalia that import valuable concepts from an Eastern Orthodox perspective. The final section reviews literature that utilizes the early Pentecostal periodicals. The goal of this survey is threefold. 1) To lay a foundation for reading of the early Pentecostal periodicals and their theological discussions. 2) To acquaint the reader with the theological issues and terminology surrounding glossolalia. 3) To show the rich theological discussions that have been largely overlooked until recently and the need for this investigation.

I. Early Literature, 1888 to 1929

While it is true that many of the first generation Pentecostals wrote 'books, pamphlets, and newspapers ... at a popular level' largely due to an 'anti-intellectualism which plagued much of the movement',[3] the following literature reveals a theological depth that has been larely ignored by scholars. Chronologically, the pieces from 1906 onward reveal the initial response of Pentecostal and non-Pentecostal scholars to the ASM revival.

Works That Predate the Azusa Street Mission Revival
These three pieces of literature written before the ASM revival provide a background for this study on glossolalia, and demonstrate the great interest in glossolalia. Charles F. Parham's pioneering pamphlet is the first formal declaration of SB having an evidence.

Hermann Gunkel, 1888
Though Pentecostals could embrace some of what Herman Gunkel's writes about glossolalia, that is not his main contribution.[4]

---

[3] Robby Waddell, 'Whence Pentecostal Scholarship? The Coming of Age of the Pentecostal Critical Tradition and a Forecast for its Future', in Steven M. Fettke and Robby Waddell (eds.) *Pentecostals in the Academy: Testimonies of Call* (Cleveland, TN: CPT Press, 2012), pp. 243-59 (244).

[4] He noted that: 1) tongues are ecstatic, Gunkel, *The Influence of the Holy Spirit*, p. 32; cf. pp. ix, 18, 31-32, 80-81, 116. 2) All Christians have the Spirit, but there are varying degrees of 'fullness', pp. 17, 42. 3) Paul was a 'pneumatic' and spoke in tongues which guided his correction of Corinth's overemphasis on glossolalia, p. 77; cf. also, pp. 25, 30-31, 81, 85-86, 88. 4) There is counterfeit and genuine

This work's significance is the observation that the Holy Spirit is known by his 'effects'.[5] This monograph is a product of Gunkel's pioneering 'reception history' or *Wirkungsgeschichte*.[6]

Carl Clemen, 1899

Carl Clemen's historical-critical method concludes that the languages of Acts 2 is a later addition to the text from a vague memory.[7] This theory would come to be called 'exalted memory' or 'cryptomnesia'.[8] He writes that genuine glossolalic 'phenomenon (is) conceivable only in the earliest period of the Christian Church' and then 'spontaneously disappeared'.[9] Further, Mk 16.17 is not original and its author had 'no definite conception of the speaking with tongues'.[10] Subsequent attempts to revitalize tongues are 'very artificial' and should not be considered a same experience as the first Christians.[11]

Charles F. Parham, 1902

The Baptism with the Holy Ghost and Speaking in Tongues, is a short pamphlet authored by Pentecostal pioneer Charles F. Parham.[12] He

---

glossolalia, p. 57. Overall, he presents a 'lively picture' of the Spirit compatible with the NT worldview, pp. 96, 127.

[5] Gunkel, *The Influence of the Holy Spirit*, pp. 25-26, 31, 39.

[6] 'Gunkel founded a "school," fathered form critical research', introduction, Gunkel, *The Influence of the Holy Spirit*, p. vii.

[7] Carl Clemen, '"The Speaking with Tongues" of the Early Christians', *The Expository Times*, 10.344 (1899), pp. 344-52 (345-46, 352).

[8] Charles Shumway, provides an explanation of the fully developed theory, Charles Shumway, 'A Study of "The Gift of Tongues"' (AB Thesis, University of Southern California, 1914), pp. 23-30; cf. Frederick G. Henke, 'The Gift of Tongues and Related Phenomena at the Present Day', *The American Journal of Theology*, 13.2 (April 1909), pp. 193-206 (205); Alexander Mackie, *The Gift of Tongues: A Study in Pathological Aspects of Christianity* (New York: George H. Doran Company, 1921), pp. 253-54; George Barton Cutten, *Speaking with Tongues, Historically and Psychologically Considered* (New Haven, London: Yale University Press; Humphrey Milford, Oxford University Press, 1927), pp. 176-81. James D.G. Dunn notes that cryptomnesia is not a panacea because it would have to be 'communal ecstasy' on the Day of Pentecost, James D.G. Dunn, *Jesus and the Spirit* (Philadelphia: The Westminster Press, 1975), p. 151. For a positive assessment of cryptomnesia, see Cyril Glyndwr Williams, *Tongues of the Spirit: A Study of Pentecostal Glossolalia and Related Phenomena* (Cardiff: University of Wales Press, 1981), pp. 34, 54, 184, 188-89.

[9] Clemen, 'The Speaking with Tongues', pp. 346, 351.

[10] Clemen, 'The Speaking with Tongues', p. 352; cf. pp. 345-56.

[11] Clemen, 'The Speaking with Tongues', p. 346; cf. pp. 349-50.

[12] Charles F. Parham, 'The Baptism with the Holy Ghost' in W.F. Carothers, *The Baptism with the Holy Ghost and the Speaking in Tongues* (Zion City, IL: Caroth-

is largely seen as the father of Pentecostalism's theology of glossolalia.[13] This brief summary will also include writings from *The Everlasting Gospel*.[14] Parham's theological significance is threefold: evidential glossolalia, missionary tongues (MT), and a biblical hermeneutic.

Parham believes that rooted in Scripture is a third experience, a SB that has an evidence: 'speaking in tongues is an inseparable part of the Baptism of the Holy Spirit distinguishing it from all previous works; and that no one has received the Baptism of the Holy Spirit who has not a *Bible evidence* to show for it'.[15] The evidence or 'Bible sign', is distinct from the 'anointing' which occurs at salvation and the WH second work view of sanctification.[16] Sanctification could not be SB because 'the Bible evidence is lacking in their lives'.[17] Wesleyan-holiness' sanctification is open to 'private interpretations as to His visible manifestation', but SB 'is a gift not a grace, (and) is not obtained in justification or sanctification'.[18]

Parham believes that all glossolalia is a specific human language given to tell the gospel in that language. These are new tongues for missionaries:[19] 'in the close of the age, God proposes to send forth men and women preaching in languages they know not a word of, which when interpreted the hearers will know is truly a message from God'.[20] This belief solidified into a litmus test for missionaries: 'if the Holy Spirit had sent out these workers, they would have been endowed with real tongues'.[21] These MT are the

---

ers, 1906 reprint; January 1902), pp. 5–18. Parham's section was previously published in January 1902, in Charles F. Parham, *Kol Kare Bomidbar: A Voice Crying in the Wilderness* (Reprint, Joplin, MO: The Joplin Printing Co., 1944), pp. 25-38.

[13] Goff, *Fields White unto Harvest*, p. 16. There is a debate among historians as to just who is the founder of Pentecostalism. Other notable candidates are: Seymour, p. 10; no human founder, 'the Holy Spirit alone had prompted this movement', p. 14; and both Parham and Seymour together, p. 15.

[14] Charles F. Parham, *The Everlasting Gospel* (n.p., 1919).

[15] Parham, 'Baptism with the Holy Ghost', p. 15 (emphasis added).

[16] Parham, *The Everlasting Gospel*, p. 70. He writes, 'the anointing is within you a well of water (artesian); the baptism lends the pressure to compel that well to flow from your inwards parts in "streams of living water"', p. 70.

[17] Parham, 'Baptism with the Holy Ghost', p. 7.

[18] Parham, 'Baptism with the Holy Ghost', pp. 7, 10.

[19] Parham, 'Baptism with the Holy Ghost', pp. 8, 11, 15.

[20] Parham, 'Baptism with the Holy Ghost', p. 11.

[21] Parham, *The Everlasting Gospel*, p. 70. After most of Pentecostalism moved away from MT, he wrote that the 'gift of tongues may develop into a real gift

same as the 'gift of tongues' that Paul notes in 1 Corinthians 12. Glossolalia's restoration is an integral sign of God's activity within history for a last day's revival.[22] Cessationists are wrong in saying 'those things were only meant for the apostles and only to be spiritually interpreted for us', because 'the same evidence would follow today as at that time'.[23]

Finally, these early pioneers were biblical literalists,[24] and Parham lays out what will be a standard Pentecostal interpretation of the Holy Spirit having an evidence. On the Day of Pentecost, Peter identifies Joel's prophecy with glossolalia: 'this is that which was spoken by Joel, the prophet'.[25] Pentecost is so pivotal and paradigmatic that Acts 2 would 'be sufficient (by itself), but it is found repeatedly, yea every time the Holy Ghost fell and the evidence was noted, it proved to be this same one of speaking in tongues'.[26] Parham sees a 'pattern' in the book of Acts (2, 10 & 19), and Paul's writings are complimentary to Luke's.[27]

Post Azusa Street Mission Revival (1906) Works

Warren F. Carothers, 1906

In the early years, Warren F. Carothers worked closely with

---

of language', apparently moving from supernatural ability to use of foreign languages 'intelligently', p. 68. This position is held so tightly that even after a lot of proof otherwise, the denomination he founded still holds this position, Goff, *Fields White unto Harvest*, p. 163.

[22] Parham's eschatology is an imminent premillennial eschatology, with emphasis on 'sealing of the Bride', which occurs with SB. This sealing will help those who are genuine 'escape the plagues and wraths of the last days' and imparts to them special powers for the end-time harvest, Parham, 'Baptism with the Holy Ghost', p. 6. Only the elect 'Man-child' (the 144,000) will be raptured, all the remaining Christians will go through tribulation until the millennial kingdom is established, McQueen, *Toward a Pentecostal Eschatology*, pp. 12-13. This special sealing is evidenced by tongues as a sign, Parham, 'Baptism with the Holy Ghost', p. 7; cf. Goff, *Fields White unto Harvest*, pp. 78-79.

[23] Parham, 'Baptism with the Holy Ghost', pp. 8, 13.

[24] Robeck, *Azusa Street*, p. 110; cf. Russell P. Spittler, 'Are Pentecostals and Charismatics Fundamentalists? A Review of American Uses of These Categories', in Karla Poewe (ed.), *Charismatic Christianity as a Global Culture* (Colombia, SC: University of South Carolina Press, 1994), pp. 103-18 (111).

[25] Parham, 'Baptism with the Holy Ghost', p. 16.

[26] Parham, 'Baptism with the Holy Ghost', p. 16.

[27] Parham, 'Baptism with the Holy Ghost', pp. 16-17. In this tract Parham sees a pattern only in Acts 2, 10 and 19. He believes that Paul's testimony of speaking in tongues and command to 'forbid not' supports his position, p. 18.

Parham, serving as his 'Field Director'.[28] Nonetheless, Carother's theology of tongues diverged from Parham's in its nature and purpose. At first, he doubted the linguistic nature of glossolalia until 'I heard a sister sing an entire hymn in German, which I readily understood in its entirety ... I came to believe them to be of God'.[29] Yet he expressed doubt about Parham's theory of MT:

> just what part of tongues is to fill in the evangelization of heathen countries is [sic] matter for faith as yet. *It scarcely seems from the evidence at hand to have had much to do with foreign mission work in New Testament times*, and yet, in view of the apparent utility of the gift in that sphere and of the wonderful missionary spirit that comes with Pentecost, we are expecting the gift to be copiously used in the foreign field. *We shall soon know*.[30]

This doubt about MT enabled Carothers to see three additional purposes for glossolalia. First, 'tongues now are praises to God in language peculiarly acceptable to Him'.[31] Second, personal edification: some pray for hours 'just for the joy and edification they receive from the heavenly exercise'.[32] His third reason is that it is a sign for unbelievers.[33] As for the Bible sign, Carothers clarified that one 'may have the Holy Spirit ... and not yet have the baptism', for example, John the Baptist.[34]

Minnie Abrams, 1906

Minnie Abrams' book (1906) about a revival at the Mukti Mission in India reveals the worldwide nature of Pentecostalism's

---

[28] Warren F. Carothers, 'Notes and Paragraphs' in *The Baptism with the Holy Ghost and the Speaking in Tongues* (Zion City, IL: Carothers, 1906). At the time of his SB, Carothers was a lawyer and pastor of Christian Witness Tabernacle in Houston, TX, Robeck, *Azusa Street*, p. 45. He would become an Executive Presbyter in the AG, was a segregationist, and did not believe Seymour should to go to Los Angeles until he had been Spirit baptized, pp. 46-50.

[29] Carothers, 'Notes and Paragraphs', pp. 19-20.

[30] Carothers, 'Notes and Paragraphs', p. 21 (emphasis added).

[31] Carothers, 'Notes and Paragraphs', p. 21.

[32] Carothers, 'Notes and Paragraphs', p. 21. He notes 1 Cor. 14.14 for biblical support.

[33] Carothers, 'Notes and Paragraphs', p. 21. He notes 1 Cor. 14.22 for biblical support.

[34] Carothers, 'Notes and Paragraphs', p. 23; cf. pp. 23-24.

origin and is among the earliest Pentecostal publications.[35] She states, 'young men and women are receiving the GIFTS of the Holy Spirit, speaking with tongues, interpreting tongues previously unknown to them; the sick are being healed, and unclean spirits cast out to prayer'.[36] After sanctification it is 'the fullness of the Holy Ghost, the fire that empowers us to preach the word in the fullness of love and with signs following'.[37] Glossolalia is a sign of empowerment: 'it was not until this manifestation of the Holy Spirit was received that they (the disciples) were empowered to preach the death and resurrection of Jesus'.[38]

Dawson A. Walker, 1906

Aware of the Welsh revival, Dawson A. Walker's work is an attempt to prove that Luke was a credible historian precisely because he does not harmonize with Paul.[39] Walker disagrees with attempts to 'elevate St. Paul at the expense of St. Luke'[40] because there are many 'forms' of glossolalia,[41] and Luke stresses

---

[35] Minnie Abrams, *The Baptism of the Holy Ghost & Fire* (Kedgaon, India: Mukti Mission Press, 2nd edn, 1906). The first edition was published in April 1906 and makes no mention of glossolalia. The second edition was published in December 1906 and is identical to the first, except for the inclusion of tongues. It may have been revised due to its popularity, or because of Abrams awareness of the ASM revival, or that 'the indigenous Indians … were already speaking in tongues', cf. Robeck, *Azusa Street*, pp. 253-54 (254). Of note is: 1) the report of tongues at the ASM revival, pp. 69-70. 2) Abrams countered cessationism by noting: that Acts 2.39 is a promise for 'all who are afar off'; that Acts 2.17-20 notes that signs are to continue until 'that great and notable day'; and that 'there are many proofs that the fire of the Holy Ghost has been given to the people of God all down through the centuries', pp. 19, 38, 68.

[36] Abrams, *Holy Ghost & Fire*, p. 3.

[37] Abrams, *Holy Ghost & Fire*, pp. 71, cf. pp. 46-47.

[38] Abrams, *Holy Ghost & Fire*, p. 38. Abrams believes the disciples received the Spirit when Jesus breathed on them (Jn 20.22); however, 'when we have come to Christ for the forgiveness of our sins we have received only the tiniest beginning of what Christ purchased for us on the cross', p. 25. She advises that 'no one should seek to have manifestations … because others have had them', p. 85. Also, 'we do not need to worry over these manifestations, nor seek to suppress them', p. 79. Finally, 'every time she put her hands upon the work at Mukti to suppress joy or strong conviction … the work of revival stopped', pp. 74-75, 80.

[39] Dawson A. Walker, *The Gift of Tongues and Other Essays* (Edinburgh: T & T Clark, 1906), pp. 27, 35, 49, 58, n.

[40] Walker, *The Gift of Tongues*, p. 4; cf. pp. 30-31.

[41] Walker, *The Gift of Tongues*, pp. 40-41.

God as the source rather than the 'precise mode of the phenomenon'.[42] Following Clemen, glossolalia on the Day of Pentecost was an ecstatic form of speech in which the speaker recalled foreign words overheard in Jerusalem.[43] Walker believes that 'the two different accounts are not mutually exclusive' and that a better understanding of psychology and exegesis will clarify the gap between Paul and Luke.[44]

George Floyd Taylor, 1907

The Spirit and the Bride[45] is significant as the 'first sustained text of pentecostal theology'.[46] Taylor, addresses a wide range of topics relevant to Pentecostal glossolalia, including its distinction from sanctification, the nature of tongues, and the gifts of the Spirit, but he takes 'special pains to answer the question, *"do all who receive the Baptism of the Spirit speak with other tongues?"*'[47]

In order for the Pentecostal perspective of evidential tongues to make sense, SB has to be separated from the WH perspective that SB is a distinct work of sanctification.[48] Taylor writes that 'sanctification is the eradication of the carnal mind; while the Baptism of the Holy Ghost is a filling: the one takes place at Calvary; while the other occurs at

---

[42] Walker, *The Gift of Tongues*, p. 46.

[43] Walker, *The Gift of Tongues*, p. 61.

[44] Walker, *The Gift of Tongues*, p. 35. Yet, at one point Walker falls back on discrediting the text of 1 Corinthians to make his supposition about an influential 'Christ party' at Corinth fit, p. 78.

[45] George F. Taylor, *The Spirit and the Bride* (Dunn, NC, 1907). Taylor was among the first to speak in tongues at the revival in Dunn, NC, in January 1907. He became the General Superintendent of the Pentecostal Holiness Church, H. Vinson Synan, 'George Floyd Taylor', in Stanley Burgess (ed.), *NIDPCM* (Grand Rapids, MI: Zondervan, rev. and expanded edn, 2002), pp. 1115-1116; cf. Robeck, *Azusa Street*, pp. 216-19.

[46] Wacker, *Heaven Below*, p. 74. Gary B. McGee notes that 'it represents the first book-length treatise on Pentecostal theology,' Gary B. McGee, '"Brought into the Sphere of the Supernatural": How Speaking in Tongues Empowered Early Pentecostals', *Encounter: Journal for Pentecostal Ministry* 4.1 (Fall 2007), pp. 1–17 (13 n. 16). Taylor himself claimed that this is the first book by someone filled with the Spirit seeking to 'place the Baptism of the Holy Spirit in its scriptural setting, and to show forth its peculiar accompaniment, the speaking in other tongues as evidencing its unmistakable reception', Taylor, *The Spirit and the Bride*, p. 9.

[47] Taylor, *The Spirit and the Bride*, p. 5 (emphasis original).

[48] A WH understanding only, 'brings its adherents into the vestibule of Pentecostal power and fulness', Taylor, *The Spirit and the Bride*, p. 8; cf. p. 88.

Pentecost'.[49] He concludes that, 'the Baptism of the Spirit has nothing to do with the sin question, but is an enduement of power for service'.[50]

Regarding the nature of glossolalia, the individual is a mere vessel being used: 'the Holy Ghost, having come into them ... (that) was giving the utterance'.[51] Tongues 'are real languages spoken by branches of the human family'.[52] Missionary tongues bridges Babel's linguistic gap:[53]

> while the 'confusion of language' will never be completely done away until the 'restoration of all things,' yet this chasm was bridged at Pentecost ... God is now augmenting the spread of the gospel by bridging and enabling his children to cross at once the chasms which they hitherto have had to cross by years of study and practice.[54]

And, 'a person who has the gift of tongues can speak other languages at will, and, no doubt, several different languages'.[55]

Even though Taylor was not taught about the evidence, he

---

[49] Taylor, *The Spirit and the Bride*, p. 75. He notes that one is an 'emptying' and the other a 'filling', p. 39: 'sanctification is a dedication; the Baptism of the Holy Spirit is an empowerment. The one is entirely ... a subtraction; the other is wholly an addition. Sanctification has to do with sin; the baptism of the Holy Spirit has to do only with the saint', p. 89. He believes that 'if the baptism of the Holy Spirit sanctifies, no one was ever sanctified until Pentecost ... (and) we know (this) to be untrue', p. 88. He also points out that the disciples were sanctified when Jesus blessed them (Lk. 24.50). Taylor's reasoning is that the disciples received their justification in Jn 20.22, pp. 75-77.

[50] Taylor, *The Spirit and the Bride*, p. 87.

[51] Taylor, *The Spirit and the Bride*, pp. 33, 34. It is the 'Holy Ghost taking the tongue' and using 'a person's tongue to speak a language', p. 36.

[52] Taylor, *The Spirit and the Bride*, p. 51. Taylor believes that Peter, Stephen, Philip, and even Jesus preached in other languages: Peter preached to the Italian band at Cornelius' home; Stephen preached to the Libertines, the Cyrenians, Alexandrians, Cilicians, and the Asians (Acts 6.9); and Philip preached to the Ethiopian (Acts 8.26-39), p. 35. 'Jesus talked to the ignorant fallen Samaritan woman at the well, doubtless in her own dialect. So, too, of the Syrophenician woman and the Gadarenes. True, the Scriptures do not have the word "tongues" in these incidents', p. 48.

[53] The ASM missionaries will be 'able to speak in any language to whom God sends, using the language thus given of God with absolute perfection', Taylor, *The Spirit and the Bride*, p. 94.

[54] Taylor, *The Spirit and the Bride*, pp. 33, 34.

[55] Taylor, *The Spirit and the Bride*, pp. 62-63.

personally experienced it upon his SB.[56] He writes that the Bible evidence 'stands out ... as a lofty mountain above the plain',[57] but because Satan can imitate it, it is not 'an unmistakable evidence'.[58] Taylor's defence of the evidence is thoroughly scriptural: 1) he begins with the promise in John's gospel that the Comforter would testify of Jesus.[59] 2) Although Paul's epistles do not overtly teach the evidence,[60] it could be argued that gifts of the Spirit always follow SB.[61] 3) 'We have an abundance of other scriptures to prove our position', such as Mk 16.17, 18,[62] the book of Acts,[63] Isa. 28.11, 12.[64] Taylor challenges critics to find any other evidence for SB in Scripture.[65]

Finally, in response to critics,[66] Taylor's retorts to the theory of cessation are noteworthy: 1) 'God never withdrew Pentecost or

---

[56] He writes that within five minutes of 'meeting the first person who had his Pentecost the Holy Ghost was talking with my tongue. Three days later a certain brother said to me that he believed all who received the Baptism of the Holy Ghost would speak in tongues. This was a surprise to me, as it was the first time that I had thought on this line', Taylor, *The Spirit and the Bride*, pp. 39-40.

[57] Taylor, *The Spirit and the Bride*, p. 68.

[58] Taylor, *The Spirit and the Bride*, p. 57.

[59] 'Any of these nine (spiritual) gifts in their normal bestowment is an evidence of Pentecost; yet no one of them is to be taken as *the testimony of the Comforter* and hence is *not the first evidence* to be expected', Jn 15.26-27, Taylor, *The Spirit and the Bride*, p. 24; cf. pp. 25-33; 38-39 (emphasis added).

[60] Taylor, *The Spirit and the Bride*, p. 48. However, he believed much could be learned about glossolalia from 1 Corinthians. For example: 1) a case could be made against the WH view of SB as sanctification because Paul called them holy when 'he had just as much proof that they were not even converted', p. 54. 2) Paul was a tongue speaker and IE can be 'implied', p. 56. 3) Tongues builds up the church, p. 72.

[61] Initial evidence is the gateway to the spiritual gifts, Taylor, *The Spirit and the Bride*, p. 63. 'I have yet to hear the first one interpreting a message spoken by the Holy Ghost who had not himself had a manifestation of tongues', p. 64. The spiritual gifts are to be sought, to be tempered by divine love, and are to build up the church or individual, pp. 63, 66-67, 70.

[62] Taylor, *The Spirit and the Bride*, p. 51.

[63] While he examines Acts, he does not refer to a pattern per se, Taylor, *The Spirit and the Bride*, pp. 35-36, 55, 87-88.

[64] Taylor, *The Spirit and the Bride*, p. 135.

[65] Taylor, *The Spirit and the Bride*, p. 46. He directly responds to why laughter and wisdom are not evidential, pp. 46-47.

[66] Taylor responds to many other criticisms of Pentecostalism. They reveal the severe social opposition of the day and are not germane to this study. For example, he responded to the charge that Pentecostals are stubborn, Taylor, *The*

any of its power from the Church; but the Church withdrew from Pentecost and lost its power',[67] 2) a careful exegesis of 1 Cor. 13.8-10 reveals that its prophecy is not yet fulfilled,[68] and 3) the latter rain concept explains historical gaps and occurrences.[69]

Thomas Ball Barratt, 1909

Thomas Ball Barratt is credited with bringing the Pentecostal message to Norway and much of Europe.[70] In this work he attempts to 'meet some of the criticisms of the day concerning the Pentecostal Movement'.[71] He articulates reasoned arguments for critics of glossolalia: 1) he argues against cessationism a full nine years before Benjamin B. Warfield even wrote, *Counterfeit Miracles*![72] 2) He believes, 'the Holy Spirit does not break or disregard the individuality of the prophet, but sanctifies it, and uses it as a channel for the message to be given'.[73] 3) Barratt believes all glossolalia is

---

Spirit and the Bride, p. 42; that all WH leaders are oppositional, p. 43; that Pentecostals are the type of people who 'have never been settled in their religious experience', p. 43; and that glossolalia is not swearing, p. 51. Taylor answered the argument of 'it's not for me', with the stinging retort: 'they (WH leaders) count their works greater than the testimony of the Holy Spirit', p. 50.

[67] Taylor, *The Spirit and the Bride*, p. 41.

[68] Prophecy will pass away for there are 'no lost souls to be saved'; tongues will pass away because there will be 'one language, hence no need of the gift of languages', and knowledge will pass away because we will no longer need to interpret the Bible, Taylor, *The Spirit and the Bride*, p. 69.

[69] Taylor, *The Spirit and the Bride*, pp. 90-99.

[70] D.D. Bundy, 'Thomas Ball Barratt', in Stanley Burgess (ed.), *NIDPCM* (Grand Rapids, MI: Zondervan, rev. and expanded edn, 2002), p. 365. Though Barrett is not a part of North American Pentecostalism per se, his writings are significant due to its early publication date and content.

[71] Thomas Ball Barratt, *The Works of T.B. Barratt* (New York: Garland Publishing, 1985 reprint; London: Elim Publishing Company, 1928). This work is a compilation of two books 'In the Days of the Latter Rain', and 'When the Fire Fell and an Outline of My Life'.

[72] Benjamin B. Warfield, *Counterfeit Miracles* (Carlisle, PA: The Banner of Truth Trust, 1976), first published in 1918. Barratt notes that the early church fathers acknowledged that the spiritual gifts have appeared throughout history, 'in *almost every great revival, also the gift of tongues*', Barratt, *Works*, p. 62, cf. pp 56-65. Also, the gifts disappeared due to neglect and institutionalism in the 3rd or 4th century, p. 62. Finally, the interpretation of τὸ τέλειον in 1 Cor. 13.10 is resolved by realizing that 'perfection ... is never attained by mortals on earth. The tongues were, therefore to last continuously in the Church', p. 159.

[73] Barratt, *Works*, p. 109. Barratt is comfortable with the term 'ecstatic worship' because there was something on the Day of Pentecost to merit the charge of drunkenness, but disagrees that the tongues-speaker ever loses his or her volition. He believes that there is a mixture of human and divine, pp. 90-93.

a real language, and that while MT is theoretically possible, 'tongues does not seem to have been intended to usurp the ordinary study of languages'.[74] 4) The function of tongues is broader than just 'power for ministry':[75] glossolalia is for praise and worship;[76] it is a miracle God uses to attract people to the gospel;[77] it is a sign,[78] and somehow helps the believer grow.[79] 5) Barratt is less clear regarding the Bible evidence: demonstrations of a 'full Pentecost ... are not always similar in their outward demonstrations',[80] because 'there are other evidences of the indwelling Spirit ... I believe that many have had ... mighty baptisms *without this sign*'.[81] Another evidence is love because, 'it is possible for Satan to counterfeit the gifts, but *not the love of God poured forth in the soul*.'[82]

D. Wesley Myland, 1910

D. Wesley Myland's book, *The Latter Rain Covenant*, is the definitive work on the latter rain metaphor which Pentecostals use to explain the reappearance of glossolalia after a gap of several centuries.[83]

---

[74] Barratt, *Works*, pp. 170-71, cf. pp. 21, 46, 83. A reason for studying foreign language, according to Barratt, is so that the interpretation of tongues during a service can be verified, p. 171. He notes that some mistakes were made with MT, p. 87.

[75] Barratt links SB to power for ministry, but sees it only as one part of two. Sanctification, the second part, rounds out the mature believer, cf. pp. 39, 44, 196, 198.

[76] Barratt, *Works*, pp. 6, 45, 82, 149.

[77] Barratt, *Works*, pp. 5, 84, 114.

[78] Barratt, *Works*, pp. 1, 20, 190.

[79] 'When the Holy Ghost floods and fills you through and through, as He filled the disciples on Pentecost, you will begin to praise and magnify God in tongues, as the Spirit giveth utterance. It may not be the "gift of tongues" you receive, spoken of in I Cor. xii., but snatches of various languages, or some celestial language that the angels and God will understand ... It may not mean that you are to become a missionary ... it was a proof and sure evidence that they had received their Pentecost ... You become lifted to a higher plane ... makes your heart a hot-bed for all the fruits of the Spirit', Barratt, *Works*, p. 21.

[80] Barratt, *Works*, p. 35.

[81] Barratt, *Works*, p. 152. Again, 'many have, we expect, received the Baptism without the outward sign', p. 209. Barratt does see this as an aberration, admitting that the human spirit can hinder through unbelief, ignorance, or unwillingness. For example, 'speaking in tongues, *when it is not prevented*, comes as a matter of course', Barratt, *Works*, p. 70. These exceptions merely prove the rule, p. 219, cf. pp. 35, 67, 70, 152-54, 190, 219.

[82] Barratt, *Works*, p. 69, cf. pp. 40, 77, 106.

[83] D. Wesley Myland, 'The Latter Rain Covenant and Pentecostal Power,' in *Three Early Pentecostal Tracts* (New York: Garland Pub., 1985).

Myland draws a parallel from the rainfall in Palestine. The early spring rains are compared to the Day of Pentecost and accompany the planting of the crops; the latter fall rains are compared to the Pentecostal revival and help to ripen the crop for harvest.[84] For Myland, glossolalia is 'the advance agent, the tell-tale of Pentecost', but he does not want to 'magnify tongues out of its legitimate place'.[85] Myland sees three purposes for glossolalia: 1) to 'subdue things and make us mind our business and look to God',[86] this is to humble and subdue oneself. 2) 'To make you witnesses'.[87] 3) To worship: 'God gives you another tongue. Indeed, the ordinary tongue could never bring the highest glory to God.'[88]

Dormeaus A. Hayes, 1914

The first major monograph on glossolalia by a non-Pentecostal after the ASM revival is by Dormeaus A. Hayes. His goal is to 'be thoroughly sympathetic, reasonable, and irenic'.[89] Hayes affirms the 'gift of tongues',[90] but sees Corinthian glossolalia as a sign of immaturity and preconditioning because, 'they naturally expected … the same ecstatic ejaculations they had seen in the heathen worshipers in their similar state'.[91] He parses NT glossolalia thus: 1) Paul's understanding and his restraints should be the norm,[92] 2) Mk 16.17 reveals little,[93] 3) tongues in the book of Acts is similar in nature to Corinth,[94] and 4) the Day of Pentecost account an outlier. It is likely that ecstasy flowed out from 'memories phrases and sentences they had heard … unconsciously … and their

---

[84] 'Spiritually, the latter rain is coming to the church of God at the same time it is coming literally upon the land and it will never be taken away from her but it will be upon her to unite and empower her, to cause her to aid in God's last work for this dispensation, to bring unity to the body, the consummation of the age, and the catching away of spiritual Israel, the Bride of Christ', Myland, 'The Latter Rain', p. 94.
[85] Myland, 'The Latter Rain', pp. 108, 112.
[86] Myland, 'The Latter Rain', p. 113.
[87] Myland, 'The Latter Rain', p. 115.
[88] Myland, 'The Latter Rain', p. 148.
[89] D.A. Hayes, *The Gift of Tongues* (New York: The Methodist Book Concern, 1914), p. 8. He attended a few meetings in Chicago, pp. 84-93.
[90] Hayes, *Gift of Tongues*, p. 112.
[91] Hayes, *Gift of Tongues*, p. 17.
[92] Hayes, *Gift of Tongues*, p. 112.
[93] Hayes, *Gift of Tongues*, pp. 19-20.
[94] Hayes, *Gift of Tongues*, pp. 119-22.

memories (which) were abnormally quickened'.[95] Hayes engages the reasons given for glossolalia by Edward Irving to affirm glossolalia and clarify his position: 1) they could be a sign to the unbeliever, but 'it might be difficult to determine whether more were helped or hindered'.[96] 2) They could be an evidence, but reason alone should be sufficient and at the very least 'the sign is of infinitely less importance than the thing signified'.[97] 3) It could be for personal edification, but then it ought 'to be banished from a public service'.[98]

Charles W. Shumway, 1914

Charles W. Shumway wrote two papers on glossolalia, a BA thesis entitled *A Study of 'The Gift of Tongues'*[99] and a doctoral dissertation entitled, *A Critical History of Glossolalia*.[100] Of the two, his thesis is the more important work because in it, he claims to interact extensively with Pentecostals and is closer geographically and chronologically to the ASM.[101] These works reveal Shumway as a sympathetic critic[102] who seeks to support the historical authenticity of the glossolalia in Acts 2.1-13 by use of psychology and history.[103] Though this study does not have the space to unpack the psychological and

---

[95] Hayes, *Gift of Tongues*, pp. 54-55. Occasionally 'convulsions of the soul have ... a volcanic upheaval ... (which brings) to the surface hidden strata of the subconscious life', pp. 107-15.

[96] Hayes, *Gift of Tongues*, p. 94.

[97] Hayes, *Gift of Tongues*, p. 96.

[98] Hayes, *Gift of Tongues*, p. 97. Simply put, 'it will be sane and serviceable, or it will be silent in the Churches', p. 116 (emphasis original).

[99] The 'The Gift of Tongues' is an examination of glossolalia from biblical, historical, and psychological standpoints.

[100] Charles Shumway, 'A Critical History of Glossolalia' (PhD Dissertation, Boston University, 1919). Shumway tries to 'determine the exact character of' tongues and 'how the essential characteristics of glossolalia are traceable in all the manifestations of the phenomenon from the establishment of Christianity to the present day', p. 1.

[101] He claims extensive correspondence with 'most of the world leaders of the movement', Shumway, 'The Gift of Tongues', preface. He also claims to have attended many Pentecostal gatherings. His dissertation is less significant in that one can see a secondary agenda overlaid onto the work.

[102] He predicted that 'the meridian of its (Pentecostalism's) strength and influence has been passed ... we feel safe in saying that after a few decades, possibly longer, this movement will be practically forgotten', Shumway, 'The Gift of Tongues', p. 192.

[103] For example, 'after the two following chapters are read, it will appear that both from the psychological phenomenon of subconsciousness, and from the phenomenon of hypermnesia, we have added evidence for accepting Acts 2:1-13 as history', Shumway, 'A Critical History', p. 36. See also, pp. 30, 117.

historical approaches to tongues, Shumway's work is presented here for its overlooked value and to represent these two methods of examining glossolalia.

Exegetically, Shumway dismisses Pentecostalism's biblical defence as being 'built upon distorted interpretations of the Bible … (and) certain minor passages of Scripture'.[104] Yet, at the same time Shumway does a credible job defending a conservative reading of both Luke and Acts 2.[105] Not only are Luke's qualifications and sources credible, but his intent can be trusted.[106] In his thesis, he not only trusts the Lucan account of tongues but openly gives it priority.[107] However, Shumway seems to limit authentic tongues to the outpouring on the Day of Pentecost.[108] 'The Corinthian glossolalia was more or less a discreditable degeneration of the gift of tongues' on the Day of Pentecost,[109] and Paul was desperately trying to stop the glossolalia at Corinth but was hindered.[110] In his dissertation,

---

[104] Shumway, 'The Gift of Tongues', p. 192. He argues that Jesus' singular comment about tongues in Mk 16.17, is not in the original and therefore 'there is no good reason whatever for insisting – as do our "Pentecostal" brethren – that is [sic] is a universal promise and applicable today', p. 2; cf. Shumway, 'A Critical History', p. 3.

[105] 'Luke carefully considered the sources'; was 'old enough to converse thoughtfully with … the eye witnesses'; was 'familiar with the nature of the tongues manifested in the home of Cornelius and at Ephesus'; and could write without getting tripped up by 'Hebrew impedimenta', Shumway, 'The Gift of Tongues', pp. 10-11; cf. Shumway, 'A Critical History', pp. 30-36.

[106] Shumway, 'The Gift of Tongues', p. 5; cf. Shumway, 'A Critical History', p. 34.

[107] He writes, 'we must avoid the error of testing the Acts section by Paul's practically non-committal description in 1 Cor. 14 … the Acts description is the standard by which to judge the discreditable events in the Corinthian society', Shumway, 'The Gift of Tongues', p. 4. He backtracks on this position in his dissertation, stating, 'it seems best to take up the Corinthian account first because it is older and first-hand, while that in Acts … is later and second-hand', Shumway, 'A Critical History', p. 4.

[108] Shumway, 'The Gift of Tongues', p. 59. For example, he notes that in Corinth there may have been 'a very small amount of the genuine speaking in tongues by a very few', Shumway, 'The Gift of Tongues', p. 64. He notes that 'several Jewish traditions respecting forms of glossolalia are found', but all of these are metaphors for the voice of God, p. 7; cf. 'A Critical History', pp. 28-35.

[109] Shumway, 'The Gift of Tongues', p. 59. He also observes that at best the Corinthian tongues 'required the services of an interpreter', Shumway, 'A Critical History', p. 24.

[110] 'In his own heart, Paul wished ardently that speaking in tongues as it was carried on at Corinth might utterly cease', Shumway, 'The Gift of Tongues', p. 65.

written on the east coast of the USA, far from the ASM revival, he reverses his early work and gives priority to Paul's glossolalia, stating that all glossolalia must meet the four tests laid out in 1 Corinthians by Paul.[111]

Shumway uses contemporary psychology to argue the genuineness of glossolalia on the Day of Pentecost.[112] After all, 'the Holy Spirit ... use (s) every possible power latent in the human being to magnify and exalt Christ'.[113] Exalted memory or cryptomnesia is the theory of a 'memory deposit' from a forgotten childhood language or causally overheard sounds or foreign words that can be recalled in an 'up-rush' of emotions:[114] 'we ... suppose that their utterances in tongues were mere snatches from the prayers of the hymnology of the Temple worship'[115] and it was these 'foreign languages which were instantly recognized by visitors from many lands'.[116] Shumway prefers xenolalia[117] because it is verifiable, whereas ecstatic glossolalia is suspect.[118] Ecstatic tongues 'readily

---

[111] Shumway, 'A Critical History', p. 12. The four tests are: usefulness, relative importance, order and propriety in public worship and control in individual cases.

[112] Two additional theories are: 1) the 'miracle of hearing', which is the psychic transfer of an impression, Shumway, 'The Gift of Tongues', pp. 50-58. A handwritten note by the author states that his position regarding this theory has modified, excluding it as a viable option, p. 50. This additional theory is not mentioned in his dissertation. 2) The theory of 'contagious influences in crowds', pp. 160-165.

[113] Shumway, 'The Gift of Tongues', p. 58.

[114] Shumway, 'The Gift of Tongues', pp. 23-30; cf. Shumway, 'A Critical History', pp. 51-68. Following the psychology of William James, he believes that it is possible to become so obsessed with a thought that a trigger, or an 'up-rush', will cause the thought to become reality – which for those seeking a personal Pentecost is ecstatic tongues, Shumway, 'The Gift of Tongues', pp. 12-18; cf. Shumway, 'A Critical History', pp. 37-50.

[115] Shumway, 'The Gift of Tongues', pp. 30, 58. In his dissertation he is somewhat open to ecstatic glossolalia, because in a polyglottal city like Jerusalem 'no amount of ... foreign language in the public worship would produce the impression that the worshippers were mad', Shumway, 'A Critical History', p. 8.

[116] Shumway, 'The Gift of Tongues', p. 2.

[117] He gives four reasons why the early church fathers thought of glossolalia as foreign languages: 1) gloss can mean word of foreign speech. 2) The theory of exalted memory supports foreign language. 3) Sometimes the tongues at Corinth were interpreted. 4) Paul's 'tongues of men and angels (1 Cor. 13.1)', Shumway, 'The Gift of Tongues', pp. 62-63.

[118] At times, Shumway is open to ecstatic glossolalia, but he is largely critical of it, Shumway, 'A Critical History', p. 19. For example, Miss Hall's testimony,

lends itself to counterfeiting and … has special attraction for those who are immature spiritually'.[119] Shumway is critical of Pentecostals 'who went to foreign fields expecting to be able to preach by miraculous power in the native languages of the people … (because there is) not one well attested instance where the success was met can be located'.[120] He even followed up on Parham's claims of xenolalia and found a local pastor in Topeka who said that, 'there were no convincing proofs produced that the "speaking in tongues" was nearly all that was claimed for it'.[121]

Historically, Shumway seeks to affirm a conservative reading of Acts 2 and its xenolalia by reviewing a continuous thread of historical occurrences culminating in Pentecostalism. The bulk of his thesis traces ecstatic movements through history to the ASM revival.[122] Pentecostal tongues are 'simply a recrudescence of others … that have budded, blossomed, faded, and disappeared'.[123]

Though not a work of theology, Shumway makes two theological observations. First, he doubts that tongues have any evidentiary value. He writes, these signs 'may have served as credentials for the Gospel in the minds of those primitive believers, but other recommendations are needed, and are much more justly required, today'.[124] Second, he notes a connection between ecstatic glossolalia and 'second advent premillennialism':

all throughout Christian history those who have come to

Shumway, 'The Gift of Tongues', pp. 137-38. Miss Hall, later renounced her experience as being of 'Satanic in origin', p. 137 n. He adds, 'the theory is current among the greater part of the "Pentecostal" following that the less control they have over their actions and speech, the more it shows the Holy Spirit to be in control of them', Shumway, 'A Critical History', p. 14.

[119] Shumway, 'The Gift of Tongues', p. 62.
[120] Shumway, 'The Gift of Tongues', p. 181.
[121] Shumway, 'The Gift of Tongues', p. 168. At times he reports 'dead ends' on his research. For example, the newspaper reporter who wrote of xenolalia in Parham's Houston crusade 'cannot now be identified', because the staff had changed (p. 171, n). He confirms a news report of xenolalia in an Indian orphanage that has 'been corroborated by other visitors', but he quickly dismisses it as a case of 'exalted memory', where the girls merely recalled sounds and prayers from the other girls who spoke different native languages (p. 185). When contacted, this reporter stood by what he wrote.
[122] Shumway, 'The Gift of Tongues', pp. 74-193; cf. Shumway, 'A Critical History', pp. 75-111.
[123] Shumway, 'The Gift of Tongues', p. 117; cf. p. 192.
[124] Shumway, 'The Gift of Tongues', p. 2.

'speak in tongues' have been ardent believers that they were living in the last days. They have believed that Christ was very soon to appear ... I have never found the least trace of a person who claimed to speak in tongues who was not a premillennial second Adventist *through and through*.[125]

The rallying cry of the ASM revival, 'Jesus is coming', arose from a literal interpretation of Scripture[126] which was coupled with an eschatological expectation: 'the return of the gifts of the Spirit ... (is) *a sign that the day of Advent*' is at hand.[127]

Bennett F. Lawrence, 1916

Bennett F. Lawrence's monograph[128] is the first official history from within an established Pentecostal denomination. Lawrence begins with the statement, it 'was the doctrine of the primitive church that there was a definite experience (of the Spirit) subsequent to regeneration'.[129] His defence is made by an analogous pattern[130] of Nicodemus, Peter, and the disciples all having salvific faith before they were Spirit baptized like the Samaritans in Acts eight.[131] The result of SB is the sign of tongues,[132] guidance of the Spirit, deeper revelation and the presence of God;[133] the outward

---

[125] Shumway, 'The Gift of Tongues', p. 21. There is one exception: an ecstatic group in Kentucky in the 1800's which had 'ecstatic song', but did not speak in tongues. He explains that an 'apparent absence of the strong millennial note ... (is) quite probably the explanation of the absence of the "tongues," as well as of "prophecy"', cf. Shumway, 'A Critical History', p. 48.

[126] Shumway, 'The Gift of Tongues', pp. 20, 173 n.

[127] Shumway, 'The Gift of Tongues', p. 129.

[128] B.F. Lawrence, *The Apostolic Faith Restored: A History of the Present Latter Rain Outpouring of the Holy Spirit Known as the Apostolic Pentecostal Movement* (St. Louis, MO: The Gospel Publishing House, 1916).

[129] Lawrence, *Apostolic Faith Restored*, p. 17.

[130] '[L]et us stop our quibbling and follow the example of our predecessors in the faith', Lawrence, *Apostolic Faith Restored*, p. 20.

[131] Lawrence, *Apostolic Faith Restored*, p. 20. Here he notes the timing of SB of Paul and the disciples at Ephesus in Acts 19.

[132] He works from the gift of tongues to the 'sign of tongues', meaning that the gifts are for edifying the church when interpreted, but 'several manifestations ... do not seem to fit the above (gift pattern) perfectly; and we have called such manifestations "the sign of tongues"', Lawrence, *Apostolic Faith Restored*, p. 27. Singing in the Spirit holds an honourable place and at times is even considered the IE in lieu of spoken glossolalia, cf. pp. 7, 93, 108.

[133] Yet, he writes 'we know that tongues are not the evidence of a mature Christian character', Lawrence, *Apostolic Faith Restored*, p. 36.

effect from the believer is a more effective witness.[134] His position on the Bible evidence is to 'observe that we do not say that the speaking in other tongues is the only evidence of the baptism, it is the initial one'.[135] Besides being an evidence, the ongoing purpose of tongues is to 'edify and bless the speaker' and, only when it is interpreted in the assembly will it bless the church.[136] As for the nature of glossolalia, xenolalia occurred on the Day of Pentecost, but it *is never reported as happening again*' in the Bible.[137] Lawrence affirms glossolalia as an eschatological sign.[138]

Conclusion to the Early Literature, 1888 to 1929

Broadly speaking, in this early literature, one can see: 1) the nascent theology of Pentecostal glossolalia and 2), anti-Pentecostal exegetical literature. However, the bulk of literature from non-Pentecostals during this time period examines tongues in history, and various psychological theories. Due to space limitations, Shumway's works are presented here as representative of most of the non-Pentecostal writings.

II. Mid-Century Literature, 1930 to 1969

There are relatively few theological works on glossolalia during this period. The non-Pentecostal works are largely exegetical and support cessationism or are psychological and give pathological definitions of glossolalia. The exceptions are notable. Meanwhile, most of the Pentecostal literature during this time was written for an informed reader rather than for scholarly pursuits. Pentecostal authors either continued to refine and develop their theology of glossolalia largely independent of non-Pentecostal influence[139] or

---

[134] Lawrence, *Apostolic Faith Restored*, pp. 22-24.
[135] Lawrence, *Apostolic Faith Restored*, p. 28.
[136] Lawrence, *Apostolic Faith Restored*, pp. 26-27.
[137] Lawrence, *Apostolic Faith Restored*, p. 26. He reports that xenolalia occasionally occurs, pp. 82-83, 103, 108.
[138] Lawrence, *Apostolic Faith Restored*, p. 31.
[139] For example, Charles Conn's *Pillars of Pentecost*, is a collection of sermons that counters two pressure points upon Pentecostal glossolalia, cessationism and psychology: to counter cessationism, he appeals to the latter rain metaphor, Charles W. Conn, *Pillars of Pentecost* (Cleveland, TN: Pathway Press, 1956), pp. 57, 66; cf. pp. 67-77. To counter the idea of tongues as a psychological pathology, he appeals to Pentecost as reversing Babel: their speech was 'in clear, precise, understandable languages ... not in unintelligible gibberish', which has no

simply wrote histories of Pentecostalism.[140]

Filled with the Fullness of God, 1930

Filled with the Fullness of God is a compilation of various authors.[141] Donald Gee notes that glossolalia is the 'utterance of those carried beyond the reach of ordinary expression by the fullness of the glory of this divine baptism in the blessed Spirit'.[142] He encourages readers to seek a 'flooding of the soul with the glory of His presence'.[143] Arthur Frodsham defines glossolalia as 'speaking sacred secrets with an absent lover that our natural mind or understanding is not allowed to enter into or grasp ... (it is) a language used in initiation into a secret society, a spiritual language for a spiritual purpose'.[144] We are to consider the difference between the incompleteness of a written letter from a faraway son or daughter as compared to a face to face conversation.[145] B.C. Miller holds that biblically there 'was some immediate evidence by which those present could determine whether the baptism of the Spirit was given' and 'that it is clear that all who receive the baptism did speak in tongues'.[146] He encourages his readers to experience SB for themselves to really understand.[147]

---

psychological explanation because they were 'supernatural' languages, pp. 53, 57. Also, Robert C. Dalton's book counters three main criticisms against Pentecostal glossolalia: 1) cessationism, Robert Chandler Dalton, *Tongues Like as of Fire: A Critical Study of Modern Tongue Movements in the Light of Apostolic and Patristic Times* (Springfield, MO: Gospel Publishing House, 1945), pp. 15-51; 2) exegetical issues, pp. 99-106, 107-13; and 3) emotionalism, pp. 59, 121; cf. pp. 52-60.

[140] Frodsham states his work is 'a fuller and more accurate account' than Lawrence's *Apostolic Faith Restored* (Frodsham, *With Signs Following*, Forward).

[141] There are testimonies by two popular preachers: Smith Wigglesworth, 'A Transformation' in *Filled with the Fullness of God* (Springfield, MO: 1930), pp. 3-14; P.C. Nelson, 'My Baptism in the HolySpirit' in *Filled with the Fullness of God* (Springfield, MO: 1930), pp. 47-55.

[142] Donald Gee, 'Immersed in the Fullness of God', in *Filled with the Fullness of God* (Springfield, MO: 1930), pp. 35-44 (41).

[143] Gee, 'Immersed', p. 40.

[144] Arthur W. Frodsham, 'What is the Use of Speaking in Tongues', in *Filled with the Fullness of God* (Springfield, MO: 1930), pp. 56-62 (59).

[145] Frodsham, 'What is the Use', p. 56.

[146] B.C. Miller, 'The Baptism in the Holy Spirit. What? When? Where?', in *Filled with the Fullness of God* (Springfield, MO: 1930), pp. 15-34 (28-29).

[147] Miller, 'The Baptism', pp. 15, 33, 34.

John Mauchline, 1938

In this article, John Mauchline believes individual ecstasy can be a rich experience that surrounds 'a revelation of truth' that may or not be translatable after the experience.[148] The seeker alone can evaluate the experience.[149] He reminds his readers that the mystic Paul discouraged the practice in Corinth and Mauchline tells his readers that not many will come into God's presence and experience the '*mysterium tremendum*'.[150]

W.H. Turner, 1939

Writing from China, W.H. Turner sets out to show that glossolalia was both scriptural[151] and historical.[152] His biblical polemics follow the pattern from the book of Acts[153] and Jesus' promises in John and Mk 16.17.[154] In Jn 16.13, 'Jesus declares twice that the Holy Spirit, when He shall have come, will SPEAK'.[155] Moreover, Mk 16.17, clearly states that the disciples were 'given a sign whereby they would know when the Holy Spirit had come, namely, He would SPEAK FOR HIMSELF'.[156]

---

[148] John Mauchline, 'Ecstasy', *The Expository Times* 49 (1938), pp. 295-96 (298). He defines ecstasy as being 'temporarily alienated from the physical and sensible world, and enters into rapport with a whole field of consciousness which is denied him in his normal state', p. 295.

[149] Mauchline, 'Ecstasy', p. 297. Or are 'self-centred', p. 298.

[150] Mauchline, 'Ecstasy', p. 299.

[151] He notes that opponents of Pentecost use 'the most unorthodox method of Bible interpretation and exegesis', and 'have succeeded in convincing themselves that it is entirely unnecessary to speak in tongues', W.H. Turner, *Pentecost and Tongues: The Doctrine and History* (Shanghai Modern Publishing House, 1939), p. 50.

[152] Spirit Baptism with tongues is 'not a new doctrine, or religious manifestation, but has always reoccurred in the church, when people have earnestly sought for the infilling of the Holy Spirit, and is therefore a normal Christian experience', Turner, *Pentecost and Tongues*, preface. He devotes three chapters to citing historical occurrences throughout church history and of the spread of the present Pentecostal revival, pp. 99-154.

[153] He cites the pattern in the book of Acts three times, Turner, *Pentecost and Tongues*, pp. 39-46; 57-71; 81-98.

[154] Turner gives as much weight to Jesus' promises in John and Mk 16.17 as he does Luke, including: 1) Jesus' command to seek the infilling and that up to Pentecost 'the Holy Ghost was not yet given', Jn 7.37-39; 2) Jesus' promise that the Holy Spirit will 'testify', that is, speak on his own behalf, Jn 15.26-27; 3) The promise of power, Lk. 24.49, Turner, *Pentecost and Tongues*, pp. 31-36; 54-56.

[155] Turner, *Pentecost and Tongues*, p. 55 (emphasis original).

[156] Turner, *Pentecost and Tongues*, p. 56 (emphasis original).

Ira Jay Martin, III, 1944

In this short exegetical survey entitled, *Glossolalia in the Apostolic Church*, Ira J. Martin seeks to 'trace the stages and development of glossolalia and its place and significance in the life of the first generation of Christians'.[157] At Pentecost, 'possession of the Spirit became the highest standard of Christian experience, and ecstatic speech became the chief evidence of this possession'.[158] The remaining passages from Acts shows that tongues 'seems to have been the final proof of the presence of the Spirit'.[159] Though Paul still practiced it twenty-five years after Pentecost and recognized it as one of the gifts of the Spirit, it is the least significant[160] and 'should have no place in the public worship'.[161] Other NT passages 'indicate a widespread persistence of this phenomenon in the early days of the Christian Church', and even if Mk 16.17 is taken as a latter addition, it still attests to glossolalia's popularity.[162] Martin makes six conclusions: 1) at the beginning, glossolalia functions as 'proof or manifestation of possession by the Spirit';[163] 2) the nature is ecstatic with occasional 'intelligible ejaculations';[164] 3) 'its value was ... not in its message, but in its demonstrative quality';[165] 4) tongues became proof 'of having received the Spirit ... (a) *sine qua non* ... for all the followers of Jesus';[166] 5) Paul 'regarded it as quite inferior to the others ... his regulations and restrictions almost eliminated it from the public worship';[167] 6) because of the pride that comes with the experience, love and the fruit of the Spirit are the standard of the Christian life, and that 'history

---

[157] Ira Jay Martin, III, 'Glossolalia in the Apostolic Church', *Journal of Biblical Literature* 63.2 (June 1944), pp. 123-30 (124).

[158] Martin, 'Glossolalia in the Apostolic Church', p. 124. Following A. Harnack, he believes that Acts 4.31 is an 'abbreviated "doublet"' and therefore assumes that some of the speaking was ecstatic, pp. 124-25.

[159] Martin, 'Glossolalia in the Apostolic Church', p. 125.

[160] Martin, 'Glossolalia in the Apostolic Church', p. 125.

[161] Martin, 'Glossolalia in the Apostolic Church', p. 126.

[162] Martin, 'Glossolalia in the Apostolic Church', p. 126.

[163] Martin, 'Glossolalia in the Apostolic Church', pp. 126-27.

[164] Martin, 'Glossolalia in the Apostolic Church', p. 128.

[165] Martin, 'Glossolalia in the Apostolic Church', p. 128.

[166] Martin, 'Glossolalia in the Apostolic Church', pp. 128-29.

[167] Martin, 'Glossolalia in the Apostolic Church', p. 129. It was something to be practiced in private devotions.

has vindicated the wisdom of Paul's attitude'.[168]

Carl Brumback, 1947

Carl Brumback's work sought to be a comprehensive account of tongues and was an important Pentecostal text for many years.[169] The first half of the book addresses the criticisms of Pentecostalism, what tongues are not.[170] Brumback then defends five theses on glossolalia:[171] 1) the pattern of tongues found in the book of Acts[172] is 'the standard for believers today … the pattern for every similar baptism or charismatic enduement' that is, the reception of power.[173] 2) God chose

---

[168] Martin, 'Glossolalia in the Apostolic Church', p. 130.

[169] Carl Brumback, *'What Meaneth This?' A Pentecostal Answer to a Pentecostal Question* (Springfield, MO: Gospel Publishing House, 1947), pp. 8, 10.

[170] 1) Glossolalia is not always xenolalia, Brumback, *'What Meaneth This?'*, pp. 35-38; 2) tongues does not erupt from humankind's subconscious or forgotten memories, pp. 39-51; 3) they did not cease upon completion of the NT canon, pp. 59-87; 4) they are not absent from church history, pp. 89-96; 5) there is a difference between having emotions and fanaticism, pp. 97-114; 6) Pentecostals are not filled with the devil, pp. 117-46; and 7), glossolalia was not 'disparaged' by Paul, pp. 147-79.

[171] Simply stated, glossolalia reveals the presence of the Spirit of God, Brumback, *'What Meaneth This?'*, p. 231, cf. p. 225.

[172] Pentecost is the pattern, Brumback, *'What Meaneth This?'*, p. 198. Because Simon saw something at Samaria (Acts 8), 'the Pentecostal "evidence doctrine" can be sustained despite the absence of mention of tongues', p. 206. At Damascus (Acts 9), Paul's filling with the Holy Spirit does not mention tongues, but his testimony in 1 Cor. 14.18 infers that 'speaking with tongues was the accepted evidence of the filling of the Spirit among the apostles and the other brethren in Jerusalem', p. 217, cf. pp. 215-7. At Caesarea (Acts 10, 11), tongues are the evidence of the Spirit's presence. He notes that non-Pentecostals 'are so absorbed by the racial and dispensational aspects of this occasion that they overlook the evidential character of the tongues', p. 220. Because there was no racial significance at Ephesus (Acts 19), it is clear that 'glossolalia was not given to authenticate Christian baptism but to … establish the supernatural fact of the infilling of the Ephesians with the Holy Ghost', p. 225.

[173] Brumback, *'What Meaneth This?'*, pp. 186, 197-98. He notes that in all the five cases in the book of Acts, 'it is evident that all spoke with tongues at some time during their Spirit-filled life'. The Pentecostal doctrine is 'almost certain' in four of the five cases, and 'is absolutely certain' in three of the five cases, pp. 229-30. In chapter 18 of *Suddenly … From Heaven* he gives the history of Fred Bosworth and the early conflict of IE. He concludes: 'it would appear that … unless one is Pentecostal in his belief concerning speaking in tongues as the evidence … he does not believe in tongues at all', because, many who take the position that tongues is only one of the evidences 'feared to commit to any form of tongues at all', Brumback, *Suddenly … From Heaven*, pp. 223-24, 223.

tongues because it is an external evidence.[174] 3) His defence of IE is: a) even though God is creative, 'there was also a uniformity in that every recipient spoke with tongues';[175] b) other gifts of the Spirit are not the initial infilling according to the pattern from Acts, especially with Peter's ironclad declaration, 'they heard them speak with tongues';[176] c) love is an evidence of the Spirit, but can only be seen over time, and 'the New Testament believers ... could tell immediately';[177] d) scriptures calls the need for a sign a weakness in faith, but at other times it is 'a mark of genuineness in the experience of others'.[178] 4) Initial evidence and the gift of tongues are distinct in purpose and operation: a) in the book of Acts, tongues was to 'make manifest to the recipient and onlooker that the Holy Ghost had been given'; and in Corinth, it was for 'the personal edification of the speaker, and, when coupled with interpretation, the edification of the hearers';[179] b) not all have the gift of tongues, but all have the potential;[180] and c) without this distinction, 'we find the apostles in Acts in conflict with these (Paul's) instructions'.[181]

---

[174] He gives three reasons: 1) 'as long as man is subject to earthly frailties, he is in need of at least a few outward symbols of truth', such as the Lord's Supper and water baptism, Brumback, *What Meaneth This?*, p. 236. 2) Tongues are a uniform evidence that reveals the personality of the Spirit, and the yieldedness of the speaker to the Spirit, pp. 239-40. 3) They are a promise of the eschatological 'completion of our redemption ... (when) all shall speak one pure and mighty human language', pp. 245-46.

[175] Brumback, *What Meaneth This?*, p. 249, cf. pp. 247-49.

[176] Brumback, *What Meaneth This?*, pp. 249-52. Tongues were 'distinctly associated with the filling with the Holy Spirit at Jerusalem, Caesarea, and Ephesus', p. 251. Prophecy played a role on one or two occasions but 'was never given as the only evidence', p. 251.

[177] Brumback, *What Meaneth This?*, p. 252.

[178] Brumback, *What Meaneth This?*, pp. 252-55.

[179] Brumback, *What Meaneth This?*, pp. 265-66.

[180] First Corinthians 12.30's implied negative, 'no, not everyone speaks with tongues', must be harmonized with Mk 16.17's 'impression that all may speak in tongues, if they will only believe', Brumback, *What Meaneth This?*, p. 267.

[181] Brumback, *What Meaneth This?*, p. 268. 'There was no demand for interpretation in Caesarea by Peter, or at Ephesus by Paul' because tongues announced 'the arrival of the Spirit', p. 269. Other discrepancies with Corinth arise without this distinction: The 120 were 'out of order' on the Day of Pentecost because more than 3 were speaking at one time; and the exultation of tongues in Acts did not make for an orderly worship service, pp. 268-70.

5) There is a distinction between personal and public glossolalia.[182]

In conclusion, Brumback believes that 'divine confirmation of the message with miraculous signs' such as glossolalia will awaken the nations to the gospel.[183] At the same time, it is a warning that without a passion for an apostolic spirituality, this great truth could be 'sealed up' for a period.[184]

C.S. Lewis, 1949

Literary giant C.S. Lewis sought an answer to the question of tongues. The problem is that glossolalia was 'an intermittent "variety of religious experience"' in history[185] and 'the very same phenomenon which is sometimes not only natural but even pathological is at other times ... the organ of the Holy Ghost'.[186] He proposes that everything supernatural is limited by our 'lower natures' ability to comprehend and receive things of a 'higher nature':[187] 'the lower medium can only be understood if we know the higher medium'; therefore, 'those who spoke with tongues ... can well understand (how) that holy phenomenon differed from the hysterical phenomenon – although be it remembered, they were in a sense exactly the same phenomena'.[188] He illustrates this principle of 'transposition' with how common bread and wine are 'trans-

---

[182] Tongues for personal devotions is prayer at a deeper level that unlocks 'our own nature to us' and accesses spiritual power, Brumback, *What Meaneth This?*, pp. 291, cf. pp. 292-98. For the public gift of tongues, see pp. 299-317.

[183] Brumback, *What Meaneth This?*, p. 323, cf. pp. 321-45.

[184] He is addressing the restoration of the miraculous here and notes the loss of even the doctrine of justification by faith for a period of time, Brumback, *What Meaneth This?*, p. 278.

[185] Clives Staples Lewis, 'Transposition' in *The Weight of Glory and Other Addresses* (San Francisco: HarperCollins Publishers, 2001), pp. 91-115 (91).

[186] Lewis, 'Transposition', p. 93.

[187] 'The critique of every experience from below, the voluntary ignoring of meaning and concentration on fact, will always have the same plausibility. There will always be evidence ... to show that religion is only psychological, justice only self-protection, politics only economics, love only lust, and thought itself only cerebral biochemistry', Lewis, 'Transposition', pp. 114, 115. Said another way, 'tongues represent "a lower structure ... penetrated with higher meaning"', Matthew Wolf in Randall Holm, Matthew Wolf and James K.A. Smith, 'New Frontiers in Tongues Research: A Symposium', *JPT* 20 (2011), pp. 122-54 (134).

[188] Lewis, 'Transposition', pp. 110, 105; cf. p. 104.

posed' into something supernatural in the Eucharist,[189] giving 'an appropriate correspondence on the sensory level'.[190]

J.G. Davies, 1952 & Robert H. Gundry, 1966

These two short articles are treated together because Robert Gundry claims his piece is a 'restatement' of J.D. Davies.[191]

Davies attempts to define the nature of glossolalia solely as the foreign speech of Acts 2 and not the ecstatic speech as in 'revivalist meetings'.[192] He believes the result of defining tongues as ecstatic speech has been to elevate Paul at the expense of Luke.[193] His primary argument is the parallel in the Septuagint (LXX) between Luke's account of the Day of Pentecost and the scattering of humankind at Babel in Gen. 11.1-9. He argues: 1) it is 'quite evident' that the Day of Pentecost is 'the reunification of mankind ... (because) the account of Pentecost is dependent upon the account of Babel';[194] 2) the Septuagint's use of parallel terms makes an obvious connection to Babel; 3) if one were to remove verses 6b-11 from Acts 2, 'the remaining narrative would still involve the identification of glossolalia with speaking in foreign tongues'.[195]

---

[189] Lewis, 'Transposition', p. 94. There are many analogies in this essay, but the two primary ones are: 1) the emotion of a sublime piece of music (higher) having the same effect in our physical being as being woozy on a roller-coaster (lower), pp. 95-98, and 2) a two-dimensional pencil drawing which attempts to represent three-dimensional reality, pp. 99-100, 109-10.

[190] Lewis, 'Transposition', p. 115. Specifically, 'if you are to translate from a language which has a large vocabulary into a language that has a small vocabulary, then you must be allowed to use several words in more than one sense', p. 99.

[191] Robert H. Gundry, 'Ecstatic Utterance (NEB)', *Journal of Theological Studies* 17.2 (1966), pp. 299-307 (299).

[192] John G. Davies, 'Pentecost and Glossolalia', *Journal of Theological Studies* 3.2 (1952), pp. 228-31 (228). He writes, 'it may be contended that the evidence of 1 Cor. 14 ... does suggest the undeniable phenomena of revivalist meetings. But why confine oneself to the (ecstatic glossolalia of) revivalist meetings?', p. 231.

[193] Davies argues: 1) one has to assume that the author of Acts was 'not a close companion of St. Paul and unacquainted with the phenomenon' or 2) that a 'hypothetical editor is responsible for interpolating the whole section, verses 6b-11', Davies, 'Pentecost and Glossolalia', p. 228.

[194] Davies, 'Pentecost and Glossolalia', p. 228. The Babel story involves the fragmentation of a single language into multiple because it was 'man-centered'; whereas at Pentecost 'there are many spoken which, nevertheless, are understood in unison by the hearers' because they spoke of 'the mighty works of God', p. 229.

[195] Davies, 'Pentecost and Glossolalia', p. 229.

Further, it is plausible that Paul understood glossolalia as foreign languages because: 1) 'interpretation' could simply mean it 'is unintelligible to the majority of people';[196] and 2) of the twenty-one instances that 'translate/interpret' (ἑρμηνεύειν) and its cognates are used, eighteen strongly suggest the translating of foreign languages.[197] He writes, 'there seems, therefore, to be no adequate reason for denying that St. Paul understood glossolalia to be speaking in foreign languages ... (and) there is no conflict between his description and the accounts in Acts 2'.[198]

Robert H. Gundry takes umbrage with the New English Bible's use of the phrase 'ecstatic utterance' instead of speaking in tongues (languages) for 1 Corinthians 12-14, and seeks to limit glossolalia solely to xenolalia.[199] Gundry believes that 'the Apostle Paul does not look upon or describe the phenomenon as ecstatic utterance, but as the miraculously given ability to speak a human language foreign to the speaker.'[200] He adds to Davies' thesis: 1) throughout the NT and Greek literature generally, tongue 'refers to meaningful human speech' and that to say that it is a technical word for obscure speech is an overstatement;[201] and 2) Luke intends to convey foreign languages in Acts 2.6-11, and 'the association of Luke with Paul makes it very likely that Luke's presenta-

---

[196] Davies, 'Pentecost and Glossolalia', pp. 229-31. Paul's discussion of musical instruments and the need for notes to be distinct from other notes is moot because Paul is making an analogy that the human voice also must produce sounds that can be understood: 'indeed, from verse 19 it is quite apparent that St. Paul considered it possible to enunciate words in a tongue, although the majority would not understand them', p. 231. Gundry says that this point is well made, Gundry, 'Ecstatic Utterance', p. 300.

[197] Davies, 'Pentecost and Glossolalia', p. 230. Including Paul's use of Isa. 28.11-12, where 'the invading Assyrians whose unintelligible language will be heard by the Israelites as judgment on them' and Paul argues that in the same way glossolalia is a sign of judgment upon unbelievers, p. 230. This theme of an unfamiliar language as a sign of judgment is found a total of four times (Isa. 28.11-12; 33.19; Deut. 28.49; Jer. 5.15).

[198] Davies, 'Pentecost and Glossolalia', p. 231.

[199] Gundry notes in a footnote that Davies 'put too much weight on the argument that Luke makes Pentecost reverse Babel', Gundry, 'Ecstatic Utterance', p. 299.

[200] Gundry says this regardless of whether or not the phenomenon is similar to either Hellenistic religions or OT Prophetism, Gundry, 'Ecstatic Utterance', p. 299.

[201] Gundry, 'Ecstatic Utterance', p. 300. He writes, 'only very strong evidence ... can overthrow the natural understanding'.

tion of glossolalia reflects Paul's own understanding of the phenomenon'.[202]

From supporting Luke's account of languages at Pentecost, Gundry turns to debunk the arguments for ecstatic speech in Corinth: 1) Paul's tongues of men and of angels[203] 'corresponds to the unreal *"all's"* in the succeeding statements' and 'indicates that he does not here claim to do so'.[204] 2) Paul's 'mysteries'[205] are unintelligible only because 'neither the speaker nor anyone else in the congregation happens to have the gift of interpretation'.[206] 3) As an 'authenticating sign' the amazement factor 'depended upon its *difference* from the ecstatic gobbledegook [sic] in Hellenistic religion'!'[207] 4) To λαλ- does not always refer to incoherent babbling in Hellenistic times.[208] 5) The charges of drunkenness and madness along with the call to orderliness[209] are not 'tell-tale indications of ecstasy'.[210] 6) Paul talks about the world having many languages

---

[202] Gundry, 'Ecstatic Utterance', p. 300.

[203] First Corinthians 13.1.

[204] Gundry, 'Ecstatic Utterance', p. 301. Such as, if I have '*all* faith', or 'give away *all* I have', or 'deliver my body to be burned', 1 Cor. 13.2-3.

[205] Cf. 1 Cor. 14.2. 'The term "mystery" certainly does not indicate ecstasy', Gundry, 'Ecstatic Utterance', p. 303.

[206] Gundry, 'Ecstatic Utterance', p. 302. 'Personal edification' for Gundry is speaking to oneself in a known language for the 'private emotions of the speaker', see also, 1 Cor. 14.9, 14-19. Corinth would not contain 'numbers of people with varied linguistic backgrounds … therefore the need for someone with the miraculous ability to translate', p. 303.

[207] Gundry, 'Ecstatic Utterance', p. 303. Gundry somewhat undercuts his own argument when he writes that neither in Acts nor in 1 Corinthians are tongues '*presented as the overcoming of a communications barrier*', rather, glossolalia is presented primarily as a '*convincing miracle, only secondarily as the communication of a message; for communication alone could be accomplished more easily without "other tongues"*', Gundry, 'Ecstatic Utterance', pp. 303-304.

[208] Gundry, 'Ecstatic Utterance', p. 304. Even Paul uses this root referring to speaking 'with the mind (1 Cor. 14.19)' over against an uninterpreted tongue; as prophetic speech that is understood (1 Cor. 14.29); and even uses this root in his prohibition of women speaking in the assembly (1 Cor. 14.34-35).

[209] Acts 2.13; 1 Cor. 14.23; 14.27.

[210] He parses both Luke and Paul here. Luke: on the Day of Pentecost in Jerusalem, there were 'Palestinian Jews who did not understand the foreign languages being spoken … mistook those languages for drunken babbling. By contrast the non-Palestinian Jews recognized the languages with astonishment', Gundry, 'Ecstatic Utterance', p. 304. This is specifically contrary to Beare's opinion that they were permanent residents of Jerusalem. Gundry believes that Luke's phrases in Acts 2: 'residents of Mesopotamia (v. 9)', 'visitors from Rome (v. 10)' along with 'proselytes (v. 10)', 'men of Judah' and 'all who dwell in Jeru-

and if the language is unknown, the speaker is foreign to him; therefore, 'it should be clear that he thinks of the gift of tongues as miraculous speaking in unlearned human languages'.[211]

William G. Bellshaw, 1963

This exegetical article seeks to give reasons for the confusion surrounding tongues.[212] William G. Bellshaw holds a cessationist view of glossolalia: tongues were necessary to accredit the first believers as a sign to unbelieving Jews, and were no longer necessary 'after the canon of the Bible was completed'.[213] He believes the fact that glossolalia is only mentioned in two books of the Bible, should give Pentecostals pause, especially since it is considered the least of the gifts.[214] The nature of glossolalia has to be xenolalia because the gift of the Holy Spirit must be something 'which could not be duplicated by human means'.[215] As a sign, glossolalia was to gain the attention of the unbelieving Jews and authenticate that the message came from God.[216] Bellshaw encourages Pentecostals to return from the excesses and accompanying 'pride and presumption'.[217]

---

salem (v. 14) 'suggest that Luke means only pilgrims who had come from elsewhere for the Festival of Pentecost and therefore residents of Jerusalem in a temporary sense', p. 300, n. 2. Paul: 1) 'if the normative practice were ecstatic, Paul's concern to avoid the charge of madness would have caused him to ban the practice outright', p. 305. 2) There was 'confusion as a result of simultaneous speaking'. 3) The ability to control oneself, to wait and keep quiet 'confirms the understanding of normative Christian glossolalia as unecstatic', p. 306.

[211] Gundry, 'Ecstatic Utterance', p. 306; cf. 1 Cor. 14.10-11.

[212] William G. Bellshaw, 'The Confusion of Tongues', BibSac 120.478 (April 1963), pp. 145-53. For example, 'a recognition of the true nature of the gift of tongues will do much to demonstrate the spuriousness of so-called exhibitions of this gift today', p. 148.

[213] Bellshaw, 'Confusion', p. 151; cf. pp. 148-52. He reasons: 1) the 'perfect one' referred to in 1 Cor. 13.9 is not Christ but the NT because the adjective's gender is neuter rather than masculine; 2) partial knowing and prophesying points directly to the 'incomplete nature of the revealed Word of God', p. 151; 3) 'With the completion of the New Testament there no longer was a need for men to be used as instrumentalities to give forth God's authoritative message', p. 151.

[214] Bellshaw, 'Confusion', p. 146.

[215] Bellshaw, 'Confusion', pp. 147-48.

[216] Bellshaw never addresses how the unbeliever is supposed to know that the person speaking is speaking a language that is unknown to the speaker, Bellshaw, 'Confusion', p. 148. It is also curious that he would limit the audience for the sign, especially in the Greek city of Corinth, Bellshaw, 'Confusion', p. 149.

[217] Bellshaw, 'Confusion', p. 153.

Frank W. Beare, 1964
Frank W. Beare concludes in his article that glossolalia is

> not regarded by any NT writer as a normal or invariable accompaniment of the life in grace, and there is no justification in the classical documents of the Christian faith for holding it to be a necessary element in the fullest spiritual development of the individual Christian or in the corporate life of the church.[218]

He arrives at this conclusion through a survey of glossolalia in the NT: 1) 'there is no reference in any of the canonical gospels to "speaking with tongues." It is never attributed to Jesus and is never promised by him'.[219] 2) There are so many problems with the book of Acts that any literal interpretation is 'patently absurd'.[220] 3) 'There can be no doubt that the main purpose of Paul is to discourage the practice of speaking with tongues among (the Corinthian) Christians'.[221] Therefore, though Paul recognizes tongues as

---

[218] Frank W. Beare, 'Speaking with Tongues: A Critical Survey of the New Testament Evidence,' *JBL* 83 (September 1964), pp. 229-46 (246).

[219] Beare, 'A Critical Survey', p. 229. Beare believes that: 1) Jesus deprecates any kind of unintelligible prayer when he says 'do not keep on babbling like the pagans (Mat. 6.7)'; 2) the longer ending in Mark is not authentic; 3) though Jesus receives the Spirit in baptism 'it does not move him to speak in tongues'; 4) Luke's Gospel is anticipatory of 'power from on high', but that power enables the speakers to 'bring conviction by their testimony'; and 5) John's rich pneumatological texts are unrelated to glossolalia, pp. 229-33.

[220] Beare, 'A Critical Survey', p. 237. For example: were there 12 or 120 present, p. 236? The tongues of fire must be 'poetic imagery', p. 236. Did they rush outside when they began to speak in tongues or did the crowd hear what was going on inside, pp. 236, 237? The multitude is symbolic as well because the entire episode of representative nations 'appears to be drawn from an astrological grouping ... according to the signs of the Zodiac', p. 237. How can one distinguish clearly a particular language when so many people were speaking at the same time, p. 237? How can Peter explain the drunken appearance as something desirable, p. 238? Additionally, following A. Harnack's theory (238), Beare believes the Acts 3 & 4 story to be more accurate than the mythical Acts 2 story which is a 'reworking under the influence of later experiences and fancy' pp. 236-37, 39. Finally, Acts 10 and 19 have different emphases from Pentecost, p. 239.

[221] Beare, 'A Critical Survey', pp. 240, 244. Three reasons for his statement: 1) 'men may be inspired by other spirits than the Spirit of God' even though they speak with tongues, so the 'test lies in the intelligible content of the utterance', p. 241. 2) The implied immaturity in 1 Corinthians 13, pp. 242, 244. 3) Paul always notes the inferior value of tongues and points to something better, pp. 243-44.

a continuing gift, it is not to be regarded as 'common to all Christians'.²²²

Hendrikus Berkhof, 1964

Hendrikus Berkhof wrote that

> for Luke, the speaking in tongues, i.e., in unknown languages, is the central gift. For Paul, on the contrary, it is a phenomenon on the fringe ... We can assume, however, that Luke would not have given the descriptions in this way unless he knew that parallel phenomena belong to the life of the Christian congregations for which he wrote.²²³

Surprisingly, he adds, 'Pentecostals are basically right when they speak of a working of the Holy Spirit beyond that which is acknowledged in the major denominations'.²²⁴

William G. MacDonald, 1964²²⁵

This short booklet was originally presented as a paper for the Evangelical Theological Society's meeting in 1963. It is a seminal work as Pentecostals and non-Pentecostals begin to dialog theologically about glossolalia.²²⁶ MacDonald's main contribution is an in-

---

²²² Beare, 'A Critical Survey', p. 246.

²²³ Hendrikus Berkhof, *The Doctrine of the Holy Spirit* (Richmond, VA: John Knox Press, 1964), pp. 87-88. He adds, 'being filled with the Spirit means to equip the individual in such a way that he becomes an instrument for the ongoing process of the Spirit in the church and the world ... the justified and sanctified are now turned, so to speak, inside out. In Acts they are turned primarily to the world; in Paul primarily to the total body of Christ', p. 89.

²²⁴ Berkhof, *The Doctrine of the Holy Spirit*, p. 87. 'The "non-Pentecostal" churches have to hear in the Pentecostal movement God summoning us, not to quench the Spirit and earnestly to desire spiritual gifts ... the Pentecostal movement is God's judgment upon a church which lost its inner growth in its outward extension ... We have to rediscover the meaning of the variety of spiritual gifts', p. 93. However, ecstasy cannot be a sign of the Spirit, 'because people in such ecstasy even can say: "Jesus is cursed"', p. 91!

²²⁵ William G. MacDonald's bio in *Paraclete* reads: 'William Graham MacDonald, ThD. Front Royal, Virginia, taught a combined 22 years at Southeastern College, Central Bible College, and Gordon College, before engaging in a full-time writing ministry', William G. MacDonald, 'Biblical Glossolalia: Theses One and Two', *Paraclete* 27.1 (Winter 1993), pp. 1-7 (2).

²²⁶ William G. MacDonald, *Glossolalia in the New Testament* (Springfield, MO: Gospel Publishing House, 1964). There have been several subsequent reprints: *The Bulletin of the Evangelical Theological Society* 7 (Spring, 1964), pp. 59-68; Watson E. Mills (ed.) *Speaking in Tongues: A Guide to Research on Glossolalia*, Grand Rapids, MI: Eerdmans, 1986, pp. 127-40.

formed Pentecostal reading of the four main passages in Acts[227] and a summary of passages in 1 Corinthians.[228] He argues that the biblical encounters of the spirit, when carefully examined in light of the *ordo salutis*, point to ongoing glossolalic fillings rather than a singular act at salvation on the Day of Pentecost, and it is therefore the same for today's believers.[229] MacDonald believes that there are external and internal manifestations. The external manifestation of tongues point to the internal dwelling of the Spirit; it is an 'attestation that the Holy Spirit was dominant *within* them', that the 'filling was prior to the speaking … (and) was consequent upon the Spirit's full possession of their faculties'.[230] He reasons further that if Pentecost is the fulfilment of the 'Father's promise and Peter's message about "the gift of the Holy Spirit" as the promise for all whom God calls is valid, then there must be something *normative* about Pentecost'.[231]

Regarding the nature of Pauline tongues, he notes that 'there is no cogent exegetical ground for making any difference in the essential character of glossolalia in Corinthians from that in Acts'.[232] However, their purposes are different: one is a sign and the other is to edify the church or individual.[233] Paul's regulation of tongues at Corinth is straightforward; nevertheless MacDonald spells it out clearly.[234]

---

[227] MacDonald's exegesis of Acts 2 reveals two Lucan metaphors, being 'filled' and speaking γλῶσσαι, MacDonald, *Glossolalia*, p. 3. He notes that four things were filled in Acts 2.1-6: the time for the Spirit to be revealed, the wind that filled the place, the multitude that filled Jerusalem, and the 120 that were filled with the Holy Spirit. γλῶσσαι is used 3 times: 1) phenomenologically of what was seen, 'fiery projections (v. 3)'; 2) the Spirit-inspired languages they spoke (v. 4), and 3) as a synonym for dialects (v. 11).

[228] For example, it contains numerous references in Greek and Latin, and an extensive chart showing how Paul carefully distinguishes between tongues for personal and public edification, MacDonald, *Glossolalia*, pp. 12-13.

[229] Specifically, Jesus breathing on the disciples (Jn 20.22) was their regeneration, Pentecost was their filling (Acts 2.4), but 'in a crisis, they *again* were "all filled with the Holy Spirit." With the result that "they spoke the word of God with boldness"', MacDonald, *Glossolalia*, pp. 2-3 (emphasis original).

[230] MacDonald, *Glossolalia*, pp. 4, 5.
[231] MacDonald, *Glossolalia*, p. 5.
[232] MacDonald, *Glossolalia*, p. 14.
[233] MacDonald, *Glossolalia*, pp. 11-14.
[234] MacDonald, *Glossolalia*, pp. 14-16.

Lastly, he counters three 'problem passages' from 1 Corinthians:[235] 1) 'where there are tongues, they will be stilled'.[236] He agrees that tongues have only a temporal existence, but, 'there is no hint here that tongues will cease *before* prophecies ... or before "knowledge" passes away, or that any of these should pass off the scene *before* the time "when that which is perfect is come"'.[237] 2) 'Do all speak in tongues?'[238] This does not refer to individuals, he writes, but regards the corporate setting and is a parallel statement to Paul's other questions: 'do all teach' or 'do all govern'.[239] 3) 'How will anyone know what you are saying'[240] is resolved by the fact that Paul insisted on an interpretation in a public setting.[241] Finally, MacDonald reminds his readers that Paul's command, 'do not forbid glossolalia ... has never been revoked'![242]

Stuart D. Currie, 1965

Stuart D. Currie seeks to discern the source and nature of biblical tongues from the early church fathers in order to determine if the present 'speaking in tongues' is the same as biblical *glossais lalein*.[243] Though he works through four possibilities,[244] he dismisses all of them and concludes that there is no way to know if contemporary speaking in tongues is the same as biblical *glossais lalein*.[245]

Conclusion to the Mid-Century Literature, 1930 to 1969

The defining element of this period is that the two streams of literature largely do not influence or engage each other, at least at a scholarly level:

---

[235] MacDonald, *Glossolalia*, pp. 16-19.
[236] 1 Corinthians 13.8.
[237] MacDonald, *Glossolalia*, p. 16 (emphasis original).
[238] 1 Corinthians 12.30.
[239] 1 Corinthians 12.14-30. MacDonald, *Glossolalia*, pp. 17-18.
[240] 1 Corinthians 14.9.
[241] 1 Corinthians 14.5, 13; cf. MacDonald, *Glossolalia*, pp. 19-20.
[242] MacDonald, *Glossolalia*, p. 20; cf. 1 Cor. 14.39.
[243] Stuart D. Currie, 'Speaking in Tongues, Early Evidence Outside the New Testament Bearing on "Glossais Lalein"', *Interpretation* 19 (1965), pp. 274-94.
[244] 1) Xenolalia, pp. 276-81; 2) non-human or angelic languages, pp. 281-84; 3) 'enigmatic' words or 'dark sayings', pp. 284-88; 4) ecstasy, pp. 288-93. Currie believes there were those who 'claimed to be Christians who did in fact utter nonsense syllables under pretended inspiration'; however, this could be confused with charlatanry, sorcery, and magic and was a 'potential source of embarrassment to the church', pp. 292, 293-94.
[245] Currie, 'Speaking in Tongues', p. 294.

for more than half of the century, because of near-universal ostracism by the larger church world, Pentecostalism developed in virtual isolation. Some Evangelicals classified Pentecostalism among the cults as late as 1950.[246]

It could also be argued that it took a few generations for scholars to be raised up from within Pentecostalism.[247] Nevertheless, just before 1970 scholars began engaging with Pentecostals and began to address subjects integral to Pentecostalism like tongues. For example, in addition to MacDonald's presentation at ETS in 1964 (above), Walter Jacob Hollenweger completed his 10-volume doctoral dissertation in 1965,[248] and Watson E. Mills wrote his dissertation: 'A Theological Interpretation of Tongues in Acts and 1 Corinthians' in 1968.[249] In 1972, it was published at a popular-level and is reviewed below.

III. Contemporary Scholarship, 1970 to 2019

After 1970, there is a veritable explosion of literature on glossolalia. Four events near 1970 mark the dawn of the present era of scholarship on the subject: 1) the founding of the Society for Pentecostal Studies,[250] 2) 'A growing number of Pentecostal scholars (who) ... strengthened Pentecostal scholarship and inspired non-Pentecostal theologians to pay more attention to the doctrine and experience of the Holy Spirit',[251] 3) The publication of *Baptism in*

---

[246] William Menzies, 'The Initial Evidence Issue: A Pentecostal Response', *AJPS* 2.2 (1999), pp. 261-78 (261).

[247] 'Editorial', *JPT* 1.1 (Jan 1992), pp. 3-5; cf. Waddell, 'Whence Pentecostal Scholarship?' p. 246.

[248] Walter Jacob Hollenweger, 'Handbuch der Pfingstbewegung' (ThD dissertation, University of Zurich, 1965).

[249] Watson E. Mills, 'A Theological Interpretation of Tongues in Acts and 1 Corinthians' (PhD dissertation, Southern Baptist Seminary, 1968).

[250] The Society for Pentecostal Studies (SPS) was founded in 1970 in Dallas, TX, William Menzies, 'Editorial', *Pneuma* 1.1 (Spring 1979), pp. 3-5 (4).

[251] F. LeRon Shults & Andrea Hollingsworth, *Guides to Theology: The Holy Spirit* (Grand Rapids, MI: Eerdmans, 2008), p. 70. Consider that 'Pentecostal scholars were given the opportunity to integrate the distinctives of Pentecostal faith with their critical research. A well-documented hallmark ... is the debate that arose in biblical studies around whether the metaphor of Spirit baptism represented initiation into the Christian community (e.g. Dunn and Max Turner) or a subsequent experience of empowerment for vocation (e.g. Roger

the Holy Spirit by James D.G. Dunn and *A Theology of the Holy Spirit* by Frederick Dale Bruner, and 4) the rise of the Charismatic Movement.[252] Due to limited space, only the most significant monographs in the area of theology will be reviewed during this period. Many important works in the area of exegesis, linguistics, psychology, and history will be engaged in the constructive section but must be omitted from this survey of literature. Eleven authors and one work with multiple authors will be reviewed.

Watson E. Mills, 1972, 1985

Watson E. Mills is a major contributor to the subject of glossolalia.[253] He is 'not a practitioner ... (but has) become part of a movement toward greater tolerance'.[254] His perspective is that 'both the New Testament narrative and church history make it impossible to deny the phenomenon',[255] so his goal is to 'set forth the theological relevance of glossolalia ... and relate the experience of tongues to the larger context of biblical theology'.[256] After examining antecedents of ecstasy,[257] the Acts accounts,[258] and the issues with

---

Stronstad and Robert Menzies)', Waddell, 'Whence Pentecostal Scholarship?' p. 246.

[252] It is recognized that the Charismatic Renewal movement predates 1970; however, by the late 1960's and early 1970's many branches of Christianity were preparing official responses to the Charismatic Renewal. For example, *Report of the Special Committee on the Work of the Holy Spirit to the 182nd General Assembly* (Philadelphia, PA: The United Presbyterian Church in the United States of America, 1970); Peter D. Hocken, 'Charismatic Movement', in Stanley Burgess (ed.), *NIDPCM* (Grand Rapids, MI: Zondervan, rev. and expanded edn, 2002), pp. 477-519 (481).

[253] Mills, 'A Theological Interpretation of Tongues in Acts and 1 Corinthians'; Watson E. Mills, *Understanding Speaking in Tongues* (Grand Rapids: Eerdman, 1972); Watson Mills, 'Glossolalia: Christianity's "Counterculture" amidst a Silent Majority', *The Christian Century* (Sep 27, 1972), pp. 949-51; Watson E. Mills, *A Theological/Exegetical Approach to Glossolalia* (Lanham: University Press of America, 1985); Watson E. Mills, *The Holy Spirit: A Bibliography* (Peabody, MA: Hendrickson, 1988).

[254] Mills, *Theological/Exegetical*, p. ix.

[255] Mills, 'Counterculture', p. 950.

[256] Mills, *Theological/Exegetical*, p. 3.

[257] Mills believes that 'frenzied speech did exist prior to the Christian era, but it is too hypothetical to postulate that this speech was the same as that in Acts and 1 Corinthians', Mills, *Understanding*, p. 24; cf. Mills, *Theological/Exegetical*, pp. 80-88. Antecedents include: 1) ancient religions, pp. 9-12. 2) OT prophets, pp. 20-23; cf. Mills, *Theological/Exegetical*, pp. 12-19. 3) Intertestamental/Hellenistic period, Mills, *Understanding*, pp. 19-21.

[258] Mills notes that: 1) symbols were important to Luke (giving of the Law on Mt. Sinai, the tower of Babel, the birth of the Messiah, and the empowering

Corinthian tongues,[259] Mills states that 'Luke redacted'[260] his accounts and wrote with theological intentions.[261] Further, Luke's accounts should be used 'to interpret glossolalia biblically for the church today ... (and) should be considered primary' because 'Corinthians deals with a particular historical situation where the concept of the *Spirit of God as power* is absent'.[262] Theologically, Mills defines glossolalia as

> the effort to express the inexpressible: the indwelling of the Spirit of God within the lives of men ... ordinary human language could not express the emotions that were aroused; therefore the believer broke forth in ecstatic speech. These may have been intelligible words or phrases ... (or) were inward groanings and sighs too deep for words.[263]

He would like to say that this indwelling occurs at salvation,[264] but at times, he recognizes, that for Luke, the 'Holy Spirit is that power

---

Spirit in Rabbinic Judaism), Mills, *Theological/Exegetical*, pp. 51-53. 2) The nature of speech on the Day of Pentecost is not as important as the fact that 'this force was none other than the Spirit of God', Mills, *Understanding*, p. 36; Mills, *Theological/Exegetical*, p. 66. 3) Caesarea and Ephesus were examples of 'the gospel breaking through the gentile barrier' where it was important to have the same experience as the disciples did on the Day of Pentecost to break down 'Jewish particularism', Mills, *Understanding*, p. 39; cf. Mills, *Theological/Exegetical*, pp. 71-73.

[259] He believes that: 1) First Corinthians is not a 'thorough, descriptive analysis of the nature and value of glossolalia' because Paul is dealing with a specific problem, Mills, *Understanding*, p. 43; Mills, *Theological/Exegetical*, p. 80. 2) In the end, a theological understanding is necessary for the charismata, especially for the gift of interpretation to have any significance, Mills, *Understanding*, p. 51; Mills, *Theological/Exegetical*, p. 94. 3) Glossolalia 'bears witness to the truth of the kerygma', but it is a sign that grew to be overemphasized at Corinth, Mills, *Understanding*, p. 54. However, tongues are not the only sign, 'or even the normal sign of the presence of God', p. 56. 4) The absence of tongues in the Romans 12 list of spiritual gifts is a 'conspicuous absence' pointing to a cleaner contextual opinion by Paul that glossolalia is not 'a necessary part of the Christian life'.

[260] Luke redacted his accounts: 1) to show the parallel with the receiving of the Law at Mt. Sinai and the reversal of tongues at Babel, Mills, *Understanding*, p. 57. 2) To fit with the Pauline expectation of order and intelligibility, p. 57. 3) Because ecstasy still is a form of communication psychologically, pp. 58, 60.

[261] Luke wanted to show 'a series of great advances for the young gospel' and that 'the gospel is dependent ... upon superhuman power', Mills, Understanding, pp. 28, 35.

[262] Mills, *Understanding*, pp. 60, 59 (emphasis added).

[263] Mills, *Understanding*, p. 38; Mills, *Theological/Exegetical*, pp. 69-70.

[264] For example, 'the Holy Spirit is the ultimate validation... of salvation', Mills, Theological/Exegetical, p. 44 (emphasis added). Despite his reservations

which enables the church to carry out her mission'.[265] Therefore, tongues 'validated the presence of the Spirit of God', but they are not intended to become a formal, a superior manifestation, or a 'kind of religious panacea'.[266] Finally, glossolalia is only one of many symbols of the Holy Spirit's presence, one that 'is relatively unimportant'.[267]

Malines Document, 1974

This 1974 document was a collaborative work by Roman Catholic scholars from around the world to address the 'Charismatic Renewal' in the RCC.[268] It outlines theological and pastoral concerns with the charismatic renewal and specifically addresses glossolalia. There are three areas relevant to current discussions of tongues-speech. First, in contrast to the Pentecostal view of SB, it states, 'there are no special classes of Spirit-bearers, no separate groups of Spirit-filled believers', one receives the Spirit upon baptism.[269] While agreeing that 'the power of the Spirit would come to visibility along the full spectrum of his charisms ... the early Church would surely make no claim to a special endowment'.[270] However, it also states that there are different 'levels' of 'awareness, expectation, and openness' within communities and individuals.[271] There should be little time between baptism and reception of the Spirit.

Second, and in agreement with Pentecostalism, 'a charism ... looks outward and ministry to the church and world rather than

---

about glossolalia at Corinth, for Paul tongues 'may well have become an essential requirement – a standard for conversion ... (and) must also demonstrate their possession of it', Mills, Understanding, p. 70 (emphasis added).

[265] Mills, *Understanding*, p. 70; cf. pp. 59-60. For example, Mills would like to say there is a 'parallel between the birth of the Messiah' and the birth of the church in Acts', Mills, *Theological/Exegetical*, p. 52. However, he knows that the better parallel is Jesus' baptism at the Jordan River: 'the disciples did not become the church at Pentecost any more than Jesus became the Son of God at his baptism'.

[266] Mills, *Theological/Exegetical*, p. 73.

[267] Mills, *Understanding*, pp. 67, 68.

[268] Leo Joseph Suenens, 'Malines Document 1, Theological and Pastoral Orientations on the Catholic Charismatic Renewal', in *The Holy Spirit, Life-Breath of the Church Book II*, 1st part (Belgium: FIAT Association, 1974), pp. 3-35.

[269] Suenens, 'Malines Document', p. 9; cf. pp. 5, 10, passim.

[270] Suenens, 'Malines Document', p. 11.

[271] Suenens, 'Malines Document', pp. 11-12. Openness to the charismata 'is in no way a sign of spiritual maturity', p. 23.

inward to the perfection of the individual'.[272] Regardless, 'these acts are performed in the power the Spirit, glorify Christian [sic], and are directed in some manner toward the building up of the Christian community'.[273] In other words, charisms are empowering and missional in nature.

Third, glossolalic prayer was 'very common in the early church' and denying the possibility of its existence today 'cannot be defended exegetically or theologically'.[274] For Luke, 'Pentecost with its baptismal and charismatic elements serves as a prototype or model in Luke for the subsequent baptismal elements'.[275] Further,

> the most central function of the charism of tongues is prayer ... It is essentially a prayer gift, enabling many using it to pray at a deeper level ... Its principal function is to be found in private prayer. There is considerable spiritual value in having a preconceptual, nonobjective way of praying ... The believer prays freely without conceptual forms.[276]

'This authentic but humble and humbling gift does not belong to the centre of the Gospel proclamation' – but praying in tongues can be 'a catalyst or trigger which opens the soul up to new dimensions of life in Christ'.[277] Spirit baptism 'for Catholics and for classical Pentecostals ... functions as a common bond at the experiential level', providing an ecumenical 'similar experience'.[278]

Walter J. Hollenweger, 1986, 1988, 1989, and 1997

Walter J. Hollenweger's legendary contribution to the field of Pentecostal studies emphases the black-oral-inclusive root of Pentecostalism and highlights glossolalia as a form of oral communication.[279] He envisions glossolalia, on the one hand, as freeing people

---

[272] Suenens, 'Malines Document', p. 9. Left open to debate was whether charisms are a new 'capacity, a new faculty which was not present before the Spirit gave the gift', or the stirring up of 'a capacity which belongs to the fullness of humanity', p. 29.

[273] Suenens, 'Malines Document', p. 29.

[274] Suenens, 'Malines Document', p. 24.

[275] Suenens, 'Malines Document', p. 20. Reference is made to Acts 1.15; 2; 10.47; 11.15; 19.6, p. 20. Mark 16.17 is also referenced, p. 30.

[276] Suenens, 'Malines Document', p. 30.

[277] Suenens, 'Malines Document', pp. 30, 25.

[278] Suenens, 'Malines Document', pp. 20, 28.

[279] The nature of glossolalia according to Hollenweger is: 1) non-pathological. 'There are nowadays no scientific grounds for explaining away speaking in

from the limits of race, culture, education, and language:

> speaking in tongues, dreams and visions help in the conscientization of the people of God ... *they liberate the people of God and free them* from dehumanizing cultural, economic and social forces. They create room for an oral theological and social debate. They unfreeze liturgical, theological and socio-political formulae and replace ... by the political literacy of the whole people of God.[280]

Conversely, glossolalia allows for God's people to speak with one voice. Tongues are

> a means of communicating without numerical sentences, a kind of atmospheric communication. When a whole congregation sings in tongues and many harmonies (without following a set piece of music), Pentecostals are building a 'cathedral of sounds,' a 'socio-acoustic sanctuary,' which is particularly important for Pentecostals who do not have cathedrals. By speaking in tongues the individual can pray without being forced to express himself or herself in semantic sentences ... It has a psycho-hygienic and spiritual function.[281]

Pentecostalism's distinctive contribution[282] of glossolalia as 'non-verbal communication should not be taken lightly'.[283] In other words, the glossolalic phenomenon may bridge the gap between '"the logic of the guts" and the "logic of the brain"'.[284]

---

tongues as a pathological form of expression', Hollenweger, *The Pentecostals*, p. 343. 2) It is 'a non-verbal archetypal form of communication' that is not always ecstatic (hot), but can at times be called 'cool' tongues, p. 344. 3) Tongues are at times connected to Christian spirituality. Here he follows W. Samarin and C. Williams: 'speaking in tongues is a human ability that may or may not be used in Christian spirituality', Walter J. Hollenweger, 'After Twenty Years' Research on Pentecostalism', *International Review of Mission* 75.297 (1986), pp. 3-12 (7).

[280] Hollenweger, 'Pentecostals and the Charismatic Movement', p. 553 (emphasis added).

[281] Hollenweger, 'After Twenty Years', p. 7.

[282] He believes like Spittler, that 'glossolalia is a human phenomenon, not limited to Christianity nor even to religious behavior ... The belief that *distinguishes* the movement can only wrongly be thought of as describing the *essence* of Pentecostalism', Hollenweger, *Pentecostalism*, p. 22 (emphasis original).

[283] Hollenweger, *The Pentecostals*, p. 344.

[284] Hollenweger, *Pentecostalism*, p. 38.

Robert P. Menzies, 2007 (1991, 1998, 2000), 2016 (2000, 2013, 2014)

Robert P. Menzies has several contributions towards a Pentecostal understanding of glossolalia. His work will be reviewed in its most recent editions.[285]

The thesis of his first piece is that an Evangelical hermeneutic presents 'a very real challenge' to Pentecostal theology and especially IE.[286] He calls for Pentecostals to rearticulate their theology[287] to overcome the three largest hermeneutical challenges: 1) a two stage SB. Spirit Baptism is seen by Evangelicals as conversion-initiation (CI) into Christ and not as Pentecostalism's power for witness.[288] Menzies argues that to keep Luke's distinctive pneumatology from being subsumed into a CI category, works of the Spirit should be seen in charismatic or prophetic terms.[289] The uniqueness of glossolalia is seen in its function to provide power for witness.[290] 2) The historical precedent in the book of Acts is weak. Pentecostals are 'unable to demonstrate that Luke intended to present in the key narratives of Acts a normative model for Christian experience'.[291] Yet Menzies argues that Luke's empowering prophetic glossolalia and Paul's personal edifying glossolalia

---

[285] There is one exception: Robert P. Menzies, 'The Role of Glossolalia in Luke-Acts', *AJPT* 15.1 (2012), pp. 47-72. This article is not reviewed because the important material is fully expanded in: Robert P. Menzies, *Speaking in Tongues: Jesus and the Apostolic Church as Models for the Church Today* (Cleveland, TN: CPT Press, 2016).

[286] Footnotes are from most recent publication: Robert P. Menzies, 'Evidential Tongues: An Essay on Theological Method', in Gary B. McGee (ed.), *Initial Evidence: Historical and Biblical Perspectives on the Pentecostal Doctrine of Spirit Baptism* (Eugene, OR: Wipf & Stock, 2007), p. 220. Also published in: 1) Robert P. Menzies, *Empowered for Witness: The Spirit in Luke-Acts* (JPTSup 6; Sheffield: JSOT Press, 1991), pp. 244-55; 2) Robert P. Menzies, 'Evidential Tongues: An Essay on Theological Method', *AJPT* 1 (1998), pp. 111-23; 3) William W. Menzies and Robert P. Menzies, *Spirit and Power: Foundations of Pentecostal Experience* (Grand Rapids, MI: Zondervan, 2000), pp. 121-32.

[287] Specifically, 1) Pentecostals should emphasize that Luke's SB is a missiological enabling and not allow our contribution to be reduced to tongues alone. 2) Pentecostals should recognize that the phrase 'initial evidence' has severe limitations, at times confusing the gift with the sign. 3) Pentecostal pastors need to stress the relevance of an expectation of missionary empowerment, Menzies, 'Evidential Tongues', pp. 231-33.

[288] Menzies, 'Evidential Tongues', pp. 221-22.

[289] Menzies, 'Evidential Tongues', p. 228.

[290] Menzies, 'Evidential Tongues', p. 229.

[291] Menzies, 'Evidential Tongues', p. 223.

are compatible. When 'one receives the Pentecostal gift, one should expect to manifest tongues ... (it) is a demonstrative sign' that the church is 'a prophetic community empowered for a missionary task'.[292] 3) What is the author's intention? When one examines the pneumatology of each biblical author, the discussion usually ends up with the question of trying to discern the author's original intent. Menzies believes that the issue of SB is a question of biblical theology while that of IE is for systematic theology.[293] Overall, 'the doctrine of tongues as the initial evidence of the baptism in the Holy Spirit flowed from a synthesis of theological insights offered by (both) Luke and Paul'.[294]

Menzies calls his next contribution 'a kind of spiritual diary' of his growing understanding of glossolalia.[295] It is a compilation and reworking of many prior articles and book chapters into three main divisions: Luke and tongues, Jesus and tongues, and Paul and tongues.[296]

In part one, Luke and tongues, Menzies believes 'Luke desired to ... establish Acts 2 as a model ... of a special type of prophetic speech'.[297] there is a 'connection between speaking in tongues and

---

[292] Menzies, 'Evidential Tongues', p. 230. Menzies logic is: Paul affirms the private manifestation for all; Luke affirms the gift is connected to speech; therefore one should speak in tongues when one receives this gift.

[293] Menzies, 'Evidential Tongues', p. 226. That Luke did not deliberately set out to demonstrate IE does not render the concept invalid.

[294] Menzies, *Speaking in Tongues*, p. xiii.

[295] Menzies, *Speaking in Tongues,* p. xiv. He calls Pentecostals to be brave and to confront their fears of disagreement, embarrassment, and excess, pp. 5-6; cf. pp. 2-12.

[296] Chapters 1 & 2 are reworked from Robert P. Menzies, *Pentecost: This Story is Our Story* (Springfield, MO: Gospel Publishing House, 2013), cf. pp. 67-85, 85-98 respectively. Chapter 3 is reworked from Robert P. Menzies, 'Jesus, Tongues, and the Messianic Reading of Psalm 16', *JPT* 23.1 (2014), pp. 29-49. Chapter 5 is reworked from Menzies, *Spirit and Power*, pp. 133-44.

[297] Menzies, *Speaking in Tongues,* pp. 18-19. The difference between the known languages of Acts 2 and subsequent ecstatic passages (10.46, 19.6) is not an issue, because even though these three contain 'different activities' Luke: 1) uses 'the same Greek terms' and 2) there is a 'literary connection', pp. 17-18. This is an evolution from Menzies' earlier position that Jenny Everts has made a 'compelling' case for the glossolalia of Acts 2 glossolalia as ecstatic, Menzies, *This Story is Our Story*, p. 74; cf. pp. 69-74; Jenny Everts, 'Tongues or Languages? Contextual Consistency in the Translation of Acts 2', *JPT* 4 (1994), pp. 71-80.

prophecy (that) is crucial for Luke's narrative'.[298] Further, Spirit-inspired speech is not limited to the founding of the church.[299] Significantly, in addition to an argument solely from the book of Acts, Menzies builds a Pentecostal polemic from three passages in Luke's gospel: 1) Luke 19.39-40[300] reveals 'a motif' close to Luke's heart: 'in these last days ... the Spirit will inspire His end-time prophets to declare God's mighty deeds ... Praise and bold witness go hand in hand, they are both the necessary and (an) inevitable consequence of being filled with the Holy Spirit'.[301] 2) Luke 10.1-16 is the account of the seventy being sent out, which springs from Moses' wish that 'all the Lord's people were prophets'.[302]

> Luke views every believer as (at least potentially) an end-time prophet, and that he will issue forth in Spirit-inspired ecstatic speech ... the Pentecostal gift, as a fulfillment of Moses' wish (Num. 11.29) and Joel's prophecy (Joel 2.28-32), is a prophetic anointing that enables its recipients to bear bold witness for

---

[298] Menzies, *Speaking in Tongues*, p. 20. The Spirit of prophecy is the 'exclusive privilege of "the servants" of God' that 'typically results in miraculous and audible speech'. 'Of the eight instances where Luke describes the initial reception of the Spirit ... five specifically allude to some form of inspired speech as the immediate result (Lk. 1.41-42; 1.67; Acts 2.4; 10.46; 19.6) and one implies the occurrence of such activity (Acts 8.15, 18). In the remaining two instances, although inspired speech is absent from Luke's account (Lk. 3.22; Acts 9.17), it is a prominent feature in the pericopes that follow (Lk. 4.14, 18-19; Acts 9.20)', n. 2.

[299] Menzies, *Speaking in Tongues*, p. 20. To think it was a special gift to help the fledging church would be to 'misread Luke's narrative', p. 21. Menzies points to how Luke modified Joel's prophecy from the LXX: 1) giving visions a prominent place, p. 22. 2) The insertion of 'and they will prophesy' into v. 18, pp. 21-22. 3) The insertion of 'signs on earth below' indicates a new 'epoch marked by "signs and wonders"', according to Luke, p. 23.

[300] Though this episode is found in all four Gospels, these verses are unique to Luke: 'some of the Pharisees in the crowd said to Jesus, "Teacher, rebuke your disciples!" "I tell you," he replied, "if they keep quiet, the stones *will cry out* (Lk. 19.39-40 NIV)', Menzies, *Speaking in Tongues*, p. 30 (emphasis added).

[301] Menzies, *Speaking in Tongues*, pp. 30-31. He notes Elizabeth's blessing, Lk. 1.42-45; Mary's Magnificat, Lk. 1.46-55; Zechariah's Song, Lk. 1.67-79; Simeon's prophecy, Lk. 2.29-32; the angels, Lk. 2.13-14; Jesus' joyful praise, Lk. 10.21-24; the triumphal entry, Lk. 19.39-40; Pentecost, Acts 2.1-13; Cornelius and his household, Acts 10.46; and the believers at Ephesus, Acts 19.6, p. 30.

[302] Numbers 11.29. For an explanation of the textual disparity between 70 or 72, see Menzies, *Speaking in Tongues*, pp. 30-31.

Jesus, and this being the case, it is marked by ecstatic speech characteristic of prophets.[303]

3) Jesus' teaching on prayer in Lk. 11.9-13 'encourages post-Pentecostal [sic] disciples to pray for a prophetic anointing ... expect(ing) glossolalia to be a normal, frequent, and expected part of this experience'.[304] Luke envisioned a wide range of prophetic responses accompanying the Spirit, such as 'joyful praise, glossolalia, visions and bold witness in the face of persecution'[305] but glossolalia was perhaps top in his expectation.[306] All Christians are therefore encouraged to pray for a prophetic anointing which will include glossolalia, because tongues remind us of our need for a 'divine enabling' and is a sign that apostolic power is available today.[307]

The most pioneering section is part two: Jesus and tongues. Here, Menzies connects glossolalia directly with Jesus. The lynchpin of his argument is a messianic reading of Psalm 16 in Acts 2.25-28: the 'early church viewed Jesus' experience of glossolalia

---

[303] Menzies, *Speaking in Tongues*, pp. 33-34. Luke has no concern about false tongues, because the community of prophets will discern true prophecy, pp. 34-35.

[304] Menzies, *Speaking in Tongues*, p. 38. Menzies comes to this conclusion because Luke amends the Matthean (Q) source of 'good gifts' given to those who ask, to read the 'Holy Spirit' is given to those who ask, pp. 35-36. He sees three implications: 1) this is for the church today because 'there is no neat line of separation dividing the apostolic church from his church or ours', p. 36. 2) This promise is clearly for members of the Christian community and not an initiatory or soteriological gift. He notes the 'repetitive character' of prayer in v. 9 to show that 'this pneumatic gift is ... to be experienced on an ongoing basis (cf. Acts 2.4; 4.8, 31; 9.17; 13.9), p. 36. 3) This is viewed by Luke as a prophetic enabling, pp. 36-37.

[305] Menzies, *Speaking in Tongues*, p. 37.

[306] His support is: 1) glossolalia in Luke's narrative 'typically accompanies the initial reception of the Spirit', Menzies, *Speaking in Tongues*, pp. 37. 2) The emphasis on asking would prompt the natural question of 'when have we received this gift' and Luke's narrative indicates that there normally is an accompanying sign, p. 94. Menzies reminds those opposed to visible signs of the long history of sacraments that emphasize visible signs in the liturgical forms of Christianity, pp. 37-38. 3) A possible reason for there being fear of the Father's good gift (vv. 11, 12) is that unlike a quiet gift, 'the gift includes glossolalia, which is noisy, unintelligible, and has many pagan counterparts', p. 38.

[307] Menzies, *Speaking in Tongues*, p. 40. In an interesting excursus in *This Story is Our Story*, Menzies notes it might be possible to be full of the Holy Spirit and not speak in tongues; however, he encourages all believers to be hungry for the full biblical experience, Menzies, *This Story is Our Story*, pp. 98-101.

... as a fulfilment of Ps. 16.9'.³⁰⁸ Luke anticipates this in Lk. 10.21, where he uses a unique phrase 'he rejoiced in the Holy Spirit' to denote not only praise but prophetic inspiration and activity³⁰⁹ and 'thanksgiving in terms reminiscent of speaking in tongues'.³¹⁰ 'Peter declares that this Psalm (16) must be interpreted as a prophecy ... concerning the Messiah ... (because) it is Jesus' tongue that rejoices and his body that is not abandoned to the grave'.³¹¹ This suggests a 'significant (Lucan) literary and theological purpose'.³¹² Menzies argues that Jesus' tongue rejoiced during his earthly ministry and not just upon his resurrection.³¹³ Overall in Luke-Acts,

a messianic reading of Ps. 16.9 that understands Jesus' own experience of glossolalia, implied in Lk. 10.21, as a fulfilment of

---

³⁰⁸ Menzies, *Speaking in Tongues*, p. 63. The best we can say is 'Luke merely implies Jesus' experience of tongues', p. 62. He suggests two reasons for the lack of explicit accounts of Jesus speaking in tongues: 1) 'there were not any traditions or stories that explicitly describe Jesus speaking in tongues', and 2) 'the early church did not view this matter with total unanimity'. Even though glossolalia was widely practiced, 'some groups were less open to this manifestation'.

³⁰⁹ Menzies, *Speaking in Tongues*, p. 48. 'Here Luke utilizes the verb ἀγαλλιάω (rejoice) ... and denotes spiritual exultation ... in praise to God for his mighty acts ... a particularly appropriate way of describing prophetic activity'; cf. Lk. 1.47; 10.21; Acts 2.26.

³¹⁰ Menzies, *Speaking in Tongues*, p. 49. 'The coupling of ἀγαλλιάω with γλῶσσα in is not unexpected, for six of the eight references to γλῶσσα in Luke–Acts describe experiences of spiritual exultation that result in praise': Lk. 1.64; Acts 2.4, 11, 26; 10.46; 19.6.

³¹¹ Menzies, *Speaking in Tongues*, pp. 50-51.

³¹² Menzies, *Speaking in Tongues*, p. 51.

³¹³ Because Luke cited non-resurrection portions of Psalm 19 in his LXX quote, Menzies argues further: 1) two people cannot be at each other's right hand, Menzies, *Speaking in Tongues*, p. 53; cf. p. 52. 2) Luke redacts into Lk. 10.21 the phrase 'he rejoiced in the Holy Spirit', pp. 53-54. 3) The conceptual link of the revelation of Jesus' status as the Son, p. 54. 4) The references to fill (πληρόω) in Luke-Acts 'encourage the reader to interpret the phrase "you fill me with joy in your presence" as referring to Jesus' ecstatic experience of the Spirit during Jesus' earthly ministry'. 5) The future verb tense 'suggest[s] that the Messiah speaks these words prior to his resurrection', pp. 54-55. 6) OT prophecy 'anticipates an ongoing fulfillment' of miracles by Jesus and his followers', p. 55. 7) 'The reason for citing the extended quotation appears to be the focus in vv. 8-9a and v. 11b on joyful, ecstatic experience, which anticipates the disciples' experience of inspired tongues-speech cited in Acts 2.33', p. 55. 8) 'Luke carefully crafted his summary of Peter's sermon with an eye to presenting Jesus' ecstatic exultation ... as both a fulfilment of prophecy ... and as anticipating the experience of the disciples', pp. 56-57.

the prophecy that the Messiah's tongue would rejoice ... serve(s) as a sign for those who are a part of the end-time community of prophets, so also tongues mark the ultimate prophet and source of this prophetic community.[314]

Glossolalia identifies 'the true people of God ... and confirms their status as members of Joel's end-times prophetic band'.[315] Regarding Mk 16.17, Jesus' singular reference to tongues, Menzies argues for its originality by noting that it shares the same source that Luke used.[316] Further, he argues for its originality along with the cryptic handling of snakes and the drinking of poison. Jesus refers to Job 20.16[317] using a Hebrew literary device called *gezerah shavah*.[318] This implies a Hebrew textual tradition that is older than the Greek tradition of today's text.[319] In short, 'the LE (long ending) passes on this saying of Jesus'.[320]

In part three, Paul and tongues, Menzies begins with a response to critics who believe that tongues are not for everyone, but were limited to a select group in Corinth.[321] He argues that Paul envisions that glossolalia is for everyone because of 'the force of the rhetorical question in 12:30b, "do all speak in tongues?" and ... the significance of Paul's wishful declaration in 14:5, "I would like every one of you to speak in tongues"'.[322] For Menzies, the thrust of Paul's distinction is public verses private glossolalia as opposed to a select group who speak in tongues in contrast to others who do not. Paul employs a similar analogy about celibacy in 7.7, according to those who want to limit glossolalia; however, Menzies reveals that there are 'three couplets, which consist of parallel

---

[314] Menzies, *Speaking in Tongues*, p. 59.
[315] Menzies, *Speaking in Tongues*, p. 58; cf. pp. 57-61.
[316] Menzies, *Speaking in Tongues*, p. 69; cf. pp. 67-72.
[317] His argument rests on Job 20.13-16, where 'we have a single text from the Old Testament that offers in a concise and vivid manner parallels to both' the poison and snakes, Menzies, *Speaking in Tongues*, p. 74.
[318] Also called a 'stichwort connection', Menzies, *Speaking in Tongues*, p. 77.
[319] Menzies, *Speaking in Tongues*, pp. 77-79. He suggests that the Hebrew literary device was lost on the Greeks who 'might well have rendered in a less specific way', p. 79.
[320] Menzies, *Speaking in Tongues*, p. 80.
[321] Menzies, *Speaking in Tongues*, pp. 90-94; cf. Menzies, *Spirit and Power*, pp. 133-44.
[322] Menzies, *Speaking in Tongues*, p. 90.

statements concerning tongues and prophecy' that point to a public / private distinction, in the context of chapter 14.[323] Menzies is confident that it was Paul's genuine wish that all were glossolalists.[324] He writes, 'once we recognize the polemical nature of Paul's words in 1 Corinthians 12-14', we see that 'Paul's attitude towards tongues as a sign might not be so different from that of Luke's after all'.[325] For support of his position, Menzies believes that Paul used a literary device called a 'diatribe' in 1 Cor. 14.22,[326] and at the very least, 'there was a group at Corinth that viewed tongues as a positive sign'.[327] Regarding the gift of tongues, and beyond devotional-glossolalia,[328] Menzies believes that communal glossolalia can be useful for praise,[329] intercession[330] and even proclamation: 'when exercised in concert with the gift of interpretation, (they) can be the vehicle through which the Holy Spirit speaks to the larger church body'.[331] He reasons that while 'tongues generally takes the form of inspired praise or thanksgiving, I am reluctant to limit it ... in a rigid fashion ... (because) there are other expressions of speaking in tongues that appear to fall outside', such as singing and praying in the Spirit corporately.[332]

---

[323] Menzies, *Speaking in Tongues*, p. 99; cf. pp. 98-101. 'The parallelism ... suggests that both prophecy and tongues are open to all within the community of believers', p. 100. And further, 'if the gift of tongues has merit in its private expression, why would God withhold it', p. 101?

[324] Menzies, *Speaking in Tongues*, p. 101.

[325] Menzies, *Speaking in Tongues*, p. 118.

[326] Menzies, *Speaking in Tongues*, pp. 111-15; cf. pp. 109-18. Menzies admits this is a very difficult passage to interpret, but that this theory 'offers a coherent explanation for the relationship between the paraphrase from Isa. 28.11-12 and the opponents' inference', pp. 111, 113. Diatribe means that Paul uses the voice of an 'imaginary opponent': 'thus, in Paul's version, the hearers refuse to listen to the unintelligible speech from "foreigners" ... (therefore) the people of v. 21 refers to believers and the point of the quotation (as understood by Paul's opponents) is to say that tongues, although ineffective for instructing Christians, serve as an authenticating, apologetic sign for unbelievers', p. 113.

[327] Menzies, *Speaking in Tongues*, p. 115. He also briefly appeals to Mk 16.17 and Acts 2.19 as having a positive sign-value for glossolalia.

[328] Menzies, *Speaking in Tongues*, pp. 126-27, 130-31.

[329] Menzies, *Speaking in Tongues*, pp. 130-39.

[330] Menzies, *Speaking in Tongues*, pp. 139-46.

[331] Menzies, *Speaking in Tongues*, p. 146.

[332] Menzies, *Speaking in Tongues*, pp. 150-51.

Initial Evidence, 1991 (2007)[333]
This compilation has several great pieces, most of which are treated elsewhere in this survey. The following three works are the sole contribution from each author.

The first contributor, Larry Hurtado, approaches glossolalia from what he calls a 'post-Pentecostal' viewpoint. He believes that a 'separate level of Spirit empowerment subsequent to regeneration, with a required "evidence" of it, seems not to be reflected at all in the New Testament'.[334] Though sympathetic to his Pentecostal roots, he believes that IE resulted from 'eisegesis'. The best case exegetically that can be made for tongues speech is that it is normal, but not the norm for all people.[335]

He believes his work shows that nowhere in the book of Acts is IE explicitly taught, nor is there any indication that Luke intended to teach how the Spirit is received, 'but rather it seems to have been to show that the Spirit prompted and accompanied the progress of the gospel at every significant juncture and was the power enabling the work'.[336] Luke is inconsistent or unconcerned about teaching SB because even the pattern in Acts occurs only 3 of 5 times.[337] Hurtado notes that Peter's argument of the 'same gift' in Acts 11.1-18 'can only indicate … the same eschatological *salvation* as the Jerusalem church'.[338]

Not only is IE not explicitly taught in Acts, but 'one would think that … Paul would have included a reference to its supposed significance as "initial evidence" of Spirit Baptism if such an understanding of tongues were current at the time'.[339] Overall, Hurtado's work in 1 Corinthians covers little new ground and he finds

---

[333] Originally published in 1991, this review is of the 2007 edition.

[334] Larry W. Hurtado, 'Normal, But Not A Norm: "Initial Evidence" and the New Testament', in Gary B. McGee (ed.), *Initial Evidence: Historical and Biblical Perspectives on the Pentecostal Doctrine of Spirit Baptism* (Eugene, OR: Wipf & Stock, 2007 reprint; Hendrickson, 1991), pp. 189-201 (192).

[335] Hurtado, 'Normal, But Not A Norm', pp. 189-92.

[336] Hurtado, 'Normal, But Not A Norm', p. 194, cf. p. 195.

[337] The pattern is only seen in Acts 2.1-4; 10.44-47; 19.1-7, while the parallel passage in Acts 4.31 (which has the disciples only speaking boldly, without mention of tongues) is ignored by Pentecostals, Hurtado, 'Normal, But Not A Norm', p. 195.

[338] Hurtado, 'Normal, But Not A Norm', p. 195 (emphasis added).

[339] Hurtado, 'Normal, But Not A Norm', p. 196.

the Pentecostal arguments 'unpersuasive'.[340] He concludes that tongues are '"normal," within the range of Christian spirituality' but disagrees that there is a 'special gift or spiritual state' that accompanies tongues. Simply put, IE is a 'sincere but misguided understanding of Scripture'.[341]

The second contributor, Donald Johns, seeks to explain why past approaches to the doctrine of IE have failed and he hopes that some fresh approaches and exegetical tools will resolve the hermeneutical issue.[342] First, the failings of past approaches are Pentecostalism's inadequate response to the CI paradigm in Paul's pneumatology.[343] Second, Pentecostalism's pattern from Acts needs more than three solid cases and the two questionable ones for this inductive reasoning method to move beyond being labelled 'inconsistent'.[344] Third is the viability and ownership of the term 'baptized in the Spirit' in light of the Luke / Paul issue.

Regarding the Luke / Paul issue, Johns observes that Luke should be read as a theologian in his own right and not through Paul's pneumatology; that Paul actually says the Spirit is received at conversion, but Pentecostal critics go beyond that to add 'and only at conversion (which Paul does not say)'; that Acts 2 'must be

---

[340] Hurtado, 'Normal, But Not A Norm', p. 196. He notes: 1) that Paul emphasizes tongues here only because the Corinthians were bent on it; 2) Paul limits the congregational gift; 3) it is not for everyone; 4) there might be some personal benefit as a distinctive form of prayer and praise; 5) Paul seeks to restrict tongues; and 6) Paul prefers the mind and intelligent speech to tongues corporately, pp. 196-99.

[341] Hurtado, 'Normal, But Not A Norm', p. 200.

[342] Donald A. Johns, 'Some New Directions in the Hermeneutics of Classic Pentecostalism's Doctrine of Initial Evidence', in Gary B. McGee (ed.), *Initial Evidence: Historical and Biblical Perspectives on the Pentecostal Doctrine of Spirit Baptism* (Eugene, OR: Wipf & Stock, 2007 reprint; Hendrickson, 1991), pp. 145-67 (145-46). He believes that the early Pentecostals 'intuitively adopted techniques that are present in contemporary biblical scholarship in a more developed and polished form', p. 148.

[343] Johns notes that Paul's pneumatology is more clearly associated with conversion-initiation whereas Luke's is that of empowerment. Pentecostals on this front need to address the 'Pauline statements about every believer having received the Spirit' and the Lucan passages 'that describe the post-Easter disciples as people who needed to receive the Spirit', Johns, 'New Directions in Hermeneutics', p. 147.

[344] The three cases are: Acts 2.1-12; 10.44-8; and 19.1-7 have a close connection between reception of the Spirit and tongues; however, Acts 8.14-9 and 9.17 (along with 1 Cor. 14.18) do not fit the pattern.

interpreted primarily within Luke's theological structures'; and that we should trust Luke in Acts 8 when he says the Samaritans 'believed' and in Acts 19 when he says they were already 'disciples'.[345]

Johns has two noteworthy ideas to resolve the past failing of the IE doctrine. First, he believes that redaction criticism will be helpful in exegeting the main Pentecostal texts. After all, redaction criticism is 'similar to what classical Pentecostals have been doing all along, drawing out the theology expressed by narrative texts'.[346] Both the arrangement and omission in the narrative do reveal a theological perspective.

The second idea is narrative theology. Johns writes,

> Luke maintained the story form in Acts because the significance of what he wanted to communicate is more directly perceived through story than through expository prose, and probably because he wanted to affect the reader in ways that could not be done by any other form than story.[347]

A story will build a group identity, structure one's world, and imaginatively draw the reader into 'a simplified understanding' of reality.[348] Stories have 'rules or principles' by which the story-world operates; in the same way, the biblical world should be paradigmatic for our world today.[349]

The third and final contributor, Henry I. Lederle, seeks to define the Charismatic position on IE from an objective or ecumenical perspective.[350] While most charismatics give tongues a prominent position, few accept it as the '*sine qua non* for Spirit baptism'.[351] Their reasons, according to Lederle, are that tongues cannot be proved as the 'first effect' of SB and that its occurrence in secular and non-Christian context makes it a non-conclusive sign rather than a definitive

---

[345] Johns, 'New Directions in Hermeneutics', pp. 148-51.
[346] Johns, 'New Directions in Hermeneutics', p. 153.
[347] Johns, 'New Directions in Hermeneutics', p. 156.
[348] Johns, 'New Directions in Hermeneutics', pp. 153-55.
[349] Johns, 'New Directions in Hermeneutics', p. 156.
[350] Henry I. Lederle, 'Initial Evidence and the Charismatic Movement: An Ecumenical Appraisal', in Gary B. McGee (ed.), *Initial Evidence: Historical and Biblical Perspectives on the Pentecostal Doctrine of Spirit Baptism* (Eugene, OR: Wipf & Stock, 2007 reprint; Hendrickson, 1991), pp. 131-41 (133).
[351] Lederle, 'An Ecumenical Appraisal', p. 132.

one.³⁵² More to this chapter's point is that contrary to other Pentecostal historians, he does not believe that it was the concept of IE that caused Pentecostalism to spread like wildfire, but rather the experience of an encounter with the Holy Spirit.³⁵³ He compares such encounter with a pearl and the concept of IE as an oyster. Pearl-like encounters are possible without the shell of the oyster.³⁵⁴

The oyster of IE is a child of the Enlightenment where there is a desire for 'empirical verification, intellectual guarantees, and linear causality'; however, 'no formal structure can contain' the richness of the Spirit.³⁵⁵ Looked at another way, 'an encounter with God should serve as the *gateway* to life in the Spirit rather than as the *goal* which can always be formally verified *once* it has been reached'!'³⁵⁶ For charismatics, Lederle notes doctrinal statements are attempts to 'domesticate' the Spirit.³⁵⁷ The Charismatics' experience presents a challenge to classical Pentecostals in that 'this ongoing experience of Christ's power and presence cannot be guaranteed by the external requirement that all need to speak in tongues'.³⁵⁸ He ends with a call for a fresh dialog between classic Pentecostals and charismatics where Pentecostals consider giving up 'outdated concepts – influenced by philosophical categories no longer adhered to' – and embracing 'many new ways of looking at old insights discovered'.³⁵⁹

Frank D. Macchia, 1992, 1993, 1998, and 2006

The collective writings of Pentecostal theologian Frank D. Macchia have added significantly to the discussion on glossolalia.³⁶⁰

---

³⁵² Lederle, 'An Ecumenical Appraisal', p. 132.

³⁵³ He has two supports for this point: First, the doctrine was surrounded by controversy from the beginning. Second, the Pentecostal communities in some countries resemble charismatics more than Pentecostals in their doctrine, Lederle, 'An Ecumenical Appraisal', p. 132.

³⁵⁴ Pearl-like encounters are possible without the shell of the oyster as seen in testimonies like that of John G. Lake, Lederle, 'An Ecumenical Appraisal', pp. 133-34.

³⁵⁵ Lederle, 'An Ecumenical Appraisal', p. 134.

³⁵⁶ Lederle, 'An Ecumenical Appraisal', p. 136.

³⁵⁷ Lederle, 'An Ecumenical Appraisal', p. 136.

³⁵⁸ Lederle, 'An Ecumenical Appraisal', p. 138.

³⁵⁹ Lederle, 'An Ecumenical Appraisal', p. 139, cf. pp. 138-40.

³⁶⁰ Frank D. Macchia, 'Sighs Too Deep for Words: Toward a Theology of Glossolalia', *JPT* 1 (October 1992), pp. 47-73; Macchia, 'Tongues as a Sign'; Frank D. Macchia, 'The Question of Tongues as Initial Evidence: A Review of Initial Evidence, Edited by Gary B. McGee', *JPT* 2 (1993), pp. 117-27; Frank D. Macchia, 'Groans Too Deep For Words: Towards a Theology of Tongues as

These writings reveal a careful construction of a theology of glossolalia with four theses: 1) glossolalia is broader and more varied than what doctrinal categories can hold. 2) Glossolalia is best thought of as a sacrament. 3) Pentecostalism's doctrine of IE, though not defined well, is not easily dismissed. 4) Tongues symbolize unity and mission.

Macchia's first thesis is that glossolalia is broader than any theological category.[361] Tongues 'will contain varying nuances of meaning among those who experience it', he writes.[362] Most early Pentecostals approached tongues through a worldview of 'revivalism on "signs and wonders" and from the experiences of God in the book of Acts as pattern'; therefore, most early reflections are clustered around evidentiary tongues.[363] Despite this handicap, underlying all discussion 'was the assumption that tongues symbolized an encounter with God ... spontaneous, free and wondrous'.[364] Tongues are a physical response to God, who freely

---

Initial Evidence', *AJPS* 1/2 (1998), pp. 149-73; Frank D. Macchia, 'Babel and the Tongues of Pentecost: Reversal or Fulfillment? – A Theological Perspective', in Mark J. Cartledge (ed.), *Speaking in Tongues: Multi-Disciplinary Perspectives* (Studies in Pentecostal and Charismatic Issues; Bletchley, Milton Keynes, England: Paternoster Press, 2006), pp. 34-51.

[361] Macchia states that 'a spiritual phenomenon was changed into a shibboleth of orthodoxy ... We cannot lock Spirit baptism into a glossolalic straightjacket so that the former becomes inconceivable apart from the latter. But ... Spirit baptism is fundamentally and integrally about what tongues symbolize', Macchia, 'Towards a Theology of Initial Evidence', p. 165. Cf. Frank D. Macchia, *Baptized in the Spirit: A Global Pentecostal Theology* (Grand Rapids, MI: Zondervan, 2006), pp. 37, 281.

[362] Macchia, 'Sighs Too Deep for Words', p. 72, cf. Frank D. Macchia, 'Blessed Beyond Measure: An Autobiographical Reflection', in Steven M. Fettke and Robby Waddell (eds.), *Pentecostals in the Academy: Testimonies of Call*, pp. 129-47 (147).

[363] Macchia, 'Sighs Too Deep for Words', p. 48. He believes that the nature of tongues is ecstatic, though he qualifies it as not being ecstatic like the ancient Greeks who lost control of themselves. He reasons for a 'meaningful way of transcending one's situation without losing conscious control of oneself', p. 64. However, the interest in the precise nature of tongues is a modern quest and would not have been a concern for the ancients, pp. 63-64.

[364] Macchia, 'Sighs Too Deep for Words', p. 48. 'The experience and praxis-orientation of Pentecostalism' is as important as the historical or exegetical, Macchia, 'Initial Evidence', pp. 126-27.

chooses to reveal himself through spontaneous tongues or a structured rite such as communion.³⁶⁵ These encounters point to an eschatological reality: 'Pentecost may be termed an eschatological theophany of God ... (in which tongues are) the transformation of language into a channel of the divine self-disclosure'.³⁶⁶ Tongues are a response to God's self-disclosure, divine down not human up: 'the closer one draws to the divine mystery, the more urgent it becomes to express oneself and, concomitantly, the less able one is to find adequate expression'.³⁶⁷ The human response is 'unclassifiable, free speech in response to an unclassifiable, free God. It is the language of the *imago Dei*' that mysteriously and creatively seeks to express the experience with God.³⁶⁸ An encounter with God renews the individual and tongues do not distinguish a greater spirituality as much as 'a new creation taking place in our midst and through us among others'. Through such encounters we 'participate in the renewal of society and creation.'³⁶⁹ 'Glossolalia, even practiced alone, must have implications for one's ability to reach out to others in koinonia', Macchia writes.³⁷⁰ Tongues, then, is a language that has koinonia in the 'mystery of human freedom before God'³⁷¹ overflowing traditional cultural, gender, or class boundaries.³⁷² Tongues should 'call us out of our self- and church-centered piety to serve in the world'.³⁷³ Macchia agrees with Murray Dempster that 'tongues in Acts always accompanies the elimination of economic, racial, and religious barriers'; glossolalia 'shocks' the institutional life of the church in such a way that

---

³⁶⁵ Macchia, 'Sighs Too Deep for Words', p. 67.
³⁶⁶ Macchia, 'Sighs Too Deep for Words', p. 57.
³⁶⁷ Macchia, 'Sighs Too Deep for Words', p. 62.
³⁶⁸ Macchia, 'Sighs Too Deep for Words', p. 62.
³⁶⁹ Macchia, 'Sighs Too Deep for Words', p. 72.
³⁷⁰ Macchia, 'Sighs Too Deep for Words', p. 67. For support he notes, 'there is a basic connection between spiritual fullness and koinonia in the New Testament that cannot be denied', p. 65. Macchia recalls Bonhoeffer's statement that a person is only known as a person within society. Finally, Paul's insistence that without love great giftedness is useless, p. 67.
³⁷¹ Macchia, 'Sighs Too Deep for Words', p. 66.
³⁷² 'It is indeed interesting that inter-racial fellowship and female ordination to the ministry in early Pentecostalism were both justified as results of the latter-day experiences of Spirit baptism and glossolalia', p. 66.
³⁷³ Macchia, 'Sighs Too Deep for Words', p. 68.

there is a resulting 'love and holiness in life', a counterculture to the institution's formalization.[374]

Macchia's second thesis is the observation of a sacramental aspect to glossolalia that can be a 'door for fruitful ecumenical dialogue with other Church traditions'.[375] Even though Pentecostals are afraid of 'institutionalization of formalizing the Spirit of God' tongues fit well with the contemporary understanding of sacrament as 'occasions for personal encounter between God and the believer'.[376] Glossolalia as a sacrament bridges the gap between the extremes of Roman Catholicism's 'visible means of grace and the Reformed accent on the sovereignty and freedom of the Spirit'.[377] On the one hand, glossolalia 'includes a visible/audible human response that signifies the divine presence'; therefore it retains the Divine sovereignty and freedom side as well as 'humanity's need for the visible and tangible'.[378] Yet tongues are a different kind of sacrament, one that 'accents the free, dramatic, and unpredictable move of the Spirit of God'.[379] Therefore, it avoids the stereotype against the Catholic sacraments as being idolatrous by placing the emphasis on God's sovereignty.[380] For example, 'there is an element of spontaneity and patient waiting for the unexpected in

---

[374] Macchia, 'Initial Evidence', pp. 120-21, 124 (Org. cite: M. Dempster, 'The Church's Moral Witness: A Study of Glossolalia in Luke's Theology of Acts', *Paraclete* 23.1 [Winter 1989], pp. 1-7).

[375] Macchia, 'Tongues as a Sign', p. 76.

[376] Macchia, 'Tongues as a Sign', p. 62. Also, 'the sacraments are not understood in this newer Catholic sacramental thought as objects containing the divine presence as a static substance ... (but) as contexts for a dynamic and personal divine/human encounter', p. 71. Macchia wishes to replace sacramental substances with liminal, Spirit-invoked ritual performances: Tom Driver finds 'that ritual is a kind of performance that suggests "alternative worlds" and nourishes "imaginative visions" of God's goals for the world ... (rituals) move in a kind of liminal space, at the edge of, or in the cracks between, the mapped regions of what we like to call "the real world"', Macchia, *Baptized*, p. 248; cf. p. 255.

[377] Macchia, 'Tongues as a Sign', p. 70. His approach here is through Paul Tillich's dialectic and its gap is resolved by defining tongues as very similar to Tillich's 'kairos' event, pp. 68-69.

[378] Macchia, 'Tongues as a Sign', p. 70. There is a 'tangible self-disclosure of the Sprit', it is a 'physical/acoustic reality used as a visible sign of this experience', Macchia, 'Initial Evidence', pp. 122, 125.

[379] Macchia, 'Tongues as a Sign', p. 63.

[380] He contrasts Catholic and protestant views as: orchestrated and institutional versus free, unplanned, countercultural, and charism, pp. 72-73. Also,

charismatic signs such as evidential tongues that is absent from ecclesiastically manipulated links to apostolic experience'.[381]

On the other hand, tongues avoid the Protestant stereotype of 'radical subjectivism' by its linking to Christ and the church.[382] Macchia favours a broad definition of the term sacrament because it relies on God taking the initiative, and calls the Pentecostal sacrament 'more "theophanic" than incarnational', like at Mt. Sinai.[383] Sacramental tongues are 'encounters with God in worship, in which we participate actively but which exceed the capacities of human thought or language'.[384] Additionally, tongues as a sacrament links the individual with Christ and is rooted in Christ's purpose for the church: 'by stressing that Spirit baptism ... is for the empowerment of the church in its witness ... Pentecostals have parted significantly from the conservative Evangelical preoccupation with subjective conversion'.[385]

His third thesis is that the initial sign (IE)[386] has significance despite the criticisms. Again, a sacramental definition will assist the doctrine. There is something special about that first encounter with God, that 'overwhelming immersion of baptism of the human psyche by the person and power of the Spirit'.[387] A sacramental connection honours the 'depth and breadth of the Spirit baptismal experience and the symbolic expression of tongues, but without the rigid, scientific, glossocentric connections'.[388] He compares it to Irving's '"root and stem" out of which all other spiritual

---

'*Spiritus Creator* working from within our structured responses to God ... sacramentality as from "below", versus the 'free move of the *Spiritus Redemptor* ... a sacramentality from "above"', p. 75.

[381] Macchia, 'Initial Evidence', pp. 118-19. Macchia's contrast here is with Catholic's apostolic succession and Evangelical's scriptural inerrancy.

[382] Macchia, 'Tongues as a Sign', p. 70.

[383] Macchia, 'Tongues as a Sign', p. 73.

[384] Macchia, 'Tongues as a Sign', p. 72.

[385] Macchia, 'Tongues as a Sign', p. 70.

[386] Macchia also prefers the term 'sign' to 'evidence' noting that an 'evidence' merely provides data for a hypothesis; whereas 'sign' has a rich theological potential and a long history of use within the church, Macchia, 'Towards a Theology of Initial Evidence', p. 153. 'Initial' should be reworked to mean the initiating of the language miracle and not SB itself, pp. 172-73.

[387] Macchia, 'Tongues as a Sign', pp. 67-68.

[388] Macchia, 'Towards a Theology of Initial Evidence', p. 156. 'I have suggested shifting to the language of "sign" (rather than "evidence," which is not a biblical term) concerning tongues and focusing on the theological rather than a legalistic connection between them', Macchia, *Baptized*, p. 36.

gifts grow'.³⁸⁹ From the beginning, early Pentecostals wrestled with how to give tongues a special place without limiting SB to a glossolalic experience.³⁹⁰ In fact, there has been a natural progression from MT to an 'in-depth prayer language or a congregational gift'.³⁹¹

To address exegetical and theological concerns about IE, Macchia makes the following points: first, the connection of tongues to SB is 'not simply a strange teaching ... without any provocation from the narrative of Acts':³⁹²

> Luke followed the Jewish tendency to associate the reception of the Spirit with inspired or prophetic speech ... Luke seems to focus on tongues because of their role in miraculously uniting a diversity of people together in a common witness and praise.³⁹³

Analogous connections of tongues to Christ can be made in the book of Acts, such as Peter's speech where Jesus had a glad tongue in Acts 2.26.³⁹⁴ These analogous connections, or links, are sufficient. He muses, 'how many questions could be raised if representatives from mainline churches were to defend their understanding of the Eucharist on the basis of the New Testament witness alone'.³⁹⁵

Second, both Luke's and Paul's view of tongues are complimentary in that,

---

³⁸⁹ Macchia, 'Tongues as a Sign', p. 69.
³⁹⁰ Macchia, 'Towards a Theology of Initial Evidence', p. 156. He notes specifically the emphasis by Carothers on praise and a reference of overcoming racial barriers in the *AF* that states, 'tell me ... can you have a better understanding of the two works of grace and baptism in the Holy Ghost?', Macchia, 'Towards a Theology of Initial Evidence', p. 157.
³⁹¹ Macchia, 'Towards a Theology of Initial Evidence', pp. 156-57, 162. He believes that the missionary tongues must be 'demythologized' if the doctrine is to be developed, pp. 162, cf. 159, 164.
³⁹² Macchia, 'Towards a Theology of Initial Evidence', p. 161.
³⁹³ Macchia, 'Towards a Theology of Initial Evidence', p. 158.
³⁹⁴ Macchia, 'Tongues as a Sign', p. 65; cf. Macchia, 'Initial Evidence', pp. 119-20. Other examples are anointing, proclamation, persecution, miracles, breaking bread, and healing, pp. 65-66. For further development of this concept see, Menzies, *This Story is Our Story*, pp. 81-85.
³⁹⁵ Macchia, 'Tongues as a Sign', p. 67; cf. Macchia, 'Initial Evidence', pp. 126-27.

Luke reminds us that not all public expressions of tongues require interpreters to be enlightening or to motivate greater commitment to God. On the other hand, Paul reminds us that restriction may be necessary if unintelligible tongues begin to dominate a service.[396]

He believes that Paul was writing to correct a situation in Corinth and that one cannot 'stretch Paul's correction ... to mean that no glossolalic utterance is of any value to others without an intelligent interpretation'.[397] Tongues have value by themselves publicly and this is where Luke compliments Paul.[398] For Luke tongues 'provide a powerful witness in public of both promise and judgment, without any explanation whatever on how such clarity is granted'.[399] Gordon Fee has proven to Macchia's satisfaction that Paul's 'least' of the gifts is not what most commentators believe it to mean, but that the best gift is what the context and Spirit desire.[400]

Third, the pathway to revision the doctrine of IE for Pentecostals has already been prepared by an early Pentecostal leader J.R. Flower. Flower's testimony of being baptized six months before he spoke in tongues was, that while he was baptized in the Spirit, he did not have the 'full manifestation' as seen in the 'biblical pattern'.[401] This, Macchia believes, shifts 'the focus from tongues as the necessary accompaniment ... to tongues as the fullness of expression toward which the experience leads'.[402]

Fourth, there is a place for IE and SB that is eschatologically missional without retreating solely to the Pauline categories of

---

[396] Macchia, 'Towards a Theology of Initial Evidence', p. 170.

[397] Macchia, 'Towards a Theology of Initial Evidence', p. 169. As support he offers Rom. 8.26, where there is a positive, public use for 'groans too deep for words' that does 'not lead to a quest for self-aggrandizement or for glory', Macchia, 'Towards a Theology of Initial Evidence', pp. 170-71.

[398] Macchia, 'Towards a Theology of Initial Evidence', pp. 169-71.

[399] Macchia, 'Towards a Theology of Initial Evidence', p. 169.

[400] The view that spiritual gifts can be ranked from the least to the greatest 'is based on faulty conclusions drawn from assumptions which are read into the text', Macchia, 'Towards a Theology of Initial Evidence', p. 170. See Gordon Fee, 'Tongues – Least of the Gifts? Some Exegetical Observations on 1 Corinthians 12-14', *Pneuma* 2 (1980), pp. 3-14.

[401] Macchia, 'Towards a Theology of Initial Evidence', p. 172. He calls Flower 'the most significant general superintendent and leader of the American Assemblies of God', p. 172; cf. Macchia, *Baptized*, p. 36.

[402] Macchia, 'Towards a Theology of Initial Evidence', p. 171.

praise and edification.[403] On the one hand, as a symbol of an encounter with God, glossolalia expresses both human weakness and divine strength in a way that cannot be codified because of its mystery, spontaneity, and artistic expression initiated by God.[404] On the other hand, doctrines function as a grammar that is helpful for explaining truths. In this case, there is an implied relationship between experiencing the presence of God and tongues right from the first Pentecostals.[405] Not only can a case be made from Acts connecting tongues with SB,[406] but the significance of glossolalia in Acts is the bringing 'together all the peoples of the earth in common praise and witness'.[407] He believes that tongues represents a uniting of the people of God as 'oracles' for vocal praise and witness.[408]

The fourth thesis in Macchia's construction of a Pentecostal theology of glossolalia is unity and mission. He affirms tongues as empowerment,[409] but contends that there is a deeper significance to tongues on the Day of Pentecost when contrasted with the

---

[403] Macchia, 'Towards a Theology of Initial Evidence', p. 167. Ultimately that is because 'it is God and not humanity who bears miraculous witness to the gospel' while with sanctification it is the individual who bears witness, p. 166; cf. Macchia, *Baptized*, p. 271.

[404] Macchia, 'Towards a Theology of Initial Evidence', pp. 167-68. We have moved glossolalia 'away from the proper place ... as an experience by formalizing it', p. 168. He reminds Pentecostals that the early Pentecostals tarrying to receive SB implies a sovereignty of God that defies a scientific cause and effect law, p. 155.

[405] Macchia says that it was 'not imported from the outside and imposed upon Pentecostal piety' but it 'was already implied from the beginning of Pentecostal experience and testimony', Macchia, 'Towards a Theology of Initial Evidence', p. 168.

[406] For support Macchia notes, H. Gunkel, R. Pesch, G. Montague, K. McDonnell, and J. Williams (Macchia, 'Towards a Theology of Initial Evidence', pp. 159-62).

[407] Macchia, 'Towards a Theology of Initial Evidence', p. 159.

[408] Macchia, 'Towards a Theology of Initial Evidence', p. 162, cf. 165. Becoming an oracle of God in these last days does not imply ability or worthiness as 'tongues reveal the limits of human speech to capture and express the mystery of God's redemptive presence'; glossolalia is 'trying to put into words what is deeper than words', p. 163. Even misguided missionary tongues pointed in the right direction, reaching beyond one's self to 'share the goodness of God across cultural and national boundaries', p. 164.

[409] Macchia, 'Initial Evidence', p. 121. He notes that this required a narrowing of its connection to sanctification, Macchia, *Baptized*, p. 83.

tower of Babel story in Genesis 11. Pentecost is more than a reversal of the scattering of languages.[410] To view Babel simply as punishment[411] is myopic because there is a rich 'positive reading' that is possible.[412] It can be argued that the scattering was God's grace upon them 'as a way of breaking the spell of idolatry and disobedience ... and filling the earth with the proliferation of life'.[413] One could say the dispersion was God's gracious way of getting humankind to spread out over the world and live freely and creatively, developing various cultures and languages as he intended from the beginning.

Tongues at the Pentecost event are really a fulfilment or a resolution of the Babel metaphor in two ways: first, the coming together at Pentecost of the Diaspora Jews is a reversal of the scattering, but there immediately follows another scattering after Pentecost, one, 'not in fragmentation, but unified by the Spirit'.[414] Second, it is important that 'the languages of Pentecost are not reversed into a single tongue'.[415] Macchia says that the Day of Pentecost glossolalia is 'not incomprehensible but *over*comprehensible' meaning that there is 'a common understanding that floods over cultural boundaries to include everyone'.[416] There is a universal experience in the midst of diversity.

This view has several implications for glossolalia: first, it affirms an 'ecumenical significance' to tongues in Acts 10 that 'requires the actual presence of Gentile participants and not just their

---

[410] Macchia, 'Babel and the Tongues of Pentecost', p. 51.

[411] Macchia acknowledges the concept of judgment in the story as well as God's grace, Macchia, 'Babel and the Tongues of Pentecost', p. 43.

[412] Macchia, 'Babel and the Tongues of Pentecost', p. 44.

[413] Macchia, 'Babel and the Tongues of Pentecost', p. 42.

[414] Key to this point is Paul's speech at the Aeropagus in Acts 17.27, in which the peoples of the world were dispersed in a way that would help them recognize God as the gift of life, breath, and being in the midst of their migrations and unique geographical and cultural settings, Macchia, 'Babel and the Tongues of Pentecost', p. 44; cf. Macchia, *Baptized*, pp. 211-18.

[415] Macchia, 'Babel and the Tongues of Pentecost', p. 44. He notes that the early Pentecostals 'turned to a notion of what may be termed the sanctification of human speech. The unruly tongue is said to be tamed and transformed into a source of telling truth, praising God, or bearing witness to Christ.' Macchia, *Baptized*, p. 83.

[416] Macchia, 'Babel and the Tongues of Pentecost', p. 44.

representation by Diaspora Jews'.[417] Tongues are 'the first ecumenical language of the church' because 'no single language or voice in the dialogue can unambiguously hold the truth'.[418] Second, the early Pentecostals started with a global theology of tongues that brought together people of various cultures and races,[419] but they were 'saddled with the mistaken assumption that tongues were used in the New Testament to preach the gospel to the nations'.[420] When MT proved to be folly, Pentecostals sought out a meaning for their glossolalic experience and 'drifted towards an ecstatic experience that marked certain Christians as being filled' with the implication that others were partially or not filled. In other words, tongues become exactly the opposite of what God intended, a point of division instead of unity.[421] Third, while giving high marks to both Pauline and Lucan nuances for tongues,[422] he opts for a rich and liberating, unfettered definition of tongues.[423]

Heidi G. Baker, 1995

Heidi G. Baker's PhD thesis reconstructs Pentecostalism's theology of glossolalia by emphasizing it as a prayer language that is a 'liberating, democratizing and unifying experience, a trans-rational devotional language of the heart' that is 'sacramental in significance'.[424] She believes that Pentecostal SB has parallels in the

---

[417] Macchia, 'Babel and the Tongues of Pentecost', p. 46; cf. Macchia, *Baptized*, p. 218.

[418] Macchia, 'Babel and the Tongues of Pentecost', p. 49; cf. Macchia, *Baptized*, p. 213.

[419] E.g. *AF* 1.5 (Jan. 1907), p. 3.

[420] Macchia, 'Babel and the Tongues of Pentecost', p. 48.

[421] Macchia, *Baptized*, p. 36. 'This is the great value of the Pentecostal emphasis on speaking in tongues. Tongues are the language of love, not reason ... the outpouring of divine love upon us is the ultimate description of Pentecost', p. 257.

[422] Macchia writes, 'Luke may give tongues a public sign value not found in Paul and Paul may grant tongues a personal/individual value not discussed in Luke. But this difference adds variety and richness to a theology of tongues', Macchia, 'Babel and the Tongues of Pentecost', p. 50.

[423] Macchia comes pretty close to saying that dogmatic statements are exclusive and idolatrous rather than liberating, diverse, and heavenly when he writes 'ideas become dogma and any diversity of tongues, heresy'. Macchia, 'Babel and the Tongues of Pentecost', p. 49.

[424] Heidi G. Baker, 'Pentecostal Experience: Towards a Reconstructive Theology of Glossolalia' (PhD Thesis, King's College, London, England, 1995), pp. ii; cf. pp. 208-33.

broader church experience. For example, the RCC has confirmation 'that takes place after personal profession of faith and after appropriate instruction';[425] and the 'early Eastern Orthodox Christians saw chrismation as an extension of Pentecost ... the Holy Spirit descends on the person baptized and seals on him the grace of baptism';[426] however, 'the Reformed tradition allows for only one beginning event of Christian life'.[427]

Baker notes that 'glossolalia may not be considered a fail-proof sign of Spirit baptism for several reasons':[428] 1) 'there is no declaration in the New Testament stating it as the only evidence', 2) 'formalization in essence denies the complete freedom and sovereignty of the Holy Spirit',[429] and 3) it 'tends to detract from the broader theological significance of glossolalic prayer'.[430] She concludes that 'Pentecostals would do well to recognize tongues (IE) not as normative, but only as a normal and legitimate symbol'.[431]

Baker's constructive work supports her thesis that glossolalic prayer is a 'liberating, democratizing and unifying experience,[432]

---

[425] Baker, 'Pentecostal Experience', p. 156.
[426] Baker, 'Pentecostal Experience', p. 161.
[427] Baker, 'Pentecostal Experience', p. 168.
[428] Baker, 'Pentecostal Experience', pp. 152-82, 200, 227.
[429] Baker, 'Pentecostal Experience', p. 180.
[430] Baker, 'Pentecostal Experience', p. 182.
[431] Baker, 'Pentecostal Experience', p. 182. Baker's position is 'that the infilling ... need not be attested to by glossolalia', and one's 'personal Pentecost is only an expectation and a commencement of the conclusive theophany of God that will come in the Parousia for all believers', pp. 234, 292. Cf. Jack W. Hayford, *The Beauty of Spiritual Language* (Nashville, TN: Thomas Nelson, 1966), pp. 93, 98.

[432] As for liberating, here quoting Macchia, 'glossolalia is an unclassifiable, free speech response to an unclassifiable, free God. It is a language of the Imago Dei''', Baker, 'Pentecostal Experience', p. 180. 'Those who pray in tongues believe they are capable of more in life because of the availability of the spirit', p. 212. Regarding democratizing, she writes, 'Glossolalic prayer may also be theologically reconstructed as an essentially democratizing practice, enabling even the least likely to proclaim the gospel ... to express themselves without learning religious phraseology that may be required of priests and pastors', Baker, 'Pentecostal Experience', pp. 213-14. As for unifying, she states, 'Glossolalia may be understood as a reversal of the tower of Babel, a type of reestablishing of international church unity ... a symbol of universal oneness and an expansion of the gospel to all peoples', Baker, 'Pentecostal Experience', p. 216.

and a trans-rational devotional language of the heart[433] which is sacramental in nature'.[434] However, and perhaps more important, is her work on kenosis and theosis. She writes that the 'practice of glossolalic prayer may be understood as emptying out of the self before God (kenosis) so that one might become full of the Holy Spirit and thereby participate in Christ's nature (theosis)'.[435]

Her definition of theosis is taken from Eastern Orthodox theologians: 'the experience and practice of glossolalic prayer symbolize the indwelling presence of God … we may see glossolalic prayer as a symbol which becomes the language of divine mystery'.[436] 'While we may not know the essence of God, it is still possible to encounter God'.[437] Glossolalia itself is the '"utterance of sounds from the depths of one's being (and) can symbolize an encounter with the divine reality" … these mystical sounds are "as sonorous forms of the divinity, as icons composed as sounds"'.[438] This encounter opens one up to greater illumination by the Holy Spirit, 'a path to a vivid awareness of things divine as well is a symbol of participation in things divine'.[439] Therefore,

> the true significance of glossolalia is in what it symbolizes theologically … a response of the total self to the prior and inef-

---

[433] 'Glossolalic prayer transcends one's own knowledge and language abilities and arises from the depth of the human spirit illuminated by the Holy Spirit', Baker, 'Pentecostal Experience', p. 219.

[434] 'In glossolalic prayer the participant focuses on God as the object of adoration, and therefore the focus moves away from language as the means of adoration … (and becomes) a "linguistic symbol of the sacred" … (that) says "God is here"', Baker, 'Pentecostal Experience', p. 228.

[435] Baker, 'Pentecostal Experience', p. 253.

[436] Baker, 'Pentecostal Experience', pp. 260-61. This 'subject could only be approached by means of the language of metaphor – the use of symbolism – and the context of prayer and wonder' because 'it is clear that the God of Orthodoxy and Pentecostalism is a living God, both transcendent and willingly immanent. He will not, therefore, fit into pre-possessed philosophical categories. The apophatic characteristic of the theological tradition of the East may also help us to perceive in some way the ongoing experience and practice of glossolalic prayer', pp. 260-61. Baker addresses Evagrius, Macarius, and Diadocus as intellectual figures of Orthodox Byzantium, Baker, 'Pentecostal Experience', pp. 269-75; Symeon The New Theologian's contribution of experience, pp. 275-80; and Gregory Palamas as representative of Hesychasm, pp. 280-84.

[437] Baker, 'Pentecostal Experience', p. 267.

[438] Baker, 'Pentecostal Experience', p. 274.

[439] Baker, 'Pentecostal Experience', p. 277. Theosis is also a process, p. 285.

fable self-disclosure of God ... The purpose of this form of prayer is not to inform, but to participate in the divine nature.[440]

In so doing, it is 'an expression of mystery'; it is 'holy speech authored by and addressed to God'.[441]

Simon Chan, 1997, 1999, and 2000

The collective works of theologian Simon Chan have shaped the recent discussion on glossolalia.[442] He believes that the theology of IE appears to be 'in tatters' for two reasons:[443] 1) the problem of using the overly scientific term 'evidence' and 2) the gap between Luke's and Paul's pneumatology.[444] Luke's understanding is phenomenological whereas Paul's is soteriological, and Chan senses that the two views must be harmonized under some larger category.[445]

Chan proposes as a solution the broad category of relationship, noting that the 'initial evidence doctrine makes the best sense only

---

[440] Baker, 'Pentecostal Experience', pp. 279-80.

[441] Baker, 'Pentecostal Experience', pp. 282, 286. 'In the end language alone is not adequate to express the depth of one's encounter with God to others. (But) Mystical and symbolic imagery advances from the incapacity of rational language to express experience', p. 292.

[442] Simon Chan, 'The Language Game of Glossolalia, or Making Sense of the "Initial Evidence"', in Wonsuk Ma and Robert P Menzies (eds.), *Pentecostalism in Context: Essays in Honor of William W. Menzies* (JPTSup 11; Sheffield: Sheffield Academic Press, 1997), pp. 80-95; Simon Chan, 'Evidential Glossolalia and the Doctrine of Subsequence', *AJPS* 2.2 (1999), pp. 195–211; Simon Chan, *Pentecostal Theology and the Christian Spiritual Tradition* (JPTSup 21; Sheffield: Sheffield Academic Press, 2000).

[443] Chan, 'The Language Game of Glossolalia', p. 80.

[444] Chan, 'The Language Game of Glossolalia', p. 81.

[445] He notes three insufficient solutions to bridge this gap: 1) Robert Menzies 'power for ministry' paradigm which he notes 'entails methodological difficulties' and is too narrow a category, Chan, 'The Language Game of Glossolalia', p. 83 n. 12, cf. p. 85. 2) Turner's non-sacramental CI view ends theologically being subsumed into the evangelical view of salvation, Chan, 'Evidential Glossolalia and the Doctrine of Subsequence', pp. 197, cf. pp. 202, 208. 3) Peter Hocken's relatively overlooked category of 'revelation' fits well with the testimonies of the early Pentecostals, Chan, 'The Language Game of Glossolalia', p. 85; cf. Peter D. Hocken, 'The Meaning and Purpose of "Baptism in the Spirit"', *Pneuma* 7.2 (1985), pp. 125-33. However, revelation was an insufficient category for the early Pentecostals because they 'testified, among other things, to the nearness of Jesus and the "revelation of the triune God in me"', Chan, 'The Language Game of Glossolalia', p. 85.

in the context of such intimacy'.[446] He writes, 'relationship is a more basic category for understanding the nature of the work of the Spirit than mission. We can understand mission in terms of relationship but not vice versa'.[447] Tongues occur within a relationship of intimacy with God and when the individual's mind and will are not overpowered by the Spirit.[448] Tongues are the natural result of being overwhelmed with God's presence, just as it is the natural to cry when one is sad, so too,

> if the *initial* baptism in the Spirit is understood as essentially denoting an experience of deep personal intimacy with the triune God in which the Spirit exercises full control, then it would be in fact quite accurate to see tongues as its natural concomitance or evidence.[449]

Chan supports his solution in four ways.

First, SB falls theologically into one of two camps, either a CI one or a sacramental one. The evangelical CI view, at its closest point of Pentecostal understanding, tends to see SB merely as an 'intensification of a pre-existing reality' which occurred at salvation.[450] Chan prefers a sacramental view that is close to Macchia's.[451] He proposes that

> a sacramental view of Spirit-baptism has the advantage of preserving the distinctiveness of the Pentecostal experience (which the two-stage theory tries to do) and at the same time grounding the experience in the doctrine of conversion-initiation.[452]

Without a sacramental view, evidential tongues become 'normal'

---

[446] Chan, 'The Language Game of Glossolalia', p. 85. He gives the analogy of two lovers who develop their own '"idiolect" known only to themselves'; or to a parent who has such a close relationship with their child that they can understand their babblings. Pentecostals 'may not always be the most spiritually mature, yet within their limited knowledge they are able to enter into a deeply meaningful level of personal engagement with their heavenly Father', Chan, 'The Language Game of Glossolalia', p. 86.
[447] Chan, *Pentecostal Theology*, pp. 45-46.
[448] Chan, 'The Language Game of Glossolalia', p. 88.
[449] Chan, 'The Language Game of Glossolalia', p. 90.
[450] Chan, *Pentecostal Theology*, p. 56.
[451] Chan, 'The Language Game of Glossolalia', p. 87.
[452] Chan, 'Evidential Glossolalia and the Doctrine of Subsequence', p. 210.

but not the 'norm'; it loses its 'distinctive qualities' in the evangelical view where the Christian life is 'one big, indistinct blob'; and Pentecostals appear to be 'spiritual elites', because the 'power for ministry' definition states only the result of Spirit-baptism and not its theological essence.[453] Chan believes in connecting evidential glossolalia sacramentally into the CI *ordo salutis*, similar to water baptism and confirmation.[454] He suggests that Pentecostals 'locate Spirit-baptism in the sacrament of holy communion' which would dovetail nicely with 'repeatable infillings'.[455]

Chan clarifies his sacramental view in three ways: 1) there is an emphasis on the divine initiative in the encounter, making it a 'symbol of a spiritual reality and not just an arbitrary sign'.[456] Indeed, it 'must always be interpreted in the context of the presence of God'.[457] However, he believes, this encounter aspect does not fit well with sacramentalism.[458] Therefore, 2) the tongues of SB are a passive or infused grace; whereas, tongues as a prayer language is a 'means of grace'.[459] Tongues

> were not the means of grace but the *fruit* of grace, the spontaneous response to the *prior* action of God ... It is this aspect of Pentecostal experience that tongues functions as 'evidence' rather than as sacramental sign.[460]

Initially tongues is a signal 'of the in-breaking of divine revelation' and subsequently 'a "prayer language" that can be exercised throughout one's life'.[461] This ascetical component is a human-

---

[453] 'Normal' not the 'norm' is the theological terminus for Menzies' Lucan theology of empowered speech. Subsuming into the evangelical view of salvation is the theological terminus for Turner's non-sacramental CI view. 'Spiritual elitism' is the result of our two-stage experience. Chan, 'Evidential Glossolalia and the Doctrine of Subsequence', pp. 197, cf. pp. 202, 208.

[454] Chan, 'Evidential Glossolalia and the Doctrine of Subsequence', p. 206.

[455] Chan, 'Evidential Glossolalia and the Doctrine of Subsequence', p. 211.

[456] Chan, *Pentecostal Theology*, p. 53.

[457] Chan, *Pentecostal Theology*, p. 55.

[458] Chan, 'The Language Game of Glossolalia', p. 87. Here the sacramental model will have to be expanded to include what he calls an 'enthusiastic concept', where 'in such an overwhelming way ... the only appropriate response is open receptivity'.

[459] Chan, *Pentecostal Theology*, p. 78. 'Pentecostal ascetics' he writes, 'will sometimes speak in tongues quite deliberately as a means of cultivating intimacy with God through an act of *anamesis* ... they simply pray and in the course of praying they will find themselves moving from activity to passivity', p. 81.

[460] Chan, 'The Language Game of Glossolalia', p. 87.

[461] Chan, *Pentecostal Theology*, pp. 77-78.

seeking God side in addition to the divine initiative side.⁴⁶² 3) Physical items can convey the spiritual, and glossolalia is no exception:

> tongues will always sound gibberish from the human perspective. Yet, out of ordinary bread and wine, out of ordinary gibberish, something happens to us: God has graced the bread and wine; God has graced the gibberish!⁴⁶³

The second way that Chan supports his category of relationship is through a Pauline CI view rather than a Lucan power view because: 'these two, while distinct experientially, are one theological reality, one great work of Christian initiation'.⁴⁶⁴ Paul's soteriological dimension includes Luke's charismatic dimension, but not the reverse, and therefore Paul's theology of glossolalia is central to the discussion of SB. The distinct Pentecostal experience is not subsumed into Paul's soteriological category when each biblical author is allowed to speak for himself.⁴⁶⁵ He notes, 'glossolalia bears a *necessary* relation to Spirit-baptism within the larger pattern of canonical meaning'.⁴⁶⁶

His third support for relationship is that 'glossolalia must be brought into a meaningful relationship to other significant theo-

---

⁴⁶² Chan writes, 'there is a basic ascetical structure in the Pentecostal understanding of spiritual progress ... the habit of tarrying ... praying, fasting, seeking the Lord are all necessary conditions', Chan, *Pentecostal Theology*, p. 76.
⁴⁶³ Chan, *Pentecostal Theology*, p. 79.
⁴⁶⁴ Chan, 'The Language Game of Glossolalia', p. 91.
⁴⁶⁵ Chan, *Pentecostal Theology*, p. 47. Chan believes that Matthew nuances believers as empowered through the abiding presence of Jesus (SB); Mark's nuance is SB as empowerment 'as well as anointing to be a servant and the sacrifice for sin'; Luke's focus is on the charismatic work in his gospel and empowerment in the book of Acts and he 'shows relatively little interest in the Spirit as the power of the spiritual, ethical and religious renewal of individual'; John sees it as 'the power to reveal God, especially in the word of Jesus' teaching and preaching'; and Paul's writings has the Spirit 'indwelling the believers who creates the character of Christ in them' in what Turner calls the 'executive power' of Christ.
⁴⁶⁶ Chan, *Pentecostal Theology*, p. 45. Historical occurrences alone fail to 'show from history that it had the same significance that modern Pentecostals have given it', p. 40. The Dunn and Menzies debate confirms to Chan that 'the Pentecostal doctrine can be vindicated if we can establish it within the larger pattern of meaning derived from the whole canon of Scripture', p. 43. Chan is careful to note that this does not undercut biblical authority in a post-modern way, but 'the church as the canonically shaped community *recognizes* the truth as it embodies or 'indwells' the Scripture', p. 44.

logical symbols' in order to reformulate the doctrine without violating the 'integrity of the Pentecostal experience'.[467] For example, he sees a parallel in the mystical tradition and notes Teresa of Avila's reception of 'spiritual delight' from God as an illustration.[468] Following George Lindbeck's cultural-linguistic theory, both a mystic like Teresa of Avila and the Pentecostal 'is operating according to its own cultural-linguistic grammar' and the sign and the thing signified have an 'integral connection'.[469] For a Pentecostal, the sign is tongues and for a mystic like Teresa of Avila, it is silence.[470] Initial evidence is 'a sub-cultural-linguistic system within the larger Christian community',[471] a 'regulative grammar' for the Pentecostal community that parallels grammars in other Christian communities such as the 'Jesus Prayer' and silence.[472] Glossolalia, he writes,

> makes even better sense when evidential tongues are interpreted within the broader context of the Christian mysticism tradition where silence signals a certain level of intimacy with God ... But ultimately, glossolalia, makes the best sense when it is understood as signifying a reality which configures gracious and powerful affection in a distinctively Pentecostal way.[473]

Fourth, Chan contends that relationships need both order and spontaneity. Chan's illustrations of spontaneity and order highlight relationship and glossolalia: just as children live in reality, yet can also experience times of play when they 'step out of the ordinary world into a different world', so Pentecostals have insisted on a

---

[467] Chan, 'The Language Game of Glossolalia', pp. 83, cf. p. 81. He has an ecumenical passion to connect with the broader Christian traditions, Chan, 'Evidential Glossolalia and the Doctrine of Subsequence', pp. 198, 201.

[468] Chan, 'Evidential Glossolalia and the Doctrine of Subsequence', p. 199.

[469] Chan, 'Evidential Glossolalia and the Doctrine of Subsequence', pp. 197, 200; cf. Chan, *Pentecostal Theology*, p. 43.

[470] Chan, *Pentecostal Theology*, p. 61.

[471] Chan, *Pentecostal Theology*, p. 62, n. 89.

[472] Chan, *Pentecostal Theology*, pp. 10, 61-62. For example, he believes that glossolalia 'represents the lower levels of passive prayer, or the transition from active to passive prayer' in the mystical tradition. Chan likens tongues to Teresa of Avila's prayer mansions, specifically the transition from the third mansion to the fourth mansion when, 'the soul becomes increasingly receptive ... (and) the soul receives 'spiritual delight' from God', pp. 59-60.

[473] Chan, *Pentecostal Theology*, p. 41.

second experience or reality separate from the normal reality.[474] Pentecostal tongues present us with a normal Christian life having both order and an unpredictable playfulness in a genuine relationship with the living God.[475]

Mark Cartledge, 1998, 2000, 2006

Mark Cartledge writes on a wide variety of aspects of glossolalia, usually from a multidisciplinary perspective.

Cartledge's first article, is in response to Cox's assessment of glossolalia in the twenty-first century. Cox believes that postmodernism's 'ecstasy deficit' will be filled by glossolalia as 'primal speech'.[476] Through a case study, Cartledge affirms the cultural shift from a fundamentalist's static form of worship to one that is open to experimentation, one that downplays hierarchy, and one that holds in tension scriptural literalism and individual experiences.[477] He believes that twenty-first century use of glossolalia will rest upon the Pentecostal's system of experientialism.

Cartledge's second article is valuable for its bibliographic and theological overview of the main scholarly positions on the nature and function of NT glossolalia.[478] Regarding the linguistic nature of tongues, all the opinions can be summarized into two broad ones: 'either (1) both Luke and Paul considered glossolalia to be unlearned human language (with perhaps angelic speech as well); or (2) they both considered the phenomenon to be inarticulate speech'.[479] Cartledge opts for the former because, while Luke's Pentecost narrative

---

[474] Chan, 'Evidential Glossolalia and the Doctrine of Subsequence', p. 208.

[475] Chan, *Pentecostal Theology*, p. 80. Chan likens the human divine relationship to a child and play. For example, children play in the real world but can create make-believe scenarios, in the same way Pentecostals have breakthroughs into a different/higher reality, p. 80, cf. p. 56. See also, Chan, 'The Language Game of Glossolalia', p. 86; Chan, 'Evidential Glossolalia and the Doctrine of Subsequence', p. 208.

[476] Mark J. Cartledge, 'The Future of Glossolalia: Fundamentalist or Experientialist?', *Religion* 28 (1998), pp. 233-44, cf. p. 234.

[477] Cartledge, 'Future of Glossolalia', pp. 237-38. He breaks from Cox in two ways: 1) his case study revealed that glossolalia may have already changed from 'an evidence of Baptism in the Spirit', to private use for prayer and edification; a reversal from public to private glossolalia, p. 239. 2) Cartledge believes that 'glossolalia will become one symbol among many used in religious practice'.

[478] Cartledge, 'The Nature and Function', pp. 135–50.

[479] Cartledge, 'The Nature and Function', p. 139. The majority of scholars see 'Corinthian glossolalia as emerging out of ecstatic unintelligible speech of Hellenistic antiquity', p. 141. This would make the ecstatic utterances of the

is clearly xenolalia and Paul's 'tongues of men' could be similar, the reverse – that the tongues on the Day of Pentecost could be understood as 'inarticulate speech' – does not fit with the text:[480]

> Luke considered glossolalia to be real unlearned human languages (xenolalia), while Paul understood glossolalia to be either a real unlearned human language (xenolalia) or a mysterious kind of heavenly language which he called 'the language of angels'.[481]

However, Paul was not interested in the 'precise linguistic nature of glossolalia' as much as he was in affirming the gift and its proper use.[482] Paul gives priority to the spiritual community over inspired individuals and objects to glossolalia without interpretation in this context.[483]

The function of tongues, in the end, is determined by whether one gives priority to Luke or Paul.[484] Luke emphasizes tongues as a sign of the end-times, the 'Spirit of Prophecy', and for Paul, it is a sign of God's blessing or curse and can be used in prayer and praise.[485] Parsing his final thoughts on Paul and tongues, Cartledge writes,

> in order to balance the extremes of the spiritual elite, Paul advocates either a more communal use of the gift (with interpretation) or a more privatized use. I would suggest that had it been used and controlled in the public context, the private context may not have been emphasized quite so much as by Paul.[486]

Delphic priestess and the frenzied speech of the Mystery Religions direct forerunners of Corinthian glossolalia. Christopher Forbes disagrees, he says that tongues were original to the early church, a *'religious novum'*, p. 142. Cartledge notes that the definition of ecstatic is important. He believes that to read back an altered state or trance-like state ignores Paul's directive of control in 1 Cor. 14.28. The Corinthian problem was 'the exaltation of glossolalia above other works of the Spirit', p. 143. Paul's correction then is that tongues are not a sign of an elite status and are at best 'a negative sign to unbelievers'.

[480] Cartledge, 'The Nature and Function', pp. 139-40.
[481] Cartledge, 'The Nature and Function', pp. 149-50.
[482] Cartledge, 'The Nature and Function', p. 139.
[483] Cartledge, 'The Nature and Function', pp. 144, 149.
[484] Cartledge, 'The Nature and Function', p. 148.
[485] Cartledge, 'The Nature and Function', pp. 149-50.
[486] Cartledge, 'The Nature and Function', p. 150.

Cartledge's third contribution is an examination of Charismatic spirituality. Glossolalia is one of the expressions in a spiritual process; a process of *'searching* for God, who once *encountered* effects change within the life of the searcher, who is then *transformed* or renewed in order to continue the journey'.[487] Tongues as 'inspired speech is a constant thread that runs right through its (Charismatic spirituality's) process and is seen at various points in the framework'; though primarily at the encounter phase, it also occurs at search or transformation phases.[488]

In his chapter on inspired speech Cartledge briefly reviews inspired speech in the OT and NT to show its connection with encountering God, noting that Jesus is called the very Word of God himself, who is then the 'prophet par excellence'.[489] The glossolalia on the Day of Pentecost is linked to a dramatic reception of God's Spirit, which is Jesus' promise of power for witnessing.[490] Experiences of encountering God are central to understanding glossolalia and are 'given expression by means of biblical categories'; in fact, these experiences cannot be described without a conceptual category.

Cartledge holds to a broad category of inspired speech, including prophecy, wisdom, knowledge, discernment, prayer, preaching, and even testimonies.[491] The common aspect here is the divine prompting one to speak, occurring usually at the encounter phase. For example, 'most prophetic speech ... is based upon a prior (though not always) revelatory experience as well as a prompting to speak'.[492] Another category for glossolalia is that of a sign.[493] In fact, initially, one may have an 'overwhelming sense of God's pres-

---

[487] Mark J. Cartledge, *Encountering the Spirit: The Charismatic Tradition* (Maryknoll, NY: Orbis Books, 2007), p. 25 (emphasis added). This process occurs within a framework of narrative, symbol, and praxis, pp. 25-32.
[488] Cartledge, *Encountering the Spirit*, p. 69.
[489] Cartledge, *Encountering the Spirit*, p. 72.
[490] Cartledge, *Encountering the Spirit*, pp. 73-4.
[491] Cartledge, *Encountering the Spirit*, pp. 78-85.
[492] Cartledge, *Encountering the Spirit*, p. 75.
[493] Cartledge believes glossolalia is a key symbol for Charismatics. He follows Hollenweger and Cox noting that glossolalia is a 'cathedral of the poor', and represent a 'liturgy (that) is continually in the making' where 'there is room for improvisation', Cartledge, *Encountering the Spirit*, pp. 29, 60, 61. Along this line, it functions to help the person identify with a particular group, p. 29.

ence and an inescapable urge to articulate the speech that is beginning to be formed in their minds'.[494]

For Cartledge, the process of transformation has an outflow in kingdom witness. Often, tongues are seen as a post-conversion empowerment for ministry by Pentecostals, but Charismatics usually differ from Pentecostals on IE.[495] They prefer a sacramental theology.[496] Regardless, tongues are considered a gateway to power.[497] This power can be called upon for spiritual warfare: 'as a key tool in the armory, speaking in tongues is used as a means of personal and corporate prayer and empowerment, enabling committed and self-sacrificial service to the community for the sake of the gospel'.[498] Finally, Cartledge notes that a glossolalic encounter 'only makes sense within … (an) eschatological framework'.[499] This means that tongues symbolize a restoration of the gifts of Pentecost that 'prepares for the imminent harvest and the return of Christ the King'.[500]

Gerald Hovenden, 2002

In this monograph, Gerald Hovenden's goals are to 'study the phenomenon of "inspired speech" in the ancient world, in order to determine (1) whether "tongues" were a feature of the ancient world's religious experience' and 2), if such a context affected the first Christians' understanding of tongues.[501] Hovenden's study not only examines the contextual backgrounds of glossolalia, he also applies the results of his findings to a fresh examination of the Lucan and Pauline texts on glossolalia. Four noteworthy items evolve: 1) glossolalia is unique to the Christian church and originated on the Day of Pentecost. 2) The 'spiritual ones' in Corinth was not just a faction within the church, but was the entire church in contrast to other lesser churches.[502] 3) Paul's restrictions on pub-

---

[494] Cartledge, *Encountering the Spirit*, p. 78.
[495] Prophecy or dance can also be initiatory evidence, Cartledge, *Encountering the Spirit*, p. 108.
[496] Cartledge, *Encountering the Spirit*, pp. 108-109.
[497] Cartledge, *Encountering the Spirit*, p. 108.
[498] Cartledge, *Encountering the Spirit*, p. 111.
[499] Cartledge, *Encountering the Spirit*, p. 114.
[500] Cartledge, *Encountering the Spirit*, p. 113.
[501] Gerald Hovenden, *Speaking in Tongues: The New Testament Evidence in Context* (JPTSup 22; Sheffield: Sheffield Academic Press, 2002), p. 3.
[502] Hovenden, *Speaking in Tongues*, pp. 166-67.

lic glossolalia were to ensure orderly worship and to not hinder evangelistic efforts. Tongues were being used insensitively and may have been confused with 'cultic worship'.[503] 4) 'There are apologetic implications of the sacramentality of tongues', which should be explored further.[504]

The most significant finding is that that there was no glossolalia-like phenomenon in the ancient world until the Day of Pentecost. Until then, 'it appears likely that the phenomenon of "speaking in tongues" was unknown'.[505] This finding is in direct conflict with Mills's thesis that 'the early Christians may well have known of a religious phenomenon not wholly different from what Luke described in the Pentecost narrative'.[506] Hovenden examined possible parallel occurrences of 'inspired speech' in the ancient pagan world right up through the NT era.[507] In all of the cases examined, the speech was either not glossolalic, was intelligible, or was produced by natural talent or an induced means.[508] Hovenden also examined inspired speech in the OT and inter-Testamental periods, which revealed that though prophecy was at times involuntary and other times contagious, the fact God spoke to his people through prophets / prophecy does not lead automatically to glossolalia or xenolalia because the prophecy was always intelligible.[509] However,

---

[503] Hovenden, *Speaking in Tongues*, p. 167. Hovenden believes contemporary tongues-speakers should ask 'what connotations the non-Christian would associate with speaking in tongues' today, p. 167.

[504] Hovenden, *Speaking in Tongues*, pp. 167-68.

[505] Hovenden, *Speaking in Tongues*, p. 164.

[506] Hovenden, *Speaking in Tongues*, p. 29 n. 122.

[507] He surveyed the following ancient documents: the Mari documents, the story of Cassandra daughter of King Priam of Troy, the encounter of Mys the Carian and Ptoan Apollo by three ancient writers, the literature of the Dionysus Cult especially Euripides' *Bacchae* and Lycophron's *Alexandra*, and the famous Oracle at Delphi was given extensive attention, Hovenden, *Speaking in Tongues*, pp. 6-26. He also surveyed the records of Alexander of Abunoteichos and the evidence from Livy from the Hellenistic mystery religions, pp. 26-30.

[508] In fact, the singular possible account of parallel phenomena may have been an imitation of the Day of Pentecost phenomena, in other words having the exact opposite influence. Alexander of Abunoteichos may have been 'deliberately imitating, in order to gain credibility, the Christian phenomenon of tongues', Hovenden, *Speaking in Tongues*, p. 28.

[509] Hovenden, *Speaking in Tongues*, pp. 31-37. Hovenden examines 1 Sam. 10.5-13; 19.20-24; and Isa. 28.9-13 extensively while many others are referenced.

Hovenden agrees with Mills and Cyril Williams that there is a discernible move within the OT prophets away from ecstatic to intelligible speech and that the psychological features associated with the glossolalists are similar to the prophets.[510] He writes, 'the Spirit motifs in Luke's writings are predominantly Jewish in origin, and owe little if anything to specifically Greek mysticism or Manic prophecy'.[511] Both Menzies and Max Turner agree that there was a Hebrew origin for a 'Spirit of prophecy' motif from which the NT understanding of glossolalia would develop.[512] Specifically, it was the expectation that God communicates to humanity through intermediaries and that 'such communication could be spontaneous and directed towards God'.[513] In fact, Hovenden implies that, rather than being influenced by its context, Christianity may have been the source of glossolalic-like phenomena world-wide.[514]

Although Hovenden's examination of Lucan tongues is thorough,[515] he believes the next significant item regards the Corinthian context. Largely flowing out of an impasse over 1 Cor.

---

[510] Hovenden, *Speaking in Tongues*, pp. 36-37. He finds, for example, that there was no 'prophetic silence' during the intertestmental period, it merely changed its form into what D. Aune categorizes as: 1) apocalyptic, 2) eschatological, 3) clerical, and 4) sapiential, cf. pp. 42-43.

[511] Hovenden, *Speaking in Tongues*, pp. 53-54.

[512] Hovenden, *Speaking in Tongues*, pp. 44-47. Menzies believes this 'Spirit of prophecy' is the traditional Jewish understanding of the Spirit, where 'the Spirit acting as the organ of communication between God and a person', p. 44. Turner is more nuanced and broader than just speech. For Turner, the Spirit of prophecy is: 1) charismatic revelation and guidance to an individual, 2) charismatic wisdom, 3) invasively inspired prophetic speech, and 4) invasively inspired charismatic praise, pp. 44-45.

[513] Hovenden, *Speaking in Tongues*, p. 53.

[514] He quotes Samarin for support: glossolalia is 'rarely found in societies that have had no contact with Christianity', Hovenden, *Speaking in Tongues*, p. 166.

[515] Hovenden, *Speaking in Tongues*, pp. 56-104. He concludes that Luke *did not* have a theological motive and the Day of Pentecost event was a real occurrence, pp. 93-94. As theological motifs, Mt. Sinai, the tower of Babel, the birth of the Messiah and the birth of the church, and the Acts thesis sentence (Acts 1.8) of receiving power for mission are merely 'backcloths' that Luke uses to explain what was intrinsic to the event itself, pp. 80, 86-88, 91 cf. pp. 89-93. Tongues, according to Luke 'represent the coming of the Spirit of prophecy' as an ecstatic experience that includes 'invasive charismatic praise' and it becomes a 'normal and possibly widespread, part of the early church's experience', pp. 102, 104. Tongues breaks down religious and social barriers, signals the end-times, and is an IE, though Hovenden would not as define IE as narrowly as Menzies would, pp. 99-102.

12.29-30 (do all speak in tongues?) between Turner and Menzies,[516] Hovenden theorizes that contextually, Paul is not referring to a faction of over-zealous tongues-speakers within the church, but that the conflict was between the Corinthians and other churches that they viewed as less spiritual.[517] The question at Corinth was not how can 'divine and demonic ecstasy be distinguished from each other',[518] viz a viz, the influence of a Hellenistic religion;[519] but rather Paul's goal was 'to remind them that (an) "inspired utterance" as such is not evidence of being "led by the Spirit" ... *all* the χαρίσματα are, therefore, indications of the Spirit's presence'.[520]

Hovenden's third finding is that Paul's restrictions on tongues at Corinth was so that the people could be instructed and to ensure that tongues were not confused with the 'anomalous speech with cultic worship' of the Hellenistic culture.[521] Paul clearly desires intelligent speech in the public assembly and tongues is 'a means of address to and praise of God'; however, the lack of order in the lists of spiritual gifts reveals Paul bringing balance to the public use of the gift, 'while at the same time affirming its value as a genuine gift of God'.[522] Paul believed tongues to be a non-ecstatic[523] 'language in the broadest sense (on occasion human, and on occasion possibly angelic)'.[524] His stress on intelligibility, especially

---

[516] Hovenden, *Speaking in Tongues*, pp. 152-59. Menzies believes Paul is referring to the public manifestation and not the private use, but Turner believes this leads to the public use being superior to the private use, p. 154. Turner does not believe Paul saw tongues as available to all believers.

[517] Hovenden cites the source of this thought from Gordon Fee (Gordon D. Fee, *The First Epistle to the Corinthians* (Grand Rapids: Eerdmans, 1987), p. 6), but Fee believes that the conflict is between the Corinthian church and Paul, Hovenden, *Speaking in Tongues*, pp. 156-57, cf. pp. 156-59.

[518] Hovenden, *Speaking in Tongues*, p. 108.

[519] There is no 'hard evidence' that the Cephas party was connected to Peter or had anything to do with tongues; and neither are there any undisputed parallels to tongues in Hellenistic religions, Hovenden, *Speaking in Tongues*, pp. 106-108.

[520] Hovenden, *Speaking in Tongues*, pp. 110-11.

[521] Hovenden, *Speaking in Tongues*, p. 167, cf. pp. 130-32.

[522] Hovenden, *Speaking in Tongues*, pp. 111, 114.

[523] Which means it was subject to regulation, Hovenden, *Speaking in Tongues*, p. 150. This is contrary to Dunn and F. Bruce who believe in a state of ecstasy, pp. 148-49 n. 202.

[524] This is contrary to Dunn and Fee who believe it was primarily angelic in nature and in agreement with V. Poythress and Forbes who believes it to be 'the

coming from a tongue-speaking ally, enables him to imply that 'tongues have no evangelistic potential'.[525] Uninterpreted tongues are a sign to unbelievers; they are a sign of 'God's displeasure and impending judgment' because of their rejection.[526]

Hovenden's fourth item is the affirmation of a sacramental element to tongues,[527] though it is rather undeveloped in his book. Also noteworthy is his work on devotional tongues[528] and his conclusion that Pauline and Lucan tongues are complimentary because they are written from two different contexts.[529] He holds to a broad interpretation of IE.[530]

William K. Kay, 2006

While this investigation does not directly address the psychological aspects of glossolalia nor psychology as an approach to the study of tongues, this significant piece by William K. Kay is presented as background and a resource to the subject.[531] Kay provides an historical overview of all the major works that examine glossolalia from a psychological perspective. Kay observes that Pentecostalism

> came into being at almost the same time as psychology and psychiatry. So while these new humanistic academic disciplines

---

miraculous ability to speak unlearned human and (possibly) divine or angelic languages', Hovenden, *Speaking in Tongues*, p. 126, cf. pp. 124-30.

[525] Hovenden, *Speaking in Tongues*, p. 131. For example, quoting Fee: 'Paul's urgency is for the Corinthians to cease thinking like children, to stop the public use of tongues, since it only drives the unbeliever away rather than leading him or her to faith', p. 146.

[526] Hovenden, *Speaking in Tongues*, p. 147.

[527] Hovenden, *Speaking in Tongues*, pp. 138-40.

[528] Hovenden, *Speaking in Tongues*, cf. pp. 132-41. Hovenden notes that Paul does not explain how tongues edifies the individual other than as speaking to God in prayer, praise, blessing, thanksgiving, and mysteries. Hovenden finds common ground among Dunn, Fee, J. Sweet, Turner, Macchia, and even Poythress and E. Käsemann.

[529] Hovenden, *Speaking in Tongues*, pp. 159-61.

[530] Hovenden, *Speaking in Tongues*, p. 151. Paul would agree that all believers have the potential to speak in tongues, though 'there is no reason to believe that Paul thought tongues a necessary sign of the presence of the Spirit. Clearly he considers a whole range of manifestations to be proofs of the Spirit's indwelling'. Potentially all may, but to press this to all 'should' speak in tongues is 'claiming too much', p. 161.

[531] William K. Kay, 'The Mind, Behaviour and Glossolalia: A Psychological Perspective', in Mark J. Cartledge (ed.), *Speaking in Tongues: Multi-Disciplinary Perspectives* (Studies in Pentecostal and Charismatic Issues; Bletchley, Milton Keynes, England: Paternoster Press, 2006), pp. 174-205.

started to explore the inner space of the psyche, a fresh supernaturalistic wave of spiritual life began to break on the shores of North America and Europe, and to bring with it a revived conception of the normal Christian.[532]

The earliest Pentecostals 'attracted the research interest of leading psychologists and psychiatrists', which 'was almost uniformly hostile'.[533] This survey reveals that as psychology advanced in its research methods and listened to other 'human and social sciences', its assessment of glossolalia and glossolalics has

> overturned most of the findings of earlier research: glossolalics are not in trace-like states when they are speaking in tongues; they do not show signs of psychopathology; they are not especially susceptible to hypnosis; they are not neurotic; evidence for social learning of glossolalia is weak; glossolalics are not especially dependent upon authority figures; glossolalia may be, but need not be, a sign of commitment to a charismatic group; the meaning of glossolalia may indeed be theologically derived, but this need not be to its detriment.[534]

Kay's research has revealed that there is still interest in research of glossolalia by a wide range of academic disciplines, and that as research methods improve, the psychological perspective is increasingly kind to a Pentecostal understanding of glossolalia. Future research might continue to reveal both theology and psychology as mutually informative.[535]

Delbert H. Tarr, 2010

Pentecostal missionary and linguist Delbert (Del) H. Tarr, Jr. collects and restates some important theological ideas so that an informed reader can understand.[536] Tarr adds to the theological conversation of glossolalia in four ways.

First, the overall thesis of the book is that

---

[532] Kay, 'A Psychological Perspective', p. 178.
[533] Kay, 'A Psychological Perspective', pp. 179, 204. There were notable exceptions such as Carl Jung, pp. 177, 181-82.
[534] Kay, 'A Psychological Perspective', pp. 204-205.
[535] Kay, 'A Psychological Perspective', p. 205.
[536] Del Tarr, *The Foolishness of God* (The Access Group, 2010). This overlooked work earns its place in this review for its rich and philosophical/linguistic depth from a widely travelled anthropologist and linguist.

> God has hidden His empowerment from those who insist on their own power ... (but) He gives it freely to those who take the risk of simple obedience and full submission ... God has hidden the precious gift of the fullness of the Holy Spirit baptism behind what seems foolish and even ridiculous (tongues) *so the wrong ones won't find it.*[537]

Just as Jesus' parables were meant to hide as well as illuminate[538] 'so He (God) has hidden the power of the Holy Spirit for the most effective witness behind the symbol of total submission and the foolishness of glossolalia'.[539] Tongues speech *'requires a sort of "emptying" of self, of relinquishing the godlike power of speech and meaning making'.*[540]

Second, Tarr's theology of glossolalia is apophatic.[541] 'I propose the phenomenon of glossolalia is *irrational by design* ... It's not logical, was not meant to be and only suffers damage to its essence in trying to force it through Aristotelian linear Euclidean constructs.'[542] Further, 'the closer one draws to the divine mystery, the more urgent it becomes to express oneself and, concomitantly, the less able one is to find adequate expression'.[543] Ultimately,

> the person who has found meaning in the symbolic exercise of tongues speech does not need to, probably cannot, articulate this overwhelming perception of God's presence in everyday language. When forced to explain it, somehow, it rather ruins

---

[537] Tarr, *The Foolishness of God*, p. 224 (emphasis original).

[538] Tarr, *The Foolishness of God*, p. 221. Tarr also compares it to Paul's 'power in weakness' theology (284) and the incarnation itself, pp. 259-67.

[539] Tarr, *The Foolishness of God*, p. 167. Further, 'He chose the foolishness of tongues as the symbol, the required "getting lost" enough, to empower us for witness so we'd be motivated to "lose our lives to find them" (Matt. 10:39)'.

[540] Tarr, *The Foolishness of God*, p. 265 (emphasis original).

[541] For example, 'conceptual models, diagrams, and verbal expressions of how God may wish to communicate with man and through man can probably never capture the totality of this process, even though they are helpful to our understanding. God is infinite and languages finite. One cannot contain him in words, Tarr, *The Foolishness of God*, p. 121 (emphasis original). Here Tarr acknowledges E. Rybarczyk's work, cf. pp. 72, 136-37, 146-47; 165; 220, 310-11, 318, 426.

[542] Tarr, *The Foolishness of God*, pp. 5, 6, 165 (emphasis original). 'The Holy Spirit is less understood from the rationalized, intellectualized Western world of our times than in the Eastern concrete-relational or psychical world of the 2/3rd World today', p. 118.

[543] Here quoting Macchia, Tarr, *The Foolishness of God*, p. 356.

or diminishes the wonder of it all ... they seek a guide who only has at heart they're getting lost.[544]

Third, 'the "oralness" of tongues speech is a form of "tolerance for ambiguity" the hyper-literalist fundamentalist cannot, nor will not accept'.[545] Christianity began as an oral religion and was only later codified, with leadership changing from a Spirit-inspired prophet to a Bible-teaching priest.[546] Real communication is far richer than words, and includes *'facial expressions, gestures, tone of voice, body posture, the distance between people, use of time* ... we are communicating feelings, values ... and more'.[547] Tongues are like 'a tiny infant (who) attempts to reach out with its cry and nonverbal gestures'.[548] She is clearly understood even though traditional words are not used. One of the more interesting linguistic illustrations was Tarr's learning to understand the 'drum talk' of West Africa:

> African peoples can use the drums to talk to each other, send messages over long distances ... understandable to the average citizen, yet when desired, (they can) drum out a more secret code understood only by the chief and the members of his court ... I could not understand 'drum talk' until I could shift my mind away from the literal, linear, print organized orientation of my European languages ... I chafed at the drummer's inability to drum according to my rules ... The message is more a general impression whose essence ... must be filled in by the receiver.[549]

---

[544] Tarr, *The Foolishness of God*, p. 285.
[545] Tarr, *The Foolishness of God*, p. 293.
[546] Here quoting Smith: 'early Christianity was not a religion of the book ... It was community centred, not around scribes but prophets ... A shift occurred whereby text received a privileged status and the original oral/aural and charismatic way of being was suppressed and all pressed and gradually declared to be defunct ... The emphasis on the letter – planted the seeds which killed and quenched the ongoing revelatory ministry of the Spirit by silencing the prophets with the Canon ... (and was fully) realized nearly 2000 years later in Protestant fundamentalism and conservative evangelicalism – textual communities *par excellence*', Tarr, *The Foolishness of God*, p. 146 (emphasis original). Also following J. Ash, 'the bishops, not the Canon expelled prophecy', p. 86.
[547] Tarr, *The Foolishness of God*, p. 124. Tarr claims 65% of communication is nonverbal, p. 138.
[548] Tarr, *The Foolishness of God*, p. 104, cf. p. 138.
[549] Tarr, *The Foolishness of God*, p. 158; cf. Del Tarr, *Double Image: Biblical Insights from African Parables* (New York: Paulist Press, 1994), pp. 151-55.

Finally, glossolalia is a significant symbol for the Christian community. Tarr believes that tongues empowers the believer as 'a deliverance from the iron cage of grammar and (is) a graceful provision to those who did not have the strength or the fluency to pray with their own words'.[550] Tongues opens 'space for verbal, extemporaneous expression of ordinary believers'.[551] However, like Seymour, Tarr believes that '"tongues as initial evidence" was not true "evidence" until it was *also evidenced* by' divine love and unity.[552] Glossolalia is a symbol of

> the need for justice and reconciliation within the body of Christ. Tongues thus represents 'a broken speech for the broken body of Christ until perfection arrives' … glossolalia is a sign that cuts through differences of gender, class, culture and language to reveal the new community of the Spirit … it is also a sign that the eschatological community of the Spirit is a present reality and that God is at work in the world.[553]

Kenneth Richard Walters, Jr, 2010

In 1983, Russell P. Spittler asked the question, 'who taught those honored forbears that the Holy Spirit needed an "evidence"?'[554] Kenneth Walter's PhD thesis answers that question.[555] In what he calls a 'detailed historiographical' study of the forces that led to nearly universal acceptance of IE among most Pentecostals, he charts five major forces: Scottish common sense realism, Christian evidence literature, camp meeting revivalism, dispensational premillennialism, and restorationism.[556]

First, Thomas Reid and Scottish common sense realism were a reaction to David Hume's philosophy that led to scepticism about

---

[550] Quoting Cox, Tarr, *The Foolishness of God*, p. 228.
[551] Tarr, *The Foolishness of God*, p. 235.
[552] Tarr, *The Foolishness of God*, p. 380.
[553] Tarr, *The Foolishness of God*, pp. 381, 383.
[554] Russell P. Spittler, 'Suggested Areas For Further Research in Pentecostal Studies', *Pneuma* 5.2 (Fall 1983), pp. 39-57 (48).
[555] Kenneth Walters, 'Why tongues? The History and Philosophy Behind the Initial Evidence Doctrine in North American Pentecostal Churches' (PhD Dissertation, Fuller Theological Seminary, 2010). Subsequently published as: Kenneth J. Walters, Jr, *Why Tongues? The Initial Evidence Doctrine in North American Pentecostal Churches* (JPTSup 42; Blandford Forum: Deo Publishing, 2016). Footnotes follow the dissertation.
[556] Walter, 'Why Tongues?', p. 16.

the world in which we live, since 'one could never be sure that one's experience had any real connection to the world outside of one's mind'.[557] Simply put, common sense realism says that one can trust their senses and experiences as a basis for truth. Common sense realism became the foundation for modern science and was so pervasive that it stood behind all theology both conservative and liberal; it was the 'lingua franca' of the time period.[558] An important outflow of common sense realism for Fundamentalism and subsequently for Pentecostalism is the inductive Bible reading method, which was seen as 'science' over the '"esoteric" interpretations of the Germans and other "liberals"'.[559] Walters claims that common sense realism provided the philosophical foundation for Pentecostal's IE doctrine.[560]

Another reaction to scepticism and Darwinism produced a body of Christian writings called 'Christian evidences literature', which purposed to 'provide "proof" of the reliability of the Bible and the divinity of Jesus Christ'.[561] This body of literature was apologetic in nature and 'provided both the logic and vocabulary for the Pentecostal doctrine of initial evidence'.[562] In reaction to Hume, these writers established that evidences are known by their effect, that eyewitnesses can make a strong case, and that miracles authenticated the person and mission of Jesus.[563] This made inner experiences, prophecy, and miracles extremely important as supporting evidence alongside the inductive method of reading Scripture. Most of the earliest Pentecostals used the terminology of Christian evidences to show that miracles authenticated new works of God.[564]

---

[557] Walter, 'Why Tongues?', p. 20.
[558] Walter, 'Why Tongues?', pp. 28, 33.
[559] Walter, 'Why Tongues?', p. 40.
[560] Walter, 'Why Tongues?', p. 231.
[561] Walter, 'Why Tongues?', p. 56.
[562] Walter, 'Why Tongues?', p. 57.
[563] Walter, 'Why Tongues?', pp. 61-68.
[564] Walters, specifically quotes Parham, Tomlinson, and D. Kerr as examples. Walters, 'Why tongues?', pp. 79, 85-86.

Walters writes 'it was at the camp meetings that people expected and experienced physical manifestations which they associated with God's gracious movement in their lives'.[565] He believes that it was out of revivalism that people expected an experience, specifically a second work of grace for sanctification called 'baptism of the Holy Spirit'.[566] In these early camp meetings, tongues was just one of several manifestations, and outsiders saw little difference between the Pentecostal manifestation of tongues and the manifestations in a WH camp meeting.[567]

Regarding dispensational premillennialism, Walters believes that it also played a strong role in the formulation of IE.[568] Even beyond empowerment for mission, he sees that tongues were a sign of the end times.[569] The restoration of tongues meant that the Lord was about to return because there was an expectation of a new Pentecost for the great end times harvest. A new Pentecost would be like the first Pentecost, *'The same causes and same conditions produce the same effects'*.[570]

The final component in the development of the doctrine of IE is restorationism, which basically leaps back in history to the pristine original. Walters claims that restorationism is a ubiquitous paradigm within American society.[571] 'It is restorationism which explains the choice of tongues as the initial physical evidence of the baptism in the Holy Spirit',[572] he writes. Wesleyan Holiness leaders 'were beginning to wonder if their restorationist reading of the scriptures might mean that they could expect a return of the experience of speaking in tongues'.[573] Among these were A.B. Simpson, R.A. Torrey, and D. Warner who helped train Seymour.[574] For example, Walters quotes Simpson: 'if you expect the healing of the sick, you must also include the gift of tongues – and if the gift

---

[565] Walters, 'Why Tongues?', p. 102.
[566] Walters, 'Why Tongues?', p. 92.
[567] Walters, 'Why Tongues?', p. 100, cf. pp. 94-99.
[568] Walters, 'Why Tongues?', p. 103.
[569] Walters, 'Why Tongues?', p. 126.
[570] Walters, 'Why Tongues?', p. 140 (emphasis original).
[571] Walters, 'Why Tongues?', p. 146.
[572] Walters, 'Why Tongues?', p. 142.
[573] Walters, 'Why Tongues?', p. 156.
[574] Walters, 'Why Tongues?', p. 155-60.

of tongues has ceased, so in the same way has the power over diseases'.[575] Adding to this is the concept of the latter rain, which helped give biblical support for restorationism.[576]

In his penultimate chapter, Walters charts the doctrine on IE from these five philosophical foundations, including the rise of language and vocabulary, and the resulting expectation through to the experience of the early Pentecostals.[577] Then, he chronicles the growth and acceptance of the theory of IE and its solidification into the established doctrine of nearly all Pentecostals.[578]

IV. Dialog Partners with an Eastern Perspective

In addition to Baker, Chan, and Tarr (above), the following authors make contributions from an Eastern perspective to the theological conversation about glossolalia.

Edmund J. Rybarczyk, 2005

Pentecostals utilized Modernism well to explain tongues, but such explanations are now dated; therefore, Edmund Rybarczyk calls for a reformulation of Pentecostal glossolalia:[579]

> Evangelicals, and now North American Pentecostals like them, have sought for so long to *explain* Christianity to the world it seems they have forgotten the depths and realities of Christianity are sometimes better simply beheld, simply encountered ... (because) words sometimes damage the mystery.[580]

In this article, he suggests that Orthodoxy's apophatic theology and postmodern philosophical constructs could help Pentecostals explain glossolalia to the world.

---

[575] Walters, 'Why Tongues?', p. 159.
[576] Walters, 'Why Tongues?', p. 162.
[577] Walters, 'Why Tongues?', pp. 180-95.
[578] Walters, 'Why Tongues?', pp. 195-212.
[579] Edmund J. Rybarczyk, 'Reframing Tongues: Apophaticism and Postmodernism', *Pneuma* 27.1 (Spring, 2005), pp. 83-104. Using reasoned arguments from Scriptures, Pentecostals concluded logically that tongues were an evidence – a 'proof', p. 83. He believes that 'Pentecostals might do better to simply embrace the paradoxical nature of tongues speech ... (as) non-rational and non-linear', pp. 95-96.
[580] Rybarczyk, 'Reframing Tongues', p. 103 (emphasis original).

First, apophatic theology 'is a category that is both latent within and implicitly familiar to Pentecostals' but it has been denigrated by modernity.[581] Therefore, a re-examination of apophaticism might be useful in restating Pentecostal glossolalia as praise and prayer. Apophatic theology is knowing by 'the way of unknowing, or the *via negativa*', that is, even though our human minds are limited to known categories, there is an understanding beyond what we know.[582]

> Human beings were created with the capacity to be mystically encountered by God ... an 'organ of vision' in our souls ... something in us that experientially-ontologically corresponds to God himself. This something is not simply our moral capacity, our rationale, or our aesthetic sense ... there is a spiritual *something* constitutive of mankind that was created in order to apprehend God.[583]

Apophaticism is 'knowing' this mystery of God, which is inexpressible.[584] 'Paul makes evident a kind of nascent apophatic theology ... (in) his teaching on tongues as Spirit-given and Spirit-motivated unintelligible praise and prayer, together with his teaching that the Spirit prays through believers'.[585] Put another way, 'man is capable of *transcending his own nature*',[586] that is, despite the fallen nature of humankind, 'God, for his own loving and mysterious reasons, re-creates us to be vehicles for unintelligible and non-rational modes of communication'.[587] For example, Paul's

---

[581] Rybarczyk, 'Reframing Tongues', p. 84.
[582] Rybarczyk, 'Reframing Tongues', p. 84. The Orthodox position holds both apophatic (unknown, yet known) and cataphatic (positive and assertive knowledge) knowledge in tension, p. 89.
[583] Rybarczyk, 'Reframing Tongues', p. 89.
[584] God, 'manifests himself in his simplicity, formed out of the formless, incomprehensible, and ineffable light. I can say nothing more. Nonetheless, *he manifests himself very clearly*. He is perfectly recognizable. He speaks and listens in a manner that cannot be expressed ... But *what can I say about what cannot be spoken about?* What the eye has not seen, with the ear has not heard, what the heart of man has never imagined: *how can any of this be expressed by words,*' Rybarczyk, 'Reframing Tongues', p. 88.
[585] Rybarczyk, 'Reframing Tongues', p. 93.
[586] Rybarczyk, 'Reframing Tongues', p. 90.
[587] Rybarczyk, 'Reframing Tongues', p. 92.

writings supports that one can communicate with God,[588] that the Spirit helps one to pray and that there is great value even in non-rational tongues.[589] In addition, there is an inexpressible response to a divine encounter articulated by glossolalia, note 'how difficult it was to describe the encounters with the resurrected Christ, his Spirit, and the transcendent – divine'.[590] He reminds his readers that Orthodoxy's theological goals differ from Pentecostal usage of apophaticism.[591]

Second, 'Postmodernism is open to non-rational and non-verbal means of knowing ... (it) rejects the tenant that all-knowing is rational, linear, or verbal'.[592] There are two categories, imaging and aesthetics, that could be utilized to explain glossolalia. Phenomenologically, glossolalia is similar to a golfer imagining the end result rather than thinking about their swing: 'the Pentecostal believer who intercedes with unintelligible utterances does not focus on the sounds her mouth is making ... (but) is fixated upon the person, community, or situation for whom or which the Holy

---

[588] 1 Corinthians 14.2. Rybarczyk does not develop this thought much, but states that more than mere communication, the Spirit actually works through the actions of people. The 'insistence that God's Spirit yearns to work in and through the believer's Spirit – characterizes the history of their movement and bears similarities to apophatic theology', Rybarczyk, 'Reframing Tongues', p. 95.

[589] 1 Corinthians 14.14-15, 18-19; Rom. 8.26-27; cf. Rybarczyk, 'Reframing Tongues', pp. 90-93. Fee believes that 'Paul and the early church had not been tampered with by the mind-set of rationalism, and he found great value in prayer that was from the heart, from within, but which did not necessarily need approval from the mind to be uttered before God', p. 91.

[590] Rybarczyk, 'Reframing Tongues', p. 90. He notes that the 'apostolic writers were not concerned to reduce every spiritual experience, miracle, vision or theophany to a plainly cause-and-effect, or rational, level'.

[591] Specific differences are: 1) Orthodoxy regularly incorporates silence in prayer, Rybarczyk, 'Reframing Tongues', p. 95. 2) Orthodoxy's goal via apophaticism is 'the transformation of the human person. By beholding God with the eyes of the soul one becomes like God', pp. 87, 88. It seeks a vision of a transcendent God, called a *'theoria*: a vision of God in one's soul ... a foretaste of the beatific vision that awaits us in eternity', p. 95. Also significant, 3) Orthodox theologians have not discussed glossolalia as apophatic speech, p. 94. 4) 'Along with the ancient ecclesial reasons for the quashing of the pneumatic gifts there is a clear disdain within Eastern Orthodoxy for Pentecostalism as an incomplete Christian expression. Orthodoxy consistently restricts the charismata to ecclesial and liturgical categories', p. 94 n. 48.

[592] Rybarczyk, 'Reframing Tongues', p. 96.

Spirit is impelling her to pray'.[593] Aesthetics and art are 'dynamic and inclusive realms for framing glossolalic practice'.[594] 'Like an artist who paints what cannot easily be put into words, tongues speaking-praying-worshipping helps the believer express to God what words cannot.'[595]

Daniela C. Augustine, 2012

Perhaps the most theologically comprehensive view of glossolalia comes from an Eastern European Pentecostal context, which developed through 'continual dialogue (with) the Eastern Orthodox tradition', and was 'inspired by the liturgical life of the underground Pentecostal movement under Communism'.[596] In this view, Pentecost was a pivotal event, making the church an 'icon on earth'[597] where glossolalia is an audible eschatological sign of 'the ultimate destiny of heaven and earth ... being called together into one holy *koinonia*', functioning as a sacrament.[598]

Following the 'Christus Victor'[599] view of the redemption of society[600] and creation, Daniela Augustine wrote that just as the last Adam

---

[593] Rybarczyk, 'Reframing Tongues', p. 100.

[594] Rybarczyk, 'Reframing Tongues', p. 101. 'God is himself an artist ... the gospel was not given as an idea, an abstract or logical *logos* as it appeared in ancient Greek thought ... (but as) Jesus, the incarnate Word of God', p. 99.

[595] Rybarczyk, 'Reframing Tongues', p. 100.

[596] Daniela C. Augustine, *Pentecost, Hospitality, and Transfiguration* (Cleveland, TN: CPT Press, 2012).

[597] Augustine, *Pentecost, Hospitality, and Transfiguration*, p. 18. She calls her view of Pentecost, an 'incarnationalist view', p. 25.

[598] Augustine, *Pentecost, Hospitality, and Transfiguration*, pp. 35-39. She uses the word sign instead of icon to describe glossolalia, especially when she later describes it as a sacrament that actually participates in what it symbolizes, pp. 37, 39.

[599] This view of the atonement is also called, the 'dynamic' or 'classic' view', cf. Gustaf Aulén, *Christus Victor: An Historical Study of the Three Main Types of the Idea of the Atonement* (New York: MacMillan Publishing Co., 1969).

[600] Her view of salvation goes beyond the individual to the whole of society. For example, 'The Church is the incarnational vehicle of this divinely ordained transfiguring of the world', Augustine, *Pentecost, Hospitality, and Transfiguration*, p. 30. Also, 'Pentecost is also a literal crossing of the bridge from the private to the public ... revealing of the sons (and daughters) of God for which creation longs and groans', p. 26, cf. p. 32.

reversed the consequences of the fall by rejecting the temptation to take a shortcut towards attaining one's calling ... (so) Pentecost reverses the consequences of Babel's imperial project, by reaffirming God's salvific work as redemption of the human community'.[601]

Both the Garden of Eden and the tower of Babel were 'shortcuts' to humanity's ultimate calling of 'deification (*theosis*)'.[602] At Pentecost, 'the Son recapitulates in Himself – into His Body, the Church'[603] and 'the creative power of the Word (like at Mt. Sinai)[604] brings about the reality of the Kingdom in the present through the voices of the Spirit-filled community'.[605]

Speech is an excellent symbol of embracing and accepting 'the other' because 'language ... lies on the borderline between oneself and the other'.[606] Therefore, 'it is no accident that the language of the other stands at the center of the Pentecost event as an expression of the prioritization of the other in the kingdom of a new humanity'.[607] Glossolalia then connects the church with her future as 'an audible sign of this eschatological unfolding with the Body

---

[601] Augustine, *Pentecost, Hospitality, and Transfiguration*, p. 42. Societal sin is the elimination of 'the other' into an 'homogenizing shortcut' which has 'dehumanizing patterns of association' contrary to God's plan of affirming diversity, pp. 31-32.

[602] 'The eastern Orthodox understanding of deification (*theosis*) as attaining the likeness of God in Christ-likeness is affirmed as the ultimate calling and purpose of all humanity ... It takes one will to create humanity, but two to sanctify it ... the synergistic collaboration between the divine and human will', Augustine, *Pentecost, Hospitality, and Transfiguration*, p. 22, cf. p. 21.

[603] Augustine, *Pentecost, Hospitality, and Transfiguration*, p. 27.

[604] Acknowledging scholarly doubts about Pentecost having a Mt. Sinai connection, she nevertheless notes two connections: 1) there is a covenant with his people. 'Pentecost marks the moment of the historical promise of covenantal renewal with God and neighbor ... (the) *telos* for humanity and the rest of creation', Augustine, *Pentecost, Hospitality, and Transfiguration*, p. 34. 2) There is flaming speech. 'God establishes in a creative speech act a covenant with His people ... His flaming words become visible to the multitude ... and later to the flames of Pentecost', p. 32.

[605] Augustine, *Pentecost, Hospitality, and Transfiguration*, p. 29.

[606] Augustine, *Pentecost, Hospitality, and Transfiguration*, p. 34.

[607] Augustine, *Pentecost, Hospitality, and Transfiguration*, p. 34.

of Christ – the mutual indwelling of heaven and earth as a foretaste of the ultimate Christic destiny'.[608] However, it is more than a mere sign of the future: 'the Spirit empowers humanity to recover the speech of the other across lines of alienation and mutual exclusion into a "covenantal conversation that fosters the root form of human relatedness: communion"'.[609] It actually 'unites the material and spiritual dimensions of existence ... transforming and transfiguring the earth into the Kingdom of God'.[610]

Glossolalia functions sacramentally by 'articulating the mystery of the union of the redeemed creation with its Creator and experiencing the in-breaking of the eschatological fullness of Christ in His Body'.[611] There is genuine power in glossolalia because it 'mediates to us the power of the invisible grace that transforms us into a visible extension of Christ on earth'.[612] It is within the context of sacramental tongues that she defines Pentecostalism's IE and ongoing gift of tongues: 'the initial surrender ... is an expression of embracing this call to oneness in Christ as our personal and communal destiny ... (and) the continual practice of speaking in tongues by the believer could be viewed as an act of *praktikê* (ascetic struggle) within the context of liturgy'.[613]

Daniel Castelo, 2017

Daniel Castelo believes 'that Pentecostalism is ... best understood as a mystical tradition of the church Catholic'.[614] He argues that mysticism is the best epistemological category[615] for Pentecostal

---

[608] Augustine, *Pentecost, Hospitality, and Transfiguration*, p. 36.
[609] Augustine, *Pentecost, Hospitality, and Transfiguration*, p. 35.
[610] Augustine, *Pentecost, Hospitality, and Transfiguration*, p. 36.
[611] Augustine, *Pentecost, Hospitality, and Transfiguration*, p. 37.
[612] Augustine, *Pentecost, Hospitality, and Transfiguration*, p. 39. Here she is building upon Macchia, and others who write that tongues are a sign that actually participate in that which they symbolize, p. 38.
[613] Augustine, *Pentecost, Hospitality, and Transfiguration*, p. 37. She defines *praktikê* as 'fasting from oneself on behalf of the other' as in Jn 3.30: 'He must become greater; I must become less'.
[614] Daniel Castelo, *Pentecostalism as a Christian Mystical Tradition* (Grand Rapids, MI: Eerdmans, 2017), pp. xv-xvi. He defines mysticism as 'the encounter with God of the Christian confession' and spirituality as 'activities and practices that anticipate both the encounter itself and the outcomes and obligations stemming from it', pp. xviii-xix.
[615] Castelo offer's Land's 'master category' of spirituality within the community as the best way to ground mysticism epistemologically, Castelo, *Christian*

theology, otherwise, 'if reduced to concepts and proposition ... (it) loses its very essence'.[616] This is 'not due to illogicality on their part, (or) owing to the emotional nature of their faith, but ... [rather that] the mystery of Yahweh ... (is) disposed to leave certain things unresolved'.[617] 'God and the experience of God are inherently irreducible at the conceptual level. Many Pentecostals have been repeatedly at a loss to articulate what it is they witness and experience in Pentecostal worship.'[618] Regarding glossolalia, Castelo believes that 'apophaticism' effectively explains the limits of what humanity can understand and communicate about God encounters.[619] He 'does not feel obligated to retain initial evidence logic',[620] but understands tongues as 'a mystical encounter' coupled with 'a mystical doctrine that support and critique one another'.[621] He offers three suggestions: 1) Pentecostals highlight testimonies involving 'the *attainment* and the *pursuit* of fullness' to downplay the reductionist tendency of the 'haves and have-nots': 'there is always more to experience and consider, given that we live this side of the eschaton'.[622] 2) To 'recognize that trials and spiritual aridity, even spiritual defeat and desolation, are a part of growth even *after* one's baptism in the Holy

---

Mystical Tradition, pp. 3-6, 18, 24. Pinnock's category of 'perfection and relationality' does not connect the bifurcation of spirituality and theology', pp. 15-16.

[616] Here quoting Hollenweger, Castelo, *Christian Mystical Tradition*, p. 4. Chan's category of biblical revelation, self, and the world also fails because 'it puts the systematician "in the driver's seat"', p. 20.

[617] Castelo, *Christian Mystical Tradition*, p. 14.

[618] Castelo, *Christian Mystical Tradition*, pp. 22-23.

[619] 'Apophaticism can serve a crucial role in countering logo-centricity ... both apophaticism and Pentecostalism are at odds with the kinds of evangelicalism ... that assume that revelation needs to be rational, and that which is rational in this particular sense is inextricably bound to an understanding that words can adequately and fittingly account for the mysteries of the faith', Castelo, *Christian Mystical Tradition*, p. 129.

[620] Castelo, *Christian Mystical Tradition*, p. 159. Further, IE logic might be 'perpetuating a masking of a more basic lacuna. Generally put, the empirical availability of tongues may have contributed to a theologically impoverished account of Spirit-baptism among classical Pentecostal American denominations.'

[621] Castelo, *Christian Mystical Tradition*, p. 160 (emphasis original).

[622] Castelo, *Christian Mystical Tradition*, pp. 161, 163. 'The Spirit-baptized life is one that lives in an ongoing paradox of attainment and pursuit because its ground and end is the triune God of Christian confession. The Spirit-baptized life is epicletic in nature – it is a way of life that is actively receptive. It is driven by a burning desire that tastes and seeks the goodness of God', p. 166.

Spirit'.[623] And 3), that 'the transformation of language can be a channel of divine self-disclosure',[624] a knowable ignorance:

> Pentecostals need to wrestle with the claim that ignorance in the spiritual life generally and Spirit-baptism in particular can be a dynamic of grace because the ignorance in question is not vacuous but distance-creating or space-accommodating for the possibility of beholding uniquely the divine splendor.[625]

Tongues-speakers 'do not know what they are saying ... (and) in some sense, *they do not need to know* what they are saying because what is happening at such moments resists and defies description ... (and points) to the superabundance of ... God'.[626]

V. Literature Utilizing the Early Periodicals

This review of literature should reveal the need for this study. It is obvious that a lot of theological discussion has occurred about glossolalia. However, an important voice has largely been missing: the testimony of the first Pentecostals. There are only seven articles that extensively research and utilize these primary sources and testimonies in the area of Pentecostalism's distinctive feature of glossolalia.[627] These articles demonstrate the richness of theological material that has yet to be fully explored. They are examined here as a conclusion to this review of literature and as an introduction to the exploration of the early Pentecostal periodicals.

Gary B. McGee, 1991, 2001, 2008

Historian Gary B. McGee carefully examined the earliest documents and wrote three articles utilizing the Pentecostal periodicals.

---

[623] Castelo, *Christian Mystical Tradition*, p. 167 (emphasis original).

[624] Castelo, *Christian Mystical Tradition*, p. 173.

[625] Castelo, *Christian Mystical Tradition*, p. 176. 'Just as the senses can neither grasp nor perceive the things of the mind ... the inscrutable One is out of the reach of every rational process. Nor can any words come up to the inexpressible Good, this One, this Source of all unity, this supra-existent Being', p. 173.

[626] Castelo, *Christian Mystical Tradition*, p. 176 (emphasis original).

[627] Though several monographs appeal to these works, only these seven articles begin with the periodicals and work towards the theology of the early Pentecostals. For example, Macchia's arguments, in 'Groans Too Deep For Words' (surveyed above), relies on the early periodicals; however, he uses them as support rather than building an argument from them.

In the first article, he specifically seeks out lesser known books, tracts, and magazines to hear the voices of popular preachers and personalities on IE.[628] As expected, McGee discovers that glossolalia was a sign of empowerment for a last day's harvest.[629] However, he also finds a rich purpose for tongues beyond its sign-value. Tongues 1) encourage holiness,[630] 2) reveal yieldedness,[631] 3) minimize the distinctions between clergy and laity,[632] and 4), provide 'a refreshing of spirit for the initiated'.[633]

As for IE, McGee discovers that the pattern from the book of Acts is popular and connected with divine healing.[634] Statements about IE are bold: 'there is no record of anyone ever speaking in tongues before he was baptized in the Holy Ghost',[635] or, does God have a new method for us or 'does He still fill them ... as He did in the days of old?'[636] There is a distinction between initial tongues and the gift of tongues, otherwise 'the Scriptures ... contradict themselves, and Paul's teachings seriously disagree with his practice'.[637] Initial tongues are not controlled by the mind and are 'unregulated by apostolic instruction'; whereas with the gift of tongues, the mind is in control and Paul's rules apply.[638] Finally,

---

[628] Gary B. McGee, 'Popular Expositions of Initial Evidence', in Gary B. McGee (ed.), *Initial Evidence: Historical and Biblical Perspectives on the Pentecostal Doctrine of Spirit Baptism* (Eugene, OR: Wipf & Stock, 2007 reprint; Hendrickson, 1991), p. 120.

[629] For example, A McPherson wrote,

when you walk down the street looking for a barber, first you look for a red and white pole, the sign, in other words. When you are looking for dinner you look for a sign that says, Restaurant. The barber's pole cannot shave you, neither can the wooden restaurant sign feed you, but they are just signs to indicate that behind those doors there is a barber who can serve you, or within the restaurant doors there is food that will satisfy your hunger. So it is with the Bible sign, the speaking in tongues. It indicates that the Comforter has come to abide within (McGee, 'Popular Expositions', p. 122; cf. p. 121).

[630] McGee, 'Popular Expositions', p. 122.
[631] McGee, 'Popular Expositions', p. 123.
[632] McGee, 'Popular Expositions', pp. 123-24.
[633] McGee, 'Popular Expositions', p. 124.
[634] McGee, 'Popular Expositions', pp. 125-27. The connection point is Mk 16.16-18.
[635] McGee, 'Popular Expositions', pp. 126-27.
[636] McGee, 'Popular Expositions', p. 127.
[637] McGee, 'Popular Expositions', p. 129, cf. pp. 127-29.
[638] McGee, 'Popular Expositions', p. 129.

McGee notes that these early pioneers tried to make their case in Scripture and not on experience alone; however, 'a person that has eaten an apple ... is better qualified to speak on the question of the kind and quality of the apple'.[639]

In his second article, McGee makes a case that 1) there was great anticipation for the 'restoration of the gift of tongues ... among radical evangelicals for over two decades' before the ASM revival,[640] and 2) that Parham's theology of MT and IE has roots that predate his formulation.[641] Regarding the failure of MT, McGee writes that by late 1906 and 1907, 'most came to recognize that speaking in tongues constituted worship and intercession in the Spirit (Rom. 8:26; 1 Cor. 14:2), which in turn furnished the believer with spiritual power'.[642]

In his third and final article utilizing the Pentecostal periodicals, McGee proposes that the early Pentecostals were not overwhelmed by the failure of MT[643] because they already had a new

---

[639] McGee, 'Popular Expositions', p. 129.

[640] Gary B. McGee, 'Shortcut to Language Preparation? Radical Evangelicals, Missions, and the Gift of Tongues', *International Bulletin of Missionary Research* 25.3 (2001), p. 122. As early as 1885, three missionaries 'put their Chinese grammar books aside and prayed for the Pentecostal gift of Mandarin and supernatural power according to Mk 16:17', p. 119. In 1889 eight men and women went to Sierra Leone 'confident of biblical promises of healing and Pentecostal tongues'. However, missionary tongues were not received, three died of malaria and the rest persevered through language study, p. 119. Simpson in 1891 'considered the possible reappearance of tongues ... (and wrote) "instances are not wanting now of its apparent restoration in missionary labours both in India and Africa"', p. 110. Later Simpson pulled away from this position. W. Godbey predicted that the 'gift of language ... (was) destined to play a conspicuous part in the evangelization of the heathen world ... (and that) all missionaries in heathen lands should seek and expect this Gift', p. 120.

[641] Pastor Walker Black preached about a 'post-conversion baptism in the Holy Spirit' as early as December 1895, and Jennie Glassey received a 'wonderful language lesson', McGee, 'Shortcut to Language Preparation', pp. 119-20. Through a mutual friend, Frank W. Sandford, Parham heard Glassy's story and even witnessed glossolalia in Durham, Maine. Parham printed Glassy's story in 1899, p. 123 nn. 26-34; cf. Goff, *Fields White unto Harvest*, p. 72; Robeck, *Azusa Street*, pp. 40-43.

[642] McGee, 'Shortcut to Language Preparation', p. 122.

[643] McGee notes that by November of 1906 hesitation was expressed for missionary tongues and its influence was greatly diminished by 1908 because of the reports coming back from the missionary field, Gary B. McGee, '"The

worldview, a 'new world of realities',[644] in which glossolalia was functionally sound. The soundness of this new worldview enabled the early Pentecostals to 'tease out' the following about glossolalia: 1) tongues are a means of deeper prayer,[645] 2) new love inspires Pentecostals to 'reach over ethnic and cultural barriers',[646] and 3) deeper worship is possible through glossolalia.[647]

Cecil M. Robeck, Jr., 1991 and Renea Brathwaite, 2010

Cecil M. Robeck is another historian who makes a significant contribution using the early Pentecostal periodicals. Robeck's first article and Rena Braithwaite's response will be treated together.

Robeck's first article traces the development of Seymour's theology of glossolalia and that of three other pioneers: Pastor Joseph Smale of New Testament Church; his associate Elmer K. Fisher; and Parham.[648] An unsigned ditty in *AF* states '*tongues are one of the signs* that go with every (Spirit-) baptized person ... *but it*

New World of Realities in Which We Live'": How Speaking in Tongues Empowered Early Pentecostals', *Pneuma* 30.1 (January 1, 2008) pp. 108-35 (115 n. 36).

[644] McGee, 'The New World of Realities', p. 108. McGee's title comes from a quote by Alfred Street, an early Pentecostal pioneer, who observes this new worldview: 'it is a mistake to think that outward signs ... are the most important part ... The real wonder is the new world of realities in which we live, the new possibilities that arise from our spirit being restored to its proper place under the guidance of the Holy Spirit', p. 130.

[645] McGee, 'Sphere of the Supernatural', p. 7. Because 'tongues-speech as a missio-linguistic tool drove the notoriety of the new movement, the concomitant role of prayer and worship was obscured', McGee, 'The New World of Realities', pp. 113-14; cf. pp. 119-20, 130. An earlier draft of 'The New World of Realities' was published as: McGee, 'Sphere of the Supernatural', p. 11

[646] McGee, 'The New World of Realities', pp. 113-14; cf. p. 130. Much has been made by other historians that Seymour had to sit outside the classroom in the hall to hear the lecture because of his race. But McGee notes that four of the ten teachers were women and one of these four was African-American, pp. 117, 18. This egalitarian spirituality within Pentecostalism 'explains in part why Pentecostalism has been so easily contextualized around the world', p. 121.

[647] McGee, 'The New World of Realities', pp. 119-20.

[648] Cecil M. Robeck, Jr, 'William J. Seymour and "The Bible Evidence"', in Gary B. McGee (ed.), *Initial Evidence: Historical and Biblical Perspectives on the Pentecostal Doctrine of Spirit Baptism* (Eugene, OR: Wipf & Stock, 2007 reprint; Hendrickson, 1991), pp. 72-95.

is not the real evidence of the baptism in everyday life'.[649] Robeck concludes that tongues were tested by four pioneers: Parham and Fisher arrive at what would become the standard North American doctrine of tongues as the IE of SB; while Smale and Seymour acknowledge the reality of tongues, they reject its evidentiary nature.[650]

Renea Brathwaite challenges Robeck's thesis.[651] Where Robeck sees an 'evolution' in Seymour's thinking, Brathwaite sees a nuancing and not an abandonment.[652] Brathwaite points out three weaknesses: 1) there is a distinction between the 19 articles signed by Seymour and unsigned articles.[653] 2) Robeck's creative use of italics (above).[654] 3) This infers that Seymour, who was kicked out of his denomination for holding to his beliefs, would knowingly allow 'blatant misrepresentations' that were contrary to the published statement of faith in *AF*.[655] Brathwaite concludes that Seymour's view was merely trying to balance 'an over-dependence on the evidentiary value of tongues'.[656]

Glen Menzies, 1998

Glen Menzies evaluates today's AG doctrine of IE with other materials of its original author, Daniel W. Kerr's doctrinal writings, to see if and how they differ.[657] Menzies writes that 'Kerr represents

---

[649] Robeck, 'William J. Seymour and "The Bible Evidence"', p. 81 (emphasis original).

[650] Robeck, 'William J. Seymour and "The Bible Evidence"', p. 88.

[651] Brathwaite, 'Tongues and Ethics', pp. 203-22.

[652] Brathwaite, 'Tongues and Ethics', pp. 204, 222. Brathwaite writes 'this is a pastoral distinction and not a new teaching that seeks to replace tongues with the fruit of the Spirit as the Bible evidence of Spirit baptism', p. 209. Margaret Poloma compares these differing approaches to Jonathan Edwards and John Wesley. Parham, like Edwards approached revival in categories of 'true' or 'false', while Seymour, like Wesley was 'willing to let the weeds grow along with the wheat (rather) than quench what they believed to be the activity of the Holy Spirit', Margaret Poloma, *Main Street Mystics: The Toronto Blessing & Reviving Pentecostalism* (Walnut Creek, CA: Altamira Press, 2003), p. 63.

[653] Brathwaite, 'Tongues and Ethics', p. 209.

[654] Brathwaite, 'Tongues and Ethics', p. 209.

[655] Brathwaite, 'Tongues and Ethics', pp. 212-13.

[656] Brathwaite, 'Tongues and Ethics', p. 222.

[657] Glen W. Menzies, 'Tongues as "The Initial Physical Sign" of Spirit Baptism in the Thought of D.W. Kerr', *Pneuma* 20.2 (1998), pp. 175–89. Menzies notes specifically, books, sermons, and doctrinal committee work, and a handwritten proposed Statement of Fundamental Truths that Kerr was commissioned to draft, pp. 180-83.

an early stage in the development of Pentecostalism ... characterized by greater fluidity ... (when) theological variety was tolerated'.[658] He believes that Kerr would hold a broader view.[659] Menzies reasons: 1) the earliest official articulation of IE was phrased: 'the full consummation of the baptism ... is indicated by the initial [physical][660] sign of speaking in tongues', implies the completion of a process.[661] 2) The word 'physical' 'seems to have lost all significance' today, but for the earliest pioneers the word physical was a specific contrast to 'spiritual' signs that were far more subjective.[662] 3) Kerr believes that 'tongues are not the only sign of the baptism' but they are 'the silencing sign'.[663] There was only one sign that served 'as an apostolic litmus test' which silenced all doubt and criticism – glossolalia.[664]

Cecil M. Robeck, Jr, 2003

In his second article, Cecil Robeck theorized that there is a rising magisterium in the AG that is indistinguishable from one in the RCC.[665] Robeck studied the early Pentecostal literature and concludes that the pioneers 'showed a remarkable ability to tolerate a variety of theological positions on subjects such as the nature of

---

[658] Menzies, 'The Initial Physical Sign', p. 189.

[659] For example, Menzies writes that 'there is certainly some doubt about whether Kerr would have been comfortable with saying, as does the Assemblies of God position paper mentioned above, that "[evidential tongues] always occurred at the very time the believers were baptized in the Spirit and not on some future occasion" ... he would almost certainly have agreed with the broader view, common among early Pentecostals', Menzies, 'The Initial Physical Sign', p. 188.

[660] The word 'physical' was said to be inadvertently absent from the published minutes, the following year's council corrected this, see p. 178 n. 12.

[661] Menzies, 'The Initial Physical Sign', pp. 178-79.

[662] Menzies, 'The Initial Physical Sign', pp. 183. For example, Flower claimed 'to have been baptized in the Spirit weeks before first speaking in tongues', p. 185; cf. n. 30. Flower writes, 'certainly, the voice of the Word and Spirit within are more sure than the sign of tongues without', p. 184.

[663] Menzies, 'The Initial Physical Sign', p. 187.

[664] Menzies, 'The Initial Physical Sign', p. 187.

[665] Cecil M. Robeck Jr., 'An Emerging Magisterium? The case of the Assemblies of God', *Pneuma* 25.2 (Fall 2003), p. 214. To be fair with Robeck concerning this piece, he categorically denies it is about the doctrine of IE, but about who makes doctrinal decisions, Robeck, 'Emerging Magisterium', p. 212. Also, Robeck pleads for both the leadership of denominations and the academy to work together as a part of Christ's Church, p. 211. To those in the academy he pleads for them to remain honest in reporting facts and not revise them for the sake of peace or advancing one's career, p. 207.

the Trinity and theories on sanctification, baptism in the Holy Spirit, and speaking in tongues'.[666] The experience of SB and glossolalia, rather than theology, was held in common.[667] Due to its primal state, there was no single theology of glossolalia among the early Pentecostals. Differences included the nature and purpose of glossolalia[668] as well as IE.[669]

Conclusion to Literature Utilizing the Early Pentecostal Periodicals.

Given the number of publications on glossolalia, it is surprising that there are only seven articles that examine what the first Pentecostals believed. The seven articles above are narrow in scope and yet reveal the theological importance of the early Pentecostal periodicals. Because of a lack of research in this area, McGee calls for this investigation:

> though the psychological and social factors of speaking in tongues and the theologies of some early leaders have been carefully explored, the earliest Pentecostal descriptions of Spirit baptism and how tongues empowered them deserve further consideration.[670]

---

[666] Robeck, 'Emerging Magisterium', p. 176. Regarding glossolalia Robeck believes doctrinal lines were fluid regarding the nature of tongues, precise terminology, and the timing of IE, pp. 177-78; cf. n. 32.

[667] Robeck, 'Emerging Magisterium', p. 177.

[668] For example, regarding the nature of tongues Robeck notes that 'W.F. Carothers saw subtle differences in purpose and use', Robeck, 'Emerging Magisterium', pp. 177-78.

[669] For example, 'many understood that if a person had not spoken in tongues, s/he had not received the baptism in the Spirit. Others were not so dogmatic on the issue of timing ... "sooner or later they will speak in tongues as the Spirit gives utterance",' Robeck, 'Emerging Magisterium', pp. 177-78; cf. p. 177 n. 32. The personal testimonies of two Pentecostal pioneers (Flower and Gee) ran counter to the established doctrine of IE, pp. 186-97.

[670] McGee, 'The New World of Realities', p. 110.

3

THE WESLEYAN-HOLINESS PENTECOSTAL PERIODICALS

I. The Azusa Street Mission Revival – *The Apostolic Faith*

A. History of the Revival

Glossolalia was experienced by many before the ASM revival facilitated exponential growth.[1] Noteworthy occurrences were Edward Irving's Catholic Apostolic Church in London,[2] the Camp Creek revival in 1896,[3] Benjamin H. Irwin's itinerate ministry,[4] and Frank Sanford's ministry in Shiloh, Maine.[5] It was at Shiloh, just outside the sleepy mill town of Durham, Maine, where the theological founder of Pentecostalism, Parham, first witnessed glossolalia.[6] Parham had asked his students in Topeka, Kansas to search the Bible for the evidence of the baptism of the Holy

---

[1] See Appendix 2.

[2] Shumway, 'The Gift of Tongues', pp. 74-142.

[3] Also called, 'Cherokee County' revival. It led to the formation of the Church of God, Cleveland, TN, Synan, *The Holiness-Pentecostal Tradition*, pp. 72-73, cf. Conn, *Like a Mighty Army*, pp. 18-45.

[4] Synan, *The Holiness-Pentecostal Tradition*, p. 52. It is also noteworthy that Irwin was the first of the WH tradition to 'conclude there was a third experience beyond sanctification called "the baptism with the Holy Ghost and fire"'. His meetings were very emotional and physical, often compared to an earlier revival in 1801 at Cane Ridge, KY, cf. pp. 12, 52.

[5] Goff, *Fields White unto Harvest*, pp. 57-59, 73-74. Sanford believed that human evangelism methods were insufficient and that the supernatural ability to speak languages was needed.

[6] Goff, *Fields White unto Harvest*, p. 73.

Ghost. They concluded that 'the indisputable proof on each occasion was, that they spake with other tongues'.[7] That evening at a watch-night service, Agnes Ozman 'began speaking in the Chinese language and was unable to speak English for three days'.[8] Parham's ministry eventually led him to Houston, Texas where Seymour attended classes and meetings.[9] At the dawn of the ASM revival, 'it is estimated that at least 1,000 people had received the Baptism in the Spirit and spoken in other tongues ... and there were some 60 preachers and workers in the State of Texas alone'.[10]

Seymour received a call to lead a new WH church in Los Angeles, but it was short lived as he was soon locked out of the church for preaching about SB as evidenced by glossolalia.[11] In his defence before his WH leaders, he affirmed his belief that only when one had spoken in tongues was one Spirit baptized.[12] Bereft of church or denomination, Seymour started holding meetings in the home of the couple he was staying with, Edward and Mattie Lee. Soon these meetings moved to the home of Richard and Ruth Asberry at 214 North Bonnie Brae Street. On April 6, 1906, Lee did not feel well and asked Seymour to pray for him, whereupon, 'he fell to the floor and spoke with tongues'.[13] They then walked over to the Asberry's home and told the nightly gathering what had happened. One of the attendees, Jennie Moore says that,

> the power of God fell and I was baptized in the Holy Ghost and fire, with the evidence of speaking in tongues ... it seemed as if a vessel broke within me and water surged up through my being, which when it reached my mouth came out in a torrent

---

[7] Goff, *Fields White unto Harvest*, p. 66.
[8] Goff, *Fields White unto Harvest*, p. 67. She later changed her name: 'I received the baptism of the Holy Ghost and spoke in other tongues, on January 1, 1901, at Topeka, Kansas Bible school. My name then was Miss Agnes N. Ozman, now Mrs. P.M. LaBerge', Mrs. P.M. LaBerge, 'Has Had The Baptism For Fifteen Years', *WE* 129 (Mar 4, 1915), p. 5.
[9] Robeck, 'William Joseph Seymour', p. 1055.
[10] Frodsham, *With Signs Following*, p. 29.
[11] Robeck, *Azusa Street*, p. 63.
[12] Robeck, *Azusa Street*, p. 63.
[13] Robeck, *Azusa Street*, p. 67.

of speech in the languages which God had given me.[14]

It was not just Lee and Moore, but 'the whole company was immediately swept to its knees as by some mighty power'.[15] So many were attracted to the meetings that within a week an unused African Methodist Episcopal Church at 312 Azusa Street was rented and the revival meetings continued there for the next three years.[16]

'The significance of Azusa lies also in the testimonies of those whose lives were transformed by an experience of an immanent God, through the Holy Spirit.'[17] However, not all who experienced the ASM fully embraced it. Most significant of these was Parham.[18] Parham's complaints were threefold: 1) the methods used by altar workers to guide seekers into glossolalia was 'over-zealous' and there was a lack of control in the meetings.[19] 2) The mixing of the races.[20] 3) Indistinct glossolalia. Because of his belief in MT, Parham insisted on clear and distinct language-like tongues. Seymour was content with less clear glossolalia believing, that as the individual learned to yield to the Spirit, their language would become distinct.[21] The list of those people whose lives were transformed at ASM would read like a 'Who's Who' of world-wide Pentecostalism. Individuals, church planters, missionaries, and founders of denominations all believed they were equipped with God's power for ministry as evidenced by tongues: 'the significance of Azusa was centrifugal – those who were touched by it took their

---

[14] J. Moore, 'Music from Heaven', *AF* 1.8 (Mar 1907), p. 3. Note the near poetic symbolism: vessel, surge, and torrent. Women tended to express themselves right from the start in more ecstatic and poetic terms.

[15] Shumway, 'The Gift of Tongues', p. 174.

[16] The most important years were 1906-1908, though the congregation continued on past Seymour's death (9-28-1922). The building was demolished in 1931 and the land lost to foreclosure in 1938, Robeck, 'Azusa Street Revival', pp. 347-49, cf. Robeck, *Azusa Street*, pp. 319-20.

[17] Robeck, 'Azusa Street Revival', p. 349.

[18] Ann Taves notes that 'Parham began distancing himself from the revival in Los Angeles in the weeks prior to his visit ... Parham told the *Topeka Daily State Journal* that his was a "dignified movement ... when any of that class [Holy Rollers] come to our meeting and begin throwing fits, we quietly have the attendants take them out"', Ann Taves, *Fits, Trances, & Visions* (Princeton, NJ: Princeton University Press, 1999), p. 329.

[19] Robeck, *Azusa Street*, pp. 140-41. 'The real gift of tongues, is never accompanied by spasms, jerks, or foolishness of any sort', p. 230.

[20] Robeck, *Azusa Street*, p. 141.

[21] Robeck, *Azusa Street*, p. 236, cf. p. 270; *AF* 2.13 (May 1908), p. 3.

experiences elsewhere and touched the lives of others'.[22]

B. The 'Bible Evidence', Glossolalia as a Sign.

This review of *AF* newspaper affirms that there was a fascination with the evidential tongues.[23] The front page of the inaugural issue summarized the importance and logic of tongues as a sign. The opening article connected the ASM revival with the Day of Pentecost through the 'Bible evidence':[24]

> Pentecost has surely come and with it *the Bible evidences* are following, many being converted and sanctified and *filled with the Holy Ghost, speaking in tongues* as they did on the day of Pentecost.[25]

A second article distinguished the WH view of SB from the Pentecostal view of SB because 'they did not have the evidence of the second chapter of Acts, for when the disciples were all filled with the Holy Ghost, they spoke in tongues as the Spirit gave utterance'.[26] Another significant article rounded out the logic with the purpose for tongues: it is the 'gift of language' or MT.[27]

1. Why Evidence?

Just as Jesus had witnesses such as the angels at his birth and at

---

[22] Robeck, 'Azusa Street Revival', p. 349. A minority and opposing view is that rather than spreading out from ASM, 'there fell simultaneously in the year 1906, in different parts of the world, what members of the movement call "a mighty outpouring of the Holy Spirit." ... simultaneously, similar groups sprang up all over the world', Dalton, *Tongues like as of Fire*, p. 9. Hollenweger holds a nuanced position that, 'the Pentecostal movement spread like wildfire over the whole world' from United States, Hollenweger, *The Pentecostals*, p. 63. However, there are indigenous religions that have 'remarkable parallels' to Pentecostalism, thus making the ground fertile for the Pentecostal message, Hollenweger, *Pentecostalism*, p. 54.

[23] 'Bible evidence' is the preferred nomenclature in the *AF*. Other synonyms include: 'sign', 'evidence', 'outward evidence', and 'the evidence', cf. 'Tongues as a Sign', *AF* 1.1 (Sep 1906), p. 2; Mrs. W.H. Piper, '"He Shall Baptize You"', *AF* 1.10 (Sep 1907), p. 4; 'Bro. Seymour's Call', *AF* 1.1 (Sep 1906), p. 1. However, it was possible to avoid the Pentecostal nomenclature altogether. For example, Antoinette Moomau, 'China Missionary Receives Pentecost', *AF* 1.11 (Oct 1907), p. 3, wrote, 'He gave me the Bible experiences, speaking through me in other tongues.'

[24] The subtitle is, 'Los Angeles Being Visited by a Revival of Bible Salvation and Pentecost as Recorded in the Book of Acts', 'Pentecost Has Come', p. 1.

[25] 'Pentecost Has Come', p. 1 (emphasis added).

[26] 'Bro. Seymour's Call', p. 1.

[27] 'Pentecost Has Come', p. 1.

the tomb, the dove at his baptism, and people at his ascension, it was natural for these early pioneers to see speaking in tongues as a 'Bible witness, a supernatural witness'.[28] First, it is significant that the preferred terminology was 'the Bible evidence'. The Bible was believed and followed. Therefore, it was important to have the same experience as the disciples on the Day of Pentecost. In fact, the paper's statement of faith reads:

> the Baptism with the Holy Ghost is a gift *of power* upon the sanctified life; so when we get it we *have the same evidence* as the Disciples received on the Day of Pentecost (Acts 2:3, 4), in speaking in new tongues. See also Acts 10:45, 46; Acts 19:6; 1 Cor. 14:21.[29]

Second, tongues at one's personal Pentecost were the sign of God's equipping power.[30] This power was a part of a world view in which the return of Christ was imminent.[31] Tongues were a restoration of apostolic power for an end-times revival.[32] One article noted that chronologically, throughout history, there had been a restoration of salvation, sanctification, healings, and now a restoration of tongues with 'the Bible evidence'.[33] This restoration of glossolalia was pragmatically connected to the sharing of the gospel with MT: 'the wonderful sign in 1906 is the restoration of tongues, which foretells the preaching of the pure gospel to all nations, which must be done before the Gentile Times end. (Matt. 24:14.)'.[34] In 'Signs of His Coming', the author reviewed biblical prophecy and affirmed the soon return of Christ, but the climax of his argument rests on the latter rain metaphor. God

> sent the latter rain to bring it into perfection, that it might be

---

[28] *AF* 1.2 (Oct 1906), p. 4.
[29] 'The Apostolic Faith Movement', p. 2 (emphasis added).
[30] 'The Apostolic Faith Movement', p. 2.
[31] McQueen, *Toward a Pentecostal Eschatology*, pp. 61-74.
[32] For example, 'Everything is Pointing Toward the Coming of the Lord', *AF* 1.4 (Dec 1906), p. 1.
[33] The author ties each of these restorations to an individual: Luther is tied to justification by faith, Wesley is tied to sanctification, Cullis is tied to the restoration of divine healing, and Parham to SB with its sign of tongues. 'The Promised Latter Rain Now Being Poured out on God's Humble People', *AF* 1.2 (Oct 1906), p. 2.
[34] *AF* 1.8 (May 1907), p. 1.

ready for harvest. And now He is pouring out the latter rain upon the church, the baptism with the Holy Ghost and fire. We are receiving the Pentecost, speaking in tongues as the Spirit gives utterance, and the wonders and signs are still following.[35]

However, it would be wrong to state that tongues were exclusively seen as a restoration of what was lost. The concept that a remnant never lost the gift of tongues was also believed.[36]

Third, tongues announced the presence of the Holy Spirit: 'tongues are like a bell, ringing the people up. They are waking up to the fact that God is in the land', testified one participant.[37] The signs of Mk 16.16-18 occurred in Los Angeles to 'prove that God is true', noted another testimony.[38] It was like living in a modern-day book of Acts because similar 'signs as on the day of Pentecost are following … the work is spreading fast'.[39] One person encouraged doubters to believe for the sake of the revival, to examine the effects of the revival, especially speaking in new tongues and deliverances from demons and healings.[40]

Fourth, though tongues were the predominate sign, other 'effects' or 'signs following' were a part of the revival. Healing, deliverance from demons or vices, divine love, and the advance of the gospel worldwide confirmed the logic of their theology. For example, one man spoke in tongues and his family thought he had lost his mind until they saw the divine love he had.[41] Even Mason acknowledged that he accepted the other signs of Mk 16.16-18 more readily than tongues at first, but changed his mind after he put aside his assumptions and experienced glossolalia for himself.[42] Another significant sign of the revival was the breaking down of racial barriers and gender barriers: 'God makes no

---

[35] 'Signs of His Coming', *AF* 1.6 (Feb/Mar 1907), p. 6. Cf. 'We realize that we are in the time of the "latter rain" preceding His coming', *AF* 1.4 (Dec 1906), p. 3; transcribed a meeting and sermon by W.J. Seymour, *AF* 1.7 (Apr 1907), p. 2.
[36] 'The Promise Still Good', *AF* 1.1 (Sep 1906), p. 3.
[37] 'Notice', *AF* 1.2 (Oct 1906), p. 4.
[38] 'Signs Follow', *AF* 1.3 (Nov 1906), p. 4.
[39] A.G. Johnson, 'Pentecost in Other Lands, In Sweden', *AF* 1.6 (Feb/Mar 1907), p. 1.
[40] *AF* 1.1 (Sep 1906), p. 2.
[41] *AF* 1.1 (Sep 1906), p. 2.
[42] C.H. Mason, 'TN Evangelist Witnesses', *AF* 1.6 (Feb/Mar 1907), p. 7.

difference in nationality ... (all) nationalities worship together'.[43] One article noted that, 'if it had started in a fine church, poor colored people and Spanish people would not have got it ... It is noticeable how free all nationalities feel'.[44]

2. Biblical Support

The article 'Tongues as a Sign' was typical of the biblical support offered throughout *AF*.[45] The premise of the article was that signs were to be expected simply because the Bible said so.[46] Mark 16.16-17 was the favourite verse used to support tongues as a sign; it: 'plainly declares that these signs SHALL follow them that believe'.[47] Tongues were unique from the OT signs because they were reserved for the Day of Pentecost to fulfil the prophecy of Joel in Acts 2.12-17 and Jesus' promise of power to witness in Acts 1.4-8.[48] However, from the Day of Pentecost onward, tongues were repeatable for believers as a sign of the Spirit's baptism following the example of Acts 10.46; 19.1-6. Throughout *AF*, the Lucan writings were quoted more extensively than the Pauline corpus, and in 'Tongues as a Sign', one lonely sentence noted Paul's nine gifts of the Holy Spirit.[49]

3. Evidence of Spirit Baptism

Glossolalia as the Bible evidence was staunchly defended.[50] For example, Durham wrote, 'I would advise all my friends to seek the

---

[43] *AF* 1.1 (Sep 1906), p. 3. 'The people are all melted together ... all one body in Christ Jesus', *AF* 1.4 (Dec 1906), p. 1

[44] 'Bible Pentecost', *AF* 1.3 (Nov 1906), p. 1.

[45] 'Tongues as a Sign', p. 2.

[46] These early pioneers expected miracles and signs to follow: 'we must believe it all ... a return to the full Gospel brings a return of the signs following them that believe', 'Signs Shall Follow', *AF* 1.4 (Dec 1906), p. 2.

[47] At times belief referred not to salvation but to the Pentecostal message, cf. 'Beginning of World Wide Revival', *AF* 1.5 (Jan 1907), p. 1.

[48] 'Sanctified Before Pentecost', *AF* 1.4 (Dec 1906), p. 2.

[49] The Pauline works are only infrequently cited. Seymour's most extensive Pauline treatment is on the importance of prophecy in the assembly over uninterpreted tongues which only edify an individual, W.J. Seymour, 'Gifts of the Spirit', *AF* 1.5 (Jan 1907), p. 2; cf. *AF* 1.6 (Feb/Mar 1907), p. 4.

[50] It was so much a part of the theology that an article questioned why the phrase 'with the Bible evidence' did not accompany every testimony of SB, but then assured its readers that 'the *Apostolic Faith* expected it would be so understood, whether it was stated or not', R.L. Lupton, 'This is That', *AF* 1.7 (Apr 1907), p. 3, reprint; the *New Acts*.

baptism in the Holy Ghost, till they get the evidence in tongues, for it always follows; I know of no exception'.[51] Seymour wrote,

> beloved, when we receive the baptism with the Holy Ghost and fire, *we surely will speak in tongues* as the Spirit gives utterance. We are not seeking for tongues, but we are seeking the baptism with the Holy Ghost and fire. And when we receive it, we shall be so filled with the Holy Ghost, that He Himself will speak in the power of the Spirit.[52]

People were encouraged to seek SB and not tongues: 'just pray the Lord to give you the baptism with the Holy Ghost', A.A. Boddy's wife advised, 'I did not ask for "tongues" but for the Holy Ghost, and He "gave me utterance," and the joy of praising God in the Spirit'.[53] Personal testimony played a supporting role as participants testified in hindsight that they did not really have the baptism until they spoke in tongues.[54] For example, George H. Taylor wrote, 'to me it was a witness that I had received the baptism, just as it was to Peter when at the house of Cornelius'.[55]

The Bible evidence was not without theological and experiential variety. The *Apostolic Faith* allowed alternative and at times conflicting positions. Seymour's article 'Counterfeits', represented a pivotal adjustment of the evidential nature of glossolalia and the other components of glossolalia.[56] Seymour was surprised that 'people have imitated the gift of tongues'.[57] What was thought to be solely from heaven now had potential to be faked. From that article onward, godly living functioned as a backup confirmation to the sign of glossolalia. For example, an unsigned article on the need for fresh anointings noted that

---

[51] W.H. Durham, 'A Chicago Evangelist's Pentecost', *AF* 1.6 (Feb/Mar 1907), p. 4.

[52] W.J. Seymour, 'The Baptism with the Holy Ghost', *AF* 1.6 (Feb/Mar 1907), p. 7 (emphasis added).

[53] Mrs A.A. Boddy, 'Testimony of a Vicar's Wife', *AF* 1.11 (Oct 1907), p. 1. For example, 'do not ask the Lord for tongues. Just pray the Lord to give you the baptism with the Holy Ghost', 'The Enduement of Power', *AF* 1.4 (Dec 1906), p. 2.

[54] 'Baptized in Minneapolis', *AF* 1.4 (Dec 1906), p. 4.

[55] George H. Taylor, 'A Witness in Michigan', *AF* 1.8 (May 1907), p. 3.

[56] W.J. Seymour, 'Counterfeits', *AF* 1.4 (Dec 1906), p. 2; cf. 'The Enduement of Power', p. 2.

[57] Seymour, 'Counterfeits', p. 2.

tongues are *one of the signs* that go with every baptized person, *but it is not the real evidence of the baptism in the every day life.* Your life must measure with the fruits [sic] of the Spirit. If you get angry, or speak evil, or backbite, I care not how many tongues you may have, you have not the baptism with the Holy Spirit.[58]

Seymour called for discernment by the Holy Spirit and encouraged an ethical testing to distinguish the true from the counterfeit. The article added that it was possible to 'lose the Spirit of Jesus, which is divine love'.[59] Even though this additional ethical component was to help distinguish the genuine from false, in the same issue Seymour affirmed the evidential nature of tongues: 'He sent the Holy Spirit to our hearts and filled us with His blessed Spirit, and He gave us the Bible evidence, according to the 2nd chapter of Acts verses 1 to 4, speaking with other tongues'.[60]

The eleventh issue highlighted another challenge to the Bible sign doctrine, delayed glossolalia. A statement of faith written as a Q & A catechism asked: 'what is the real evidence that a man or woman has received the baptism of the Holy Ghost?'[61] It then answered divine love and the fruit of the Spirit, stating these are

> *the real Bible evidence in their daily walk and conversation*; and the outward manifestations; speaking in tongues and the signs following; casting out devils, laying hands on the sick and the sick being healed, and the love of God for souls increasing in their hearts.[62]

After affirming the ethical confirmation, the article states:

> the baptism of the Spirit is a gift of power on the sanctified life, and when people receive it, *sooner or later* they will speak in tongues as the Spirit gives utterance. A person *may not speak in tongues for a week after the baptism,* but as soon as he gets to praying

---

[58] This article appears directly under the subscription information, in a location normally reserved for the statement of faith or an editorial. 'To The Baptized Saints', *AF* 1.9 (June 1907), p. 2 (emphasis added).

[59] 'To The Baptized Saints', p. 2.

[60] W.J. Seymour, 'Letter to One Seeking the Holy Ghost', *AF* 1.9 (Jun 1907), p. 3.

[61] 'Questions Answered (*AF*)', 1.11 (Oct 1907), p. 2. This issue of the statement of faith is in a question and answer, catechetical-type of format.

[62] 'Questions Answered (*AF*)', p. 2 (emphasis added).

or praising God in the liberty of the Spirit, the tongues will follow.[63]

Throughout the *AF* one finds testimonies which imply or explicitly state a delay in tongues after SB.[64] For example, Mrs. J.E. Smith of Wolcott, NY wrote: 'I will say I have been wonderfully filled with the Holy Ghost but have not received the speaking in tongues'.[65] Nevertheless, Seymour affirmed tongues as the evidence of SB in the final issue calling it 'the Azusa standard':

> the Azusa standard of the baptism with the Holy Ghost is according to the Bible in Acts 1:5, 8; Acts 2:4 and Luke 24:49 ... Hallelujah to the Lamb for the baptism of the Holy Ghost and fire and speaking in tongues as the Spirit gives utterance ... when you get your personal Pentecost, the signs will follow in speaking with tongues as the Spirit gives utterance.[66]

The Azusa Standard was: 'when you have received your baptism, He, the Holy Ghost, will speak through you in tongues';[67] however, glossolalia had to be confirmed by divine love and the fruit of the Spirit.

4. Defining Spirit Baptism within the Wesleyan-Holiness Movement

An important early theological issue was the distinction between Pentecostal SB and the WH position of sanctification. Wesleyan-holiness people who accepted the Pentecostal message continued to affirm their experiences of salvation and sanctification and simply added a third experience of SB that was evidenced by glossolalia.[68] However, some WH people persisted that SB was sanctification and chose to reject tongues. It became a major point

---

[63] 'Questions Answered (*AF*)', p. 2 (emphasis added).

[64] Ambiguous examples: 'At Chambersburg, Pa., about 25 got baptized and some spoke in tongues, some saved, sanctified and healed', *AF* 1.10 (Sep 1907), p. 1; 'last Thursday, two sisters being shaken and nearly spoke in tongues', Mary Martin, 'London, England', *AF* 1.11 (Oct 1907), p. 1.

[65] Mrs. J.E. Smith, *AF* 1.12 (Jan 1908), p. 4.

[66] W.J. Seymour, 'The Baptism of the Holy Ghost', *AF* 2.13 (May 1908), p. 3. Seymour writes, 'stop quibbling and come to the standard that Jesus laid down for us in Acts 2'.

[67] *AF* 1.7 (Apr 1907), p. 3.

[68] W.A. Love, 'A Holiness Preacher Who Received Pentecost', *AF* 1.6 (Feb/Mar 1907), p. 7.

of conflict.[69] For example, F.E. Hill walked out of the Nazarene Church which forbade 'speaking in tongues or testifying on the line of the baptism with the Holy Ghost upon the sanctified life' and started his own church.[70] Exegetically, for support, if the pattern from Acts was not used, Mk 16.17 was employed.[71] Theologically, the Pentecostals carefully clarified that SB was not a work of grace like justification or sanctification, but was 'the gift of power ... it gives you power to speak in the languages of the nations'.[72] This was an emotionally-charged issue on both sides. One article likened the WH position to the prodigal son's elder brother who disliked the music and dancing which celebrated the restoration of the lost son.[73] Reflecting on his regional situation, Cashwell noted that some have been so 'gulled here (to) take it by faith' that their faith was nearly gone.[74]

C. Missionary Tongues[75]

'God is solving the missionary problem, sending out new-

---

[69] One testimony cryptically reports, 'there was some trouble about the Bible evidence to the baptism with the Holy Ghost, but as soon as that was straight, God began to work', 'Victory in Oakland', *AF* 1.3 (Nov 1906), p. 1.

[70] 'Vernon Mission', *AF* 1.3 (Nov 1906), p. 1.

[71] Some WH people rejected Mk 16.17 due to textual issues. To counter their argument, one article delved into the transmission and validation of the various ancient manuscripts and concluded that the present day experience affirms the variant reading; therefore, 'do not let any man riddle your Bible for you or cut out any part of it', 'Shall We Reject Jesus' Last Words?', *AF* 1.2 (Oct 1906), p. 2. For a fuller examination of how the early Pentecostal's interpreted and defended Mk 16.9-20, see John Christopher Thomas and Kimberly Alexander, '"And The Signs Are Following": Mark 16.9-20', *JPT* 11.2 (April 2003), pp. 147-70. They call for a 'reappropriation' of this passage.

[72] 'The Enduement of Power', p. 2.

[73] 'The Elder Brother', *AF* 1.2 (Oct 1906), p. 2.

[74] 'Hundreds Baptized in the South', *AF* 1.6 (Feb/Mar 1907), p. 3. This might have been the result of a powerless sanctification or Irwin's belief in multiple baptisms in the south-eastern part of the States. Here Cashwell notes specifically the baptisms of fire, dynamite, and lyddite, which are Irwin's thesis, Synan, *The Holiness-Pentecostal Tradition*, p. 57, cf. pp. 51-58. The *AF* reports that Irwin's magazine, *Live Coals,* espoused the Pentecostal sign after seeing that the Bible distinguished between tongues as a gift and as a sign, 'Transformed by the Holy Ghost', *AF* 1.6 (Feb/Mar), p. 5, reprint; *Apostolic Evangel*, Royston, GA. A few issues later the *AF* reports that through Cashwell's effort 'a great number of the officials and members of the Fire-Baptized Holiness Church have given up their man-made theories about Pentecost and gone down and received the genuine Pentecostal baptism, with the Bible evidence following', A.E. Robinson, *AF* 1.8 (May 1907), p. 2.

[75] Other monikers are the 'gift of language' and the 'Pentecostal gift'.

tongued missionaries on the apostolic faith line' quipped one writer who aptly summarizes both the theology and logic of the theory of MT.[76] God inspired xenolalia enables people to share the gospel without having to learn a foreign language.[77] For example, 'many are speaking in new tongues, and some are on their way to the foreign fields, with the gift of the language'.[78] One can see two areas of weakness with the theory from the start: 1) lack of credible verification,[79] and 2) participants who were braggadocios about the number of languages they could speak.[80] However, even though many of the testimonies were second-hand, throughout *AF* there were enough foreign-language speakers who claimed to have heard the gospel or received a revelation from God in their native language that xenolalia received a measure of credibility while the theory of MT would be tested and be discarded.[81]

1. The Theory of Missionary Tongues

The theory of MT was popularized at Parham's 1901 Bible school in Topeka, KS:

instantly the Lord took his vocal organs, and he was preaching

---

[76] *AF* 1.3 (Nov 1906), p. 2.

[77] For example, a brother Lee comments, 'Friends, I did not go to college to get this language. It is the Holy Ghost that speaks. He can talk the languages of the nations', 'A Catholic That Received Pentecost', *AF* 1.3 (Nov 1906), p. 4.

[78] 'Pentecost Has Come', p. 1.

[79] Consider: 'a Mohammedan, a Soudanese by birth, a man who is an interpreter and speaks sixteen languages, came into the meetings at Azusa Street and the Lord gave him messages which none but himself could understand. He identified, interpreted and wrote a number of the languages', *AF* 1.1 (Sep 1906), p. 1.

[80] For example, 'I now speak eleven or twelve languages', Andrew Johnson, 'Letter From Bro. Johnson', *AF* 1.2 (Oct 1906), p. 3. 'I must have spoken seven or eight languages to judge from the various sounds and forms of speech used', 'Baptized In New York', *AF* 1.4 (Dec 1906), p. 3. Cashwell writes, 'five preachers received the baptism and some of them have two or three languages already and can preach sermons and pray in the tongues', G.B. Cashwell, 'Pentecost in North Carolina', *AF* 1.5 (Jan 1907), p. 1.

[81] George Berg's writings appear often in *AF* in connection with xenolalia and he professes to know a couple of tribal languages of India. Overhearing xenolalia convinced him of its truth: 'there are very few that get the native accent by study, but this man spoke the beautiful accent of that country ... That convinced me that the Holy Ghost was giving languages in this place', Geo. E. Berg, *AF* 1.5 (Jan 1907), p. 4.

the Word in another language ... this man has preached in different languages over the United States, and men and women of that nationality have come to the altar and sought God.[82]

Biblically, it was hoped that MT were God's equipping to share the good news around the world according the biblical pattern on the Day of Pentecost, in Acts 2.4-11.[83] Other passages thought to support the practice are, Isa. 28.11[84] and 1 Cor. 13.1.[85] There were several pragmatic components to the theory: 1) the language one spoke pointed to the place of one's calling. One man spoke French, for example, 'was given a vision of Paris and called there'.[86] Later though, Seymour encouraged people not to 'puzzle' themselves about which language they were speaking.[87] 2) Because it was a real language for sharing the good news, it should be a clear and identifiable one.[88] However linguistically, great latitude was afforded xenolalia because of the wide variety of languages in the world:

> there are 50,000 languages in the world. Some of them sound like jabber. The Eskimo can hardly be distinguished from a dog bark. The Lord lets smart people talk in these jabber-like languages. Then He has some child talk in the most beautiful Latin

---

[82] 'The Pentecostal Baptism Restored', *AF* 1.2 (Oct 1906), p. 1; cf. *AF* 2.13 (May 1908), p. 2. McGee traces the roots of the theory back to 1885 in McGee, 'Shortcut to Language Preparations', pp. 119-22.

[83] For example, 'when He sent them out after Pentecost ... they had seventeen nationalities that heard the gospel in their own tongue without confusion. (Acts 2:9-11) He is doing the same today', 'The Baptism with the Holy Ghost', *AF* 1.11 (Oct 1907), p. 4.

[84] E.g. 'Pentecost At Middle States, In Potterbrook, Pa', *AF* 1.6 (Feb/Mar 1907), p. 3; 'This Is That', p. 3; 'From The Bible School in Mukti, India', *AF* 1.12 (Jan 1908), p. 1.

[85] 'Pentecost in England', *AF* 1.8 (May 1907), p. 1. Though contemporary scholarship places a great deal of emphasis on the psychological nature of glossolalia, this survey of *AF* reveals very little reflection on the subject. For example, 'ecstasy' is used only three times and then as a dramatic highlight or in poetic fashion. 'Tongues of men and angels' is believed to be used only once, 'When Jesus Comes', *AF* 1.5 (Jan 1907), p. 2; 'The Pentecostal Revival', *AF* 1.13 (May 1908), p. 4.

[86] 'At Azusa Mission', *AF* 1.8 (May 1907), p. 2.

[87] Seymour, 'The Baptism with the Holy Ghost', p. 7.

[88] For example, when the 'Holy Ghost falls upon them and they rise to their feet speaking in a clear language as the Spirit gives utterance', 'Pentecost In San Jose', *AF* 1.4 (Dec 1906), p. 1; cf. Cashwell, 'Pentecost In North Carolina', p. 1.

and Greek, just to confound professors and learned people.[89]

The languages people used were not limited to spoken languages as some were thought to have received sign-language for the deaf.[90] 'Writing in tongues' was initially thought to be possible but it was judged to be unbiblical.[91] 3) It was expected that the sounds would be indistinct at first, but as an individual yielded themselves to the Spirit, the language would become clear. For example, 'he now began to speak with the tongue yielded to Him, at first in a stammering way, finally flowing out in a clear, distinct language which sounded like Chinese'.[92] 4) Completing the linguistic family of MT was the recognition that English could be a 'foreign tongue' when one was overseas.[93]

Expectation of successful world evangelism was high as 'missionaries for the foreign fields, equipped with several languages, are now on their way'.[94] For example, 'G.W. Batman and wife are saved, sanctified and baptized with the Holy Ghost and have the

---

[89] *AF* 1.7 (Apr 1907), p. 4. One 'Indian' language was described as 'chanting songs', *AF* 1.4 (Dec 1906), p. 3. Another example is when the poor young girls in Mukti, India are given 'the sacred language of the Brahmans, the priestly class of India', 'Pentecost in Mukti, India', *AF* 1.10 (Sep 1907), p. 4.

[90] F.R. Townsend, 'Pentecostal Testimonies', *AF* 1.6 (Feb/Mar 1907), p. 8; cf. 'Ye Are My Witnesses', *AF* 1.8 (May 1907), p. 4; *AF* 1.1 (Sept 1906), p. 1. There are three testimonies of the deaf being healed: 'Fire Falling At Oakland', *AF* 1.1 (Sept 1906), p. 4; *AF* 1.3 (Nov 1906), p. 2; 'The deaf have had their hearing restored', *AF* 1.1 (Sept 1906), p. 1.

[91] 'We do not read anything in the Word about writing in unknown languages, so we do not encourage that in our meetings. Let us measure everything by the Word, that all fanaticism may be kept out of the work. We have found it questionable whether any real good has come out of such writing', *AF* 1.10 (Sep 1907), p. 2; cf. T. Junk, 'Pentecost in Seattle', *AF* 1.4 (Dec 1906), p. 1; Johnson, 'Pentecost in Other Lands, In Sweden', p. 1; Townsend, 'Pentecostal Testimonies', p. 8.

[92] W.H. Standley, 'Worth Tarrying For', *AF* 2.13 (May 1908), p. 3.

[93] 'Quite a number had received the ability to speak in English, a language before unknown to them', while others received languages from other parts of India or completely unidentifiable, Albert Norton, 'Natives In India Speak In Tongues', *AF* 1.7 (Apr 1907), p. 2.

[94] 'Fire Still Falling', *AF* 1.2 (Oct 1906), p. 1. There are two other testimonies on the same page of people going to Africa anticipating God to use them. Another typical testimony would be: 'I received my Pentecost and the gift of tongues, and am speaking in many different languages. I am soon expecting to start around the world preaching full salvation as I go, trusting my heavenly Father to supply all my needs', H.M. Turney, 'Alaska Brother Proves Acts 1.8', *AF* 1.4 (Dec 1906), p. 3.

gift of languages. They are all packed up for Monrovia, Liberia, Africa.'[95] Furloughing veteran missionaries who studied and learned a foreign language rejoiced 'to find "the more excellent way"',[96] while others thought it was an answer to prayer.[97] This passion for missions extended to non-English speakers in America as well.[98] There was even a testimony in Spanish followed by an English translation in the *AF*.[99] Tom Hezmalhalch went into great detail about one Native American preacher's sermon and the interpretation that was revealed to him.[100] His testimony ended with a call for people to pray for these unreached Native Americans.

Because initially glossolalia was the gift of a real language, translation was possible. Often there was an interpretation[101] that happened spontaneously or in response to prayer.[102] These interpretations usually centred on the Lord's soon return or were a call for repentance. For example, 'Jesus is coming again soon. Do not reject His voice. Don't reject Him, don't reject Him. He was nailed on the cross for you',[103] or 'God is love, and Jesus is coming soon'.[104]

2. The Doctrine Develops

Initially, Seymour fully supported the theory of MT, but he slowly

---

[95] 'Notice' (*AF*), p. 4. The Batmans are said to have the 'power from on high and the fitness of the gift of tongues', 'En Route to Africa', *AF* 1.4 (Dec 1906), p. 4.

[96] G.A. Cook, 'Pentecostal Power In Indianapolis', *AF* 1.6 (Feb/Mar 1907), p. 3.

[97] 'When I heard them speaking in tongues, I thought, now is the time for me to get the Chinese language. I had been in a Chinese Mission, and had been praying for the language for nearly four years', M.F. Mayo, 'A Peniel Worker Baptized', *AF* 1.8 (May 1907), p. 4.

[98] 'Spanish Receive the Pentecost', *AF* 1.2 (Oct 1906), p. 3. Cf. 'Preaching to the Spanish', *AF* 1.3 (Nov 1906), p. 4.

[99] 'Spanish Receive the Pentecost', p. 3.

[100] T. Hezmalhalch, 'Among The Indians At Needles, California', *AF* 1.5 (Jan 1907), p. 3.

[101] Mrs. Nora Wilcox, 'In Denver, Colo.', *AF* 1.8 (May 1907), p. 1.

[102] 'The interpretation is unlocked by prayer. I am glad the Lord has some things the devil cannot find out. If not, anyone could unlock the mysteries of Christ', 'Unlocked By Prayer', *AF* 1.8 (May 1907), p. 3.

[103] *AF* 1.4 (Dec 1906), p. 1, cf. 'In Minneapolis, Minn.', *AF* 1.9 (Sep 1907), p. 1. 'The interpretation of many of the messages in nearly every language spoken by the Holy Ghost in unknown tongues is that Jesus is coming', *AF* 1.8 (May 1907), p. 3.

[104] Mrs. Pearl Bowen, 'Akron Visited With Pentecost', *AF* 1.5 (Jan 1907), p. 1.

redefined it to mean prophetic speech, though he never went so far as to exclude the possibility of genuine xenolalia. In the first issue Seymour wrote an article on the five-fold gospel[105] where he states that SB occurred upon the sanctified life and enabled one to 'lift up Christ to the world in all His fullness ... (and) in His power to speak all the languages of the world'.[106] By the third issue he cautioned people from going abroad: 'some think they must go out because they have the tongues but those are good for Los Angeles or anywhere else. The Lord will lead you by His small voice.'[107] In the same issue, the Meads who were missionaries to Africa for 20 years before the ASM revival, lent credibility and caution to MT.[108] S.J. Mead noted that he was 'conscious' the whole time and God 'flooded (him) with Divine love; and I commenced to speak as I would sing a new song'.[109] But then added,

> many ask, 'Do you think these tongues will be used in a foreign field?' As for myself *I cannot say*. My God is able, this I know ... I believe God is about to repeat many of the miracles and wonders wrought in the early history of the church.[110]

Earlier, his wife had corroborated some tongues as a difficult African dialect and then offered an interpretation,[111] yet Mr. Mead's

---

[105] Though he clearly has the five-fold gospel in mind theologically, Seymour does not mention the Second Coming in this short article, W.J. Seymour, 'The Precious Atonement', *AF* 1.1 (Sep 1906), p. 2. A similar article in the second issue gives pastoral logic to the order of justification, sanctification, and SB, W.J. Seymour, 'The Way Into The Holiest', *AF* 1.2 (Oct 1906), p. 4. He does not mention the full five-fold gospel, including the Second Coming, until the 5th issue, W.J. Seymour, 'Behold The Bridegroom Cometh!', *AF* 1.5 (Jan 1907), p. 2. On the same page there is an unsigned article condemning the doctrine of the annihilation of the wicked, 'Annihilation of the Wicked', *AF* 1.5 (Jan 1907), p. 2. He notes the soon return again in the 9th issue, W.J. Seymour, 'Testimony And Praise To God', *AF* 1.9 (Jun 1907), p. 4.

[106] Seymour, 'The Precious Atonement', p. 2.

[107] W.J. Seymour, 'In Money Matters', *AF* 1.3 (Nov 1906), p. 3.

[108] S.J. & A.K. Mead, 'New-Tongued Missionaries For Africa', *AF* 1.3 (Nov 1906), p. 3.

[109] Mead & Mead, 'New-Tongued Missionaries For Africa', p. 3.

[110] Mead & Mead, 'New-Tongued Missionaries For Africa', p. 3 (emphasis added).

[111] 'Message Concerning His Coming', *AF* 1.2 (Oct 1906), p. 4.

vague answer (above) was significant for its lack of full endorsement.[112]

In the fourth issue there is a pivotal article in which Seymour recognizes the possibility of counterfeit glossolalia: 'we should know a tree by its fruit. Wherever we find the real, we find the counterfeit also.'[113] He is surprised that 'people have imitated the gift of tongues' after they were 'tested' and 'found wanting'.[114]

In the fifth issue Seymour gave priority to interpreted tongues as prophecy in the corporate setting over the concept of MT. He wrote that God 'can speak in any language He chooses to speak', but 'prophecy is the best gift to the church, for it builds up the saints and edifies them and exalts them to higher things in the Lord Jesus'.[115] The article encouraged the Pauline boundaries in the assembly of 1 Corinthians 14, and ended pragmatically:

> we all used to break out in tongues; but we have learned to be quieter with the gift. Often when God sends a blessed wave upon us, we all may speak in tongues for awhile, but we will not keep it up while preaching [sic] service is going on, for we want to be obedient to the Word, that everything may be done decently and in order and without confusion.[116]

The doctrine of MT did not change quickly because the editors allowed additional testimonies to be printed as the theory was being tested. For example, George E. Berg writes,

> in regard to the languages given here, I can testify that they are real languages, because I have interpreted not less than five messages given by different persons, spoken in languages of

---

[112] A month later, he reportedly identified the specific tribe of one xenolaliac occurrence, then interpreted it into English and then repeated it again in the tribal tongue, *AF* 1.4 (Dec 1906), p. 4.

[113] Seymour, 'Counterfeits', p. 2. He specifically mentioned practitioners of Christian Science, Theosophy, and Spiritualism. Another WH preacher testifies in the subsequent issue that at ASM 'I saw the real and I saw the counterfeit, the wheat and chaff', J. Jeter, 'There Is Something in This For Jesus', *AF* 1.6 (Feb/Mar 1907), p. 6.

[114] Seymour, 'Counterfeits', p. 2. He uses the word 'imitate' twice in this article referring to people imitating a genuine work of God.

[115] Seymour, 'Gifts of the Spirit', p. 2.

[116] Seymour, 'Gifts of the Spirit', p. 2.

British, India, which languages I know personally, having lived in India.[117]

In the sixth issue Seymour again took the emphasis off foreign languages and put it onto intelligent speech:

> do not seek for tongues but the promise of the Father ... Beloved, if you do not know the language that you speak, do not puzzle yourself about it, for the Lord did not promise us He would tell us what language we were speaking, but He promised us the interpretation of what we speak.[118]

In the ninth issue one can see the theory of MT being separated from xenolalia. On the one hand, Seymour defined the 'other tongues' of Acts 2.1-4, to be known languages.[119] On the other hand, two significant items indicated a change in the doctrine of MT: 1) missionary A.G. Garr reported from the field that reaching the missionaries is the key to missions because 'they know all the customs of India *and also the languages*. The only way the nations can be reached is by getting the missionaries baptized with the Holy Ghost.'[120] 2) The outcome of an investigation by the CMA into a glossolalic episode at one of its churches in Chicago was published.[121] The report stated that,

---

[117] Geo. E. Berg, 'Baptized with the Holy Ghost', *AF* 1.4 (Dec 1906), p. 3; cf. 'The Heavenly Anthem', *AF* 1.5 (Jan 1907), p. 3; 'God Is His Own Interpreter', *AF* 1.5 (Jan 1907), p. 3.

[118] Seymour, 'The Baptism with the Holy Ghost', p. 7.

[119] Seymour, 'Letter to One Seeking the Holy Ghost', p. 3.

[120] A.G. Garr, 'From Distant Lands, The Work in India', *AF* 1.9 (Jun 1907), p. 1 (emphasis added).

[121] This testimony probably refers to an outpouring of the Spirit at their annual Convention in Cleveland, OH when Henry Wilson was charged to investigate, 'From Other Pentecostal Papers', *AF* 1.8 (May 1907), p. 3. If this is the same investigation, it concludes that the experience of tongues is 'scriptural'. The CMA and its close relationship to the Pentecostal movement is noted often: 'Many Witnesses to the Power of the Blood and of the Holy Ghost, In Homestead, PA', *AF* 1.7 (Apr 1907), p. 1; M.L. Ryan, 'Pentecost In Spokane, Wash.', *AF* 1.7 (Apr 1907), p. 4; 'In The Last Days', *AF* 1.9 (Jun 1907), p. 1; 'The Promise of the Father And Speaking with Tongues In Chicago', *AF* 1.9 (June 1907), p. 3; Gideon Ziegler, 'The Lord Is Speaking in the Earth Today, Swanton, Ohio', *AF* 1.12 (Jan 1908), p. 1; 'Fires Are Being Kindled, Jerusalem', *AF* 2.13 (May 1908), p. 1; 'Fires Are Being Kindled, India', *AF* 2.13 (May 1908), p. 1; 'Chinese Filled with the Holy Spirit', *AF* 2.13 (May 1908), p. 4. Respecting the close relationship, there is a correction that reads, 'the Christian Alliance did

the tongues they speak in *do not seem to be intended as a means of communication between themselves and others*, as on the Day of Pentecost, but corresponds more closely with that described in the 14th [sic] of 1 Corinthians, 2nd verse, and seems to be a means of communication between the soul and God.[122]

A respected fellowship like the CMA stating that glossolalia is not a means of communication was significant. The report affirmed the phenomenon as biblical, having usefulness in praise, prayer, and as a sign.[123]

Their singular view of the nature of glossolalia was slowly splitting into the view that there are two types of tongues, xenolalia and glossolalia. They discovered that not all glossolalia was xenolalia; nevertheless, enough native speakers testified to hearing something in their own language from God that these pioneers left room for genuine xenolalia. For example, a testimony in the twelfth issue affirmed that glossolalia was not for communication:

> they who have received the gift of tongues are not using them for delivering messages from the Scriptures, except those who have received the gift of interpretation. They pray and praise God, and sometimes sing hymns in unknown tongues.[124]

But, there were several testimonies about speaking in another language throughout the twelfth issue[125] and even in the final issue.[126] In the end, Seymour's final article on SB emphasized power for

---

not come into the work or discontinue their meetings, as might have been understood' in a prior issue, 'Correction', *AF* 1.12 (Jan 1908), p. 2.

[122] 'The Promise of the Father and Speaking with Tongues in Chicago', p. 3 (emphasis added).

[123] Ironically, the next issue of *AF* reported that at the CMA's annual convention a young lady was filled with the Spirit and spoke in an African tongue. It read that the language 'was recognized by missionaries from Africa as being the very language of the part of Africa to which the sister was expecting to go', *AF* 1.10 (Sep 1907), p. 1.

[124] 'From The Bible School In Mukti, India', p. 1.

[125] F. Crawford, 'The Lord Is Speaking in the Earth Today, Minneapolis and St. Paul', *AF* 1.12 (Jan 1908), p. 1; A.J. Rawson, 'The Lord Is Speaking in the Earth Today, Lynn Mass.', *AF* 1.12 (Jan 1908), p. 1; W.H. Standley, 'Testimonies', *AF* 1.12 (Jan 1908), p. 3.

[126] For example: 'A Policeman's Testimony', *AF* 2.13 (May 1908), p. 1; Sister John Woodruff, 'A Mother's Experience of Pentecost', *AF* 2.13 (May 1908), p. 3; Standley, 'Worth Tarrying For', p. 3; A.H. Argue, 'Italians and Indians Receive the Holy Ghost, *AF* 2.13, p. 4.

130 *Toward a Pentecostal Theology of Glossolalia*

miracles and mission that flow out of unity and purity, and that speaking in tongues was 'the Azusa standard' of Bible evidence, but this standard was not defined as the ability to speak foreign languages.[127]

3. Testimonies of Missionary Tongues

A considerable number of testimonies by native speakers lent credibility to the theory of MT before it was separated from rare cases of xenolalia.[128] For example, one of the more dramatic stories was of a man who spoke in tongues to a police officer and was thrown in jail and then later was taken to the hospital as insane, but 'one of the attendants interpreted one of the languages that I spoke as the Kru language, a tribe in Africa that he was acquainted with'.[129] Then, before being institutionalized as insane, he preached in tongues to a review board, whereupon one of the judges understood his speech as Italian and released him. Another testimony was from a medical doctor who had spent time in India. He wandered into a service and through great conviction over a period of days 'got the whole thing'. He was so touched when he identified the Marathi language that he left his medical practice and returned to India as a missionary.[130] These who heard, spoke, or witnessed such occurrences were not shaken by the fact that MT did not work exactly as they had anticipated because there were other biblical purposes for glossolalia besides MT.

D. Purposes for Glossolalia

In addition to its evidential value, glossolalia had other biblical purposes, such as empowerment, prayer, praise, and revelation.

1. Empowerment

'The Baptism with the Holy Ghost is *a gift of power* upon the sanctified life; so when we get it we have the same evidence as the

---

[127] Seymour, 'The Baptism of the Holy Ghost', p. 3.

[128] The *AF* even published Sister Rosenthal's address at the end of her testimony as if to say, 'go talk to her', Sister Rosenthal, 'The Miracle of Speaking in Tongues', *AF* 1.9 (Jun 1907), p. 2.

[129] 'Arrested For Jesus' Sake', *AF* 1.4 (Dec 1906), p. 3. Lucy Farrow testified upon her return from Liberia that, 'the Lord had given her the gift of the Kru language and she was permitted to preach two sermons to the people in their own tongue', 'Pentecostal Missionary Reports', *AF* 1.11 (Oct 1907), p. 1.

[130] T. Hezmalhalch, 'In Indianapolis, Ind.', *AF* 1.7 (Apr 1907), p. 1.

Disciples received on the Day of Pentecost', read the *AF's* statement of faith.[131] The primary purpose for tongues according to these early Pentecostals was to validate God's empowering. Power was connected to speech through the glossolalist's need, through biblical support, and through a built in correspondence.

In their testimonies one often reads two words, 'lack' and 'more'. These Pentecostal pioneers believed that their Christian experience did not match what they read in the NT.[132] There was a lack of 'true Pentecostal power' that sent Parham searching until he had 'more of the power of God'.[133] Veteran missionaries to Africa wrote, 'we felt the lack of the power and love in the service of our Master, and we commenced seeking that power from Him'.[134] The means to receive power was to admit one's need and seek God like the disciples on the Day of Pentecost.[135] Lack of power motivated them to seek and cry out for more: 'we want all the signs that it may prove that God is true. It will result in the salvation of many souls'.[136] Glossolalia 'gave me more power in speaking for Christ', wrote Mrs. Boddy.[137]

The Bible promised power, so they expected power: 'we have the promise of the same power today'.[138] Like the Apostles, the purpose for receiving power was to fulfil the great commission.[139]

---

[131] 'The Apostolic Faith Movement', p. 2 (emphasis added). Cf. 'The Spirit Follows the Blood', *AF* 1.1 (Sep 1906), p. 3.

[132] Turney, 'Alaska Brother Proves Acts 1:8', p. 3; Durham, 'A Chicago Evangelist's Pentecost', p. 4; Louis Osterberg, *AF* 1.7 (Apr 1907), p. 4; Standley, 'Worth Tarrying For', p. 3.

[133] 'Pentecost Has Come', p. 1. This lack of power is noted in the statement of faith because some confused sanctification for 'the Baptism and failed to reach the glory and power of a true Pentecost', 'The Apostolic Faith Movement', p. 2. 'More' is an important word in *AF*, one testimony points out that the 150 filled in Los Angeles are more than the 120 on the Day of Pentecost, *AF* 1.1 (Sep, 1906), p. 1.

[134] Ardell K. Mead, 'Sister Mead's Baptism', *AF* 1.3 (Nov 1906), p. 3. They were acutely aware of a lack of power: 'we have heard the funeral of the Gospel preached, the power of nobody unto nothing, now we are preaching the power of God unto salvation', *AF* 1.4 (Dec 1906), p. 1

[135] 'Seven Months of Pentecostal Showers', *AF* 1.4 (Dec 1906), p. 1.

[136] 'Signs Follow', p. 4.

[137] Mrs A.A. Boddy, 'Testimony of a Vicar's Wife', p. 1.

[138] 'The Promise Still Good', p. 3.

[139] 'Tongues as a Sign', p. 2; cf. Seymour, 'Letter to One Seeking the Holy Ghost', p. 3.

The promises of Acts 1.8 and Lk. 24.49, were often quoted.[140] Jesus' baptism at the River Jordan was interpreted as an equipping baptism and the logic went: if Jesus needed the power, so do his disciples today.[141] The article, 'The Enduement of Power' was typical of the teaching regarding tongues as a sign of power:[142] SB is 'a gift of power ... (that) makes you a witness unto the uttermost parts of the earth. It gives you power to speak in the languages of the nations'.[143]

There are two built-in points of correspondence between tongues and power: anointed speech and the restoration of spiritual gifts. First, the power they sought was for anointed preaching[144] and testimony:[145] 'the gift of tongues was a sign and a powerful and a practical witnessing agency'.[146] In other words, if the Holy Spirit could take control of the tongue for glossolalia, God could also provide the anointing for sharing the Good News. Seymour wrote, 'the baptism with the Holy Ghost gives us power to testify to a risen, resurrected Savior', because 'when the Holy Ghost life comes in, the mouth opens, through the power of the Spirit in the heart'.[147] Glossolalia, whether as xenolalia or ecstatic tongues, was a demonstration of power itself.[148] Some even reported that 'the Holy Ghost came in mighty power, causing me to laugh as I have never done in my life'.[149] In their enthusiasm, sometimes these pioneers promoted 'Pentecostal power' more than the

---

[140] There are only a couple of references to Zech. 4.6, *AF* 1.3 (Nov 1906), p. 2; Seymour, 'Counterfeits', p. 2.

[141] 'Pentecostal Notes', *AF* 1.10 (Sep 1907), p. 3; Seymour, 'The Baptism of the Holy Ghost', p. 3.

[142] W.J. Seymour's 'Receive Ye the Holy Ghost', *AF* 1.5 (Jan 1907), p. 2.

[143] 'The Enduement of Power', p. 2.

[144] 'Gracious Pentecostal Showers Continue to Fall', *AF* 1.3 (Nov 1906), p. 1.

[145] 'We do preach in testifying', writes Seymour, 'In Money Matters', p. 3.

[146] A.H. Post, 'Testimony of a Minister', *AF* 1.5 (Jan 1907), p. 4.

[147] W.J. Seymour, 'River of Living Water', *AF* 1.3 (Nov 1906), p. 2; Seymour, 'The Baptism with the Holy Ghost', p. 7; cf. A.S. Copley, 'Pentecost in Toronto', *AF* 1.5 (Jan 1907), p. 4; Mrs. James Hebden, 'This is the Power of the Holy Ghost', *AF* 1.6 (Feb/Mar 1907), p. 4.

[148] 'What use is it unless understood ... but in the mighty power and demonstration of the Holy Ghost', 'Missions in Los Angeles', *AF* 1.7 (Apr 1907), p. 2.

[149] A.A. Boddy, 'Reports from England', *AF* 1.9 (Jun 1907), p. 1.

gospel of salvation.[150] For the most part however, there was 'a missionary spirit for saving souls'.[151]

Second, the restoration of tongues signalled a restoration of all the gifts of the Holy Spirit. If tongues were restored, then apostolic-like power was also restored: 'now I feel a power for witnessing I never had before and an assurance of power in service'.[152] At SB the glossolalic received confidence that they could be used for any of the 'signs following'.[153] Georgetta Jeffries wrote, 'I praise Him for the power in the sign He gave me of speaking in tongues ... I praise God for the healing power'.[154] Florence Crawford wrote,

> I am filled with wonder, love, and praise that God would permit me to see the workings of His mighty power in these last days. O to think we have lived to see the return of the apostolic power and to see the gifts restored back to the church.[155]

The restoration of tongues affirmed the NT worldview of an unseen spiritual battle: 'apostolic power will mean apostolic persecution. Hell with all its power will be turned loose'.[156] Consider the report from one Pentecostal camp meeting: 'the enemy came in as an angel of light, and we had a battle with the powers of darkness; but it was turned into victory after all'.[157] Spiritual battles required confronting demons with Pentecostal power.[158] Though there is counterfeit power, like Ananias and Sapphira, 'God's power was mightier than all the forces of hell, so their sin found them out'.[159]

---

[150] 'The Promised Latter Rain Now Being Poured out on God's Humble People', p. 1; cf. G.A. Cook, 'The Pentecostal Power In Indianapolis', *AF* 1.6 (Feb/Mar 1907), p. 3.

[151] W.J. Seymour, 'The Holy Ghost and the Bride', *AF* 2.13 (May 1908), p. 4.

[152] A.B. Shepherd, 'Pentecostal Testimonies', *AF* 1.6 (Feb/Mar 1907), p. 8.

[153] 'Pentecost With Signs Following', *AF* 1.4 (Dec 1906), p. 1.

[154] Georgetta Jeffries, 'Another Witness', *AF* 1.4 (Dec 1906), p. 1.

[155] F. Crawford, 'Testimony And Praise To God', *AF* 1.9 (Jun 1907), p. 4.

[156] *AF* 1.2 (Oct 1906), p. 3; cf. J.G. Bourman, 'A Businessman's Testimony of Pentecost', *AF* 1.5 (Jan 1907), p. 4.

[157] 'Everywhere Preaching The Word', *AF* 1.10 (Sep 1907), p. 1.

[158] 'Pentecostal Power in San Diego', *AF* 1.5 (Jan 1907), p. 1. 'O to think He has given us this power and these words of the Father that bring instant healing, and rebuke demons and bring salvation to poor perishing souls', 'Electric Messages From The Field', *AF* 2.13 (May 1908), p. 2.

[159] Seymour, 'Counterfeits', p. 2.

For Seymour, power was defined more broadly than just tongues. It was an infusion of 'divine power' that invested the individual with 'heavenly authority':[160]

> when you have the Holy Ghost, you have an empire, a power within yourself ... So when we get the power of the Holy Ghost, we will see the heavens open and the Holy Ghost power falling on earth, power over sickness, diseases and death.[161]

Overtly seeking power had it pluses and minuses. To outsiders Pentecostals sounded braggadocios, but their own self-perception was that of genuine awe and humility at being used by God. For example, 'we are only in the A.B.C. [sic] of this wonderful power of God that is to sweep over the world'.[162] Another shared, 'if we all keep low down at the feet of Jesus and give Him all the honor and glory, (that) all the power and signs of Pentecost will be restored'.[163] Durham assessed that Seymour's power was 'in his weakness'.[164] 'Power came only through heart purity', noted one testimony.[165] Yet, Pentecostals offered demonstrations of power. They looked down on those merely 'theorizing' and offered a 'public testimony of His power'.[166] They were critical of 'the feebleness of the so-called sanctified' (WH people) because they 'failed to reach the glory and power of a true Pentecost'.[167] Pentecostal power was often contrasted with powerless 'formal' Christianity. A minister of the Church of England confessed that 'we are altogether too formal, we need the power of the Holy Spirit' and even credits the demise of the Welsh revival with an attempt

---

[160] W.J. Seymour, 'The Holy Spirit Bishop of the Church', *AF* 1.9 (Jun 1907). p. 3.

[161] Seymour, 'The Baptism of the Holy Ghost', p. 3.

[162] 'Hallelujah for the Prospect', *AF* 1.2 (Oct 1906), p. 4. 'Power with God meant deep humility in our dealings with our fellow creatures', G.A. Cook, 'Receiving the Holy Ghost', *AF* 1.3 (Nov 1906), p. 2.

[163] *AF* 1.4 (Dec 1906), p. 3.

[164] Durham, 'A Chicago Evangelist's Pentecost', p. 4.

[165] 'In Allegheny, PA', *AF* 1.7. (Apr 1907), p. 1. 'When we see people that are not bringing forth the fruits of the Spirit, it matters not how many tongues or how much power to move mountains they may have, the Lord says they are nothing', *AF* 1.12 (Jan 1908), p. 3.

[166] *AF* 1.1 (Sep 1906), p. 2; 'Baptized in New York', p. 3.

[167] A.G. Garr, 'Pentecost in Danville, VA', p. 2; 'The Apostolic Faith Mission', *AF* 1.10 (Sep 1907), p. 2.

'to graft it (the Spirit's power) on to their creeds and formalism'.[168]

2. Prayer

Without much thought as to the nature of tongues, glossolalia was assumed to be horizontal speech towards men either as xenolalia or prophecy, or it was vertical speech with God. In contexts where it was not a sign of empowerment, the glossolalic was often able to discern whether her inspired speech was prayer or praise. Many reported a deeper level of prayer and worship as a result of glossolalia:

> they do not speak in tongues in the assembly, but when in prayer; they become intense in their supplication; they are apt to break out in the unknown tongue, which is invariably followed by ascriptions of praise and adoration which are well-nigh unutterable.[169]

This deeper prayer through glossolalia could occur in the public setting, as in the example above, or in a private one: 'while in secret prayer at my bedside, I was led of the Spirit to pray in an unknown language for nearly all the world'.[170] The article, 'Prayer', stated succinctly the reasoning of praying in tongues and revealed that the early Pentecostals had incorporated Paul's theology of glossolalia in Rom. 8.26: 'prayer is the Spirit making intercession through you. Sometimes, it is in groanings that cannot be uttered. He takes your whole being and commences prevailing through you.'[171]

3. Praise

If the language one spoke was neither a human language nor prayer, it was praise to God according to Acts 10.46.[172] Cashwell wrote, 'I began to speak in tongues and praise God. A brother interpreted some of the words to be, "I love God with all my

---

[168] S.J. Mead, 'On the Way to Africa', *AF* 1.6 (Feb/Mar 1907), p. 5.
[169] 'The Promise of the Father and Speaking with Tongues in Chicago', p. 3.
[170] 'Arrested for Jesus' Sake', p. 3.
[171] 'Prayer', *AF* 1.12 (Jan 1908), p. 3.
[172] 'Speaking in Tongues', *AF* 1.13 (May 1908), p. 4. For example, 'he went to the altar ... and arose drunk on the new wine of the kingdom, magnifying God in a new tongue', 'Other Points', *AF* 1.10 (Sep 1907), p. 1.

soul'".[173] Praise was often the lubricant and result of an encounter with God.[174] Lucy Leatherman testified that she was seeking the Baptism and that her praise brought her through 'the wound in His side' and the Lord said 'Praise Me', whereupon she 'began to praise Him in an unknown language'.[175] One article compared the coming of the Holy Spirit to the singers and trumpeters giving praise when the Lord's presence came down at the dedication of Solomon's Temple:

> when they praised the Lord in unison, the house was filled with the glory of the Lord. He will fill the room and you shall be baptized with the Holy Ghost and with fire, and God will give you a new tongue as a trumpet in singing or speaking.[176]

Praise occurred in private, at work,[177] or in a public worship setting, and when it was the latter occurred, it was occasionally interpreted as praise for the audience.[178] A.A. Boddy took a more Pauline view of tongues according to a reprinted tract. He wrote that 'men and women and even children (are) magnifying God in tongues' or 'speaking mysteries to God for their own strengthening':[179] 'what I felt and realized of the sorrow and love of Jesus was beyond all expression, finding vent only in another "tongue"'.[180]

4. Revelation

It could be argued that revelation as a theological category could include all the purposes listed above. However, because glossolalia signalled the presence of God many experienced revelations:

---

[173] G.B. Cashwell, 'Came 3,000 Miles For His Pentecost', *AF* 1.4 (Dec 1906), p. 3; cf. Tom Anderson, 'Pentecostal Testimonies', *AF* 1.6 (Feb/Mar 1907), p. 8.

[174] Garr, 'Pentecost in Danville, VA', p. 2; cf. *AF* 1.8 (May 1907), p. 2. 'It was not long till the flood of joy began and all over the room they were praising and glorifying God in different tongues', 'The "Latter Rain" in Zion City, Ill', *AF* 1.9 (Jun 1907), p. 1.

[175] 'Pentecostal Experience', *AF* 1.3 (Nov 1906), p. 4.

[176] 'Type of Pentecost. II Chron. 5', *AF* 1.7 (Apr 1907), p. 3.

[177] Two back-to-back testimonies told of being overcome while at work finding expression in glossolalia, *AF* 2.13 (May 1908), p. 1.

[178] For example, 'Holy Ghost Singing', *AF* 1.1 (Sep 1906), p. 4.

[179] 'Pentecost in England', p. 1.

[180] 'Reports from England', p. 1.

'many have seen visions of Jesus and of heavenly fire'.[181] Another simply says, 'the Christians have seen their God', as an explanation of the tongues.[182] This divine and human encounter elicited a verbal response. Myrtle K. Shideler had an ecstatic experience and received a revelation of 'which there are not words enough in the English language to express'.[183] 'When He comes in, He comes talking', summarized one writer.[184] At other times, 'it means that the Spirit hushes all the flesh … let all flesh be silent before Him'.[185] Often the Spirit revealed sin.[186] Tongues not only revealed God's mysteries to his people but also hid the meaning from Satan.[187]

Overall, Pentecostals believed they were on solid biblical ground for glossolalia in many ways; nevertheless, the first battle for Pentecostalism regarded sanctification's relationship to SB.

E. Sanctification and Divine Love

The issues of sanctification and divine love were broadly discussed in connection with glossolalia.

1. Sanctification

Sanctification was tied to glossolalia in two ways; it sequentially preceded SB and only a sanctified person could be Spirit baptized.

Separating sanctification from SB was an early priority because most WH groups believed the baptism of the Spirit to be the same as sanctification.[188] They could not imagine God using a dirty vessel for the grand task of world evangelism. One had to be cleansed before they could be used. The *AF* stated, 'they could not receive

---

[181] 'Pentecost in Australia', *AF* 2.13 (May 1908), p. 1.
[182] 'The Pentecostal Revival', p. 4.
[183] This ecstatic-like testimony starts with her being 'glued to the floor' because of the power of God. She begins to speak a few 'broken sentences' in tongues and then receives her unspeakable revelation. She bursts into spontaneous praise and adoration, whereupon she has either a second or a fuller revelation that includes Jesus himself, Myrtle K. Shideler, 'Received Her Pentecost', *AF* 1.5 (Jan 1907), p. 3.
[184] 'Pentecost In Other Lands', *AF* 1.6 (Feb/Mar 1907), p. 1.
[185] *AF* 1.6 (Feb/Mar 1907), p. 5.
[186] *AF* 1.4 (Dec 1906), p. 3.
[187] 'Unlocked by Prayer', p. 3.
[188] 'Bro. Rosa's Testimony', *AF* 1.2 (Oct 1906), p. 1; 'One Church', p. 3; 'A Holiness Preacher Who Received Pentecost', p. 7.

the Spirit if they were not clean'.[189] Therefore, sequentially and pragmatically, 'the Baptism with the Holy Ghost is a gift of power upon the sanctified life'.[190]

This point was emphasized in the opening lines of the first issue:

> Pentecost has surely come and with it the Bible evidences are following, many being *converted* and *sanctified* and *filled* with the Holy Ghost, speaking in tongues as they did on the day of Pentecost.[191]

Seymour testified how he had thought the baptism of the Spirit was sanctification, but learned otherwise.[192] The reason for emphasizing this point was clear:

> too many have confused the grace of Sanctification with the endowment of Power, or the Baptism with the Holy Ghost; others have taken 'the anointing that abideth' for the Baptism, and failed to reach the glory and power of a true Pentecost.[193]

Spirit baptism, like the Day of Pentecost, is an equipping power evidenced by 'speaking in new tongues' providing a 'new language'.[194]

This WH-Pentecostal position on sanctification did not waver in *AF*.[195] The Pentecostal view of SB did not ask WH people to disregard their belief and experience of an evidential sanctification, but added a third experience beyond the two works of grace (justification and sanctification):

---

[189] 'The Apostolic Faith Mission', *AF* 2.13 (May 1908), p. 2; cf. 'Cured of Doubts and Fears', *AF* 1.9 (Jun 1907), p. 2.

[190] 'The Apostolic Faith Movement', p. 2. This one appears to be part of a brief doctrinal section under the circulation information. It is repeated verbatim in *AF* 1.3 (Nov 1906), p. 2, *AF* 1.10 (Sep 1907), p. 2; and in modified forms in *AF* 1.11 (Oct 1907), p. 2, and *AF* 2.13 (May 1908), p. 2.

[191] 'Pentecost Has Come', p. 1 (emphasis added).

[192] See, 'Bro. Seymour's Call' and 'Pentecost Has Come', p. 1.

[193] This appears in what could be considered a statement of faith, entitled 'The Apostolic Faith Movement'. It appears under the subscription information, p. 2.

[194] 'The Old-Time Pentecost', *AF* 1.1 (Sep 1906), p. 2; 'Two Works of Grace And The Gift of the Holy Ghost', *AF* 1.1 Sep 1906), p. 3.

[195] Surprisingly, Durham's testimony does not include any mention of sanctification at this point, Durham, 'A Chicago Evangelist's Pentecost', p. 4.

those who have received the baptism with the Holy Ghost testify that they had a clear evidence of sanctification first. Hundreds testify that they received the Bible evidence of speaking in a new tongue.[196]

In fact, SB and the vocal nature of tongues complimented the WH doctrine of sanctification. Seymour wrote that, 'when we get the baptism with the Holy Spirit, we have something to tell, and it is that the blood of Jesus Christ cleanseth from all sin'.[197] Unlike justification or sanctification, 'the baptism with the Holy Ghost is not a work of grace but a gift of power. Sanctification is the second and last work of grace.'[198]

There are two other nuances of sanctification in *AF*. First, it was a sealing for the Second Coming:

> the only people that will meet our Lord and Savior Jesus Christ and go with Him into the marriage supper of the Lamb, are the wise virgins – not only saved and sanctified, with pure and clean hearts, but having the baptism with the Holy Ghost.[199]

This does not appear to be a strong theme,[200] and the eschatology in the newspaper seems inconsistent.[201] Second, some drew a hard line between fruit of the Spirit and SB: 'when we are sanctified, we have ... the fruits of the Spirit; but when we are baptized with the Holy Ghost, He comes in with His gifts'.[202]

---

[196] 'Gracious Pentecostal Showers Continue to Fall', p. 1.

[197] Seymour, 'River of Living Water', p. 2.

[198] 'The Enduement of Power', p. 2.

[199] Seymour, 'Behold, the Bridegroom Cometh!', p. 2; cf. 'Preserved and Sealed', *AF* 1.6 (Feb/Mar 1907), p. 7: 'He cleanses from all unrighteousness and afterwards pours in oil. And when He fills you up with oil, then He sends you out to proclaim His precious Word. This oil keeps us pure and sweet and preserved.'

[200] 'Sanctification makes us holy, but the baptism with the Holy Spirit empowers us for service after we are sanctified, and seals us unto the day of redemption', 'Questions Answered', *AF*, p. 2; cf. Seymour, 'Receive Ye the Holy Ghost', p. 2.

[201] For example, in a lengthy unsigned article, the author wrote, 'to have part in the rapture we must be sanctified and holy and live the life of a full overcomer' with no mention of SB, 'Full Overcomers', *AF* 1.12 (Jan 1908), p. 2.

[202] *AF* 1.6 (Feb/Mar 1907), p. 5.

Nevertheless, the walk of a sanctified person grew to be a distinguishing mark of SB parallel to glossolalia. Again, the acknowledgement of the potential of counterfeit tongues in the fourth issue appears to have been seminal.[203] Seymour notes that there were real and counterfeits in the Kingdom of God, but reminded true believers to walk in the light and to remember that Jesus' blood cleanses from all sin, that spiritual discernment is required.[204] In the final issue, Seymour affirms that tongues will occur at SB, it is the 'Azusa standard'; however, the article also emphasized that a genuine SB will reveal itself in unity with other believers, sanctification and divine love.[205] Even his call for the Shekinah glory to rest upon Spirit baptized people like the fiery tongues of Pentecost did not appear to be a statement on glossolalia but rather purity.[206] These ethical qualities are in addition to the missionary thrust of Pentecostal SB.[207]

2. Divine Love

Another distinguishing mark was divine love. Durham wrote, 'the first thing that impressed me was the love and unity that prevailed in the meeting, and the heavenly sweetness that filled the very air that I breathed'.[208] Many connected divine love to the inspired speech at SB, similar to a motive or impetus to speak.[209] Cashwell's testimony was typical: 'He filled me with His Spirit and love, and I am now feasting and drinking at the fountain continually and speak as the Spirit gives utterance'.[210] One Nazarene brother

---

[203] Seymour, 'Counterfeits', p. 2.

[204] Seymour does not use the word spiritual discernment, he notes 'the Holy Spirit would reveal to every one of the true children that had the Pentecostal baptism, and put a heavy rebuke upon the counterfeit', Seymour, 'Counterfeits', p. 2.

[205] 'The Baptism of the Holy Ghost', p. 3. He writes, the 'Apostolic Faith means one accord, one soul, one heart', and 'He will find pure channels to flow through sanctified avenues for His power', and finally, 'a sanctified person is cleansed and filled with divine love'.

[206] It is nestled in between two sections entitled, 'The Baptism Falls on a Clean Heart' and 'The Holy Ghost Flows Through Pure Channels'.

[207] 'The Holy Ghost and the Bride', p. 4.

[208] Durham, 'A Chicago Evangelist's Pentecost', p. 4. It was the love and singing in the Spirit that created a longing in his heart for more.

[209] For example, Ardell K. Mead testified that, 'the Spirit 'flooded (me) with Divine love; and I commenced to speak as I would sing a new song', Mead, 'Sister Mead's Baptism', p. 3.

[210] Cashwell, 'Came 3,000 Miles', p. 3.

viewed it as the main spiritual result of SB: 'it was a baptism of love. Such abounding love! Such compassion seemed to almost kill me with its sweetness! ... This baptism fills us with divine love.'[211] Another connected it with the power of SB:

> the Pentecostal power, when you sum it all up, is just more of God's love. If it does not bring more love, it is simply a counterfeit ... Pentecost makes us love Jesus more and love our brothers more. It brings us all into one common family.[212]

Others were content to leave it undefined theologically and saw divine love as a part of the atmosphere of the Holy Spirit. For example, 'I have entered into the deeper experience. Have received the speaking, singing, and reciting poetry in a number of languages' wrote pastor J.T. Boddy, and each time I receive 'something new, with love and all the fruits of the Spirit increased, and adoration to Jesus intermingled'.[213]

Divine love, like the fruit of the Spirit, was considered a more reliable sign than tongues. For example, 'when we see people that are not bringing forth the fruits of the Spirit, it matters not how many tongues or how much power to move mountains they may have, the Lord says they are nothing'.[214] As a genuine mark, divine love cannot be counterfeited, though it can be lost through backsliding.[215] Seymour connected divine love with sanctification and not SB: 'a sanctified person is cleansed and filled with divine love, but the one that is baptized with the Holy Ghost has the power of God'.[216] In one article, the editorial staff replied that the real evidence of SB is divine love and the fruit of the Spirit. However the next sentence revealed the struggle to develop a consistent theological position. They wrote that divine love and the fruit of the Spirit, are

---

[211] *AF* 1.1 (Sep 1906), p. 1.
[212] *AF* 2.13 (May 1908), p. 3.
[213] J.T. Boddy, 'Pentecostal Testimonies', *AF* 1.6 (Feb/Mar 1907), p. 8.
[214] *AF* 1.12 (Jan 1908), p. 3. 'If you find people that get a harsh spirit, and even talk in tongues in a harsh spirit, it is not the Holy Ghost talking. His utterances are in power and glory and with blessing and sweetness', *AF* 2.13 (May 1908), p. 2.
[215] *AF* 1.4 (Dec 1906), p. 4. Love was the first mark of the Spirit to go when someone backslid while tongues could remain for a while before melting away.
[216] Seymour, 'The Baptism of the Holy Ghost', p. 3.

the real Bible evidence in their daily walk and conversation; and the outward manifestations; speaking in tongues and the signs following; casting out devils, laying hands on the sick and the sick being healed, and the love of God for souls increasing in their hearts.[217]

These two distinguishing marks for these Pentecostals were more pragmatic than theological. It is as if they were saying, 'show me what you do rather than tell me what you believe'.[218]

F. The Heavenly Anthem

There was one component of glossolalia that was greeted with much favour, the heavenly anthem (HA). Jennie Moore, the future wife of Seymour, was the first woman to speak in tongues at the cottage prayer meeting on Bonnie Brae Street in Los Angeles when the Spirit first fell on Monday, April 9th, 1906. She described the encounter:

> I sang under the power of the Spirit in many languages, the interpretation both words and music which I had never before heard ... the Spirit led me to the piano, where I played and sang under inspiration, although I had not learned to play.[219]

The HA[220] was a part of the ASM revival from the beginning, and there were numerous testimonies and accounts throughout *AF*. A careful reading revealed a consensus regarding HA's inspiration, general nature, direction, emotional affect, and purpose. For example, note how the first published account of the HA reads very close to Moore's testimony, 'the Lord is giving new voices, he translates old songs into new tongues, he gives the music that is being sung by the angels and has a heavenly choir all singing the same heavenly song in harmony'.[221]

---

[217] 'Questions Answered (*AF*)', p. 2.
[218] For example, 'we are not fighting men or churches, but seeking to displace dead forms and creeds and wild fanaticisms *with living, practical Christianity.* "*Love, Faith, Unity*" are our watchwords, and "Victory through the Atoning Blood" our battle cry', 'The Apostolic Faith Movement', p. 2 (emphasis added).
[219] Moore, 'Music from Heaven', p. 3.
[220] Other monikers are the 'heavenly song', 'singing in the Spirit', 'singing in tongues', 'chorus of tongues', the 'heavenly choir', the 'heavenly chant', or 'heavenly chorus' but an article in the fifth issue entitles the phenomena as 'the Heavenly Anthem', 'The Heavenly Anthem', p. 3.
[221] *AF* 1.1 (Sep 1906), p. 1.

First, the HA was believed to be inspired-speech, because it was in 1 Cor. 14.15. When one sang in this fashion, it was under the direction of the Holy Spirit: 'no one but those who are baptized with the Holy Ghost are able to join in – or better, the Holy Ghost only sings through such in that manner', read one testimony.[222] An even bolder statement read that the HA defies 'all the power of human [sic] to imitate'.[223] It was considered a gift of the Spirit without any reflection upon it not being among Paul's specific lists. For example, 'the gift of singing and playing instruments in the Spirit has been given'.[224]

Second, the HA was a spontaneous new song sung either in a heavenly language or in xenolalia, but occasionally it occurred with a familiar hymn or melody, with one report of a 'Christmas carol in tongues'.[225] Mason says, 'He has sung hundreds of songs (through me). I do not have time to go back over one to practice it, for the next will be new'.[226] For these early Pentecostals, it was heaven come down to earth: 'she started singing in the same tongue (Chinese-like). What heavenly music! It sounded very much like an angel's voice coming rolling [sic] over the balconies of heaven.'[227]

Third, one can discern a deep emotion in these reports and testimonies. There was an overflowing joy, like someone going to one's own wedding,[228] or an awe-inspiring beauty[229] that could last for hours.[230] One writer said it was an 'indescribable experience and must be passed through to appreciate it'.[231] Though spontaneous, it was controllable by the speaker. J.T. Boddy, wrote,

---

[222] 'The Heavenly Anthem', p. 3.
[223] 'Bro. Ryan Receives His Pentecost', *AF* 1.3 (Nov 1906), p. 3. cf. C. Eckert, 'Pentecost at a Funeral', *AF* 2.13 (May 1908), p. 3.
[224] *AF* 1.3 (Nov 1907), p. 4.
[225] 'The Heavenly Anthem', p. 3.
[226] C.H. Mason, 'Testimonies', *AF* 1.12 (Jan 1908), p. 4.
[227] 'A Policeman Receives Pentecost', *AF* 2.13 (May 1908), p. 1.
[228] Mason, 'TN Evangelist Witnesses', p. 7.
[229] It is the 'most ravishing and unearthly music', wrote one eyewitness, Durham, 'A Chicago Evangelist's Pentecost', p. 3, cf. Eben Lind, 'Healed By The Lord', *AF* 1.9 (Jun 1907), p. 3.
[230] Boddy, 'Personal Testimonies', p. 8, cf. Kathleen Scott, 'Testimonies', *AF* 1.12 (Jan 1908), p. 4.
[231] G.H. Lester, 'Testimonies', *AF* 1.12 (Jan 1908), p. 4.

> I have entered into the deeper experience. Have received the speaking, singing, and reciting poetry in a number of languages, with power to use one or two at will in public services or with private persons when the Lord leads.[232]

There are only a couple reports of being overwhelmed in song to the point of losing control in an ecstatic fashion. An example from Kilsyth, Scotland read,

> an engine driver was making his way home, and his legs gave way. The power of God fell on him, and they supported him to Brother Murdoch's [sic] kitchen where many have received the baptism, and he was soon 'through,' singing as the Spirit gave him utterance, and has been singing ever since.[233]

Fourth, theologically, the HA was a synonym for SB's IE. It was the Bible evidence in song not speech. For example, one report read, 'a 10 year old was the first to get the baptism, he began clapping his hands and singing "Jesus Savior, pilot me"'.[234] Another read, the Holy Spirit 'gave me the Bible evidence of speaking and singing in tongues'.[235] It was believed that God determined the evidence; 'He will manifest His power in the demonstration of speaking *or* singing in tongues, just as the Holy Ghost chooses'.[236] At times it was like God priming the pump with the HA before seekers would effortlessly speak in tongues.[237] For example, one man 'began a song without words for a time (worshiping in the Spirit) then a few utterances in tongues, and so on till he spoke most fluently'.[238] Missionary Antoinette Moomu's testimony sounded similar. She wrote that after a complete sanctification, 'I was charged with the power of God and my soul flooded with glory. The Spirit sang praises unto God. Glory to Jesus. He gave

---

[232] Boddy, 'Personal Testimonies', p. 8.

[233] 'Pentecostal Outpouring in Scotland', *AF* 2.13 (May 1908), p. 1. 'When singing or speaking in tongues, your mind does not take any part in it', 'Honor The Holy Ghost', *AF* 2.13 (May 1908), p. 2.

[234] 'Pentecost Among the Young People', *AF* 1.4 (Dec 1906), p. 3.

[235] R.J. Scott, 'What Pentecost Did for One Family', *AF* 1.6 (Feb/Mar 1907), p. 7, cf. 'Humble Sister', *AF* 1.8 (May 1907), p. 4.

[236] *AF* 1.12 (Jan 1908), p. 3 (emphasis added). 'The Lord sings and speaks through you in another tongue', 'Pentecostal Notes', p. 3.

[237] Hebden, 'This is the Power of the Holy Ghost', p. 4.

[238] *AF* 1.8 (May 1907), p. 1.

me the Bible experiences, speaking through me in other tongues.'²³⁹ Another wrote, 'It is so solemn and yet so heavenly and deepen's [sic] one's hunger' for the Holy Spirit.²⁴⁰ And a grieving mother's heart was healed of the pain over her young child's death when she joined in singing with the 'voice divine'.²⁴¹ Female writers tended to write in more poetic language. For example, springtime and the accompanying birdsong were perhaps the most sublime definition of the HA: 'the flowers all bud out in their souls, and they commence singing in tongues like the birds, showing us that the Holy Ghost brings spring to our hearts, and the blossoms and the fruit commence growing.'²⁴²

Fifth, the HA normally occurred in a public worship setting where the direction of the speech was upwards to God in praise. Often there was a desire to translate the praise horizontally, like prophecy to the hearers.²⁴³ One eyewitness wrote that she sang a song in tongues which she then interpreted as the 'Doxology'.²⁴⁴ At times it was even thought to be a specific portion of Scripture sung in a foreign language.²⁴⁵

These pioneers usually saw the HA as parallel to speaking in tongues. Yet, as controversial as tongues were in that day, Frank Bartleman wrote that the HA's near unanimous approval 'seemed to still criticism and opposition, and was hard for even wicked men to gainsay or ridicule'.²⁴⁶

G. Tongues as a Gift of the Holy Spirit
Though the Pauline components of glossolalia were not fully developed in *AF*, at times one can see glimpses of Paul's writings.

---

²³⁹ Moomau, 'China Missionary Receives Pentecost', p. 3.
²⁴⁰ 'From Distant Lands', p. 1.
²⁴¹ C. Eckert, 'Pentecost at a Funeral', p. 3.
²⁴² *AF* 1.11 (Oct 1907), p. 2.
²⁴³ 'Message in Tongues Interpreted', *AF* 1.6 (Feb/Mar 1907), p. 7, cf. *AF* 1.10 (Sep 1907), p. 4.
²⁴⁴ LA. Sims, *AF* 1.6 (Feb/Mar 1907), p. 8.
²⁴⁵ 'The Heavenly Anthem', p. 3, cf. 'A Missionary Family', *AF* 1.8 (May 1907), p. 2.
²⁴⁶ Bartleman, *An Eyewitness Account*, p. 63. One singular reference in *AF* could be read as negative. It encourages people not to sing for 'fancy' but under the anointing, cf. *AF* 1.12 (Jan 1908), p. 2. Robeck notes two negative accounts outside of the *AF*. One from a newspaper reporter, but the most notable would be Parham who downplayed it as just another 'negro chant', Robeck, *Azusa Street*, pp. 150-58.

First, while some seem unaware of a distinction between the Bible sign and gift of tongues,[247] others saw a distinctions: 'at first I find that I had tongues as a sign, now as one of the gifts'.[248] Their nomenclature itself was imprecise, and how this spiritual gift functioned in the congregation was unfamiliar.[249] For example, note how fuzzy this testimony was: 'I myself have received the gift and speak in many different tongues'.[250] Here, the gift of tongues could refer to evidential tongues,[251] MT,[252] the Holy Spirit himself,[253] or to what Paul referenced in 1 Corinthians 12-14.[254] The third issue of the *AF* clearly distinguished between 'the Bible evidence ... (and) the '"gift of tongues" or "divers tongues" and the interpretation', but this distinction was not consistently published.[255] Nevertheless, the following was generally accepted about the gifts of the Spirit in *AF*: 1) because eight of the nine gifts were exercised before Pentecost, tongues were somehow unique.[256] 2) It is a 'free gift ... the promise of the Father',[257] a 'good gift'.[258] 3) 'The Lord is restoring *all the gifts* to His church' because '*all the gifts* of the

---

[247] Levi Lupton, 'Holiness Bible School Leader Receives Pentecost', *AF* 1.6 (Feb/Mar 1907), p. 5.

[248] Hebden, 'This is the Power of the Holy Ghost', p. 4; cf. Post, 'Testimony of a Minister', p. 4; 'Transformed by the Holy Ghost', p. 5; A.B. Shepherd, *AF* 1.6 (Feb/Mar 1907), p. 8.

[249] 'We all used to break out in tongues; but we have learned to be quieter with the gift', Seymour, 'Gifts of the Spirit', p. 2. Seymour pioneered the praxis of glossolalia in the congregational setting and as such, had to deal with aberrations such as those who wanted to preach in tongues, 'Unlocked by Prayer', p. 3.

[250] E.C. Ladd, 'In Des Moines', *AF* 1.6 (Feb/Mar 1907), p. 3. Cf. Maggie Geddis, 'Found The Pearl of Great Price', *AF* 1.6 (Feb/Mar 1907), p. 4.

[251] 'The Promised Latter Rain Now Being Poured out on God's Humble People', p. 1; 'Spanish Receive the Pentecost', p. 3; 'Baptized in New York', p. 3; 'This Is That', p. 3.

[252] *AF* 1.1 (Sep 1906), p. 1; H.M. Allen, 'When the Holy Ghost Speaks', *AF* (Oct 1906), p. 2; 'Pentecost in India', p. 1; 'En Route to Africa', p. 4.

[253] *AF* 1.1 (Sep 1906), p. 1; Seymour, 'River of Living Water', p. 2; 'The True Pentecost', *AF* 1.4 (Dec 1906), p. 2; 'Bearing His Reproach', *AF* 1.5 (Jan 1907), p. 2.

[254] 'Came From Alaska', AF 1.3 (Nov 1906), p. 2; 'The Enduement of Power', p. 2; Post, 'Testimony of a Minister', p. 4.

[255] 'Gracious Pentecostal Showers Continue to Fall', p. 1; cf. 'Transformed by the Holy Ghost', p. 5.

[256] 'Tongues as a Sign', p. 2; 'Sanctified Before Pentecost', p. 2.

[257] Ophelia Wiley, 'Sermon From A Dress', *AF* 1.2 (Oct 1906), p. 2; Seymour, 'The Way Into The Holiest', p. 4; *AF* 1.4 (Dec 1906), p. 1.

[258] *AF* 1.4 (Dec 1906), p. 1; Seymour, 'Gifts of the Spirit', p. 2.

Spirit ... are for the church today'.²⁵⁹ 4) 1 Corinthians 12-14 provided the guidelines for use of the gift:²⁶⁰ 'we have learned to be quieter with the gift ... (so) that everything may be done decently and in order' reveals a desire to follow the Pauline directives to Corinth.²⁶¹ Finally, 5), public prophecy was required to have an interpretation, which revealed a Pauline understanding of 'the best gift to the church, for it builds up the saints'.²⁶² The concept of edifying oneself through glossolalia was infrequent in *AF*.²⁶³

II. Early Southern Pentecostalism – *The Bridegroom's Messenger*

A. History of the Revival

Undoubtedly, the central figure for Pentecostalism in the south was Gaston B. Cashwell. He brought the revival fire back from Los Angeles; led what would be the East Coast revival centre; influenced many WH leaders to experience SB; and even brought several WH denominations into the Pentecostal camp. He was called 'the apostle of Pentecost in the south' due to his barnstorming revival tours across the south.²⁶⁴

Cashwell's ministry led him from the Methodist Episcopal Church to the Holiness Church of North Carolina where he was an influential evangelist.²⁶⁵ He heard about the ASM revival though the *Way of Faith* periodical and went to Los Angeles

---

²⁵⁹ *AF* 1.2 (Oct 1906), p. 4 (emphasis added). Cf. 'Editors Receive the Pentecost', *AF* 1.3 (Nov 1906), p. 3; Post, 'Testimony of a Minister', p. 4; Crawford, 'Testimony And Praise To God', p. 4.

²⁶⁰ 'The True Pentecost', p. 2; 'Other Pentecostal Saints', *AF* 1.4 (Dec 1906), p. 3; 'Questions Answered (*AF*)', p. 2.

²⁶¹ Seymour, 'Gifts of the Spirit', p. 2. This is in contrast to 'those who have "Tongues"' at Keswick and (were) 'unable and unwilling to control them when moved by the Spirit', 'Tongues at Keswick', *AF* 1. 6 (Feb/Mar 1907), p. 2.

²⁶² Seymour, 'Gifts of the Spirit', p. 2; cf. *AF* 1.1 (Sep 1906), p. 1; 'Pentecost in India', *AF* 1.3 (Nov 1906), p. 1.

²⁶³ Possibly as few as two: Seymour, 'Gifts of the Spirit', p. 2; *AF* 1.6 (Feb/Mar 1907), p. 4.

²⁶⁴ H.V. Synan, 'Gaston Barnabas Cashwell', in Stanley Burgess (ed.), *NIDPCM* (Grand Rapids, MI: Zondervan, rev. and expanded edn, 2002), pp. 457-58 (457).

²⁶⁵ Stephens notes that this migration took roughly nine years and that Cashwell was a large man with a booming voice and a 'powerful presence', Stephens, *The Fire Spreads*, p. 201, cf. Synan, *The Holiness-Pentecostal Tradition*, p. 113.

specifically to 'seek for the baptism of the Holy Ghost'.[266] At first Cashwell was shocked by the interracial and 'fanatical' nature of the revival, but wrote 'as soon as I reached Azusa Mission, a new crucifiction [sic] began in my life and I had to die to many things'.[267] Overcoming his racism, he insisted that Seymour pray for him and soon found what he was seeking:

> the Lord opened up the windows of heaven and the light of God began to flow over me in such power as never before ... I began to speak in tongues and praise God. A brother interpreted some of the words to be, 'I love God with all my soul.' He filled me with His Spirit and love ... and speak as the Spirit gives utterance, both in my own language and in the unknown language.[268]

Upon his return to the south, Cashwell led a month-long revival[269] in Dunn, NC where thousands of WH people and many leaders[270] experienced SB. The revival was so strong that 'the Fire-Baptized Holiness Church (FBHC), and the Pentecostal Free-Will Baptist Church entered the pentecostal movement' though it.[271] Subsequent whirlwind tours by Cashwell and other recent converts quickly brought about the Holmes Bible and

---

[266] Cashwell, 'Came 3,000 Miles', p. 3; cf. Synan, *The Holiness-Pentecostal Tradition*, p. 113.

[267] Cashwell, 'Came 3,000 Miles', p. 3; cf. Synan, 'Gaston Barnabas Cashwell', p. 457.

[268] Cashwell, 'Came 3,000 Miles', p. 3.

[269] Synan, *The Holiness-Pentecostal Tradition*, p. 114; cf. Robeck, *Azusa Street*, p. 218. Stephens marks this revival as the genesis of the Pentecostal movement in the south, Stephens, *The Fire Spreads*, p. 2. Stephens believes that the intense interest stems from: 'a negative, apocalyptic' premillennial eschatology that rejects civic improvement in this world, p. 138; an extensive 'print culture', pp. 111-14, 198-201; a Christianity that matches 'authentic Holy Ghost religion ... (where) tongues speech was the ultimate evidence of both Spirit empowerment and the coming of Jesus', p. 187; and a 'competitive drive against holiness fellowships', p. 222.

[270] 'The key to the amazing spread of the Pentecostal movement in the south was the receptive attitude of the various holiness leaders in the months from 1906 through 1908. The winning of King, Tomlinson, and Mason was crucial to the Pentecostal advance', wrote Synan. Synan, *The Holiness-Pentecostal Tradition*, p. 128.

[271] Synan, 'Gaston Barnabas Cashwell', p. 457; cf. Robeck, *Azusa Street*, pp. 218-19.

Missionary Institute,²⁷² two future founders of the Assemblies of God,²⁷³ and influenced the Church of God (Cleveland, TN) toward the Pentecostal movement.²⁷⁴ His own denomination was the last group to be brought into the Pentecostal movement, whereupon it changed its name to the Pentecostal Holiness Church.²⁷⁵

B. Gaston B. Cashwell and Elizabeth A. Sexton as Editors

There was a subtle difference between how Cashwell and Sexton reported on the revival. Early issues of *TBM,* largely followed the themes and interests of the *AF*.²⁷⁶ The initial thirteen issues with Cashwell as editor were a snapshot of the leading edge of the expanding revival and largely focused on the revival's effects in the United States.²⁷⁷ Even though Seymour and Cashwell envisioned a world-wide revival,²⁷⁸ Sexton morphed *TBM* from a regional to an international revival report: 'follow His footprints around the globe and you will realize more fully that "the field is the world," and that He is stepping from continent to continent, and from zone to zone, to hasten the preparation for the great and terrible day of the Lord'.²⁷⁹ In *TBM,* missionaries reported

---

²⁷² Stephens noted that 'by 1908 hundreds of energetic evangelists were crisscrossing the South, preaching tongues and converting thousands', Stephens, *The Fire Spreads*, p. 203.

²⁷³ M.M. Pinson and H.G. Rogers, Alexander, *Pentecostal Healing*, p. 86.

²⁷⁴ Synan, 'Gaston Barnabas Cashwell', p. 457; Synan, *The Holiness-Pentecostal Tradition*, pp. 123-24.

²⁷⁵ Synan, 'Gaston Barnabas Cashwell', p. 458; cf. Synan, *The Holiness-Pentecostal Tradition*, pp. 117-23.

²⁷⁶ There was even a friendly letter of encouragement by Seymour stating 'wherever this blessed gospel goes through His Spirit-filled servants – a fruitful field grows up right away', Seymour 'Letter from Bro. Seymour', p. 2.

²⁷⁷ During the same exact time period there were only three issues of *AF* (October 1907, January and May 1908) while fourteen issues of *TBM* were published by Cashwell, though issue 1.10 (March 15ᵗʰ, 1908) is not extant.

²⁷⁸ Many furloughing missionaries were filled with the Spirit at ASM and new ones were sent out, Robeck, *Azusa Street*, pp. 235-80. Also, the titles of articles indicate an expansive world-view: 'Beginning of World Wide Revival', p. 1; 'Pentecost Both Sides of the Ocean', *AF* 1.6 (Feb/Mar 1907), p. 1; 'Everywhere Preaching the Word', p. 1; 'The Lord Is Speaking in the Earth Today', p. 1; 'Fires Are Being Kindled By The Holy Ghost Throughout The World', *AF* 2.13 (May 1908), p. 1.

²⁷⁹ E.A. Sexton, 'Editorials, What Hath God Wrought?', *TBM* 2.46 (Sep 15, 1909), p. 1; e.g. E.A. Sexton, 'Editorials, The Great White Harvest', *TBM* 2.38 (Jun 1, 1909), p. 1; E.A. Sexton, 'Editorials, Africa For Christ', *TBM* 3.68 (Aug

both their success and struggles.[280]

Sexton's view was that SB was not just to evoke 'sweet heavenly melody and high-sounding praises' but worshipful obedience[281] to tell the whole world:

> the great and last call of God has been given to the church in the Pentecostal movement. It is a call to push the missionary work; and this means that every nation must be visited with the living, saving Gospel of our Lord Jesus; and that those who are sent must measure up to the Bible standard, equipped as the disciples were after Pentecost.[282]

Sexton challenged her readers, 'O beloved, God is evidently calling for Spirit-filled workers who would lay down their lives for the gospel'.[283] Those called to foreign lands needed to speak in tongues and be totally committed.[284] The *Bridegoom Messenger* staff

---

15, 1910), p. 1; E.A. Sexton, 'Editorials, Another Year of Service If The Lord Tarry', *TBM* 4.72 (Oct 15, 1910), p. 1.

[280] Regarding success: 'In Estonia ... the gift of "tongues" is heard quite often in the meetings ... they are most often uttered by young women, less frequently by men', 'Speaking in Tongues In Russia', *TBM* 3.47 (Oct 1, 1909), p. 3; 'The Pentecostal revival is rolling on in Wales ... fifteen to twenty received the baptism of the Bible sign of "tongues!" Nine received in one meeting', D.E. Evans, 'Pentecost in Wales', *TBM* 3.47 (Oct 1, 1909), p. 1. Regarding struggles: 'There is not one open door here where we can give this precious truth to the people', Lucy M. Leatherman, 'Pentecost In Jerusalem, Palestine', *TBM* 1.16 (Jun 15, 1908), p. 1; 'Missions to Mohammedans are the most difficult of all Christian missionary enterprises ... we must break the influence of Mohammedanism or we shall ourselves be broken', 'Africa The Battle Ground', *TBM* 4.88 (Jun 15, 1911), p. 4.

[281] E.A. Sexton, 'Editorials, "And Ye Would Not"', *TBM* 2.31 (Feb 1, 1909), p. 1. Popular missionary Thomas Junk notes that 'it pays to be obedient and go all the way with the Lord', Thomas Junk, 'From Bro. Thos. Junk', *TBM* 3.53 (Jan 1, 1910), p. 1.

[282] E.A. Sexton, 'Editorials, Increasing Missionary Activity', *TBM* 3.69 (Sep 1, 1910), p. 1.

[283] E.A. Sexton, 'Editorial, Going with a Message', *TBM* 4.76 (Dec 15, 1910), p. 1.

[284] Often, the sole credential for several new missionaries is 'the baptism of the Holy Spirit after the manner of the day of Pentecost', Albert Norton, 'The New Missionaries', *TBM* 1.31 (Feb 1, 1909), p. 2. Some cautioned against tongues as the sole criterion: 'do not think ... That because you received the spirit with the sign of the new tongues that you must necessarily drop your present occupation (1 Cor. 7:20-24) and go right out preaching', 'Good Advice', *TBM* 3.60 (Apr 15, 1910), p. 2. For example of total commitment: 'my work here is till Jesus comes or I am called home. I never shall see the home land

took responsibility for missionary offerings and distribution[285] and passed on practical advice, such as the need for passports.[286] From her editorial desk Sexton saw the world. She gave a large amount of space to foreign missions which reflected her theology of tongues: from Jerusalem to the ends of the earth.

C. Glossolalia and Sanctification

1. The Bible Evidence[287]

Without question the expected biblical sign of SB was glossolalia, because it was clear from the pattern from the book of Acts[288] and Mk 16.17. Early Pentecostals relied heavily on Mk 16.17 as Jesus' singular explicit reference to glossolalia.[289] Cashwell wrote that Bro. McManning 'was filled with the Holy Ghost and spoke in tongues, *as all do who receive Him*';[290] they will 'have the same effect and give the same evidence that He did on the day of Pentecost and down through the apostles'.[291] One article, similar to a statement of faith, noted that 'we teach that all who receive the Pentecostal baptism of the Holy Ghost speak with other tongues as the

---

again till I see it from the clouds', Thomas Junk, 'Bro. Thos. Junk's Letter', *TBM* 3.59 (Apr 1, 1910), p. 2.

[285] Mrs. G.B. Cashwell acted as 'Secretary and Treasurer' until, at least, December 1st, 1908. See report, *TBM* 2.27 (Dec 1, 1908), p. 2. Eventually, Miss Sadie Wightman was added as a missions editor, 'Missionary Editor', *TBM* 8.167 (Feb 1, 1915), p. 2.

[286] Editor, 'To Out-Going Missionaries', *TBM* 5.105 (Mar 1, 1912), p. 2; cf. 5.111 (Jun 1, 1912), p. 3.

[287] The most common term used in *TBM* was 'Bible evidence'. Other descriptors include: the 'same evidence', the 'real Bible evidence', a 'necessary evidence', and also the 'infallible evidence', cf. G.B. Cashwell, 'Editorials (2)', *TBM* 1.6 (Jan 15, 1908), p. 1; Eli Gardner, 'A Great Mistake', *TBM* 3.61 (May 1, 1910), p. 4; Mrs. A.J. Hough, 'My Pentecostal Baptism', *TBM* 4.83 (Apr 1, 1911), p. 3; K.E. England, 'Latter Rain Falling', *TBM* 6.136 (Jul 1, 1913), p. 2.

[288] 'The Holy Ghost In Samaria', *TBM* 1.16 (Jun 15, 1908), p. 4.

[289] 'I expect to see the last of Mark verified out in the east of Canada', C.E. Kent, 'Asks for Prayer', *TBM* 1.2 (Nov 1, 1907), p. 2; cf. E.D. Gatlin, 'Bonneau, S.C.', *TBM* 1.9 (Mar 1, 1908), p. 3; Christine Eckman, 'Speaking in Tongues', *TBM* 2.30 (Jan 15, 1909), p. 4; E.A. Sexton, 'Editorial, And These Signs Shall Follow Them That Believe #1', *TBM* 7.151 (Mar 1, 1914), p. 1; A.W.F., 'Gospel Manuscripts', *TBM* 8.160 (Aug 15, 1914), p. 4; Ella J. Staley, 'My Testimony', *TBM* 9.180 (Mar 1, 1916), p. 4; and E.A. Sexton, 'Editorial, And These Signs Shall Follow Them That Believe #2', *TBM* 9.186 (Sep 1, 1916), p. 1.

[290] G.B. Cashwell, 'The Victory at Pleasant Grove Camp Meeting', *TBM* 1.2 (Nov 1, 1907), p. 1 (emphasis added).

[291] Cashwell, 'Editorials (2)', p. 1.

Spirit gives them utterance'.[292] Boddy wrote that 'none are satisfied unless they have the sign of tongues'.[293] There were numerous examples in the early issues.[294] Some even retracted their opposition to the doctrine after having experienced it.[295] One stated, 'what a great loss it would have been to me to have stopped short of the real Bible evidence ... press on and get God's best'.[296] Tongues were the litmus test, with only a few exceptions. For example, G.W. Hall testified of a young boy who danced in the Spirit for his evidence,[297] and there were a few testimonies of a delay between SB and evidential glossolalia, but far fewer than in *AF*.[298]

For the believer, evidential tongues was to 'prove that the Holy Ghost has taken possession of the Temple ... that the promise has been fulfilled'.[299] Those promises included that one had received the same power that the apostles received[300] for a 'larger witness for Jesus';[301] that they were now 'especially equipped for the Master's kingdom';[302] and to prove that 'we are his sent ones'.[303] Thomas B. Barrett summarizes, that 'where tongues ... are bestowed, we have a special and gracious evidence of the Holy Spirit's indwelling presence (Acts x.46)'.[304]

---

[292] 'Questions and Answers (*TBM*)', *TBM* 1.7 (Feb 1, 1908), p. 2.

[293] A.A. Boddy, 'Conference of Pentecostal Saints at Hamburg, Germany', *TBM* 2.32 (Feb 15, 1909), p. 2.

[294] H.H. Goff, 'H.H. Goff's Letter', *TBM* 1.1 (Oct 1, 1907), p. 2; Fannie Winn, 'How God has Blessed the Work of Our Missionaries in China', *TBM* 1.16 (Jun 15, 1908), p. 2.

[295] H.M. Turney, 'An Explanation', *TBM* 2.33 (Mar 1, 1909), p. 2; B.F. Duncan 'Athens, Ga', *TBM* 3.60 (Apr 15, 1910), p. 3.

[296] Gardner, 'A Great Mistake', p. 4; cf. England, 'Latter Rain Falling', p. 2.

[297] G.W. Hall, 'Pentecost Among the Holiness Baptists', *TBM* 1.22 (Sep 15, 1908), p. 2.

[298] For example, 'I received the baptism of the Holy Ghost in April 10th, 1908, but the first manifestation I received was in January – the same year', W.J. Harvey, 'Key West, Fla', *TBM* 2.38 (May 15, 1909), p. 4; cf. H.M. Turney, 'From England', *TBM* 2.32 (Feb 15, 1909), p. 4.

[299] Lizzie Frazer, 'Portion of a Letter from India', *TBM* 1.6 (Jan 15, 1908), p. 4.

[300] E.A. Sexton, 'Editorials, A Tract That Will Interest You', *TBM* 2.37 (May 1, 1909), p. 1

[301] J.A. Culbreth, 'The Baptism and Evidence of Pentecost Foreshadowed', *TBM* 1.8 (Feb 15, 1908), p. 2.

[302] T.B. Barratt, 'Standard of Truth Taught in This Revival', *TBM* 4.86 (May 15, 1911), p. 4.

[303] B. Bernsten, 'From Brother B. Bernsten', *TBM* 3.52 (Dec 15, 1909), p. 1.

[304] Barratt, 'Standard of Truth Taught in This Revival', p. 4

Tongues were also a sign to the unbeliever according to 1 Cor. 14.22. This Pauline component was an advancement from *AF's* nearly exclusive Lucan theology.[305] Tongues convinced some unbelievers[306] and hardened others:[307] 'when Pentecost comes around, and people get the sign, and don't accept the Holy Ghost, they get further off'.[308]

2. Sanctification and Divine Love

The early Pentecostal experience of glossolalia elicited a re-examination of sanctification from two vantage points: soteriology and as a sign.

Soteriologically, that tongues now accompanied SB meant that many WH people had to redefine their sanctification experience. What they thought was SB was now a separate sanctification experience.[309] This distinction was emphasized more in the *AF* than in *TBM*. The driving force of this redefinition of sanctification was the glossolalic experience; if one did not speak in tongues it was presumed to be a sanctification experience.[310] This created an issue with timing: 'some are stumbling over the fact, that many receive the baptism soon after being saved, and use this for a basis

---

[305] There was an awareness of the different contexts for Paul and Luke: remember that 1 Corinthians was written 'partly to correct the wrong use of the gifts. In the book of Acts there were no rules laid down for the speaking in tongues because it was the utterance of God himself, and who will instruct God', E.K. Fisher, 'Stand for the Bible Evidence', *TBM* 2.40 (Jun 15, 1909), p. 2?

[306] *TBM* 1.11 (Apr 2, 1908), p. 2.

[307] 'It was intelligible only to those who were in sympathy with the speaker, while the unbelievers scoffingly ascribed it to madness or excess of wine', '"Tongues"', *TBM* 2.30 (Jan 15, 1909), p. 4 (reprint from *Household of God*); cf. Flavius Lee, 'Signs Shall Follow Them That Believe', *TBM* 3.47 (Oct 1, 1909), p. 4.

[308] It is unclear here if the author is referring to unbelievers or anti-Pentecostals, R.B. Hayes, 'Bethel, N.C.', *TBM* 1.17 (Jul 1, 1908), p. 3

[309] J.H. King, 'Answers to Questions as Requested', *TBM* 1.4 (Dec 15, 1907), pp. 2, 3; A.H. Butler, 'From Bro. Butler', *TBM* 1.5 (Jan 1, 1908), p. 4; H.M. Barth, 'Justification, Sanctification, and the Baptism of the Holy Ghost', *TBM* 1.6 (Jan 15, 1908), p. 2.

[310] 'There is a baptism of the Holy Ghost for God's children different from what we receive when entirely sanctified, and that it is followed by the speaking in an unknown tongue', E.G. Murrah, 'Three Epochs In My Life', *TBM* 1.1 (Oct 1, 1907), p. 3. 'This cleansing is the first phase of sanctification … not the baptism of the Holy Ghost as some teach', R.M. Evans, 'Nassau, N.P., Bahama Islands', *TBM* 5.114 (July 15, 1912), p. 3.

of their argument against the necessity of being sanctified prior to receiving the gift of the Holy Ghost'.[311] The timing problem was typified in Caesarea (Acts 10, 11) where justification, sanctification, and SB occurred almost simultaneously. Sexton ably responded to the Caesarean problem. First, their hearts were 'purified by faith' and they had 'devout Christian character'.[312] Second, 'we are persuaded that God has sanctified and prepared them for the baptism'.[313] Third, 'sanctification is, in a sense, comprehended in justification ... (it) may, and no doubt should begin at the same time'.[314] It was this last point of bundling sanctification and justification too tightly that would lead to the 'finished work' controversy.[315] There is a teaching ... (that) at the moment of conversion, (one is) both justified and sanctified, and that they must then tarry for the baptism of the Holy Ghost. The sign by which they may

---

[311] E.A. Sexton, 'Sanctification And The Gift of the Holy Ghost', *TBM* 2.29 (Jan 1, 1909), p. 2; H.M. Barth, 'Sanctification – The Yielded Life' *TBM* 5.117 (Sep 1, 1912), p. 2.

[312] Acts 15.9, E.A. Sexton 'Editorials, Some Questions Answered', *TBM* 2.45 (Sep 1, 1909), p. 1.

[313] E.A. Sexton, 'Editorial, Sanctification', *TBM* 4.89 (Jul 1, 1911), p. 1.

[314] E.A. Sexton, 'Editorials, Sanctification The Necessary Preparation For The Pentecostal Baptism', *TBM* 3.65 (Jul 1, 1910), p. 1.

[315] The FW controversy began in February 1910 with Durham preaching at 'old Azusa', M.M. Pinson, 'Field Notes From Bro. M.M. Pinson', *TBM* 4.84 (Apr 15, 1911), p. 3. Initially, Durham testified to 'sanctification as a second work', but later changed his position and testimony to accommodate his 'Baptist roots', Alexander, *Pentecostal Healing*, p. 150, cf. n. 470. At the ASM, 'Durham preached that 'the finished work of Christ on Calvary provided not only for the forgiveness of sins but for the sanctification of the believer ... (and that) the believer need only appropriate the benefits of the finished work of Calvary', Richard M. Riss, 'Finished Work Controversy', in Stanley Burgess (ed.), *NIDPCM* (Grand Rapids, MI: Zondervan, rev. and expanded edn, 2002), pp. 638-39 (638). Despite calls for unity, this rift would continue for roughly 35 years even though Durham died in 1912, cf. A.A. Boddy, 'A Suggested Resolution', *TBM* 5.118 (Sep 15, 1912), p. 2; 'we believe that Mr. Boddy's desires to heal division in Los Angeles has been in great measure accomplished', Rev. L.J. Mead, 'Rev. A.A. Boddy in Los Angeles', *TBM* 5.118 (Sep 15, 1912), p. 3. 'Both sides often adopted extreme positions', greater unity finally came as Pentecostals began working closer together after WWII, when 'those who believed in sanctification as a second work of grace began to refer to the experience of entire sanctification as an eradication of one's sinful nature, not merely a complete surrender to God. Finished work advocates ... (who) often minimized the need for experiential sanctification' began to see the need of a more experiential sanctification, Riss, 'Finished-Work Controversy', p. 639; cf. Brumback, *Suddenly ... From Heaven*, pp. 99-106, esp. pp. 105-106; Synan, *The Holiness – Pentecostal Tradition*, pp. 149-51.

certainly know that the work is accomplished is the speaking in tongues.[316]

Overall, the theology of glossolalia itself was not an issue during this controversy because both sides held that SB was subsequent to salvation; was not a 'third work of grace'; and that sanctification was not SB.[317]

Evidentially, sanctification had both passive and active facets connected with glossolalia. The logic was that only a fully cleansed person could be completely yielded to the Holy Spirit and thus speak with tongues. R.B. Hayes wrote,

> when we got to the place that we gave up everything and everybody, unloaded everything, got free from every entanglement, of bondage, died to church creeds, leadership and got little in our own sight, the criticizing spirit all gone, then we received the blessed baptism of the Holy Ghost and spoke in tongues as the Spirit gave utterance.[318]

In other words, tongues were evidence of a fully yielded and sanctified life. One had to be a fully cleansed temple before the Holy Spirit would enter in SB or to be used in the spiritual gifts.[319] Not having a cleansed temple was cited as a source for 'counterfeit baptisms and counterfeit manifestations'.[320]

---

[316] H.A. James 'Justification-Sanctification, The Finished Work of Christ In The Soul', *TBM* 5.108 (Apr 15, 1912), p. 1.

[317] E.A. Sexton, 'Editorials, Doctrine of the Pentecostal Movement' *TBM* 2.37 (May 1, 1909), p. 1; cf. Sexton, 'Editorials, Sanctification The Necessary Preparation', p. 1; E.A. Sexton, 'Editorials, Sound Doctrine', *TBM* 3.60 (Apr 15, 1910), p. 1; Pinson, 'Field Notes From Bro. M.M. Pinson', p. 3.

[318] R.B. Hayes, 'Slack up in Pentecostal Saints', *TBM* 4.87 (Jun 1, 1911), p. 3; 'So when the Holy Spirit has complete control we find Him using our tongues', Sexton, 'Sanctification And The Gift of the Holy Ghost', p. 2.

[319] G.B. Cashwell, 'Speaking in Other Tongues', *TBM* 1.1 (Oct 1, 1907), p. 2; Sexton, 'Sanctification And The Gift of the Holy Ghost', p. 2; 'Letter From Thomas Junk', *TBM* 2.42 (Jul 15, 1909), p. 1.

[320] Editor, 'A Word of Warning', *TBM* 2.30 (Jan 15, 1909), p. 2. A full year before the start of the 'Finished Work Controversy', Sexton noted that another source of the counterfeit was that 'many of us have been taught that sanctification meant sinless perfection. While this is the purpose of its working ... it does not mean we are overcomers because we are sanctified. The work of transformation must go on until we are made like Him' (Editor, 'A Word of Warning', p. 2).

However, tongues were proven to be an unreliable sign so divine love and the fruit of the Spirit became the undeniable sign.[321] Sexton wrote that, speaking in tongues is the distinguishing evidence of the baptism, 'provided it is accompanied with the fruit of the spirit. Gal 5:22-23'.[322] One writer stated that he cannot say of a stranger,

> this man is baptized in the Holy Ghost because he speaks in tongues. He would have to see also divine love ... divine love is always and absolutely a necessary and only certain evidence accompanying the true baptism ... 'tongues' are a sign of His mighty entrance, but love is the evidence of His continuance in controlling power.[323]

Mack M. Pinson, who would later follow the FW side of the controversy, called for more love to be actually lived out.[324] In February, 1913, eight European leaders[325] of the Pentecostal movement put their names to a declaration at an International Pentecostal Council. Their declaration affirms evidential tongues[326] if accompanied by the fruit of the Spirit, and then adds: 'we do not teach that all who have been baptized in the Holy Ghost, *even if they should speak in tongues*, have already received the fullness of the blessings of Christ implied in this Baptism'.[327] Divine love and the fruit of the Spirit were concomitant and supporting evidences to glossolalia that, if missing, rendered the claim to SB void or in progress.

---

[321] 'Real love must express itself in service; which is the proof of love', Hattie M. Barth, 'The Love of Christ', *TBM* 1.2 (Nov 1, 1907), p. 1.

[322] Sexton, 'Editorials, Doctrine of the Pentecostal Movement', p. 1.

[323] 'Tongues: The Pentecostal Sign', *TBM* 4.77 (Jan 1, 1911), p. 2.

[324] Pinson, 'Field Notes From Bro. M.M. Pinson', p. 3.

[325] Boddy and C. Polhill, England; G. Polman, Holland; Barratt, Norway; Emil Hamburg, J. Paul, and C.O. Voget, Germany; and Anton B. Reuss, Switzerland.

[326] We believe that SB is 'the coming upon and within of the Holy Spirit to indwell the believer in His fullness, and it is always borne witness to by the *fruit of the Spirit and the outward manifestation*, so that we may receive *the same gift as the disciples* on the day of Pentecost', emphasis mine, 'International Pentecostal Council Issues Declaration', *TBM* 6.126 (Feb 1, 1913), p. 1.

[327] 'International Declaration', p. 1 (emphasis added).

D. Missionary Tongues

1. Xenolalia

The Bridegroom's Messenger wrestled more openly with MT than did *AF*. Right from the start, the definition of glossolalia was sharpened to distinguish xenolalia from glossolalia. Cashwell defined the 'gift of tongues' as 'divers kinds of tongues of many languages' according to 1 Corinthians 12-14 in contrast to just 'speaking in tongues' or the 'manifestation' of tongues.[328] For example,

> we see clearly that the baptism of the Holy Ghost is not the gift of tongues ... when we receive the baptism of the Holy Ghost, we will speak in a tongue unknown to us; but when we receive the gift of tongues we will have divers kinds of languages and will speak and be understood.[329]

At times, articles and testimonies supported the theology of MT and at other times, failures were plainly stated.

Missionary tongues were so widely anticipated that people dreamed of speaking in a foreign language[330] and a phonetic transcription of tongues was even included on the first page of the first issue.[331] Testimonies from *AF* or other publications were reprinted for support.[332] The theology of MT in *TBM* initially continued a calling to a specific field by identifying the language one spoke;[333] the ability to speak a number of

---

[328] One editorial noted that Spirit-inspired speech is not the ability to learn a language in college and that a careful reading of 1 Corinthians 12-14 revealed 'the difference between speaking in tongues and the gift of tongues', Cashwell, 'Speaking in Other Tongues', p. 2.

[329] G.B. Cashwell, 'Editorials, The Word Fulfilled', *TBM* 1.8 (Feb 15, 1908), p. 1; cf. 'Questions and Answers (*TBM*)', p. 2.

[330] I.W. Ogle, 'Ocala, Fla.', *TBM* 1.7 (Feb 1, 1907), p. 3.

[331] 'Sept. 6th 5 A.M.', *TBM* 1.1 (Oct 1, 1907), p. 1.

[332] 'The Miracle of Speaking in Tongues', *TBM* 1.4 (Dec 15, 1907), p. 4, reprint; 'The Miracle of Speaking in Tongues', *AF* 1.9 (Jun 1907), p. 2. Cf. 'Work in Africa', *TBM* 1.14 (May 15, 1908), p. 1, reprint; *AF* 1.11 (Oct 1907), p. 1.

[333] 'Quite a number of them have received the gift of tongues, and have gone to the foreign fields as missionaries to the people whose language God has given them', E.A. Sexton, 'Editorials', *TBM* 1.2 (Nov 1, 1907), p. 1; cf. M. Perry, 'Good Tidings from Marion, N.C.', *TBM* 1.4 (Dec 15, 1907), p. 1; E.F. Landis, 'Pentecost in South China', *TBM* 1.9 (Mar 1, 1908), p. 2.

languages,³³⁴ or even 'any language' at will,³³⁵ including sign language for the deaf;³³⁶ and affirmed that the source of this foreign speech was the Holy Spirit.³³⁷ It confirmed that the apostolic age continues to the present.³³⁸ Ideally, testimonies included some verification of the language. For example, one occurrence of xenolalia was labelled 'unquestionable' by native Norwegian and Swedish speakers.³³⁹ If a native speaker was not present, the next best thing were missionaries who understood the language.³⁴⁰

However, MT were challenged by actual reports from the mission field. Even in the first issue of *TBM*, it is reported that 'not many of the gifts have been restored to the Church yet ... (some) thought they had the Gift of Tongues [sic]' but they only had a 'manifestation' of the Spirit.³⁴¹ Azusa Street missionaries like the well-known Garr also challenged the doctrine:

> I am not able to preach to the people in their native tongue; but we have an excellent interpreter, an educated Chinese, who has

---

³³⁴ 'Miss Lucy Villars', *TBM* 1.2 (Nov 1, 1907), p. 4; 'Report of Pentecost from Marvels in India', *TBM* 1.5 (Jan 1, 1908), p. 1; Lewis Sawgalsky, 'Experience and Testimony of Lewis Sawgalsky', *TBM* 4.94.3 (Sep 15, 1911), p. 3.

³³⁵ S.O. Lee, 'Cerro Gordo, N.C.', *TBM* 1.7 (Feb 1, 1908), p. 3. 'Suddenly the Holy Spirit came to his temples, baptized them then and there. Brother Colyar spoke fluently in Chinese, and has ever since been able to talk at will with all Chinamen he has met. He and his family are now on their way to China, to use, as missionaries, the new tongue was the Holy Ghost is given them', 'Received the Chinese Language', *TBM* 1.39 (Jun 1, 1909), p. 1.

³³⁶ F.M. Britton, 'Letter From Bro. Britton', *TBM* 1.5 (Jan 1, 1908), p. 2.

³³⁷ Mrs. Littleton could not identify her language or even tell if it was a language but wrote, 'I do know the Holy Ghost was talking through me', 'Mrs. E.C. Littleton's Testimony', *TBM* 1.1 (Oct 1, 1907), p. 3.

³³⁸ Culbreth, 'Pentecost Foreshadowed', p. 2. Culbreth noted that Pentecost and the present tongues are a reversal of confusion of languages. Another reference to Babel simply noted that 'God sent the tongues', affirming that God was the source of language, J. Reid, 'Concerning the Tongues', *TBM* 1.3 (Dec 1, 1907), p. 3; cf. V.P. Simmons, 'Tongues', *TBM* 5.109 (May 1, 1912), p. 1.

³³⁹ H. VanLoon 'Harford, Ontario', *TBM* 1.7 (Feb 1, 1908), p. 3.

³⁴⁰ 'The missionaries themselves have understood several words that the Spirit spoke through me in other tongues', T.J. McIntosh, 'Macao, China, August 22, 1907', *TBM* 1.1 (Oct 1, 1907), p. 4; cf. Geo. Hansen, 'A Good Letter From Shanghai, China', *TBM* 3.51 (Dec 1, 1909), p. 4; C.J. Montgomery, 'Speaking in Tongues', *TBM* 4.77 (Jan 1, 1911), p. 4 (reprint from *TOF* 3011 (Nov 1910), pp. 253-55..

³⁴¹ Unsigned article, *TBM* 1.1 (Oct 1, 1907), p. 1.

received the baptism of the Spirit and speaks in tongues; and the people get about all that is preached to them in that way.[342]

The reality on the field was that glossolalia was rarely a foreign language that one could employ at will. Verification was usually subjective. For example, M.D. Sellers wrote that even if tongues were not a language he would still believe it because 'I can see that it's God'.[343] Sexton admitted some failures were made, but added that the

> Pentecostal light which they carried with them, and the good they have accomplished greatly outweighs every blunder or mistake on their part ... if but one of our missionaries can use 'new tongues' in their field of labor ... the fact is established forever.[344]

The human-side was faulted for any shortcomings. Missionary Lizzie Frazer believed she would speak in the Marathi language 'when I am humble enough and perfectly free in spirit'.[345]

The concerns regarding xenolalia came to a climax in the eleventh issue, with a response to a widely known letter accusing Pentecostal missionaries in general and one young man in particular of failure.[346] In his front page editorial, Cashwell addressed the young man in a fatherly fashion. Cashwell encouraged him to pray, to wait, and to yield to the Holy Spirit, and then added: 'while we did not then believe that the gift of language had come to you, *we dared not* put our hands upon God's anointed'.[347] An article by John

---

[342] A.G. Garr, 'News from China', *TBM* 1.7 (Feb 1, 1908), p. 1.
[343] M.D. Sellers, 'Letter from Brother Sellers', *TBM* 1.8 (Feb 15, 1908), p. 4.
[344] E.A. Sexton, 'Editorials, Raised Us Up Together', *TBM* 1.9 (Mar 1, 1908), p. 1.
[345] 'A Testimony', *TBM* 1.9 (Mar 1, 1908), p. 3.
[346] E.A. Sexton noted that this letter came from Macao, China and was addressed to Rev. J.M. Pike, editor of *The Way of Faith* newspaper, E.A. Sexton, 'To Our Readers', *TBM* 1.11 (Apr 1, 1908), p. 2. One of Pike's criticisms was that this letter was to be 'a "private letter" to us, (but) has been published widely in England, Canada and United States and has the appearance of a determined effort to destroy the influence of this young missionary, and to cut off the means necessary for his support in the field', J.M. Pike, 'A Plea For Charity And Forbearance', *TBM* 1.11 (Apr 1, 1908), p. 2.
[347] Cashwell said he prayed regularly for unity and 'that all the gifts be restored speedily', G.B. Cashwell, 'Editorials, Let Us Take Courage', *TBM* 1.11 (Apr 1, 1908), p. 1 (emphasis added).

M. Pike responded to the critics. Pike believed that

> God was doing a 'new thing' in bestowing the gift of tongues to facilitate the work of the world's evangelization ... we [sic] could not be persuaded that He had yet bestowed 'the gift of tongues' upon any to preach the gospel to the heathen in their own tongue.[348]

However, Pike adds that 'this did not discourage them or deter them from persisting in their God-given task'. They reached the English speakers and 'the heathen through interpreters'.[349] He called his Pentecostal readers to press on because it was the 11th hour and the work was so large. He challenged critics to have forbearance and love because 'a place can be found for any'.[350] Yes, it was a serious 'mistake' on this young man's part but it 'has not arrested his message or hindered his work'.[351] In the same issue, China-missionary T.J. McIntosh wrote so emotionally about his desire to speak to his hearers in their native language (via tongues), that when Cashwell read his letter, he wrote 'I wept and prayed ... I am expecting the gift of tongues just as much as I expect to see Jesus'.[352]

Subsequent issues revealed a more reserved doctrine of MT. First, there is a straightforward acknowledgement that tongues do 'not seem to be an enabling ... a continuous use of foreign language without practice or study'.[353] Second, there was a greater at-

---

[348] Pike, 'A Plea For Charity And Forbearance', p. 2. This article was first printed in *The Way of Faith*, and is noted here as a reprint.

[349] Pike, 'A Plea For Charity And Forbearance', p. 2. Sexton agreed and stated that her desire in this issue was 'to answer these unfair statements by pointing to the mighty working of God through these same missionaries', Sexton, 'To Our Readers', p. 2.

[350] Pike was hesitant of all independent missionaries and would have preferred this young man work in cooperation with others, but noted that because of the shortness of time God is 'engaging the "irregulars"', Pike, 'A Plea For Charity And Forbearance', p. 2.

[351] Pike, 'A Plea For Charity And Forbearance', p. 2.

[352] G.B. Cashwell, 'Editorials, Have Faith In God', *TBM* 1.12 (Apr 15, 1908), p. 1. McIntosh wrote, 'Oh! How we would love to speak to these poor people. Of course, God speaks with our tongues, but not their language', T.J. McIntosh, 'Letter From Brother McIntosh', *TBM* 1.11 (Apr 1, 1908), p. 1.

[353] 'The Value of Speaking in Tongues', *TBM* 1.12 (Apr 15, 1908), p. 4.

tempt to verify the testimonies. For example, Presbyterian overseer W.T. Ellis heard 'girls speaking in other tongues, some in English, some in Greek, some in Hebrew' and other languages.[354] Calling himself an 'unbiased witness', Ellis noted that it was 'a story far surpassing in its marvel, anything we have hitherto heard'.[355] One testimony was even signed by fifteen Chinese who 'acknowledge that the Holy Ghost spoke through the Chinese language to them through Mrs. George Hanson'.[356] Third, from early 1909 onward, some testified to hearing only a portion of a known language. This indicates a development in the doctrine that allows for tongues occasionally being a known language and more generally being an unknown tongue. For example, 'there were about fifteen Indians at this camp meeting … he spoke three different sentences in their language'.[357] Sexton called people to 'lay aside your prejudice now, do away with your unjust judgment' because so little was known about these 'wonderful visitations of God'.[358] A very pragmatic tension emerged: when xenolalia occurred it was joyfully received as the gift of tongues;[359] but tongues were not normally presumed to be foreign languages. Sexton's response to WH critics was an excellent summary:

we believe it would be of great profit to reprint some of the

---

[354] Elizabeth A. Sexton, 'Set Thine Heart To Understand', *TBM* 1.14 (May 15, 1908), p. 1. For English as a foreign language cf. Mrs. Blanche Hamilton, 'A Portion of A Letter From C. And M. A. Missionary To A Friend In Florida', *TBM* 1.17 (Jul 1, 1908), p. 2.

[355] He was an overseer for the Presbyterian Mission Board and was in India inspecting on this occasion and called himself an 'unbiased witness', Sexton, 'Editorials, Set Thine Heart To Understand', p. 1.

[356] Bau Yien-Ching, 'Witness to The Chinese Language Spoken as The Spirit Gave Utterance', *TBM* 3.70 (Sep 15, 1910), p. 2.

[357] 'Spoke in an Indian Language', *TBM* 2.1 (Jan 1, 1909), p. 4. One testimony notes that a Hindu 'did not know enough of all these languages to get the connection … (but) all at once he burst forth saying, "she is now speaking my language"', to infer that the tongues speech was in a known language, but that this individual did not know that tribal language well enough, so the Spirit had to switch to a better known language, J.O. Lehman, 'Johannesburg, South Africa', *TBM* 2.14 (Jun 1, 1909), p. 2.

[358] Sexton, 'Editorials, Set Thine Heart To Understand', p. 1.

[359] Numerous testimonies of xenolalia were published after the pragmatic solution. For example, German was reported in, 'A Remarkable Testimony', *TBM* 1.13 (May 1, 1908), p. 4; English in, T.B. Barratt, 'In Norway', *TBM* 1.13 (May 1, 1908), p. 4; Kru in 'Work in Africa', p. 1.

many cases known where speaking in tongues, as the Spirit gives the utterance has been understood by someone familiar with the language spoken. We gather from 1 Cor. 14:2 that not all speaking in tongues may be understood by man.[360]

2. Language Acquisition

Concomitant with the theological wrestling of xenolalia was the acknowledgment on the field of the need to learn foreign languages: 'we cannot speak Arabic ... we could not do much but sing and shout God's praises and bear witness to the love and joy which can only come through Jesus Christ our Lord'.[361] Nevertheless, testimonies, beginning in 1909, reveal a pragmatic adaptation: 'Father has not given us the language out right, but has wonderfully, so wonderfully helped us, so that in the few months we not only can talk pretty well, but also read His word in Chinese, certainly not fluently, but better and better every day'.[362] Until the language was mastered, interpreters were engaged.[363] Testimonies began to include prayer requests[364] and reports of intensive study[365]

---

[360] She recalls twelve instances of xenolalia that are of 'reliable authority', E.A. Sexton, 'The Unknown Tongue is Sometimes Known', *TBM* 3.66 (Jul 15, 1910), p. 1.

[361] Fannie Winn, 'Letter from Sister Fannie Winn', *TBM* 1.16 (Nov 15, 1908), p. 4.

[362] 'God is Blessing in China', *TBM* 2.32 (Feb 15, 1909), p. 1. 'They realize that one great need is to learn the language quickly', A. Norton, 'From Brother Norton', *TBM* 2.35 (Apr 1, 1909), p. 1. Even at one of the best documented sites of xenolalia, the Mukti Mission, India, it is reported that the 'lady missionaries ... seem to be making good progress in the study of the language', Manoramabai, 'Mukti, Mission, Kedgaon', *TBM* 3.63 (Jun 1, 1910), p. 2.

[363] There was a reluctance to use interpreters: 'we have many reasons for not preaching through an interpreter; first ... we don't know what he is saying; second, they do not interpret as we wish it to be given; third, ... he wants a large sum of money', Geo. M. Kelly, 'Work in a Chinese Village', *TBM* 5.109 (May 1, 1912), p. 1. However, pragmatically they were engaged until the language was learned, cf. Garr, 'News from China', p. 1; Pike 'A Plea For Charity And Forbearance', p. 2; 'Use of the Gift of Tongues', *TBM* 2.40 (Jun 15, 1909), p. 1.

[364] 'We covet your prayers for ... each dear missionary in the study of the language', Lillian Garr, 'From Sister Garr', *TBM* 4.81 (Mar 1, 1911), p. 2. Cf. Olive Maw, 'God Needs Workers in His Vineyard', *TBM* 1.22 (Sep15, 1908), p. 3; Amos Bradley, 'From Central America', *TBM* 3.49 (Nov 1, 1909), p. 2.

[365] 'We are getting the language very fast, the people say, but of course, it seems slow to us. I can do most any kind of business in the stores that I want to do, and can talk some to the people about Yisu (Jesus) and His Mukti (salvation)', R.E. Massey, 'Letter From Brother Massey', *TBM* 2.34 (Mar 15, 1909), p. 2; cf. R.E. Massey, 'Pentecostal Fire Falling at Bahraich, India', *TBM* 2.36 (Apr

to learn the language with the goal of preaching in the local language.[366] Study of foreign languages was supported biblically: 'we are doing some very hard studying these days in the language. We desire to "show ourselves approved unto God," but we must "study" to do it'.[367] However, the presumption of xenolalia was so high, that some were disappointed: 'brother and sister Cram have gone home to the United States. Did not get the language'.[368] By early 1910, Barratt, addressed the issue forthrightly:

> we are perfectly assured that ... there will in all countries be abundant evidence of the fact that the Holy Spirit knows all languages, and is able to speak these through his believing people. Still we would point out the fact, that the speaking in tongues does not seem to have been intended to usurp the ordinary study of languages.[369]

Theologically, Barratt believed glossolalia's 'chief object on the day of Pentecost was that of giving Peter's sermon a miraculous background, and invest the disciples with divine authority'.[370]

E. Purposes For Glossolalia

1. Empowerment

At the heart of their distinctive theology, these early Pentecostals connected glossolalia with an equipping power.[371] Not surprisingly, *TBM* continued this foundational theology from the *AF*. Restoration of the apostolic message required apostolic power. The apostles had,

---

15, 1909), p. 1; R.E. Massey, 'How God is Blessing in India', *TBM* 3.48 (Oct 15, 1909), p. 2; 'Studying the Chinese Language', *TBM* 3.71 (Oct 1, 1910), p. 4; R. Atchison, 'Brother Robt. Atchin Writes', *TBM* 4.90 (Jul 15, 1911), p. 2, *et al.*

[366] Winn, 'How God Has Blessed the Work', p. 2; Bradley, 'From Central America', p. 4; R.E. Massey, 'From India', *TBM* 2.45 (Sep 1, 1909), p. 1; Lillian Garr, 'Portion of a Letter from Sister Garr', *TBM* 3.58 (Mar 15, 1910), p. 2.

[367] Amos Bradley, 'From Amos Bradley', *TBM* 3.62 (May 15, 1910), p. 3.

[368] B. Bernsten, 'From China', *TBM* 3.51 (Dec 1, 1909), p. 3. A. Anderson notes that only 'a minority returned to the USA disillusioned', Allan Anderson, 'The Vision of the Apostolic Faith: Early Pentecostalism and World Mission', *Swedish Missiological Themes*, 97.3 (2009), pp. 295-314 (300).

[369] T.B. Barratt, 'Instances of the Speaking in Known Tongues Through the Holy Spirit', *TBM* 3.54 (Jan 15, 1910), p. 3.

[370] Barratt, 'Instances of the Speaking in Known Tongues', p. 3.

[371] 'The promise of the tongues in this verse (Acts 1.8) is an equipping for service', Reid, 'Concerning The Tongues', p. 3.

> credentials adequate for its (the gospel's) accomplishment ... power for service, for extending this kingdom, and the subjection and ultimate overthrow of Satan's ... We must demand and have a Pentecost to-day [sic], which will tally in every essential, with the original pattern! ... Demons must be cast out, those of all tongues must be addressed in their own language, sick must be healed, the unbelieving must see signs and know of the truth 'this is that.' ... We must be 'filled with all the fullness of God.'[372]

The reason for this strong connection to the past, is that 'our means were too meager and our methods inadequate for the great work of the evangelization of our sin-cursed world ... God has heard our prayer'.[373] Glossolalia somehow equipped for more effective speech: 'since I have received my Pentecost, I have more power and liberty to speak to souls about Jesus than I did before'.[374]

Tongues were also an initiation into the ability to use all sorts of Spiritual gifts. 'After Pentecost, added power came upon them all', wrote Sexton, 'and many signs and wonders were done through His name'.[375] Spiritual power in the Kingdom of God required a corresponding death to self so that one could be used as a conduit:

> He does not give us power. We are still as weak as ever. He has the power, and it is He that continues to exercise it, but He gives us 'authority' to claim the exercise of His power, and as we do this in our helplessness, His strength is made perfect in our weaknesses. We have the faith and He has the power.[376]

---

[372] J.E. Sawders, 'The Pentecostal Standard', *TBM* 1.4 (Dec 15, 1907), p. 4.

[373] E.A. Sexton, 'Editorial, Entering The Fifth Year of Service', *TBM* 5.95 (Oct 1, 1911), p. 1.

[374] Thomas B. Epps, 'Another Witness', *TBM* 1.5 (Jan 1, 1908), p. 3.

[375] E.A. Sexton, 'Editorial, Power of The Name of Jesus', *TBM* 4.91 (Aug 1, 1911), p. 1. 'I am sure there has been a spiritual power operating within me since I received the Pentecostal baptism, that I did not experience before that time', N.J. Holmes, 'One Year of Pentecostal Experience', *TBM* 1.18 (Jul 15, 1908), p. 4; cf. E.A.S., 'Editorials, The Great Pentecostal Revival', *TBM* 2.33 (Mar 1, 1909), p. 1.

[376] 'Christ Has The Power', *TBM* 5.119 (Oct 15, 1912), p. 1. Cf. *TBM* 1.13 (May 1, 1908), p. 2. Sexton sees a corresponding rest: 'the Pentecostal baptism brings us to know more perfectly "The rest which remaineth for the people of

Death to self was also a part of 'character development'[377] or preparing the bride for the Second Coming;[378] a sanctifying and equipping power signalled by glossolalia.

2. Prayer

The Bridesgroom's Messenger continued and refined the *AF*'s theology that glossolalia was occasionally Spirit-inspired prayer back to God. Typical testimonies were based on Paul's groaning in the Spirit in Rom. 8.26:

> the Spirit Himself does the praying in us. It is the Christ enthroned on a surrendered life groaning out the agonies of the great intercessor at God's right hand. It is God in the earth pleading with God in the heavens on behalf of God and man.[379]

This glossolalic prayer was thought to be more effective because it was Spirit-led.[380] For example, W.M. Tallent wrote, 'I began to pray in the unknown tongue and the child was healed'.[381] Such power was sacred and mysterious.[382] It not only reached back to the apostles[383] but forward to heaven: 'how we do love to talk to

---

God." Our activity in service is by the power of the Spirit in us, we cease from our own labors. He worketh in us and our own labor is made "Peaceful activity",' E.A. Sexton, 'Editorials, River of Water of Life', *TBM* 3.48 (Oct 15, 1909), p. 1.

[377] A.S. Worrell, 'Wonderful Times Coming', *TBM* 1.9 (Mar 1, 1908), p. 4.

[378] N.J. Holmes, 'Altamont Bible And Missionary Institute', *TBM* 1.20 (Sep 15, 1908), p. 4.

[379] A.S. Copley, 'The Prayer of the Righteous', *TBM* 2.35 (Apr 1, 1909), p. 2; cf. Sarah D. Wooten, 'Testimony of Sister S.D. Wooten', *TBM* 2.46 (Sep 15, 1909), p. 3; Lillian Garr, 'Brother And Sister Garr In India', *TBM* 3.59 (Apr 1, 1910), p. 1; F.F. Bosworth, 'Pentecost at Dallas, Texas, With Signs Following', *TBM* 4.88 (Jun 15, 1911), p. 3.

[380] 'When I pray in a tongue the Holy Spirit is praying through me, and His praying through me must be of great use', Mrs. M.K. Norton, 'A Letter From Mrs. M.K. Norton', *TBM* 1.5 (Jan 1, 1908), p. 4.

[381] W.M. Talent, 'Brother Tallent's Letter', *TBM* 1.9 (Mar 1, 1908), p. 3.

[382] 'Most of them pray at times in "tongues," but they are so lost in praise and prayer when this takes place that one feels it is too sacred to be discussing as to the origins', 'Pandita Ramabai's Work', *TBM* 1.16 (Jun 15, 1908), p. 1.

[383] 'I know that what the Pentecost God in His mercy gave me is the same kind of blessing as that received by the disciples at Pentecost in Jerusalem', T.B. Barratt, 'Scenes In A Scandinavian Meeting, Where Pastor Barratt Labors', *TBM* 2.39 (Jun 1, 1909), p. 1.

Him by secret prayer! This communion is as sweet at heaven, yea, it is a foretaste of that delectable land.'[384]

One significant article broadens to the concept of glossolalic-prayer of Rom. 8.26, by defining it sacramentally: when praying in tongues, one '"feeds himself." Yes, for it is a feeding on spiritual food, of which our soul and body experience the blessing and power'.[385] So that the sacramental component is not missed, the author compares praying in tongues to receiving the elements in Holy Communion:

> when we are edifying ourselves by speaking in tongues, we are at the same time fed by His flesh and by His blood, and this being fed by His flesh and blood brings us into closer communion with Him ... Then we realize the power of this being fed also in our soul and in our body. Our soul becomes quieter, stronger ... Our body is fed. The life which is in the flesh and blood of Christ flows through our body.[386]

This sacramental component is singular to this article, but that it was reprinted from the *Confidence* periodical represents a willingness to recognize a broad definition of their glossolalic experience. Her article, which defined tongues speech as speaking mysteries to God, ended with a call to holiness, especially holiness of speech.[387]

3. Praise

Those who testified in *TBM* often assumed that glossolalia was praise. Though they did not know exactly what they were saying, they somehow knew it was praise: 'the power of God fell upon me and soon the Holy Spirit was praising Jesus in other tongues ... I knew I was worshiping Jesus in spirit and in truth'.[388] Evan Roberts was confident of the result, but vague about the exact nature of God-directed glossolalia:

---

[384] E.G. Murrah, 'Macon, GA., April 27, 1908', *TBM* 1.14 (May 15, 1908), p. 4.

[385] Mrs. Polman, 'Speaking in Tongues (*TBM*)', *TBM* 7.146 (Dec 15, 1913), p. 4, reprint; Mrs. Polman, 'Speaking in Tongues', *Confidence* 8.6 (Aug 1913), pp. 151-52.

[386] Polman, 'Speaking in Tongues (*TBM*)', p. 4.

[387] Polman, 'Speaking in Tongues (*TBM*)', p. 4.

[388] C.E. Ritchie, 'The Comforter Has Come', *TBM* 3.49 (Nov 1, 1909), p. 3.

when we receive an anointing of the Holy Spirit and He speaks, praises, or adores God through us in an unknown tongue, we are invigorated, energized and revived ... those who have never received such an anointing can never understand the blessedness of it.[389]

Glossolalic praise was an overflow of the Spirit's presence, which often began by praising God in one's native tongue. For example,

a dear baptized sister came and kneeling behind me, began to praise the Lord in a whisper, then I remembered to try to speak a word of praise and glory to Jesus, that was the sweetest moment of my life when my tongue went off in a language I knew nothing about.[390]

Those who experienced glossolalic praise described an overflowing richness where, 'all English seems inadequate',[391] and 'wave after wave still flooded my soul so that I could not sleep much, but praised the Lord all night'.[392]

4. Revelation

Testimonies often included the words 'revelation' or 'mystery'[393] to describe their experience. Spirit baptism and its accompanying tongues initiated the believer 'into the deeper things'.[394] Revelations were across many areas of spirituality: 'since the fuller baptism of the Spirit ... there has also come a deeper sense of the realness of God, of the life of the Word, of the love of the Spirit and the supremacy of Christ'.[395] Testimonies included revelations

---

[389] Evan Roberts, '"Believe Not Every Spirit"', *TBM* 6.131 (Apr 15, 1913), p. 2.

[390] Mrs. M.C. Stewart, 'Benson, S.C.', *TBM* 1.13 (May 1, 1908), p. 3.

[391] 'Tongues In The Air', *TBM* 5.97 (Nov 1, 1911), p. 3.

[392] Littleton, 'Mrs. E.C. Littleton's Testimony', p. 3.

[393] 'Quite a number of those who have received the Pentecostal baptism have been given revelations and visions and dreams', E.A. Sexton, 'The Situation', *TBM* 1.4 (Dec 15, 1907), p. 2. 'This baptism in the Holy Spirit is a mighty inspiration and revelation ... how wonderful are the deeper revelations of Jesus', A.H. Post, 'Letter From Bombay, India', *TBM* 2.25 (Nov 1, 1908), p. 1. 'And so the tongues seem to be today in connection with this "Latter Rain" baptism that is letting the saints into the mysteries of these last days', Frank Bartleman, 'Letter From F. Bartleman', *TBM* 1.9 (Mar 1, 1908), p. 2.

[394] 'Amos 4:4', *TBM* 5.96 (Oct 15, 1911), p. 4.

[395] D. Wesley Myland, 'A Personal Word', *TBM* 4.89 (Jul 1, 1911), p. 2.

of Jesus, the ability to discern the 'false from the true',[396] a greater understanding of the Bible,[397] and insight into someone's past so that they could repent.[398] As with the *AF*, there is no discernible pattern of revelation upon speaking in tongues; rather, it is an occasional and varied accompaniment.

5. Tongues as a Gift of the Holy Spirit

Paul's gift of tongues in *TBM* was developed further than in the *AF*.[399] Tongues as a congregational gift was separated from Luke's ecstatic encounter. Starting with a simple biblical hermeneutic,[400] and still giving primacy to the book of Acts and Mk 16.15, the Pauline passages were incorporated as complimentary to the Lucan passages. Personal testimonies regularly contained phrases like, 'tongues are a sign *to unbelievers*'[401] and 'the gift of interpretation', revealing a greater incorporation of Pauline glossolalia than in the *AF*.[402]

In a significant article in the first edition of *TBM*, Cashwell made several points about tongues speech, but did so from 1 Corinthians 12-14 rather than Acts. First, he distinguished between the glossolalia of SB and the gift of the Spirit, which he viewed as xenolalia.[403] Second, the gift was more than a heightened natural linguistic ability, but a supernatural gift that offers spiritual insight; it is the ability to really 'see' and 'understand'.[404] Third, the Pauline

---

[396] Worrell, 'Wonderful Times Coming', p. 4; cf. R.E. Massey, 'Pentecostal Convention In Fyzabad, India' *TBM* 3.56 (Feb 15, 1910), p. 4.

[397] Mok Lai Chi, 'Testimony of Mok Lai Chi', *TBM* 3.52 (Dec 15, 1909), p. 4.

[398] M.M. Pinson, V.W. Kennedy, and William Lyons, 'Meeting at Clinton, S.C.', *TBM* 2.39 (Jun 1, 1909), p. 2.

[399] 'Questions and Answers (*TBM*)', p. 2.

[400] E.A. Sexton called the Bible our 'guide book' when defending against fanaticism. E.A. Sexton, 'Pentecostal Light', *TBM* 1.1 (Oct 1, 1907), p. 3; cf. Cashwell, 'Editorials, The Word Fulfilled', p. 1.

[401] Emphasis added, indicating a Pauline rather than a Lucan phrase, 'The Supernatural', *TBM* 1.9 (Mar 1, 1908), p. 1.

[402] She quotes 1 Cor. 14.13 and writes, 'I prayed to God to give me the interpretation, and my prayer was answered ... I know what He is speaking about'. Mrs. Julia White, 'Atlanta, GA.' *TBM* 1.13 (May 1, 1908), p. 3.

[403] Cashwell, 'Speaking in Other Tongues', p. 2.

[404] Cashwell, 'Speaking in Other Tongues', p. 2.

restrictions apply. For the gift to be useful in the church it must be interpreted, otherwise it is no better than unknown Latin in the RCC. Outside the church the gift is a sign to the unbeliever.[405] Fourth, and significantly, Cashwell noted that Paul's views could inhibit and restrict Luke's views on glossolalia if not properly understood. He cautioned against too narrow a Pauline understanding: It was 'the cunningness of the Devil' to 'explain the 2, 10, and 19 chaps. of Acts by the 14 chap. of 1st Cor., and to keep the people in ignorance'.[406]

The articles and testimonies confirm the merging of a Pentecostal understanding of both Lucan and Pauline glossolalia. First, these pioneers understood the nuances between Paul's gift of tongues from Luke's ecstatic speech:

> failure to see the difference between the speaking in tongues as the Spirit gives utterance ... and the gift of tongues ... has perplexed many honest seekers after the truth. When no differences are made, Scripture seems to contradict Scripture, and there is no harmony; but when the distinction is made, all is clear and there is perfect harmony.[407]

Biblically, the actual operation of the gift of tongues necessitated the revival of another gift, the gift of interpretation. E.A. Sexton called this gift, 'one of the most important of all the gifts of the Spirit', not only because it was 'very solemn and impressive',[408] but because it allowed the meeting to comply with the Pauline restrictions in 1 Corinthians 14. People with this gift were sought out.[409]

---

[405] 'But the Holy Ghost moves upon many to speak for a sign to the unbeliever. Isaiah 28:11-13. 1st Cor. 14:21-22', Cashwell, 'Speaking in Other Tongues', p. 2.

[406] Cashwell, 'Speaking in Other Tongues', p. 2.

[407] R.E. McA., 'Difference Between Speaking in Tongues and the Gift of Tongues', *TBM* 4.88 (Jun 15, 1911), p. 4 (reprint from *TGR* 1 (May 1911), p. 4).

[408] E.A. Sexton, 'Editorials – Interpretation of Tongues', *TBM* 2.23 (Oct 1, 1908), p. 1. 'The first time, we do not always get the interpretation, but we lay a special stress on the necessity of praying for the interpretation and with wonderful results', Barratt, 'Pastor Barratt's Letter', *TBM* 1.16 (Jun 15, 1908), p. 4.

[409] 'We have an interpreter who interprets all that is spoken in tongues', 'Oklahoma City', *TBM* 1.27 (Dec 1, 1908), p. 2. 'Pray that God will give us an

Second, all believers could 'become messengers of supernatural speech';[410] therefore, Paul's gift of the Spirit allowed for a greater human role than Luke's ecstatic speech:

> speaking in tongues as the Spirit gives utterance is the direct operation of the Holy Ghost upon the vocal organs ... But the gift of tongues ... 'is entrusted to your wisdom,' and may be used at will, and must be governed according to first Corinthians 14th chapter.[411]

In other words, Lucan-like ecstatic speech 'does not need controlling' (and is uncontrollable), but with the Pauline-like gift of tongues, the speaker has the 'power to control the gift and avoid confusion in the assembly'.[412]

Third, because of this human component, greater order and evaluation of the spirit-inspired speech was required in the assembly. The Pauline restrictions were embraced to counter the devil's counterfeits[413] and oddities such as 'rebuking in tongues'[414] and personal prophecies.[415] 'The Holy Ghost never tells us to do

---

interpreter of what is said in tongues, in that we may step out on God's promises fully and wholly', Nolia Pennington, 'A Girl's Testimony And Call', *TBM* 1.20 (Sep 15, 1908), p. 3.

[410] V.P. Simmons, 'What is the Baptism of Fire?' *TBM* 3.55 (Feb 1, 1910), p. 4. There is 'a general gift of prophecy in the church, while some are very specially called of God to be prophets', Pastor Barratt, 'Prophecy', *TBM* 2.44 (Aug 15, 1909), p. 2.

[411] McA., 'Difference Between', p. 4. Being used 'at will' was a common early phrase though it probably meant at the Spirit's leading and not just anytime, cf. Mrs. Lorena Cotton, 'Letter From Sister Cotton', *TBM* 1.22 (Sep 15, 1908), p. 4; Mary Courtney, 'Portion of Letter to a Friend', *TBM* 3.50 (Nov 15, 1909), p. 4.

[412] McA., 'Difference Between', p. 4.

[413] 'We need to look out for the lying spirits. I refuse to accept messages that are given in tongues or any other way, if they are not in harmony with the Word of God. There are three spirits at work everywhere: the Holy Spirit and evil spirit and human spirit ... (we need to) weigh all messages and prophesying and everything by the Word', M.M. Pinson, 'Prove All Things', *TBM* 3.52 (Dec 15, 1909), p. 2; cf. Barratt, 'Pastor Barratt's Letter', p. 4.

[414] 'Rebuking in Tongues', *TBM* 3.56 (Feb 15, 1910), p. 2. This author contends a biblical precedent for rebuking from 2 Tim. 4.1-2, but notes that 'rebuking in tongues' as it is presently being practiced is not in the Bible. The author urges caution because 'we knew it was of the devil and the unsavoury fumes of the pit attended it'.

[415] If personal messages are given, 'there must be a response in the hearts of those who are Spirit filled, those were living holy lives ... I did not believe

anything contrary to the Word'.[416] The corporate guidelines of 1 Corinthians 14, were warmly embraced for the sake of order and biblical compliance.[417]

F. Eschatological Glossolalia

For the early Pentecostals, glossolalia was theologically related to eschatology. Tongues were linked so intrinsically with eschatology that Sexton wrote, 'our Pentecostal experience is enriched daily by the anticipation of His coming'.[418] A heightened eschatological urgency can be sensed in *TBM*.[419] For example, 'everything seems to be focusing to a climax of some undefined event. Ominous forebodings of the culmination of things seem to be felt by saint and sinner.'[420] Though there was no singular eschatological system, they believed that 'the Pentecostal baptism is, *somehow*, connected with the preparation for the appearing of the Lord'.[421] Biblical metaphors gave logic to their eschatological perspective; glossolalia connected with three in particular:

First, the latter rain was the primary metaphor. It explained glossolalia's sudden reappearance. The restoration of tongues

---

them unless they were confirmed by the word of God, and given by holy men filled with the Spirit. That is our conviction', '"Personal Messages: Their Dangers"', *TBM* 5.106 (Mar 15, 1912), p. 4.

[416] H.F. Roberts, 'Try The Spirits', *TBM* 2.31 (Feb 1, 1909), p. 4. Only one article tried to nuance Paul's admonition: 'the instructions given in 1 Cor. 14, only refer to times of teaching, not to altar services, or seasons of tarrying for the baptism of the Holy Ghost', Courtney, 'Portion of Letter to a Friend', p. 4.

[417] For example, see, V.P. Simmons, '"Hath Raised"', *TBM* 3.51 (Dec 1, 1909), p. 3.

[418] E.A. Sexton, 'Editorials, Hath Raised Us Up', *TBM* 1.9 (Mar 1, 1908), p. 1.

[419] Not that this was absent in *AF*, but eschatology was overshadowed by the experience of SB, glossolalia, and the revival itself. Note the urgency: 'since Pentecostal power to love has come into our hearts, the world is our parish, and God is hastily equipping and thrusting out people into all parts of the world. They are giving up all for Jesus', E.A. Sexton, 'Editorials, The Bridegroom's Messenger One Year Old Oct. 1', *TBM* 1.22 (Sep 15, 1908), p. 1.

[420] E.A. Sexton, 'Editorials, Wonders of the World', *TBM* 1.19 (Aug 1, 1908), p. 1.

[421] E.A. Sexton, 'And There Shall Be No More Curse', *TBM* 1.16 (Jun 15, 1908), p. 1 (emphasis added). McQueen notes that 'no single view (of eschatology) had become solidified by the end of 1920', McQueen, *Toward a Pentecostal Eschatology*, p. 77, cf. pp. 96-97.

equated with an equipping for a final world-wide, end-times revival; it was 'the key to the present revival'.[422] Xenolalia was initially thought to be God's equipping for these end times missionaries:

> if Jesus tarries until we have to learn all the languages of the world in colleges, He will not come soon ... The gift of languages of the world is of more importance today than ever before, for the efforts of education on this line have thus far proven a failure.[423]

Obedience to the Spirit's calling was critical because the Lord's return depended upon human effort.[424] Even though support for MT slowly diminished, a passion for a world-wide last day's mission remained.

Though there were other signs that would indicate the end,[425] glossolalia was like a trumpet blast preceding the Lord's return (1 Thess. 4.16-17).[426] Glossolalia was called the 'Bible trademark of heaven' that indicated that these were the last and 'perilous days'.[427] Even the rejection of glossolalia by some WH people[428] and others was seen as the hardening of hearts that would occur in the end times. Andrew H. Argue asked, 'are God's people going to fail to give the unbeliever this sign in these closing days?'[429] Biblically, the urgency was fuelled by passages like Mt. 24.14, and the latter rain

---

[422] 'The Value of Speaking in Tongues', p. 4.

[423] 'Colleges vs. Gifts of the Spirit', *TBM* 1.1 (Oct 1, 1907), p. 1.

[424] 'When the Gospel of the kingdom shall be preached as a witness to all nations then the end shall come. Let's be faithful to our trust', B.S. O'Neal, 'Atlanta, Sept. 26, 1907', *TBM* 1.1 (Oct 1, 1907), p. 3; cf. Britton, 'Letter from Bro. Britton', p. 2; G.B. Cashwell, 'Letter From G.B. Cashwell', *TBM* 2.33 (Mar 1, 1909), p. 2.

[425] Earthquakes, for example, are foretold in Mt. 24.7. This sign is amplified in 'Earthquakes in Divers Places', *TBM* 1.4 (Dec 15, 1907), p. 4. This short note reports recent earthquakes around the word and then quotes Mt. 24.7-8 as support for the Lord's soon return. Miracles and healings are another example, E.A. Sexton, 'Editorials, "O, Man"', *TBM* 1.18 (Jul 15, 1908), p. 1.

[426] Mrs. E.L. Murrah, 'My Testimony', *TBM* 1.5 (Jan 1, 1908), p. 3.

[427] R.B. Hayes, 'Perilous Times', *TBM* 1.6 (Jan 15, 1908), p. 1. Author noted these verses for support: Acts 2.17; Mk 16.17; and 2 Tim. 3.1.

[428] G.B. Cashwell, 'Editorials (1)', *TBM* 1.5 (Jan 1, 1908), p. 1.

[429] A.H. Argue, 'Is "Speaking with New Tongues" An Essential Sign?', *TBM* 11.205 (n.d., likely, July 1918), p. 2.

passages of Joel 2.28-31 and Acts 2:16-20.[430] Glossolalia and the frequent cry 'Jesus is coming', according to Sexton, were 'the first rays of light, (a) harbinger of the full blaze of a glorious day about to break on the slumbering church'.[431]

Second, that God preserved a remnant of tongues-speech is the another metaphor. It was often used to counter cessationism.[432] Interestingly, there is no indication that they saw a parallel between God preserving a remnant of Israel in the OT with a remnant of tongues-speech; instead, they turned to church history for support. Starting with the early church fathers like St. Chrysostom[433] and going throughout history to the present day, they found that 'instances like these are constantly coming to light'.[434] V.P. Simmons,[435] was a frequent contributor to this remnant metaphor. He wrote articles on the history of tongues that traced tongues speech through the centuries up to the present day revival;[436] articles on previously undiscovered pre-ASM occurrences of glossolalia;[437] and he believed that historians coloured their

---

[430] 'The Value of Speaking in Tongues', p. 4. Cf. Cashwell, 'Editorials, An Explanation', p. 1; Mrs. M.K. Norton, 'A Letter From Mrs. M.K. Norton', *TBM* 1.5 (Jan 1, 1908), p. 4.

[431] E.A. Sexton, 'Editorials, Jesus Is Coming', *TBM* 1.7 (Feb 1, 1908), p. 1. Cf. Sexton, 'Editorials, "O, Man"', p. 1

[432] Bertha B. Kahrs, 'The Nine Gifts', *TBM* 4.76 (Dec 15, 1910), p. 4.

[433] 'What An Ancient Writer Says On The Gift of Tongues', *TBM* 2.42 (Jul 1, 1909), p. 2.

[434] V.P. Simmons, 'Another Fact Concerning The Speaking in Tongues In A.D. 1844', *TBM* 3.65 (Jul 1, 1910), p. 1.

[435] Not much is known about him. One Mary B. Simmons of Frostproof, FL gave her testimony of SB in *AF*, perhaps this is his wife or daughter. Mary B. Simmons, 'Testimonies', *AF* 1.12 (Jan 1908), p. 4.

[436] V.P. Simmons, 'History of Tongues', *TBM* 1.3 (Dec 1, 1907), p. 2; 1.7 (Feb 1, 1908), p. 4; V.P. Simmons, 'History of Tongues – Additional Testimony', *TBM* 1.12 (Apr 15, 1908), p. 2. In addition to the tracts themselves, advertisements appear in *TBM* 1.8 (Feb 15, 1908), p. 2; 1.9 (Mar 1, 1908), p. 2; and 1.11 (April 1, 1908), p. 2.

[437] His first new discovery was of an occurrence in 1855 among the 'Gift Adventists' in Providence, RI, V.P. Simmons, 'By V.P. Simmons', *TBM* 2.34 (Mar 15, 1909), p. 2. In 1875, it continued among the 'Gift Adventists' more broadly, V.P. Simmons, 'Bro. V.P. Simmons of Frostproof, Florida', *TBM* 2.46 (Sep 15, 1909), p. 2. His final discovery was of an occurrence at a camp meeting in New England in 1844, eleven years earlier than the 'Gift Adventist' outpouring, Simmons, 'Speaking in Tongues In A.D. 1844', p. 1.

accounts to exclude glossolalia.[438]

Hattie Barth had a poignant perspective on the remnant metaphor. For her the remnant not only connected with the historical past, but also with the eschatological future: 'the ages overlap like links in a chain ... Pentecost itself really belongs to the next dispensation ... every sign is a foretaste of that coming age'.[439] To Barth, glossolalia was a glimpse of the unity that is in heaven contrasted with the divisions of Babel. She encouraged her readers to 'live in advance of our time'.[440] Both the restoration and remnant metaphors were embraced dialectically[441] and helped to explain glossolalia as an eschatological phenomenon.

Third, the bride of Christ was the last metaphor which connected glossolalia and eschatology: 'the Pentecostal baptism has come to prepare the saints for the gifts of the Spirit that the work may be done that Jesus said before his return'.[442] The title, *TBM*, reveals this strong eschatological connection.[443] Initially, tongues were an equipping of the bride:

> I saw that this outpouring of the Spirit was not only to restore to the church signs and wonders, but also to get ready the Bride for the return of the Bridegroom, and that as I was heir to all the promises (through Jesus) the 'Latter Rain' experience was for me.[444]

Simmons wrote that the reason for the ongoing gift of interpre-

---

[438] 'They evidently consider tongue talking a fanaticism, a weakness, to be kept out of sight; but in some way it will out [sic], and readers will know that their biographers and compilers are not impartial writers', V.P. Simmons, 'Historians Dodging Tongues', *TBM* 2.39 (Jun 1, 1909), p. 2; E.A. Sexton concurs, cf. Editor, 'Editorials, Early Methodism', *TBM* 3.70 (Sep 15, 1910), p. 1.

[439] Hattie M. Barth, 'The Things of the Kingdom', *TBM* 2.34 (Mar 15, 1909), p. 4. Cf. also, Alexander, *Pentecostal Healing*, pp. 91-93; McQueen, *Toward a Pentecostal Eschatology*, pp. 91-92.

[440] Barth, 'The Things of the Kingdom', p. 4.

[441] Sexton, 'Editorial, Some Interesting Facts about the Pentecostal Movement', *TBM* 4.79 (Feb 1, 1911), p. 1, for example, wrote about the worldwide impact of the latter rain and then traced the remnant of tongues speech throughout history in the same article.

[442] Unsigned article, *TBM* 1.1 (Oct 1, 1907), p. 1; cf. M.W. Moorhead, 'Brother Max Wood Moorhead's Letter', *TBM* 5.120 (Nov 1, 1912), p. 4.

[443] TBM's banner reads that 'while the bridegroom tarried, they all slumbered and slept. And at midnight there was a cry made: Behold, the Bridegroom cometh; go ye out to meet him (Mt. 25.5-6, KJV).'

[444] Eckman, 'Speaking in Tongues', p. 4.

tation was so 'that all nine of the spiritual gifts are continued' for preparing the Church 'for (its) translation'.[445] Later, tongues became a part of the premillennial eschatology that narrowed the bride of Christ from all believers to just the overcomers.[446] Tongues became a part of this remnant-bride worldview: 'this is the period for gathering a remnant 'out of every kindred, and tongue, and people, and nations ... for a witness unto (not conversion of) all nations (Matt. 24:14)'.[447]

G. The Nature of Glossolalia

In *TBM,* reflections on the nature of glossolalia were implicit and pragmatic.

1. The Heavenly Anthem

The testimonies about the HA in *TBM* resemble those in *AF.* First, the HA was God-inspired speech. Clyde Brawner said, 'the Holy Ghost fell on me and began to singing [sic] in other tongues'.[448] At times it was a gift of the Spirit for the congregation and had an interpretation,[449] at other times it was a sign of SB: 'those who get the baptism of the Spirit in my meeting speak and sing in other tongues as the Spirit gives utterance'.[450] Second, though generally spontaneous and new in nature, at times the melodies were from a familiar tune and could be either in English or a foreign tongue.[451] Third, the HA was awe inspiring. C.E. Kent wrote, 'when we speak or sing in heaven's own language, how the

---

[445] V.P. Simmons, 'Questions Concerning Tongues', *TBM* 1.14 (May 15, 1908), p. 2.

[446] McQueen believes that 'the role of the Holy Spirit was shifted from empowerment for mission to preparation of the bride of Christ' as a result of a tension between their Pentecostal experience and the developing eschatology, McQueen, *Toward a Pentecostal Eschatology,* p. 97; cf. p. 96.

[447] E.A. Sexton, 'The Prince of Peace', *TBM* 7.162 (Sep 15, 1914), p. 1.

[448] Clyde Brawner, 'Cocoanut Grove, Fla', *TBM* 1.1 (Oct 1, 1907), p. 2. Supporting the belief of divine origin are testimonies, such as, 'frequently six to ten people would be singing in the foreign tongues without discord', F.M. Britton, 'Pentecostal Work in Florida', *TBM* 1.1 (Oct 1, 1907), p. 4.

[449] 'Pentecost in Corinna, ME', *TBM* 1.9 (Mar 1, 1908), p. 1.

[450] M.M. Pinson, 'Birmingham Report', *TBM* 1.3 (Dec 1, 1907), p. 1; cf. John Goins, 'Pentecostal Work at Florence, Ala', *TBM* 1.2 (Nov 1, 1907), p. 2.

[451] Suzie A. Duncan, 'What The Movement Is', *TBM* 4.75 (Dec 1, 1910), p. 4.

beauties fade out of the old earth and its passing scenes'.[452] Finally, the direction of these inspired songs were generally vertical towards God, but occasionally horizontal as prophecy. Sometimes both vertical and horizontal in direction: 'a good many of the Chinese have also received their Pentecost, and are singing, praising and praying in new tongues ... Mr. Hamill sings most wonderfully, and Mr. Quick interprets for him'.[453]

2. Passive Speech and the Source of Glossolalia

Most noticeable regarding the nature of tongues in the Cashwell editions was the near uniformity of the testimonies that stated their experience of SB in a passive way. Instead of saying 'I spoke in tongues', as was common in *AF*, most testimonies were phrased like, 'he took my tongue and testified for Himself',[454] or 'spoke for Himself',[455] or 'spoke through me',[456] though some were poetically passive.[457] Even the phrase 'received the baptism' has a passivity about it.[458] With this view, the human vocal cords were a mere conduit for divine action and speech. Montgomery's testimony represents this concept:

> the brain seemed entirely passive, the words not coming from that source at all, but from an irresistible volume of power

---

[452] C.E. Kent, 'Letter From C.E. Kent', *TBM* 1.6 (Jan 15, 1908), p. 3.

[453] Landis, 'Pentecost in South China', p. 2.

[454] Mrs. J.B. Kilgore, 'Largo, Fla', *TBM* 1.7 (Feb 1, 1908), p. 3; cf. Molet Turner, 'Testimony', *TBM* 1.15 (Jun 1, 1908), p. 3; V.W. Kennedy, 'Saved, Sanctified, Baptized And Called to the Foreign Field', *TBM* 2.35 (Apr 1, 1909), p. 3; passim.

[455] Goins, 'Pentecostal Work at Florence, Ala', p. 2; E.B. LaBaw, 'Danville, Illinois', *TBM* 2.6 (Apr 15, 1909), p. 3; passim.

[456] H. Bush, 'Hermon, Cal', *TBM* 1.3 (Dec 1, 1907), p. 2; cf. L.S.P., 'The Gates of Answered Prayer', *TBM* 1.3 (Dec 1, 1907), p. 4; Mrs. L.F. Bott, 'Sister Poit's Testimony', *TBM* 1.4 (Dec 15, 1907), p. 3.

[457] 'He graciously answered and poured into my innermost being a glorious flood of living water which gushed up and overflowed in mighty hallelujahs and praises to God in the Spirit's own tongue', Mrs. W.F.E. Story, 'Orlando, FLA., March 27, 1908', *TBM* 1.12 (Apr 15, 1908), p. 3; cf. Murrah, 'Three Epochs', p. 3; R.B. Hayes, 'Anderson, S.C.', *TBM* 1.9 (Mar 1, 1908), p. 3.

[458] R.E., M.E., and John Paul Massey, 'American Mission, Fyzabad, U. P., India' *TBM* 3.54 (Jan 15, 1910), p. 4; E.C. Childer, 'Pierce, Florida', *TBM* 3.55 (Feb 1, 1910), p. 3; Herman E. Tower, 'Maryville, TN', *TBM* 3.59 (Apr 1, 1910), p. 3.

within, which seem to possess my whole being, spirit, soul and body ... that He was speaking 'heavenly mysteries' through me was most delightful.[459]

In time there was criticism for this overly passive voice in the publication:

> we have been criticized for the testimony so often heard in our assemblies: 'that the Spirit spoke for himself.' That it should be referred to as the individual speaking as the Spirit gives utterance ... No doubt mistakes have been made.[460]

Her defence was that the 'Spirit of God may so possess the human as to speak through him words of inspiration and power'.[461] Thereafter, the passive voice was less pronounced. The logic of divine origin for glossolalia was that 'language can emanate only from an intelligence, and since the language does not exist in the mind of persons thus speaking, it must come from a superior mind'.[462] As a conduit, it was important for an individual to yield full control. Because 'I was using my tongue constantly and my lips', the Holy Spirit said, 'that He could not use them, so long as I had them in my use or possession'.[463]

There was a more moderate position: human essence was present and cooperated with the divine Spirit. Some compared it to being drunk: 'I spoke in tongues for a long time, and I acted as one drunk on wine'.[464] Bartleman described it thusly, 'the "baptism with the Holy Ghost" sinks our minds into Christ ... (it) deals with the hitherto undefined realm of the religious self'.[465] But the issue

---

[459] Carrie Judd Montgomery, 'Mrs. Carrie Judd Montgomery', *TBM* 2.32 (Feb 15, 1909), p. 3. Cf. E.A. Sexton, '"Who Hath Believed Our Report?"', *TBM* 1.15 (Jun 15, 1908), p. 1.

[460] E.A. Sexton, 'Editorials, "As The Spirit Gave Them Utterance"', *TBM* 3.71 (Oct 1, 1910), p. 1.

[461] Sexton, 'Editorials, "As The Spirit Gave Them Utterance"', p. 1.

[462] W.H. Piper, 'The Sovereignty of God', *TBM* 2.46 (Sep 15, 1909), p. 4.

[463] Eli Gardner, 'God's Banner Over Them Was Love', *TBM* 2.40 (Jun 15, 1909), p. 4.

[464] Alfred Weigle, 'Pentecostal Testimony', *TBM* 3.50 (Nov 15, 1909), p. 3; cf. J.G. Rawlings, 'What God Can Do for a Drunkard', *TBM* 2.39 (Jun 1, 1909), p. 4; E.L. Slaybaugh, 'An Interesting Testimony And God's Call to Africa', *TBM* 3.58 (Mar 15, 1910), p. 3.

[465] F. Bartleman, 'Report of Camp Meeting, Alliance Ohio', *TBM* 1.18 (Jul 15, 1908), p. 2.

was not straightforward at all because humans could counterfeit the genuine.

Counterfeit tongues was readily acknowledged in *TBM*.[466] D.W. Griffin divided tongues into three categories: 'false tongues' which were demonically inspired; 'flesh tongues' which were in one's own strength and feelings like at Corinth; and finally, 'faith tongues' which were 'the direct gift of the Holy Spirit ... where your will is in line with the divine and where you have one motive or moving power – the glory of God'.[467] Simmons believed that speaking in genuine tongues helped discern demonic activity so that it could be cast out.[468] He mentions that Mk 16.17 is more than just a list of signs; tongues speech helps to 'cast out devils'.[469] This human side called for discernment on the part of believers, but also gave an explanation for any failings.[470] Because the source of glossolalia could be either divine, fleshly, or demonic, these early pioneers had to defend the nature of their glossolalia.

3. The Language(s) of Glossolalia

Because it was clear that not all tongues speech was xenolalia, a reasonable answer had to be given to the critics who said it, 'is contrary to reason and common sense, for the Holy Ghost to speak through us, and neither we, nor anyone else know what is being said'.[471] Occasionally, Evangelical commentators were quoted to give support and reason. For example, F. L. Godet noted it is 'a tongue which no man understands, so that what he says remains a mystery ... a sort of spiritual soliloqua'; P. Schaff noted that 'a new experience always expresses itself in appropriate language ... (it) broke through the confines of ordinary speech and burst out in ecstatic language of praise'.[472] H. Bushnell claimed not

---

[466] 'Counterfeits', *TBM* 1.18 (Jul 15, 1908), p. 1; B.S. O'Neal, 'A Sanctified Mind', *TBM* 2.29 (Jan 1, 1901), p. 4; V.P. Simmons, 'Casting Out Devils', *TBM* 3.57 (Mar 1, 1910), p. 2.

[467] D.W. Griffin, 'Tongues', *TBM* 4.79 (Feb 1, 1911), p. 4.

[468] Simmons, 'Casting Out Devils', p. 2.

[469] Simmons, 'Casting Out Devils', p. 2.

[470] 'Serious mistakes have been made by very precious Saints, as well as false teachers' but the root case is 'the want of perfect oneness among the brethren', E.A. Sexton, 'Editorials, Pentecost', *TBM* 2.38 (May 15, 1909), p. 1.

[471] Murrah, '"They Overcame By The Blood of the Lamb And The Word of Their Testimony"', *TBM* 1.19 (Aug 1, 1908), p. 2.

[472] '"Tongues"', p. 4.

to understand 'the great mystery of language' in tongues, but suggested that its unknown quality has 'greater dignity and propriety, for just the reason that they require another gift to make them intelligible' and that they are a 'symbol to the world of the possibility of a divine access to the soul'.[473] He reasoned that revelation needs not only God to speak but the hearer to have some response that others can see.

However, the more organic Pentecostal response was to respond that tongues were either xenolalia,[474] angelic, or heavenly speech,[475] or that it was like the Corinthian glossolalia and does not need to be a language at all:

> it is often asked what profit is there in 'speaking in tongues?' ... The Holy Spirit is in communication with the spirit of the believer. This is very edifying; it strengthens and enlarges his spirit, causing him to magnify God more and more. It results in giving him an inner and very intimate knowledge of his creator.[476]

III. The Church of God in Christ – *The Whole Truth*

A. History of the Revival

Charles H. Mason encountered the holiness doctrine from a northern missionary,[477] and together with his friend, C.P. Jones, 'cause (d) no small stir' with their dynamic holiness preaching.[478] Jones and Mason 'traveled and itinerated ... much more widely than most other African-Americans in the region'.[479] Soon they were 'expelled from the National Baptist Convention'[480] and formed the COGIC.[481] The COGIC was significant in that it 'was

---

[473] 'Dr. Bushnell On Supernatural Manifestations of the Spirit', *TBM* 3.53 (Jan 1, 1910), p. 4 (reprint from *TLR*).
[474] V.P. Simmons, 'The Exercise of Tongues', *TBM* 3.63 (Jun 1, 1910), p. 4; cf. Sexton, 'Editorials, "As The Spirit Gave Them Utterance"', p. 1.
[475] Simmons, 'The Exercise of Tongues', p. 4
[476] W.S. Lake, 'How I Received The Pentecostal Blessing', *TBM* 6.124 (Jan 1, 1913), p. 3.
[477] Stephens, *The Fire Spreads*, p. 77.
[478] Clemmons, 'Charles Harrison Mason', p. 866.
[479] Stephens, *The Fire Spreads*, p. 77.
[480] Alexander, *Pentecostal Healing*, p. 115.
[481] Synan, *The Holiness-Pentecostal Tradition*, p. 71.

the first southern holiness denomination to become legally chartered' and was also interracial.[482]

Soon, Mason was drawn[483] to the ASM revival and during the six weeks he was there[484] he was filled with the Spirit and developed a lifelong friendship with Seymour.[485] Meanwhile, Mason's church was already acquainted with Pentecostalism because of the ministry of Glen A. Cook, so it was fully behind Mason when he returned.[486] However, Jones 'did not want to add this new teaching to the church' and they debated for four months. Mason 'viewed the baptism in the Holy Spirit as a normative, empowering experience that came upon those who had previously been sanctified' including speaking in tongues as IE.[487] Their separation occurred in August 1907 with the denomination split roughly half between Mason and Jones.[488]

The new Pentecostal COGIC played an important role by ordaining whites as well as blacks. Between 1906 until 1914, 'scores of white ministers joined Mason's church'.[489] However, the south was becoming a more 'difficult place for African-Americans to live. Whites were increasingly moving to disenfranchise blacks in the region.'[490] In 1914, because of 'the difficult climate of southern racism, the white membership called for separation, which culminated in the Hot Springs organizational meeting of the Assemblies of God (AG)'.[491] There, Mason preached one of the

---

[482] Synan, *The Holiness-Pentecostal Tradition*, p. 71.

[483] He realized 'they did not have the power described in the New Testament, though they may see the sick healed, the dead raised, or even demons exorcised', Alexander, *Pentecostal Healing*, p. 116.

[484] Robeck, *Azusa Street*, p. 219.

[485] Robeck, *Azusa Street*, p. 39. Robeck reports that Seymour sought Mason's advice regarding his relationship to Clara Lum. Mason advised against such a relationship, 'in an era of Jim Crow', p. 310.

[486] Robeck, *Azusa Street*, p. 220; cf. Alexander, *Pentecostal Healing*, p. 116.

[487] Alexander notes that Jones 'was not convinced that tongues was the initial evidence', Alexander, *Pentecostal Healing*, p. 116; cf. Robeck, *Azusa Street*, p. 221.

[488] Robeck, *Azusa Street*, p. 221, cf. Clemmons, 'Charles Harrison Mason', p. 866.

[489] Synan, *The Holiness-Pentecostal Tradition*, p. 70.

[490] Robeck, *Azusa Street*, p. 219.

[491] Alexander, *Pentecostal Healing*, p. 117. There are four possible reasons: '1) cultural racism held by white Pentecostals; 2) racial segregation in the broader culture (e.g. Jim Crow laws); 3) theological differences over sanctification (COGIC held to a second-work position, while Bell and other AG founders

inaugural sermons[492] of the AG and 'maintained warm fellowship with the white Pentecostals' thereafter.[493]

COGIC continued to grow,[494] and 'at least 10 other church bodies owed their origins to Mason's church'.[495] Mason desired and prayed for 'above all things a religion like the one he heard about from the old slaves and seen demonstrated in their lives'.[496] Pentecostalism fit nicely, both 'preserving the "spiritual essence" and the "prayer tradition" of black religious experience'.[497] It is said that Seymour and Mason began 'one of the most powerful expressions of Black religion in the world'.[498] Because of his long life, 'Mason stamped his personality on his church far more emphatically than any other holiness leader'.[499]

B. Confirmation of Normative Pentecostalism

Though it would be unwise to extrapolate too much from a single issue, three elements of normative Pentecostalism are clear in the singular extant edition of *TWT*.

First, SB with evidentiary tongues was in harmony with early Pentecostalism. Included in *TWT's* statement of faith is Mk 16.17, 'they shall speak with new tongues'. Young reported that 'many are getting saved, sanctified and baptized with the Holy Ghost and fire, with Bible evidence of speaking in tongues' in the north.[500] One article focused on SB and affirmed the separation of sanctification from SB as two events and the evidentiary nature of

---

held to a finished-work position); 4) ecclesiological differences (COGIC had an episcopal system with bishops, and the AG held strong Congregationalist commitments', William J. Molenaar, 'Christian Unity: A Founding Principle of the Assemblies of God', *Heritage* 34 (2014), pp. 57-65 (61).

[492] Robeck, Azusa Street, p. 39; cf. Synan, *The Holiness-Pentecostal Tradition*, p. 172.

[493] Clemmons, 'Charles Harrison Mason', p. 866.

[494] Clemmons reports 5,500 congregations with 482,000 adherents in 1961, Clemmons, 'Charles Harrison Mason', p. 867.

[495] Clemmons, 'Charles Harrison Mason', p. 867.

[496] Clemmons, 'Charles Harrison Mason', p. 865.

[497] Clemmons, 'Charles Harrison Mason', p. 866.

[498] Clemmons, 'Charles Harrison Mason', p. 867.

[499] Synan, *The Holiness-Pentecostal Tradition*, p. 71. 'Mason served as Bishop of the church from its organization in 1896 until his death in 1961', Alexander, *Pentecostal Healing*, p. 114.

[500] D.J. Young, *TWT* 4.4 (Oct 1911), p. 4.

tongues:⁵⁰¹

> every place we read where the spirit came upon the people or the person it was a similar experience, and I am so glod [sic] to know that when we believe on him like they believed and surrender to him like they did and tarry for the power, it will come on us just like it came on them … Jesus said these signs shall follow the believers … they shall speak with new tongues.⁵⁰²

The above quote also reveals they desired to have the same experience as the biblical Pentecost.

Second, singing a new song by the Holy Spirit played a large role in Mason's ministry during their Annual Convocation. Spirit-song occurred eight days of the convention.⁵⁰³ Sadly, the writing was ambiguous, and glossolalia was not specifically stated; additionally, often a translation was given in English. In one case, it was sung to a familiar tune, 'Glory to God'.⁵⁰⁴ Also, 'we were taught to sing in the Spirit on this beautiful Sabbath morning' could imply a human source for the Spirit-song. ⁵⁰⁵ Mason's testimony of glossolalic singing in the *AF* was unambiguous.⁵⁰⁶

Third, there was a testimony of a child giving direction for the service via glossolalia: 'the Spirit in an unknown tongue spoke through little sister Velda Young, on the first night, and ask everyone to keep hands off, and let the Lord work in the meeting, and

---

⁵⁰¹ 'The Spirit of God Upon Us', *TWT* 4.4 (Oct 1911), p. 4. They were sanctified when Jesus breathed on them, Jn 20.22, 23, and then it states, 'he tells them ye shall receive power after the Holy Spirit come upon you. And so they did tarry in Jerusalem'. There are two additional didactic articles: 1) the editor, Justus Bowe, provides an untitled article that affirms the reality of hell, *TWT* 4.4 (Oct 1911), p. 2. 2) An unsigned and untitled teaching that encourages people to have a 'true heart' towards God by turning from deceitfulness, p. 2.

⁵⁰² 'The Spirit of God Upon Us', p. 4.

⁵⁰³ It is listed on days, 4, 7, 11, 13, 15, 18, 19, and 27, 'Report of the Annual Convocation', *TWT* 4.4 (Oct 1911), pp. 1, 3.

⁵⁰⁴ 'Report of the Annual Convocation', p. 1.

⁵⁰⁵ 'Report of the Annual Convocation', p. 1. '"Glory to God" was sung in the spirit by our pastor today. The Lord had sent him to us, and *as the Spirit sang out* in him the new song of praise *today the Lord gave us such a wonderful instruction* through Elder C.H. Mason', is another example of unclear scripting (emphasis added).

⁵⁰⁶ 'I surrendered perfectly to Him and consented to Him. Then I began singing a song in unknown tongues, and it was the sweetest thing to have Him sing that song through me', Mason, 'TN Evangelist Witnesses', p. 7.

great would it be [sic]'.[507] The leaders followed this prophetic word and reported, 'so we did and so was the work greater than we've known for the short time of five days'.[508]

IV. Church of God (Cleveland, TN) – *The Church of God Evangel*

A. History of the Revival

The Church of God (CG) traces its history back earlier than the ASM revival. Their story 'begins in the mountains of southern Appalachia in 1886 with a small group of Baptist reformers who adopted a restorationist view of the church'.[509] Richard G. Spurling, Jr., established the Christian Union (CU) with the guiding principle that the church was visible and corporate.[510] Of the four churches that formed and loosely fellowshipped with the CU, only one survived beyond the first ten years.[511]

In 1895 a WH revival broke out in Camp Creek, NC,[512] and the effects of 'the Spirit (were) similar to those recorded in the book of Acts'[513] including tongues.[514] This revival energized Spurling's followers. In 1899, evangelists from Irwin's Fire Baptized Holiness Association (FBHA) would 'set ablaze this revival and bring it to

---

[507] 'Report of the Children's Meeting', *TWT* 4.4 (Oct 1911), p. 4.

[508] 'Report of the Children's Meeting', p. 4.

[509] Wade H. Phillips, *Quest to Restore God's House: A Theological History of the Church of God (Cleveland, TN), Volume I 1886-1923* (Cleveland, TN: CPT Press, 2014), p. xvi. This work is ground-breaking in that it varies from the denomination's accepted history (e.g. Conn, *Like a Mighty Army*) and that it so quickly was accepted as a scholarly correction to the historical record.

[510] See Phillips, *Quest*, pp. 97-98 for the 'core principles' of the CU.

[511] Phillips, *Quest*, p. 85, cf. pp. 74-91.

[512] It was located in the Shearer Schoolhouse in Cherokee County, Synan, *The Holiness-Pentecostal Tradition*, p. 72.

[513] Phillips, *Quest*, p. 107. This revival was not the direct result of the CU but 'the groundwork (was) laid by Spurling and his followers', p. 108. Contrary to Conn, who recorded that 'the two groups became one', Conn, *Like a Mighty Army*, p. 20, cf. pp. 13-20.

[514] Phillips writes that '"Speaking in tongues" was not at first recognized as a significant and distinct manifestation … (though) eyewitnesses later recalled occurrences of tongues speech in their meetings', Phillips, *Quest*, p. 107, cf. Conn, *Like a Mighty Army*, p. 24, cf. pp. 22-24. There were testimonies of glossolalia 'sometime between 1885 and 1886' in the CU, p. 107, n. 4.

fever pitch'.⁵¹⁵ Wade Philips argues that glossolalia was a part of Irwin's theology by April 1899⁵¹⁶ and that the FBHA is the real beginning of American Pentecostalism.⁵¹⁷ On May 15th, 1902 the group was renamed the Holiness Church at Camp Creek (HCCC)⁵¹⁸ and on June 13, 1903, they added their most significant member, Ambrose J. Tomlinson.⁵¹⁹

---

⁵¹⁵ Phillips, *Quest*, p. 119, cf. pp. 119-72. Phillips notes that the peak of the FBHA coincided, timing-wise, with its introduction at Camp Creek, p. 153.

⁵¹⁶ Phillips notes two significant theological points: 1) 'Irwin had distinguished as early as April 1899 the manifestation of "tongues of fire" on the day of Pentecost in Acts 2.3 from the manifestation of the various dialects in verse four', Phillips, *Quest*, p. 138. 2) 'Irwin's reference to "ecstatic speech" as a result of the baptism of *lyddite* predates by eight months Charles Fox Parham's introduction of SB with its connection to speaking in tongues at Topeka, Kansas in January 1901', p. 136.

⁵¹⁷ 'Further research and reflection in the recent years on the historical and theological evidence has led us to conclude that the beginning of the Pentecostal movement should indeed be located in the fire-baptized holiness movement, particularly in the light of what was proclaimed and experienced in 1899-1900 with the proliferation of *glossolalia* and other spiritual gifts', Phillips, *Quest*, p. 139. His arguments are: 1) the FBHA 'movement simply metamorphosed into a new form under a new name – the Pentecostal movement', p. 125; 2) both sought spiritual power to advance the gospel, p. 127; 3) 'Parham himself was introduced not only to a post-sanctification "third work blessing" but also to glossolalia in fire-baptized meetings', p. 136, cf. p. 143; 4) and theologically, 'the developing theology of tongues speech in the Pentecostal movement (Parham's and Seymour's) ... began to sound remarkably similar to what Irwin taught in 1889–1900', p. 138. Counter arguments are: 1) Only following Azusa were tongues 'both anticipated and consciously understood to be the initial and conclusive evidence of Spirit-baptism', pp. 141-42. Conn wrote, 'what had happened the simple, rustic Christians could not then understand ... how long it was before the realization of what happened to the group is not certain, but it could not have been long', Conn, *Like a Mighty Army*, p. 24. 2) Goff notes that though Parham was influenced by FBHA, Parham 'dismissed it as 'mere "chatter", "jabber", and "babble", for he claimed the ability to distinguish between known languages and mere "gibberish"', Phillips, *Quest*, p. 137; 3) The wave of revival clearly flowed from Azusa Street and not from Camp Creek. For example, in 1908 A.J. Tomlinson invited G.B. Cashwell for 'more knowledge on the subject as well as the experience itself', Conn, *Like a Mighty Army*, p. 84. Synan does call the Camp Creek revival 'the greatest instance of speaking with other tongues before 1906', Synan, *The Holiness-Pentecostal Tradition*, p. 111.

⁵¹⁸ Phillips, *Quest*, p. 168, cf. pp. 167-72.

⁵¹⁹ Phillips, *Quest*, p. 210; cf. pp. 173-223; Conn, *Like a Mighty Army*, pp. 44-50, Harold D. Hunter, 'Ambrose Jessup Tomlinson', in Stanley Burgess (ed.), *NIDPCM* (Grand Rapids, MI: Zondervan, rev. and expanded edn, 2002), pp. 1143-45; Alexander, *Pentecostal Healing*, p. 96. Synan calls Tomlinson 'a mystical Quaker from Indiana. A restless wanderer', Synan, *The Holiness-Pentecostal Tradition*, p. 74.

Originally from Westfield, IN, Tomlinson found his way to Culberson, NC, doing colportage work.[520] In his formative years he was influenced by many people[521] and everyone quickly recognized his leadership skills.[522] Soon after joining the HCCC, Tomlinson was elected its pastor.[523] The HCCC slowly grew in adherents, in the number of churches, and thanks to the FBHA, in its theological vocabulary.[524] Tomlinson's leadership grew as well: 'by 1904 Tomlinson was pastor of three out of four affiliated congregations and edited … a periodical titled *The Way*'.[525]

In 1906 a 'General Assembly'[526] was so popular that it became an annual event.[527] The HCCC 'did not claim to be a part of the Pentecostal movement before 1906'[528] even though its 'Pentecostal doctrine continued to grow with the emphasis … on spiritual gifts,

---

[520] Tomlinson sold for both the American Bible Society and the American Tract Society, Hunter, 'Ambrose Jessup Tomlinson,' p. 1143; cf. Phillips, *Quest*, p. 173.

[521] Phillips spells out a significant Quaker influence, Phillips, *Quest*, pp. 175-79. Frank W. Stanford's ministry at Shiloh in Durham, ME was a major influence as well, with Tomlinson even being re-baptized and joining his movement, pp. 194-201; cf. Hunter, 'Ambrose Jessup Tomlinson', p. 1144; Synan, *The Holiness-Pentecostal Tradition*, p. 75. Stephens believes that it was 'Cashwell's paper and his ceaseless evangelism (that) helped guide the Church of God (Cleveland) … into the pentecostal fold', Stephens, *The Fire Spreads*, p. 203; cf. Phillips, *Quest*, p. 234. Noticeably missing from Phillips' list is Montgomery's influence on divine healing, Hunter, 'Ambrose Jessup Tomlinson,' p. 1143.

[522] For example, he was not content to peddle Bibles and tracts, during this time he also organized an orphanage and published *Samson's Foxes*, a paper that 'featured articles and news from the WH movement and the healing movement and appeals to assist the needy', Hunter, 'Ambrose Jessup Tomlinson,' pp. 1143-44; cf. Phillips, *Quest*, pp. 185-92.

[523] Phillips, *Quest*, pp. 205, 217; cf. Conn, *Like a Mighty Army*, pp. 44, 52.

[524] Phillips, *Quest*, pp. 119-67. Conn notes that these 'twenty years had inserted into the modern Christian vocabulary terms like "Pentecostal," "unknown tongues," and "divine perfection," and "sanctification," whose meanings had been lost in a maze of theological garble', Conn, *Like a Mighty Army*, p. 55.

[525] By 1904 there were four congregations in three states and three mission stations, Phillips, *Quest*, p. 217. Hunter, 'Ambrose Jessup Tomlinson,' p. 1144.

[526] Phillips, *Quest*, pp. 218, 223-26; cf. Conn, *Like a Mighty Army*, pp. 61-62; cf. Alexander, *Pentecostal Healing*, pp. 96-97.

[527] Conn, *Like a Mighty Army*, pp. 61, 62.

[528] It was not 'until after the dispute over speaking in tongues in 1909-1910 … that the Church of God clearly identified itself with the Pentecostal movement', Phillips, *Quest*, p. 233. This dispute was also over Tomlinson's autocratic style of leadership, pp. 233, 238-44.

divine healing, and the baptism of the Holy Ghost'.[529] In 1907 the HCCC was renamed the Church of God.[530] In 1908 Tomlinson sought out Cashwell and invited him to preach at a nearby church during the CG General Assembly. There Tomlinson was filled with the Spirit with the evidence of glossolalia on January 10, 1908.[531] After 'he received his baptism, all the Church of God ministers were then Holy Ghost baptized men, for all the others had received the experience – some as much as twelve years earlier'.[532] The CG continued to grow these early years through hard work, sacrifice,[533] and revival:[534]

> there were remarkable spiritual manifestations. Many afflicted persons were healed ... frequent messages were given in tongues and interpreted ... this speaking forth in ecstasy was by no means unusual but was rather the expected nature of the services.[535]

Today, the CG has grown to become one 'of the oldest and largest pentecostal bodies'.[536]

B. As 'The Spirit Gives Utterance'

Like other Pentecostal periodicals of the time, the *COGE* held firmly to evidentiary glossolalia, although the preferred terminology was the phrase to speak 'as the Spirit gives utterance'.[537] This

---

[529] Conn, *Like a Mighty Army*, p. 75.

[530] Conn, *Like a Mighty Army*, p. 74.

[531] Phillips, *Quest*, pp. 235-36; cf. Synan, *The Holiness-Pentecostal Tradition*, pp. 123, 124.

[532] Conn, *Like a Mighty Army*, p. 85. Robeck states that 'by 1908 ... several Wesleyan-holiness denominations embraced the message of the Azusa Street Mission and its revival', listing CG among these denominations, Robeck, *Azusa Street*, p. 10, cf. p. 219.

[533] For example, R.M. Evans, 'sold his home in Durant ... and his few cows, hogs, and chickens. With the money from these, he bought a wagon and team of mules ... (and) drove (them) more than three hundred miles to Miami ... where he ... sold the mules' and thus provided his passage to the Bahamas to evangelize, Conn, *Like a Mighty Army*, p. 112.

[534] Conn, *Like a Mighty Army*, pp. 85-154, cf. C.W. Conn, 'Church of God (Cleveland, TN)', in Stanley Burgess (ed.), *NIDPCM* (Grand Rapids, MI: Zondervan, rev. and expanded edn, 2002), pp. 530-34 (531).

[535] Conn, *Like a Mighty Army*, pp. 136, 137.

[536] Conn, 'Church of God (Cleveland, TN)', *NIDPCM*, p. 530.

[537] W.F. Bryant, 'A Pentecostal Funeral', *COGE* 1.1 (Mar 1, 1910), p. 8. Other phrases to identify the evidentiary nature are: the 'Bible evidence' and simply

phrase distinguished evidentiary tongues from the gift of tongues.[538] Tongues as an evidence of SB was clearly defended and explained in the pages of the *COGE*.

Theological reflection about IE and glossolalia was largely limited to what the Bible stated. Tomlinson wrote that it was important 'to have an experience that will measure up to the word of God'.[539] Evidential tongues were 'plain' to all who read the Bible with an 'unprejudiced mind' because it was a clear 'Bible doctrine'.[540] A.E. Street set out to prove from Scripture that one could be filled with the Spirit without speaking in tongues, but discovered that 'the Bible is too plain'.[541] Tomlinson went so far as to write that in 'the sacred book of books … it is as much of a command to receive the Holy Ghost and talk in other tongues as it is to be baptized with water or take the bread and wine to commemorate the Lord's death till he comes again'.[542] The earnest desire was to relive Pentecost: 'it was almost like Pentecost repeated, with over one hundred exercised by the power of the Spirit, at one time … talking in tongues, praising God, shouting, preaching, praying exhorting, and glorifying God'.[543] It was important that SB be immediately verifiable to the entire group as in T.S. Payne's report: 'one lady received the Holy Ghost for *we heard her* speak in tongues

---

'the evidence', cf. Edith Brawner, 'Maitland, Fla (1)', *COGE* 1.5 (May 15, 1910), p. 7; 'The Church of God', *COGE* 1.12 (Aug 15, 1910), p. 3.

[538] 'The first thing Mr. Wheatlake does is to confuse the speaking in tongues as the Spirit gives utterance with the "gift of tongues"', A.J. Tomlinson, 'Beautiful Light of Pentecost', *COGE* 8.18 (May 12, 1917), p. 1.

[539] A.J. Tomlinson, 'What is the Evidence of the Baptism with the Holy Ghost?', *COGE* 1.19 (Dec 1, 1910), p. 1.

[540] A.J. Tomlinson, 'Speaking in Tongues', *COGE* 5.51 (Dec 26, 1914), p. 1. One could say that at times the noun 'Bible' was used as an adjective to signify divine authority, for example, 'we know the baptism of the Holy Ghost and tongues as the evidence is a Bible doctrine', A.J. Tomlinson, 'More About The Church', *COGE* 1.9 (Jul 1, 1910), p. 1.

[541] A.E. Street, 'What is Pentecost', *COGE* 5.30 (Jul 25, 1914), p. 6.

[542] A.J. Tomlinson, 'We Would Not Know', *COGE* 6.15 (Apr 10, 1915), p. 1.

[543] 'Camp meetings at Cleveland', *COGE* 1.16 (Oct 15, 1910), p. 4; cf. A.J. Tomlinson, 'Pentecostal Shower', *COGE* 1.2 (Mar 15, 1910), p. 1; A.J. Tomlinson, 'Pentecostal Experience Accompanied with Tongues', *COGE* 1.4 (Apr 15, 1910), p. 1; Henry Watts, 'Vance, Ala.', *COGE* 6.16 (Apr 17, 1915), p. 2; J. Wilson Bell, 'Kingston, Jamaica, B.W.I.', *COGE* 8.35 (Sep 8, 1917), p. 4.

and magnify God'.[544] S.J. Heath explained that 'to be a witness one must speak, write or give a sign. The Holy Ghost never comes into a person without speaking in an unknown tongue.'[545]

Exegetically, evidential glossolalia was rooted in the traditional Pentecostal reading of the book of Acts.[546] In addition to Acts and Mk 16.17, it was believed that Jesus taught evidential tongues in Jn 15.26, 16.13, giving the *COGE* the strongest Johannine footing of all the early Pentecostal periodicals.[547] People often based their testimony on Jesus' teaching that the Holy Spirit would 'speak for himself'.[548] Mrs. E.L. Hammond even stated that Jesus was a glossolalic: 'I was running the references and found where Christ spoke in other tongues'.[549] Tomlinson explained that 'the Holy Ghost is a person that can talk ... (Jesus said) the Holy Ghost would "testify" when He came'.[550]

Explicit doctrinal statements were rare in the *COGE*, and when they were made, were straightforward and without nuance.[551] One such statement read that the CG 'stands for the whole Bible rightly

---

[544] T.S. Payne, 'Evangelistic', *COGE* 5.7 (Feb 14, 1914), p. 8 (emphasis added). Cf. C.F. Bright, 'Valdesta, Ga.', *COGE* 5.32 (Aug 8, 1914), p. 6; Jennie Lacy, 'Shady Grove, Miss.', *COGE* 6.36 (Sep 4, 1915), p. 4.

[545] S.J. Heath, 'Shall We Recognize the Holy Ghost?', *COGE* 10.24 (Jun 14, 1919), p. 4.

[546] Tomlinson, 'What is the Evidence of the Baptism with the Holy Ghost?', p. 1; W.G. Anderson, 'Thoughts On The Church', *COGE* 5.13 (Mar 28, 1914), p. 5; A.J. Tomlinson, 'All Will Speak In Tongues', *COGE* 7.5 (Jan 29, 1916), p. 1; F.J. Lee, '"Is The Present Tongues Movement of God?"', *COGE* 7.9 (Feb 26, 1916), p. 1; A.J. Tomlinson, 'The Holy Ghost And Tongues', *COGE* 9.14 (Apr 6, 1918), pp. 1, 2.

[547] R.M. Evans, 'Missionary', *COGE* 1.1 (Mar 1, 1910), p. 7; Tomlinson, 'What is the Evidence of the Baptism with the Holy Ghost?', p. 1; A.J. Tomlinson, 'Receive the Holy Ghost', *COGE* 6.9 (Feb 27, 1915), p. 1; A.J. Tomlinson, 'Receive the Holy Ghost', *COGE* 6.16 (Apr 17, 1915), p. 1; Tomlinson, 'All Will Speak In Tongues', p. 1; Lee, '"Is The Present Tongues Movement of God?"', p. 1.

[548] E.g. Joe Bowker, 'Charlotte, Tenn.', *COGE* 6.52 (Dec 25, 1915), p. 3.

[549] Mrs. E.L. Hammond, 'Oakland, Fla.', *COGE* 6.3 (Jan 16, 1915), p. 2.

[550] Tomlinson, 'Speaking in Tongues', p. 1; cf. A.J. Tomlinson, 'The Holy Ghost', *COGE* 6.21 (May 22, 1915), p. 1.

[551] There is only one explicit doctrinal statement in the *COGE*: 'The Church of God', *COGE* 1.12 (Aug 15, 1910), p. 3. Phillips notes that this 'teaching' was written by a 'Committee composed of Tomlinson, Spurling, Lemons, and McClain', Phillips, *Quest*, p. 369, n. 203. Because of the infrequency of such statements, ministers were encouraged to 'preserve this copy of the Evangel for future references'.

divided', followed by twenty-five doctrines in a single sentence with Scripture references.⁵⁵² Those relevant to glossolalia stated:

> the baptism with the Holy Ghost subsequent to cleansing: The enduement of power for service: Matt. 3:11, Luke 24:49-53, Acts 1:4-8 ... the speaking in tongues as the evidence of the baptism with the Holy Ghost: John 15:26, Acts 2:4, Acts 10:44-46, Acts 19:1-7 ... the full restoration of the gifts to the church: 1 Cor. 12:1-7-10-28-31 [sic], 1 Cor. 14:1 ... signs following believers: Mark 16:17-20, Rom. 15:18-19, Heb. 2:4.⁵⁵³

Glossolalia evidenced only the initial infilling. It was 'not intended to mean a permanent or continuous evidence ... but only to establish the fact that the Spirit has come in at the time He comes in'.⁵⁵⁴ It was 'the one and only decisive evidence',⁵⁵⁵ the singular sign: 'we are not afraid to declare in the face of every foe that all will speak in tongues when they are baptized with the Holy Ghost and fire'.⁵⁵⁶ The sign was verification of God's equipping power. 'And what better method could He adopt' wrote Tomlinson, 'that we may know when the work is finished?'⁵⁵⁷

The evidential nature of SB was often challenged by critics.⁵⁵⁸ Occasionally, Tomlinson advocated separation from those who

---

⁵⁵² 'The Church of God', p. 3.

⁵⁵³ 'The Church of God', p. 3. An earlier doctrinal statement contains 18 points. Spirit Baptism is defined as the 'full restoration of the gifts ... an experience for people today, the same as for the Apostles (Luke 24:49; Matthew 28:19, 20; Acts 2:39)', Phillips, *Quest*, p. 367.

⁵⁵⁴ Tomlinson, 'What is the Evidence of the Baptism with the Holy Ghost?', p. 1.

⁵⁵⁵ Lee, '"Is The Present Tongues Movement of God?"', p. 1.

⁵⁵⁶ Tomlinson, 'All Will Speak in Tongues', p. 1; cf. Street, 'What is Pentecost', p. 6.

⁵⁵⁷ Tomlinson, 'What is the Evidence of the Baptism with the Holy Ghost?', p. 1.

⁵⁵⁸ 'Quite a number of Pentecostal papers come to my office, but it has been a long time since I saw an article ... that taught clearly that all will speak in tongues when they are baptized with the Holy Ghost ... People are flooding me lately with letters in teachings against the tongues as evidence of the baptism ... We mean to sound the message of the "tongues" unto all the ends of the earth. All will speak in other tongues when they are baptized with the Holy Ghost', A.J. Tomlinson, 'The Experience Is Real', *COGE* 7.8 (Feb 19, 1916), p. 1.

denied glossolalia.[559] He warned his pastors not to let just anyone preach as there are deceivers who 'teach a good deal of the doctrine, but say that the speaking with other tongues is not necessarily the evidence of the baptism with the Holy Ghost, and that not all will speak with tongues who received the baptism'.[560] There was a fear that if tongues were not ongoing, the CG would decline or fragment:

> while our experiences are still fresh and sweet, they may not continue so if we should fail to emphasize the tongues ... if the Spirit does not manifest Himself occasionally by using your tongue as He did when He first came in, how do you know that He still remains?'[561]

The strong defence of glossolalia and the fear of losing it were connected to a deep reverence and belief that tongues were the voice of the Holy Spirit. For example,

> some teachers say: 'just claim the Holy Ghost and you will have Him' ... It is a shame to teach honest souls that the Holy Ghost is of such little consequence that they will not know when He comes ... when He comes into our being we are very conscious of the fact; others will know it too, as they hear Him make the utterance in other tongues.[562]

C. Responses to the Critics

In addition to evidential tongues, other aspects of the theology of glossolalia in the *COGE* were polished and clarified in response to her critics. For example, the charge of cessationism was countered by: 1) noting occurrences within church history,[563] 2) appealing to

---

[559] A.J. Tomlinson, 'Mysterious Fellowship', *COGE* 10.40 (Oct 4, 1919), p. 1.

[560] A.J. Tomlinson, 'Warning And Advice', *COGE* 1.12 (Aug 15, 1910), p. 1; cf. A.S. Worrell, 'The Crisis Now On', *COGE* 1.16 (Oct 15, 1910), p. 5; A.J. Tomlinson 'Loyalty To Christ', *COGE* 7.18 (Apr 29, 1916), p. 1.

[561] A.J. Tomlinson, 'Emphasize the Tongues', *COGE* 9.7 (Feb 17, 1918), p. 1.

[562] Andrew McFail, 'Big Clifty, Ky.', *COGE* 8.37 (Sep 22, 1917), p. 3; cf. A.J. Tomlinson, 'Strange Ideas and Doctrines', *COGE* 7.26 (Jun 24, 1916), p. 1.

[563] A.J. Tomlinson, 'The Opposition Weakening', *COGE* 8.9 (Mar 3, 1917), p. 1.

the latter rain hermeneutic,⁵⁶⁴ and 3) with the belief that there is an all or nothing aspect to spiritual manifestations:

> if we accept part of the Bible and the manifestations of the Spirit part of the way why not take all ... isn't there sufficient proof that the apostles and early church spoke in tongues? Is there one particle of evidence that the speaking has been done away?⁵⁶⁵

In response to the criticism that speech had to be intelligible to edify, Tomlinson noted that tongues 'does not always require intelligent teaching or expression'.⁵⁶⁶ He further argued that there would be no need for a gift of interpretation if the audience knew what was said. He believed that 'when one speaks to himself in an unknown tongue, although he may not understand the words spoken, he is edified'.⁵⁶⁷

Some critics used Paul's 'do all speak in tongues?'⁵⁶⁸ to mean that not everyone will do so. In keeping with the established Pentecostal distinction between glossolalia as a sign and as a gift, Tomlinson's reply was:

> we do not claim that *the gift of tongues* is evidence of the baptism of the Holy Ghost ... (rather, it is) tongues *as the Spirit gave utterance* as the evidence of the baptism of the Holy Ghost and no one ever received this blessed baptism without the tongues.⁵⁶⁹

The charge that tongues were 'of the devil' caused Lee to acknowledge and address counterfeit tongues.⁵⁷⁰ Counterfeit tongues were seen in the context of a spiritual battle and were often countered by prayer and confrontation: 'during this meeting

---

⁵⁶⁴ Lee, '"Is The Present Tongues Movement of God?"', p. 1.
⁵⁶⁵ Sam C. Perry, 'Why Reject Speaking in Tongues', *COGE* 8.39 (Oct 6, 1917), p. 3.
⁵⁶⁶ A.J. Tomlinson, 'Edification And Comfort', *COGE* 8.20 (May 26, 1917), p. 1.
⁵⁶⁷ A.J. Tomlinson, 'The Gift of Tongues', *COGE* 8.24 (Jun 23, 1917), p. 1.
⁵⁶⁸ 1 Corinthians 12.30.
⁵⁶⁹ A.J. Tomlinson, 'Confidence Unshaken', *COGE* 8.21 (Jun 2, 1917), p. 1 (emphasis added). Cf. Sam C. Perry, 'What is the Use of Speaking in Tongues #2?', *COGE* 9.16 (Apr 20, 1918), p. 3.
⁵⁷⁰ Lee, '"Is The Present Tongues Movement of God?"', p. 1.

the devil came up as an Angel of light speaking in tongues and claiming the gifts but the Lord gave the victory over the power of the devil'.[571] Tomlinson theorized that Satan and manipulative individuals could speak with tongues.[572] R.M. Evans pointed out that to focus on counterfeits weakens the 'confidence in *the sign* of the incoming and abiding Comforter'.[573] Readers were encouraged to know the genuine which was identifiable by the fruit of the Spirit: 'if the fruits of Spirit … (are) the experience of the one that talks in tongues, who could say that he was actuated by the Devil in talking in tongues?'[574] However, it was contended that to understand glossolalia, one had to experience it: 'only those who have talked in other tongues … know anything about it'.[575] There was a 'deep dwelling place' of spiritual knowledge that 'none should try to claim … without the Holy Ghost', wrote Tomlinson.[576]

D. Signs and Wonders

The CG distinguished itself from other Pentecostal groups by signs and wonders. It claimed to be 'the only religious institution that stands for the Bible rightly divided, with *all* the signs, gifts and graces'.[577] Evidential glossolalia was seen as a gateway experience, opening up the glossolalic to have faith and power for all the signs

---

[571] E.L. Simmons, 'Tarpon Springs, Fla.', *COGE* 6.50 (Dec 11, 1915); cf. D.F. Baldree, 'To Backsliders', *COGE* 8.7 (Feb 17, 1917), p. 4; Perry, 'What is the Use of Speaking in Tongues #2?', p. 3.

[572] A.J. Tomlinson, 'Tongues, Tithes, Knowledge', *COGE* 8.29 (Jul 28, 1917), p. 1; A.J. Tomlinson, 'Pray! Pray! Pray!', *COGE* 5.16 (Apr 18, 1914), p. 2!

[573] R.M. Evans 'Does Satan Speak In Tongues?' *COGE* 9.25 (Jun 22, 1918), p. 4 (emphasis added).

[574] Lee, '"Is The Present Tongues Movement of God?"', p. 1; cf. Sam C. Perry, 'Why Does Satan Hate the Speaking in Tongues', *COGE* 10.51 (Feb 1, 1919), p. 3.

[575] Tomlinson, 'The Opposition Weakening', p. 1; cf. Sam C. Perry, 'What is the Use of Speaking in Tongues #1?', *COGE* 8.40 (Oct 13, 1917), p. 3; Tomlinson, 'The Holy Ghost And Tongues', pp. 1, 2.

[576] A.J. Tomlinson, 'Dwell Deep', *COGE* 8.51 (Dec 29, 1917), p. 1.

[577] A.J. Tomlinson, 'Editorial', *COGE* 8.23 (Jun 16, 1917), p. 2 (emphasis added). Cf. A.J. Tomlinson, 'Missionary Sunday', *COGE* 8.10 (Mar 10, 1917), p. 1. Alexander noted that while 'Tomlinson did have fellowship with other Pentecostals … the Church of God was the *true* church and the Bible church', Alexander, *Pentecostal Healing*, p. 100, n. 153 (emphasis original). Phillips believes the emphasis on signs and wonders was two-fold: 'Tomlinson sought for extraordinary powers and manifestations that would confirm not only his own apostolic calling and position but also the corporate identity … as being the true restoration of the apostolic church', Phillips, *Quest*, p. 351.

and wonders. Though all the signs of Mk 16.17-18 were claimed some signs were given more prominence than others.[578]

Glossolalia was *the* Bible evidence, an initiation into a life characterized by *all* the Bible signs, especially Mk 16.17-18.[579] Note how Tomlinson bundles all these signs together and considers them to be of equal rank:

> it would be in the extreme to emphasize the sign of casting out devils and disregard the other signs, or laying hands on the sick and leave off the tongues or taking up of serpents ... each of these signs has its place among the signs but not alone ... neither must we make a hobby of the signs and neglect the gifts and fruits of the Spirit.[580]

In an article titled 'Sensational Demonstrations', Tomlinson reasoned that signs and wonders were scriptural;[581] were a sign of God's 'approval';[582] and were a 'a means of preaching the gospel' because they had an attractional aspect.[583] Practically speaking, some signs were given greater prominence.[584] For example, healing

---

[578] W.H. Rogers, 'Walhalla, S.C.', *COGE* 7.44 (Oct 28, 1916), p. 3.

[579] Tomlinson notes that the signs of Mk 16.17-18 were 'done with the deepest reverence and faithfulness ... (so that) the Scriptures are proven true', A.J. Tomlinson, 'Persistent Faith', *COGE* 7.51 (Dec 16, 1916), p. 1.

[580] A.J. Tomlinson, 'Extremes and Extremists', *COGE* 7.37 (Sep 9, 1916), p. 1; cf. A.J. Tomlinson, 'Faith is Developing', *COGE* 5.46 (Nov 21, 1914), pp. 1-2.

[581] A.J. Tomlinson, 'Sensational Demonstrations', *COGE* 5.38 (Sep 19, 1914), p. 1. 'Quite a number of our people here had been demonstrating this sign (snake handling) as indicated in Mark 16:18, and that it had been very effective for good', Tomlinson, 'Sensational Demonstrations', p. 2; cf. A.J. Tomlinson, 'Another Good Opportunity', *COGE* 7.35 (Aug 26, 1916), p. 1; A.J. Tomlinson, 'True Signs that Follow', *COGE* 11.15 (Apr 10, 1920), p. 1.

[582] Tomlinson, 'Sensational Demonstrations', p. 1; Mrs. Clyde Haynes, 'Great Revival In Chattanooga,' *COGE* 6.27 (Jul 3, 1915), p. 3. Cf. A.J. Tomlinson, 'The Present Situation', *COGE* 6.10 (Mar 6, 1915), p. 1; Mrs. Mary Howell, 'The Church of God', *COGE* 8.3 (Jan 20, 1917), p. 4.

[583] Tomlinson, 'Sensational Demonstrations', p. 1; cf. W.D. Collins, 'Signs', *COGE* 8.18 (May 12, 1917), p. 3; Sam C. Perry, 'The Power of God', *COGE* 9.7 (Feb 16, 1918), p. 3; A.J. Tomlinson, 'One Heart And One Soul', *COGE* 10.17 (Apr 26, 1919), p. 1.

[584] Z.R. Thomas lists running, dancing, leaping, trembling, being slain in the spirit, and speaking in other tongues among the 'different ways the spirit operates on our mortal bodies', Z.R. Thomas, 'Operations of the Holy Spirit', *COGE* 5.24 (Jun 13, 1914), pp. 5, 7.

was a prominent sign along with the faith to avoid taking medicine.[585] Snake handling[586] was another prominent sign for a short time (1914-1917):[587]

> she went down in prayer and the power of the Lord fell on her and she picked the snake up in the name of the Lord and handled it in all shapes that she could think of and then started home with it in her hands. She put the serpent down three times and took it up again … the fourth time she laid it down her mother struck it with an ax.[588]

Minority voices regarding snake handling were rarely printed in the *COGE* during the window of this study.[589] The power to handle live coals[590] or hot objects[591] was also frequently mentioned by Tomlinson.[592] For example, 'ten were dancing under the power and

---

[585] Cf. Alexander, *Pentecostal Healing*, pp. 101-13.

[586] Tomlinson, 'Sensational Demonstrations', p. 1; A.J. Tomlinson, 'Love God and One Another' *COGE* 10.17 (Apr 26, 1919), p. 1; A.J. Tomlinson, 'Snake Bitten Child Report', *COGE* 11.38 (Sep 18, 1920), p. 1. Snake-handling was even given tacit approval at the 11th (1915) General Assembly when the *COGE* reported, 'no serpents were brought in, but there was plenty of power to have taken up the most poisonous reptile if it had made its appearance', 'The 11th Annual Assembly', *COGE* 6.46 (Nov 13, 1915), p. 2.

[587] It appears in *COGE* extensively during 1914-1917. Perhaps the earliest accounts is J.B. Ellis, 'Oneonta, Ala.', *COGE* 5.19 (May 9, 1914), p. 8; cf. Phillips, *Quest*, pp. 350-58.

[588] R.D. Atnipp, 'Poplar Bluff, Missouri', *COGE* 6.35 (Aug 28, 1915), p. 2; cf. *COGE* 5.40 (Oct 4, 1914), p. 6; G.M. Green, 'Crab Orchard, Tenn.', *COGE* 6.32 (Aug 7, 1915), p. 3; S.W. Patterson, 'Report From Sobel, Tenn.', *COGE* 6.38 (Sep 18, 1915), p. 4; Henry Kinsey, 'Report', *COGE* (Aug 5, 1916), p. 3, *et al.*

[589] One unsigned notice read, 'it had been rumored that a snake was going to be brought there for the saints to handle. Jesus said (Matt. 12:39) "an evil and adulterous generation seeketh after a sign: and no sign shall be given …"', *COGE* 5.36 (Sep 5, 1914), p. 3. Michael J. McVicar notes that following Tomlinson's departure in 1922, snake handling gradually ceased being a distinctive and eventually was condemned in 1939, Michael J. McVicar, 'Take Away the Serpents from Us', *Journal of Southern Religion* 15 (2013), http://jsr.fsu.edu/issues/vol15/mcvicar.html.

[590] Roy L. Cotnam, 'Sale Creek, Tenn.', *COGE* 5.17 (Apr 25, 1914), p. 5.

[591] Chimneys and globes are mentioned, Mrs. Martha Crowder, 'Foster Falls, Va.', *COGE* 6.1 (Jan 2, 1915), p. 3.

[592] Even at the 1914 General Assembly there was a 'demonstration of God's presence by the wonderful manifestation of the "like as of fire," and other displays of his power and glory', A.J. Tomlinson, 'The New Building', *COGE* 5.47 (Nov 21, 1914), p. 1; cf. A.J. Tomlinson, 'The Assembly', *COGE* 5.45 (Nov 14,

speaking and singing in tongues ... eight of us ran to the fire and took up handfuls of live coals without being burned'.[593] Some saw fire in the sky[594] or a supernatural fire like Moses' burning bush.[595] Less prominent were the signs of casting out of demons[596] and the drinking of poison.[597] An occasional reference to the deaf being healed presented some challenges. The deaf requested prayer for healing[598] and could be Spirit baptized with tongues.[599] However, though some deaf were healed,[600] many of the healing re-

---

1914), p. 1; A.J. Tomlinson, 'Extracts From An Address', *COGE* 5.60 (Dec 19, 1914), p. 1.

[593] Lillie Tilghman, 'Hardy Station, Miss.', *COGE* 6.37 (Sep 11, 1915), p. 2.

[594] Scott Hayes, 'Strange Sight at Archadale, Ala.' *COGE* 1.18 (Nov 15, 1910), p. 4; V.W. Kennedy, 'Fire and Pillars of Smoke', *COGE* 1.18 (Nov 15, 1910), p. 5; Sallie O. Lee, 'Calhoun, Ga.', *COGE* 6.42 (Oct 16, 1915), p. 2; Mrs. Christina Smith, 'Atlanta, Ga.', *COGE* 6.50 (Dec 11, 1915), p. 4.

[595] Aaron A. Smith, 'Wimauma Camp Meeting', *COGE* 5.24 (Jun 13, 1914), p. 4. Biblical reasoning for the handling or sighting of fire were 1) John the Baptist's 'Holy Ghost *and fire*' (emphasis added). Tomlinson connected it to John the Baptist's statement that 'Jesus would baptize the people of Holy Ghost and fire', A.J. Tomlinson, 'Fire, and Like as of Fire', *COGE* 7.48 (Nov 25, 1916), p. 1; cf. W.A. Walker, 'In The Fire', *COGE* 5.15 (Apr 11, 1914), p. 7; E. Hayes and wife, 'A Report', *COGE* 5.21 (May 23, 1914), p. 6. 2) It is 'a kind of deliverance from fire exhibited in Daniel 3', *COGE* 14.11 (Mar 17, 1923), p. 4; cf, Alexander, *Pentecostal Healing*, p. 106. 3) The live coals from a seraph that touched Isaiah's lips (Isa. 6.6, 7), J.W. Buckalew, 'Report From Brewster, Fla', *COGE* 5.38 (Sep 19, 1914), p. 8; A.J. Tomlinson, 'Baptized with the Holy Ghost And With Fire', *COGE* 9.13 (Mar 30, 1918), p. 1

[596] W.M. Rumler, and wife, 'Convention Report', *COGE* 7.24 (Jun 10, 1916), p. 2. Cf. Baldree, 'To Backsliders', p. 4; J.A. Williams, 'Report', *COGE* 7.25 (Jun 17, 1916), p. 3.

[597] On the one hand, the drinking of poison was discouraged: 'if the Bible had said *they "shall" drink* deadly poison, that would have been done also, but since it says *"if they shall* drink any deadly thing, it shall not hurt them"', A.J. Tomlinson, 'The Church of God', *COGE* 7.27 (Jul 1, 1916), p. 1 (emphasis added). On the other hand, it was a Bible sign that required a 'special anointing', A.J. Tomlinson, 'Drinking Deadly Poison', *COGE* 8.14 (Apr 14, 1917), p. 1; cf. M.S. Lemons, 'Thy Word Is Truth', *COGE* 7.23 (Jun 3, 1916), p. 4.

[598] Manerva Mitchel, 'South Pittsburg, Tenn.', *COGE* 5.29 (Jul 18, 1914), p. 5; Mrs. Ida Poe, 'Hixon, Tenn.', *COGE* 6.43 (Oct 23, 1915), p. 2; Clator Sapp, 'Wess, Ky.', *COGE* 10.38 (Sep 20, 1919), p. 4.

[599] 'Editorial Notes' *COGE* 6.27 (Jul 3, 1915), p. 2; M.S. Lemons, 'Chattanooga, Meeting', *COGE* 6.28 (Jul 10, 1915), p. 2; L.L. Turner, 'Report', *COGE* 6.43 (Oct 13, 1915), p. 4; S.C. Luther, 'Oppy, Ky.', *COGE* 9.14 (Apr 6, 1918), p. 3.

[600] Johnie Cagle, 'Ooltewah, Tenn.', *COGE* 6.34 (Aug 21, 1915), p. 4; N.M. Kinney, 'Lindale, Ga.', *COGE* 6.50 (Dec 11, 1915), p. 4; G.T. Stargel, 'Report', *COGE* 7.30 (Jul 22, 1916), p. 2; F.J. Ewart, 'God's Fig Tree Budding', *COGE*

ports were second-hand or were found to be false after investigation.[601] Frequent contributor L. Howard Juillerat believed that the deaf would finally be made whole during the millennial.[602]

E. Testimonies

Because there were 325 issues read during the window of this study, a brief review of some testimonies will help the reader hear the voice of the people and will reveal the practical theology of glossolalia that developed regarding: 1) longing and victory, 2) pre-glossolalic stages, 3) the emotion or affect, and 4) glossolalia and grief.

J.W. Douglass wrote, 'I just got so hungry it didn't seem that I could endure much longer without the baptism of the Holy Ghost'.[603] This hunger went hand in hand with personal surrender and at the same time a passionate pursuit of the Holy Spirit.[604] For example, W.M. Lowman wrote,

> the Lord spoke to me and said, 'if you want the Holy Ghost you must clean out the temple so I can come in.' ... I threw the plug (of tobacco) away ... stopped every mean thing in my life ... (and) after three days and nights without ceasing to call upon God I received the Holy Ghost and spoke with other tongues as the experience came.[605]

One's first experience with glossolalia was a deep experience for the average person and not just a doctrine.[606] For example, 'the reason I know I have this precious comforter is because He talks for Himself as the Spirit gives utterance, in other tongues, just as

---

8.28 (Jul 21, 1917), p. 3; H.W. Poteat, 'Wilmington, Del.', *COGE* 9.26 (Jun 29, 1918), p. 4; M.W. Letsinger, 'Afton, Tenn.', *COGE* 10.22 (May 31, 1919), p. 4.

[601] M.S. Lemons, 'A Solemn Warning to Persecutors', *COGE* 1.9 (Jul 1, 1910), p. 3; A.J. Tomlinson, 'Marvelous Healings', *COGE* 5.14 (Apr 4, 1914), p. 2; J.C. Underwood, 'From Bro. Underwood', *COGE* 5.38 (Sep 19, 1914), p. 4.

[602] I. Howard Juillerat, 'The Ages', *COGE* 9.11 (Mar 16, 1918), p. 4.

[603] J.W. Douglass, 'Gardner, Florida', *COGE* 5.29 (Jul 18, 1914), p. 8; cf. Geo. T. Brouayer, 'Chattanooga, Tenn.', *COGE* 1.9 (Jul 1, 1910), p. 6.

[604] H.J. Brady, 'Request for Prayer', *COGE* 5.18 (May 2, 1914), p. 4; G.W. Peeples, 'Lake Butler, Fla.', *COGE* 6.22 (May 29, 1915), p. 2.

[605] W.M. Lowman, 'Hiwassee, Va.' *COGE* 1.13 (Sep 1, 1910), p. 8.

[606] Ella Simmons, 'Boyett, Fla.', *COGE* 1.5 (May 1, 1910), p. 7; Lula M. Chambers, 'Culbertson, N.C.', *COGE* 1.11 (Aug 1, 1910), p. 7; Park Lacy, 'Scobey, Miss.', *COGE* 6.3 (Jan 16, 1915), p. 4.

He said He would in Acts 2:4, and John 15:16'.[607] H.V. Freeman's experience was typical, 'I was under the power for hours when I began speaking in tongues as in Acts 2:4'.[608] Bursting into often loud[609] glossolalia was described as a victory: 'Sunday night four more came through to victory, shouting and talking in tongues'.[610] The most frequent mention of tongues in the *COGE* was simply a revival report noting the number of people who spoke in tongues.[611] The next frequent mention was praise or thanksgiving for God's wonderful provision. For example, S.W. Patterson wrote, 'I praise God for my Pentecost with Bible evidence of speaking in other tongues'.[612]

Probably out of kindness or as a way of making sense of the experience for those who did not speak in tongues, there were occasions where the term 'stammering lips' was used to soften the hardness of the evidentiary language.[613] For example, Luda Clark's eulogy stated, 'she made her way toward the baptism so close that she received the stammering lips'.[614] Nevertheless, it was assumed that one would push through to the genuine fluency, like Mrs.

---

[607] D.R. Holcomb, 'Dora, Ala.', *COGE* 7.5 (Jan 29, 1916), p. 2.

[608] H.V. Freeman, 'Rock Island, Tenn.', *COGE* 6.8 (Feb 20, 1915), p. 4.

[609] John X. Smith, 'Letter of a Baptist to His Wife', *COGE* 1.9 (Jul 1, 1910), p. 2; A.J. Tomlinson, 'The Great Assembly', *COGE* 7.42 (Oct 14, 1916), p. 1. Cf. 'Manifestations of the Spirit', p. 5; James Cline, 'Elkhurst, W. Va.', *COGE* 6.24 (Jun 12, 1915), p. 2. Initial Evidence could also occur quietly, cf. Julia McCallie Divine, 'My Inheritance', *COGE* 1.5 (May 1, 1910), p. 5.

[610] Walter Harden, 'Empire, Ala.', *COGE* 7.47 (Nov 18, 1916), p. 3; cf. 'Another Battle Abroad', *COGE* 1.7 (Jun 1, 1910), p. 4; M.S. Lemons, 'A Report', *COGE* 5.19 (May 9, 1914), p. 5.

[611] For example, 'there were 35 who received the baptism of the Holy Ghost with the sign speaking in other tongues as the spirit gave utterance', 'Great Meeting at Gintown, Ala.', *COGE* 1.15 (Oct 1, 1910), p. 5; cf. H.L. Trim, 'Evangelistic Tour', *COGE* 5.17 (Apr 25, 1914), p. 4; M.S. Lemons, 'Jefferson City, Tenn.', *COGE* 6.2 (Jan 9, 1915), p. 1, *et al.*

[612] Rev. S.W. Patterson, 'Sobel, Tenn.', *COGE* 1.6 (May 15, 1910), p. 5, cf. Mittie Tubbs, 'Amor, Miss', *COGE* 6.36 (Sep 4, 1915), p. 2; Mrs. Maggie Osment, 'Cleveland, Tenn.', *COGE* 6.38 (Sep 18, 1915), p. 2; Walter Byerler, 'Dayton, Tenn.', *COGE* 6.46 (Nov 13, 1915), p. 2; Lamb H. Lanier, 'Deer Park, Fla.', *COGE* 7.27 (Jul 1, 1916), p. 3; Martha Marrisett, 'Jefferson City, Tenn.', *COGE* 7.41 (Oct 4, 1916), p. 4, *et al.*

[613] W.P Benefield, 'Midland City, Ala.', *COGE* 1.16 (Oct 15, 1910), p. 8; Bartley L. Hicks, 'A Spiritual House', *COGE* 11.47 (Nov 27, 1920), p. 4.

[614] 'Another One Gone', *COGE* 8.4 (Jan 27, 1917), p. 3.

Brinson-Rushire: 'I spoke in a stammering tongue as the Spirit gave utterance ... as the Spirit continued to work in me a few days a real language was given'.[615]

Joy was the usual emotional result of tongues speech. J.D. Williams described it as 'unspeakable joy and happiness – the half can never be told. Joy, joy, from my head to my toes'.[616] Others described their SBs as times of 'joy and peace',[617] or 'the happiest hours I ever spent'.[618] The emotional affect was often extended to all who were at the assembly, using phrases like, '*we* had a happy time',[619] or 'it makes *us* feel so good',[620] or '*we* certainly had a grand time'.[621]

At times, tongues were connected with the transition from life to death, from the earthly to the heavenly:[622] 'when I leave this old sinful world', wrote Florence Long 'I want to go talking in tongues'.[623] It is hard to decipher whether glossolalia was giving comfort or functioned as a rite of passage because the testimonies were so simply stated: 'He left this world speaking in tongues and praising God'[624] or 'she praised God and talked in other tongues until she became unconscious'.[625] Nevertheless, the written

---

[615] Mrs. Brinson-Rushire, 'Taiafu, Shantung, China', *COGE* 6.44 (Oct 30, 1915), p. 3.

[616] J.D. Williams, 'Miami, Fla.', *COGE* 5.18 (May 2, 1914), p. 4, cf. Mrs. E.R. Simmons, 'The Word of God', *COGE* 6.19 (May 8, 1915), p. 3.

[617] Rinah E. Ranming, 'Short Testimonies', *COGE* 5.18 (May 2, 1914), p. 2; cf. E.C. Childers, 'Brewster, Fla.', *COGE* 6.4 (Jan 23, 1915), p. 4.

[618] Myrtie Fricks, 'Craneater, Ga.', *COGE* 6.7 (Feb 13, 1915), p. 3.

[619] Bell Scoggins, 'Marco, Fla.', *COGE* 6.2 (Jan 9, 1915), p. 2 (emphasis added).

[620] E.H. and Clara Pearson, 'Kentwood, La.', *COGE* 6.47 (Nov 20, 1915), p. 1 (emphasis added).

[621] Bertha Hilbun, 'Kentwood, La.', *COGE* 5.60 (Dec 19, 1914), p. 2 (emphasis added).

[622] Ed. 'Asleep In Jesus', *COGE* 8.10 (Mar 10, 1917), p. 3; Her Pastor, 'Gone Home', *COGE* 8.31 (Aug 11, 1917), p. 4; J.B. Ellis, 'Gone To Rest', *COGE* 9.47 (Nov 23, 1918), p. 4; 'Obituaries', *COGE* 10.23 (Jun 7, 1919), p. 4; 'Obituaries', *COGE* 10.23 (Jun 7, 1919), p. 4; 'Obituaries', *COGE* 10.28 (Jul 12, 1919), p. 3.

[623] Mrs. Florence Long, 'Sale Creek, Tenn.', *COGE* 6.34 (Aug 21, 1915), p. 3.

[624] Harry Long, 'Sale Creek, Tenn.', *COGE* 6.30 (Jul 24, 1915), p. 1.

[625] C.C. Walker, 'Transported From Belmont, N.C. To Heaven', *COGE* 7.16 (Apr 15, 1916), p. 3.

testimony of glossolalia indicates that it brought peace to the speaker and their loved ones during these times of grief.[626]

F. Sanctification

Rooted in the WH wing of Pentecostalism, the *COGE* held firmly to the threefold pattern of justification, sanctification, and SB; however, some testimonies revealed a lack of understanding of the tradition's teaching.

Similar to other WH groups that transitioned to Pentecostalism, it was necessary to clarify that SB was subsequent to and different from sanctification.[627] A.L. Tarpley's testimony was typical: 'I thought I got the baptism of the Holy Ghost when sanctified, but as soon as I heard Pentecost preached and speaking in other tongues I saw at once that I didn't have that experience … I saw they had something that I did not have'.[628] Sanctification was a prerequisite for SB: 'the Evangel will stand square for two works of grace … sanctification subsequent to regeneration … (and) the baptism of the Holy Ghost as an enduement of power on the sanctified life'.[629] Freeman clarified it further:

> sanctification is holiness, the baptism of the Holy Ghost is the enduement with power; sanctification is the cleansing: the baptism is the filling … sanctification causes you to magnify and praise Jesus: but the Holy Ghost magnifies God in new tongues and sings and praise through you himself.[630]

It was inconceivable that one could be filled with God's Spirit and not be holy:

> we must be pure in heart and life by the redeeming blood of Jesus. None but a pure heart can bear the fruits and powers of

---

[626] 'Gone Home', *COGE* 7.6 (Feb 5, 1916), p. 1; Ella Simmons, 'Gone To Be At Rest', *COGE* 8.4 (Jan 27, 1917), p. 3; Georgia Broughton, 'Gone To Be With Jesus', *COGE* 8.5 (Feb 3, 1917), p. 2.

[627] Phillips, *Quest*, p. 147.

[628] A.L. Tarpley, 'Hyatt Tenn.', *COGE* 1.8 (Jun 15, 1914), p. 4; cf. Mrs. C.L. Silver, 'Burnside, Ky.', *COGE* 1.8 (Jun 15, 1910), p. 7; Minnie Lee Newton, 'Shelby, N.C.', *COGE* 8.47 (Dec 1, 1917), p. 4.

[629] AJ Tomlinson, 'From The Old to the New', *COGE* 7.53 (Dec 30, 1916), p. 4; cf. A.J. Tomlinson, 'Confusion of Scriptures', *COGE* 5.23 (Jun 6, 1914), p. 2.

[630] H.V. Freeman, 'McMinnville, Tenn.', *COGE* 6.25 Jun 19, 1915), p. 2; cf. J.B. Lucas, 'Mooreville Mississippi', *COGE* 1.10 (Jul 15, 1910), p. 5.

Pentecost. Uncleanness or sin of any kind, in thought, word or act is destructive to the Spirit's work within the human heart and life.'[631]

Doctrinally, SB was an equipping of power, but testimonies occasionally pointed to a completion of the sanctification process[632] or a 'keeping power'.[633] For example, my 'husband has served the Lord 25 years. When we went to hear the evangelist, he used tobacco. He talked in tongues and threw away his tobacco';[634] or 'praise God for the wonderful baptism with the Holy Ghost and fire which burns up all sin and leaves room for nothing but hallelujahs to God';[635] and 'when the Holy Ghost comes he tames that unruly member which is the tongue ... and makes us speak kindly, brings peace in homes'.[636] Occasionally, the entire three stage process was collapsed into one event: 'she went down on her knees a sinner and came up talking in tongues'.[637]

G. Purposes for Glossolalia

1. Power

From the first extant issue of the *COGE*, Tomlinson recognized that 'the Holy Spirit was given to the disciples ... to give them power to accomplish just what they did accomplish. He is given us today for the same purpose'.[638] Tongues were 'one of the smallest things connected with this blessing ... Jesus said, "Ye shall receive

---

[631] Sam C. Perry, 'Sanctification', *COGE* 5.44 (Oct 31, 1914), p. 6; cf. 'A few Words of Warning', *COGE* 5.40 (Oct 4, 1914), p. 4; Perry, 'What is the Use of Speaking in Tongues #2', p. 3.

[632] For example, the power that the Holy Spirit gives is 'power over all temptation', Mrs. P.T. Collier, 'Love Thy Neighbor', *COGE* 6.21 (May 22, 1915), p. 2.

[633] 'I am praising God for the Holy Ghost, and the Bible witness of talking in tongues ... For a power that keeps me free from sin every day', Annie May Duncan, 'Jefferson City, Tenn.', *COGE* 6.14 (Apr 3, 1915), p. 1; cf. Lura Clevenger, 'Jefferson City, Tenn.', *COGE* 6.14 (Apr 3, 1915), p. 3.

[634] Mrs. A.B. Sherrill, 'Spring City, Tenn.', *COGE* 5.15 (Apr 11, 1914), p. 8.

[635] Gladston Hackney, 'Soddy, Tenn.', *COGE* 5.17 (Apr 25, 1914), p. 7. Or, 'burns up all base desire', Beatrice B. Smith, 'Testimony', *COGE* 5.33 (Aug 15, 1914), p. 5.

[636] John Burk, 'Cliff View, Va.', *COGE* 7.10 (Mar 4, 1916), p. 2; cf. E.J. Boehmer, 'Salvation Is Real', *COGE* 6.23 (Jun 5, 1915), p. 3.

[637] W.W. Rose, 'White Stone, Ga.,' *COGE* 6.30 (Jul 24, 1915), p. 4.

[638] A.J. Tomlinson, 'Apology for Above Title', *COGE* 1.1 (Mar 1, 1910), p. 1.

power." Not merely power to profess, or to make a display, but power to be, and overcome; power to do the things of Jesus Christ'.[639] Usually, it was power to 'testify for Jesus Christ';[640] however, SB with tongues opened an individual up to all the spiritual gifts:

> speaking in tongues is certainly an exhibition of power ... however the goal is to do something. To stop with that and do nothing else is to lose the real value of the great blessing of God's presence that makes the tongues possible ... (it) brings into a man the entire range of the workings of the Holy Spirit himself who is thus ready to work in all his completeness the nine works of the Spirit.[641]

SB was transformative power so that men were 'astonished at what is being done'.[642] Everyone had the potential to work signs and wonders; everyone could share the good news regardless of their education.[643] W.F. Hesson's testimony was typical:

> this baptism gives power for service, and makes you a worldwide witness ... (it) leads into intercessory prayer as you never experienced it before ... (it) prepares you for service in this world and seals you unto the world to come.[644]

Not everyone was called overseas, so the Spirit's power also equipped the individual for use in his own neighbourhood. For example, Mrs. R.D. Atnipp wrote, 'the Lord wonderfully sanctified me and filled me with the Holy Ghost with Bible evidence ... we are having services at my home and we are praying for workers, and that lost souls may be saved.'[645] The Spirit would 'separate' out some especially called to go into all the world.[646] This power was

---

[639] Sam C. Perry, 'There Are Other Things As Well', *COGE* 9.19 (May 11, 1918), p. 3.
[640] Sam C. Perry, 'Filled With The Spirit', *COGE* 7.13 (Mar 25, 1916), p. 3.
[641] Street, 'What is Pentecost', p. 6.
[642] Z.D. Simpson, 'Ethelsville, Ala.', *COGE* 5.14 (Apr 4, 1914), p. 5, cf. 'All Need the Holy Ghost', *COGE* 1.5 (May 1, 1910), p. 2.
[643] 'All Need the Holy Ghost', p. 2.
[644] W.F. Hesson, 'Seeking The Baptism', *COGE* 5.23 (Jun 6, 1914), p. 5.
[645] Mrs. R.D. Atnipp, 'Poplar Bluff, MO.', *COGE* 5.39 (Sep 26, 1914), p. 5.
[646] 'This does not mean all shall go ... some should go and the Holy Ghost is faithful to separate ... too many go without being separated', Hesson, 'Seeking The Baptism', p. 5.

concomitant with tongues-speech. 'One man who had never prayed before, and had been a vile sinner for 50 years, was saved, sanctified and baptized with the Holy Ghost. He spoke in tongues, *and exhorted* for two hours.'[647]

2. Prayer

In the *COGE,* there was scant theological reflection on how glossolalia lead one into deeper prayer. Normally, Rom. 8.26 was simply referenced as praying in the Spirit,[648] and occasionally it was acknowledged that such prayer was 'according to the will of God'.[649] In addition to intercession, glossolalic prayer was the backdrop or environment for seekers of SB. Mrs. C.L. Thigpen's anecdote was typical:

> we all knelt down and the power of prayer fell upon me, and the Spirit made intercession with groanings that could not be uttered. The husband was knocked down by the power ... he got up and prayed and praised for the Holy Ghost, and it was not long before he was knocked down again, and in about an hour came through speaking in tongues.[650]

Perry noted that prayer 'is a very natural exercise to the soul ... (it) is a necessary accompaniment of the baptism of the Holy Ghost'.[651]

3. Praise

Though it was only occasionally stated in the *COGE,* another purpose for tongues was magnifying God. 'The Spirit of God came upon me in great power and I began to speak in a language other than my own ... I found myself in an attitude of praise and I was

---

[647] Mrs. Minnie Hall, 'Punta Gorda, Fla.', *COGE* 1.3 (Apr 1, 1910), p. 6 (emphasis added).

[648] A.J. Tomlinson, 'Holy Ghost and Us', *COGE* 7.50 (Dec 9, 1916), p. 1; A.J. Tomlinson, 'Some Bible Teachings and Counsel', *COGE* 8.4 (Jan 27, 1917), p. 2.

[649] 'Camp Meeting at Arcadia, Fla.', *COGE* 1.19 (Dec 1, 1910), p. 5.

[650] Mrs. C.L. Thigpen, 'Mentone, Ala.', *COGE* 1.18 (Nov 15, 1910), p. 5; cf. H.S. Harris, 'Cascilla, Miss.', *COGE* 7.35 (Aug 26, 1916), p. 4; L.J. Davis, 'Canton, N.C.', *COGE* 6.15 (Apr 10, 1915), p. 4.

[651] Perry, 'Filled With The Spirit', p. 3; cf. A.J. Tomlinson, 'Soul Travail And Prevailing Prayer', *COGE* 8.32 (Aug 18, 1917), p. 1.

made to sing'.⁶⁵² Like other early Pentecostal periodicals, giving praise to God primed the pump for SB: 'she began to praise Him and in a few moments she was speaking the sweetest language I ever heard, also singing in tongues was in the program'.⁶⁵³ Also, evidentiary tongues were considered praise to God. For example, 'two received the baptism of the Holy Ghost for we heard them speak with tongues and magnify God'.⁶⁵⁴

4. Revelation

Tongues speech upon SB opened the door to revelations from God that normally would be hidden from the human mind. Tomlinson compared this to the Urim and Thummim (Ex. 28.30): 'a means by which some things will be revealed that otherwise will never be known'.⁶⁵⁵ Many times this revelation was of Jesus himself: 'as the Holy Ghost came in with his wonderful illuminating and revealing power, as I beheld his majesty and beauty',⁶⁵⁶ or,

> I was caught away in the Spirit for about one hour. I saw a blaze go from my mouth to heaven and I received the Holy Ghost just then ... I was alone with Christ in spirit. I spoke in other tongues as the spirit gave utterance.⁶⁵⁷

Because there was an emphasis on Jesus' teaching that the Spirit would 'testify of himself', actual communication or conveyance of information was inferred slightly more than from other Pentecostal groups.⁶⁵⁸ Sam Perry wrote, 'the Holy Ghost will testify to himself through the lips of the believer ... sometimes (with) visions, bodily emotions and great mental illuminations'.⁶⁵⁹ The

---

⁶⁵² Rachel Wheeler, 'Woodstock, Ga.', *COGE* 8.40 (Oct 13, 1917), p. 3.
⁶⁵³ Mrs. I.V. Powers, 'A Wonderful Experience', *COGE* 1.13 (Sep 1, 1910), p. 8.
⁶⁵⁴ I.H. Marks, 'Marco, Fla.', *COGE* 5.18 (May 2, 1914), p. 6; cf. Mrs. Cora A. Nelson, 'Champaign, Ill.', *COGE* 6.2 (Jan 9, 1915), p. 4.
⁶⁵⁵ A.J. Tomlinson, 'More About the Gifts', *COGE* 5.20 (May 16, 1914), pp. 2, 3.
⁶⁵⁶ C.A. Freeman, 'Lithia, Fla.', *COGE* 1.9 (Jul 1, 1910), p. 6; cf. Goldman Ingram, 'Cleveland, Tenn.', *COGE* 5.11 (Mar 14, 1914), p. 8
⁶⁵⁷ Lottie Barnett, 'Unicoi, Tenn.', *COGE* 7.11 (Mar 11, 1916), p. 4.
⁶⁵⁸ Andy Rue, 'Athens, Tenn.', *COGE* 1.8 (Jun 15, 1910), p. 5; cf. Sam C. Perry, 'The Baptism of the Holy Ghost', *COGE* 7.15 (Apr 8, 1916), p. 3.
⁶⁵⁹ Sam C. Perry, 'How Can I Know', *COGE* 7.1 (Jan 1, 1916), p. 3.

Spirit revealed 'love, mercy, and power',[660] the ability to 'tell some of the people things they had done',[661] about tongues itself,[662] and a great variety of other spiritual things. 'The Holy Ghost will reveal things that we need to know if we'll obey him ... to know a thing that is spiritual and living it must come through and by the Holy Spirit.'[663] Note how glossolalia was the entryway into more revelation when Tomlinson wrote,

> one of the great beauties and glories in this last experience (SB) is that it is always accompanied with the speaking in other tongues ... it is only the beginning. When the Holy Ghost comes he begins to instruct and teach.[664]

5. Gifts of the Spirit

The Pentecostal outpouring of tongues signalled the restoration of all the spiritual gifts, including the vocal gifts of the Spirit in 1 Corinthians 12-14, including: tongues, interpretation, and prophecy. Tongues and interpretation were the equivalent of prophecy that was preceded by glossolalia.

Tongues and interpretation in the public gatherings were often reported[665] and were straightforward in their hermeneutic: if someone spoke in tongues for the first time, it was considered the evidence of SB. Subsequent occurrences were either a message from God for the whole congregation or were for personal edification. Tomlinson wrote, 'there is a difference between speaking with other tongues as the Spirit gives the utterance as described in the second chapter of Acts, and the gift of tongues which Paul gives instructions in the fourteenth chapter First Corinthians'.[666] Tongues and interpretation were two separate gifts that functioned in tandem. Tongues when exercised in a public assembly required

---

[660] Tomlinson, 'More About The Gifts', p. 2.
[661] W.E. Evans, 'Report', *COGE* 8.22 (Jun 9, 1917), p. 3.
[662] Tomlinson, 'Tongues, Tithes, Knowledge', p. 1.
[663] W.G. Anderson, 'Baptized with the Holy Ghost', *COGE* 6.37 (Sep 11, 1915), p. 3.
[664] A.J. Tomlinson, 'Converted, Sanctified, and Baptized with the Holy Ghost', *COGE* 6.51 (Dec 18, 1915), p. 1.
[665] Cf. W.W. Spears, 'Benhaden, Fla', *COGE* 5.7 (Feb 14, 1914), p. 4; Tomlinson, 'The Assembly', p. 3; C.R Curtis, 'Lake Park, Ga.', *COGE* 5.60 (Dec 19, 1914), p. 1.
[666] Tomlinson, 'The Gift of Tongues', p. 1.

an interpretation to edify the congregation and to comply with Paul's restrictions.[667] For example, 'she came speaking in tongues, under the mighty power of God, and gave a part of the interpretation to two of the workers',[668] or, 'God looked upon unworthy me in pity and gave me the interpretation of the message in tongues I had given under the power of the Spirit'.[669] On occasion, it was believed that one person in each church possessed the gift: 'the Lord has given the gift of interpretation to a sister, who interprets our messages, for which we thank Him and praise Him'.[670] However, the phenomena of God speaking 'wonderful messages ... through those lips of clay' was more important than an individual's possession of a spiritual gift.[671] For example, 'messages began to flow and interpretations were given. Oh, it was wonderful to listen to God talking to His people through *the saints*'.[672] The speaker believed that they were speaking at the behest of the Spirit. Mother Cress' testimony is typical: 'the Spirit told me to stand up and He would fill my mouth. I obeyed and the Spirit spoke through me first in my own language, then in another tongue, then again in my own language.'[673]

Against a critic who argued that tongues were the least important gift, it was countered that you cannot go by a biblical ranking, because 'according to his theory then charity is a minor grace because it is given last ... (in) 1 Cor. 13:13' and tongues would be extremely high according to Jesus' list in Mk 16.17-18.[674] In the end, 'if God knows what is best for his people, the Church cannot be at its best without these gifts'.[675]

---

[667] A.J. Tomlinson, 'Hold Steady Now', *COGE* 8.19 (May 19, 1917), p. 1; A.J. Tomlinson, 'On The Bible Line', *COGE* 2.23 (Jun 16, 1917), p. 1; A.J. Tomlinson, 'Samson And His Exploits', *COGE* 10.39 (Sep 27, 1919), p. 1.

[668] 'An Indian Woman's Message', *COGE* 1.3 (Apr 1, 1910), p. 7.

[669] Flora E. Bower, 'Miami, Fla.', *COGE* 1.14 (Sep 15, 1910), p. 5.

[670] Edmund S. Barr and Wife, 'Nassau', *COGE* 1.4 (Apr 15, 1910), p. 6; cf. A.G.S., 'Boaz, Ala.', *COGE* 7.9 (Feb 26, 1916), p. 3. Bertha Hendricks even prayed specifically for this gift, Bertha Hendricks, 'Harriman, Tenn.', *COGE* 5.9 (Feb 28, 1914), p. 8.

[671] L.A. Ray, 'Gone Home', *COGE* 8.28 (Jul 21, 1917), p. 4.

[672] 'Field Notes', *COGE* 3.14 (Sep 15, 1912), p. 7 (emphasis added). Cf. Ellen Jones, 'Ethelsville, Ala.' *COGE* 5.13 (Mar 28, 1914), p. 6; Mrs. W.E. Lord, 'Preston, MD.', *COGE* 5.15 (Apr 11, 1914), p. 6.

[673] Mother Cress, 'Abilene, Kan.', *COGE* 1.14 (Sep 15, 1910), p. 6.

[674] A.J. Tomlinson, 'Covet The Best Gifts', *COGE* 8.25 (Jun 30, 1917), p. 1.

[675] Tomlinson, 'Covet The Best Gifts', p. 1.

The content of the Spirit's message through the gift of interpretation (and prophecy) was occasionally stated in the *COGE*. Usually, the Spirit stated that Jesus was about to return,[676] or encouraged people,[677] or warned people.[678] However, the majority of the testimonies highlighted the phenomenon itself – that God has spoken.

6. Personal Edification

Tomlinson encouraged people to speak in tongues for their personal edification as a separate function of the Holy Spirit from IE or the public gift of tongues following 1 Cor. 14.14. To have experienced a full SB and then not speak in tongues occasionally was to live 'beneath their privilege' and to be 'without this special kind of edification that God has provided for your good'.[679]

H. Eschatology and Tongues

The return of glossolalia signalled the beginning of the end times. Tongues were part of a prophetic environment that warned of the end times and prepared the church for the Lord's return.

Mrs. E.N. Howell saw the present outpouring of tongues as 'a sign or token of a new era' similar to the era changes at the tower of Babel and at Pentecost.[680] Perry noted there were 'many signs which are to come in the last days'[681] and 'many are seeing in the present conditions the signs of Jesus' coming'.[682] The return of glossolalia was the preeminent sign[683] 'proving that we are in the

---

[676] W.M. Coleman, 'Hill View, Tellico Mountains Tenn.', *COGE* 1.7 (Jun 1, 1910), p. 5.

[677] W.F. Bryant, 'The Mountain Work', *COGE* 1.9 (Jul 1, 1910), p. 4; Milton Padget, 'Bahama Islands', *COGE* 5.50 (Dec 19, 1914), p. 3.

[678] For example, 'a message was given by the Holy Ghost that the door of mercy was going to be closed and that someone would be cut off', Minnie Ivens, 'Mentone, Ga.,' *COGE* 6.30 Jul 24, 1915), p. 4.

[679] A.J. Tomlinson, 'What If You Have Not?', *COGE* 10.13 (Mar 29, 1919), p. 1; cf. Tomlinson, 'Edification And Comfort', p. 1.

[680] Mrs. E.N. Howell, 'Windsor, Fla.', *COGE* 1.7 (Jun 1, 1910), p. 6.

[681] Sam C. Perry, 'Jesus Is Coming', *COGE* 5.39 (Sep 26, 1914), p. 6; Lula L. Jones, 'Clearwater, Fla.', *COGE* 6.17 (Apr 24, 1915), p. 4.

[682] Sam C. Perry, 'The Need of the Hour', *COGE* 6.5 (Jan 30, 1915), p. 3.

[683] AJ Tomlinson, 'Extracts From Discourse Delivered At Assembly', *COGE* 6.48 (Nov 27, 1915), p. 1; cf. A.J. Tomlinson, 'Guilty Or Not Guilty', *COGE* 7.41 (Oct 4, 1916), p. 1.

last days ... declaring the coming of Jesus is near'.[684] The latter rain metaphor gave logic to tongues reappearance.[685] Most testimonies saw tongues as an eschatological sign without a lot of theological reflection. For example,

> I am praising God for baptizing me with the Holy Ghost with the Bible evidence of speaking in other tongues ... I am ready and looking for the coming of Jesus with my lamp trimmed and burning, oil in my vessel and ready to meet the bridegroom when he comes'.[686]

Tongues were a call 'to the marriage supper of the Lamb'.[687]

Further, the environment of tongues speech was often concomitant with prophetic speech about the return of Jesus. Some examples are: I 'began singing in the Spirit and speaking other tongues. I feel that Jesus wants me to sound the alarm that he is coming soon',[688] and 'the power fell and we had a wonderful time, shouting, dancing, and talking in tongues. The Spirit spoke through me saying, "He is coming! He is coming"!'[689] Note the urgency when both glossolalia and eschatology are combined: 'it can be well remembered that when Pentecost was first preached that many of us were afraid that Jesus would come before we got the baptism of the Holy Ghost. His coming seems to be the theme of everyone.'[690]

Eschatological tongues played a role in preparing for the coming of Jesus. Tomlinson saw broadly that 'justification, sanctification, the baptism of the Holy Ghost evidenced by speaking in other tongues as the Spirit gives utterance, divine healing and the Church of God ... (altogether were) mainly to prepare people for

---

[684] Sam C. Perry, 'Be Ye Also Ready', *COGE* 5.47 (Nov 21, 1914), pp. 6, 7; cf. Tomlinson, 'Extracts From Discourse Delivered at Assembly', p. 1.

[685] A.J. Tomlinson, 'The Holy Ghost And Fire', *COGE* 9.30 (Jul 27, 1918), p. 1.

[686] E.C. Caddell, 'Kimberly, Ala.', *COGE* 6.16 (Apr 17, 1915), p. 2; cf. Ella New, 'Woodstock, Ga.', *COGE* 5.18 (May 2, 1914), p. 6.

[687] Howell, 'Windsor, Fla.', p. 6.

[688] Mrs. Nettie Way, 'Chattanooga, Tenn.', *COGE* 5.39 (Sep 26, 1914), p. 5.

[689] Belle Scoggins, 'Atlanta, Ga.', *COGE* 7.8 (Feb 19, 1916), p. 4.

[690] M.S. Lemons, 'Something To Think About', *COGE* 7.3 (Jan 15, 1916), p. 3; cf. Chas. E. Lockard, 'Cedar Grove, Ky.', *COGE* 8.41 (Oct 20, 1917), p. 4.

the great event – the coming of Christ'.[691] At times, however, the average person viewed the Bible sign as the final set in the process of preparation: 'I received the Holy Ghost over a year ago, hallelujah, with the Bible evidence of speaking in tongues as the spirit gives utterance. I praise him for ever getting me ready for His coming.'[692]

Finally, tongues were so thoroughly connected with eschatology that Tomlinson speculated that at

> the sounding of the trumpet when the dead in Christ shall be brought forth from their graves singing that strange and beautiful song, the strains of which have never fallen on mortal ear … the tongues as the Spirit gives utterance will be brought into use in a way scarcely thought of before.[693]

I. The Nature of Glossolalia

1. Missionary Tongues and Xenolalia

Missionary tongues and Xenolalia were not as pronounced as in other publications. While one can find anecdotal accounts, and there was a desire for MT, the *COGE's* position was similar to other Pentecostal publications. Tomlinson and the *COGE* followed the tension in periodicals like *TBM* and *AF*: while leaving room for genuine and rare occurrences,[694] it was not the norm.[695] Occasionally there was a report of someone's glossolalia being a

---

[691] A.J. Tomlinson, 'Christ Is Coming', *COGE* 6.29 Jul 17, 1915), p. 2; cf. A.J. Tomlinson, 'Be Careful And Wise', *COGE* 6.34 (Aug 21, 1915), p. 1.

[692] J.H. Lance, 'Dawson, Ala.', *COGE* 6.25 Jun 19, 1915), p. 4.

[693] Tomlinson, 'Tongues, Tithes, Knowledge', p. 1. Speculation and strong opinion were common for Tomlinson. For example, because tongues speech was so common, he was looking forward to some of the CG members being translated like Elijah to instill the fear of God in people, A.J. Tomlinson, 'Translation Power', *COGE* 9.9 (Mar 2, 1918), p. 1.

[694] We 'often hear people speak in other tongues and the messages are often understood by those who have the knowledge of other languages … if we cut out the manifestations and demonstrations of the Holy Ghost in our meetings and homes we will fall into dead formality in only a very few days', A.J. Tomlinson, 'Faith, Love, And Power', *COGE* 9.16 (Apr 30, 1918), p. 1. Tomlinson pointed to the other signs when confronted with an occurrence of missionary tongues that was debunked, Tomlinson, 'On The Bible Line', p. 1

[695] 'It is not stated (in the Bible) that the other tongues were understood as they were by the different nationalities (as) in the first instance', Tomlinson, 'The Opposition Weakening', p. 1.

known language.⁶⁹⁶ For example, 'another native boy (South African) came and received the baptism of the Holy Ghost, and spoke in the English language, which was unknown to him'.⁶⁹⁷ And a missionary noted a special anointing to speak in Chinese with greater fluency than her studies had provided:

> I had prayed … that the Lord would open my ears and loose [sic] my tongue and … He most blessedly answered prayer and the Chinese noticed right away the great change … it was hard to get back to my English, but instead it was easier to use Chinese praises and blessings … He was answering prayer and making the Chinese language mine.⁶⁹⁸

Occasionally, someone testified of xenolalia: 'the first night I received the baptism of the Holy Ghost with the Bible evidence. The Spirit sang through me, and later spoke in five or six different languages'⁶⁹⁹ or 'now I am saved sanctified and filled with the blessed Holy Ghost, and when He came He testified in a language I knew nothing about'.⁷⁰⁰ Perry would go so far as to say that 'there is absolutely no evidence to sustain' the idea that tongues were used for preaching.⁷⁰¹

2. Heavenly Anthem

The HA was very well received for its beauty and divine source, and was considered both a spiritual gift and the equivalent of evidential glossolalia. Susan McKinney's testimony was typical: 'we had a glorious Pentecostal shower the last night at the meeting, with singing in tongues and dancing'.⁷⁰²

---

⁶⁹⁶ Edith Brawner, 'Maitland, Fla (2).', *COGE* 1.15 (Oct 1, 1910), p. 6; W.A. Wilcox, 'Mater, Ky.', *COGE* 8.42 (Oct 27, 1917), p. 2.
⁶⁹⁷ *COGE* 1.3 (Apr 1, 1910), p. 4; cf. D.F. Baldree, 'Fargo, Ga.', *COGE* 8.26 (Jul 7, 1917), p. 4.
⁶⁹⁸ Mrs. P.R. Rushin, 'Missionary', *COGE* 8.29 (Jul 28, 1917), p. 2.
⁶⁹⁹ C.R. Curtis, 'A Word of Testimony', *COGE* 1.1 (Mar 1, 1910), p. 6; cf. Eary A. Nelson, 'Allentown Pennsylvania', *COGE* 1.8 (Jun 15, 1914), p. 6.
⁷⁰⁰ Mrs. Lunie Thomas, 'Lula, Fla.', *COGE* 1.15 (Oct 1, 1910), p. 8.
⁷⁰¹ Perry, 'What is the Use of Speaking in Tongues #2', p. 3.
⁷⁰² Susan McKinney, 'Chokoloskee, Fla.', *COGE* 5.3 (Jan 17, 1914), p. 8; cf. J.W. Buckalew, 'Report from Bro. Buckalew', *COGE* 5.8 (Feb 21, 1914), p. 5; Lorena Cotton, 'Safety Harbor, Fla.', *COGE* 6.3 (Jan 16, 1915), p. 2; Editorial Notes, *COGE* 6.20 (May 15, 1915), p. 2.

Testimonies of the HA gave it high praise. For example, it was 'the most beautiful of melodies to the glory of God',[703] and 'I have never heard anything so beautiful and soul-ravishing in my life'.[704]

The HA was the Holy Spirit using human vocal organs to speak and praise. Tomlinson stated that 'the heavenly chorus' is 'the singing by the lips of the Holy Ghost through human lips as he played upon the vocal cords'.[705] The presence of God was sensed during the HA: 'all of a sudden someone was up singing in other tongues. The moment she began singing the power of God struck me in both hands, and ran to my elbows. *I was convinced of it being the word of God*'.[706] One article noted that 'no one can possibly join in when it is sung, except those who are baptized in the Holy Spirit; and even the baptized saints can sing in this chorus only as the Spirit moves upon them to do so'.[707]

The HA was considered the functional equivalent of the Bible sign for the uninitiated. For example, she 'received the Holy Ghost at home. The Spirit took her tongue and she began to sing in another language, and she said it was the sweetest music she ever heard.'[708] But for the Spirit-baptized believer, the HA was a gift: 'I received the gift of the Holy Ghost and sang in an unknown tongue'.[709]

Occasionally, atypical things occurred in the environment of the HA. Some claimed to understand what was being sung in glossolalia. For example, 'it was thought that my wife sung from the seventh to the fourteenth Psalms',[710] and 'God gave us the interpretation ... she fell in the aisle and soon began to sing in the Spirit, and then, oh how the Spirit did speak through her the wonderful things of God'.[711] Some noted the ability to play the organ without study. For example, 'one sister played the organ under the

---

[703] Howard B. Tutter, 'Mansfield, Illinois', *COGE* 6.5 (Jan 30, 1915), p. 4.
[704] 'Manifestations of the Spirit', p. 4.
[705] A.J. Tomlinson, 'Supernatural Occurrences', *COGE* 1.5 (May 1, 1910), p. 1.
[706] T.L. McLain, 'The Latter Rain', *COGE* 1.1 (Mar 1, 1910), p. 5 (emphasis added).
[707] 'Manifestations of the Spirit', p. 4.
[708] Evans, 'Report', p. 4.
[709] Jonah L. Shelton, 'Ruskin, Tenn.', *COGE* 1.15 (Oct 1, 1910), p. 5.
[710] Milton Padgett, 'Miami, Fla.', *COGE* 1.6 (May 15, 1910), p. 3.
[711] W.F. Bryant, 'Work In The Tellico Mountains of TN', *COGE* 1.7 (Jun 1, 1910), p. 8.

power, and she did not know a thing about playing, but the Spirit carried her there'.[712]

3. Passive Speech and the Nature of Glossolalia

At times, the *COGE* expressed a belief that the Holy Spirit completely took over an individual upon SB and that she was completely passive. Though it was never the subject of a thorough examination by the contributors to the *COGE*, there was a great deal of difficulty expressing the interaction between the human and divine. W.G. Anderson noted the overwhelming nature of IE:

> every one who has been baptized with the Holy Ghost and spoke in other tongues know [sic] that there was at least a short period in which there was no consciousness of what was going on and as to whether the soul was in the body or out of the body God only could know ... talking in tongues is not possible for man to do it is God who talks.[713]

Many testified that the Spirit 'spoke' for himself,[714] but some phrased it as an overpowering of the person. For example, 'the blessed Holy Comforter came and testified by taking my tongue and using it in speaking in an unknown language'.[715] Mary Etta Hooper compared it to dying for a period of time.[716] Tomlinson taught that 'the Holy Ghost has complete control and utters words through lips of clay independent of any effort of the individual'; whereas, when exercising the gift of tongues one 'can control the speaking'.[717] At times Tomlinson would seem to say that the human was overwhelmed by the divine, but then clarifies the indescribable interaction between the two:

---

[712] W.L. Reynolds, 'Carrollton, Ala.', *COGE* 6.8 (Feb 20, 1915), p. 4; cf. Geo. T. Brouayer, 'Whitebluff, Tenn.', *COGE* 7.2 (Jan 8, 1916), p. 2; Clifford Bishop, 'Brooksville, Fla.', *COGE* 8.1 (Jan 6, 1917), p. 3.

[713] Anderson, 'Baptized with the Holy Ghost', p. 3.

[714] For example, 'He has filled me with the blessed Holy Ghost, who speaks for Himself', Mary Wood, 'Nassau, N.P., Bahama Islands', *COGE* 1.4 (Apr 15, 1910), p. 6; cf. Azille Pirkle, 'Chickamauga, Ga', *COGE* 1.18 (Nov 15, 1910), p. 7; Bowker, 'Charlotte, Tenn.', p. 3; passim.

[715] Rev. J.D. Reneker, 'Orlando, Fla.', *COGE* 1.12 (Aug 15, 1910), p. 7.

[716] 'I went down for the Holy Ghost at 9 o'clock Monday night and I died until 5 o'clock Tuesday evening. When I came back to this world I was speaking in tongues'. Mary Etta Hooper, 'Cocoa, Fla.', *COGE* 7.34 (Aug 19, 1916), p. 3.

[717] Tomlinson, 'The Holy Ghost', p. 1.

when the Holy Ghost comes into our bodies to abide, He always gives the utterance ... He both moves our bodies and uses our tongues in some language to suit Himself ... There are two persons in one body ... How the soul feasts while in *special communion* with the Holy Ghost. *You talk to him and then he talks to you. Your physical ear may not understand His words but your soul will be flooded with the sweetness and glory of heaven.*[718]

Note the difficulty others had: 'I hardly realized what happened for some time; but after a while I found myself',[719] and 'He came in He talked for Himself and I know all about it, for I was there'.[720] Most were aware that they were speaking but were unaware of the content.[721] However, Mrs. Naomi Murphy knew that the Spirit 'began to talk about Jesus'.[722] Tomlinson added that 'the Spirit does not keep such control all the time. He leaves a person to himself a good deal of the time and here is where wisdom is needed.'[723]

V. The International Pentecostal Holiness Church – *The Pentecostal Holiness Advocate*

A. History of the Revival

The International Pentecostal Holiness Church (IPHC) was the result of the merger of the Fire-Baptized Holiness Church (FBHC), the Pentecostal Holiness Church (PHC), and the Tabernacle Pentecostal Church (TPC).[724] These three denominations were established before the ASM revival and believed in 'a "second

---

[718] Tomlinson, 'Holy Ghost and Us', p. 1 (emphasis added).
[719] C.A. Rowland, 'Hayesville, N.C.', *COGE* 8.46 (Nov 24, 1917), p. 4.
[720] H.L. Gillet, 'Parrish, Fla.', *COGE* 5.45 (Nov 14, 1914), p. 7.
[721] For example, 'the blessed Holy Ghost came in and took my tongue and used it. He spoke something, that I don't know what it was,' Mrs. B.A. Carter, 'Manatee, Fla.', *COGE* 6.4 (Jan 23, 1915), p. 3.
[722] Mrs. Naomi Murphy, 'Pittsburgh, Ga.', *COGE* 1.12 (Aug 15, 1910), p. 6.
[723] A.J. Tomlinson, 'The Holy Ghost And Wisdom', *COGE* 9.31 (Aug 3, 1918), p. 1; cf. A.J. Tomlinson, 'To The Praise of His Glory', *COGE* 10.16 (Apr 19, 1919), p. 1.
[724] H. Vinson Synan, 'International Pentecostal Holiness Church' in Stanley Burgess (ed.), *NIDPCM* (Grand Rapids, MI: Zondervan, rev. and expanded edn, 2002), pp. 798-801 (799). The first merge was between the FBHC and the PHC on January 31, 1911 and the second merge occurred in 1915 between the PHC and the TPC, Synan, 'IPHC', *NIDPCM*, p. 800; cf. Synan, *Old Time Power*, p. 128.

work of grace" following conversion'.⁷²⁵ They had been impacted by either the National Holiness Association's (NHA) work⁷²⁶ or other sanctification-oriented 'non-Wesleyan preachers',⁷²⁷ and believed that 'a fresh outpouring of the Holy Spirit was the greatest need of the church'.⁷²⁸ These 'small holiness groups joined the ranks of the Pentecostal movement after 1906 under the ministry of Gaston Barnabas Cashwell', where they experienced and 'accepted the Pentecostal "initial evidence" teaching'.⁷²⁹ Each of these three churches had its own story.

First, the FBHC⁷³⁰ originated out of the Iowa Holiness Association, where in 1895, Irwin 'sought for and received an experience that (John) Fletcher referred to as a "baptism of burning love"'.⁷³¹ Irwin believed it was a '"third blessing" for all the sanctified, (and was) called the "baptism of fire"'.⁷³² Theologically, this

---

⁷²⁵ Synan, *Old Time Power*, p. 6.

⁷²⁶ Synan calls the WH Movement, 'the mother of the modern Pentecostal revival', Synan, *Old Time Power*, p. 7. The NHA was founded in 1867 to 'revive and spread the experience of entire sanctification', p. 23 It was denounced in 1894 by the Methodists for two reasons: 1) 'the independent nature of the National Holiness Association', and 2) the Methodists began to 'question the doctrine of sanctification as a second blessing', pp. 31-32; cf. pp. 35, 38; Dayton, *Theological Roots*, pp. 35-108; Stephens, *The Fire Spreads*, pp. 15-55; Synan, *Holiness-Pentecostal Tradition*, pp. 22-43.

⁷²⁷ For example, N.J. Holmes, a Presbyterian minister and the founder of the TPC, was 'filled with the baptism of the Holy Ghost', as a 'definite experience of sanctification' after a visit to D.L. Moody, Synan, *Old Time Power*, p. 126. Synan notes there were other 'champions of sanctification' who were outside of the normal Methodist family but aligned theologically: Charles G. Finney, John H. Noyes, A.B. Earle, and William E. Boardman, Synan, *Old Time Power*, p. 19.

⁷²⁸ Synan, *Old Time Power*, p. 8.

⁷²⁹ Synan, 'International Pentecostal Holiness Church', pp. 799, 800. Synan finds it significant that 'the 1911-1915 mergers ... indicated a doctrinal unity ... (and) no doctrinal compromises necessary', Synan, *Old Time Power*, p. 129.

⁷³⁰ Originally called the Fire-Baptized Holiness Association, it changed its name to the FBHC in 1902, Synan, *Old Time Power*, p. 60.

⁷³¹ Synan, 'International Pentecostal Holiness Church', p. 799. Synan notes that, 'according to his (Irwin's) reading of Fletcher, many early English Methodists testified to an experience beyond salvation and sanctification which they called "the baptism of burning love"', Synan, *Old Time Power*, p. 45.

⁷³² Synan, 'International Pentecostal Holiness Church', p. 799; cf. Stephens, *The Fire Spreads*, pp. 179-85; Synan, *The Holiness-Pentecostal Tradition*, pp. 51-60; Goff, *Fields White unto Harvest*, pp. 54-57.

idea that the baptism of the Holy Ghost is an experience separate from both regeneration or sanctification is probably the most important doctrinal contribution of the movement. This later became the basic foundation of the Pentecostal Movement, with the single addition of glossolalia as the 'initial evidence'.[733]

Irwin was a dynamic speaker who attracted thousands and influenced many future leaders of the Pentecostal movement, including Joseph H. King and possibly Parham.[734] Despite strict holiness standards, Irwin's teaching found fertile soil in the hearts of 'Holiness people who were dissatisfied with their experience of sanctification (and) were strongly attracted to a teaching that offered more'.[735] The classical WH movement condemned Irwin's *more*, calling it the 'third blessing heresy', or 'third blessingism', forcing Irwin to start his own organization in August, 1898.[736] The FBHC grew rapidly, especially in the South and Midwest, and Irwin incorporated several scientific-sounding spiritual experiences[737] into meetings that 'were (already) characterized by shouting and dancing before the Lord'.[738] When Irwin fell into sin in 1900, the FBHA was at its peak.[739] His fall exposed two weaknesses in the movement: its dependence upon a single dynamic personality and that

---

[733] Synan, *Old Time Power*, p. 61; cf. Phillips, *Quest*, pp. 138-39.

[734] Historians disagree on the level of influence Irwin and the FBHC had on Parham. Here they are listed from lesser to greater influence: Goff, *Fields White unto Harvest*, p. 56; Synan, *Old Time Power*, p. 54; Stephens, *The Fire Spreads*, p. 189; Phillips, *Quest*, pp. 136, 135.

[735] For example, no neckties, adornment or eating of pork, Synan, *Old Time Power*, pp. 51, 119, 125. Synan, *Old Time Power*, p. 47.

[736] Synan, *Old Time Power*, p. 47; cf. H.V. Synan, 'Fire-Baptized Holiness Church' in Stanley Burgess (ed.), *NIDPCM* (Grand Rapids, MI: Zondervan, rev. and expanded edn, 2002), p. 640.

[737] Irwin gave these post sanctification experiences scientific names like the baptism of dynamite, lyddite, oxidite, and selenite, in an effort to draw analogies of power from contemporary discoveries. For an irenic and full explanation, see Phillips, *Quest*, pp. 128-35.

[738] Synan, 'International Pentecostal Holiness Church', p. 799. Synan notes the existence of 'emotional phenomena that had characterized the Cane Ridge revivals earlier in the century. Those receiving "the fire" would often shout, scream, speak in other tongues, fall into trances, receive the holy dance and holy laugh, and even get the "jerks"', Synan, *Holiness-Pentecostal Tradition*, p. 52.

[739] At that time the FBHC was in 'ten American states and two Canadian providences', Synan 'FBHC', *NIDPCM*, p. 640.

the seeking of 'ever greater experiences of religious excitement' would strain credibility and eventually become unscriptural.[740] Seminary-trained King succeeded Irwin and 'had the discouraging task of seeing most of the organization crumble away'.[741] However, in 1907, through the ministry of Cashwell, the ASM's revival resuscitated the FBHC.[742] King received his Pentecostal baptism with other tongues[743] and in 1908, 'the church amended its doctrine to include the Pentecostal view on tongues, thus becoming the first official Pentecostal denomination in the U.S.'[744] King served as IPHC's general superintendent from 1917 to 1946.[745]

Second, the PHC[746] was founded as the Holiness Church of North Carolina (HCNC) by evangelist Ambrose B. Crumpler who was 'determined to bring the holiness movement to his native state'.[747] Two years after 'the holiness movement had been officially discredited in southern Methodism' (1896), a revival broke out under Cumpler's ministry 'that rivaled the great awakenings of the antebellum camp meeting era'.[748] Significant among those

---

[740] Synan, *Old Time Power*, p. 55

[741] Synan, *Old Time Power*, p. 59. King was elected on July 2, 1900. He was a graduate from the School of Theology at U.S. Grant University (now University of Chattanooga), he was an evangelist in Georgia, then the 'ruling elder of Ontario and pastor of the Toronto church when the call came to assume the editorship of *Live Coals* in March 1900', p. 58.

[742] Synan notes that 'the ministers of the Fire-Baptized Holiness Church were especially interested in hearing Cashwell', Synan, *Old Time Power*, pp. 101-102. He also notes the dynamic effect of the ASM revival on the western states, pp. 116-18.

[743] Synan, Old Time Power, p. 102. Cf. Synan, Holiness-Pentecostal Tradition, p. 117.

[744] Synan 'FBHC', *NIDPCM*, p. 640.

[745] H.V. Synan, 'Joseph Hillery King' in Stanley Burgess (ed.), *NIDPCM* (Grand Rapids, MI: Zondervan, rev. and expanded edn, 2002), pp. 822-23. His long tenure was interrupted once from 1941-45, when another led the PHC.

[746] Several names preceded IPHC: the Pentecostal Holiness Church of North Carolina (1900), then the HCNC (1901), then the Pentecostal Holiness Church (1909), and finally it was changed to IPHC in 1975, Synan, 'International Pentecostal Holiness Church', pp. 799-800.

[747] Synan, 'International Pentecostal Holiness Church', p. 799.

[748] Synan, *Old Time Power*, p. 68.

touched was G.F. Taylor.[749] Crumpler was a dynamic preacher who 'declared he had not committed a sin since his "second blessing"'[750] and was critical of Methodism's lack of holiness.[751] He broke with the Methodist Church in 1899[752] over holiness and issued a call to 'several independent holiness groups … for a meeting in Fayetteville to organize a new denomination', called the HCNC.[753] Crumpler settled in Goldsboro, North Carolina, built a large congregation and published a bimonthly paper called *The Holiness Advocate*.[754] News of the ASM revival in 1906 'electrified' holiness people and 'the "tongues" doctrine quickly became the number one issue within holiness circles'.[755] When Cashwell held a meeting in Dunn, North Carolina on December 31, 1906,[756]

---

[749] Synan, *Old Time Power*, p. 73. Taylor would go on to found the Falcon Holiness School, publish Sunday School materials, serve as General Superintendent (1917-19), and become the founding editor for the *Pentecostal Holiness Advocate*, cf. Synan, 'George Floyd Taylor', pp. 1115-16.

[750] Synan writes, 'this claim made him (Crumpler) famous and controversial. It became the central attraction of his meetings and stirred up passions pro and con', Synan, *Old Time Power*, p. 69; cf. pp. 71, 73.

[751] Crumpler was fond of calling the Methodist church 'the church of the holy refrigerator,' or 'the old theater-going, whiskey-drinking, card-playing, tobacco-using, secret lodge-loving, oyster-frying, ice cream supper, dancing church', Synan, *Old Time Power*, p. 74.

[752] Crumpler had an on/off relationship with the Methodist church, breaking with the church twice (1898 & 1899) cf. Synan, *Old Time Power*, pp. 73-79. He rejoined the Methodist church because he was 'determined to overturn Rule 301' which required evangelists to get prior local pastoral approval before ministering in a location, H.V. Synan, 'Ambrose Blackman Crumpler', in Stanley Burgess (ed.), *NIDPCM* (Grand Rapids, MI: Zondervan, rev. and expanded edn, 2002), p. 566. After he lost control of the HCNC, 'he returned to the Methodist Church, where he remained for the rest of his life', p. 566.

[753] Synan, *Old Time Power*, p. 79. 'It is not known if this was called as a session of the "North Carolina Holiness Association"' or a call to reformulate Crumpler's first denomination, 'The Pentecostal Holiness Church', which had not met since 1897; cf. pp. 75, 76.

[754] Synan, *Old Time Power*, pp. 80-82.

[755] Synan, *Old Time Power*, p. 94.

[756] Synan writes, 'every holiness preacher on the East Coast, it seemed, wanted to investigate the new doctrine to actually see and hear for himself an Azusa recipient as he spoke in the strange new tongues', Synan, *Old Time Power*, p. 98. The Dunn revival was so significant to the Pentecostal movement that Synan calls the Dunn revival, 'Azusa Street East', Synan, *Holiness-Pentecostal Tradition*, p. 114, cf. pp. 114-17.

Crumpler did not attend[757] but his 'preachers listened in awe as Cashwell spoke with other tongues ... and scores of people quickly received the Pentecostal baptism and spoke in other tongues "as the Spirit gave utterance"'.[758] Taylor received his Pentecost there and in 1907 'published a ringing defense of the new Pentecostal doctrine entitled *The Spirit and the Bride*', which proved timely.[759] Timely because Crumpler's attitude toward glossolalia changed from 'cautiously welcoming' to 'taking an extremely strong editorial position against the "tongues crowd"'.[760] 'After a great struggle' in 1908, 'Crumpler walked out of the life of the church he had founded'.[761] In 1909, the HCNC renamed itself the PHC.[762] The FBHC and the PHC merged on January 31, 1911, taking the name of the latter.[763]

Third, the TPC[764] was formed when Nickles J. Holmes 'accepted the second blessing teaching of D.L. Moody'[765] and 'received a definite experience of sanctification' in 1896.[766] That brought him into conflict with the Presbytery Synod of South Carolina; whereupon he left the Presbyterian Church 'to found an independent congregation' in 1898.[767] Other Presbyterian churches in the area, mostly South Carolina, that had been touched by the WH movement followed Holmes' lead.[768] He started the Holmes

---

[757] Synan writes, 'Crumpler, who was previously engaged to hold a meeting in Florida during the same month of the Dunn revival ... let it be known ... he was going to oppose it. However, in Crumpler's absence, most of his preachers received the experience and accepted Cashwell's doctrine of initial evidence', Synan, *Old Time Power*, p. 101.

[758] Synan, *Old Time Power*, p. 99; cf. Robeck, *Azusa Street*, pp. 216-19.

[759] Synan, *Old Time Power*, p. 107; cf. Synan 'Taylor', *NIDPCM*, p. 1115.

[760] Synan, *Old Time Power*, pp. 100, 106.

[761] Synan, *Old Time Power*, pp. 105, 108.

[762] Synan, *Old Time Power*, p. 110.

[763] Synan, 'International Pentecostal Holiness Church', p. 800.

[764] The TPC was originally named Brewerton Independent Presbyterian Church then the Tabernacle Presbyterian Church and then changed to the TPC 'in keeping with its new doctrinal position', Synan, *Old Time Power*, p. 127, cf. p. 126.

[765] Synan, 'International Pentecostal Holiness Church', p. 799.

[766] Synan, *Old Time Power*, p. 126.

[767] Synan, 'International Pentecostal Holiness Church', p. 799.

[768] Synan, 'International Pentecostal Holiness Church', p. 799.

Bible and Missionary Institute[769] in 1898 and sent out several missionaries.[770] This small group also accepted the Pentecostal 'teaching under the ministry of G.B. Cashwell and Taylor'.[771] The TPC merged with the PHC in 1915.[772]

H. Vinson Synan wrote that the IPHC 'would have a heavy southern accent, with by far the largest concentration of strength in the Southeast'.[773] Nevertheless, 'the church did grow to be one of the most respected and influential churches in the Pentecostal movement'.[774]

B. The 'Initial Evidence'

In the first edition of the *PHA,* Taylor made it clear that 'the church and paper stand for the Baptism of the Spirit to be received subsequent to heart cleansing, and that the initial evidence of this Baptism is the speaking in tongues as in Acts 2:4'.[775] It is believed that statement is the first use of the phrase 'initial evidence', a full eleven years after the ASM revival.[776] The official doctrinal statement came a few months later:

> we believe also that the Pentecostal Baptism of the Holy Ghost and fire is obtainable by a definite act of appropriating faith on the part of the fully cleansed believer, and that the initial evidence of the reception of this experience is speaking with

---

[769] It is 'now known as Holmes College of the Bible, (and) is the oldest Pentecostal educational institution in the world', H.V. Synan, 'Nickels John Holmes' in Stanley Burgess (ed.), *NIDPCM* (Grand Rapids, MI: Zondervan, rev. and expanded edn, 2002), p. 730.

[770] Synan, *Old Time Power,* pp. 126-29.

[771] Synan, *Old Time Power,* p. 126.

[772] Synan, 'International Pentecostal Holiness Church', p. 800.

[773] Synan, *Old Time Power,* p. 129.

[774] Synan, *Old Time Power,* p. 135.

[775] G.F. Taylor, 'Our Policy', *PHA* 1.1 (May 3, 1917), pp. 9-10 (9); cf. G.F. Taylor, 'Basis of Union: Chapter XV, The Baptism of the Holy Ghost', *PHA* 1.38 (Jan 17, 1918), pp. 8-9. The *PHA* was consistent in capitalizing the word 'baptism' when referring to SB because it signified the abiding presence of the Holy Spirit in the believer. Taylor wrote, 'the phrase "Baptism of the Holy Ghost" is not found in the Bible, but we build the phrase from the words of John the Baptist', G.F. Taylor, 'Basis of Union: Chapter XV, the Baptism of the Holy Ghost', *PHA* 1.38 (Jan 17, 1918), pp. 8-9.

[776] Cf. Robeck, 'William J. Seymour and "The Bible Evidence"', p. 89.

other tongues as the Spirit gives utterance (Luke 11:13; Acts 1:5; 2:1-4; 8:17; 10:44-46; 19:6).[777]

Yet there must have been pressure to 'back down' from this position as seen by the consistent defence of IE's terminology, exegesis, and theological arguments.[778]

First, 'initial evidence' was the primary phrase used by the leaders in their teachings. However, others phrases such as the 'first sign', the 'first miraculous manifestation', and the 'first evidence'[779] were used to highlight the points that tongues are not 'the **greatest** phase of the Baptism' and that '*other* Bible evidences, or rather results' should follow the believer.[780] The phrase, 'as the Spirit gives utterance' was used consistently to distinguish evidentiary tongues from the gift of tongues and was the preferred nomenclature in testimonies.[781]

Second, the *PHA* paralleled other Pentecostal periodicals in using the pattern from the book of Acts. Taylor wrote that 'in every place in the New Testament where there is a record of one receiving the Baptism of the Holy Spirit, there is a record of the speaking in tongues as the Spirit gave utterance'.[782] Even Acts 8 'is

---

[777] G.F. Taylor, 'Basis of Union: Chapter XVII, Initial Evidence', *PHA* 1.40 (Jan 31, 1918), pp. 4-5; cf. G.F. Taylor, 'Editorial: Examination Questions', *PHA* 6.28 (Nov 9, 1922), p. 4; F.M. Britton, 'We Believe #1', *PHA* 6.43 (Feb 22, 1922), p. 2.

[778] G.F. Taylor, 'Editorial Thoughts #2', *PHA* 1.20 (Sep 13, 1917), p. 1; G.F. Taylor, 'Editorial: Do All Speak with Tongues', *PHA* 3.10 (July 3, 1910), pp. 8-10; G.F. Taylor, 'Editorial: Speaking in Tongues', *PHA* 3.11 (Jul 10, 1919), pp. 8-10. 'There is a tendency among some people today to let up on the real evidence of the Baptism of the Holy Ghost ... let us all stand by the old landmarks and let those people who come through in our meetings know that if they did not speak in tongues they did not get the Baptism of the Holy Ghost', O.C. Wilkins, 'Reports', *PHA* 3.36 (Jan 1, 1920), p. 15.

[779] J.H. Pate, 'Goldsboro, N.C.', *HA* 6.4 (Jun 1, 1906 [?]), p. 3; Taylor, 'Editorial: Speaking in Tongues', p. 8; G.F. Taylor, 'Editorial: Our Church History #2', *PHA* 4.47 (Mar 24, 1921), p. 9.

[780] Taylor, 'Editorial: Speaking in Tongues', p. 8 (bold original, italics added).

[781] For example, 'in 1 Cor. 14, Paul is comparing the gift of tongues with the gift of prophesy, and that has nothing to do with the speaking in tongues as the Spirit gives utterance', Taylor 'Editorial: Speaking in Tongues', p. 8; Lewis Sawgalsky, 'Testimony and Experience of Lewis Sawgalsky, Converted Jew', *PHA* 1.6 (Jun 7, 1917), p. 5.

[782] Taylor, 'Editorial: Speaking in Tongues', p. 10; G.F. Taylor, 'Sunday School Lesson: Peter and John in Samaria – Acts 8:4-39', *PHA* 3.40 (Jan 29, 1920), p. 2; W.H. McCurley, 'The Baptism of the Holy Ghost', *PHA* 1.23 (Oct

strongly in favor'.[783] In a retort to opponents, Taylor begs, 'for one single Bible instance where any of these (other spiritual gifts) were given as the "initial evidence or result" of the Baptism apart from speaking in tongues'.[784] Additionally, both Jn 15.26 and Mk 16.17, 18 were foundational. Though Jesus was not thought to speak in tongues,[785] Jn 15.26 was seen as prophetic, a 'thus saith the Lord' passage[786] that was now fulfilled: 'I praise God for being filled with the Holy Ghost, like they got on the day of Pentecost. I praise God that when He came *He testified, just like He said he would*.'[787] Based on this passage, F.M. Britton believed that tongues were expected on the Day of Pentecost:

> if it had not been that they were expecting the Holy Ghost to speak when He came they would no doubt have claimed Him before or by the time they got back to Jerusalem, because they had as much as any holiness man you ever saw without speaking in other tongues.[788]

4, 1917), pp. 2-3, 6; Taylor, 'Basis of Union: Chapter XVII, Initial Evidence', pp. 4, 5.

[783] Taylor, 'Editorial: Speaking in Tongues', p. 10. The argument of Deane Alfred and Adam Clarke, is that that the Samaritans 'saw' something that caused Simon to want the ability to convey the Holy Spirit, Taylor, 'Peter and John in Samaria – Acts 8:4-39', p. 2. Additional to Alfred and Clarke's exegetical argument, F.M. Britton parallels Acts 8 to Acts 11 and concludes 'that as the two lessons are paralleled into separate meetings ... they must have been both the same in speaking in other TONGUES', F.M. Britton, 'We Believe #4', *PHA* 6.49 (Apr 5, 1922), pp. 3-4.

[784] Taylor, 'Editorial: Do All Speak with Tongues', p. 10; cf. Taylor, 'Editorial: Speaking in Tongues', p. 10.

[785] G.F. Taylor, 'Question Box #357', *PHA* 3.7-8 (Jun 12 & 19, 1919), p. 11. An exception was Emma Bullin, who had a vision where 'I heard Jesus singing and speaking in tongues', Emma Bullin, 'Testimonies', *PHA* 5.23 (Oct 6, 1921), p. 14.

[786] 'We have several passages that would sustain our position without twisting the meaning a particle ... John 15:26 says "When the Comforter is come ... he shall testify of me." Here is a "Thus saith the Lord"', Taylor, 'Editorial: Do All Speak with Tongues', p. 10; cf. J.A. Culbreth, 'The Comforter', *HA* 6.4 (Jun 1, 1906 [?]), p. 5; C.F. Noble, 'Questions Answered', *PHA* 3.23 & 24 (Oct 2 & 9, 1919), p. 5; J.G. Kimrey, 'Do All Speak with Tongues?', *PHA* 4.6 (Jun 10, 1920), p. 2; W.M. Branch, 'The Baptism of the Holy Ghost', *PHA* 4.32 (Dec 9, 1920), pp. 3, 4; Marie Thompson, 'Pentecost as a Preparation for Work', *PHA* 5.1 (May 5, 1921), p. 13. F.M. Britton, 'We Believe #2', *PHA* 6.44 (Mar 1, 1922), p. 2.

[787] Coy Lawson, ' Winston-Salem, N.C.', *PHA* 1.38 (Jan 17, 1918), p. 11.

[788] Britton, 'We Believe #2', p. 2.

Mark 16.17, 18 was another significant passage,[789] but it was used to highlight a balanced view of tongues in contrast to excesses of those who longed for signs and wonders.[790]

Third, though evidential tongues were primarily supported from the pattern in the book of Acts, two facets were theologically driven. Both of these were seen in the earlier writings by Crumpler, who was reluctant to embrace the Bible sign.[791] Crumpler saw little difference between SB and sanctification because they 'are so closely connected and related that they are really treated in Scripture as one'.[792] Also, tongues were not the sole evidence of SB: 'we see no reason why the outpouring of the blessed Spirit should not be accompanied by the *manifestation of all His gifts* in these days'.[793] Even though Crumpler had a glossolalic-experience, these positions would lead him eventually to walk away from his own denomination.[794] To be theologically feasible Taylor had to separate

---

[789] Taylor affirmed its place in the book of Mark despite the textual issues, G.F. Taylor 'Editorial: Mark 16:9-20 Examined', *PHA* 2.17 (Aug 22, 1918), pp. 8-10 (8).

[790] G.F. Taylor, 'Question Box #10', *PHA* 1.2 (May 10, 1917), pp. 12, 13; C.F. Noble, 'Christianity, Men and Methods #5', *PHA* 1.37 (Jan 10, 1918), p. 2: Taylor 'Editorial: Mark 16:9-20 Examined', p. 8; G.F. Taylor, 'Editorial: Mark 16:9-20 Reviewed', *PHA* 2.18 (Aug 29, 1918), pp. 8-10 (8); G.F. Taylor, 'Question Box #324', *PHA* 2.48 (Mar 27, 1919), p. 6; G.F. Taylor, 'Question Box #665', *PHA* 4.39 (Jan 27, 1921), p. 10; R.B. Beall, 'The Holy Spirit Is a Person', *PHA* 1.3 (May 17, 1917), p. 2; Noble, 'Questions Answered', p. 5.

[791] Crumpler wrote: 'we are not able to accept some of the teaching, especially that which affirms that *all who receive* the Baptism of the Spirit *will necessarily* speak with new tongues', A.B. Crumpler, 'Press the Revival – Reject the Counterfeit', *HA* 6.4 (Jun 1, 1906 [?]), p. 4 (emphasis added). Possibly as early as June 1, 1906 (edition is undated), J.A. Culbreath stated that the IE issue was 'waiting for a settlement', but in support of IE encouraged readers not fear 'a "third blessing"' and 'never stop short of the same manifestation of Pentecost', Culbreth, 'The Comforter', p. 5.

[792] A.B. Crumpler, 'The Baptism of Fire', *HA* 6.5 (Jun 15, 1906), p. 4; cf. A.B. Crumpler, 'The Work of the Holy Spirit', *HA* 6.5 (Jun 15, 1906), p. 4.

[793] A.B. Crumpler, 'Editorial: Extracts and Comments', *HA* 7.3 (May 15, 1907), p. 1. Emphasis mine. A prior edition states 'every Bible scholar that follows this believer in God's word will find that the first sign that follows the ones that receive the Holy Ghost was the speaking in "tongues"', Pate, 'Goldsboro, N.C.', p. 3.

[794] A.B. Crumpler, 'Editorial: He Satisfies: He Abides', *HA* 7.4 (Jun 1, 1907), p. 1; G.F. Taylor, 'Basis of Union: Who Are We?', *PHA* 1.24 (Oct 11, 1917), pp. 4-6; G.F. Taylor, 'Editorial: Our Church History #1', *PHA* 4.46 (Mar 17, 1921), pp. 8-9.

evidentiary glossolalia from both sanctification and the gift of tongues.

To answer the question, 'do all speak in tongues' upon SB? Taylor explained that the 'plain language of Acts 2:4' really meant 'all'.[795] Further, Taylor had to show that the tongues as a sign and as a gift were distinct theologically even though they were identical in essence. Paul advocated for a wide distribution of spiritual gifts based on 1 Cor. 12.7-31 for the common good; whereas, the book of Acts revealed a single initiatory sign for everyone Spirit baptized.[796] Taylor articulated that if Acts 2.4

> was the (Pauline) *gift of tongues*, it is exceedingly strange that all the one hundred and twenty received the same gift ... if God really means to give diversity of gifts as the initial evidence of the Baptism, it is exceedingly strange that He failed to do so in the very first case.[797]

Further, if it was the gift of tongues at Ephesus (Acts 19), it was curious that Paul 'raised no objections to the whole twelve speaking in tongues at one time', which was contrary to his own guideline in 1 Cor. 14.27.[798] Therefore, to those who argued that any of the nine gifts could suffice as an evidence of SB, Taylor concluded that 'if all who receive the Baptism in Apostolic day spoke in other tongues, *it is logical* that all who receive the Baptism today will do the same'.[799] Finally, a pragmatic defence was that 'the only preachers that have ever been successful in getting persons through to Pentecost have been those who have stood for speaking in tongues as the evidence'.[800]

---

[795] G.F. Taylor, 'Question Box #79', *PHA* 1.18 (Aug 30, 1917), p. 8; cf. G.T. Alady, 'Testimonies', *PHA* 1.19 (Sep 6, 1917), p. 13; G.F. Taylor, 'Editorial: Speaking in Tongues', p. 9.

[796] 'I do not see that *all receive* any one of these nine gifts. The Spirit divides the gifts as He pleases, and He may not please to give one of these gifts to *every one*', Taylor, 'Editorial: Speaking in Tongues', p. 9 (emphasis added). His argument from 1 Cor. 12.11 emphasizes that 'all these are the work of one and the same Spirit, and he gives them to each *one just as he determines*'.

[797] Taylor, 'Editorial: Speaking in Tongues', p. 9. Further, if Acts 2.4 'was the gift of tongues there is a serious conflict between Acts 2:4 and 1 Cor. 12'.

[798] G.F. Taylor, 'Editorial: 1 Corinthians 14', *PHA* 5.3 (May 19, 1921), p. 8; cf. Taylor, 'Editorial: Speaking in Tongues', p. 9.

[799] Taylor, 'Editorial: Speaking in Tongues', p. 10 (emphasis added).

[800] Taylor, 'Editorial Thoughts #2', p. 1.

C. Responses to Critics

1. Signs and Wonders

Because they covered roughly the same geographic area, the PHC faced competition and criticism from its neighbour the CG. These early issues of the *PHA* revealed an ecclesiology and a function for signs and wonders in contrast to the CG.[801] The CG claims

> they are the only church that preaches the whole Bible, and that certain unscriptural signs must follow them or they will be lost ... (they say) we as a church have compromised, and *we don't believe in the signs of tongues*, healing ... they claim to go beyond us in signs, by handling snakes and coals of fire, hot lamp chimneys, stovepipes, etc.[802]

Mark 16.17, 18 was carefully explained several times to counter such excesses. For example, two of Mark's signs were 'for the benefit of others – casting out devils, and healing the sick; two signs (were) for the benefit of the believer – taking up serpents, and drinking deadly things'.[803] However, glossolalia was the natural consequence of the

> incoming of the glorified 'Word.' (John 1:1, 14; 7:39) ... it is the *inevitable result* of a certain cause ... The early church did not speak in tongues just to display power; they spoke in tongues as the *inevitable result* of their Baptism, and the blessings that followed were the God-given overplus.[804]

Contributors to the *PHA* had strong words for believers who

---

[801] 'This paper undertakes to assist the church in its work, but not to *magnify the church* out of due proportion ... (but to) use great caution *not to ridicule any other church*. The editor knows several who have undertaken to build up their organization at the expense of others', Taylor, 'Our policy', p. 10; cf. G.F. Taylor, 'Editorial thoughts #1', *PHA* 1.1 (May 3, 1917), p. 1; C.F. Noble, 'Christianity, Men, and Methods #1', *PHA* 1.22 (Sep 27, 1917), pp. 3-4 (3); W.J. Noble, 'Beware the Church of God', *PHA* 1.24 (Oct 11, 1917), p. 3; G.F. Taylor, 'Sunday School Lesson', *PHA* 3.28 (Nov 6, 1919), pp. 2, 3; S.W. Sublett, 'The Church', *PHA* 4.19 (Sep 9, 1920), pp. 2, 3.

[802] Noble, 'Beware the Church of God', p. 3 (emphasis added).

[803] Taylor, 'Question Box #10', pp. 12, 13.

[804] Taylor, 'Question Box #10', p. 13 (emphasis added).

sought signs.[805] For example, because of Jesus' admonition that an adulterous generation seeks a sign, tongues were not to be sought: 'we are not to get our eyes on the sign, but the One who will show the sign ... we are to see the signs follow us ... (but) we are not to follow the signs at all'.[806] However, God did provide signs. There was Noah's rainbow and the virgin birth, so too 'the sign of the Baptism of the Holy Ghost ... is speaking in tongues as the Spirit gives utterances'.[807] Tongues are 'a token or manifestation of the Spirit to show you He has come to abide forever ... to let you know He has come'.[808] This glossolalia 'should be held sacred, and should not be used for show'.[809]

2. Cessation

Cessationism was largely countered by appeals to Scripture[810] and not just experience.[811] For H.C. Webb cessationism was a non-issue because spiritual 'gifts were concomitants of the (ongoing) gospel;'[812] cessationists 'quote no Scripture in support' and conveniently forget that 'Paul said, "forbid not to speak in tongues"'.[813] He mused in a retort, 'why not believe also that the Epistles written to the churches were intended only for that generation of Christians then living, and therefore nothing preached

---

[805] For example, they had 'another spirit', Noble, 'Christianity, Men, and Methods #1', p. 3; a 'heathenish practice', Noble, 'Christianity, Men and Methods #5', p. 2; they are 'playing with demons', R.M. Ramlie, 'Osceola, Ark.', *PHA* 2.14 (Aug 1, 1918), p. 12; it is 'next to blasphemy', Taylor 'Editorial: Mark 16:9-20 Reviewed, p. 8; and is a commitment to 'presumptuous things', Taylor, 'Question Box #665', p. 10.

[806] C.F. Noble, 'Christianity, Men, and Methods #2', *PHA* 1.24 (Oct 11, 1917), p. 12; cf. C.F. Noble, 'Christianity, Men, and Methods #4', *PHA* 1.29 (Nov 15, 1917), p. 14.

[807] W.O. Akers, *PHA* 5.37 (Jan 12, 1922), p. 2; cf. Z.A. Sutphin, 'Our Weekly Sermon: The Holy of Holies', *PHA* 4.10 (Jul 8, 1920), p. 3.

[808] C.F. Noble, 'Christianity, Men and Methods #3', *PHA* 1.28 (Nov 8, 1917) p. 6.

[809] Taylor 'Editorial: Mark 16:9-20 Reviewed', p. 9.

[810] W.J. Martin, 'Our Weekly Sermon: Acts 12:5', *PHA* 6.9 (Jun 29, 1922), p. 4.

[811] 'These are days of conflicting theories, and largely on individual experiences ... We must not interpret the Word of God by our experiences, but every experience must be interpreted in the light of God's Word – the infallible rule of our faith and practice', A.B. Crumpler, 'Bible Repentance', *HA* 7.4 (Jun 1, 1907), p. 1.

[812] H.C. Webb, 'Spiritual Gifts', *PHA* 2.44 (Feb 27, 1919), pp. 6-7 (7).

[813] Webb, 'Spiritual Gifts', pp. 6-7.

or written by the apostles is binding on any Christian now?'.[814] A query about the prophecy that tongues will cease (1 Cor. 13.8) was answered that 'in heaven or in the age to come there will be but one language, and so tongues will be unnecessary'.[815] The latter rain was still a popular biblical metaphor for SB[816] but it was not as prominent a response to cessationism as with the earlier periodicals.[817]

3. Counterfeits

Taylor wrote, 'we do not say that all who claim to speak in tongues have the Baptism; but what we say is that all who receive the Baptism will speak in tongues as the Spirit gives utterance'.[818] That is because 'the devil counterfeits everything good'; the genuine tongues begets counterfeits.[819] 'These demons know everybody, and they can exactly mimic the voice ... (and) there are many examples in the New Testament of evil spirits speaking through men'.[820] The genuine can be discerned from the counterfeit by revelation or by the lack of love and unity.[821] Taylor bluntly stated that,

> there are those who speak in tongues, *but are void of love*, and surely such speaking in tongues is as sounding brass, or tinkling cymbal ... are they speaking by the power of the Holy Spirit? They are not ... (but) by the spirit of the devil.[822]

The genuine could also be discerned by holiness: 'we know the devil can sing, pray, testify, talk in tongues, shout, and preach; but

---

[814] Webb, 'Spiritual Gifts', p. 7.
[815] G.F. Taylor, 'Question Box #911', *PHA* 5.46 (Mar 16, 1922), p. 14.
[816] G.F. Taylor, 'Question Box #1335', *PHA* 7.30 (Nov 22, 1923), p. 6.
[817] F.M. Britton, 'We Believe #3', *PHA* 6.47 (Mar 22, 1922), pp. 4, 5.
[818] G.F. Taylor, 'Sunday School Lesson: Peter and Cornelius – Acts 10:1-11:18', *PHA* 3.41 (Feb 5, 1920), p. 3.
[819] Byon A. Jones, 'Our Weekly Sermon: Anti-Pentecost', *PHA* 6.19 (Sep 7, 1922), p. 2.
[820] G.F. Taylor, 'Basis of Union, Chapter XXVI: Spiritualists', *PHA* 1.52 (Apr 25, 1918), p. 4.
[821] G.F. Taylor, 'Sunday School Lesson: Love – 1 Corinthians 13', *PHA* 3.7 & 8 (Jun 12 & 19, 1919), pp. 2-3; A.L. Sisler, 'Holiness God's Plan', *PHA* 4.15 (Aug 12, 1920), p. 2.
[822] Taylor, 'Sunday School Lesson: Love – 1 Corinthians 13', pp. 2-3; G.F. Taylor, 'Editorial: Essentials #1', *PHA* 4.36 (Jan 6, 1921), pp. 8-10; G.F. Taylor, 'Editorial: Essentials #2', *PHA* 4.37 (Jan 13, 1921), p. 9 (emphasis added).

he cannot live holy'.[823]

At a lesser level, there were pretenders[824] and godly people who could speak evil with their tongues. Such speech was like gangrene according to Taylor.[825] For example: 'oh, Jesus trim off the evil speaking from our tongues'[826] and 'pray that the Lord will keep my tongue from speaking evil words, and that I may do the Lord's will'.[827] And it was possible for some who wanted to make a show and 'strain a point to shout, or talk in tongues' while 'in the flesh'.[828] The solution for this was to

> yield your members to God as his instruments of righteousness … let's hold the doors of our lips, and only let the Holy Ghost himself speak through us as he will. I do not only believe we speak with other tongues as the Spirit gives utterance, in other tongues, but I do believe He ought to have the complete control of our tongue to speak in English, and let Him speak alone and be controlled by Him.[829]

D. Testimonies

The content and style of the testimonies in the *PHA* were very similar to other early Pentecostal periodicals, especially the *COGE*. Spirit Baptism was simply added to the phraseology of earlier second-work testimonies in the *PHA*. For example, a typical early *HA* testimony was: 'I want to praise God that I am still saved and sanctified and healed'.[830] A typical later *PHA* was: 'I am glad I have the old time religion, saved, sanctified, and *baptized with the Holy Ghost, with the evidence of speaking with other tongues as the spirit gives utterance*'.[831] Nevertheless, other themes are clearly seen through the voice of these early pioneers.

The most common references to glossolalia in the testimonies were those of gratitude and praise for the experience, like Robert

---

[823] H.S. Brooks, 'Testimonies', *PHA* 3.52 (Apr 22, 1920), p. 14.
[824] E.D. Norton, 'Testimonies', *PHA* 6.14 (Aug 3, 1922), p. 13.
[825] G.F. Taylor, 'Editorial: Eating Cankers', *PHA* 5.35 (Dec 29, 1921), pp. 4-5; cf. R.B. Beall, 'The Advocate and it's Editor', *PHA* 5.32 (Dec 8, 1921), p. 3.
[826] Mrs. Le McDaniel, 'Testimonies', *PHA* 5.6 (Jun 9, 1921), p. 15.
[827] Mrs. Mary E. Rowe, 'Request For Prayer', *PHA* 6.20 (Sep 14, 1922), p. 5.
[828] G.F. Taylor, 'Editorial', *PHA* 2.7 (Jun 13, 1918), p. 9
[829] C.F. Noble, 'Reports', *PHA* 3.14 (Jul 31, 1919), p. 6.
[830] F.J. Cain, *HA* 6.3 (May 15, 1906), p. 2.
[831] D.M. Dennis, 'Testimonies', *PHA* 2.47 (Mar 20, 1919), p. 15 (emphasis added).

Bartlett: 'I am so glad because I have the evidence of speaking in tongues as the spirit gave me utterance'.[832] The second most common reference were the revival reports that usually included the number of people who spoke in tongues.[833] Insightful for this study were the testimonies that described their experience apart from the standard phraseology. For example, Elwood Dobbins was amazed that 'the blessed Holy Ghost came in and spoke through the lips of clay in other tongues'.[834] Others elaborated on the confirmation of the Holy Spirit's presence:

> some people say they do not know whether they received the Holy Ghost or not, but if they received it like I did, they will know when they get it, for he will take control of your tongue and speak through you ... I went to the altar and had only been there a short while until the Holy Ghost begun to sing through me. That was the sweetest music I ever heard. I could not help singing, and I did not want to help it.[835]

Some commented on the Holy Spirit's communication. He 'spoke for Himself',[836] 'testified for Himself',[837] and 'talked for Himself'[838] about the 'mysteries of God'[839] or 'testified of Jesus'.[840] Sadie Turlington even broke into glossolalia while writing out her testimony:

> I just pressed my case up to God for the Baptism of the Holy Ghost according to the Bible evidences, for I knew He had

---

[832] Robert Bartlett, 'Testimonies', *PHA* 2.26 (Oct 24, 1918), p. 8.

[833] For example, 'there were fifty saved, fifteen sanctified as a second work of grace, eight receive the Holy Ghost, and spoke in other tongues as the spirit gave utterance (Acts 2:4)', J.F. Ramsey, 'Evangelistic Notes', *PHA* 1.12 (Jul 19, 1917), p. 10.

[834] Elwood A. Dobbins, 'Testimonies', *PHA* 6.32 (Dec 7, 1922), p. 15.

[835] Lizzie Miller, 'Testimonies', *PHA* 3.6 (Jun 5, 1919), p. 14.

[836] B.C. Sellers, 'Reports', *PHA* 1.8 (Jun 21, 1917), p. 7; G.H. Montgomery, 'From The Holmes Bible and Missionary Institute', *PHA* 6.45 (Mar 8, 1922), p. 7.

[837] Mrs. Virginia Hayes, 'Testimonies', *PHA* 6.4 (May 25, 1922), p. 7. This phrase followed the example of testimonies in the *PHA*, cf. Ada H. Barnes, 'The Witness Stand', *HA* 7.3 (May 15, 1907), p. 2; Sudie Turlington, 'My Experience', *PHA* 7.3 (May 15, 1907), p. 2.

[838] A.C. Knight, 'Greensboro, N.C.', *PHA* 1.44 (Feb 28, 1918), p. 5.

[839] Mrs. Cora Barnett, 'Nicholson, GA', *PHA* 1.43 (Feb 21, 1918), p. 12.

[840] D.M. Dennis, 'Marion, S.C.', *PHA* 1.28 (Nov 8, 1917), p. 9.

never testified for Himself with tongue, and nothing anooi onomyrd [sic] my tongue, and nothing short of this would ever satisfy me.[841]

The glossolalist's emotion was usually joy. For example, glossolalia 'starts the joy bells ringing in my soul' wrote Mrs. Annie Brott.[842] There often was a section entitled 'Our Dead' that honoured those who 'died in the faith'.[843] Remembrances of SB,[844] and public displays of glossolalia helped friends and relatives mourn.[845] There were many accounts of the dying speaking or singing in tongues just moments before their death. For example, 'in her last hours she remained shouting, praising the Lord, and talking in tongues, until the death angel took her away',[846] and 'she shouted and talked in tongues 10 minutes before she died'.[847] Mrs. M.E. Oden

> shouted and praised the Lord for gifts, and Jesus appeared to her in a vision and she spoke to Him. The Spirit sang through her in other tongues, 'The Eastern Gates,' 'Hallelujah Bells,' 'If You Don't Bear the Cross You'll not Wear the Crown,' and many other beautiful songs that we had never heard.[848]

---

[841] Turlington, 'My Experience', p. 2.

[842] Mrs. Annie Brott, 'Testimonies', *PHA* 3.37 (Jan 8, 1920), p. 15; cf. Katie Parker, 'My Experience', *HA* 6.4 (Jun 1, 1906), p. 6; Crumpler, 'Editorial: He Satisfies: He Abides', p. 1; F.M. Britton, *PHA* 1.22 (Sep 27, 1917), p. 12; J.O. Lehman, 'Letter from S.A.', *PHA* 2.27 (Oct 31, 1918), p. 13; O.E. Sproull, 'The Blessing of Sorrow', *PHA* 6.8 (Jun 22, 1922), p. 4.

[843] G.R. Thomas, 'Tribute to the Memory of Mrs. Rebecca Harrison', *PHA* 2.28-29 (Nov 7 & 14, 1918), p. 14; T.M. Bizzell, 'Testimonies', *PHA* 2.36 & 37 (Jan 2, 9, 1919), p. 12.

[844] J.L. Oliver, 'Our Dead: Mrs. Zadie Farmer', *PHA* 2.52 (Apr 24, 1919), p. 16; cf. W.J.A. Russum, 'Our Dead: Sister N.E. Dudley', *PHA* 3.27 (Oct 30, 1919), p. 7; D.B. Causey, 'Our Dead: MC. D. Brown', *PHA* 4.32 (Dec 9, 1920), p. 6.

[845] Mrs. C.A. Stroud 'Our Dead: Gertrude Johnson', *PHA* 2.42 (Feb 13, 1919), p. 10; His Brother, 'Our Dead: Noel Earl Sutphin', *PHA* 3.37 (Jan 8, 1920), p. 6; 'Our Dead', *PHA* 3.43 (Feb 19, 1920), p. 6.

[846] Sam D. Page, 'In Memory of Our Darling Sister', *PHA* 2.30 & 31 (Nov 21 & 28, 1918), p. 14.

[847] Mrs. N.E. Greenwood & Mrs. J.P. Spain, 'Our Dead: Sister Melton', *PHA* 5.6 (Jun 9, 1921), p. 11.

[848] Mrs. M.E. Oden, 'Our Dead: Eula Melvin', *PHA* 3.7 & 8 (Jun 12 & 19, 1919), p. 16; cf. Mrs. E.D. Reeves, 'Our Dead: Spencer', *PHA* 3.34 (Dec 18,

Tongues provided courage and faith during times of suffering, E.D. Reeves wrote 'our faith is made stronger by her death'.[849] Deathbed glossolalia occasionally preceded a plea for the dying's loved ones to turn to faith[850] or a prophetic word.[851] One young man arose from the dead speaking in tongues and was commissioned to 'tell his father and mother that this is the right gospel'.[852]

E. Sanctification
Two theological facets of glossolalia touched upon the doctrine of sanctification: is SB sanctification? And, 'can God use a dirty vessel?'

In the very first edition of the *PHA* Taylor wrote that SB was 'subsequent to heart cleansing',[853] a third work of grace in the fivefold WH tradition that was distinct from justification and sanctification. References to this difficult theological issue were not as numerous as expected;[854] however, there were some hints of the ongoing debate. For example, Mrs. F.H. Davis wrote that 'the M.P. Holiness Church is here and there are some good Christians in it too, but they will not have the tongues, as they claim they receive the Holy Ghost at sanctification'.[855] Also, J.A. Synan wrote,

I thought according to the doctrine of the holiness folks that I

1919), p. 12; H.O. Harris, 'Myrtius Rebecca Roland', *PHA* 5.21 (Sep 22, 1921), p. 7.

[849] E.D. Reeves, 'Our Dead: Mrs. Helen Reese', *PHA* 3.47 (Mar 18, 1920), p. 7. For honesty about suffering and glossolalia cf. Minnie Finely, 'Our Dead: Parks Sorrow', *PHA* 5.44 (Mar 2, 1922), p. 4. For those claiming no pain, cf. S.D. White, 'Our Dead: Mrs. M.J. Fort', *PHA* 5.37 (Jan 12, 1922), p. 6; A.H. Butler, 'Our Dead: Sister Francis Elks', *PHA* 5.47 (Mar 23, 1922), p. 11.

[850] L.R. Graham, 'Our Dead: Malissis Jan Tew Crabtree', *PHA* 2.48 (Mar 27, 1919), p. 13; A Friend, 'Mrs. W.T. Freeman', *PHA* 5.24 (Oct 13, 1921), p. 8.

[851] Mrs. A.H. Butler, 'Obituary', *PHA* 1.33 (Dec 13, 1917), p. 7.

[852] David Niswander, 'Testimonies', *PHA* 3.10 (Jul 3, 1919), p. 13.

[853] Taylor, 'Our Policy', p. 9.

[854] There is no mention of SB or tongues in the two 'Basis of Union' articles on entire sanctification, where one would expect a mention of this distinction, G.F. Taylor, 'Basis of Union, Chapter XII: Entire Sanctification', *PHA* 1.35 (Dec 27, 1917), pp. 4, 5; G.F. Taylor, 'Basis of Union, Chapter XIII: The Second Work of Grace', *PHA* 1.36 (Jan 3, 1918), pp. 2, 3; cf. G.F. Taylor, 'Basis of Union, Chapter 1: Who Are We?', *PHA* 1.24 (Oct 11, 1917), p. 4.

[855] Mrs. F.H. Davis, 'Testimonies', *PHA* 3.47 (Mar 18, 1920), p. 13; cf. McCurley, 'The Baptism of the Holy Ghost', p. 2; E.C. Bolen, *PHA* 1.25 (Oct 25, 1917), p. 9; Mrs. Lena Swann, 'Bessemer, Ala', *PHA* 1.43 (Feb 21, 1918), p. 7; E.H. Blake, 'Our Weekly Sermon', *PHA* 6.8 (Jun 22, 1922), pp. 2, 3..

had received the Holy Ghost, but when I heard a Pentecostal sermon preached from Acts 2:4, and witnessed the demonstrations, shouting, dancing, and speaking in tongues I could see they had something more than I had ... I have not spoken in tongues.[856]

In the WH schema of the *ordo salutis* the three parts were neatly divided up,[857] even at the popular level.[858] For example: 'I am still saved, sanctified, and baptized with the Holy Ghost with the initial evidence of speaking in other tongues as the spirit gives utterance'[859] or 'I praise God this day finds me saved, sanctified, and the precious Holy Ghost still abides with the Bible evidence of speaking in other tongues as the Spirit gives utterance according to Acts 2:4'.[860]

Logically, sanctification had to precede SB in order for the genuine Holy Spirit to abide in the believer:

the experience of sanctification *prepares us for* the Baptism of the holy Ghost, and to preach or teach, that we can receive the Baptism of the Holy Ghost without being sanctified ... (is to) be possessed with inbred sin ... (and) at enmity against God ... and lay(s) the foundation for an awful spirit of deception and a *counterfeit baptism*.[861]

Therefore, there were numerous appeals to put away tobacco,[862] 'worldly amusements',[863] and to overcome sin.[864] In fact, Taylor believed the standard for fellowship should not be tongues, because

---

[856] J.A. Synan, 'Testimonies', *PHA* 3.43 (Feb 19, 1920), p. 13.

[857] H.C. Webb, 'Baptized Into One Body', *PHA* 4.30 (Nov 25, 1920), pp. 2-3.

[858] Remarkably, two early and knowledgeable writers defended against the conversion/initiation view of SB long before Dunn wrote *The Baptism in the Holy Spirit* (Westminster Press, 1970). Cf. D.B. Southern, 'The Baptism of the Holy Ghost', *PHA* 4.1 (May 6, 1920), pp. 3-4; Webb, 'Baptized Into One Body', pp. 2-3.

[859] J.B. Horton, 'Testimonies', *PHA* 6.52 (Apr 26, 1922), p. 12.

[860] Mrs. Allie Surglon, 'Testimonies', *PHA* 6.8 (Jun 22, 1922), p. 13.

[861] A.H. Butler, 'Our Weekly Sermon', *PHA* 6.50 (Apr 12, 1922), p. 3 (emphasis added). Britton, 'We Believe #2', p. 2.

[862] F.M. Britton, 'The Indwelling Spirit', *PHA* 1.5 (May 31, 1917), p. 3; G.W. Stanley, 'Reports', *PHA* 6.9 (Jun 29, 1922), p. 11.

[863] H.E. Oxendine, 'Our Weekly Sermon: Holiness', *PHA* 5.48 (Mar 30, 1922), p. 2; cf. H.H. Morgan, 'Shine', *PHA* 5.43 (Feb 23, 1922), p. 4.

[864] Bell Lewis, 'Testimonies', *PHA* 5.43 (Feb 23, 1922), p. 13.

'sanctification as a second definite work of grace is the balance wheel to the experience and doctrine of the Christian church'.[865] Spirit baptism was not just about power, or tongues, or 'the gifts of the Spirit as recorded in the 12th of 1st Corinthians, but the coming of the Holy Ghost HIMSELF to abide with us forever'[866] and 'entering into the very closest relations and fellowship with God'.[867] It was the abiding Spirit, or Jesus himself, who spoke through the believer:

> the Baptism of the Holy Ghost is the bringing of the glorified Jesus into our hearts and lives ... they (the apostles) were filled with the glorified Word. This glorified Word began to manifest itself through the vocal organ. This is one reason why they spake in tongues.[868]

At times, this view caused a bifurcation of the Spirit's indwelling into two parts, where just 'because we have received the Spirit (sanctification) is not proof that we have received the Spirit Himself (SB)'.[869]

F. Purposes for Glossolalia

Compared with other early periodicals, the purpose for tongues in the *PHA* was more implicit than explicit. However, a careful examination revealed the same purposes for glossolalia as the other periodicals, that is: power, prayer, praise, and revelation.

1. Power

'We see where Jesus told his disciples that they should receive power after the Holy Ghost had come on them', wrote Mrs. P.S. Foster, 'it seems that after we receive the Baptism of the Holy Ghost we are better equipped to work for God and can tell more about his wonderful works'.[870] Further, Jesus promised spiritual power and modelled it after his baptism at the Jordan River: 'the purpose of the Holy Spirit's coming upon Jesus at this particular

---

[865] Taylor, 'Editorial Thoughts #2', p. 1.
[866] Southern, 'The Baptism of the Holy Ghost', p. 3.
[867] Webb, 'Baptized Into One Body', pp. 2-3.
[868] G.F. Taylor, 'Sunday School Lesson: The Holy Spirit Our Helper', *PHA* 2.51 (Apr 17, 1919), pp. 2, 3; cf. Beall, 'The Holy Spirit Is a Person', p. 2.
[869] Beall, 'The Holy Spirit Is a Person', p. 2.
[870] Mrs. P.S. Foster, 'Modern Pentecostal Missionary Work', *PHA* 5.1 (May 5, 1921), p. 14.

time was to anoint Him for service. Jesus did His work through the power of the Spirit.'[871] Most believed that SB was to facilitate evangelism: 'last Monday night the power of God fell in such a wonderful way that the people shouted and danced, and talked in tongues, and sinners rush to the altar until the altar was full'.[872] However, testimonies that mentioned power usually referred to powerful altar experiences.[873] Only a few stated they could share their faith more effectively. Glossolalia was not the power in itself, but a sign of the Spirit's power within. Mrs. Ethel Cook poignantly wrote that 'the Baptism is the gift of power on a clean life'.[874]

2. Prayer

Taylor's response to the question 'what is the good of speaking in other tongues' highlighted prayer as the foremost reason for tongues: '(1 Cor. 14:4). It is always good to edify yourself in him ... It is always good to speak to God (1 Cor. 14:2) ... (1 Cor. 14:14, 15). It is always good for your spirit to pray ... It is good to let the Holy Spirit speak through you. (Acts 2:4).'[875] 'There is praying in tongues', he wrote, 'but then the understanding is unfruitful.'[876] He explained that prayer could go beyond human reason and vocabulary to praying in the Spirit.

3. Praise

R.B. Beall noted it was 'usually overlooked' that the purpose of tongues was to 'praise and glorify' God.[877] He clarified that

> speaking in tongues as the Spirit gave utterance was used as *a doxology or praise* ... (whereas) the speaking in tongues with the

---

[871] W.J. Noble, 'Sunday School Lesson: Baptism and Temptation of Jesus', *PHA* 4.22 (Sep 30, 1920), p. 4.

[872] R.B. Beall, 'Notice', *PHA* 2.45 &46 (Mar 6 & 13, 1919), p. 11

[873] For example, 'we began to pray and the power began to fall on the saints and brother Jesse Banks began to talk in tongues, and the first thing I knew I was shouting, and I sang in tongues and danced under the power of God', Nora Dawson, 'Testimonies', *PHA* 4.7 (Jun 17, 1920), p. 12.

[874] Mrs. Ethel Cook, 'Testimonies', *PHA* 3.6 (Jun 5, 1919), p. 12; cf. Joseph F. Barnett, *PHA* 1.25 (Oct 25, 1917), p. 7; cf. Lucinda Banister, 'Testimonies', *PHA* 3.37 (Jan 8, 1920), p. 16.

[875] G.F. Taylor, 'Question Box #595', *PHA* 4.19 (Sep 9, 1920), p. 10.

[876] Taylor, 'Editorial: 1 Corinthians 14', p. 9.

[877] Beall, 'The Holy Spirit Is a Person', p. 3.

gift is different; it is not so much a doxology or praise, but *a sign* to unbelievers, Mark 16:17; 1 Cor. 14:22.[878]

Testimonies such as Brother Glenn's confirmed that praise was one of the purposes for glossolalia: 'he would rejoice, speak in tongues, and praise God'.[879]

4. Revelation

Occasionally, there were revelations of Jesus when speaking in tongues.[880] Taylor wrote

> this Pentecostal Baptism ... brings to the heart a revelation of the son of God. It is the glorified Jesus coming back to dwell in us. It is Jesus crowned within. It is a revelation of the Trinity to the soul. It is the Father, Son, and Holy Spirit coming to dwell with us and in us forever.[881]

Testimonies affirmed that revelation occasionally accompanied glossolalia. For example, Mollie Kenny wrote that 'when I yielded to the Lord he showed me a large ball of fire, and just above that I saw the head of Jesus'.[882] Emma Bullin was walking and talking in tongues when 'I saw Jesus in the Spirit looking down on the whole human family full of love, pity, and tender mercy'.[883] However, Crumpler had a vision of 'the awful doom of the soul lost in hell' that was concomitant with his IE.[884]

G. Tongues as a Gift of the Holy Spirit

Another purpose for glossolalia was the public gift of tongues. The *PHA* presented the most thorough explanation on the gifts

---

[878] Beall, 'The Holy Spirit Is a Person', p. 3 (emphasis added). Cf. Taylor, 'Editorial: Our Church History', p. 9.

[879] W.J. Martin, 'Our Dead: Owen S. Glenn', *PHA* 5.23 (Oct 6, 1921), p. 11; cf. A.H. Butler, 'Kingston, N.C.', *PHA* 2.16 (Aug 15, 1918), p. 11; Fletcher Ackerman, 'Testimonies', *PHA* 3.11 (Jul 3, 1919), p. 11; R.L. Stewart, 'Our Dead: Mrs. Mary Anne Fisher', *PHA* 3.45 (Mar 4, 1920), p. 11.

[880] W.A. Cramer, 'Pentecost at Cleveland', *HA* 6.4 (Jun 1, 1906), p. 4; Ackerman, 'Testimonies', p. 11.

[881] Taylor, 'Basis of Union: Chapter XV, the Baptism of the Holy Ghost', p. 9.

[882] Mollie Kenny, 'Testimonies' *PHA* 1.12 (Jul 19, 1917), p. 15.

[883] Bullin, 'Testimonies', p. 14.

[884] Crumpler, 'Editorial: He Satisfies: He Abides', p. 1.

of tongues to date. First, Luke's view of glossolalia was complimentary with Paul's:[885]

> Paul was teaching on the same line with Peter, as he spoke on the day of Pentecost after one hundred and twenty received the Holy Ghost and began to speak in other tongues ... Paul was teaching the doctrine of Repentance, Justification, Sanctification, the *Baptism of the Holy Ghost*, Divine Healing, *and the Nine Spiritual Gifts*.[886]

Second, IE was the doorway to the spiritual gifts. 'After this filling, we believe there are several gifts of the Spirit, that all these gifts are under the control of the person receiving them, and that the gift of tongues is one of them.'[887]

Third, that the gift of tongues differed from IE was addressed multiple times.[888] 'A person with the gift of tongues can speak any language on earth at will.'[889] 'He may speak any language under the sun at his own discretion. Though I do think that the one who has the gift of tongues will be led by the Spirit as to when to exercise the gift.'[890] Also, the tongues of IE did not need to be interpreted. Even though all glossolalia could be interpreted, 'I have my doubts whether it all should be interpreted ... (because) some things are spoken directly to God, and need to be interpreted'.[891] The regulation by Paul in 1 Cor. 14.27, was for 'those who have the gift of tongues as a gift ... it does not refer to speaking in tongues as the

---

[885] 'Paul never tried to regulate those who spoke in tongues as the spirit gives utterance', G.F. Taylor, 'Question Box #839', *PHA* 5.27 (Nov 3, 1921), p. 5.

[886] S.E. Stark, 'Paul's Doctrine', *PHA* 1.12 (Jul 19, 1917), p. 3 (emphasis added). Cf. Taylor, 'Editorial: Do All Speak with Tongues', p. 9; Taylor, 'Editorial: 1 Corinthians 14', pp. 8-9.

[887] Taylor, 'Editorial: 1 Corinthians 14', p. 8; cf. Webb, 'Baptized Into One Body', p. 2.

[888] G.F. Taylor, 'Question Box #32', *PHA* 1.9 (Jun 28, 1917), p. 15; G.F. Taylor, 'Question Box #732', *PHA* 4.47 (Mar 24, 1921), p. 10; Taylor, 'Editorial: 1 Corinthians 14', pp. 8, 9; Taylor, 'Question Box #839', p. 5; G.F. Taylor, 'Question Box #1108', *PHA* 6.37 (Jan 11, 1923), p. 10.

[889] Taylor, 'Question Box #32', p. 15. 'There seems to be no limit to the number of languages that might be so spoken', 'Editorial: 1 Corinthians 14', p. 8.

[890] Taylor, 'Question Box #1008', p. 10.

[891] G.F. Taylor, 'Question Box #33', *PHA* 1.9 (Jun 28, 1917), p. 15; cf. G.F. Taylor, 'Question Box #618', *PHA* 4.26-27 (Oct 28 & Nov 4, 1920), p. 10.

Spirit gives utterance'.[892]

Fourth, a closely related gift, the gift of interpretation, was 'absolutely independent of the mental powers', wrote Taylor: 'I never know it is until I say it'.[893] 'Interpretation is not translation. Men translate from one language to another with their understanding, but interpretation is given just like speaking in tongues';[894] whereupon, 'he gives his vocal organs to the Holy Spirit, and the Spirit gives interpretation'.[895] The HA could receive an interpretation.[896]

Finally, the orientation of speech for the gift of tongues was two-directional: vertically, it was communication with God for prayer[897] and personal edification.[898] Horizontally, tongues in the public setting were to be interpreted and were 'equal to the message through prophecy'.[899] This public setting for tongues and interpretation was what Paul restricted to two or three occurrences.[900] Also horizontal, occasionally, tongues were a sign to the sinners of their hard-hearts:[901] 'when I yielded to the Lord he ... gave out a message in tongues to the lost sinners, but some just stood back as hard-hearted as the devil would want them to'.[902]

H. Eschatology and Glossolalia

Compared to other early periodicals, glossolalia was not as strongly connected with eschatology. Some exceptions were that Crumpler saw tongues as evidence of the restoration of spiritual gifts

---

[892] Taylor, 'Question Box #732', p. 10.
[893] G.F. Taylor 'Question Box #41', *PHA* 1.10 (Jul 5, 1917), p. 15.
[894] G.F. Taylor, 'Question Box #1055', *PHA* 6.22 (Sep 28, 1922), p. 9.
[895] G.F. Taylor, 'Question Box #815', *PHA* 5.18 (Sep 1, 1921), p. 5.
[896] C.E. White, 'Testimonies', *PHA* 3.27 (Oct 30, 1919), p. 14.
[897] 'Often the intensity of the prayer was so great that it is impossible to express it with the understanding, and then is when the Spirit prays. (Rom. 8:26)', Taylor, 'Editorial: 1 Corinthians 14', p. 9.
[898] G.F. Taylor, 'Question Box #458', *PHA* 3.46 (Mar 11, 1920), p. 10; cf. Taylor, 'Question Box #1055', p. 9.
[899] Taylor, 'Editorial: 1 Corinthians 14', p. 9; cf. Britton, 'We Believe', pp. 4, 5.
[900] Taylor, 'Question Box #839', p. 5.
[901] Taylor expounded, 'there are some people who have hardened their hearts against God in the truth. God has given them every kind of a warning but they will not yield. In Isaiah 28:9-13 we read that God speaks to this class in other tongues as a sign that the final doom was near at hand', Taylor, 'Editorial: 1 Corinthians 14', p. 9; cf. Taylor, 'Question Box #595', p. 10.
[902] Mollie Kenny, 'Children's Corner', *PHA* 1.12 (Jul 19, 1917), p. 15.

through SB in 'this dispensation', but did not elaborate.[903] Britton noted that 'men and women in all generations had the Holy Spirit ... in the measure that belonged to their day and dispensation'.[904] Tongues was the dividing line between the former rain and the later rain: 'there was not any speaking in tongues as the Spirit gives utterance in the old dispensation, but all that received the Holy Ghost in His personal abiding fullness spoke in other tongues'.[905] Della Cobb noted that 'it will take more than' tongues 'to meet Jesus in the air ... we have to live the life and give Him the praise due Him'.[906] And Zebrum Sutphin noted that tongues were a part of the eschatological message: 'blessed indeed will it be for Jesus to come and find his servant or servants preaching the Baptism of the Holy Ghost with the same evidence that God stamped upon it at the beginning (with other tongues as the spirit gave utterance)'.[907]

I. Nature of Glossolalia

1. Singing in the Spirit

Singing in the Spirit was most often reported as an altar experience similar to Nora Dawson's: 'we began to pray and the power began to fall on the saints and brother Jesse Banks began to talk in tongues, and the first thing I knew I was shouting, and I sang in tongues and danced under the power of God'.[908] Singing in tongues was the functional equivalent for IE; it was tongues with a melody: 'I sure did get a blessing in my cup and saucer both run over ... The Holy Ghost talked in tongues and sang in tongues through me. I know I have got him.'[909] Sometimes the song was a

---

[903] Crumpler 'Editorial: Extracts and Comments', p. 1.
[904] Britton, 'We Believe', p. 4.
[905] Britton, 'We Believe', p. 4.
[906] Della Cobb, 'Who Will Be in the Air', *PHA* 6.48 (Mar 29, 1922), pp. 4-5.
[907] Zebrum Sutphin, 'Coming of the Son of Man', *PHA* 2.8 (Jun 20, 1918), p. 2.
[908] Nora Dawson, 'Testimonies', p. 12.
[909] Mrs. Fletcher Bowen, 'Testimonies', *PHA* 2.19 (Sep 5, 1918), p. 13; cf. Parker, 'My Experience', p. 6; Mrs. Florence Anderson, 'The Witness Stand', *HA* 7.4 (Jun 1, 1907), p. 2; Miller, 'Testimonies', p. 14; O.M. Millsap, 'Reports', *PHA* 3.41 (Feb 5, 1920), p. 13; Mrs. A. Gamble, 'Testimonies', *PHA* 3.52 (Apr 22, 1920), p. 14; Mrs. Nora Scarce, 'Testimonies', *PHA* 4.2 (May 13, 1920), p. 16.

familiar tune[910] and at other times a new song.[911]

2. Passive Speech

The *PHA* held the same idea as the *GOGE* that an individual was completely passive during IE:

> when one receives the Baptism of the Holy Ghost the Spirit speaks himself with the human tongue without any effort whatever on the individuals part any more than he must yield not only his tongue, but his entire being to the Holy Ghost.[912]

This was in order that the Holy Spirit could do the speaking:

> when we receive the Holy Ghost like they did at Pentecost, the Holy Ghost himself does the speaking. It is not us, but him. We find in St. John 15:26 these words … 'He shall testify of me.' We see from the reading of these words, that the Holy Ghost speaks himself.[913]

Testimonies affirmed this passive nature for IE. For example, E.J. Jarrett wrote, 'it seemed to me like my tongue was cloven tongues, then he began to speak. I could do nothing only open my mouth, and He did the rest',[914] and J.C. Conley wrote, 'the first thing I knew, I lost sight of everything and the next thing I knew the Holy Ghost had come and I was speaking in other tongues'.[915]

3. Xenolalia

Neither MT nor xenolalia were a notable part of the anecdotal or theological conversation in the *PHA*, but they were not totally absent either. For example, Lewis Sawgalsky boasted, 'it will be easy for wife and I to preach Christ in our country, as we can speak about thirteen different languages, *besides the many that the Holy Ghost*

---

[910] Scarce, 'Testimonies', p. 16; Oden, 'Our Dead: Eula Melvin', p. 16; Ackerman, 'Testimonies', p. 11; Reeves, 'Our Dead: Spencer', p. 12; Scarce, 'Testimonies', p. 16.

[911] Taylor, 'Editorial: Our Church History', p. 9; cf. Cramer, 'Pentecost at Cleveland', p. 4; J.H. King, 'A Timely Warning', *PHA* 5.11 (Jul 14, 1921), p. 2.

[912] Taylor, 'Question Box #1108', p. 10; cf. Taylor, 'Question Box #839', p. 5.

[913] Branch, 'The Baptism of the Holy Ghost', p. 4.

[914] E.J. Jarrett, 'Testimonies', *PHA* 3.31 & 32 (Nov 27 & Dec 4, 1919), p. 14.

[915] J.C. Conley, 'Testimonies', *PHA* 3.51 (Apr 15, 1920), p. 15.

speaks through us'.[916] In one playful article, C.F. Noble reported that 'there were two Chinese boys in South Carolina heard [sic] a sister speak in their own language while engaged in prayer'.[917] He also noted that the Holy Spirit speaks all the languages of the world, but that tongues were intentionally 'unknown'.[918] He believed it possible that God could grant the ability to read or write known foreign languages, just like Daniel interpreted the handwriting on the Babylonian wall.[919] Generally though, missionaries were expected to study the local language:

> I'm improving daily in my Chinese and am able to speak quite freely now. Me and my colporteurs stand on the street corners and preach for hours at a time. It is a joy unspeakable to be able to tell the story of Jesus to the Chinese in their own language.[920]

Overall, the examples listed here were rare compared to the earlier periodicals and R.B. Beall admitted that, 'some have made sad mistakes … because they had the gift of tongues and spoke the language of a certain nation (thought they) must go to that nation, but this is not Scripture'.[921]

---

[916] Sawgalsky, 'Testimony and Experience of Lewis Sawgalsky', p. 5 (emphasis added).

[917] Noble, 'Questions Answered', pp. 3-5 (3); cf. Anderson, 'The Witness Stand', p. 2.

[918] Noble, 'Questions Answered', pp. 3-4; cf. G.F. Taylor, 'Question Box #928', *PHA* 5.48 (Mar 30, 1922), p. 10.

[919] Noble, 'Questions Answered', p. 3.

[920] W.H. Turner, 'Missionary Department', *PHA* 5.31 (Dec 1, 1921), p. 3. Also, 'if we are called as a missionary, we are not to suppose that his coming is so near we have no time to prepare for our work, but must rush out without preparation. If you are called to any work, first prepare yourself for it, and if Jesus comes while you are preparing you will be just as ready as you would be if you are doing that work', G.F. Taylor, 'Looking For Jesus', *PHA* 1.29 (Nov 15, 1917), p. 9.

[921] Beall, 'The Holy Spirit Is a Person', pp. 3-4; cf. Bertha C. Doering, 'Missionary Department', *PHA* 4.33 (Dec 16, 1920), p. 12.

4

THE FINISHED WORK PENTECOSTAL PERIODICALS

'From 1906 to 1910, the Pentecostal movement fit decidedly within the Wesleyan stream of theology' and then

> in 1910, William Durham modified his theology, accommodating it to his Baptist roots. This new Pentecostal soteriology disclaimed sanctification as a second definite work of grace, seeing justification and sanctification as occurring at the moment of conversion. He based his theology on what he called the Finished Work of Christ on the cross.[1]

Durham had 'a strongly polemic temper',[2] and pushed the issue relentlessly.[3] His theology would eventually cause Pentecostalism to coalesce into three camps: WH, FW, and Oneness Pentecostal-

---

[1] Alexander, *Pentecostal Healing*, p. 150. Richard M. Riss cites the 'Keswick movement in England and the Christian Missionary Alliance' as exceptions to the WH view of sanctification, Riss, 'Finished Work Controversy', p. 638. William K. Kay notes that 'there were two relevant doctrinal schemes in circulation' at the time, WH and Keswick's higher life, William K. Kay, *Pentecostalism: A Very Short Introduction* (New York: Oxford University Press, 2011), p. 59.

[2] Menzies, *Anointed To Serve*, p. 76. For example, he strongly warned against Pentecostal churches organizing into a denomination, William Durham, 'Warning', *PT* 1.5 (Jul 1910), pp. 9-10.

[3] There is a possibility that he was just responding in kind to his opponents, Bartleman, *Azusa Street*, p. 175. Durham's writings fit with Spittler's assessment of Fundamentalism: 'Fundamentalism reacted in an intellectual style ... argumentative, logical, rational ... (and) the Bible presented inerrant factual truth', Spittler, 'Are Pentecostals and Charismatics Fundamentalists?', p. 107.

ism.⁴ Recent scholarship has shown that sometimes the WH and the FW streams share a common theology and at other times they diverge.⁵

I. Advocate and Bridge-Builder⁶ – *Triumphs of Faith*

A. History of Carrie Judd Montgomery

As a result of the newly discovered 'prayer of faith'⁷ Carrie Judd was healed from a nervous disease.⁸ She received hundreds of inquiries about 'faith cures' after her own healing was reported in the local newspaper.⁹ This prompted her to write a book called *The Prayer of Faith*.¹⁰ It was 'revolutionary' and became wildly successful because it 'was one of the earlier books published on divine healing'.¹¹ Even more letters arrived after its publication and at the

---

⁴ Brumback, *Suddenly From Heaven*, p. 105; cf. pp. 101-105.

⁵ Alexander discovered that 'the understanding of salvation and how it is obtained has directly affected the way each group theologized about healing', Alexander, *Pentecostal Healing*, p. 195. McQueen's examination of eschatology noted a distinct difference between the two streams. He concludes that the FW eschatology quickly became 'fossilized' and is less dynamic than WH's because of 'a single reference point' for salvation, McQueen, *Toward a Pentecostal Eschatology*, p. 203. Green found no distinction between the two traditions regarding the Lord's Supper, Green, *Towards a Pentecostal Theology of the Lord's Supper*, p. 178. Finally, Melissa Archer notes that both streams 'present a unified portrait of worship', Archer, *'I Was in the Spirit on the Lord's Day'*, p. 117.

⁶ 'Her contribution to the Pentecostal movement can ... be described generally in two broad roles; enthusiastic advocate and bridge-builder between movements', Daniel Albrecht, 'Carrie Judd Montgomery: Pioneering Contributor to Three Religious Movements', *Pneuma* 8.1 (1986), pp. 101-19 (111).

⁷ Her father read about Sarah Mix's account of healing in the newspaper and wrote to her about how she was healed. Mix immediately wrote back and instructed her about prayer and faith. At an agreed upon day and time, Sarah, Carrie, and her father prayed together, Jennifer A. Miskov, *Life on Wings: The Forgotten Life and Theology of Carrie Judd Montgomery (1858-1946)* (Cleveland, TN: CPT Press, 2012), pp. 19-23; cf. p. 303; Alexander, *Pentecostal Healing*, p. 26.

⁸ Miskov, *Life on Wings*, p. 21. Miskov reports that Carrie Judd was healed of hyperesthesia, 'a condition of the nerves' on February 2, 1879, p. 15.

⁹ Miskov, *Life on Wings*, p. 25. The *Buffalo Commercial Advertiser* of Buffalo, NY, ran the story on Oct. 20, 1880, Warner, 'Carrie Judd Montgomery', p. 904.

¹⁰ Carrie F. Judd, *Prayer of Faith* (Chicago and New York: Fleming H. Revell Company, 1880).

¹¹ Miskov, *Life on Wings*, p. 26. Miskov reports that by 1893, 40,000 copies had been sold and it was translated into French, Dutch, German, and Swedish, pp. 26-27. Miskov notes that it was the timing of Montgomery's story along

urging of her brother, she started the monthly publication *TOF*.¹² About that same time, she opened a healing home¹³ and spoke wherever she was invited.¹⁴ The timing and focus of her ministry 'brought her into the leadership circle of the growing faith movement'.¹⁵ Over the years her personal network of friends grew to become a virtual who's who of the healing and Pentecostal movements.¹⁶

Carrie Judd Montgomery was so 'busy running her various ministries¹⁷ that she did not have the time or energy to consider the new signs at Azusa Street', but her new husband, businessman George Montgomery, investigated it in the fall of 1906.¹⁸ Carrie

---

with her writing talent, otherwise, 'her story might have just been another … healing among a stack of many', p. 29.

¹² Miskov, *Life on Wings*, p. 27. First edition was January 1881. In 1899, Montgomery wrote the periodical 'is a monthly journal, purely undenominational, and devoted to the promotion of Christian Holiness and Divine Healing (from a scriptural standpoint alone)', p. 28.

¹³ She 'was at the beginning of the tide of healing homes' and predated John G. Lake's famous healing room by twenty years, Miskov, *Life on Wings*, pp. 35, 49. Even Parham would follow her pattern for a healing home, Miskov, *Life on Wings*, p. 35.

¹⁴ Miskov notes that C.J.M. avoided the debate about women in ministry and spoke wherever invited (Miskov, *Life on Wings*, pp. 53-54). She also became a friend and mentor to many of the famous women preachers of her day, Elizabeth Sisson, Maria B. Woodworth-Etter; Catherine Booth; missionary Minnie Abrams; Amie Semple McPherson, pp. 53-54; 72-79; 86; 131-35 (respectively).

¹⁵ Warner, 'Carrie Judd Montgomery', p. 904.

¹⁶ In addition to the friends listed in the notes above were A.B. Simpson, Charles Cullis, William E. Boardman, Elizabeth Baxter, Warner, 'Carrie Judd Montgomery', pp. 904-905. She was even 'named recording secretary to the board' of the CMA when it was organized in 1885 by Simpson, p. 905. After the ASM revival, she expanded her circle of friends to include Pentecostal pioneers, such as: Bartleman, Seymour, Boddy, Frodsham, Zelma Argue, and Francisco Olzábal, Miskov, *Life on Wings*, pp. 47, 135-38.

¹⁷ Albrecht calls her a symbolic 'religious entrepreneur', Albrecht, 'Carrie Judd Montgomery', p. 101. Her endeavours included: prison ministry, a healing home, special projects with the Salvation Army, a refuge home, camp meetings, ministerial training school, and an orphanage, Miskov, *Life on Wings*, pp. 85, 86, 86-93, 92, 95-97, 97-99, 100-105.

¹⁸ Miskov, *Life on Wings*, p. 112. It is unknown exactly when George Montgomery visited the ASM revival, but the first mention of the revival in *TOF* appears in December 1906. An editor's note simply says, 'my husband had recently visited Los Angeles and attended some of these meetings', Editor's Note, to F. Bartleman, 'Letter From Los Angeles', *TOF* 26.12 (Way of Faith) (Dec 1906), pp. 247-52 (247).

'saw that there was something more' and was soon Spirit baptized and speaking in tongues.[19] She became a founding member of the AG[20] but was careful not to sever her many friendships with non-Pentecostals, acting instead as a 'Pentecostal ambassador' and living out her belief that divine love and unity were more important than manifestations of the Spirit.[21]

B. Pre-Azusa Hints of Glossolalia

Through its large and independent subscription list, the *TOF* helped to lay the groundwork for the Pentecostal movement.[22] Even before the ASM revival, phrases like 'baptized in the Spirit',[23] 'former and latter rains',[24] and 'Pentecost/al'[25] were common parlance in *TOF*.[26] *Triumphs of Faith* promoted the idea that the gift of divine healing was still possible through faith; however, the restoration of one spiritual gift inferred the restoration of all the

---

[19] Miskov, *Life on Wings*, p. 117; cf. pp. 114-17; Carrie Judd Montgomery, '"The Promise of the Father (#1)": A Personal Testimony', *TOF* 28.7 (Jul 1908), pp. 145-49; Carrie Judd Montgomery, 'Speaking in Tongues: A Personal Testimony', *TOF* 30.11 (Nov 1910), pp. 253-55.

[20] She is listed as a 'founder' by default. Albrecht notes that 'she was listed as an A/G charter member because of her affiliation with' the COGIC, where she received ordination papers on 11/1/1914, Albrecht, 'Carrie Judd Montgomery', p. 118 n. 65. Her first self-sought credentials with the AG were on 30/11/1917, when she renewed what had been rolled over from the COGIC.

[21] Miskov, *Life on Wings*, p. 139; cf. pp. 130-31. 'While Carrie supported the Pentecostal movement, she did not cut ties with other religious organizations … Simpson invited her to speak at his meeting up until the end of his life regardless of her new affiliation', pp. 126, 131.

[22] Dayton calls the spiritual environment pre-ASM dry tinder that was 'awaiting the spark that would set it off', Dayton, *Theological Roots*, p. 174.

[23] Theodore L. Cuyler, 'The Effectual Prayer', *TOF* 26.1 (Jan 1906), pp. 8-11 (11); Charles G. Finney, 'Power From on High', *TOF* 26.11 (Nov 1906), pp. 217-20 (218-19); Clement C. Cary, 'How Some Revivals Were Brought About', *TOF* 26.11 (Nov 1906), pp. 228-31 (230).

[24] E. Sisson, 'A Call To Prayer For A World-Wide Revival', *TOF* 26.3 (Mar 1906), pp. 57-61 (58).

[25] W.W. Foulston 'How the New Pentecost is Coming', *TOF* 31.3 (Mar 1911), pp. 63-66, reprint; *The Concentrated Life* (Sept 1906). Montgomery editor's note states she was unaware of the ASM revival and Ramabai's work in India, p. 63.

[26] Miskov notes that 'as early as 1885, Carrie spoke at a conference that encouraged people to seek "a special baptism of the Holy Spirit"', Miskov, *Life on Wings*, p. 229; cf. 228-32.

spiritual gifts.²⁷ Here are three pre-ASM revival examples in *TOF* that hint of glossolalia.

First, eight months before the ASM revival, Adam Clark, sounded thoroughly Pentecostal when he wrote that Spirit-led vocalization was the most effective type of prayer:

> the Spirit ... leads the saints to express themselves in words, groans, sighs or tears ... the unutterable groan is big with meaning, and God understands it, because it contains the language of his own Spirit. Some desires are too mighty to be expressed; there is no language expressive enough to give them proper form and distinct vocal sound.²⁸

Second, three months before the ASM revival, Montgomery wrote that often, full healing occurred in the presence of Jesus, where 'no human eloquence can avail ... (and) all earthly wisdom stilled. The power of human speech taken away [sic] that the *heavenly tongue* may be given instead'.²⁹

Third, one month before the ASM revival, Elizabeth Sisson pleaded for intercessors who would pray for a great revival because, during the Welsh revival,³⁰ 'we realised we were in the last days' and 'we were knee-deep in another mighty Pentecost'.³¹ Her call highlighted Joel's promise that 'we might expect a literal outpour [sic] of God's Spirit upon all flesh' during the latter rain.³²

C. Azusa Fire Spreads to *TOF*

Montgomery's introduction of tongues to her audience was cautious and measured.³³ The first intentional mention of glossolalia

---

²⁷ 'Scripture on Sickness and Healing', *TOF* 27.4 (Apr 1907), pp. 88-90.

²⁸ Adam Clark, 'He Maketh Intercession', *TOF* 25.8 (Aug 1905), pp. 188-89 (189).

²⁹ Editor, 'The Touch of His Healing Hand', *TOF* 26.1 (Jan 1906), p. 2 (emphasis added).

³⁰ Using the Welsh revival as a baseline, she believed this latter rain revival would be so great that it would 'throw the revival in Wales into the shade' of history, Sisson, 'A Call To Prayer', pp. 59-60.

³¹ Sisson, 'A Call To Prayer', pp. 57, 59. Sisson, worked at William Boardman's healing home in London from time to time. It 'was ... the place where Andrew Murray experienced his healing', Miskov, *Life on Wings*, p. 33.

³² Sisson, 'A Call To Prayer', p. 58.

³³ Alexander observes that despite her entrepreneurial spirit, 'she did not enter into these new arenas without caution', Alexander, *Pentecostal Healing*, p. 27. 'Negative opinions were balanced by a growing group of friends from

in *TOF* likely occurred in October, 1906, and was rather cryptic: 'there is a state of deep, divine fervor described in Scripture as a "hot heart," "fervent, or boiling in spirit," and having a *"tongue of fire"*'.[34] The article called its readers 'to walk between the two extremes of cold formality ... and wild ranting fanaticism'.[35] Montgomery clearly used this article to reaffirm her boundaries. For example, the piece noted that 'true fire ... will have its demonstrations, but does not emphasize them, nor measure its sanctity by them, nor prescribe them to others, nor condemn others for not having them'.[36]

In December, 1906 Montgomery introduced glossolalia to her readers with two articles – one by Bartleman and the second by A.S. Worrell – but she wrote special notes from the editor that functioned as bookends for both.[37] The first bookend stated 'my husband has ... attended some of these meetings ... and is convinced that *the work is of God*'.[38] Then, the first sentence of Bartleman's article reads, 'I believe the Lord would have me mention a few facts, especially in regard to the feature of the "tongues" in our meetings'.[39] Bartleman pointed out that there were counterfeit tongues, but that the existence of these counterfeits only proves the existence of the genuine.[40] Cautious to not 'unduly exalt' tongues above the 'Giver of the gift', he then answered the question 'of what practical use are tongues?' First, though hesitant of xenolalia, he noted, 'there have been a few cases where they have worked salvation among foreigners within our own borders'.[41] Second, the gift of tongues when interpreted, has been

---

around the world who reported a personal Pentecost', Albrecht, 'Carrie Judd Montgomery', p. 109.

[34] 'True And False Fire', *TOF* 26.10 (Oct 1906), pp. 195-98 (195) (emphasis added).

[35] 'True And False Fire', pp. 195, 197.

[36] 'True And False Fire', p. 197.

[37] Bartleman, 'Letter From Los Angeles', p. 247; A.S. Worrell, 'The Movements in Los Angeles', *TOF* 26.12 (*Gospel Witness*) (Dec 1906), pp. 256-57 (257).

[38] Editors note, Bartleman, 'Letter From Los Angeles', p. 247.

[39] Bartleman, 'Letter From Los Angeles', p. 247.

[40] Bartleman, 'Letter From Los Angeles', pp. 247-48.

[41] Bartleman, 'Letter From Los Angeles', p. 248. Note his caution: 'it has not yet been proven of just what practical value the present gift of tongues will be in foreign fields', and 'the tongues have played their part already ... and we do well to walk softly at such time as this', pp. 248, 251.

'praises to God, exhortations, (and) warnings'.[42] Third, 'God is trying to attract our attention'. Fourth, the 'heavenly choir' is 'the very foretaste of the rapture that we shall soon realize when He shall call for us'.[43] The second piece, by Worrell, confirmed 'there are *real gifts of tongues* here in Los Angeles' as well as counterfeits.[44] Following Worrell's account, the final bookend reads, 'we do not stand for this whole movement, but only for the part that is of God'.[45] Compared with other early Pentecostal periodicals examined above, there are far fewer references to glossolalia.

D. Testimonies

The personal testimonies in TOF are much longer than in other early Pentecostal periodicals. In fact, most are article length. Even though this limited the testimonies in each issue, what was published was carefully selected and often had more theological weight than the brief and often repetitious testimonies found in other periodicals. Therefore, personal testimonies will not be treated separately, but are incorporated into this survey of TOF below.

E. The Evidence and Divine Love

Perhaps more than any other early periodical, Montgomery provided space for various opinions about the evidentiary nature of glossolalia.[46] Though Montgomery eventually embraced IE, she allowed the discussion to play out in her periodical for some time

---

[42] Bartleman, 'Letter From Los Angeles', p. 249.
[43] Bartleman, 'Letter From Los Angeles', pp. 251-52.
[44] Worrell, 'The Movements in Los Angeles', p. 256. He went to Los Angeles 'to investigate the facts' and visited four revival centres in Los Angeles in 1906, p. 257.
[45] Editor's note in Worrell, 'The Movements in Los Angeles', p. 257.
[46] Montgomery waited at least nine issues between hearing of glossolalia's restoration ('True And False Fire', p. 195) and publishing an article about glossolalia's sign-value, A.A. Boddy, 'These Signs Shall Follow', *TOF* 27.6 (Jun 1907), pp. 138-40 (139). The most popular phrase was simply 'the evidence', A.T. Lange, 'The Glory That Excelleth', *TOF* 29.11 (Nov 1909), pp. 250-55. Other phrases include: 'first evidence', 'immediate evidence', 'Bible evidence', and 'unmistakable evidence', cf. Mrs. G.A. Murray, 'Evidences of A Real Pentecostal Baptism', *TOF* 30.9 (Sep 1910), pp. 205-209 (206); W. Bramwell, 'How Rev. William Bramwell Received Entire Sanctification', *TOF* 31.4 (Apr 1911), p. 82; Ellen M. Winter, 'A Plea For The Love And Unity of the Spirit', (*Word and Work*) *TOF* 32.9 (Sep 1912), pp. 195-99 (198); E.M. Stanton, 'The Effect of the Divine Indwelling', *TOF* 34.7 (Jul 1914), pp. 160-61 (161).

and balanced the divisive doctrine of an evidence with a call for unity and love.

1. 'The Evidence'

Those who doubted or denied the sign value of tongues tended to give theological and pastoral reasons for their position.[47] For example, Worrell believed there was an 'an undue importance attached to speaking in tongues' especially if it were 'regarded as *the decisive proof* that one has received his Pentecost'.[48] His reasons: Satan can counterfeit tongues, it causes pride and an unteachable spirit, and it ignores 'the work of the Spirit in the development of Christ-life in the Trinity-filled believer'.[49] Later, he endorsed I. May Throop's testimony of a progressive Spirit-baptism as a great 'representative of this Pentecostal experience'.[50] Abrams refused to say that tongues were 'the only sign':[51]

> while all may and should receive the sign,[52] yet we dare not say that no one is Spirit-baptized who has not received the sign. Yet we see the same gifts and graces and power for service in those who hold these different beliefs ... the Scriptures do not warrant our pronouncing judgment on those who do not speak

---

[47] For example, A.T. Lange experienced God's presence without glossolalia so strongly that he called it his SB. Eight months later, his subsequent tongues-experience 'added nothing to the glory and joy in the spirit of worship, to the sense and vision of His glorious presence' of his previous SB, Lange, 'The Glory That Excelleth', pp. 250-55.

[48] A.S. Worrell, 'The Pentecostal Movement in Los Angeles', *TOF* 27.8 (Aug 1907), pp. 179-81 (179) (emphasis added).

[49] Worrell, 'The Pentecostal Movement in Los Angeles', p. 180.

[50] A.S.W. 'Remarks', *TOF* 28.11 (Nov 1908), p. 132. Throop wrote, I 'knew that I had the Holy Spirit' but not like 'the people of Azusa Street', I. May Throop, 'A Partial Experience', *TOF* 29.6 (Jun 1909), pp. 129-32 (129). She 'tarried' for her Pentecost and then grasped it by faith. 'I was perfectly conscious of having received the baptism of the Holy Ghost; but I was also conscious that I had not received the fire, neither had I received the new tongue', p. 131. Five days later, there was 'a chattering first, then the Heavenly song, then the song in an unknown tongue ... God had taken possession of my body, even that unruly member – my tongue'.

[51] Miss Minnie Abrams, 'India', *TOF* 28.11 (Nov 1908), pp. 260-62 (260). 'It is evident that most of the Christians in Apostolic times did speak in tongues', p. 261.

[52] Abrams encouraged everyone to press on until they receive 'the fullness of this Pentecostal blessing', Abrams, 'India', p. 261.

in tongues.⁵³

She did not want the evidence to be divisive and advocated for working together in love.⁵⁴ George B. Studd believed there was a preoccupation with signs⁵⁵ and could not 'subscribe to this for one moment' because

> many, very many, precious saints of God have received and rejoiced in the conscious indwelling presence, comfort, sanctifying power and guidance of the Holy Spirit; but they have not yet seen their privilege nor obtained the blessing of that *full possession* which He takes of the body as well as the soul.⁵⁶

He reasoned that less than full possession of the Holy Spirit was possible because the church had 'lost its original purity and power … the full truth has only been restored to us by degrees'.⁵⁷

However, even doubters of the evidence noted that tongues functioned as a gateway experience for other gifts of the Spirit. Worrell believed that all the gifts were possible 'after the Pentecostal experience has begun'.⁵⁸ A CMA article noted that 'the "tongue" is *but the beginning* of God's work … the great object and value of such baptisms and of the gifts of the Spirit is that we may be used in the salvation of the perishing souls'.⁵⁹ Mrs. G.A. Murray believed that '*the first evidence* … was that of speaking with other tongues'; however, 'while the utterance in unknown tongues is one of the evidences of a spiritual baptism, it is not a sufficient proof in itself'.⁶⁰ For her the 'crowning evidence' was unity and love.⁶¹

---

⁵³ Abrams, 'India', p. 261.
⁵⁴ Abrams, 'India', p. 261.
⁵⁵ George B. Studd, 'Floods of Blessing', *TOF* 33.6 (Jun 1913), pp. 125-29 (126).
⁵⁶ George B. Studd, 'The Holy Ghost Received', *TOF* 31.2 (Feb 1911), pp. 41-42 (41) (emphasis added). Later, Studd sounded as if he embraced IE, cf. George B. Studd, 'And There Was a Voice', *TOF* 34.8 (Aug 1914), pp. 182-86 (185).
⁵⁷ Studd, 'The Holy Ghost Received', p. 42.
⁵⁸ Worrell, 'The Pentecostal Movement in Los Angeles', p. 180.
⁵⁹ CMA Report (1907), 'Work In South China', *TOF* 29.1 (Jan 1909), pp. 9-12 (11) (emphasis added).
⁶⁰ Murray, 'Evidences of a Real Pentecostal Baptism', pp. 206, 207 (emphasis added).
⁶¹ Murray, 'Evidences of a Real Pentecostal Baptism', pp. 207-208. Her other evidences are typical: power for witnessing and holiness, joy in worship, unselfishness, and prayer, pp. 206-208.

Those who embraced a sign-value for tongues tended to emphasize specific biblical passages[62] and personal testimonies. For example, Boddy believed that the signs of Mk 16.17-18 would be given to 'true believers ... (and) certainly present among Spirit-filled Christians' as promised by Jesus himself and seen in the writings of Luke and Paul.[63] Boddy was a strong proponent of evidential glossolalia, stating, 'we consider it the Pentecostal movement, because God is giving the same sign, the speaking with tongues, as he did in the beginning at Jerusalem and at Ephesus and at Caesarea'.[64] Cecil Polhill called tongues a distinctive 'Pentecostal sign' and his friend experienced a 'wonderful manifestation of Pentecostal power, including and evidenced by the speaking in other tongues'.[65] Albert Norton wrote,

> I was kept from becoming an earnest seeker by the thought ... that I might have the fullest baptism of the Spirit without any utterance in tongues; and that I had in all probability have this fullest baptism in a wonderful experience ... all I needed now was to have that experience revived.[66]

However, after meeting some Pentecostal missionaries, Norton re-examined Scripture and came to believe 'that when the full baptism came I would have an utterance in another tongue', which he did.[67] E.M. Stanton attempted to distinguish between sign and symbol.[68] If the glossolalia in Acts 'were mere symbols' they could be removed from the narrative without damaging it; however,

---

[62] Several authors appealed to Scripture without landing on either side of the IE discussion, and therefore added very little to the debate; cf. Thos. M. Jeffreys, 'Faith in The Spoken Words of God' (*The Overcoming Life*), TOF 30.1 (Jan 1910), pp. 10-14 (14); E.T. Slaybaugh, 'What are the Manifestations of the Spirit for the Edifying of the Body of Christ?', TOF 30.2 (Feb 1910), pp. 31-32; 'Trusting God Beforehand', TOF 32.1 (Jan 1912), pp. 21-22.

[63] Boddy, 'These Signs Shall Follow', p. 139.

[64] A.A. Boddy, 'Pentecostal Outpouring', TOF 32.11 (Nov 1912), pp. 231-35 (231-2).

[65] Cecil Polhill, 'This is That', TOF 28.5 (May 1908), pp. 100-104 (100).

[66] Albert Norton, 'Rain in the Time of the Latter Rain', TOF 29.9 (Sep 1909), pp. 195-200 (196).

[67] Norton, 'Rain in the Time of the Latter Rain', p. 197; cf. p. 195 for an account of Spirit–baptism.

[68] He quotes A. Kyper that symbols had a less essential quality to the narrative than signs: 'symbols ... are intended to represent, or indicate something or call attention to it, hence they may be omitted without them suffering the matter

tongues appears as a part of the narrative, a real constitutent [sic] of the event ... and that it was repeated at Caesarea and Ephesus is an evidence that it was not a mere symbol but that it belonged inseparably to the baptism of the Holy Ghost.[69]

Stanton called glossolalia the 'immediate effect of the divine incoming and indwelling', which is an evidence to the speaker himself.[70] Horace Bushnell observed that tongues were so foolish looking and sounding, that 'for just that reason it has the stronger evidence when it occurs'.[71]

Montgomery's own testimony caused her to be less dogmatic about the evidence. On the one hand, she saw signs and wonders as thoroughly biblical.[72] On the other hand, she was not bothered by a delay between the embrace of SB by faith and the actual reception of the Spirit.[73] This followed the pattern of her personal healing, when she first accepted SB 'by faith' and, within a week, spoke 'a few scattered words in an unknown tongue and then burst into a language (that) came pouring out in great fluency and clearness'.[74] Faith was emphasized because 'without the operation of faith' there are no results.[75] In fact, at times, faith itself became the

---

itself ... if these signs were mere symbols, the event would have been the same without them; but the absence of the sign of other tongues would have modified the character of subsequent history completely', Stanton, 'The Effect of the Divine Indwelling', p. 160.

[69] Stanton, 'The Effect of the Divine Indwelling', p. 160. 'The speaking with tongues is not simply the sign or evidence of the baptism, but (is) a part of the divine baptism itself, B.H. Irwin, 'My Pentecostal Baptism – A Christmas Gift', *TOF* 27.5 (May 1907), pp. 114-16 (114).

[70] Stanton, 'The Effect of the Divine Indwelling', p. 161.

[71] Horace Bushnell, 'Dr. Bushnell On Supernatural Manifestations of the Spirit', *TOF* 29.2 (Feb 1909), pp. 36-37 (36); cf. Studd, 'And There Was a Voice', p. 185.

[72] Carrie Judd Montgomery, 'God Is Confirming His Word By Signs and Wonders', *TOF* 33.5 (May 1913), pp. 97-99 (99).

[73] Mrs. Belle Marshall, 'Deliverance of an Insane Sister', *TOF* 27.1 (Jan 1907), pp. 11-13 (11); John Salmon, 'Baptized with the Holy Ghost', *TOF* 28.11 (Nov 1908), pp. 258-60; S.R. Break, 'The Latter Rain Fullness, A Personal Testimony', *TOF* 29.4 (Apr 1909), pp. 82-83; Ethel L. Opie, 'Healed and Baptized', *TOF* 34.7 (Jul 1914), pp. 155-57 (156).

[74] Montgomery, '"The Promise of the Father (#1)"', p. 148. She dated her SB as 29 June 1908 when she spoke in tongues and not her earlier experience or stand of faith, p. 149; cf. Miskov, *Life on Wings*, p. 247

[75] F.F. Bosworth, 'The Wonders of Faith', *TOF* 33.10 (Oct 1913), pp. 231-35 (234).

evidence:[76] 'the Spirit is received by faith in Jesus ... the Holy Ghost must be accepted without feeling *or evidence of any kind*, except simply the word of promise'.[77] However, for those with weak faith, signs would be granted.[78]

2. Divine Love

Throughout the IE debate, Montgomery's strongest words were for those who spoke in tongues and lacked love.[79] Lack of love caused '"fleshly manifestations" ... (and) repel(led) other hungry seeking souls'.[80] Montgomery began her personal testimony by stating, 'there was much that did not appeal to me ... (some people) seemed to get in the way of the Spirit ... became lifted up ... (caused) confusion ... (and) failed to walk in Scriptural lines', and only after she heard of a godly friend's SB did she '"thirst" for the fullness'.[81] Because love was the 'foundation and root' of the Spirit[82] it was possible to determine between a true and counterfeit experience:

> the real test is divine love ... some of the 'tongues' heard in these days are brassy and metallic and without the sweetness and benediction of the Spirit in them. Praise God for the true 'tongues' of heavenly adoration proceeding from a heart filled with love to God and man, which glorify him.[83]

The genuine Spirit of God within will be recognized by divine love and not by 'the exercise of gifts'. Divine love 'is the very Creator

---

[76] 'Living Faith', *TOF* 30.10 (Oct 1910), pp. 222-23.

[77] 'The Gift of the Holy Ghost – How Received?' (*Our Monthly*) *TOF* 29.12 (Dec 1909), pp. 280-82 (281) (emphasis added).

[78] Carrie Judd Montgomery, '"Little Faith" and "Great Faith"', *TOF* 31.3 (Mar 1911), pp. 49-63 (54); cf. M. Boddy, 'Trials of Faith, Leading to the Manifestation of the Sons of God', *TOF* 31.3 (Mar 1911), pp. 66-68; 'Trusting God Beforehand', pp. 21-22.

[79] Miskov, *Life on Wings*, pp. 254-58.

[80] Carrie Judd Montgomery, 'The Editor in Los Angeles, Calif.', *TOF* 30.2 (Feb 1910), pp. 27-28 (27).

[81] Montgomery, '"The Promise of the Father (#1)"', p. 146.

[82] Carrie Judd Montgomery, 'Touch Not Mine Anointed', *TOF* 30.3 (Mar 1910), pp. 52, 53; cf. 'Life at the Home of Peace', *TOF* 32.1 (Jan 1912), pp. 12-16.

[83] Carrie Judd Montgomery, 'Service for the King', *TOF* 30.10 (Oct 1910), pp. 217-20 (220).

Himself in us'.⁸⁴ Genuine glossolalia, rooted in love, reverses Babel's divisions and brings unity.⁸⁵

At times, Montgomery implied that strong doctrinal statements created separation. For example, 'we feel that minor differences of doctrine should not be allowed to separate'.⁸⁶ Consider Ellen Winter's snapshot of the situation:

> not a few Christian leaders are trying to 'unite' the members on some points of doctrine that they are making a specialty … some of them insist that speaking in tongues is the Bible evidence, while others hold that the possession of any of the other gifts of the spirit, without tongues, maybe proof of the baptism … let me magnify the wisdom and grace of God that place the love chapter between the twelfth and fourteenth chapters of 1 Cor., like meat in a sandwich.⁸⁷

Unity will not be attained through doctrinal statements but through 'divine love circulating through the whole body of Christ'.⁸⁸ Therefore, Montgomery reasoned that 'love, perfect Divine love is the only and most necessary sign of the baptism of the Holy Spirit. But other gifts, such as … to speak with tongues … are not to be discarded.'⁸⁹

F. Responding to the Critics

Despite the fact that Montgomery's aim was divine love and unity, she cautiously introduced her large independent readership to glossolalia. Whether it was intentional or not, after an issue that was especially tongues-centric or polemic in nature, she would downplay or have a complete absence of glossolalia in the next issue.⁹⁰ This balancing act required *TOF* both to defend speaking

---

⁸⁴ Mrs. M. Baxter, 'In The Last Day', *TOF* 33.1 (Jan 1913), pp. 5-7 (70).
⁸⁵ Mrs. Polman, 'Testimony of Mrs. Polman', *TOF* 30.2 (Feb 1910), p. 43.
⁸⁶ Montgomery, 'The Editor in Los Angeles', p. 28.
⁸⁷ Winter, 'A Plea For The Love And Unity of the Spirit', p. 198.
⁸⁸ Carrie Judd Montgomery, 'For this Cause', *TOF* 30.12 (Dec 1910), pp. 265-68 (266).
⁸⁹ 'Word From India', *TOF* 29.2 (Feb 1909), pp. 39-40 (39).
⁹⁰ For example, issue 33.5 (May 1913) has two significant articles on glossolalia: Montgomery, 'Confirming His Word', pp. 97-99; Kent White, 'Baptized with the Holy Ghost And Fire', *TOF* 33.6 (May 1913), pp. 99-103. The subsequent issue does not mention tongues specifically, and even includes a call to

in tongues and to be self-critical of Pentecostal excesses. *Triumphs of Faith* addressed the role of signs and manifestations, cessationism, and counterfeit tongues.

According to W. Berhard, it was 'the evident supernatural element in the movement' that was 'a great stumbling block' and raised the broader question of 'the supernatural or miraculous' signs and manifestations in general.[91] However, the appeal to the Bible for support was common: 'let's cease trying to justify ourselves with bodily manifestations as the manifestations of the Spirit of God ... and with open hearts, face the word of God and measure up to it'.[92] 'An insatiate hunger for a manifestation of the Spirit's power', wrote Theodore Cuyler, was the natural outflow of 'a tremendous responsibility for (lost) souls'.[93] Tongues and divine healing[94] were the primary manifestations of the Holy Spirit in *TOF*, but 'holy laughter'[95] and groaning[96] were also mentioned.

Triumphs of Faith recognized that cessationism posed a threat to the gifts of the Spirit and glossolalia.[97] *Triumphs of Faith* dealt with cessation much like the other periodicals and appealed to Scripture and church history for defence. For example, because Mk 16.17-18 was in 'doubt', one author turned to 'the corresponding closing passages in other evangelists' and found that the word of God was to be preached with signs following; that the word 'was attested by the "sign", or visible evidence, of perfected bodily restoration'.[98] It was reasoned that because healings still occurred, tongues also

---

prayer so that 'we shall not be so occupied with manifestations', Studd, 'Floods of Blessing', p. 126.

[91] C. Berhard, 'Supernatural Gifts', TOF 31.9 (Sep 1911), pp. 199-204 (201).

[92] Slaybaugh, 'What are the Manifestations of the Spirit', p. 32; cf. Morton Plummer, 'The Fear Test', *TOF* 33.8 (Aug 1913), pp. 190-91; Montgomery, 'Speaking in Tongues', *TOF* 30.11 (Nov 1910), pp. 253-55; Miskov, *Life on Wings*, pp. 251-54.

[93] Cuyler, 'The Effectual Prayer', p. 11; cf. Horace Bushnell, 'Reflected Light', *TOF* 27.11 (Nov 1907), pp. 243-45 (243).

[94] Etta Costellow, 'Pentecostal Blessing', *TOF* 31.7 (Jul 1911), pp. 179-80; 'A Visit From Rev. A.A. Boddy', *TOF* 32.9 (Sep 1912), p. 216.

[95] Opie, 'Healed and Baptized', p. 156.

[96] 'A Cyclone of Power And Glory In Answer To Prayer', *TOF* 28.1 (Jan 1908), pp. 11-12.

[97] 'It is now commonly assumed that miracles and all similar externalities of divine power have been discontinued, because ... the canon of Scripture is closed up', Bushnell, 'Reflected Light', p. 243.

[98] 'Scripture on Sickness and Healing', p. 90.

continued. Historically, miracles and glossolalia were 'lost for all the centuries' because men were not faithful and 'spasmodic in their faith and spirituality'.[99] Bushnell noted that the theory of cessation fails because, 'miracles continued for two hundred and fifty years after' they should have ended.[100]

Satan 'can devise ... (and will) counterfeit, oppose and destroy the work of the Holy Spirit'; satanic tongues are possible.[101] However, the counterfeit implies a genuine.[102] The following advice was given regarding counterfeit glossolalia: seek God wholeheartedly;[103] pray for the 'spirit of discernment';[104] the fruit of the Spirit is the 'proper foundation' for the gifts of the Spirit, especially, divine love and humility;[105] the devil's counterfeit will be 'cold, formal, lifeless' and have no power, while the genuine will be 'full of praise to Jesus, and glowing with his matchless love';[106] and finally, 'the blood of Christ ... and the Spirit of God who has been poured out on them according to his promise, are able to keep them from errors'.[107] One pastor did not teach about tongues as a 'protection against all counterfeit and spurious imitation'; nevertheless, 'they received powerful premonitions of the Latter Rain ... (which were) fully affirmed and witnessed to by a manifestation in tongues'.[108] Two authors mentioned that 'blasphemy of the Holy Spirit' was 'to ascribe to Satan the mighty working of the

---

[99] Bushnell, 'Reflected Light', p. 244; cf. Bessie Porter Head, 'Many Kinds of Voices', *TOF* 28.11 (Nov 1908) pp. 254-58; 'Work In South China', p. 9;

[100] Bushnell, 'Reflected Light', p. 243; cf. 'Pentecost In The Year 1830', *TOF* 29.2 (Feb 1909), pp. 41-42; 'A Wonderful Work', *TOF* 27.6 (Jun 1907), pp. 128-29; E. Sisson, 'Extract from Andrew Murray's New Book', *TOF* 29.3 (Mar 1909), p. 72; Berhard, 'Supernatural Gifts', pp. 201-202.

[101] J.M. Pike, 'Pentecostal Movement', *TOF* 30.11 (Nov 1910), pp. 250-51; cf. 'Work In South China', pp. 10-11.

[102] Foulston, 'How the New Pentecost Is Coming', pp. 63, 65; cf. A.S. Worrell, 'An Open Letter to the Opposers of this Pentecostal Movement', *TOF* 27.11 (Nov 1907), pp. 246-49 (246).

[103] V.P. Simmons, 'Is It Reasonable', *TOF* 29.10 (Oct 1908), pp. 222-23 (222).

[104] 'Work In South China', pp. 10-11.

[105] 'Try the Spirits', *TOF* 30.6 (Jun 1910), pp. 133-34; cf. Bertha Pinkham Dixon, 'The Latter Rain', *TOF* 28.5 (May 1908), pp 115-19.

[106] Worrell, 'An Open Letter to the Opposers', p. 249; cf. J.O. Lehman, 'Reports from Regions Beyond', *TOF* 29.2 (Feb 1909), pp. 37-39 (38).

[107] 'Word From India', pp. 39-40.

[108] Gerard A. Bailly, 'Calvary Leads to Pentecost', *TOF* 30.2 (Feb 1910), pp. 41-43 (42).

Holy Spirit in many of these Pentecostal people'.[109]

G. Sanctification

Montgomery's view on sanctification either never neatly fit into either category or changed from Wesleyan's 'complete in a moment' to the FW's 'ongoing process'.[110] Regardless, 'sanctification is the necessary preparation for receiving the gift of the Holy Ghost' with tongues.[111] *Triumphs of Faith* called Pentecostals to higher standards of holiness.[112] Further, one must strive for more holiness, being daily filled with the Spirit. Note Montgomery's poetic language when she writes, do not neglect

> to press through … until the vessel is FILLED with oil … our bodies must be holy and separated from the lusts of the earth … when your body gets full of the oil of the Holy Spirit your lips and tongue get filled also, and the new tongues drop off your lips like honey; you will be distinctly conscious that it is the Heavenly Dove who is speaking through you in other tongues … but after receiving the baptism there must be a continuous act of faith, always drinking of Christ in order to keep filled.[113]

---

[109] Worrell, 'An Open Letter to the Opposers', p. 247; cf. 'Word From India', pp. 39-40.

[110] Miskov believes that even before her SB she mixed both Keswick and Wesleyan terms and concepts along with Phoebe Palmer's theology to 'act in faith to take hold of what was already available, confess what has been receive, and stand on God's word as the evidence', Miskov, *Life on Wings*, p. 238. For support of her WH side see, Carrie Judd Montgomery, 'Letter From Mrs. Montgomery (#3)', *TOF* 29.9 (Sep 1909), pp. 207-209 (207); Bramwell, 'How Rev. William Bramwell Received Entire Sanctification', p. 82. For support to her FW side see, Carrie Judd Montgomery, 'Sanctification and the Baptism of the Holy Spirit', *TOF* 31.11 (Nov 1911), pp. 241-44 (243); Carrie Judd Montgomery, 'The Remnant of the Oil', *TOF* 31.12 (Dec 1911), pp. 265-70. Her own unique view of sanctification is best pictured as measures of the Spirit and the call for 'more', cf. Miskov, *Life on Wings*, pp. 235-40, 266-73.

[111] E.A. Sexton, 'Sanctification And The Gift of the Holy Ghost' *TOF* 29.9 (Sep 1909), pp. 200-203.

[112] 'This movement demands of its promoters, pure hearts, clean lives, perfect love, earnest zeal, the deepest self-denial, abounding liberality, intense spirituality, perfect obedience to God', (*Way of Faith*) 'Intensified Opposition', *TOF* 29.12 (Dec 1908), pp. 278-79 (278).

[113] Carrie Judd Montgomery, 'The Promise of the Father (#2)', *TOF* 37.1 (Jan 1917), pp. 1-6 (4-5) (capitals original). Cf. A.S. Worrell, 'The Season of the Latter Rain', *TOF* 34.2 (Feb 1914), pp. 42-43.

Whether writing about healing, sanctification, or the presence of the Holy Spirit, Montgomery believed that there was always 'more' available.[114]

H. Purposes for Glossolalia

The purposes for glossolalia in *TOF* followed those of other periodicals.

1. Power

Though not as prominent as other periodicals, tongues-speech was connected with power in *TOF*.[115] For example, 'the power of the Spirit came upon the preacher, and he began to pray, bursting forth in an unknown tongue',[116] or 'the Holy Ghost has the power to equip you for every emergency'.[117] However, *TOF* was careful to note that the power for ministry was not from tongues but from having God's Spirit within.[118] Tongues were merely the sign of full Spirit possession:[119]

> don't take it as power because you speak in tongues ... don't take that for the power ... there is a place to get where you know the Spirit is upon you, so you will be able to do the works which are wrought by this blessed Spirit of God in you, and the manifestation of His power shall be seen.[120]

Power was not resident within the individual but was the 'giving out from ourselves *of freshly-received Divine life*'.[121]

---

[114] Montgomery, 'Sanctification And The Baptism of the Holy Spirit', p. 243; cf. Montgomery, 'The Remnant of the Oil', pp. 265-70; Miskov, *Life on Wings*, pp. 268-73.

[115] Miskov's assessment is that SB's main purpose for Montgomery was empowerment for service 'with hints of eradication included (a Wesleyan influence)', Miskov, *Life on Wings*, p. 244; cf. pp. 240-44.

[116] Minnie F. Abrams, 'God's Wonderful Working in India', *TOF* 32.4 (Apr 1912), pp. 78-81 (80).

[117] Smith Wigglesworth, 'Spiritual Gifts', *TOF* 34.11 (Nov 1914), pp. 248-52 (249-50); cf. 'The Dhond Revival', *TOF* 28.9 (Sep 1908), pp. 196-200.

[118] 'Testimony', *TOF* 28.11 (Nov 1908), pp. 243-44 (244).

[119] Henry Varley, 'Fullness of the Holy Ghost', *TOF* 27.7 (Jul 1907), pp. 160-62; 'A Prayer', *TOF* 27.6 (Jun 1907), p. 140; cf. Miskov, *Life on Wings*, p. 245.

[120] Smith Wigglesworth, 'What Wilt Thou Have Me To Do', *TOF* 34.10 (Oct 1914), pp. 227-30 (228-29).

[121] Varley, 'Fullness of the Holy Ghost', p. 160 (emphasis added). Cf. C.F. Ladd, 'Power for Service', *TOF* 29.3 (Mar 1909), pp. 69-70 (69).

2. Prayer

Tongues offered a new and deeper way to pray, indeed 'it is Jesus praying through us, by the Holy Spirit ... remember it is Jesus praying through you'.[122] For example, even though she was thousands of miles away, one missionary recounted that they 'were told in tongues to pray for me; all this shows a new the power of intercessory prayer'.[123] These prayers were viewed as spiritual warfare in the unseen realm:

> how blessed when your whole being feels the prayer of the Spirit working within you mightily! You are conscious of having a force within you of unalterable desire, the groanings, which cannot be uttered, of the Holy Ghost in the midst.[124]

Glossolalic-groaning was occasionally seen as deep intercession for holiness[125] or a personal need, but usually it was intercession for the lost.[126] The Holy Spirit, 'pled through her for souls ... with groanings and tears and evidences upon her face of great interior suffering'.[127] At times revelation was given 'to identify themselves with the person prayed for'.[128]

3. God's Presence: Greater Worship and Revelation

First, similar to other early periodicals, *TOF* envisioned glossolalia as a means of richer worship and a response to God's revelation: 'there has been an increased spirit of praise, and a worshiping of the blessed Trinity, the increased revelation of Christ and His

---

[122] LBY, 'That Your Prayers Be Not Hindered', *TOF* 33.1 (Jan 1913), pp. 17-18 (17); cf. 'Days of Blessing in India', *TOF* 27.4 (Apr 1907), pp. 95-96; Ramabai, 'Showers of Blessing', *TOF* 27.12 (Dec 1907), pp. 267-69.

[123] Alma E. Doering, 'A Missionary's Testimony', *TOF* 31.6 (Jun 1911), pp. 124-27 (126).

[124] 'The Imperative Mood And The Present Tense of Faith', *TOF* 31.3 (Mar 1911), pp. 69-72 (70); cf. Miss Abrams, 'Intercessory Prayer', *TOF* 29.1 (Jan 1909), pp. 16-17 (16); Emma Krater, 'A Word from India', *TOF* 33.2 (Feb 1913), pp. 30-31 (31).

[125] 'A Cyclone of Power', pp. 11-12.

[126] Miss E. Sisson, 'God's Prayer House', *TOF* 29.10 (Oct 1908), pp. 230-34 (234); Break, 'The Latter Rain Fullness, A Personal Testimony', p. 83; Carrie Judd Montgomery, 'Letter from Mrs. Montgomery (#2)', *TOF* 29.5 (May 1909), pp. 112-18.

[127] Editor, 'Pentecostal Outpouring and Beulah', *TOF* 28.9 (Sep 1908), p. 195.

[128] Abrams, 'Intercessory Prayer', p. 16.

finished work ... has needed a new medium of praise. This God has given us in the new tongues'.[129] Grace Dempster testified that 'praise and worship swelled up within and sought expression, but words cannot be found which satisfied until the Holy Spirit Himself gave utterance through other tongues'.[130] The revelation was of a deeper understanding of the Bible[131] or was a 'fresh, deep, mighty revelation of Himself'.[132]

Second, Montgomery envisioned further experiences with God that were inexpressible, even with glossolalia:

> there is ... an experience beyond service and beyond prayer, and that is a revelation of His own personality to such an extent that there is nothing but adoring worship filling our being. Usually it is a blessed experience to be able to speak in tongues, to let the heavenly song flow out, but there are times when even tongues cease, when His presence is so all-pervading in the atmosphere so heavenly that I cannot talk at all in any language, but the power of His blessed Spirit upon me is so marvelous that it seems as though I were almost dwelling in heaven.[133]

This desire for the presence of God was described as a 'hunger' for God.[134]

---

[129] Carrie Judd Montgomery, 'A Year With the Comforter', *TOF* 29.7 (Jul 1909), pp 145-47 (146-47).

[130] Grace S. Dempster, 'That I May Know Him', *TOF* 30.2 (Feb 1910), pp. 28-31 (31); cf. Max Wood Moorhead, 'A Personal Testimony', *TOF* 28.9 (Sep 1908), pp. 203-205; Carrie Judd Montgomery, 'Be Filled With the Spirit', *TOF* 29.9 (Sep 1909), pp. 193-95 (193); Costellow, 'Pentecostal Blessing', pp. 179-80; Mrs. Henry S. Morgan, 'Healed by the Power of God', *TOF* 34.4 (Apr 1914), pp. 76-77 (77).

[131] 'This Is That', *TOF* 28.5 (May 1908), pp. 100-104 (102); Carrie Judd Montgomery, 'Some Important Changes', *TOF* 28.12 (Dec 1908), pp. 267-69 (268).

[132] Head, 'Many Kinds of Voices', p. 256; Lange, 'The Glory that Excelleth', pp. 252-53.

[133] Carrie Judd Montgomery, 'The Life on Wings: The Possibility of Pentecost', *TOF* 32.8 (Aug 1912), pp. 169-77 (175-6); cf. Carrie Judd Montgomery, 'The Quickening Life of the Indwelling Spirit', *TOF* 29.10 (Oct 1908), pp. 217-19 (217). Miskov believes that for Montgomery it was possible to speak in tongues and not have one's 'full baptism', Miskov, *Life on Wings*, pp. 258-60. 'While Carrie personally associated one's Spirit Fullness with tongues, her teaching was *sometimes inconsistent* with this', p. 262 (emphasis added).

[134] Miss Cora Hansen, 'Testimony', *TOF* 28.9 (Sep 1908), pp. 202-203; Moorhead, 'A Personal Testimony', p. 203; Chas. T. Hettiaratchy, 'In His "Banqueting House"', *TOF* 30.3 (Mar 1910), pp. 66-69 (66).

Finally, tongues were a symbol of the liminal overlap between God and humankind. While other early periodicals wrote simply about the Holy Spirit dwelling in and speaking through the individual, *TOF* produced at least two articles that enriched the theology of divine presence and glossolalia. First, 'this gift of tongues … is designed to be a symbol to the world of the possibility and fact of a divine access to the soul, and a divine operation in it'.[135] Second, Mrs. Polman explicitly envisioned glossolalia as sacramental, an intermingling of the human and divine:

> the Holy Spirit uses this gift of tongues to bring us into closer communion with God … He gave us the gift of tongues to receive spiritual food. And are not we fed when we come into communion with the Holy One? … We also feel the depth of blessing which is in eating His flesh and drinking His blood … so, when we are edifying ourselves by speaking in tongues, we are at the same time fed by His flesh and by His blood, and this being fed by His flesh and blood brings us into closer communion with Him … as it were, married to Him, and become one flesh, one bone with Him.[136]

Perhaps this was what the pioneers were aiming to say when they wrote that 'the Spirit teaches them to speak … in unbroken communion with God',[137] or the Holy Spirit 'speaks for Himself'.[138]

4. Tongues as a Gift of the Holy Spirit

Public glossolalia is a biblical gift of the Spirit that somehow edifies the Church and, when interpreted, is the equivalent of prophecy.[139] The practice in the local church should follow the boundaries established in 1 Corinthians 14.[140] Readers were encouraged to seek God and not the gift: 'the more we realize that God has

---

[135] Bushnell, 'Supernatural Manifestations', p. 37.

[136] Mrs. Polman, 'Speaking in Tongues (*TOF*)', *TOF* 33.10 (Oct 1913), pp. 235-37 (236-37); cf. Mrs. Polman, 'Speaking in Tongues', *BGM* 7.146 (Dec 15, 1913), p. 4, reprint; Mrs. Polman, 'Speaking in Tongues', *Confidence* 8.6 (Aug 1913), pp. 151-52.

[137] 'Word From India', p. 40.

[138] Stanton, 'The Effect of the Divine Indwelling', p. 161.

[139] Carrie Judd Montgomery, 'Edifying The Body of Christ', *TOF* 32.6 (Jun 1912), pp. 121-24 (123); Wigglesworth, 'Spiritual Gifts', pp. 249-50.

[140] 'Try The Spirits', pp. 133-4; Montgomery, 'Confirming His Word', pp. 97-99.

furnished us with a gift, the more completely we will be united with Jesus, so that people will be conscious of Him rather than of His gift'.[141] One article made a sharp distinction between the gifts of the Spirit and OT miracles because

> the personal gift of the Holy Ghost as at Pentecost, was not possible before His (Jesus') own ascension and glorification ... the gift of the Spirit ... since the Day of Pentecost, was and is something totally distinct from anything before that time, a new and loftier dispensation.[142]

Finally, though 'rebuking' a person in tongues was condemned in one article,[143] two testimonies 'rebuked' the demonic powers and saw a spiritual victory.[144]

I. The 'Latter Rain'

'The latter rain' was a significant metaphor that accounted for glossolalia's return and at the same time signalled that the end-times were near.[145] The latter rain was more prominent here than in other early Pentecostal periodicals. It was used to describe the current season of revival: 'we are living in the time of the actual physical rain, and also in the time of the latter spiritual rain. Joel ii:23 is a wonderful picture of a Pentecostal meeting.'[146] It connected the current revival with Pentecost[147] and greater torrents of the 'latter

---

[141] Wigglesworth, 'Spiritual Gifts', pp. 249-50; cf. Berhard, 'Supernatural Gifts', p. 199; cf. Break, 'The Latter Rain Fullness, A Personal Testimony', pp. 82-83.

[142] S.P. Jacobs, 'The Spirit Before Pentecost', *TOF* 31.9 (Sep 1911), pp. 213-14.

[143] 'The Spirit of Long-Suffering', *TOF* 30.6 (Jun 1910), pp. 130-32 (131).

[144] Smith Wigglesworth, 'The Confidence That We Have in Him', *TOF* 34.8 (Aug 1914), pp. 177-79; Mabel C. Scott, 'In The Beginning – God', *TOF* 34.8 (Aug 1914), p. 186.

[145] Boddy, 'Pentecostal Outpouring', pp. 234-35; A.B. Simpson, 'Gospel Healing', *TOF* 34.4 (Apr 1914), pp. 80-86 (85); Julia Morton Plummer, 'The Bridegroom Cometh', *TOF* 34.7 (Jul 1914), pp. 165-66 (165); cf. Miskov, *Life on Wings*, p. 258.

[146] Boddy, 'Pentecostal Outpouring', p. 233; cf. Carrie Judd Montgomery, 'Letter From Mrs. Montgomery (#2)', *TOF* 29.4 (Apr 1909), pp. 73-80 (74); Montgomery, 'Letter From Mrs. Montgomery (#2)', p. 112; 'Tongues Are For A Sign (#2)', *TOF* 30.1 (Jan 1910), pp. 23-24; Sadie Cody, 'The Work And Workers', *TOF* 32.11 (Nov 1912), pp. 228-29 (229).

[147] 'This is That', p. 104.

rain' were prayed for: 'let us be determined to give God no rest and no men rest until we have the revival all around us. Use letters, conversation etc. "Ask of the Lord Rain in the time of the Latter Rain" (Zech. X., 1) He says, and He will send it.'[148]

J. The Nature of Glossolalia
The nature of tongues in *TOF* was ecstatic and mysterious, and at times it was a song or a known language.

1. Ecstatic and Mysterious

When speaking in tongues, 'the believer did the talking' but the 'Spirit gives the utterance', according to Fred F. Bosworth.[149] Glossolalia occurred when the human

> spirit was wrapt into a state of ecstasy by the immediate communication of the Spirit of God. In this ecstatic trance the believer was constrained by irresistible power to pour forth his feelings of thanksgiving and rapture in words; yet the words which issued from his mouth were not his own.[150]

Polhill noted that the believers' understanding of glossolalia changed from 'to speak in a foreign language not previously studied' to be an 'ecstatic and worshipping voice ... an inexpressible longing of their hearts (that) was not satisfied until this new tongue was given'.[151] Though ecstatic, 'tongues ... are as real to Him (God), as the spoken tongues of the world'.[152]

2. Heavenly Singing

The 'heavenly singing' often occurred when 'the tide (of) gladness reaches its climax ... (and) all who have received the Pentecostal baptism join in and it is like music of the angels'.[153] The singing

---

[148] Cecil Polhill, 'The Pentecostal Movement In The Foreign Mission Field', *TOF* 29.4 (Apr 1909), pp. 80-81 (81).

[149] F.F. Bosworth, 'Power in the Holy Ghost', *TOF* 34.11 (Nov 1914), pp. 244-47 (246-47); cf. Geo. E. Berg, 'My Pentecostal Baptism', *TOF* 30.11 (Nov 1910), pp. 251-53.

[150] Conybeare and Howson, 'The Gift of Tongues', *TOF* 29.7 (Jul 1909), p. 168.

[151] 'This is That', pp. 101-102.

[152] Bushnell, 'Supernatural Manifestations', p. 37.

[153] Mrs. F. Kies, 'The Morning Prayer Service at Beulah Heights', *TOF* 33.10 (Oct 1913), pp. 221-22.

was generally thought to be praise that overlapped the praise in heaven.[154] Through the gift of interpretation, Abrams 'found the same words of praise being spoken through various ones in different languages'.[155] Heavenly singing was the equivalent of the glossolalia of IE.[156] Montgomery was known for her singing in the Spirit[157] and so appreciated its sound that she wrote of one occasion that the song was 'so wonderful that it thrilled my heart to its depth'.[158]

3. Xenolalia

Xenolalia is a small but regular feature throughout the window of this examination. However, *TOF* published testimonies of xenolalia long after the other early Pentecostal periodicals had ceased regularly publishing accounts.[159] Similar to testimonies in other periodicals, they listed the languages they spoke,[160] noted cases when non-English speakers spoke colloquial English,[161] and addressed the supernatural aspect of tongues.[162] Some writers longed for 'missionary tongues'[163] to facilitate the gospel and noted the sign value of

---

[154] 'She sang praises to God in new tongues ... and together we praised in tongues until we seemed we were in Heaven', Mrs. Herbert Dyke, 'Healing Through the Great Physician', *TOF* 33.7 (Jul 1913), p. 156.

[155] Abrams, 'Intercessory Prayer', p. 16.

[156] Cora Doucette, 'Healing of Soul And Body', *TOF* 27.12 (Dec 1907), pp. 286-87.

[157] Kies, 'The Morning Prayer Service at Beulah Heights', pp. 221-22; Montgomery, '"The Promise of the Father (#1)"', p. 148; Carrie Judd Montgomery, 'Behold, I Make All Things New', *TOF* 33.1 (Jan 1913), pp 3-4 (4); Dyke, 'Healing Through the Great Physician', p. 156.

[158] Carrie Judd Montgomery, 'As Dying, And Behold We Live', *TOF* 34.5 (May 1914), p. 98. One exception to a beautiful melody had 'a deep guttural language', Mrs. C. Nuzum, 'From Every Nation, Kindred And Tongue', *TOF* 34.2 (Feb 1914), pp. 29-30 (30).

[159] In the periodicals listed above, accounts past 1909 were rare. McGee noted that by late 1906 and early 1907 accounts of glossolalia emphasized 'worship and intercession in the Spirit', McGee, 'Shortcut to Language Preparation', p. 122. However, here they appear as late as, Grace Agar, 'Life More Abundant', *TOF* 34.2 (Feb 1914), pp. 27-29 (28).

[160] Irwin, 'My Pentecostal Baptism – A Christmas Gift', pp. 114-17; Mary B. Mullen, 'A New Experience', *TOF* 28.9 (Sep 1908), pp. 213-14.

[161] *TOF* 27.5 (May 1907), p. 105; Albert Norton, 'The Gift of the Holy Ghost', *TOF* 28.1 (Jan 1908), pp. 14-16 (14-15).

[162] Bushnell, 'Supernatural Manifestations', p. 37.

[163] Lizzie Fraser, 'Testimony', *TOF* 29.1 (Jan 1909), pp 12-13; Lehman, 'Reports From Regions Beyond', pp. 37-38; J.O. Lehman, 'Johannesburg, South Africa', *TOF* 29.9 (Sep 1909), p. 213.

xenolalia.¹⁶⁴ Two interesting accounts explained that the hearers did not 'understand all the words', but grasped enough to identify the language and get a rudimentary understanding, revealing a level of critical judgment towards xenolalia.¹⁶⁵ Perhaps accounts of xenolalia were given greater latitude because of Montgomery's own testimony of SB, when she 'spoke and sang in unknown tongues (there seemed three or four distinct languages)'.¹⁶⁶ Later she went to great lengths to verify what 'seemed like Chinese' by a 'credible witness'.¹⁶⁷ Missionary tongues were an exception to the rule and not the norm: at first we thought that 'the gift was for the preaching of the gospel to foreigners' but now we see it as a sign, where 'unbelievers are brought face-to-face with the supernatural and evidence of "the powers of the world" to come'.¹⁶⁸

K. Affect – Joy and Laughter

Joy is an emotion that stands out when reading *TOF*: 'it is far beyond the power of pen to describe or tongue to express the unspeakable joy that comes from Himself as He perfectly subdues and endues'.¹⁶⁹ Laughter was an outflow of joy, but it was also a means of learning to yield to the Spirit, a foreshadowing of full glossolalia like 'stammering lips'. For example,

> I wanted all the Lord had for me ... as we bowed our heads in prayer the Holy Spirit came upon me and holy laughter (Ps.

---

¹⁶⁴ Norton, 'The Gift of the Holy Ghost', p. 15; 'Extract from a Christian Workers Letter', *TOF* 28.11 (Nov 1908), p. 249; 'Tongues Are For A Sign', pp. 23-24.

¹⁶⁵ Doering, 'A Missionary's Testimony', p. 126; Norton, 'The Gift of the Holy Ghost', pp. 14-15.

¹⁶⁶ Montgomery, '"The Promise of the Father (#1)"', p. 148. Miskov notes that Montgomery 'did not rely upon the manifestation of tongues to enable her to speak foreign languages' but had experienced xenolalia, Miskov, *Life on Wings*, p. 251; cf. pp. 250-51.

¹⁶⁷ Montgomery, 'Speaking in Tongues', p. 253. The credible witness for Montgomery was Harriette M.T. Shimer, 'a missionary of the Society of Friends who had been working in China for the past seven years' wrote a verification that 'Mrs. Montgomery ... repeatedly prayed and sang in Chinese', p. 255. This article was reprinted as a tract: Carrie Judd Montgomery, *Speaking in Tongues* (Framingham, MA: Christian Workers Union, n.d.). For other attempts of verification, cf. Sadie Cody, 'The Work and Workers', pp. 228-29; *TOF* 34.2 (Feb 1914), pp. 28-29.

¹⁶⁸ Berhard, 'Supernatural Gifts', p. 204.

¹⁶⁹ Mullen, 'A New Experience', p. 214; cf. Mrs. Frances Kies, 'A Year As "Door Keeper"', *TOF* 34.4 (Apr 1914), p. 87.

cxxvi:2) ... (later) when he again came upon me in holy laughter, and as I just let go of my tongue and vocal organs He took possession, speaking and singing so sweetly in His own language.[170]

One very reserved man had a dream that he would have uncontrollable laughter upon his baptism and then did.[171] However, there was little theological reflection on laughter other than its occurrence.

II. Pre-Assemblies of God – *The Pentecost*

A. History of J. Roswell Flower

J. Roswell Flower's parents[172] became disillusioned with John A. Dowie's[173] community in Zion, IL and moved to Indianapolis, IN where they attended the CMA church.[174] 'The Pentecostal message came to Indianapolis from the ASM revival in Jan. 1907 through the ministry of Cook' where Flower surrendered his life and 'became active in ministry'.[175] At the time, Flower was working for a seed company and studying to become a lawyer. At the age of 20 he started *The Pentecost* and 'his contributions clearly demonstrate his familiarity with many personalities and facets of the emerging Pentecostal movement'.[176] Flower added his name to those calling for organization of what would become the AG.[177] He attended

---

[170] Opie, 'Healed and Baptized', p. 156; cf. Marshall, 'Deliverance of an Insane Sister', p. 12 ; A.C., 'Pentecostal Outpouring in England', *TOF* 29.1 (Jan 1909), p. 15; Hettiaratchy, 'In His "Banqueting House"', pp. 66-69; F.F. Bosworth, 'Letter From Dallas, Texas', *TOF* 34.3 (Mar 1914), p. 72; Grace C. Agar, 'Missionary Gleanings', *TOF* 34.9 (Sep 1914), pp. 209-10 (209); Mrs. May Evans, 'Healed of Cancer', *TOF* 34.12 (Dec 1914), pp. 271-72.

[171] W.W. Simpson, 'Notes From Kansu', *TOF* 33.3 (Mar 1913), pp. 53-55.

[172] See Brumback, *Suddenly From Heaven*, pp. 10-11, for the story of Mr. and Mrs. George L. Flower.

[173] Edith L. Blumhofer, 'John Alexander Dowie', in Stanley Burgess (ed.), *NIDPCM* (Grand Rapids, MI: Zondervan, rev. and expanded edn, 2002), pp. 586-87.

[174] Gary B. McGee, 'Joseph James Roswell Flower and Alice Reynolds', in Stanley Burgess (ed.), *NIDPCM* (Grand Rapids, MI: Zondervan, rev. and expanded edn, 2002), pp. 642-44 (642).

[175] McGee, 'Flower', *NIDPCM*, p. 642.

[176] McGee, 'Flower', *NIDPCM*, p. 642.

[177] The first call appeared in: 'General Convention of Pentecostal Saints and Churches of God In Christ', *WW* 9.12 (Dec 20, 1913), p. 1. His support was published one issue before the convention in *WW* 10.3 (Mar 20, 1914), p. 1. It appears that Flower was in search of a suitable affiliation. Note *TP's* attempts at finding a suitable association: two issues state this paper was the 'Official

the Hot Springs, AR meeting and held 'almost continuous positions of leadership from the inception of the Assemblies of God until his retirement, exercising an important stabilizing ministry during formative years'.[178]

B. The 'Full Consummation' of Spirit Baptism

Perhaps it was Flower's personal SB that caused him to hold a theologically nuanced and pastoral approach to the Bible sign.[179] In fact, his views diverged slightly from the standard view of IE in three ways. First, Flower 'shifted the focus from tongues as the necessary accompaniment of the reception of SB to tongues as the fullness of expression toward which the experience leads'.[180] Question: 'is the baptism in the Holy Spirit the finishing touch of the Christian experience? Ans. No. It is the top layer of the foundation of such experiences.'[181] As such, there was theological room for various experiences leading up to fullness. For example, 'stammering lips' were a type of proto-glossolalia that occurred before fullness. One missionary to Africa wrote, 'a white brother in our cottage meeting here last Friday night was near the confirmation of his baptism – stuttering and stammering, yet he did not let go'.[182] Also, there could be various 'anointings' that were not

---

organ of the Christian Assembly, corner Alabama and New York streets, Indianapolis, Indiana', *TP* 1.3 (Nov 1908), p. 4; *TP* 1.4 (Dec 1908), p. 8. Issue five notes that it was the 'Official organ of the Apostolic Faith Mission, cor. Alabama and New York strs., Indianapolis, Indiana', *TP* 1.5 (Jan/Feb 1909), p. 6. The very next issue states that 'we have moved *The Pentecost* from Indianapolis to Kansas City, Mo. It is about two years since I first met Brother Copley and since that time our hearts have slowly been *joined together* in a peculiar and wonderful manner', *TP* 1.6 (Apr/May 1909), p. 6 (emphasis added).

[178] Menzies, *Anointed To Serve*, p. 66. He served as founding secretary and secretary 1914-16 and 1935-59, and Foreign Missions Secretary from 1919 to 1925, Brumback, *Suddenly From Heaven*, pp. 167-68.

[179] 'Bible evidence' is the phrase used to describe the sign value of glossolalia in *TP*, e.g. H.M. Allen, 'The Bible Evidence', *TP* 1.3 (Nov 1908), p. 5.

[180] Macchia, 'Towards a Theology of Initial Evidence', p. 172.

[181] Flower, 'The Apostolic Question Box', *TP* 1.9 (Aug 1909), p. 9. It is unclear who authored this piece, though Flower was the Editor and Copley was the Associate Editor. In a later tract, Flower wrote, 'the receiving of the Holy Spirit was not considered a crowning experience for the believer – the culmination of Christian perfection – but an initial experience', Flower's tract, 'Is it Necessary to Speak In An Unknown Tongue' (Toronto, Canada: Full Gospel Publishing House, 1954 [?]), pp. 7-8.

[182] Ida F. Sackett, 'Words From Johannesburg', *TP* 2.4 (Mar 1, 1910), p. 8; cf. A.W. Brenzinger, 'Victory in Biglerville, Pa', *TP* 1.8 (Jul 1909), p. 2.

SB.[183] Finally, there were varying degrees of 'fullness'. For example, 'by this manifestation (tongues) ... it is known whether believers enjoy Pentecostal or *pre-pentecostal fullness*'.[184]

Second, *TP* was comfortable printing testimonies which noted a delay between when one 'received the Spirit by faith'[185] and when the sign of tongues occurred.[186] For example, Mary Lindley wrote, 'I accepted the promise the 11th day of last October and received the baptism in the Holy Spirit *and a few weeks later* the Spirit spoke for Himself through my lips in another tongue'.[187] Most notable among the testimonies of delayed tongues was the editor himself.[188] He claimed the baptism by faith and days later, 'the Lord ... gave me a big blessing, but no tongues'.[189] Later, in Kansas Citywhile alone in prayer, the Lord gave me *a few words in tongues* and I spoke them. Instantly the power of God struck me and ...

---

[183] Mrs. N. Mc -, 'A Timely Testimony', *TP* 2.5 (Apr 1, 1910), p. 3; cf. A.S. Copley, 'Sanctification', *TP* 1.2 (Sep 1908), p. 7. However, the editors note that 'the New Testament certainly makes no distinction between the anointing of the Spirit and the baptism in the Spirit. They are one and the same thing', *TP* 2.5 (Apr 1, 1910), p. 4.

[184] A.S. Copley, 'The Threefold Standard', *TP* 1.1 (Aug 1908), p. 8 (emphasis added).

[185] The position of *TP* is identical to Montgomery's noted above. For example, 'faith brings the answer', *TP* 2.5 (Apr 1, 1910), p. 4; 'speaking in new tongues is not promised to them who tarry for tongues, but to them that believe', *TP* 2.9 & 10 (Sep/Oct 1910), p. 11. Flower claimed both his sanctification and SB by faith, J. Roswell Flower, 'God Honors Faith', *TP* 2.3 (Feb 1910), p. 1.

[186] Ruth Angstead, 'A Grand Experience', *TP* 1.2 (Sep 1908), pp. 1-2 (1); 'Nuggets for Seekers', *TP* 1.3 (Nov 1908), p. 6; Sackett, 'Words From Johannesburg', p. 8; Mrs. N. Mc -, 'A Timely Testimony', p. 3.

[187] Mrs. Mary Lindley, 'The Beginning of Days for Me', *TP* 2.2 (Jan 1910), pp. 1, 3 (p, 3) (emphasis added).

[188] Flower's testimony was published three times after the founding of the AG: 1) J. Roswell Flower, 'How I Received the Baptism in the Holy Spirit (#1)', *PE* 982 (Jan 21, 1933), pp. 2-3 and 'How I Received the Baptism in the Holy Spirit (#2)', *PE* 983 (Jan 28, 1933), pp. 6-7; 2) J. Roswell Flower, 'How I Received the Baptism in the Holy Spirit (#3)', *PE* 2000 (Sep 7, 1952), pp. 5-7; and 'How I Received the Baptism in the Holy Spirit (#4)', *PE* 2001 (Sep 14, 1952), pp. 5, 12-13; 3) J. Roswell Flower, 'How I Received the Baptism in the Holy Spirit (#5)', *PE* 4132 (Jul 18, 1993) pp. 18-20. Macchia notes that the final retelling 'omits Flower's description of the delay in his experience between Spirit baptism and tongues', Macchia, 'Towards a Theology of Initial Evidence', p. 172; cf. Robeck, 'Emerging Magisterium', pp. 186-93. The 1933 and 1952 retellings are nearly identical with only minor changes. The 1993 retelling receives a substantial editing, omitting that SB, like healing, is obtained by faith, J. Roswell Flower, 'How I Received the Baptism in the Holy Spirit (#5)', pp. 18-20 (20).

[189] Flower, 'God Honors Faith', p. 1.

I was filled with joy unspeakable and full of glory. Then for a whole month I had to stand right there believing God. He gave me much joy and peace *but no tongues*.[190]

Later, 'God confirmed His Word' with signs following.[191] Overall, Flower answered delayed glossolalia with pastoral care:

> praise Him and tongues will invariably follow ... let us not discourage that one by telling him that he has not received the baptism simply because he has not spoken in another language. Let us not assume the place of God ... the voice of the Word and Spirit within are more sure than the sign of tongues without.[192]

Third, while Flower believed that glossolalia was the Bible evidence after the pattern in Acts,[193] he was nevertheless open to other signs of the Holy Spirit's presence:

> too much stress on speaking in tongues as the Bible evidence weakens the argument. To insist that this is the only evidence of the baptism in the Holy Spirit is to compel us to accept all speaking in tongues as divine. Whereas some is purely human and others certainly satanic. The Scripture is beautiful and safeguards itself. It records at least three signs of the Spirit's presence ... '**speak with tongues** and **magnify God**' (Acts 10:46) ... 'spake with tongues and **prophesied**' (Acts 19:6) ... we do not need to have a new tongue to magnify the Lord or to prophesy ... let us not stress any gift or doctrine out of due proportion ... when the Comforter comes, He will make Himself known, and evidence His presence.[194]

Because tongues were the final rather than first evidence of fullness, there was theological room for other signs of the Spirit's indwelling that led to that fullness. However, eventually,

---

[190] Flower, 'God Honors Faith', p. 1 (emphasis added).
[191] Flower, 'God Honors Faith', p. 1. The fullest published testimony (1933) notes: signs of joy, holy laughter, and the casting out of a demon, Flower, 'How I Received the Baptism in the Holy Spirit (#2)', pp. 6-7 (7).
[192] *TP* 2.5 (Apr 1, 1910), p. 4; cf. *TP* 2.9 & 10 (Sep/Oct 1910), p. 11.
[193] 'Caution to Seekers', *TP* 1.6 (Apr/May 1909), p. 9; J.O. Lehman, 'The Evidence of the Baptism in the Holy Spirit', *TP* 1.12 (Nov 1909), p. 2.
[194] *TP* 2.11 & 12 (Nov/Dec 1910), p. 9; cf. Lehman, 'The Evidence of the Baptism in the Holy Spirit', p. 2. Initial Evidence 'is beyond controversy'.

all those who are baptized with the Holy Spirit will either at the time of their baptism or shortly afterwards speak in tongues, yet we must with great care and humility teach this truth not too dogmatically or we shall be before we are aware, preaching tongues and thereby obscure the Christ.[195]

Finally, H.M. Allen disliked the scientific term 'Bible evidence' even though he fully embraced the concept as biblical.[196]

C. Responding to Critics

The Pentecost dealt lightly with two areas of criticism, the origin of tongues and cessation. Glossolalia could have a satanic origin.[197] As noted above, tongues could not be the singular sign of SB otherwise all tongues speech, including fleshly and demonic would be divine.[198] Such thinking would 'weaken the argument' of spiritual signs and cause 'well-meaning but untrained people to sometimes exalt this gift above measure, (and) pass beyond the Spirit into the flesh, become selfish and hence fanatical'.[199] Glossolalia could have a human origin, such as having a seeker repeat the same word or sound repetitiously. Such fleshly origins were 'dangerous':

> our duty is to tarry for the enduement with power, the fullness of God, by a wholly yielded attitude of the entire being to God ... many times seekers are rushed through. *They do get some kind of tongues*, but do not get the baptism; hence there is a lack of love and humility.[200]

To counter the claim that 'speaking in tongues is from the pit',

---

[195] Lehman, 'The Evidence of the Baptism in the Holy Spirit', p. 2. In a short tract Flower clarified: 'it would seem that there are varying measures of the Spirit experienced by believers ... (which) is determined by the willingness or ability of the person to yield to the Holy Spirit's possession ... it would be decidedly wrong for such a consecrated believer to declare that he had not received the Holy Spirit, even though he had not spoken in tongues. However his experience ... is still somewhat short of the pattern as set forth in the Acts ... without denying anything that God has done for him in the past, the individual may yield still further ... (then) *there will be inspired utterance*', Flower, 'Is it Necessary to Speak In An Unknown Tongue', pp. 13-15 (emphasis added). He distinguished between a baptism and 'an "inbreathing" of the Holy Spirit'.
[196] Allen, 'The Bible Evidence', p. 5.
[197] 'Why?', *TP* 1.7 (Jun 1909), p. 2; *TP* 1.9 (Aug 1909), p. 10.
[198] Lehman, 'The Evidence of the Baptism in the Holy Spirit', p. 2.
[199] Flower, 'The Apostolic Question Box', p. 9.
[200] 'Caution to Seekers', p. 9 (emphasis added).

several safeguards were posited.[201] First, genuine tongues should follow the biblical precedents, flow out of a humble heart and edify.[202] The yielded heart was to seek God and not tongues.[203] Second, the fruit of the SB person was a key indicator of the genuineness (or not) of their glossolalia.[204] Flower retooled Gamaliel's sage advice here, that 'if the work be of God, it shall stand. If not, it shall fail'.[205]

Cessationism was addressed in passing by two writers. Julia Divine noted several outpourings of tongues-speech in Church history. She called these 'oases' that 'brought refreshing from the presence of the Lord'.[206] An unnamed writer mused that some say 'the age of miracles is passed', but at the same time say 'the Holy Spirit is needed by all believers'.[207] This subtly implied that the Holy Spirit was not limited to 'one dispensation' or was solely 'for the Jews', undercutting reasons for cessation.

D. Purposes for Glossolalia

TP had several implied purposes for glossolalia similar to the periodicals above, though discussing the purpose for tongues did not seem to be a priority.[208] The following reasons for glossolalia were inductively culled from *TP* rather than didactically stated.

1. Power, Prayer, and Praise

First, glossolalia was intimately connected with power and the missionary call:

---

[201] 'Why?', *TP* 1.7 (Jun 1909), p. 2.

[202] Flower, 'The Apostolic Question Box', p. 9; *TP* 2.9 & 10 (Sep/Oct 1910), p. 11.

[203] Mrs. Minnie Quinn, 'Testimony', *TP* 1.1 (Aug 1908), p. 2; Alice M. Reynolds, 'Note From Indianapolis', *TP* 1.8 (Jul 1909), p. 11. Lehman notes that if someone wants the baptism but does not want tongues 'it shows at once that their will is not surrendered to God's will, for it is God's will that you shall speak in tongues', Lehman, 'The Evidence of the Baptism in the Holy Spirit', p. 2.

[204] 'Why?', p. 2.

[205] J. Roswell Flower, 'An Important Warning', *TP* 2.5 (Apr 1, 1910), p. 6.

[206] Mrs. Julia McCallie Divine, 'Spiritual Manifestations and the Churches', *TP* 1.3 (Nov 1908), p. 5.

[207] *TP* 2.5 (Apr 1, 1910), p. 4.

[208] One solitary paragraph stated: 'what is the use of tongues? ... prophecy is (now) fulfilled ... the human heart truly is satisfied only when it satisfies the heart of Jesus Christ fully by letting Him have His way absolutely ... personal upbuilding ... (it) builds up the church ... (and) it is a sign to the unbelieving', Flower, 'The Apostolic Question Box', p. 9.

the baptism of the Holy Ghost does not consist in simply speaking in tongues ... it fills our souls with the love of God for lost humanity, and makes us much more willing to leave home ... when we have tarried and receive that power, then, and then only are we fit to carry the gospel. When the Holy Spirit comes into our hearts, the missionary spirit comes with it; they are inseparable.[209]

Second, Copley noted that the Spirit prays through us: 'the Spirit Himself maketh superlative intercession for us with groanings inexpressible (Rom. 8:26 Int.) O, Lord, teach us to pray and teach us how to let the spirit pray through us'.[210] Third, 'The messages in tongues were largely praises'.[211]

2. Xenolalia

Xenolalia was another stated reason for tongues.[212] *The Pentcost* published accounts of MT during a fourteen month window, and then went silent on the subject. In the very first issue (Aug 1908) it reported that 'one dear man got saved, sanctified and baptized in about 10 minutes ... for several hours, praising God in tongues, speaking in German and Dutch languages he never knew before'.[213] One testimony even professed to a miracle of hearing:

the Lord withheld the gift of tongues from us. Here (Hailua, Hawaii) most of the people were Japanese, Portuguese, Chinese and natives, who cannot speak nor understand English tongues. We asked the Father in Jesus name to give them interpretation of our tongue. Glory, he did![214]

The Pentecost reported that 'we have just received word that Brother O'Reilly, in South America, is speaking in languages and being un-

---

[209] J.R. Flower, 'Editorial', *TP* 1.1 (Aug 1908), p. 4.
[210] A.S. Copley, 'Pentecost in Type', *TP* 1.8 (Jul 1909), pp. 7-8 (7).
[211] Mrs. Melvia Booker, 'Impressions', *TP* 1.10 (Sep 1909), pp. 2-3 (2); cf. Anna Holmquist, 'The Lord Hath Helped', *TP* 2.9 & 10 (Sep/Oct 1910), pp. 9, 16 (16).
[212] 'Why?', p. 2.
[213] J.O. Lehman, *TP* 1.1 (Aug 1908), p. 7; cf. Bro. Murray, 'The Use of Tongues', *TP* 1.3 (Nov 1908), p. 6; W.H. Standley, 'A Tardy Experience', *TP* 1.3 (Nov 1908), p. 7.
[214] F.E. Yoakum, 'Pentecostal Miracle', *TP* 1.4 (Dec 1908), p. 14.

derstood. As soon as we get more information will make announcement.'[215] The next issue questioned, 'how can the Jew be reached unless he ... hears the speaking in tongues in his own language by people who never learned the language?'[216] Four testimonies in subsequent issues were of xenolalia.[217] For example, 'Mrs. Hanson spoke in Chinese, yet did not know her own message ... the astonished student ... heard his own Mandarin tongue'.[218] The final account (Oct 1909) of xenolalia came from Antoinette Moomau who reported that 'one Chinese woman came through to her baptism speaking in clear English and she could not speak a word of English naturally'.[219] After October, 1909 there is no mention of MT in the remaining eleven extant issues of *TP*.

E. The Nature of Glossolalia

1. Heavenly Anthem

Similar to reports in other periodicals, the HA was more easily embraced than spoken-tongues, and was more readily identified as inspired. Copley wrote

> the sublimest (manifestation) ... is the anthem of the so-called 'heavenly choir.' Where the Holy Spirit has His way fully, He often utters unnameable, indescribable sounds through surrendered voices and lips ... the ecstasy at such moments is inexpressively glorious.[220]

If someone were able to sing in tongues, they would be counted among the Spirit-baptized; it was their Bible evidence. For example, 'one of our dear people here has received her baptism. She has the Bible evidence ... she induced them to let her sing of Jesus and of His blood. As she began to sing, she received her

---

[215] *TP* 1.6 (Apr/May 1909), p. 6.
[216] *TP* 1.7 (Jun 1909), p. 6.
[217] Brenzinger, 'Victory in Biglerville, Pa', p. 2; Mrs. M.E.H., *TP* 1.9 (Aug 1909), p. 4.
[218] Mrs. Woodbury, 'Tongues Heard and Understood', *TP* 1.9 (Aug 1909), p. 2
[219] Sisters Moomau and Phillips, 'Report From China', *TP* 1.11 (Oct 1909), p. 3.
[220] A.S. Copley, 'Pentecost in Type (Part 2)', *TP* 1.11 (Oct 1909), pp. 5-6 (6); cf. Angstead, 'A Grand Experience', pp. 1-2 (1).

baptism.'²²¹ The HA also attested to the Holy Spirit's presence in the meeting: 'the power of God fell on the meeting and many were speaking and singing in tongues'.²²²

2. Inspired Human Speech

According to one unnamed author in *TP*, glossolalia was people talking at the inspiration of the Holy Spirit, they were not a passive mouthpiece through whom the Holy Spirit spoke:

> the phrases, 'He spoke for Himself,' 'He spoke through me,' 'He will speak through me,' are not scriptural ... it is not the Spirit but the people talking in tongues. It is true, the Spirit furnishes the language – the 'utterance' – but the people furnish the subject.²²³

Many testimonies either refrained from saying 'He spoke for Himself', or were revised to have a more active human part. For example, Mrs. Minnie Quinn, wrote, 'I spoke in tongues as the Spirit gave utterance', or, 'I praised God when the Spirit gave utterance in an unknown tongue to me', and 'I spoke in two languages'.²²⁴ However, the author did give leeway for the Spirit to operate:

> to be sure, God might give the message. The Greek for the word 'utterance' would include the subject matter as well as the language, and it is entirely possible that the Spirit might, not only furnish the language but also furnish the subject matter, as He certainly does and the gift of prophecy. But if we are to judge by Scripture examples, this must be very rare.²²⁵

Testimonies where the individual was a passive tool of the Holy Spirit were published as well.²²⁶

---

²²¹ 'Baptized and Healed', *TP* 2.11 & 12 (Nov/Dec 1910), p. 5; cf. Grace Gilliam Mitchel, 'My Testimony for Christ', *TP* 1.11 (Oct 1909), p. 6; Amanda Smith, 'Testimonials', *TP* 2.4 (Mar 1, 1910), p. 3.

²²² Mrs. S.A. Smith, 'Pentecost in TN', *TP* 1.2 (Sep 1908), p. 8; cf. Alice M. Reynolds, 'The Indianapolis Work in General', *TP* 1.6 (Apr/May 1909), p. 11; L.B. Sly, 'Pentecost in Youngstown, Ohio', *TP* 1.7 (Jun 1909), p. 10.

²²³ *TP* 2.9 &10 (Sep/Oct 1910), p. 11.

²²⁴ Quinn, 'Testimony', p. 2; Martha J. Lewis 'Pentecost for Nine Years', *TP* 1.3 (Nov 1908), p. 7; H.H. Jones, *TP* 1.10 (Sep 1909), p. 4.

²²⁵ *TP* 2.9 &10 (Sep/Oct 1910), p. 11.

²²⁶ 'Nuggets for Seekers', p. 6; Reynolds, 'Note From Indianapolis', p. 11.

III. Rise of the Finished Work – *Pentecostal Testimony*

A. History of William H. Durham

Though William H. Durham only served for five years as a Pentecostal pastor and evangelist before dying of pneumonia in 1912, his FW doctrine would identify the FW denominations and provide the foundation for Oneness Pentecostalism.[227] Though some would be won over to the FW position, Durham seemed to have given voice to large numbers of people who did not embrace the WH position.[228] Coming from a Baptist background, Durham pastored at Chicago's North Avenue Mission when he heard about the revival in Los Angeles. At Azusa, Seymour prophesied over him that wherever Durham would preach, 'the Holy Spirit would fall upon the people'.[229] This proved to be true because his powerful preaching drew thousands.[230] At his Chicago revival, it was not at all uncommon to hear people at all hours of the night speaking in tongues and singing in the Spirit.[231] He also influenced others who would become leaders in the movement[232] and networked with ethnic minority Pentecostal leaders.[233] William W. Menzies

---

[227] William Durham, 'Personal Testimony of Pastor Durham', *PT* (Mar 1909), pp. 5-7; Brumback, *Suddenly From Heaven*, p. 100; Riss, 'Finished Work Controversy', p. 639; Richard M. Riss, 'William H. Durham', in Stanley Burgess (ed.), *NIDPCM* (Grand Rapids, MI: Zondervan, rev. and expanded edn, 2002), pp. 594-95 (594); David A. Reed, 'Oneness Pentecostalism', in Stanley Burgess (ed.), *NIDPCM* (Grand Rapids, MI: Zondervan, rev. and expanded edn, 2002), pp. 936-44 (936-37).

[228] Goss, *The Winds of God*, p. 204; Bartleman, *Azusa Street*, pp. 169-79.

[229] Durham, 'Personal Testimony of Pastor Durham', p. 7 (reprint in *PT* 2.3 (Jun 1912), p. 4); Riss, 'William H. Durham', p. 594.

[230] Riss, 'William H. Durham', p. 594.

[231] William Durham, 'The Great Chicago Revival', *PT* 2.2 (May 1912), pp. 13-14; cf. William Durham, 'How The Work Is Progressing', *PT* 1.5 (Jul 1910), p. 15; Brumback, *Suddenly From Heaven*, p. 69; Goss, *The Winds of God*, pp. 199-204.

[232] Riss, 'William H. Durham', p. 594. Notable among the early leaders are: Argue, E.N. Bell, Howard Goss, and McPherson. Cf. Durham, 'How The Work Is Progressing', p. 15; Menzies, *Anointed To Serve*, pp. 65, 76. Brumback believes the Chicago revival also impacted William Piper and the Stone Church, Brumback, *Suddenly From Heaven*, pp. 70-71.

[233] His work among ethnic minorities include: Daniel Berg (founded AG in Brazil), Luigi Fancescon (Italians), F.A. Sandgren (Scandinavians), and Urshan (Persian). Durham took note of the multiple ethnicities touched in the Chicago revival and wrote, 'if I ever saw the proof that God is no respecter of persons,

notes that 'God used Durham there (Midwest) much as He did Cashwell in the south'.²³⁴

B. The Finished Work and Spirit Baptism

Durham had two theological passions that show up throughout *PT*: the FW and SB.²³⁵ For example, the

> Pentecostal Testimony stands for *real full salvation* (FW) in Christ, and for the *real baptism of the Holy Spirit*. *False* theories concerning the baptism will be exposed ... we stand, and shall continue to stand for unity of all God's people in the Spirit, not in the *flesh*. *We cannot afford to purchase unity by sacrificing the Truth of God*.²³⁶

1. The Finished Work

Even though Durham himself had a second-work of sanctification experience, after his own SB he reformulated his theology to adapt 'it to his Baptist roots ... This new Pentecostal soteriology disclaimed sanctification as a second definite work of grace, seeing justification and sanctification as occurring at the moment of conversion'.²³⁷ Durham became highly critical of the WH second work of sanctification,²³⁸ especially because he viewed it as an

---

I saw it here. Old and young, black and white, without respect to creed or nationality, the people who went to seek God were met with His mighty power and baptized in the Spirit', Durham, 'The Great Chicago Revival', p. 13.

²³⁴ Menzies, *Anointed To Serve*, p. 65.

²³⁵ William Durham, 'The Two Great Experiences', *PT* 1.8 (Aug 1911), pp. 5-7 (6); William Durham, 'The Progress of the Work In General', *PT* 2.1 (Jan 1912), p. 1; Durham, 'The Great Battle of Nineteen Eleven', p. 7; Durham, 'The Great Chicago Revival', p. 14.

²³⁶ Durham, 'Editorial', p. 1 (emphasis added). Note the sharp line here: God 'used it (IE) to *draw a line between* those who had the baptism and those who had not', William Durham, 'Speaking in Tongues Is The Evidence of the Baptism in the Holy Spirit', *PT* 2.2 (May 1912), pp. 9-11 (11) (emphasis added).

²³⁷ Alexander, *Pentecostal Healing*, p. 150. Alexander notes that the memorial edition 'omits the account of his sanctification experience', n. 470.

²³⁸ His two primary criticisms are: 1) there is 'not even one Scripture that teaches that sanctification is a second work of grace', William Durham, 'Sanctification', *PT* 1.8 (Aug 1911), pp. 1-3 (1); cf. Durham, 'The Two Great Experiences', p. 6; William Durham, 'An Open Letter To My Brother Ministers In And Out of the Pentecostal Movement. A Strong Appeal', *PT* 1.8 (Aug 1911), pp. 12-13 (13); William Durham, 'The Finished Work of Calvary: Identification with Jesus Christ Saves and Sanctifies', *PT* 2.1 (Jan 1912), pp. 1-3. 2) 'Experience, and not Scripture is used to prove the experience', Durham, 'Sanctification', p. 1. 3) Durham's opponents mischaracterize his position, William

incomplete view of salvation.[239] Sanctification, he believed, was complete upon justification and then one lived a life of 'continual dependence on Jesus Christ ... (an) overcoming life'.[240]

Durham's FW doctrine touched glossolalia in two ways: first, tongues signified that in SB the person was 'sealed unto the day of redemption ... (a) seal of a finished salvation in Jesus Christ';[241] however, he would not go so far as to say 'only those who had the baptism and spoke in tongues were saved'.[242] This was accomplished by two clear receptions: 'the truth is, sinners receive Christ, and believers, and believers only, receive the Holy Spirit'.[243] Though it is unclear exactly what he meant by 'seal' of the Spirit, he compared it to the sign-value of circumcision: 'this sealing did not make him (Abraham) righteous, but was an external sign, a testimony'.[244]

Second, Durham argued that sanctification experiences should not be called the baptism of the Holy Spirit. 'Many of us have called our experiences by the wrong name',[245] and then questioned '"what am I to do with my experience?" Brother, change its name.'[246] One testimony implied that leading people into SB was

---

Durham, 'Some Other Phases of Sanctification', *PT* 2.2. (May 1912), pp. 7-9 (9).

[239] He writes that with the WH position 'men are *partly saved* in conversion, and that it takes a second work of grace to complete the job', Durham, 'The Two Great Experiences', p. 6.

[240] Durham, 'Sanctification', p. 2; cf. Durham, 'The Great Battle of Nineteen Eleven', pp. 6-8; William Durham, 'The Great Need of the Hour', *PT* 2.1 (Jan 1912), pp. 10-11 (10).

[241] Durham, 'The Two Great Experiences', p. 6; cf. Durham, 'The Progress of the Work In General', p. 1.

[242] William Durham, 'False Doctrines', *PT* 2.2 (May 1012), pp. 6-7 (6); cf. William Durham, 'Sealed With The Spirit (incomplete article)', *PT* (Mar 1909), p. 12.

[243] Durham, 'False Doctrines', p. 6.

[244] Durham, 'Sealed With The Spirit', p. 12. This sealing is compared to a corporate logo today, a 'Bible brand', William Durham, 'A Word To Ministers, From A Minister', *PT* (Mar 1909), pp. 10-12 (11); William Durham, 'The Great Crisis Number Two', *PT* 1.5 (Jul 1910), pp. 1-4 (3).

[245] Durham, 'Sanctification', p. 1.

[246] William Durham, 'The Second Work of Grace People Answered', *PT* 1.8 (Aug 1911), pp. 7-9 (9); cf. Durham, 'The Two Great Experiences', p. 6. Durham notes that sanctification could also mean 'set apart for a holy use' and not just cleansing, Durham, 'The Second Work of Grace People Answered', p. 8; cf. Durham, 'Some Other Phases of Sanctification', pp. 7-8.

easier when people were unaware of 'the second work theory'.²⁴⁷ Durham did not elaborate, but perhaps he believed that in such cases, a clarification of terms was not necessary.

2. The Evidence²⁴⁸

'Many honest souls oppose the truth of God', wrote Durham, 'telling them they could have the Holy Ghost and not speak in tongues, or that they already had the baptism and all they need to do is wait for the evidence of tongues'.²⁴⁹ Durham disagreed and became a staunch defender of evidentiary glossolalia.²⁵⁰ He even called it the dividing 'line between those who had the baptism and those who had not'.²⁵¹ He reasoned that this was either 'a genuine outpouring of the Holy Spirit, or it is the basest fraud the world has ever seen'.²⁵² His defence of the evidence may have been a reaction to the spirituality and cultural background of his day. First, he saw few Christians living a vibrant life: 'there is neither fanaticism nor counterfeit in the denominational churches of this day; the reason is they are dead'.²⁵³ Further, 'higher criticism' and 'intellectual knowledge' were weakening the faith of future ministers.²⁵⁴ He viewed the revival and its accompanying sign as a restoration of biblical Christianity for the end times.²⁵⁵ Second, he stood for a living relationship with God against the influence of the popular new scientific method. He believed there was

---

²⁴⁷ William Durham, 'A Great Revival In Dallas, Texas', *PT* 1.8 (Aug 1911), p. 14.
²⁴⁸ 'The evidence' is used to describe evidential glossolalia. Durham used the moniker, 'the Bible evidence' in his testimony, Durham, 'Personal Testimony of Pastor Durham', p. 7.
²⁴⁹ Durham, 'An Open Letter To My Brother Ministers', p. 12.
²⁵⁰ Durham, 'Criticisms Answered', p. 11.
²⁵¹ Durham, 'Speaking in Tongues is the Evidence of the Baptism in the Holy Spirit', pp. 9-12 (11); cf. William Durham, 'The Winnipeg Convention', *PT* 2.1 (Jan 1912), pp. 11-12 (12).
²⁵² Durham, 'The Great Crisis Number Two', p. 3.
²⁵³ William Durham, 'What is the Evidence of the Baptism in the Holy Ghost, No. 3', *PT* 2.1 (Jan 1912), pp. 4-6 (5); cf. William Durham, 'The Great Crisis: The Finished Work Is Hastening It', *PT* 2.2 (May 1912), pp. 4-6 (5).
²⁵⁴ Durham, 'A Word to Ministers, from a Minister', p. 10.
²⁵⁵ Durham, 'The Great Crisis Number Two', p. 4; Durham, 'An Open Letter To My Brother Ministers', p. 13; William Durham, 'The Gospel of Christ', *PT* 2.1 (Jan 1912), pp. 8-10 (9); Durham, 'The Great Crisis: The Finished Work Is Hastening It', p. 6.

an attempt on the part of the scientific world to rule God out entirely, or to leave us only a vague, mysterious, impartial God ... (but) we have this clear unmistakable *proof* of the word of God concerning the baptism of the Holy Ghost ... the blessed Holy Spirit simply comes upon and into our souls and bodies and takes possession and speaks through us, as a *proof* that is the real Bible brand.[256]

A case could be made that Durham (along with others)[257] co-opted the language of science for apologetic and evangelistic engagement with his culture.[258] Terms like 'proof' and 'evidence' are frequent in *PT*:[259] 'we believe the speaking in tongues to be the *evidence* of the baptism of the Holy Ghost. God is *confirming* this doctrine with the signs [sic]'.[260]

If scientific proof of SB was demanded, then Durham was happy to oblige. Three extant articles with nearly identical arguments laid fact upon fact toward the logical conclusion that SB 'is always a definite experience. It is invariably accompanied by the speaking in other tongues as the spirit gives utterance.'[261] His arguments were: fact one, 'the most Spiritual persons were the first to be baptized, and speak in tongues'.[262] In contrast, 'the dishonesty of those who opposed the movement did much to convince me of its genuineness', because they charged 'the Pentecostal people with what they neither believed nor taught ... (and) they began to ridicule the manifestations of the Spirit in the movement'.[263] Fact two eliminated doubt. Durham asked the Azusa workers

---

[256] Durham, 'The Great Crisis Number Two', pp. 2-3.

[257] Sisson, 'A Call To Prayer For A World-Wide Revival', p. 60; Perry, 'Why Reject Speaking in Tongues', p. 3.

[258] Spittler, 'Suggested Areas For Further Research In Pentecostal Studies', p. 48; cf. H.D. McDonald, *Theories of Revelation: An Historical Study 1860-1960* (London: Uwin Brothers, 1963).

[259] Durham, 'A Word to Ministers, from a Minister', p. 10; Durham, 'The Great Chicago Revival', p. 13.

[260] Durham, 'Editorial', p. 1. 'Evidence' is used at least 30 times, e.g. William Durham, 'Manifestations Number II', *PT* 1.5 (Jul 1910), pp. 7-9; William Durham, 'Doctor Dixon Answered', *PT* 1.5 (Jul 1910), pp. 12-14; Durham, 'Evidence, No. 3', pp. 4-6; Durham, 'Evidence of the Baptism', pp. 9-11.

[261] Durham, 'The Two Great Experiences', p. 6.

[262] William Durham, 'Fragment', *PT* (Mar 1909), p. 5; cf. Durham, 'Evidence of the Baptism', p. 10; Durham, 'Personal Testimony of Pastor Durham', p. 6.

[263] Durham, 'Evidence, No. 3', pp. 4-5.

if everyone had spoken in tongues, they replied they had, and I will confess that I was disappointed, as it would've been a great relief to me if I could've found one who had received just what the rest did except the tongues, but I could not.[264]

Fact three was Durham's own personal journey which led him from opposing it 'with all my might' to writing that 'God gloriously baptized me in his Holy Spirit, and O! How He did speak through me in tongues!'[265] Fact four was that the Bible gave 'this as the sign in every case'.[266] Even though Durham believed that all one 'had to do was to read Acts 2:4, and measure their experience by it, as this is God's only standard',[267] the experiences of the disciples in Acts 10, 11, and 19 were 'a sign whereby they knew beyond a doubt that the Holy Ghost had fallen'.[268] Fact five was the personal testimony of thousands who, when Spirit baptized, spoke in tongues. Further, 'whenever they cease in any place to teach that the tongues are the evidence the power of God lifts and they have very few baptisms anymore'.[269] As Durham saw it, there was no middle ground: 'if the tongues are the evidence, and men reject that part of the message, they are rejecting that much of the message of God'.[270]

Durham applied the Bible evidence standard to himself and his close friends. Both he and Bell had multiple experiences before they testified to a full SB: Durham felt 'a mighty current of power' go through him, fell to the floor and then later physically shook before his third encounter when he spoke in tongues.[271] Bell was filled with joy and a 'holy laughter filled my mouth', and then was given one word to shout, 'glory' before his third encounter when

---

[264] Durham, 'Fragment', p. 5; cf. Durham, 'Evidence, No. 3', p. 4.
[265] Durham, 'Fragment', p. 5; cf. Durham, 'Personal Testimony of Pastor Durham', pp. 6, 7.
[266] Durham, 'Fragment', p. 5.
[267] Durham, 'Evidence, No. 3', p. 5.
[268] Durham, 'Fragment', p. 5; cf. Durham, 'Tongues Is The Evidence of the Baptism', p. 11.
[269] Durham, "Speaking in Tongues is the Evidence of the Baptism in the Holy Spirit', pp. 10-11.
[270] Durham, 'An Open Letter To My Brother Ministers', p. 12.
[271] Durham, 'Personal Testimony of Pastor Durham', p. 7.

he too spoke in tongues.[272]

C. Responding to Critics

In addition to his passionate writings on the evidence and the FW, Durham did address some general criticisms of glossolalia. He wrote,

> whenever there is a revival of considerable power there are sure to be manifestations ... when signs and wonders cease it is a sure evidence that the church has drifted away from God, and that God has withdrawn His presence from it ... His return is evidence and accompanied by signs and wonders ... (however) there never was a genuine work in progress that Satan did not get some counterfeit in to it.[273]

He countered cessation with an appeal to history and encouraged people to judge for themselves the genuineness of the present revival.[274] He warned that ascribing to Satan what is an actual work of the Spirit is 'blaspheming the Holy Spirit'.[275]

In one article Durham answered the criticism of A.C. Dixon, the pastor of Moody Church.[276] First, Dixon believed that Pentecost was a miracle of hearing not speaking[277] and that it was unrepeatable. Durham responded that Dixon ignored Peter's account in Acts 10.47 and the retelling in Acts 11.15, where Peter specifically stated, 'it was the speaking in other tongues ... that convinced both Peter and those with him'. Further, he noted that Dixon left off the adjective 'other' in his writing, as if people simply spoke 'in a different way in the same language'.[278] Second, Dixon believed that tongues were 'ecstatic ... (and) expressed emotion without

---

[272] E.N. Bell, 'Testimony of A Baptist Pastor', *PT* (Mar 1909), pp. 8-10 (10); cf. E.N. Bell, 'Sermon Given By Bro. E.N. Bell', *WE* 113 (Oct 30, 1915), p. 3; cf. Bro. E.N. Bell, 'Sermon', *WE* 113 (Oct 30, 1915), p. 3.
[273] Durham, 'Manifestations Number II', pp. 7-8.
[274] Durham, 'Manifestations Number II', pp. 7-8.
[275] Durham, 'Manifestations Number II', p. 8.
[276] Durham, 'Doctor Dixon Answered', pp. 12-14.
[277] Durham does not counter this argument. He writes, 'the Scriptures say distinctly that they spake in other tongues, to our mind there is no room whatever for doubting that they really spake in other tongues', Durham, 'Doctor Dixon Answered', p. 12.
[278] Durham, 'Doctor Dixon Answered', p. 12.

thought'.²⁷⁹ The gift of interpretation was 'someone would stand up and explain to the people that the one speaking in tongues was not crazy, but simply so happy that he had lost control of himself'.²⁸⁰ Durham responded that it was a travesty to downplay a gift of the Holy Spirit to happy emotionalism. When Durham spoke in tongues,

> I spoke as the Spirit gave utterance ... it was the operation of the Holy Ghost that caused the speaking in tongues ... I am just as apt to speak when under a burden for the lost, or for the work of the Lord, or when in earnest prayer, as when I am rapturously happy.²⁸¹

Third, 'Dixon makes the astonishing statement that speaking in tongues was a sign of unbelief rather than faith'.²⁸² Durham reminds Dixon of Jesus' promise that 'these signs shall follow them that believe' and that by Paul's own admission he would be the 'greatest unbeliever'.²⁸³

D. The Finished Work as *The Pentecostal Testimony's* only Distinction

In the five extant issues²⁸⁴ of *PT* only the emphasis on the FW is unique. Beyond that, the testimonies and articles reveal that Durham held views of glossolalia in keeping with other Pentecostal periodicals. For example, IE is dogmatically supported and the purposes for tongues are: praise,²⁸⁵ prayer,²⁸⁶ and as a sign.²⁸⁷ The nature of glossolalia could be the HA²⁸⁸ or glossolalia. Durham

---

²⁷⁹ Durham, 'Doctor Dixon Answered', p. 13.
²⁸⁰ Durham, 'Doctor Dixon Answered', p. 13.
²⁸¹ Durham, 'Doctor Dixon Answered', p. 13.
²⁸² Durham, 'Doctor Dixon Answered', p. 14.
²⁸³ Durham, 'Doctor Dixon Answered', p. 14.
²⁸⁴ The memorial issue, *PT* 2.3 (Jun 1912), has only a few revival reports and ministry updates that are new. All the significant articles were reprints of prior editions.
²⁸⁵ Bell, 'Testimony of A Baptist Pastor', p. 10.
²⁸⁶ Durham, 'Doctor Dixon Answered', p. 13.
²⁸⁷ Durham, 'A Word To Ministers, From A Minister', p. 11.
²⁸⁸ Durham, 'Personal Testimony of Pastor Durham', p. 6; cf. William Durham, 'Our Canadian Tour', *PT* 1.5 (Jul 1910), pp. 5-6 (5); William Durham, 'The Miraculous, Instantaneous Healing of Mabel Snipes, From Consumption', *PT* 1.5 (Jul 1910), pp. 6-7 (6); Durham, 'Manifestations Number II', p. 7; Durham, 'How The Work Is Progressing', p. 15; William Durham, 'The Great Revival At Azusa Street Mission – How It Began And How It Ended', *PT* 1.8

does not address the role of the human will in glossolalia other than to say it is not 'ecstatic',[289] that the Holy Spirit speaks through the individual,[290] and one should not seek tongues but SB.[291]

IV. Pre-Assemblies of God – *Word and Witness*

A. Eudorus N. Bell

Eudorus N. Bell sought and received his SB during a requested leave of absence from his Baptist church.[292] He was 'one of the better educated Pentecostals during this period',[293] and his first Pentecostal pastorate was in Malvern, AK during which time he became the editor of *WW*.[294] He would be among the first to call for the organization of the AG and was elected as its first general chairman.[295] 'When he was rebaptized during the early years of the Oneness controversy, it both shocked and pleased Pentecostals who were divided over the issue. Trinitarians, however, were relieved when he returned to their camp.'[296] Brumback believed Bell

---

(Aug 1911), pp. 1-4 (3); Durham, 'The Winnipeg Convention', p. 11; William Durham, 'Los Angeles Convention', *PT* 2.1 (Jan 1912), pp. 12-13 (13).

[289] Durham, 'Doctor Dixon Answered', p. 13.

[290] Durham, 'The Gospel of Christ', p. 8.

[291] Durham, 'A Word To Ministers, From A Minister', p. 11. The full quote reads, 'is the baptism in the Holy Spirit the finishing touch of a Christian experience? ... No. It is the *top layer of the foundation* of such an experience ... they are exhorted to go on to perfection'.

[292] While Bell was a pastor in Fort Worth, TX, he received his SB at North Avenue Mission, Chicago, IL, under the ministry of Durham, Brumback, *Suddenly From Heaven*, p. 69; cf. Bell, 'Testimony of A Baptist Pastor', pp. 8-10 (10); Bell, 'Sermon Given By Bro. E.N. Bell', p. 3.

[293] Wayne E. Warner, 'Eudorus N. Bell', in Stanley Burgess (ed.), *NIDPCM* (Grand Rapids, MI: Zondervan, rev. and expanded edn, 2002), p. 369. He attended 'Stetson University in the 1890s, Southern Baptist Theological Seminary (1900-1902), and the University of Chicago (B.A., 1903)'.

[294] Brumback, *Suddenly From Heaven*, p. 164.

[295] A position Bell held in 1914 and again in 1920-23. He also served as General Secretary 1919-1920 and pastored from 1917-1919, Warner, 'Eudorus N. Bell', p. 369.

[296] Warner, 'Eudorus N. Bell', p. 369; cf. Brumback, *Suddenly From Heaven*, pp. 195-99; Menzies, *Anointed To Serve*, pp. 114-18. Even though Bell 'published articles and editorials denouncing the New Issue ... he accepted baptism in the name of Jesus Christ as a valid alternative, (but) opposed any requirement to be rebaptized', Reed, 'Oneness Pentecostalism', p. 937. In the summer of 1915 he was rebaptized at a camp meeting in Jackson, TN, Brumback, *Suddenly From Heaven*, pp. 195-96. By November 1915, Flower wrote that Bell had 'been desir-

flip-flopped because of spiritual exhaustion and the desire to have a successful meeting. Brumback writes,

> He found himself 'in a corner' ... Bell had been working day and night ... [which] made it almost impossible for him to pray ... At the camp meeting, Bell received the impression that, if he did not preach Acts 2:38, the camp would be the worst.[297]

Agreeing with Brumback, Menzies states, 'he had been swept away out of fear of losing influence'.[298]

B. 'The Evidence'

'The evidence' or the 'Bible evidence'[299] in the *WW* was a 'great essential doctrine'[300] that 'does for us exactly what it did for' the earliest Christians.[301] At times, *WW* reads as though the discussion was beyond 'the evidence', at least by its contributors. For example, 'the sign of receiving the baptism is, *beyond controversy*, (it is) speaking in other tongues as the Spirit gives utterance'.[302] O.P. Brann wrote that his SB was 'such a clear definite evidence ... I can positively say no one receiving the experience will ever again have a shadow of doubt about this being the evidence and sign

---

ing to be released from the editorial chair for one year, and offered his resignation', J.R. Flower, 'A Change of Editors', *WW* 12.11 (Nov 1915), p. 4. Eventually, it was Bell's 'firm Trinitarian belief' that kept him 'from enlisting in the new movement'. By the 3rd General Council, Fall 1916, Bell was back in favour with the AG when it was 'faced with the unpleasant task of setting doctrinal limits' contrary to a founding principle that it would not create an organization 'that legislates or forms laws and articles of faith', Warner, 'Eudorus N. Bell', p. 938.

[297] The meeting went 'flat' so he announced his baptism, Brumback, *Suddenly From Heaven*, p. 199.

[298] Menzies, *Anointed To Serve*, p. 118.

[299] The preferred nomenclature is 'the evidence', with quite a few references to the 'Bible evidence'. Bell states, 'THE SPEAKING IN OTHER TONGUES AS THE SPIRIT OF GOD GIVES THE UTTERANCE IS THE INDISPUTABLE EVIDENCE OF THE BAPTISM WITH THE HOLY SPIRIT', E.N.B., 'What is the Evidence of the Baptism In The Spirit', *WW* 9.6 (Jun 20, 1913), p. 7.

[300] L.C. Hall, 'The Great Crisis Near at Hand', *WW* 9.11 (Nov 20, 1913), p. 1.

[301] Geo. G Brinkman, *WW* 10.5 (May 20, 1914), pp. 1-2 (1).

[302] C.W. Doney, 'The Gospel of the Kingdom', *WW* 10.3 (Mar 20, 1914), p. 2 (emphasis added). Consider Pinson's remark, 'all the leading preachers and workers stood together that ... when God saves a man he is ready for baptism in the Spirit and when baptized he will speak in tongues', M.M. Pinson, 'Trip to the Southwest', *WW* 8.6 (Aug 20, 1912), p. 1.

God has set'.[303] Nevertheless, contributors reaffirmed that the sign value of tongues was scriptural, that it was the 'first of the gifts' among multiple experiences, and that the terminology used to express it was insufficient.[304]

The evidence was so thoroughly believed to be biblical that the testimonies in *WW* developed a unique 'shorthand' to signify this rootedness. The most frequently used shorthand phrase was 'as in Acts 2.4'. For example, Harry Van Loon testified that 'fifteen on this one day were baptized in the Spirit and came through speaking in other tongues *as in Acts 2:4*'.[305] Other shorthand phrases were, 'as the Spirit gave utterance',[306] 'as in Acts 10:44-46',[307] as 'in Acts 2:4; 10:45; and 19:6',[308] 'as they did on the day of Pentecost',[309] 'as at first',[310] 'according to the book of Acts',[311] and the phrase, 'Bible evidence'.[312] Contrary to those who labelled glossolalia the 'TONGUE HERESY' and the 'DELUSION OF THE DEVIL',

---

[303] O.P. Brann, 'O.P. Brann Baptized', *WW* 10.3 (Mar 20, 1914), p. 4.

[304] Andrew L. Fraser, 'A Contrast in Values', *WW* 10.8 (Aug 1914), p. 3.

[305] Harry Van Loon, 'Oakland, Cal.', *WW* 8.8 (Oct 20, 1912), p. 1. This phrase was used extensively, cf. Editor, 'God Working Still In The land', *WW* 8.10 (Dec 20, 1912), p. 3; 'Bro Sweaza, MO', *WW* 9.12 (Dec 20, 1913), p. 3; J.M.C., 'Paxton, Fla.', *WW* 10.5 (May 20, 1914), p. 3; Carry Dyer, 'Charlton, Iowa', *WW* 12.7 (Jul 1915), p. 1.

[306] 'Glory In Unity At The Eureka Springs Camp!', *WW* 8.6 (Aug 20, 1912), p. 1; Herbert Buffum, 'Topeka, Kan', *WW* 9.5 (May 20, 1913), p. 3; M.M. Pinson, 'Cazadero Camp Meeting', *WW* 10.10 (Oct 1914), p. 1; E.F Cunningham and Wife, 'Maud, ILL', *WW* 12.9 (Sep 1915), p. 3.

[307] F.R. Anderson, 'Morgan Center, IA', *WW* 9.3 (Mar 20, 1913), p. 2; Wm. A. Summers, 'Sinners Deeply Convicted', *WW* 12.5 (May 1915), p. 8; W.T. Robbins, 'Prayer Answered', *WW* 12.8 (Aug 1915), p. 2; Wm. T. Robbins, 'God Wonderfully Works At Fagan, KY.', *WW* 12.9 (Sep 1915), p. 7.

[308] M.M. Pinson, 'Sanctified In Christ', *WW* 9.1 (Jan 20, 1913), p. 4; Clyde Bailey, 'Grand View, Ind.', *WW* 10.3 (Mar 20, 1914), p. 1; Editor, 'A New Creation', *WW* 8.8 (Oct 20, 1912), p. 2; 'All Round Christians', *WW* 9.1 (Jan 20, 1913), p. 2.

[309] F.M. Couch, 'God Working in Egypt', *WW* 8.6 (Aug 20, 1912), p. 3; cf. Daniel C.O. Opperman, 'Gleanings From The Foreign Mission Field', *WW* 9.5 (May 20, 1913), p. 4; Wm H. Merrin, 'Topeka Camp Glorious', *WW* 10.10 (Oct 1914), p. 1.

[310] 'Frank Denney', *WW* 12.7 (Jul 1915), p. 6.

[311] Mrs. F.L.P., 'Osborne, Kan.', *WW* 10.5 (May 20, 1914), p. 3.

[312] S.A. Jamieson, 'God Still In Dallas', *WW* 9.2 (Feb 20, 1912), p. 2; Mary DeWeese, 'Springfield, MO', *WW* 9.5 (May 20, 1913), p. 3; Mrs. Annie Green, 'Baptized 28 Years Ago', *WW* 10.1 (Jan 20, 1914), p. 2; W.M. Coleman, 'The Mountain Work', *WW* 12.5 (May 1915), p. 7.

J.E. Longdon challenged his readers to 'read the following references in your Bible, and hear God's own answer to this question'.[313] Longdon then noted there were 'three witnesses' in Acts: Jews, Romans, and Greeks 'all alike at once spoke with other tongues when baptized with the Holy Ghost'.[314]

Similar to other Pentecostal periodicals, there were testimonies in *WW* that came close to full SB but fell just short of glossolalic speech.[315] For example, 'my wife also nearly received hers. The Spirit moved her lips and whispering the words [sic]'[316] and 'one who had utterance in tongues before but not fully satisfied, has come out fully'.[317] E.N. Bell noted that he had multiple experiences before his SB.[318] After differentiating between the evidence and gift of tongues, Andrew L. Fraser wrote that tongues 'is **not the least** of the gifts, but **it is the first** of the gifts … it is the steppingstone … to higher things'.[319] Glossolalia was the entry point to 'greater responsibility'.[320] Also, 'unscriptural methods', such as having a candidate repeat a sound or phrase over and over until they spoke gibberish was condemned.[321] Likewise counterfeits were rejected.[322] The seeker was encouraged that yieldedness was

---

[313] J.E. Longdon, 'Are Tongues a Heresy?', *WW* 9.6 (Jun 20, 1913), p. 6.

[314] Longdon, 'Are Tongues a Heresy?', p. 6. Here Longdon alludes to Moses' requirement for multiple witnesses in Deut. 17.6; 19.15 (cf. Mt. 18.16; 2 Cor. 13.1; and Heb. 10.28), but he expands this concept from the witness of three individuals to the three people groups of Jews, Romans, and Greeks in Acts 2.4; 10.44-47; 19.2. Longdon also includes Jn 15.26 in this list. Cf. 'The Sign Will Follow', *WW* 9.10 (Oct 20, 1913), p. 2.

[315] Standley, 'Worth Tarrying For', p. 3; Benefield, 'Midland City, Ala.', p. 8; Brinson-Rushire, 'Taiafu, Shantung, China', p. 3; 'Another One Gone', p. 3; Hicks, 'A Spiritual House', p. 4; and Flower, 'The Apostolic Question Box', p. 9.

[316] J.G. Gray, 'His Wedding Garments', *WW* 12.5 (May 1915), p. 3.

[317] W.W. Simpson, 'W.W. Simpson', *WW* 12.5 (May 1915), p. 6.

[318] 'Those who thus press on with God, walking in the Spirit of holiness, will have many blessed experiences … the writer had fully half a dozen blessed experiences while seeking the baptism, and very many more since', Editor, 'A New Creation', p. 2; cf. 'Editorials – Avoid Extremes', *WW* 9.11 (Nov 20, 1913), p. 2.

[319] Fraser, 'A Contrast In Values', p. 3 (emphasis original).

[320] Fraser, 'A Contrast In Values', p. 3.

[321] P.M. Stokely, 'Is It You?', *WW* 9.8 (Aug 20, 1913), pp. 2-3 (2).

[322] A.S. Worrell, 'Wonderful Times Coming', *WW* 10.7 (Jul 20, 1914), p. 1, Reprint, *TBM* 1.9 (Mar 1, 1908), p. 4.; Editor of *Baptist Watchman*, 'Speaking with Tongues', *WW* 9.10 (Oct 20, 1913), p. 4. Bell even called for healings to be verified before submitting them for publishing, as 'a single mistake of this kind

critical to receiving their SB.³²³

Bell acknowledged that the terminology regarding glossolalia was affecting the theological discussion. For example,

> the phraseology (of the evidence) is often woefully at fault ... to declare, without modification, that just tongues is always the certain evidence of the baptism with the Holy Ghost leaves the way open for every devil possessed or demon possessed person in the world to claim the baptism of the Holy Ghost ... we advocates of this truth *must hedge about more carefully our statements* about tongues being the evidence of the baptism.³²⁴

Bell advised including the phrase, 'as the Spirit of God gives utterance' as a qualifying phrase. Further, such terminology must also be accompanied by a life of 'love, joy, holiness, obedience to God ... (to) show that they are true, clean children of God'.³²⁵ Finally, the experience with God was only a beginning and was beyond words:

> we thank God for the waves of power and glory that sweep over and envelop our being in this blessed experience ... *when no longer words in our vocabulary can do justice* to the occasion, and we 'begin to speak in other tongues as the spirit gives utterance' ... But this experience is not the end of Christian development. It is only the beginning of a life in which the Holy Ghost has undertaken to work out God's purpose in us.³²⁶

C. Critics and Intramural Theological Pressures

Outside theological pressure caused Pentecostals to address cessation, while within Pentecostalism there was an intramural debate between the WH and FW positions of sanctification. In *WW,* one

---

in print discredits hundreds of genuine testimonies in the same paper', E.N. Bell, 'Revival News in Home Land', *WW* 9.10 (Oct 20, 1913), p. 2; cf. Editor, 'Exaggerations', *WW* 9.2 (Feb 20, 1912), p. 3.

³²³ Brann, 'O.P. Brann Baptized', p. 4; E.N.B., 'A Statement', *WW* 12.6 (June 1915), p. 4.

³²⁴ E.N.B., 'What is the Evidence of the Baptism In The Spirit', p. 7 (emphasis added).

³²⁵ Bell, 'What is the Evidence of the Baptism In The Spirit', p. 7.

³²⁶ W.T. Gaston, 'The Ministry of the Spirit', *WW* 9.6 (Jun 20, 1913), p. 6 (emphasis added).

can see a another intramural theological debate emerge that brought pressure on glossolalia: the 'New Issue (Oneness)'.[327]

1. Cessationism

Though cessationism was addressed occasionally in articles only one editorial by Bell responded directly to cessationism.[328] W.T. Gaston added that tongues were scriptural and that cessationists 'err greatly, NOT KNOWING THE SCRIPTURES'.[329] Gaston and Bell explained that Paul in 1 Cor. 13.8-12, compared the coming 'perfection' as seeing Jesus face to face in contrast to today's imperfect mirror or childlike-ignorance.[330] Bell parsed 1 Cor. 13.8 to mean that tongues

> and all the other gifts of the Spirit belong to this present age of imperfection, and are given for the building up and perfecting of the saints. When the saints get out of the present world TRAINING CAMP, are graduated into perfection, light and knowledge of Christ's presence on earth again, they will no longer need the tongues, and they shall cease, just as the word says. Not NOW, Paul says, but THEN![331]

Other arguments to counter the claims of cessationists were: 1) one cannot ignore the testimony of present-day tongues-speakers;[332] 2) nor their godly character;[333] and 3):

> there has been a growing tendency not only among critics, but also among Bible expositors generally, to eliminate the supernatural from the Bible as far as possible … (and to) deny the miracles of Christ and the apostles … how will they account for those who speak so as to be understood in languages which

---

[327] Reed, 'Oneness Pentecostalism', pp. 936-44; Brumback, *Suddenly From Heaven*, pp. 191-210; Menzies, *Anointed To Serve*, pp. 111-21.
[328] Editor, 'Editorials: Tongues Cease', *WW* 10.10 (Oct 1914), p. 2.
[329] He refers to: Isa. 28.11; 1 Cor. 14.21; Mk 16.17; Acts 2.4; 10.45-46; 19.6, W.T. Gaston, 'The Unknown Tongues', *WW* 9.3 (Mar 20, 1913), p. 4.
[330] Gaston, 'The Unknown Tongues', p. 4; Editor, 'Editorials: Tongues Cease', p. 2.
[331] Editor, 'Editorials: Tongues Cease', p. 2.
[332] Gaston, 'The Unknown Tongues', p. 4.
[333] Editor of *Baptist Watchman*, 'Speaking with Tongues', p. 4.

they had never learned?'[334]

2. Sanctification

WW followed other Pentecostal periodicals by distinguishing SB from sanctification. Pinson confessed his evolution of thought: 'yea, nearly all of us called it (sanctification) the baptism with the Holy Ghost; but when we found out we never had the baptism, we confessed our mistake like all honest people ought to do'.[335] The WH position of a second, instantaneous work of grace was not believed to be scriptural;[336] nevertheless, there were numerous calls for holy living after glossolalia. These calls sometimes blurred the distinction between the two camps. For example, Bell wrote:

> hundreds are getting saved, baptized with the Spirit and talking in tongues as the Spirit gives utterance ... so far so good, but what is next? ... CONTINUED CONSECRATION ... it is one thing to have an *instantaneous cleansing* of the heart and quite another thing to get wrought into the practice in everyday life and walk the truth implied in such heart cleansing.[337]

Despite disagreement, there were several calls for unity. For example, Flower wrote that 'unity of spirit was absolutely necessary in the realization of Pentecost, and it is absolutely necessary in the continuation of Pentecost. No unity – no Pentecost. Unity – Pentecost.'[338] H.M. Savage stated that because both sides 'heal the sick, speak with tongues, and cast out demons ... then they surely must have something from God ... let us be careful how we speak of one of God's children ... the divisions and strifes [sic] are not of God'.[339]

---

[334] Editor of *Baptist Watchman*, 'Speaking with Tongues', p. 4; cf. Editor, 'The Good of Speaking with Tongues', *WW* 8.6 (Aug 20, 1912), p. 4.

[335] Pinson, 'Sanctified In Christ', p. 4; cf. 'Editorials – Avoid Extremes', p. 2.

[336] E.N. Bell, 'Editorial – Cleansing And Holiness', *WW* 8.6 (Aug 20, 1912), p. 2; Pinson, 'Sanctified In Christ', p. 4.

[337] E.N.B., 'The Baptism, What Next', *WW* 9.5 (May 20, 1913), p. 2 (emphasis added); cf. E.N.B., 'The Second Blessing', *WW* 9.12 (Dec 20, 1913), p. 2.

[338] J.R.F., 'Wiser Than Children of Light', *WW* 12.5 (May 1915), p. 1; cf. Arch P. Collins, 'To the Saints', *WW* 8.8 (Oct 20, 1912), p. 2.

[339] H.M. Savage, 'An Honest Inquiry', *WW* 10.4 (Apr 20, 1914), p. 2. Bell published Savage's article immediately after his own article on the FW. Bell then encourages his readers to 'note' Savage's moderating tone and call for mutual respect, Editor, 'The Finished Work', *WW* 10.4 (Apr 29, 1914), p. 2.

3. The 'New Issue' (Oneness)[340]

The 'new issue', rooted in the Acts 2.38 baptismal formula, insisted that baptism was to be 'in the name of Jesus' to be salvific, thereby challenging the orthodox view of the Trinity.[341] Many articles in *WW* addressed the new issue and glossolalia became a secondary, but logical, part of the controversy.[342] WH Pentecostals viewed Durham's FW theology as collapsing justification and sanctification into one event. Birthed by FW proponents[343] the new issue further collapsed Spirit-baptism into one event, making justification, sanctification, and SB a single event that was evidenced by glossolalia. For example, 'some want us to teach a man is not a child of God until he gets the baptism of the Holy Ghost. This is clearly unscriptural.'[344] Even before the AG was formed, many determined that 'there is not one hint of tongues being the evidence of regeneration or the new birth'.[345] Further, even

---

[340] It was 'originally called the "New Issue" or "Jesus Only," by 1930 the movement's self-designation was "Jesus Name," "Apostolic," or "Oneness" Pentecostalism', Reed, 'Oneness Pentecostalism', p. 936.

[341] 'The name Jesus was the object of devotion. For many, the name itself became a source of spiritual power', Reed, 'Oneness Pentecostalism', p. 936.

[342] J.R.F, 'Wiser Than Children of Light', p. 1; E.N. Bell, 'To Act In The Name of Another (WW)', *WW* 12.5 (May 1915), pp. 2-3; The Executive Presbytery, 'Preliminary Statement', *WW* 12.6 (June 1915), p. 1; E.N. Bell, 'The Sad New Issue', *WW* 12.6 (June 1915), pp. 2-3; E.N. Bell, 'The Great Outlook', *WW* 12.6 (June 1915), p. 4; E.N. Bell, 'The "Acts" On Baptism In Christ's Name Only', *WW* 12.7 (Jul, 1915), pp. 1-2; E.N.B., 'Scriptural Varieties On Baptismal Formula', *WW* 12.7 (Jul, 1915), pp. 3, 6; E.N. Bell, 'There Is Safety In Counsel', *WW* 12.10 (Oct 1915), p. 1. Brumback believes the first response to the new issue came from E.N. Bell, 'Baptized Once For All', *WE* 83 (Mar 27, 1915), pp. 1, 3; Brumback, *Suddenly From Heaven*, pp. 191-210 (193-94). There is an untimely gap of extant issues of *WW* between November 1914 and April 1915.

[343] 'The New Issue pioneers had been disciples of Durham' and though he tried to draw attention to Christ's atoning work, he 'also sowed the seeds of a radical Christocentric alternative that reasoned that, if there is only one name (Jesus) to be used in baptism, that name must be given by God in biblical revelation, and it must reflect the radical unity of God's being', Reed, 'Oneness Pentecostalism', pp. 936-37.

[344] Editor, 'Sonship and the Baptism', *WW* 9.6 (Jun 20, 1913), p. 4; cf. Presbyters, 'Personal Statement', *WW* 12.10 (Oct 1915), p. 4.

[345] Editor, 'The New Birth And The Baptism With The Spirit', *WW* 9.11 (Nov 20, 1913), p. 2; cf. Seely D. Kinne, 'The New Birth And The Baptism', *WW* 10.1 (Jan 20, 1914), p. 3; Fraser, 'A Contrast In Values', p. 3. The Holy Spirit was resident in the disciples before the Day of Pentecost in some fashion, but the Spirit came 'in a *new way* on that day', Editor, 'The New Birth And The

though the disciples waited in Jerusalem following Jesus' command,

> it is never once necessary *in a special formula* to invoke the name of Jesus Christ in order for one filled with and under the power the Spirit to speak in there [sic] supernatural tongues ... a little prayer to the Father or a little praise to Jesus serving just as well to make them break forth to speaking with other tongues, as any special invoking of any particular name ever could do.[346]

D. Purposes for Glossolalia

Like other Pentecostal periodicals listed above, glossolalia enhanced prayer[347] and was a sign that the believer had spiritual power to 'vanquish all the forces of hell and possess the land'.[348] However, there was only one article that addressed the purpose of tongues directly. In that article, it was significant that Bell began with tongues as 'one of the Christian "signs" ... a sign of faith *not the only sign*, but one of them ... they are a sign that the gift of the Holy Spirit has been poured out upon the speaker'.[349] Clearly, in his mind, the evidence was one of the primary purposes for tongues. He then restated what many other Pentecostals have written before, that tongues play a role in bringing the lost to Christ:

> tongues are for **sign** ... to them that **believe not** ... tongues are one of God's signs whereby he miraculously speaks to unbelievers. Many have, to the knowledge of the writer by this means, been turned to God and saved ... Reader, are you one that ... despite all God's miraculous talking to you through 'other tongues and lips' ye will not still believe?[350]

E. The Nature of Glossolalia

According to *WW,* tongues 'do not originate in our minds, but are

---

Baptism With The Spirit', p. 2 (emphasis added). This premise begs the question, just how does the Holy Spirit indwell before and after SB? Especially when Bell writes, 'without this baptism in the Spirit one is left in an ABNORMAL condition what Jesus calls in John 14:18 "comfortless" or "orphans"', Editor, 'Sonship and the Baptism', p. 4.

[346] Bell, 'To Act In The Name of Another (WW)', p. 3.
[347] D.C.O.O., 'Revival In Houston', *WW* 9.3 (Mar 20, 1913), p. 1.
[348] W.T. Gaston, 'Onward, Yet Tested', *WW* 9.6 (Jun 20, 1913), p. 6; cf. E.N.B., 'A Statement', p. 4.
[349] Editor, 'The Good of Speaking with Tongues', p. 4.
[350] Editor, 'The Good of Speaking with Tongues', p. 4.

indited [sic] by the Holy Ghost'.[351] They were 'ecstatic utterances, utterances which were probably unintelligible to the person himself, and which generally – not always – he was unable to interpret it to others'.[352] In other words, the person of the Holy Spirit enters into humankind and 'gives (them) power to speak in tongues or languages never learned'.[353]

1. Xenolalia and Language Study

Many testified that they heard glossolalia in a known language. Once Bell added this note following a testimony: 'this Bro. is himself a Scandinavian and understands the Swedish himself, and ought certainly to know whether this woman was speaking in the Swedish or not'.[354] But at the same time there was no hint of MT.[355] In fact, Bell was relentless in his call for missionaries to 'settle down to learn the language'[356] and missionaries openly spoke of their need for learning the local language, their struggle with language study, and their admiration for those who knew the local language.[357] He noted that 'much harm is done and much false

---

[351] Gaston, 'The Unknown Tongues', p. 4.

[352] Fraser, 'A Contrast In Values', p. 3.

[353] Brinkman, *WW* 10.5, pp. 1-2 (1).

[354] Carl Carlson, 'Language Recognized', *WW* 9.9 (Sep 20, 1913), p. 1

[355] 'John and Dora Crouch', *WW* 9.2 (Feb 20, 1912), p. 2; R.L. Holmes, 'His Works in Arizona', *WW* 9.8 (Aug 20, 1913), p. 4; 'Lee Floyd, Texas', *WW* 9.12 (Dec 20, 1913), p. 3; J.E. Simmons, 'Factoria, Kan.', *WW* 10.1 (Jan 20, 1914), p. 1; Samuel G. Garner, 'Samson, Ala.', *WW* 10.7 (Jul 20, 1914), p. 2; A.H. Argue, 'Great Blessings In Western Canada', *WW* 10.8 (Aug 1914), p. 3; Will C. Trotter, 'God Mightily Works In Portland', *WW* 12.6 (June 1915), p. 3; Z.W. Bullock, 'Victory In Revival', *WW* 12.7 (Jul 1915), p. 5; W.M. Harrison, 'Understood In French (WW)', *WW* 12.7 (Jul 1915), p. 5.

[356] Editor, 'A Word to Foreign Missionaries', *WW* 8.8 (Oct 20, 1912), p. 3; cf. E.N.B., 'Too Much Returning. Why Is It? The Remedy', *WW* 9.9 (Sep 20, 1913), p. 2; E.N. Bell, 'God's Work in Foreign Lands', *WW* 9.11 (Nov 20, 1913), p. 4. Two other of Bell's guidelines for missionaries are reflected in standard AG practice today: 1) no privately owned property in foreign lands, E.N. Bell, 'Editor's Note', *WW* 9.7 (Jul 20, 1913), p. 1, and 2) 'it is more and more evident that some sort of system and testing missionaries according to the word of God shall prevail and only those should be approved for the foreign fields who first make good at home', E.N.B., 'Note', *WW* 10.4 (Apr 29, 1914), p. 4.

[357] *WW* 8.8 (Oct 20, 1912), p. 4; Hugh Cadwalder, 'The Staying Kind Needed in Egypt', *WW* 8.10 (Dec 20, 1912), p. 2; Elmer B. Hammond, 'God In Other Lands', *WW* 8.10 (Dec 20, 1912), p. 4; Hugh Cadwalder, 'Minieh, Egypt', *WW* 8.10 (Dec 20, 1912), p. 4; Sis. Harrison, 'Foreign Lands Feel His Presence', *WW* 9.1 (Jan 20, 1913), p. 2; Sister Aston, 'Foreign Lands Feel His Presence', *WW* 9.1 (Jan 20, 1913), p. 2; 'Bro. Faukner', *WW* 9.2 (Feb 20, 1912), p. 2; Almyra

teaching given out by the interpreter misrepresenting to the people what the missionary has really said'.[358]

2. Heavenly Anthem

Glossolalia could also be sung. Bosworth described the HA as 'beautiful poetry' sung 'extemporaneously under the inspiration and power of the Holy Ghost'.[359] Similar to other Pentecostal periodicals, the HA was readily accepted as divine song. For some, it was heaven come to earth. For example, 'last night the heavenly choir sang in a wonderful way',[360] or 'God ... let down the heavenly host to play and sing for us. Many of the saints and many sinners heard the heavenly choir'.[361] Others testified that the Holy Spirit enabled the singer to do things she could not do without a special anointing.[362] For example, 1) three testimonies noted that the HA was xenolalia;[363] 2) one 'young girl' played the organ and sang in the Spirit under the power of God;[364] and 3) and one 'old war

---

Aston, 'From Sis. Aston', *WW* 9.3 (Mar 20, 1913), p. 1; Sarah A. Smith, 'Jerusalem, Palestine', *WW* 9.8 (Aug 20, 1913), p. 1; Almira Aston, 'Nowaganj, India', *WW* 9.9 (Sep 20, 1913), p. 4; Bro. Bass, 'From Bro. Bass', *WW* 9.11 (Nov 20, 1913), p. 3; Florence Bush, 'From Florence Bush', *WW* 9.11 (Nov 20, 1913), p. 3; H.A. Goss, 'On The Way', *WW* 9.12 (Dec 20, 1913), p. 3; E.N. Bell, 'En Route To Persia', *WW* 9.12 (Dec 20, 1913), p. 4; 'John D. James', *WW* 10.4 (Apr 29, 1914), p. 4; 'W.F. Dugmore', *WW* 10.7 (Jul 20, 1914), p. 4; 'B.A. And Mrs. Schoeneich', *WW* 12.6 (June 1915), p. 7; 'Paul D. Van Valen', *WW* 12.8 (Aug 1915), p. 3; 'W.D. Grier', *WW* 12.9 (Sep 1915), p. 6; 'Tommy F. Anderson', *WW* 12.9 (Sep 1915), p. 6; 'Mr. and Mrs. F.H. Gray', *WW* 12.11 (Nov 1915), p. 6; 'Willa B. Lowther, China', *WW* 12.11 (Nov 1915), p. 6.

[358] Editor, *WW* 10.4 (Apr 29, 1914), p. 4.

[359] F.F. Bosworth, 'The God of All The Earth Working At Dallas', *WW* 8.10 (Dec 20, 1912), p. 1.

[360] Will C. Trotter, 'Manifestation of glory In Portland, Ore.', *WW* 12.9 (Sep 1915), p. 7.

[361] A.B. Robinson and Wife, 'Opp, Alabama', *WW* 12.10 (Oct 1915), p. 5; cf. Maude M. Delany, 'God's Mighty Power', *WW* 8.8 (Oct 20, 1912), p. 3; A. Blackburn, 'Whitsuntide Convention At Sunderland, England', *WW* 10.7 (Jul 20, 1914), p. 2.

[362] D.G. Dailey, 'Baptist Minister's Experience', *WW* 10.1 (Jan 20, 1914), p. 3; Mrs. A.R. Flower, 'Indianapolis Tent Meeting', *WW* 10.7 (Jul 20, 1914), p. 2; A.W. Orwig, 'Program Versus The Holy Ghost And Vice Versa', *WW* 10.8 (Aug 1914), p. 2; Wm. H. Merrin, 'The City Stirred', *WW* 12.5 (May 1915), p. 7; Pastor Geo. H. Hicks, 'Revival Now On', *WW* 12.10 (Oct 1915), p. 5.

[363] John A. Preston, 'Brookshire, Tex.', *WW* 9.10 (Oct 20, 1913), p. 3; cf. Josephine Planter, 'Tunis, N. Africa', *WW* 9.8 (Aug 20, 1913), p. 1; W.L. Wood, 'Bro. Wood In Los Angeles', *WW* 12.7 (Jul 1915), p. 5.

[364] E.N. Bell, 'Good Dothan Camp', *WW* 12.11 (Nov 1915), p. 3.

horse ... (who) can't sing a tune, not even a campfire tune, but oh the heavenly music that rolls from him in other tongues, verse after verse, while on his knees before the Lord'.³⁶⁵ Finally, only the redeemed could join in singing the HA.³⁶⁶

F. Testimonies

In addition to testimonies that revealed a unique shorthand to explain the biblical rootedness of the evidence (noted above), two additional thoughts emerged from testimonies. First, two testimonies hinted at a rudimentary sacramentalism. For example, L.V. Roberts noted that 'several have also been healed through laying on of hands as in Mark 16:17–18 and handkerchiefs as in Acts 19:12'.³⁶⁷ Roberts connected the sacred handkerchiefs and tongues speech in Acts and Mark as signs of God's 'fresh blaze'. Second, there was one testimony of deathbed glossolalia: 'as the end drew on heaven came so near that he saw the Golden city and heard the angels singing ... he passed on sweetly praising God in other tongues'.³⁶⁸

V. The Assemblies of God – *The Pentecostal Evangel* ³⁶⁹

A. History of the Assemblies of God

'The Assemblies of God did not come into existence as a "pentecostalized" Holiness group';³⁷⁰ rather, as early as 1909, there were loosely-affiliated clusters of independent Pentecostals all across

---

³⁶⁵ E.N. Bell, 'Falfurrias, Tex.', *WW* 9.6 (Jun 20, 1913), p. 5.
³⁶⁶ D.C.O. Opperman, 'God Stretching Out His Hand To Heal', *WW* 9.10 (Oct 20, 1913), p. 1.
³⁶⁷ L.V. Roberts, 'Fresh Blaze in Indianapolis', *WW* 9.2 (Feb 20, 1913), p. 3.
³⁶⁸ Chlora P. Johnson, 'Senath, MO', *WW* 9.8 (Aug 20, 1913), p. 2; cf. J.H. James, 'Asleep In Jesus', *WW* 10.4 (Apr 29, 1914), p. 1. Publication of death notifications was limited to 'well known' missionaries or minister after July 1915, Editor, 'Pertaining To Death Notices', *WW* 12.7 (Jul 1915), p. 4.
³⁶⁹ Because this periodical had several names during the period of this study, the abbreviation of *PE* will be used throughout the primary text and formal citations will be used in the footnotes.
³⁷⁰ Alexander, *Pentecostal Healing*, p. 160. It was 'neither locally defined nor organized around a Wesleyan view of holiness', E.L. Blumhofer and C.R. Armstrong, 'Assemblies of God', in Stanley Burgess (ed.), *NIDPCM* (Grand Rapids, MI: Zondervan, rev. and expanded edn, 2002), pp. 333-40 (333).

the country[371] 'who had come from Baptist backgrounds'[372] and would later embrace Durham's FW theology. Their stated reasons for organizing in 1913 were: 1) a 'better understanding' of doctrine, 2) to 'conserve the work', 3) cooperation in foreign missions work, 4) to obey *'the laws of the land'*, and 5) 'a general Bible Training School'.[373] Many believe that left unstated was the theological divergence from the WH view of sanctification and racial issues.[374] Their informal relationships were developed through camp meetings, short-term Bible schools, and Pentecostal periodicals.[375]

---

[371] 'By 1909 there were at least four regional associations of independent Pentecostal ministers and churches. Three of these employed the name "Apostolic Faith." Parham's original group in Kansas; the Crawford Fellowship in the Northwest; and the Texas-Arkansas group headed by E.N. Bell and H.A. Goss', Menzies, *Anointed To Serve*, p. 90. The fourth group was named the 'Church of God in Christ, but issued credentials separately from Mason's group', p. 91; cf. Brumback, *Suddenly From Heaven*, pp. 152-56. Blumhofer and Armstrong added to these four the Elim Fellowship and CMA groups from New York, and Dowie's Christian Catholic Church from Chicago, Blumhofer and Armstrong, 'Assemblies of God', p. 333. Blumhofer also includes Piper's Stone Church and Durham's North Avenue Mission, Chicago, IL as having significant regional followings, Blumhofer, *The Assemblies of God*, pp. 199-200.

[372] Alexander, *Pentecostal Healing*, p. 160; cf. p. 161. Perhaps, the explanation is as simple as those who 'did not hold to a belief in a second work of grace after conversion ... those who had been Baptists or Presbyterians', Riss, 'Finished Work Controversy', p. 639.

[373] 'General Convention of Pentecostal Saints and Churches of God In Christ', p. 1 (emphasis original).

[374] On the one hand, though 'many of these white ministers had been ordained by African-American Charles H. Mason of the Church of God in Christ, in reality, they were already having fellowship along racial lines. These two distinctions, one racial and one theological, led these Pentecostals to call for an organizational meeting', Alexander, *Pentecostal Healing*, p. 160, cf. Alexander, *Black Fire*, pp. 177, 269-77; Howard N. Kenyon, 'Black Ministers in the Assemblies of God', *AG Heritage* (Spring, 1987), pp. 10-13, 20. On the other hand, history may never resolve the reason why Mason would even attend the founding council of the AG, Robeck, *Azusa Street*, p. 35; cf. Willie T. Millsaps, 'Willie T. Millsaps Remembers C.H. Mason at Hot Springs', *AG Heritage* 4.2 (Summer 1984), p. 8. For example, it is curious that the *PE* quoted awkwardly Mason: Mason is 'a real prophet of God ... [who] blessed the council in its actions for God. So I repent. I have never seen anything *more manifestly approved* of God. Whatever the future may have in store for us none present doubted but that God was in our midst thus far, guiding, approving, and leading His people on', 'Hot Springs Assembly; God's Glory Present', *WW* 10.4 (Apr 20, 1914), p. 1; 'General Council Special', *WW* 10.5 (May 20, 1914), p. 1 (emphasis original). The worst example of racial insensitivity in the early *PE* is: W.F. Carothers, 'Attitude of Pentecostal Whites to the Colored Brethren In The South', *WE* 103 (Aug 14, 1915), p. 2.

[375] Menzies, *Anointed To Serve*, pp. 87-92 (emphasis original).

The call for organization was first made by five men on Dec. 20, 1913 in *WW*,[376] but within three months, twenty-nine other 'recognized Pentecostal leaders' added their support.[377] Though Bell and Flower would remain influential, an egalitarian attitude prevailed at the beginning of the AG until a series of theological crises would cause the rise and fall of some these early leaders.[378] These crises progressively shaped how the AG would codify glossolalia as SB's IE, thus a brief review of these crises and the first, third, fourth, and sixth General Councils is necessary.[379]

First, there was a decidedly anti-organizational attitude[380] and it was feared that 'reliance upon the might and power of ecclesias-

---

[376] 'This call is for all the churches of God in Christ, to all Pentecostal or Apostolic Faith Assemblies who desire with united purpose to co-operate in love and peace to push the interest of the kingdom of God everywhere ... only for those saints who believe in the baptism with the Holy Ghost with sings [sic] following, Acts 2:4; 10:46; 19:6; Mark 16:16-1 [sic]; 1 Cor. 12:8-11. Neither is this meeting for any captious, contrary, divisive or contentious person', 'General Convention of Pentecostal Saints and Churches of God In Christ', p. 1. The five original signers were: M.M. Pinson, A.P. Collins, Goss, D.C.O. Opperman, and E.N. Bell.

[377] Blumhofer, *The Assemblies of God*, p. 200; cf. Menzies, *Anointed To Serve*, p. 93.

[378] Blumhofer notes that with each theological crisis, leadership trended away from 'Parham's earlier colleagues' to 'men with backgrounds in the Christian Missionary Alliance ... a higher percentage of northern and Eastern men', Blumhofer, *The Assemblies of God*, pp. 236-37. This in turn 'attracted new adherents who were pleased with the council's trend toward doctrinal stability', p. 238. The emerging leadership 'began to distance itself from ... Pentecostals, like Ewart, Cook, or Frank Bartleman, who were essentially restless, unstable, and visionary, always pursuing more revelations', p. 237. In the first four years, ten executive presbyters withdrew or had been dismissed from the AG, p. 243. cf. D. William Faupel, *The Everlasting Gospel: The Significance of Eschatology in the Development of Pentecostal Thought* (JPTSup 10; Sheffield: Sheffield Academic Press, 1996), p. 302.

[379] The second and fifth General Council were historically minor. The second General Council (November 15-29, 1914 at the Stone Church, Chicago, IL) notes significant growth and authorizes moving the publishing house to St. Louis from Findlay, OH. Cf. *Combined Minutes of the General Council* (St. Louis, MO: The Gospel Publishing House, 1914); Menzies, *Anointed To Serve*, p. 107; Blumhofer, *The Assemblies of God*, pp. 211-13. The fifth General Council (September 9-14, 1917, St. Louis, MO) authorizes Bell to move the publishing from St. Louis, MO to Springfield, MO, Blumhofer, *The Assemblies of God*, p. 239.

[380] 'We ... do not believe in identifying ourselves as, or establishing ourselves into, a sect, that is a human organization that legislates of forms laws and articles of faith and has jurisdiction over its members and creates unscriptural lines of fellowship and disfellowship', *Minutes of the General Council* (1914), p. 4; cf. Blumhofer, *The Assemblies of God*, pp. 199-200.

tical machinery would replace reliance upon the Spirit of God'.[381] Independent-minded ecclesiology could have scuttled cooperation at the founding General Council;[382] however, 'fear of hierarchical authority was dispelled by articulating the principle of local church autonomy',[383] and the principle of being a 'voluntary, cooperative fellowship'.[384] They 'adopted neither a constitution nor a doctrinal statement;' however, they did adopt a 'Preamble and Resolution of Constitution' that included a recognition of Jesus' divinity and work of salvation, 'Scriptures ... as the all-sufficient rule for faith and practice', and a call for unity.[385] Seeking to use the Bible alone as the sole authority, the AG, in 'typical restorationist fashion ... refused to bind by creed, affirming simply that the Bible was its sufficient rule of faith and practice ... (however interpretation was) not necessarily static'.[386]

The new issue[387] presented itself as the second crisis. That issue was a West Coast 'novelty until January, 1915, when Glen Cook

---

[381] Brumback, *Suddenly From Heaven*, pp. 156-61.

[382] The first General Council was April 2-12, 1914, at the Grand Opera House in Hot Springs, AK, *Minutes of the General Council of the Assemblies of God* (1914); Menzies, *Anointed To Serve*, pp. 97-105; Brumback, *Suddenly From Heaven*, pp. 156-57; Blumhofer, *The Assemblies of God*, pp. 198-211.

[383] The AG's purpose 'is neither to legislate laws of government, nor usurp authority over said various Assemblies of God, nor deprive them of their Scriptural and local rights and privileges', *Minutes of the General Council* (1914), p. 4; cf. Menzies, *Anointed To Serve*, p. 95; Blumhofer and Armstrong, 'Assemblies of God', p. 334.

[384] Brumback, *Suddenly From Heaven*, p. 163.

[385] Blumhofer and Armstrong, 'Assemblies of God', p. 334; cf. Brumback, *Suddenly From Heaven*, pp. 176-77. *Minutes of the General Council* (1914), p. 4.

[386] Blumhofer, *The Assemblies of God*, p. 209; cf. 'In Doctrines', *CE* (Aug 1, 1914), p. 2. 'In a statement on doctrine, Bell articulated a view of Scripture that allowed "new light": "We must keep our skylights open so as not to reject any new light God may throw upon the old Word. We must not fail to keep pace in life or teaching with the light from heaven."'

[387] McAlister at the April 1913 camp at Arroyo Seco observed that baptism was in the name of Jesus alone in the book of Acts, Blumhofer, *The Assemblies of God*, pp. 221-23. This was picked up by John G. Scheppe and soon 'led rapidly to the virtual denial of the Trinity, a type of Modal Monarchianism', Menzies, *Anointed To Serve*, pp. 111-12. Durham's assistant Ewart, 'spent nearly a year brooding over the implications of the new doctrine ... (before he) preached his first "Jesus Only" sermon', p. 112. Oneness proponents 'gradually came to posit a three stage conversion experience': repentance, 'baptism in Jesus' name, and SB were three elements of one experience. They further came to reject Orthodox language about the Trinity', Blumhofer, *The Assemblies of God*, p. 225

undertook an evangelistic tour eastward'.[388] Then there were 'wholesale defections' with 'nearly all the leaders of the Assemblies of God falling prey to the new enthusiasm in whole or in part'.[389] Attempting to bring unity. Bell carefully constructed articles in *WW* and the *WE* on baptism and doctrinal history.[390] The executive presbytery urged prayer[391] and offered an 'official presbytery statement' on rebaptism.[392] But, in the summer of 1915,[393] when Bell himself was rebaptized in Jesus' name, Flower influenced the executive presbytery to call for a third Council.[394] The third General Council[395] decided to 'wait patiently for another year before arriving at a definite conclusion, allowing time for prayerful study of the word of God'[396] and it ended on an 'irenic note'.[397]

---

[388] Menzies, *Anointed To Serve*, p. 113.

[389] Menzies, *Anointed To Serve*, p. 115; cf. Blumhofer, *The Assemblies of God*, p. 225.

[390] Blumhofer, *The Assemblies of God*, pp. 229-30. Cf. E.N. Bell, 'Baptized Once For All', *WE* 83 (Mar 27, 1915), pp. 1, 3; D.W. Kerr, 'Spontaneous Theology', *WE* 86 (Apr 17, 1915), p. 3; E.N. Bell, 'To Act In The Name of Another (#1)', *WE* 88 (May 1, 1915), pp. 1-2; E.N. Bell, 'To Act In The Name of Another (#2)', *WE* 89 (May 8, 1915), p. 1; E.N. Bell, 'The Great Outlook', *WE* 92 (May 29, 1915), pp. 3-4; E.N. Bell, 'The Sad New Issue', *WE* 93 (Jun 5, 1915), pp. 1, 3; E.N. Bell, 'The "Acts" On Baptism In Christ's Name Only', *WE* 94 (Jun 12, 1915), pp. 1, 3; E.N. Bell, 'Scriptural Varieties On Baptismal Formula', *WE* 97 (Jul 3, 1915), pp. 1, 3.

[391] Blumhofer, *The Assemblies of God*, p. 230. They encouraged the constituency to 'work these problems out on their knees before God and with the Bible in their hands', E.N. Bell, 'Editorial Statement', *WW* 12.6 (Jun 1915), pp. 2-3.

[392] Blumhofer, *The Assemblies of God*, p. 231. Cf. The Executive Presbytery, 'Preliminary Statement', *WE* 91 (May 22, 1915), p. 1.

[393] The camp ran July 23 to August 1, 1915, H.G. Rogers, 'The Third Interstate Encampment of the Assemblies of God, Jackson, Tenn', *WW* 12.7 (Jul, 1915), p. 8.

[394] Menzies, *Anointed To Serve*, p. 115; cf. Brumback, *Suddenly From Heaven*, pp. 197-98.

[395] October 1-10, 1915, Turner Hall, St. Louis, MO, 'Minutes of the General Council' (St. Louis, MO, 1915); cf. Menzies, *Anointed To Serve*, pp. 115-16; Brumback, *Suddenly From Heaven*, pp. 200-203.

[396] Blumhofer, *The Assemblies of God*, p. 234.

[397] Menzies, *Anointed To Serve*, pp. 116, 117. They agreed that: 1) baptism was required of all Christians and that 'slight variations' in formula were inconsequential, 2) there was no scriptural example of 're-baptism', 3) 're-baptizing should not be pressed upon the saints by the preacher' except for the individual's conscience and not the baptismal formula, itself, 4) division and strife would result from 'requiring any fixed and invariable formula', 5) guest ministers must respect the will of the local pastor in this matter, and 6) 'this Council refuses to attempt to bind the consciences of men on this matter, refuses to draw any line of Christian fellowship or of ministerial fellowship on either side

Though this decision 'staved off decisive action ... it was not a permanent solution'.[398] 'Oneness proponents became more aggressive' and a fourth General Council was called.[399] At this Council, 'in spite of a solemn vow expressed at Hot Springs that the Assemblies of God would never adopt a formal creed', they nevertheless drew up a statement of fundamental truths.[400] 'The doctrinal statement as adopted militated against the Oneness views', which resulted in 156 Oneness ministers withdrawing.[401]

The sixth General Council[402] in 1918, addressed SB's evidential glossolalia. In addition to being questioned and challenged in nearly every periodical reviewed above,[403] Fred F.

---

of the question over the matter of a baptismal formula, so long as the person concerned on either side keeps in a sweet Christian spirit, is not factious, does not tear up assemblies or does not disregard the Scriptural officers in charge of local assemblies. We extend to both sides a welcome hand of fellowship so long as they are Christian in spirit and in conduct, but if either side depart from such spirit and conduct we cannot fellowship such conduct or spirit' 'The Discussion of the Formula to be Used in Water Baptism', *Minutes of the General Council* (1915), pp. 5-6.

[398] Menzies, *Anointed To Serve*, p. 116; cf. Blumhofer and Armstrong, 'Assemblies of God', p. 334.

[399] Blumhofer, *The Assemblies of God*, p. 234. Blumhofer wrote, 'oneness people tended to regard themselves as more spiritual than those who failed to embrace their teaching', p. 235. Menzies wrote, 'appeared to be troublemakers, causes of dissension and discord', Menzies, *Anointed To Serve*, p. 117; cf. Brumback, *Suddenly From Heaven*, p. 203. The fourth council was October 1916, at Bethel Chapel, St. Louis, MO, 'Minutes of the General Council' (St. Louis, MO, 1916); cf. Menzies, *Anointed To Serve*, p. 118; Brumback, *Suddenly From Heaven*, p. 204; Blumhofer, *The Assemblies of God*, pp. 235-38.

[400] Menzies, *Anointed To Serve*, p. 118. It also sought to 'satisfy those with holiness sympathies as well', Blumhofer and Armstrong, 'Assemblies of God', p. 334.

[401] Menzies, *Anointed To Serve*, p. 120; Brumback, *Suddenly From Heaven*, p. 209; Blumhofer, *The Assemblies of God*, p. 236.

[402] Springfield, MO, September 4-11, 1918, 'Minutes of the General Council' (Springfield, MO: Gospel Publishing House, 1918); cf. Menzies, *Anointed To Serve*, p. 124; Blumhofer, *The Assemblies of God*, pp. 239-43.

[403] Synan notes that Pentecostalism's antecedent, the FBHC 'did not claim it (tongues) as the only evidence', Synan, *The Holiness-Pentecostal Tradition*, p. 116; cf. Blumhofer and Armstrong, 'Assemblies of God', p. 335. There was a 'test case' in 1907 and 'A.G. Canada suggested that any of the gifts could be the immediate, empirical evidence', Menzies, *Anointed To Serve*, p. 125. So, in February 1907, no mention was made of tongues as 'the crowning biblical evidence' yet when they preached in San Antonio, TX, 'they all likewise spoke in tongues as the Spirit gave utterance', Goss, *The Winds of God*, p. 10; cf. pp. 101-104; Brumback, *Suddenly From Heaven*, pp. 216-17. Menzies cites that his own mother was a part of a similar test case in Pittsburgh, PA, cf. p. 126, fn #9.

Bosworth[404] published a tract that caused the issue to be formally addressed. This tract laid out practical[405] and two theological arguments against a dogmatic glossolalic evidence: 1) 'there is not a solitary passage of Scripture upon which to base this doctrine',[406] because: a) the glossolalia at Pentecost and Corinth were identical in essence,[407] and b) tongues as a sign was not taught in any of the Epistles.[408] 2) Tongues are a sign for unbelievers and 'FAITH is the evidence' for believers.[409] There was 'vigorous debate' as the sixth General Council took up Bosworth's challenge, but in the end, Bosworth 'was gracious enough to not seek to press his views on the Council'.[410] The Council formally resolved that 'we

---

[404] Bosworth was filled with the Spirit under Parham's ministry at Dowie's Zion City, IL. Later, he pioneered a church at the epicenter of a 1912 revival in Texas. He attended the first General Council and served as an executive presbyter from November 1914 until his resignation in 1918, Richard M. Riss, 'Fred Francis Bosworth', in Stanley Burgess (ed.), *NIDPCM* (Grand Rapids, MI: Zondervan, rev. and expanded edn, 2002), pp. 439-40 (439).

[405] Non-theological arguments included: 1) 'I am absolutely certain that many who receive the most powerful baptism for service do not receive the manifestation of speaking in tongues. And I am just as certain ... that many who SEEMINGLY speak in tongues, are not, nor have ever been, baptized in the Spirit', Fred F. Bosworth, *'Do All Speak with Tongues?'* (New York, NY: The Christian Alliance Publishing Company, n.d.), p. 3. cf. p. 4; 2) there are hundreds of great soul-winners throughout history 'without the gift of tongues', p. 5; 3) there are Spirit-baptized people who lack an 'assuring faith', p. 13; 4) mechanical methods are used to twist known language into glossolalia, pp. 15-16; 5) some people received 'the gift of interpretation when they were baptized', p. 19; and 6), the 'shallowness and instability of many of the converts who profess the baptism', p. 20.

[406] Bosworth, *'Do All Speak with Tongues?'*, pp. 4, 8-14, 16-17. He believes it was 'assumed from the fact that in three instances recorded in the Acts they spoke in tongues' but this is not a 'conclusive proof', p. 9. Clearly, Bosworth reads Luke though a Pauline lens, and takes up the cessationist hermeneutic that God used tongues as a sign in Acts solely to show the advance of the gospel beyond the Jews and were not normative for the church, pp. 9-12.

[407] Bosworth, *'Do All Speak with Tongues?'*, pp. 5-8. The xenolalia on the Day of Pentecost was 'the real gift of tongues' (6), and yet, 'the greatest phase' of speaking in tongues was 'the spontaneous life of intercession ... groanings that cannot be uttered', pp. 20-21.

[408] Bosworth, *'Do All Speak with Tongues?'*, p. 9; cf. pp. 8-13.

[409] Bosworth, *'Do All Speak with Tongues?'*, pp. 10, 12-14. Bosworth does address Mk 16.17, which most Pentecostals used for Jesus' endorsement of tongues. He writes that 'Jesus ... never taught the doctrine that all would speak in tongues', p. 17. Because there is only one reception of the Holy Spirit, p. 14. Bosworth addresses Jn 15.26-27, but with a weak argument, p. 12.

[410] Menzies, *Anointed To Serve*, p. 129; cf. Blumhofer, *The Assemblies of God*, p. 241.

consider it inconsistent and unscriptural for any minister to hold credentials with us who thus attacks as error our distinctive testimony'.[411]

B. 'The Sign' and 'The Evidence'

In the *PE*,[412] a vast amount of ink was used to promote, defend, and answer questions about evidential glossolalia; it was the 'great essential doctrine' of the AG:[413] 'if ... we are wrong in our position', wrote Flower, 'the denominational bodies would possibly take us in if we would drop this one point of contention ... the very life of the Pentecostal movement hinges on this point'.[414] The following paragraphs attempt to systematize the arguments about the sign from numerous articles within the *PE*.

---

[411] The full resolution reads, be it 'resolved, That this Council considers it a serious disagreement with the Fundamentals for any minister among us to teach contrary to our distinctive testimony that the baptism of the Holy Spirit is regularly accompanied by the initial physical sign of speaking in other tongues, as the spirit of God gives the utterance, and that we consider it inconsistent and unscriptural for any minister to hold credentials with us who thus attack as error our distinctive testimony', Minutes of the Sixth Annual Meeting of the General Council, 'Saturday Afternoon, Sept. 7th, 1918', pp. 7-8 (8).

[412] 'Evidence' was the most common scientific term used. However, there are examples like W.H. Pope who noted that tongues were 'the **immediate result**' of SB, W.H. Pope, 'Why I Believe All Who Receive the Full Baptism Will Speak in Other Tongues', *CE* 244 & 245 (Jun 15, 1918), pp. 6-7 (7) (emphasis original). W.T. Gaston noted that when the Ephesian disciples in Acts 19 spoke in tongues, it was 'as a direct first result of the SAME CAUSE', SB, W.T. Gaston, 'The New Birth And Baptism in the Holy Ghost', *CE* 296 & 297 (Jul 12, 1919), pp. 1-2, 9 (9). Note the scientific terminology even with human senses: 'it is not reason nor philosophy that makes you recognize rain is rain in the natural; it is the evidence of your senses', A.E.L., 'Pictures of Pentecost In The Old Testament', *WE* 212 (Oct 27, 1917), pp. 6-7.

[413] Hall, 'The Great Crisis Near at Hand', p. 1. Durham called it the 'pivotal doctrine', Wm. H. Durham, 'What is the Evidence of the Baptism of the Holy Ghost', *CE* 250 & 251 (Aug 10, 1918), pp. 2-3 (2). This article was later published as a tract: *Wm. H. Durham, What is the Evidence?* (Springfield, MO: Gospel Publishing House, nd). Sisson argued that the movement's growth 'with all this hedge of weirdness, mysticism, and unpopularity about them' in some way confirms its truthfulness, Elizabeth Sisson, 'A Sign People – What Meaneth This?', *CE* 270 & 271 (Jan 11, 1919), pp. 2-3, 9 (2).

[414] J.R. Flower, 'The Evidence of the Baptism', *PE* 336 & 337 (Apr 17, 1920), p. 4. The temptation to compromise on this point must have been tremendous. McPherson reportedly said, 'they will build me tabernacles from coast-to-coast if I will just shade my message a little and not insist on the speaking in other tongues as the Spirit gives utterance as the accompanying outward evidence of the Spirit's invisible presence', S.H.F., 'From The Pentecostal Viewpoint', *PE* 350 & 51 (Jul 24, 1920), p. 8.

1. The Nature and Limitations of Tongues as a Sign

First, there was consideration about the nature and limitations of tongues as a symbol. Salib Boulos concluded that biblically, 'speaking in tongues has an interconnection with the baptism of the Holy Spirit'.[415] That interconnection was 'the Holy Ghost, coming upon us, and into us … He announced his arrival and His presence by speaking through these disciples in other tongues as He gave them utterance. (Acts 2:4.).'[416] Or, as colloquially stated, 'He spoke for Himself'.[417] Boulos added that 'the sign is not the thing it signifies. So, tongues are not the baptism, but the evidence.'[418] Aimee Semple McPherson crafted two poignant illustrations to help readers understand this distinction: 1) a restaurant and its sign. Just as the restaurant's sign does not satisfy hunger, 'so (too) tongues are just an outward sign that indicate the presence within of the blessed Spirit of God … when you are filled with him, the signs will most certainly follow'.[419] 2) Just as a stamp on an envelope is not the letter itself, tongues 'were a necessary appendage to the baptism'.[420] Therefore, one 'must not seek the sign, but the divine person Himself; not the "Tongues," but the Holy Comforter. The sign will follow.'[421]

---

[415] Salib Boulos, 'In Defense of the Truth', *PE* 320 & 321 (Dec 27, 1919), pp. 10-11 (11).

[416] A.A. Boddy, 'The Holy Ghost For Us', *WE* 205 (Sep 1, 1917), pp. 1-2, 8 (2); cf. Durham, 'What is the Evidence', p. 3; E.N. Bell, 'Questions and Answers', *PE* 320 & 321 (Dec 27, 1919), p. 5; Mrs. Frank Hodges, 'The Enemies In The Land', *PE* 328 & 329 (Feb 21, 1920), pp. 6-7 (6).

[417] 'F.H. Gray and Wife', *CE* 73 (Jan 9, 1915), p. 4; A.P. Collins, 'A Baptized Baptist Preacher', *CE* 75 (Jan 23, 1915), p. 1; Pastor Earl W. Clark, 'Italians Receive The Spirit In Washington, D.C.', *WE* 130 (Mar 11, 1916), p. 13; Alma, 'And Your Daughters Shall Prophecy', *WE* 142 (Jun 3, 1916), p. 11.

[418] Boulos, 'In Defense of the Truth', p. 11.

[419] S.H.F., 'From The Pentecostal Viewpoint', p. 8.

[420] Aimee Semple McPherson, 'What is the Evidence of the Baptism of the Holy Ghost', *PE* 312 & 313 (Nov 1, 1919), pp. 6-7 (7).

[421] Boddy, 'The Holy Ghost For Us', p. 2; cf. B.F. Lawrence, 'Article VII(a) – The Gift of Tongues, and the Pentecostal Movement', *WE* 142 (Jun 3, 1916), pp. 4-6 (5); David H. McDonnell, 'The Pentecostal Baptism – Its Foundation', *CE* 282 & 283 (Apr 5, 1919), pp. 2-3 (2); Stanley H. Frodsham, 'Why We Know The Present Pentecostal Movement Is of God', *CE* 300 & 301 (Aug 9, 1919), p. 4-5 (5). C.E.R. believed that some people tended to 'rely upon the gifts or emotions solely as evidence of equipment for service'; however, 'the "gifts" are but a stimulus to the awakening and not an anchor to hold us in steady uniformity for real service', C.E.R., 'Spiritual Intoxication', *CE* 76 (Jan 30, 1915), p. 2.

2. Who is the Sign For?

Second, exactly who the sign was for became an issue because, 1) the cessationist argument limited its sign value to the early church, and 2) others insisted that because tongues were a 'sign for unbelievers' (or the Jews)[422] there was no need for any evdience because faith was the sole evidence for believers.[423] A minority opinion was that tongues were a sign of judgment for unbelievers;[424] however, most contributors to the *PE* insisted that tongues were a sign for both unbelievers and believers.[425] For example, 'not only will you know when the Holy Ghost comes in to abide, but the onlooker will see you shake under the power of God and hear you speak with tongues'.[426] Consider the urgency here: 'if God's people fail in these dark days to give the unbeliever this sign, who will give it to him?'[427] Boulos asked 'when did they (the first Christians) know that the promise was fulfilled? The answer is plain from the book of Acts.'[428] The believers were assured that they received the same gift as the first Christians because they received the same sign.[429] The sign signified that 'the blessed Spirit (was) in control'.[430]

3. Biblical Support

Third, a major discussion concerned the biblical support for signs. Glossolalia was frequently called the 'Bible sign'. For example, Bell wrote,

> the baptism in the Holy Spirit, (is) accompanied now, as in Bible

---

[422] John Kellner, 'The One True Baptism with the Holy Ghost', *CE* 300 & 301 (Aug 9, 1919), pp. 6-7 (6); 'The One True Baptism', p. 6.

[423] B.F. Lawrence, 'Article VII(b) – The Gift of Tongues, and the Pentecostal Movement', *WE* 143 (Jun 10, 1916), pp. 4-7 (4); W.W. Simpson, 'The Baptism In The Spirit – A Defense', *WE* 198 (Jul 14, 1917), pp. 2-6 (5); A.E.L., 'Pictures of Pentecost In The Old Testament', *WE* 212 (Oct 27, 1917), pp. 6-7 (7).

[424] R.W. Hudson, 'The Personality of the Holy Spirit and Other Observations', *CE* 75 (Jan 23, 1915), p. 3.

[425] W.T. Gaston, 'The Baptism According to Acts 2:4', *CE* 302 & 303 (Aug 23, 1919), p. 3.

[426] Kellner, 'The One True Baptism with the Holy Ghost', pp. 6-7 (6).

[427] A.H. Argue, 'Is Speaking with New Tongues An Essential Sign?', *PE* 358 & 359 (Sep 18, 1920), p. 2-3.

[428] Boulos, 'In Defense of the Truth', p. 10.

[429] Pope, 'Why I Believe', p. 6; E.N. Bell, 'Questions and Answers #903', *PE* 366 & 367 (Nov 19, 1920), p. 5.

[430] Pope, 'Why I Believe', p. 7; Durham, 'What is the Evidence', p. 2.

times, always with the speaking in tongues ... something miraculous will happen to cause you and all others present to know from the **Bible sign** that you have '**received the Holy Ghost**'.[431]

Though 'no passage out and out says it is necessary for tongues to accompany the baptism in the Holy Ghost', acknowledged W.H. Pope 'yet we believe the Bible *incidentally teaches it* nevertheless'.[432] Primarily, most authors in the *PE* followed the pattern from the book of Acts for the defence of evidential tongues:[433] 'in the 2nd, 10th and 19th chapters of Acts it plainly states that all who received the baptism ... spoke in other tongues'.[434] 'Three times in this one letter of Acts,' wrote Pope, 'it describes how they acted or what they did when the Spirit comes, each time telling of the tongues'.[435] J. Tunmore called it 'the **divine pattern** of the baptism of the Holy Ghost'.[436] Bell and others claimed that

> there is **not one case in the New Testament** where a believer ever spoke with tongues for the **first time**, except when the Spirit first came upon him ... the Bible points out as the sign that which is **always is** the sign – **not the gift of tongues**, but the speaking only as the Holy '**Spirit gives utterance**'.[437]

---

[431] E.N. Bell, 'Baptism With The Spirit With Speaking in Tongues', *WE* 84 (Apr 3, 1915), pp. 3-4 (3).

[432] Pope, 'Why I Believe', p. 6 (emphasis added).

[433] Bell, 'Baptism With The Spirit With Speaking in Tongues', pp. 3-4; E.N. Bell, 'Questions and Answers #95 & 96', *WE* 157 (Sep 16, 1916), p. 8; G.R. Polman, 'As The Spirit Gave Them Utterance', *WE* 178 (Feb 24, 1917), pp. 5-6 (5); Simpson, 'The Baptism In The Spirit – A Defense', p. 4; Pope, 'Why I Believe', p. 7; Durham, 'What is the Evidence', p. 2; Gaston, 'The New Birth And Baptism in the Holy Ghost', p. 2; Frodsham, 'Why We Know', p. 5; Kellner, 'The One True Baptism', p. 6; Boulos, 'In Defense of the Truth', p. 10; Arch P. Collins, 'Review of Dr. W.B. Riley's Tract "Speaking with Tongues"', *PE* 336 & 337 (Apr 17, 1920), pp. 8-9 (8); Argue, 'An Essential Sign?', p. 2.

[434] B.F. Lawrence, 'Article II – Modern Tongues in Bible Light', *WE* 122 (Jan 8, 1916), pp. 4-5 (4).

[435] Pope, 'Why I Believe', p. 7.

[436] J. Tunmore, 'Some Good Things Said At The Recent Council', *CE* 256 & 257 (Oct 5, 1918), p. 3 (emphasis original).

[437] Bell, 'Baptism With The Spirit With Speaking in Tongues', p. 4; cf. Pope, 'Why I Believe', p. 7; Boulos, 'In Defense of the Truth', p. 11.

McPherson noted that on the Day of Pentecost,[438]

> the first evidence He gave of His indwelling was to speak through their lips (giving utterance Himself), in other tongues – languages they had never learned ... You will never find an instance where the Spirit spoke through a human being in tongues up to this time ... (and) it had been prophesied by Isaiah.[439]

To these early Pentecostals, the pattern from Acts proved that 'the outpouring which took place on the day of Pentecost can and shall be repeated'.[440]

After the pattern from Acts, Isa. 28.11-12 and 1 Cor. 14.21 were frequently cited to prove that God said '*He would speak to this people* by stammering lips and another tongue' as a sign.[441]

Like their contemporaries, the *PE* looked for support of signs from Jesus himself.[442] For example, they questioned if Jesus taught or spoke in tongues. Flower reported that Jesus 'did not speak in tongues' but in Aramaic,[443] and Bell added that Jesus 'talked in several languages ... he had the Spirit without measure, and could have used any language in earth or heaven ... (but) *little is gained* over the purely theoretical problems of whether or not Jesus

---

[438] There is an interesting interpretation of the Day of Pentecost in the *PE*: glossolalia occurred in the upper room and then the apostles went outside and spoke xenolalia before the people, Pope, 'Why I Believe', p. 7; cf. Polman, 'As The Spirit Gave Them Utterance', p. 5; Simpson, 'The Baptism In The Spirit – A Defense', p. 5.

[439] McPherson, 'What is the Evidence', p. 6.

[440] Andrew D. Urshan, 'The Baptism of the Holy Ghost', *WE* 205 (Sep 1, 1917), pp. 5-7 (5).

[441] Bell, 'Baptism With The Spirit With Speaking in Tongues', p. 3 (emphasis added). Cf. Burt McCafferty, 'The Time of the Latter Rain', *WE* 187 (Apr 28, 1917), pp. 4-5 (5); Urshan, 'The Baptism of the Holy Ghost', p. 6; A.E.L., 'Physical Manifestations of the Spirit', *CE* 248 & 249 (Jul 27, 1918), pp. 2-3 (2); pp. 5-7; Gaston, 'The New Birth And Baptism in the Holy Ghost', p. 1; McPherson, 'What is the Evidence', p. 6; J.T.B., 'The Gifts of the Spirit', *PE* 336 & 337 (Apr 17, 1920), pp. 6-7 (6); Argue, 'An Essential Sign?', p. 2.

[442] Jesus' teaching on SB was far more extensive than IE. For example, Jesus taught it is okay to ask for the Holy Spirit (Lk. 11.13) and that he will send the Spirit (Jn 4.10; 7.37-39), Simpson, 'The Baptism In The Spirit – A Defense', pp. 2-6.

[443] J.R.F., 'Did Jesus Speak In Tongues', *CE* 73 (Jan 9, 1915), p. 2; cf. E.N. Bell, 'Questions and Answers #254', *WE* 203 (Aug 18, 1917), p. 9. Though Jesus' mother was thought to have spoken in tongues, Alice Flower, 'Growing Stronger', *CE* 248 & 249 (Jul 27, 1918), p. 12.

talked in supernatural tongues'.[444] An argument could be made that Isa. 28.11-12[445] was a more popular defence than Mk 16.16-17[446] of the ongoing nature of glossolalia. However, Mk 16.16-17 proved that Jesus prophesied that tongues were a sign that would follow the believer. Finally, Jesus' baptism was paradigmatic for believers. As 'a voice from heaven endorsed him and his message' at the Jordan River, so too, 'when the child of God is baptized in the Holy Ghost, and given the power to obey the commission to witness, he speaks in other tongues by heavenly inspiration'.[447]

4. Glossolalia as the Singular Sign?

Fourth, some believed that any of the nine gifts of the Spirit could be an evidence of SB. Joseph Turnmore responded that, if the Holy Spirit could have chosen any of the nine gifts, 'why was it that **all** the waiting company on the day of Pentecost **spoke in tongues** as the Spirit gave utterance?'[448] It would have been an excellent time to prove the point of diversity. J.T. Boddy reasoned that tongues carried 'more evidence of the divinely supernatural than does any one of the nine gifts of the Spirit' because 'the possessor of this gift ... is in no uncertainty about it, for he has the witness in himself'.[449] Lawrence wrote, 'we do not say that speaking in other tongues is the only evidence of the baptism, only the initial one, further we do not say that the gift of tongues is the evidence'.[450]

---

[444] E.N. Bell, 'Questions and Answers #693', *CE* 292 & 293 (Jun 14, 1919), p. 5 (emphasis added). Cf. Collins, 'Review of Dr. W.B. Riley's Tract', p. 9.

[445] W. Jethro Walthall, 'Letter From A Brother Minister', *WE* 133 (Apr 1, 1916), pp. 8-9; A.R. Wilson, *WE* 117 (Nov 27, 1916), p. 1; Pastor R.J. Craig, 'Woodworth-Etter Meeting, Sidney, Iowa', *WE* 153 (Sep 30, 1916), p. 15; E.N. Bell, 'Question And Answers #237', *WE* 201 (Aug 4, 1917), p. 9; E.N. Bell, 'Some Important Questions Answered', *CE* 282 & 283 (Apr 5, 1919), p. 3; Paul C. Boucher, 'Broken Arrow, Okla.', *PE* 318 & 319 (Dec 13, 1919), p. 14;

[446] Lawrence, 'Article II', p. 4; Pope, 'Why I Believe', p. 7; Thomas Atterberry, 'They Shall Speak with New Tongues', *PE* 320 & 321 (Dec 27, 1919), pp. 2-3.

[447] 'In The House of God', *WE* 157 (Sep 16, 1916), pp. 6-7, 9 (7).

[448] 'Joseph Turnmore', *CE* 260 & 261 (Nov 2, 1918), p. 3. Gaston wryly asked, 'was he not giving what he wanted to (on the day of Pentecost) ... How shall we account for the strange fact, that they **all** again received this **one same gift**', Gaston, 'The New Birth And Baptism in the Holy Ghost', pp. 1-2.

[449] J.T.B., 'The Gifts of the Spirit', pp. 6-7 (6).

[450] Lawrence, 'Article II', pp. 4-5.

5. A Universal Sign?

Fifth, was glossolalia the sign for everyone, after all, Paul wrote, 'do all speak in tongues (1 Cor. 12.30)?' Usually, proponents of glossolalia as an evidence appealed to the context of 1 Corinthians, believing that Paul addressed the gifts of tongues and not tongues as a sign, which was for all believers.[451] As simple as it sounds, they noted that 'all' meant all:

> the word says, 'THEY were ALL filled and began to speak with other tongues' ... Two things are positively asserted in this passage of 'they all,' namely the FILLING with the Holy Ghost and the speaking with other tongues ... It doesn't read in Acts 2:4 that 'they all were filled and SOME began to speak with tongues,' as many wrongly teach.[452]

Also, Kerr noted that Paul 'did not commit himself to a position on the question of speaking in tongues which would contradict the history of tongues in the book of Acts'.[453] After the 1918 General Council, W. Jethro Walthall and his Holiness Baptist Association were used as examples of the reasonableness of the AG's position.[454] Even though he had a glossolalic experience upon his SB, Walthall disagreed with the AG's position

> that speaking in tongues is the (singular) sign of the baptism of the Holy Spirit, while we have always maintained that all supernatural manifestations, including tongues, are confirmatory signs of the preached word in its fullness as in Mark 16:15 – 20.[455]

---

[451] J.T.B., 'Do All Speak with Tongues', *PE* 336 & 337 (Apr 17, 1920), p. 4; Gaston, 'The Baptism According to Acts 2:4', p. 3.

[452] E.N. Bell, 'Questions and Answers #94', *WE* 156 (Sep 9, 1916), p. 8; cf. E.N. Bell, 'Questions and Answers #31 & 32', *WE* 128 (Feb 26, 1916), p. 8; Bell, 'Questions and Answers #95 & 96', p. 8; Pope, 'Why I Believe', p. 7.

[453] D.W. Kerr, 'Do All Speak In Tongues', *CE* 270 & 271 (Jan 11, 1919), p. 7.

[454] Brumback, *Suddenly From Heaven*, pp. 13, 220. In addition to Walthall's example, for three months following the Council, the *PE* broke with its normal format and includes a personal testimony of SB with IE on each front page, J.W. McIntyre, 'Muldrow, Okla.', *CE* 256 & 257 (Oct 5, 1918), p. 1; William W. Parks, 'Forrester, Okla.', *CE* 258 & 259 (Oct 19, 1918), p. 1; Josephine Ross, 'Howe, Okla.', *CE* 260 & 261 (Nov 2, 1918), p. 1. Normal formatting returned with the 268 & 269 (Dec 12, 1918) issue.

[455] Walthall, 'Letter From A Brother Minister', p. 9.

He thought 'the record of incidences were in favor', and that 'the preponderance of Bible evidence (was) in their favor'; however, it was 'based upon rather far-fetched conclusions drawn from proof texts'.[456] Upon reflection, Walthall found it significant that, when the Holy Spirit fell in his congregations, 'our people began to speak in other tongues, *without ever having come in contact* with others who spoke, or with the minister who taught it definitely'.[457] He changed his position and merged his fellowship with the AG, stating: 1) that after talking with his people and doing Spirit-led research, 'it became so simple and plain as the Spirit himself began to show me',[458] and 2) 'by following the (biblical) record I saw that the universality of speaking with tongues had a more weighty testimony supporting it than that of the testimony of the universality of (water) baptism'.[459] As for fillings *sans* tongues, the phrases 'coming up to the Bible standard'[460] and 'normal'[461] were common in the *PE* and indicated that a variety of experiences were possible, but they were not to be called the SB. These pre-tongues experiences were viewed in a positive light. For example, 'a dear fellow missionary received *a gracious anointing of the Spirit* ... she did not speak clearly in tongues, but had the beginning of utterance and songs and prayer in the Holy Ghost'.[462] Nevertheless, the sign of a full and complete SB was to speak clearly and 'not merely babble'.[463] One seeker was 'not fully satisfied, (but now) has come up

---

[456] W. Jethro Walthall, 'A New Chapter In My Experience', *WE* 152 (Aug 12, 1916), pp. 5-6, 9 (5).

[457] Walthall, 'Letter From A Brother Minister', p. 9 (emphasis added). Cf. B.F. Lawrence, 'Article III(a) – The Experiences of W. Jethro Walthall', *WE* 138 (May 6, 1916), pp. 4-5.

[458] Walthall, 'A New Chapter In My Experience', p. 5.

[459] W. Jethro Walthall, 'Do All Speak with Tongues Who Receive The Baptism?', *CE* 248 & 249 (Jul 27, 1918), p. 6.

[460] Bell, 'Questions and Answers #95', p. 8; Pope, 'Why I Believe', p. 6; Durham, 'What is the Evidence', pp. 2-3.

[461] Walthall, 'A New Chapter In My Experience', pp. 5-6; Pope, 'Why I Believe', pp. 6-7; 'A Statement of Fundamental Truths Approved By The General Council of the Assemblies of God, October 2-7, 1916 (#1)', *WE* 169 (Dec 16, 1916), p. 8; Kerr, 'Do All Speak In Tongues', p. 7; Gaston, 'The New Birth And Baptism in the Holy Ghost', pp. 1-2, 9; S.H.F., 'From The Pentecostal Viewpoint', p. 8.

[462] Violetta Schoonmaker, 'Missionary Gleanings', *PE* 316 & 317 (Nov 29, 1919), p. 12; cf. Collins, 'A Baptized Baptist Preacher', p. 1.

[463] Ernest L. Whitcomb, 'North Bergen, N.J.', *PE* 346 & 47 (Jun 26, 1920), p. 14.

full', another had 'stammering lips' for 10 days.[464] Alice Flower said that if her own mother had 'known how to yield she would have spoken forth his praise in other tongues then and there' but only 'had the beginning of utterance'.[465] Therefore, the term 'full consummation' occurred naturally in the first statement of fundamental truths:

> the *full consummation* of the baptism of believers in the Holy Ghost and fire, is indicated by the initial sign of speaking in tongues, as the Spirit of God gives utterance. Acts 2:4. This wonderful experience is distinct from and subsequent to the experience of the new birth. Acts 10:44-46; 11:14-16; 15:8, 9.[466]

Even after Bosworth challenged evidential tongues at the 1918 General Council, the term 'full consummation' was reaffirmed:[467] 'we re-affirmed our position that the *full consummation* of the baptism in the Holy Ghost is invariably accompanied by the initial physical sign of speaking with other tongues as the Spirit of God gives the one baptized utterance'.[468]

7. Consummation of the Beginning

Finally, 'the baptism of the Holy Ghost is not the end, but the beginning of a blessed life. Always more to follow!'[469] Glossolalia

---

[464] 'The Latter Rain In Atlantic City, N.J.', *WE* 166 (Nov 25, 1916), p. 14 (emphasis added). Cf. B.F. Lawrence, 'Article V – Details From Various Sources', *WE* 140 (May 20, 1916), pp. 4-5; Walthall, 'A New Chapter In My Experience', p. 9.

[465] 'W.W. Simpson', *WE* 87 (Apr 24, 1915), p. 4; 'The Latter Rain In Atlantic City, N.J.', p. 14; Alice R. Flower, 'My Mother's Healing', *WE* 189 (May 12, 1917), p. 5.

[466] 'A Statement of Fundamental Truths Approved By The General Council of the Assemblies of God, October 2-7, 1916 (#2)', *WE* 170 (Dec 23, 1916), p. 8 (emphasis added). Cf. 'The Missionary Conference', *WE* 209 (Oct 6, 1917), pp. 10-11 (10); D.W. Kerr, 'Paul's Interpretation of the Baptism In Holy Spirit', *CE* 252 & 253 (Aug 24, 1918), p. 6.

[467] 'We re-affirmed our position that the full consummation of the baptism in the Holy Ghost is invariably accompanied by the initial physical sign of speaking with other tongues as the Spirit of God gives the one baptized utterance', 'Minutes of Last Council Now Ready', *CE* 266 & 267 (Dec 14, 1918), p. 14; cf. S.H.F., 'The 1918 General Council', *CE* 256 & 257 (Oct 5, 1918), pp. 2-3 (3).

[468] 'Minutes of Last Council Now Ready', p. 14 (emphasis added).

[469] Boulos, 'In Defense of the Truth', pp. 10-11.

was called 'the infant sign of the baptism experience'.[470] But if we 'continue to ask, to seek and to knock ... He is going to lead us out into fullness, powers, glories, revelations of His unspeakable love ... that we now hardly dare to dream of'.[471] One may experience further blessings but these should not be labelled. For example, Bell commented on Acts 4.31: 'there is no warrant at all in this passage for calling this a baptism of fire nor for seeking this as a baptism of fire'.[472] 'We need to be constantly filled with the Holy Ghost', Flower noted because 'we have leaked out'.[473] Finally, 'the Scriptures do not teach that you have to continue talking in tongues the rest of your life ... leave this matter with the Lord'.[474]

8. The Terminology of the Evidence Doctrine

A review of the evidential terminology used in the *PE* is in order. The most frequent monikers are simply 'sign' and 'evidence' followed by the 'Bible evidence',[475] or simply 'the evidence'.[476] Other phrases in chronological order include: 'Pentecostal evidence',[477] 'outward evidence',[478] 'indisputable evidence',[479] 'full evidence',[480] 'initial physical evidence',[481] 'external physical

---

[470] Pope, 'Why I Believe', p. 7.
[471] C.E. Simpson, 'A Methodist Minister's Personal Testimony', *CE* 300 & 301 (Aug 9, 1919), pp. 2-3, 7 (7).
[472] E.N. Bell 'Questions and Answers #25', *WE* 126 (Feb 12, 1916), p. 8.
[473] J.R.F., 'Be Filled With The Spirit', *WE* 197 (Jul 7, 1917), p. 8; cf. E.N. Bell 'Questions and Answers #118', *WE* 172 (Jan 13, 1917), p. 9. G. Kirke claimed to be 'rebaptized' in the Holy Spirit, G. Kirke, 'Remarkable Revival At Thornton Heath, London', *CE* 262 & 263 (Nov 16, 1918), pp. 8-9 (8).
[474] E.N. Bell, 'Questions and Answers #905', *PE* 366 & 367 (Nov 19, 1920), p. 5; Durham, 'What is the Evidence', p. 2.
[475] E.g. M.T. Draper, 'The Gospel In A Nut Shell', *WE* 157 (Sep 16, 1916), p. 14;
[476] E.g. McPherson, 'What is the Evidence of the Baptism of the Holy Ghost', p. 7.
[477] E.V. Jennison, 'Hutchinson, Kansas', *WE* 103 (Aug 14, 1915), p. 1.
[478] 'Rightly Dividing The Word of Truth', *WE* 121 (Jan 1, 1916), p. 10.
[479] B.F. Lawrence, 'Article X – Apostolic Faith Restored: My First Visit to the Azusa Street Pentecostal Mission, Los Angles, California', *WE* 131 (Mar 18, 1916), pp. 4-5, 7 (4).
[480] Craig, 'Woodworth-Etter Meeting, Sidney, Iowa', p. 15.
[481] 'Essentials To Pentecost', *CE* 260 & 261 (Nov 2, 1918), pp. 2-3 (p. 3). The phrase, 'initial physical sign' occurs eleven months prior: E.N. Bell, 'Questions and Answers #305', *WE* 217 (Dec 1, 1917), p. 8.

sign',[482] 'first evidence',[483] 'conclusive evidence',[484] and the 'convincing evidence'.[485] Conspicuously absent in the *PE* is the term 'initial evidence'. Therefore, while evidentiary terminology was common at the time, the phrase 'initial physical evidence' occurs twelve years after the raw expressions of the ASM revival, and the phrase 'initial evidence' is beyond the window of this study.[486]

C. Critics and Intramural Theological Pressures

The early Pentecostal pioneers faced a lot of persecution. Consider this testimony: 'over fifteen are coming to the mission, and after a struggle against their old teaching that healing and especially "tongues" are heresy, they are now seeking the baptism'.[487] This section will explore some of the theological arguments by critics.

1. Cessationism

Contributors to the *PE* acknowledged the

> tremendous storm of opposition from the scribes and high priests of our day ... that class of stiff-necked professors ... who regard the promises and references to the supernatural in the Bible, as belonging only to the early days of the church.[488]

Most Pentecostal polemicists, like Bell, noted that after the Apostles, glossolalia

> gradually declined in power and frequency as the church backslid into error and sin and came under the control of the state. But all along, during the past centuries, wherever saints got warmed up in love and unity and close enough to God, the Lord has poured out his Spirit on some with signs following as

---

[482] E.N. Bell, 'Questions and Answers #648', *CE* 284 & 285 (Apr 19, 1919), p. 5.
[483] McPherson, 'What is the Evidence', p. 6.
[484] McPherson, 'What is the Evidence', p. 7.
[485] 'Some Simple Thoughts Concerning Pentecost', *PE* 370 & 371 (Dec 11, 1920), p. 3.
[486] The first occurance of the term 'initial evidence' occurs on May 3rd, 1917 in the *PHA*: Taylor, 'Our Policy', p. 9.
[487] Bro. Will Trotter, 'Fellowship In Christ', *WE* 184 (Apr 7, 1917), p. 3.
[488] W.T. Gaston, 'The Baptism of the Holy Ghost', *CE* 298 & 299 (Aug 9, 1919), p. 4.

on the day of Pentecost.[489]

This enabled them to counter the argument with occurrences from church history[490] and allowed them to reason that the decline or absence of tongues was caused by human 'sin and unbelief' or 'lack of light on the Scriptures'.[491] Both Alice Flower and Bell interpreted Paul's 1 Cor. 13.10, 'when perfection comes', to mean when 'we shall see the king in all his beauty and perfection' and when 'we shall truly see him "face-to-face"'.[492] Further, neither prophecy nor knowledge has passed away yet.[493] McPherson simply called it 'unscriptural'.[494] A.R. Wilson argued that, if the day of 'tongues has passed' then so has the 'day for preaching the gospel' and healing because according Mk 16.15-18, they are interconnected.[495]

2. Sanctification

Thus far, the primary issue that connects sanctification and glossolalia has been to distinguish SB from the WH second work.[496] For example, 'it has been made plain that what we had called the

---

[489] E.N. Bell, 'Questions and Answers #11', *WE* 122 (Jan 8, 1916), p. 8.

[490] C.E.R., 'Spiritual Intoxication', p. 2; Bell, 'Questions and Answers #11', p. 8; Lawrence, 'Article VII(a)', p. 6; Andrew Urshan, 'Are The Days of Miracles Passed?', *WE* 180 (Mar 10, 1917), pp. 4-5 (5); E.N. Bell, 'Questions and Answers #717', *CE* 296 & 297 (Jul 12, 1919), p. 5; Atterberry, 'They Shall Speak with New Tongues', pp. 2-3; Bell, 'Questions and Answers (*PE*)', p. 5; Boulos, 'In Defense of the Truth', p. 10. Inadvertently they pass on incorrect quotes from Augustine and Chrysostom to support their polemic, Pope, 'Why I Believe', p. 7; S.H.F., 'Sunday School Lesson', *CE* 294 & 295 (Jun 28, 1919), pp. 12-13 (12).

[491] E.N. Bell (Dec 27, 1919), p. 5; E.N. Bell, 'Questions and Answers #685', *CE* 290 & 291 (May 31, 1919), p. 5; cf. B.F. Lawrence, 'Article I – Back to Pentecost', *WE* 121 (Jan 1, 1916), pp. 4-5; Bell, 'Questions and Answers #11', p. 8; Elizabeth Sisson, 'Acts–Two–Four–Past And Present', *WE* 217 (Dec 1, 1917), pp. 2-3; Bell, 'Questions and Answers #717', p. 5.

[492] Alice Reynolds Flower, 'Rightly Dividing The Word of Truth', *WE* 150 (Jul 29, 1916), p. 10; E.N. Bell, 'Questions and Answers #317', *WE* 219 (Dec 15, 1917), p. 9; cf. 'The Manifestation of Tongues', *PE* 336 & 337 (Apr 17, 1920), p. 7.

[493] J.T.B., 'A Divine Sandwich', *PE* 350 & 51 (Jul 24, 1920), pp. 2-3 (2).

[494] McPherson, 'What is the Evidence', p. 7.

[495] Wilson, *WE* 117, p. 1.

[496] Flower, 'The Evidence of the Baptism', p. 4; E.N. Bell, 'Questions and Answers #786', *PE* 318 & 319 (Dec 13, 1919), p. 5; E.N. Bell, 'Questions and Answers #799', *PE* 326 & 327 (Feb 7, 1920), p. 5. More broadly, SB endued the beginner 'to live a true life in Christ', 'As a Presbyterian Now Sees It', *CE* 65 (Oct 31, 1914), pp. 1-2 (1).

baptism of the Holy Spirit was not the baptism, for the reason that the scriptural sign ... did not follow'.[497] However, several articles in the *PE* promoted that tongues-speech could stimulate holiness. For example, one person reported that when 'I heard, for the first time, (some) one speak in another tongue my heart was pierced in an instant ... (I believed) that the baptism in the Spirit would give me more satisfaction hour by hour around-the-clock than sin ever had'.[498] A.G. Ward theorized that the Spirit would speak to and through the glossolalic about 'the fullness of the life of the glorified Christ ... as we yield through death and deep interior crucifixion of our fine parts to the indwelling of the Holy Ghost'.[499]

Another popular connection with sanctification was that the Spirit would clean up an individual's speech much like the live coal that touched Isaiah's lips:

> a live coal of the Holy Spirit's fire came down on that day of Pentecost, to cleanse and equipped for service the 120 waiting disciples ... Can a tongue that has been taken hold of by the Holy Ghost ever be used again to speak lying, angry, selfish or trifling words?[500]

Glossolalia recreated or renewed speech for the new dispensation: 'Adam's tongue was tainted ... but in this new era the tongue is being cleansed, is being sanctified, made new. The new tongue belongs to the new era the new creation, the redeemed world.'[501]

3. Counterfeit and Demonic Glossolalia

The criticism of demonic tongues and counterfeits was dealt with in a manner common to other periodicals of its day. First, Boddy noted that, 'there are not nearly so many counterfeits as some

---

[497] Atterberry, 'They Shall Speak with New Tongues', pp. 2-3.
[498] 'The Works of God: The Good of Tongues', *WE* 160 (Oct 7, 1916), pp. 4-5.
[499] A.G. Ward, 'Soul Food For Hungry Saints', *PE* 310 & 311 (Oct 18, 1919), p. 8.
[500] A.E.L., 'Pictures of Pentecost In The Old Testament', pp. 6-7; cf. Alice E. Luce, 'Lips Cleansed And Consecrated', *PE* 346 & 47 (Jun 26, 1920), pp 1-2; S.H.F., 'Sunday School Lesson', p. 13; Alice Flower, 'The Holy Spirit Our Helper', *CE* 284 & 285 (Apr 19, 1919), p. 12; E.N. Bell, 'Questions and Answers #877', *PE* 358 & 359 (Sep 18, 1920), p. 5.
[501] 'The Restoration of All Things', *WE* 202 (Aug 11, 1917), pp. 8-9 (8).

think … (some people just) do strange things'.[502] Existence of counterfeits was acknowledged and called for discernment,[503] but at the same time, 'only a *genuine* thing can be *counterfeited*'.[504] Studd noted that 'when I suggested that, notwithstanding, "speaking in tongues" was surely a scriptural experience, I was told that this was all spurious. As I thought it over, I said that if there was spurious, there must be also the genuine'.[505] Fear of receiving a demonic spirit hindered people from receiving God's Holy Spirit.[506] Second, there were only two articles that directly addressed tongues having a possible demonic source: 1) 'it is presumed Satan knows all languages, and could cause one really already possessed with demons to talk in tongues through the demons in him, but such a person will always be lacking in all the genuine **fruits** of the Holy Spirit'.[507] 2) Further,

> no person can be caused by Satan to speak with tongues except one who is already demon possessed … every real spirit medium is a demon possessed person … But all these things are only counterfeits of the real blessed work of the Holy Ghost … there is a different ring to one speaking in tongues as the blessed spirit of God gives utterance.[508]

This charge of tongues having a demonic origin divided churches: 'we formerly belonged to the Baptist gospel mission but our names have been cast out as evil because we received the baptism of the Holy Spirit with the evidence of speaking in tongues'.[509]

---

[502] Boddy, 'The Holy Ghost For Us', p. 8.
[503] 'The Manifestation of Tongues', p. 7. Dr. Worrell, believes that godly character and the positive spiritual effects of SB, despite 'the devil's counterfeits', presents non-Pentecostal Christianity with 'a real crisis'. The article does not enumerate further, Lawrence, 'Article VII(b)', pp. 4-7.
[504] B.F. Lawrence, 'Article VIII – Reminiscences of An Eyewitness', *WE* 128 (Feb 26, 1916), pp. 4-5.
[505] George B. Studd, 'My Convictions', *WE* 148 (Jul 15, 1916), pp. 4-6 (4).
[506] Hodges, 'The Enemies In The Land', p. 6.
[507] Bell, 'Baptism With the Spirit with Speaking in Tongues', p. 4 (emphasis original).
[508] E.N. Bell, 'Questions and Answers #856', *PE* 348 & 49 (Jul 10, 1920), p. 6.
[509] 'L.M. Anglin', *WE* 117 (Nov 27, 1915), p. 4.

4. The 'New Issue'

In addition to disagreement over the Trinity and baptismal formula,[510] the new issue forced a theological clarification of glossolalia. First, the *PE* affirmed that SB was subsequent from justification. Bell noted that Oneness proponents

> have logically concluded from their false premise that the Birth of the Spirit and the Baptism by Christ with the Spirit are one and the same. Also, as they hold the Baptism is accompanied by speaking in other tongues, it necessarily follows in their teaching that if one never spoke in tongues, he is not born of the Spirit.[511]

According to Bell, 'the normal order is repentance, faith and baptism in water, (and) then to receive the Spirit',[512] while Sisson believed that 'any other order then the God-given pattern is abnormal'.[513] Durham, whose work would be foundational to Oneness theology, rebuffed the idea that justification and SB were the same experience long before the new issue. He wrote that men

> teach that the Holy Spirit is received when we are christened in infancy or confirmed in youth ... (or) received in conversion ... (or finally) in sanctification ... But not one of them (these) will stand a scriptural test ... Not one of them has any sign that distinguishes his experience from the rest. **The only difference is in their theory.** So when God's true standard is lifted

---

[510] E.N. Bell, 'Questions and Answers #139', *WE* 177 (Feb 17, 1917), p. 9; E.N. Bell, 'Questions and Answers #273', *WE* 210 (Oct 13, 1917), p. 7.

[511] E.N. Bell, 'The Baptism and the Rapture', *PE* 316 & 317 (Nov 29, 1919), p. 8. The first mention of salvific glossolalia by Oneness Pentecostals in the *PE* occurs in July 1917: Bell answers the question, 'what do the "New Issue" folks believe?' He responds that 'they do not all believe alike ... some hold the Apostles had no life from God, were not born again until the Holy Ghost fell on the day of Pentecost and that no one now is born-again or begotten of God until baptized in the Holy Ghost and speaks with tongues ... others of them hold the above, except as to the tongues', E.N. Bell, 'Questions and Answers #235', *WE* 200 (Jul 28, 1917), p. 9.

[512] E.N. Bell, 'Question And Answer Department', *WE* 96 (Jun 26, 1915), p. 3. Bell does allow for God's sovereignty: 'but God has a right to baptize them with the Spirit at any time he sees fit, as he did at the house of Cornelius'. Cf. E.N. Bell, 'Questions and Answers #144', *WE* 178 (Feb 24, 1917), p. 11.

[513] Sisson, 'Acts–Two–Four–Past And Present', p. 3; cf. Simpson, 'The Baptism In The Spirit – A Defense', p. 3.

up, it reflects on all these so-called experiences where men are taught that they are to claim, but to really expect to receive nothing.[514]

Second, when and in what fashion does one receive the Holy Spirit? The *PE* clearly distinguished between an indwelling Spirit received at salvation and an empowering Spirit with the sign of tongues:

> in conversion or the new birth, the Holy Spirit operates upon us ... We are quickened or made alive, the Spirit is present and works within us, but the New Testament never calls this **the receiving of the Holy Spirit as a gift** ... They (the disciples) later received the Holy Spirit as a separate experience ... In such an experience believers also get '**filled** with the Holy Ghost' and speak with other tongues.[515]

Such a position raised a question. Exactly when did the disciples receive salvation? Boddy believed that

> they received the resurrection life of the Lord Jesus, the Spirit of Christ as their new life ... on that Easter Eve were born of the Spirit – Christ's Spirit – but on that first Whit-Sunday they received a further blessing: they were filled with the Spirit, immersed in the Holy Ghost, endued with power from on high.[516]

According to Bell, the pre-Pentecost disciples had 'the promise for the Spirit to be IN them in the sense Jesus was speaking of was still future to them', but they did not have the Spirit as we do at salvation today; they lived 'in the lapping over of the two ages'.[517] Further, Jesus' breathing on the disciples in Jn 20.21-23 'was *merely symbolic* of the mighty wind that came on the day of Pentecost';

---

[514] Durham, 'What is the Evidence', p. 2.
[515] Bell, 'Some Important Questions Answered', p. 3; cf. Sisson, 'Acts–Two–Four–Past And Present', p. 3; Kerr, 'Do All Speak In Tongues', p. 7; S.H.F., 'As On Us At The Beginning', *CE* 282 & 283 (Apr 5, 1919), p. 3; Gaston, 'The New Birth And Baptism in the Holy Ghost', p. 1; 'Some Simple Thoughts Concerning Pentecost', p. 3.
[516] Boddy, 'The Holy Ghost For Us', p. 1; cf. E.N. Bell, 'Questions and Answers #90', *WE* 154 (Aug 26, 1916), pp. 8-9; Simpson, 'The Baptism in the Spirit – A Defense', pp. 2-6.
[517] Bell, 'Questions and Answers #90', p. 8.

however, it does reveal two receptions of the Holy Spirit.[518]

Given the salvific nature of water baptism and tongues in the Oneness paradigm, it was interesting to discover that testimonies of people who spoke in tongues as they came up out of the water were printed in the *PE after* the new issue divided the fellowship. For example, 'one came out of the water speaking in tongues'.[519]

5. Divine Love

Though not a major focus in the *PE*, the following two points were made regarding divine love and glossolalia: first, love was a necessary component of tongues-speech, in fact, 'love is a mightier witness of the Spirit's indwelling than the gift of speaking in tongues'.[520] 'In the acme of true Pentecostal experience is the centering of that more excellent way.'[521] Because for us 'to have a big outward show, speaking with other tongues ... is no adequate substitute for the love of God'.[522] Second, unity will not come through doctrine, but by love.[523]

6. Rudimentary Sacramentalism

There was an implied rudimentary sacramentalism in the *PE*. First, the action of tarrying for SB was a holy action. For example, Stanley Frodsham instructed that 'when a seeker is tarrying for the power, the Spirit frequently convicts of many things that would

---

[518] Bell, 'Baptism with the Spirit with Speaking in Tongues', p. 3 (emphasis added). After renouncing his rebaptism in Jesus' name Bell believes John 20 was a 'parallel with the commission in Matt. 28:19 and Mark 16:15 ... there is no difference in meaning between these two sayings ... Jesus commissioned them in John 20:21 to 23, to receive the Spirit and to go; but they did not receive the Spirit at that moment', Bell, 'Questions and Answers #90', pp. 8-9.

[519] J.A. McPhail, 'Coffeyville, Kans.', *PE* 312 & 313 (Nov 1, 1919), p. 23; cf. W.M. Harrison, 'Understood In French (WE)', 96 (Jun 26, 1915), p. 1; E.N. Bell, 'Davis City Camp-Meeting Report', *WE* 105 (Aug 28, 1915), p. 2; Chas. Williamson, 'Humphrey, Ark.', *CE* 308 & 309 (Oct 4, 1919), p. 9; P.M. Joyner, 'Union City, Tenn.', *PE* 310 & 311 (Oct 18, 1919), p. 14; Mary Chapman, 'Victory In Madras', *PE* 366 & 367 (Nov 19, 1920), p. 10.

[520] 'Hints From A Missionary Letter', *WE* 98 (Jul 10, 1915), p. 2; cf. Boddy, 'The Holy Ghost For Us', p. 2.

[521] 'Placing The Emphasis', *WE* 109 (Sep 25, 1915), p. 4; cf. J.T.B., 'A Divine Sandwich', p. 2.

[522] Alice Flower, 'Love', *CE* 292 & 293 (Jun 14, 1919), p. 12.

[523] Will Trotter, 'Revival of Love Needed', *WE* 84 (Apr 3, 1915), p. 1; cf. Wm. F.P. Burton, 'A Great Pentecostal Outpouring in Central Africa', *PE* 340 & 341 (May 15, 1920), pp. 1-3 (3).

hinder his incoming. This is "the way of holiness".[524] The individual would then seek to live a holy life by faith. Tarrying was another sacramental act of yieldedness:

> and to those who tarry for the baptism of the Holy Spirit the promise is abundantly fulfilled. When the comforter comes in to abide, when he has subdued the whole being to his control, and he takes possession of the yielded lips, speaking through them in other tongues the praises and glories of Jesus ... it is joy unspeakable and full of glory.[525]

Second, in addition to the action of water baptism and participation in communion, objects could be sacramental items.[526] For example, handkerchiefs, when anointed, when prayed over, had the power to facilitate SB: 'I want your prayers in the anointing of his handkerchief, first that I may receive the divine anointing to speak with tongues, to lay hands on the sick and pray for them, or to do anything God has for me to do'.[527] Frank Favacuia noted an anointed handshake in his testimony:

> after tarrying for the baptism for a time, I felt it was no use and got up to go away. In departing a brother shook hands with me, and it seemed as if I had received a shock of electricity, and in two minutes I was speaking in an unknown tongue.[528]

The action of speaking in tongues was a sacred overlapping of two realities:

> supernatural manifestations in the physical realm are no new phenomena ... when He has taken full possession He speaks

---

[524] S.H.F., 'Our Distinctive Testimony', *PE* 320 & 321 (Dec 27, 1919), pp. 8-9 (8); cf. Bell 'Questions and Answers #25', p. 8; Bell, 'Some Important Questions Answered', p. 3; Kerr, 'Do All Speak In Tongues', p. 7; 'Some Simple Thoughts Concerning Pentecost', p. 3.

[525] A.E. Luce, 'Prayer For The Watersprings', *CE* 246 & 247 (Jun 29, 1918), pp. 4-5 (5).

[526] There is at least one mention of foot washing in the *PE* as an 'ordinance', P.A. Hill, 'A Testimony', *WE* 214 (Nov 10, 1917), p. 16.

[527] August Feick, 'Woodworth-Etter Meetings At Los Angeles, Cal.', *WE* 180 (Mar 10, 1917), p. 16; cf. Will C. Trotter, 'The Power Falling At Portland, Ore.', *WE* 219 (Dec 15, 1917), p. 14; J.L.L., 'Toronto's Most Joyous Sect Is the Pentecostal Assembly', *CE* 300 & 301 (Aug 9, 1919), p. 8.

[528] Frank Favacuia, 'From Miry Clay To Solid Rock', *PE* 338 & 339 (May 1, 1920), p. 8.

through the yielded lips in other tongues, as promised in Isa. 28:11, 12 (see 1 Cor. 14:21) … (and) the results even in the physical realm of His indwelling and enduement are more blessed than tongue can express, and only those who are wholly yielded to Him can taste their sweetness.[529]

Tongues overlapped between the phenomenal (sacred) and nominal (secular) realities. Another example would be those who spoke in tongues upon their deathbed, heaven and earth overlapped to give the survivors hope:

> she was speaking in tongues and interpreting up to the last, and had hardly been brought back (to life) when she began again in the Spirit. It was the most blessed deathbed I had ever witnessed. Heaven was so near and real.[530]

D. Purpose

Many writers attempted to give theological meaning to glossolalia in the *PE*.[531] By this time the theology of glossolalia had moved well beyond the somewhat naïve purpose of MT that was seen in the early *AF*.[532] In fact, one unnamed author observed that when tongues were viewed only

> as a medium of communication with people of foreign languages … (they) appear as of little practical value … (but) with an understanding of the private use of the gift of tongues as a medium of expressing the heart's deepest emotions, a greater field of usefulness opens up before us.[533]

The following purposes for tongues, both private and public, were observed in the *PE*.

---

[529] A.E.L., 'Physical Manifestations of the Spirit', pp. 2-3; cf. Bell, 'Questions and Answers #90', pp. 8-9.

[530] S.M. Ulyate, 'Brought Back To Life By Prayer', *PE* 318 & 319 (Dec 13, 1919), p. 8; cf. 'Bro. Moody At Rest', *CE* 284 & 285 (Apr 19, 1919), p. 7; 'Bro. C.G. Robinson With Christ', *PE* 330 & 331 (Mar 6, 1920), p. 12.

[531] Elder R.B. Chamber's overall hermeneutical grid was eschatology, Elder R.B. Chambers, 'Wherefore The Tongues', *WE* 127 (Feb 19, 1916), pp. 5-6. The editor noted a 'four-fold purpose': 1) sign to believer, 2) edification, 3) praise, 4) and a sign to unbelievers, Atterberry, 'They Shall Speak with New Tongues', pp. 2-3.

[532] McGee believes that the theology of 'missionary tongues' was debunked by late 1906 and early 1907, McGee, 'Shortcut to Language Preparation', p. 122.

[533] 'The Manifestation of Tongues', p. 7.

1. Power

Following the biblical promise of being 'clothed with power from on high', glossolalia was principally a sign of God's power for evangelism. For example, 'the object for which we are baptized is to "**endue us with power** from on high" to "**witness**" for Jesus (Luke 24:49; Acts 1:8)'.[534] Supernatural power was needed to reach the lost which in turn helps to 'hasten the return of the Lord'.[535] For example, 'may the blessed work continue, and this greater evangelism proceed with great power and demonstration of the Spirit, sweeping in the sinners by the thousand'.[536] However, the Holy Spirit's power was multi-purposed. SB was

> not only to speak in tongues as an evidence of His indwelling, but to fill us with God, power to resist temptation, power to lead clean, pure, holy lives, power to witness boldly for our Savior King and to overcome at all times and in all conditions.[537]

Flower noted that Pentecostal power unifies – 'forming them into a body of men and women with one purpose, one hope, (and) one faith' – so that they will be transformed into 'an aggressive body (of) people with a message … to all the earth'.[538]

2. Prayer

Using one's own vocabulary and intelligence to pray was a necessary practice for the Christian but at times public prayers could devolve into a 'circus', or 'a big outward show'; whereas, 'it is the

---

[534] Bell, 'Baptism With The Spirit With Speaking in Tongues', p. 4; cf. Boddy, 'The Holy Ghost For Us', p. 2; Wm. J. Taylor, 'The Menace of Spiritism', *PE* 338 & 339 (May 1, 1920), pp. 6-7 (7).

[535] Editor, 'The Time of Thy Visitation', *WE* 82 (Mar 20, 1915), p. 1.

[536] Editor, 'Three Mighty Outpourings', *WE* 81 (Mar 13, 1915), p. 1; cf. B.F. Lawrence, 'Article XI – The Work Spreads to India', *WE* 132 (Mar 25, 1916), pp. 4-5, 8. The second General Council pledged that 'as a Council … we commit ourselves and the movement for the greatest evangelism that the world is ever seen. We pledge our hearty co-operation, prayers and help to this end', J.R.F. 'A Greater Evangelism', *CE* 79 (Feb 27, 1915), p. 1. This spiritual power does not override human volition, E.N. Bell, 'Questions and Answers #111', *WE* 169 (Dec 16, 1916), p. 9; W.F. Carothers, 'His Baptism Renewed', *WE* 153 (Aug 19, 1916), p. 14.

[537] Mrs. John W. Ingham, 'Glorious Convention at Pretoria, South Africa', *WE* 149 (Jul 22, 1916), p. 9.

[538] J.R.F., 'A Greater Evangelism', p. 1.

prayer in secret ... (that) brings the great open reward Jesus promised. It may be a prayer in another tongue; but God understands, and the answer is certain and sure.'[539] Alice R. Flower believed that glossolalic-prayers were more effective:

> so many of God's children today have testified to the wonderful stimulus the outpouring of the Holy Spirit has given to their prayer life ... but it means cooperation with God on our part ... fluency in speaking (is not) essential to prayer. When words fail and we can only groan out our hearts to God perhaps our prayer is most big with meaning and will prove most efficacious. The greater and deeper the desire from God the less likely we will be to adequately express it. Someone has said, 'We have two intercessors, one in heaven and one in the heart. Christ for us, the Spirit within us.'[540]

When interceding though tongues, there was a point when the intercessor could feel the full burden of the lost people's perdition and experience what was called 'soul travail' and then began 'pleading for souls'.[541] At this point 'the English vocabulary was altogether inadequate, so that groanings which cannot be uttered were brought forth'.[542] For example, 'the Holy Spirit is given to lead the baptized believer into deeper experiences, such as intercession and travail of the soul for the lost and dying souls'.[543]

3. Praise and Revelation

Similar to the above periodicals, glossolalia was concomitant with a recognition of God's presence that often resulted in praise or revelation. Garfield T. Haywood reported, 'so great was the manifestation of God's presence that all the assembly joined in the

---

[539] Alice Flower, 'Prayer', *CE* 290 & 291 (May 31, 1919), p. 12.

[540] Flower, 'Rightly Dividing The Word of Truth', p. 10.

[541] Edward Armstrong, 'The Newark Convention', *WE* 88 (May 1, 1915), p. 4. Mrs. Priscilla Wilkes, 'Healed And Baptized In The Spirit', *WE* 153 (Sep 30, 1916), pp. 6-7. This is sometimes called the 'Spirit of intercession', Della Goodrich, 'Stirring Word From Central America', *WE* 152 (Aug 12, 1916), p. 13; cf. B.F. Lawrence, 'Article XIII – Pastor Barrett and the Work in Europe', *WE* 135 (Apr 15, 1916), pp. 4-5.

[542] Armstrong, 'The Newark Convention', p. 4; cf. B.F. Lawrence, 'Article IX – The Pentecostal or "Latter Rain" Outpouring in Los Angeles', *WE* 130 (Mar 11, 1916), pp. 4-5, 8; Lawrence, 'Article XI', pp. 4-5, 8.

[543] Urshan, 'The Baptism of the Holy Ghost', p. 6.

welcome chorus ... a young man ... threw up both hands and fell backwards on the floor speaking in other tongues'.[544] Frodsham noted that,

> God has given them utterance in languages supernatural and supernal, and that they have at last found an adequate way of expressing their love and praise to God ... there is something more blessed than words can express in speaking in other tongues.[545]

One 'bright young woman ... was so filled with a sense of the presence of God that ... she found herself voicing them in another tongue, on the street, in subdued tones, yet freely, clearly and without effort, all the way home'.[546] Sission wrote that 'with tongues, He is making ready a worshiping, adoring people, whose prayers fall so quickly into praises that while they are yet praying ... they are caught away in the worship and praise and adoration in tongues'.[547] Many testimonies noted the purpose of glossolalia was praise. For example, 'twenty-three were filled with the Holy Ghost and spake in tongues and *glorified God*',[548] or 'the power of God fell on the saints and they were standing all over the hall with her hands in the air *praising and magnifying the Lord* in tongues'.[549] One author noted that the very nature of tongues was an idiolect of praise and thanksgiving: 'as the soul of a loving mother grows hungry and longs to hear an expression of love from the thoughtless child who is ever receiving but never giving ... so our Father in heaven loves to have wafted to Him ... a real note of praise and

---

[544] Eld. G.T. Haywood, 'Pentecost At Apostolic Faith Assembly', *CE* 79 (Feb 27, 1915), p. 1.

[545] S.H.F., 'Our Distinctive Testimony', p. 8.

[546] B.D. Landon, 'Youngstown, Ohio', *CE* 290 & 291 (May 31, 1919), p. 9; cf. Leonard W. Coote, 'The Testimony of An English Business Man In Japan' *CE* 296 & 297 (Jul 12, 1919), pp. 6-7 (7).

[547] Elizabeth Sisson, 'Much Incense', *WE* 151 (Aug 5, 1916), p. 6.

[548] J.H. Lane, 'Earle, Ark.', *PE* 324 & 325 (Jan 24, 1920), p. 9 (emphasis added).

[549] Will C. Trotter, 'The Pentecostal Work In Portland, Ore.', *WE* 174 (Jan 27, 1917), p. 16 (emphasis added). Cf. Bro. Andrew Urshan, 'Thirsting After God', *WE* 161 (Oct 21, 1916), p. 6; Brother Andrew Urshan, 'Word From The Missionaries', *WE* 161 (Oct 21, 1916), p. 12; J.H. Gray, 'Yokohama, Japan', *CE* 278 & 279 (Mar 8, 1919), p. 7; Homer G. Wilson, *PE* 316 & 317 (Nov 29, 1919), p. 14; 'Mrs. Mary W. Chapman', *PE* 346 & 47 (Jun 26, 1920), p. 13. Passim.

thanksgiving'.[550] Glossolalia may lead to further revelations from God: 'the Spirit ... leads (us) into a knowledge and deep experience of Him who is to come. The baptism is the forerunner of the deeper experience of the work of the Spirit.'[551]

4. Tongues as a Gift of the Holy Spirit

The gift of tongues and its companion gift, the gift of interpretation, were addressed in typical Pentecostal fashion. Bro. Rickard called the restoration of this prophetic voice of God to his people 'the supreme miracle of the age'.[552] Often the interpretation was reprinted for the common good: 'messages are being given in tongues with interpretation, calling sinners to come to God and declaring that Jesus is coming soon'.[553] Or, 'the power of God fell and the interpretation to a message given in tongues was "be not afraid. It is I [sic]"'.[554]

1 Corinthians was the rulebook to be followed for this public gift.[555] Paul's unique theology of tongues: 1) 'classified and harmonized' these operations of the Spirit,[556] 2) and was 'mostly corrective' providing the 'design and scope of the promise of the Father'.[557] Yet because 'the Spiritual condition of the Corinthians was not as it ought to be ... 1 Cor. 14 is not our basis, but this is written for our learning; it is an instruction for the right use of the

---

[550] Atterberry, 'They Shall Speak with New Tongues', p. 3.
[551] 'The Importance of Receiving The Holy Spirit', *CE* 282 & 283 (Apr 5, 1919), p. 6.
[552] Bro. Rickard, 'Days of Revelation', *WE* 112 (Oct 23, 1915), p. 3; cf. A. Blackburn, 'Report of the Bradford Pentecostal Convention', *WE* 90 (May 15, 1915), p. 1; E.N. Bell, 'Question and Answers #80', *WE* 149 (Jul 22, 1916), p. 8; L.E. Brown and T.O. Anderson, 'Stowers, North Dakota', *WE* 212 (Oct 27, 1917), p. 14. E.N. Bell, 'Questions and Answers #185', *WE* 217 (Dec 1, 1917), p. 8.
[553] James Shurron, 'Koshkonong, Missouri', *WE* 124 (Jan 22, 1916), p. 14; cf. A.E. Wilson, 'Saints of Benton, Ark. Melted', *WE* 123 (Jan 15, 1916), p. 15; 'Message in Tongues', *WE* 115 (Nov 13, 1915), p. 3; A.E.L., 'Pictures of Pentecost In The Old Testament', p. 6; C.W. Doney, 'Prayer And Bible Conference', *CE* 276 & 277 (Feb 22, 1919), p. 5. Passim.
[554] Elder Daniel Lynn, 'Victory At Greenforest, Ark.,' *WE* 135 (Apr 15, 1916), p. 16; cf. 'A Message Given In Tongues and Interpretation: Given At The Council', *WE* 111 (Oct 16, 1915), p. 2; Stanley H. Frodsham, 'The Renewed Mind', *WE* 158 (Sep 23, 1916), pp. 6-7 (6); 'A Little Cloud Out of the Sea The Size of A Man's Hand', *CE* 286 & 287 (May 3, 1919), p. 4. Passim.
[555] E.N. Bell, 'Question and Answers #80', p. 8.
[556] Kerr, 'Paul's Interpretation of the Baptism', p. 6.
[557] Kerr, 'Paul's Interpretation of the Baptism', p. 6.

tongues'.[558] From practical experience, contributors to the *PE* discerned that 1) SB opened one up to be used in any other of the spiritual gifts,[559] and 2) that personal prophesies were to be discouraged.[560]

5. Eschatological Sign

Similar to other periodicals, testimonies of interpreted tongues often foretold Jesus' soon return:

> for the first two or three years nearly all, if not all who came through speaking in tongues said in their first utterance, 'Jesus is coming soon. Get ready.' In [sic] a tongue they did not know, to themselves unawares, made known to them by bystanders, by someone present whose language they spoke, or by one who could interpret tongues.[561]

Occasionally these interpretations were apocalyptic in nature: 'stirring messages in tongues and interpretation are being given, warning the people about the terrible things that are soon coming upon the earth'.[562] Like other early Pentecostal periodicals, the *PE* attached a strong eschatological connection to glossolalia. First, tongues were a sign of the new dispensation.[563] Second, the rejection of tongues was a sign of the end times.[564] Third, R.B. Chambers compared tongues to the bells on Aaron's robes, which

---

[558] Polman, 'As The Spirit Gave Them Utterance', pp. 5-6.

[559] Arthur W. Frodsham, 'The Gifts of the Spirit', *PE* 320 & 321 (Dec 27, 1919), p. 1.

[560] E.N. Bell, 'Questions and Answers #723', *CE* 298 & 299 (Jul 26, 1919), p. 5; cf. 'Mistaken Message in Tongues', *WE* 87 (Apr 24, 1915), p. 4.

[561] Sisson, 'A Sign People', p. 3; cf. Studd, 'My Convictions', p. 6; Mrs. Susie Woods, 'Further Report of Mrs. Etter's Petoskey Meeting', *WE* 151 (Aug 5, 1916), p. 11; Mrs. J.W. Snyder, 'Four Years Ago Last January', *WE* 151 (Aug 5, 1916), p. 15; R.O. Miller, 'A Letter From Rolla, MO', *WE* 158 (Sep 23, 1916), p. 15; Robt. J. Craig, 'What The Pentecostal Saints Are Doing in San Francisco', *WE* 204 (Aug 25, 1917), p. 16; James O. Sharron, 'Fellowship In Christ', *WE* 207 (Sep 15, 1917), p. 14; Lewis Short, 'Lucky, Ark.', *CE* 244 & 245 (Jun 15, 1918), p. 13; Robt. Gillespie, 'Revival At Pentecostal Assembly of God Mission, Vancouver', *PE* 344 & 35 (Jun 12, 1920), p. 14.

[562] Craig, 'Woodworth-Etter Meeting, Sidney, Iowa', p. 15.

[563] S.H.F., 'The Latter Rain', *WE* 178 (Feb 24, 1917), pp. 8-9; 'When Shall We Rise To Meet The Lord?', *WE* 184a (Apr 10, 1917), p. 2; McCafferty, 'The Time of the Latter Rain', p. 5.

[564] 'The Personal Return of Our Lord Jesus Christ', *WE* 190 (May 19, 1917), p. 4.

signalled the priests going out and coming into the Temple, to an imminent return of Christ. Tongues are

> God's appointed sign, when Christ, our high priest ENTERED INTO heaven ... before the Lord, we may expect the SAME SIGN, the SAME SOUND, when He cometh out; this is why we have the tongues with us today, peeling forth the sound of His out coming, for He is nearing the door.[565]

Significantly, glossolalia's return signalled the end times:

> if the baptism of the Holy Ghost accompanied with the sign of speaking in tongues constituted the early rain, why not the same accompany the Latter Rain? ... The coming of the Lord and the latter rain are inseparably connected.[566]

E. The Nature of Glossolalia

Ultimately, the nature of tongues was a mingling of the supernatural and natural. Whether it was the sign or gift of tongues, xenolalia, or sign language for the deaf,[567] it was the 'Spirit giving utterance'.[568] The following categories examine various aspects of the nature of tongues.

---

[565] Chambers, 'Wherefore The Tongues', p. 5. W.P Robinson connected the signs Mk 16.17 with the eschatological signs of Mt. 24.29, W.P. Robinson, 'Vera, Texas', *CE* 76 (Jan 30, 1915), p. 1. Chairman, J.W. Welch, wrote: 'to emphasize the cry, he has given the bride a new tongue to utter it, yea to whisper it, so the world shall not hear it, and the enemy cannot understand it', J.W. Welch, 'Just A Word From The General Office', *WE* 212 (Oct 27, 1917), pp. 9-10 (9); cf. Atterberry, 'They Shall Speak with New Tongues', p. 3.

[566] Argue, 'An Essential Sign?', p. 3.

[567] There was a fascinating discussion about whether sign-language for the deaf could be an IE if the one so anointed signed with their hands instead of using verbal-glossolalia. Bell's answer focused in on: 1) whether it was a genuine sign-language and 2) if the person knew sign-language. In Bell's estimation the value was in its *unknown quality* and not the status of the audience at all, E.N. Bell, 'Questions and Answers #36', *WE* 129 (Mar 4, 1916), p. 8.

[568] D.R. Stover, 'Mansfield, IL', *CE* 73 (Jan 9, 1915), p. 3; cf. Wm. H. Merrin, 'An All-Day Service', *CE* 75 (Jan 23, 1915), p. 2; 'T.B. Smith and Wife', *CE* 78 (Feb 20, 1915), p. 4; Luis Standlee, 'God's Healing Power', *CE* 79 (Feb 27, 1915), p. 3; Pastor J. Rosselli, 'Broken Arrow, Okla.', *WE* 94 (Jun 12, 1915), p. 1; 'Geo. M. Kelly', *WE* 95 (Jun 19, 1915), p. 4; 'S. Smith', *WE* 112 (Oct 23, 1915), p. 4; Raymond May and J.C. Green, 'Good Meeting Near Crockett, Tex.', *WE* 131 (Mar 18, 1915), p. 15; Arthur S. Adams, 'Codell, Kansas', *WE* 136 (Apr 22, 1916), p. 15; Bro. and Sister C.J. Studd, 'A Blessed Work In Stormville, New York', *WE* 139 (May 13, 1916), p. 14; W.H. Offiler, 'Greetings From Seattle', *WE* 140 (May 29, 1916), p. 14; W.G. Dunlap and Wife, 'A Note of Praise', *WE*

1. Mysteriously Human and Divine

These early Pentecostals wrestled with describing the nature of their experience. On the one hand, they observed a human side. For example, they condemned those who 'taught' people how to speak in tongues, which confirmed the individual's part in pushing air over their vocal cords.[569] On the other hand, they recognized a divine source to glossolalia. Flower noted that the human 'mind can lie passive and listen and wonder as another force apart from itself uses and manipulates the tongue'.[570] However they were reluctant to go so far as to use the term ecstasy. In fact, there is only one possible use of ecstasy in the classic sense, indicating a loss of personal volition:[571] with tongues, 'the believer rises above the natural into the realm of the supernatural in adoring and worshiping God ... it is a state of ecstasy'.[572] Glossolalia was not 'mere gibberish' but was either a heavenly language or a known language that the Holy Spirit spoke through or in cooperation with the

---

143 (Jun 10, 1916), p. 14; S.A. Thorp, 'The Lord of Glory', *WE* 145 (Jun 24, 1916), p. 14; Mrs. Sarah Storey, 'Before They Call I Will Answer', *WE* 129 (Mar 4, 1915), p. 15; Bro. Charles Henry, 'Overlooked Reports', *WE* 165 (Nov 18, 1916), p. 14; Edith Davis, 'The Works of God: A Testimony To Healing From Wales', *WE* 166 (Nov 25, 1916), p. 2; Bro. W.B. Carelock, 'Blessing At Three Creeks, Arkansas', *WE* 167 (Dec 2, 1916), p. 17; Bro. W.B. Carelock, 'Blessing At Three Creeks, Ark.', *WE* 170 (Dec 23, 1916), p. 16; H.E. Hanson, 'Dublin, Texas', *WE* 208 (Sep 29, 1917), p. 14; R.H. Davis, 'Davenport, IA', *WE* 209 (Oct 6, 1917), p. 14; F.A. Hale, 'A Word From San Antonio, Tex.', *WE* 220 (Dec 22, 1917), p. 14; Carrie Pride, 'Reports From The Field', *WE* 234 & 235 (Apr 6, 1918), p. 14; J.B. Moody, 'Reports From The Field', *WE* 236 & 237 (Apr 20, 1918), p. 14; Frank Lindblad, 'Reports From The Field', *CE* 248 & 249 (Jul 27, 1918), p. 14; Frank Lindblad, 'Reports From The Field', *CE* 254 & 255 (Sep 7, 1918), p. 6; Paul M. Joyner, 'Victory In TN', *CE* 256 & 257 (Oct 5, 1918), p. 14; E.R. Fitzgerald, 'Reports From The Field', *CE* 274 & 275 (Feb 8, 1919), p. 12.

[569] E.N. Bell, 'Questions and Answers #202', *WE* 187 (Apr 28, 1917), p. 9; E.N. Bell, 'Questions and Answers #612', *CE* 274 & 275 (Feb 8, 1919), p. 5.

[570] Flower, 'The Evidence of the Baptism', p. 4. In context, Flower notes that the 'tongue ... is in very close relationship to the mind' and is encouraging yieldedness to the Spirit because it is difficult to 'yield over the control of this member to another influence'. Cf. B.F. Lawrence, 'Article IV – The Work of the Spirit in Rhode Island', *WE* 124 (Jan 22, 1916), pp. 4-5.

[571] Gaston, 'The New Birth And Baptism in the Holy Ghost', pp. 1-2, 9. All other uses of 'ecstasy' are quotes by non-Pentecostals, Lawrence, 'Article VII(a)', pp. 4-6; B.F. Lawrence, 'Article III(a) – Tongues in History', *WE* 123 (Jan 15, 1916), pp. 4-5 (5).

[572] Kerr, 'Do All Speak In Tongues', p. 7.

individual:[573] 'when He takes full possession of the yielded vessel. He will take the lips and speak through them in other tongues the praises and glories of Jesus.'[574] However, Sisson, who had studied several languages and 'knew a little bit about the construction of languages' thought tongues were a bit 'wriggly' and 'without much construction'.[575] Given its indescribable nature, contributors defaulted to mystery when describing it.[576] Two profound metaphors attempted to unpack the mystery: 1) that of lovers who have a special idiolect,[577] and 2) that of a mother and child.[578]

2. Xenolalia and Language Study

The practical theology of tongues in the PE included xenolalia but without any hint of MT.[579] In fact, the number of xenolaliac testimonies were surprising given the absence of testimonies in Flower's prior periodical (TP) after October, 1909.[580] However, by this time, Pentecostal missionaries were more culturally sophisticated and valued the study of the local language:[581] 'I have gone to

---

[573] Wm. C. Schell, WE 115 (Nov 13, 1915), p. 1; cf. W.W. Childers, 'God blessing in Puxico, MO', CE 74 (Jan 16, 1915), p. 4; Alva J. Walker, 'A Testimony', WE 176 (Feb 10, 1917), p. 14; E.N. Bell, 'Questions and Answers #727', CE 298 & 299 (Aug 9, 1919), p. 5.

[574] Alice E. Luce, 'What Does The World Demand', PE 334 & 335 (Apr 3, 1920), p. 3; cf. A. Gregory Wilkinson, 'Filled with the Holy Spirit', WE 211 (Oct 20, 1917), p. 7.

[575] Elizabeth Sisson, 'Pentecostal Light', WE 205 (Sep 1, 1917), p. 7.

[576] Cf. 'The Manifestation of Tongues', p. 7; Simpson, 'A Methodist Minister's Personal Testimony', p. 3; Walthall, 'Do All Speak with Tongues Who Receive The Baptism?', p. 6.

[577] A.P. Collins, 'Three More Points', CE 272 & 273 (Jan 25, 1919), p. 4.

[578] Lawrence, 'Article VII(a)', p. 6.

[579] The one exception might be a missionary who prayed for understanding of the language and God answered her prayer: 'right there the Lord gave her the Spanish-language so that she could speak it and understand their speech', S.H.F., 'Pisgah As I Have Seen It', WE 181 (Mar 17, 1917), pp. 2-4 (4).

[580] Henry M. Oatrandor, 'Visions', CE 76 (Jan 30, 1915), p. 1; Mrs. Vivian Strickland, 'From Five to Seventeen', CE 77 (Feb 13, 1915), p. 1; Harrison, 'Understood in French (WE)', p. 1; W.J. Higgins and Wife, 'Victory In Revival', WE 96 (Jun 26, 1915), p. 1; Mary W. Chapman, 'In Madras and Travancore, India', WE 186 (Apr 21, 1917), p. 13; Mrs. Catherin Cragin, 'Paul Cragin of Bolivia', WE 233 (Mar 23, 1918), p. 9; Mrs. H.J. Johns, 'He Set The Captive Free', CE 280 & 281 (Mar 22, 1919), p. 7; Miss Jessie Wengler, 'The Missionary Department', PE 330 & 331 (Mar 6, 1920), p. 12.

[581] Geo. M and Margaret Kelly, 'Days of Blessing', CE 75 (Jan 23, 1915), p. 4; J.E. Osborn, 'Brother and Sister Hansen', CE 77 (Feb 13, 1915), p. 4; 'Sarah A. Kugler', CE 78 (Feb 20, 1915), p. 4; 'Gideon Dahlstein', CE 79 (Feb 27,

school to study this language, which is very hard. Have gone for one year and we see the need of another, to speak the language correctly as interpreter in His work.'[582] Second, these accounts seem to be recorded precisely because tongues in a known language were unusual or rare. For example,

> in the midst of his talk the power of God came on him and he felt the impulse to speak in tongues which he held back for a time. But finally it became so strong that he spoke. When he finished, a young man in the audience arose and said that Carl had spoken in French, and he could interpret it.[583]

Third, xenolalia was a sign to unbelievers:

> he dated his conversion to the night before when he heard Bro. Bosworth speak in German. He, being a German, understood ... Bro. Bosworth told him that he did not know a sentence in German and this put such a conviction on this man that he could not throw it off ... tongues are for a sign, not to them that believe but to them that believe not.[584]

At times, it was also a sign for believers by confirming its divine

---

1915), p. 4; Almyra Aston, 'Nanpara, India', *CE* 79 (Feb 27, 1915), p. 4; 'Flora A. Halland and Mother', *WE* 86 (Apr 10, 1915), p. 4; Beatrice Bernauer, 'Teaches a Sunday School Class In Japan', *WE* 94 (Jun 12, 1915), p. 4; 'Tommy F. Anderson', *WE* 104 (Aug 21, 1915), p. 2; 'Willa B. Lowther', *WE* 112 (Oct 23, 1915), p. 4. Also, missionaries who spoke the language were seen as more effective: 'W.D. Grier', *CE* 73 (Jan 9, 1915), p. 4; 'Susan B. Chester's Girls', *CE* 75 (Jan 23, 1915), p. 4; Mrs. E.A. Bernauer, 'A Little Missionary In Japan', *WE* 83 (Mar 27, 1915), p. 4; B. Berntesen, 'The Work In North China', *WE* 93 (Jun 5, 1915), p. 4; 'Bertha Sutley', *WE* 95 (Jun 19, 1915), p. 4; J.D. Wells, 'The Chico Camp-Meeting', *WE* 104 (Aug 21, 1915), p. 1; 'W.D. Grier', *WE* 117 (Nov 27, 1915), p. 4; Edw. Armstrong, 'Duluth, Minn. Convention', *WE* 118 (Dec 4, 1915), p. 1; F.H. Gray, 'Always Abounding in The Work of the Lord', *WE* 187 (Apr 28, 1917), p. 13.

[582] Marie Jurgensen, 'Marie Jurgensen', *WE* 118 (Dec 4, 1915), p. 4.

[583] 'A Visitation of God In The Great Prisons', *WE* 192 (Jun 2, 1917), p. 11; cf. S.H.F. 'Sunday School Lesson', *CE* 276 & 277 (Feb 22, 1919), p. 12.

[584] R.P. Hines, 'Tongues Are For A Sign', *WE* 85 (Apr 10, 1915), p. 2; cf. Kelly Campbell, 'Green Forest, Ark.', *WE* 120 (Dec 18, 1915), p. 3; cf. 'Sister Etter Has Success In Los Angeles, Calif.', *WE* 116 (Nov 20, 1915), p. 1; 'The Works of God: Speaking in Tongues Understood In South Africa And Other Places', *WE* 163 (Nov 4, 1916), pp. 4-5 (4); 'George H Hicks', *WE* 170 (Dec 23, 1916), p. 16.

origin 'in the mouth of two or three witnesses'.[585] Lawrence recorded an account from a non-believing, secular reporter who validated the xenolalia as 'impartially' as possible and declared it a 'wonder'.[586]

3. Heavenly Anthem[587]

The HA was noted often in testimonies. These descriptions illustrated the difficulty participants had in describing their experience of singing the HA. Testimonies like, 'she spoke and sang in tongues',[588] nuanced the human side while testimonies like, 'the heavenly anthem was sung ... (and) the Spirit spoke through him in other languages' nuanced the divine.[589] Significantly, Sisson described it as 'the wordless heavenly anthem' to indicate this unknown divine facet.[590] Some, like Priscilla Wilkes, spoke of new abilities: 'the power came upon me and I preached a sermon and prayed and sang in other tongues ... *I never could sing in the natural*, but now the Spirit let me sing and the people said that it was grand'.[591] Singing the HA was equivalent to tongues spoken upon IE.[592] At other times, it indicated the nearness of God and his kingdom: 'such singing, such praying in the Spirit I never did hear

---

[585] Will C. Trotter, 'God Mightily Works In Portland', *WE* 92 (May 29, 1915), p. 1; 'Remarkable Moving of Spirit of God At St. Paul Minn.', *WE* 172 (Jan 13, 1917), p. 15. Burton, 'A Great Pentecostal Outpouring in Central Africa', p. 2.

[586] 'The Works of God: Christians in India Are Given "Gift of Tongues"', *WE* 145 (Jun 24, 1916), pp. 4-6 (6). Cf. J.L.L., 'Toronto's Most Joyous Sect', p. 8.

[587] Other monikers used in the *PE* are: 1) 'singing in the Spirit', W.L. Wood, 'Bro. Wood In Los Angeles', *WE* 96 (Jun 26, 1915), p. 1; 2) 'singing in other tongues', Wilkes, 'Healed And Baptized In The Spirit', pp. 6-7; 3) 'singing a new song', Sarah Haggard Payne, 'The Fulfillment of A Life Dream', *WE* 172 (Jan 13, 1917), pp. 4-5 (5); and 4) 'heavenly music', George Hansen, 'The Porto Rican Revival', *WE* 220 (Dec 22, 1917), p. 11.

[588] W.D. Smith, 'Big Creek, Ark.', *WE* 88 (May 1, 1915), p. 4.

[589] Mrs. J.F. Greer, 'The Essex, Mo., Revival', *WE* 133 (Apr 1, 1915), p. 15; cf. F.A. Denton, 'Baptized And Rejoicing', *WE* 84 (Apr 3, 1915), p. 2; Lawrence, 'Article X', p. 4.

[590] Sisson, 'A Sign People', p. 2. Sisson's unique word choice here parallels what Augustine may have called glossolalia, see Appendix 2.

[591] Wilkes, 'Healed And Baptized In The Spirit', p. 7 (emphasis added). Cf. Hansen, 'The Porto Rican Revival', p. 11.

[592] Agnes Shirlaw, 'A Healing And A Revelation of the Soon Coming of Jesus', *WE* 189 (May 12, 1917), p. 4 (emphasis added). Cf. Will C. Trotter, 'The Portland Camp Meeting', *WE* 202 (Aug 11, 1917), p. 16; E.L. Bants, 'Reports

before. As we sang, wave after wave of the Holy Spirit came down and swept through the church until it seemed the Angels were in our midst taking part in the singing.'[593] 'Beyond words to describe'[594] and 'more beautiful than tongue can tell or words to express',[595] indicated the limitation of human speech in the divine presence.

F. Testimonies

The numerous personal testimonies in the *PE* followed the general pattern of testimonies in the other early Pentecostal periodicals, and notable testimonies have been included in the summary above. The greatest number of testimonies in the *PE* affirmed that their experience matched the apostles in the book of Acts. Several types of shorthand developed to convey this scriptural rootedness: 'Bible evidence',[596] 'scriptural evidence',[597] 'received the baptism as in Acts 2:4',[598] 'spoke with other tongues as in Acts

---

From The Field', *CE* 280 & 281 (Mar 22, 1919), p. 14; B.S. Moore, 'In The Regions Beyond', *CE* 260 & 261 (Nov 2, 1918), p. 10; B.C. Williams, 'Los Angeles, Calif.', *PE* 314 & 315 (Nov 15, 1919), p. 14.

[593] J.H. James, 'Torrents of Blessing', *CE* 78 (Feb 20, 1915), p. 3; cf. Hansen, 'The Porto Rican Revival', p. 11.

[594] Payne, 'The Fulfillment of A Life Dream', p. 5.

[595] Shirlaw, 'A Healing And A Revelation', p. 4.

[596] Howard Prather, 'A Testimony', *CE* 73 (Jan 9, 1915), p. 1; Merrin, 'The City Stirred', p. 1; John A. Westman, 'Revival Outpourings', *WE* 98 (Jul 10, 1915), p. 3; Mrs. Ethel Peace, 'A Few Testimonies', *WE* 101 (Jul 31, 1915), p. 1; 'baptizing one in the Spirit, with Pentecostal evidence', Jennison, 'Hutchinson, Kansas', p. 1; Rev. E.J. Douglas, 'Great Revival Spirit At Dyer, Tenn.', *WE* 116 (Nov 20, 1915), p. 4; Daniel Berg, 'Over 300 Baptized In The Spirit', *WE* 136 (Apr 22, 1916), p. 12; W.S.P., 'Healed And Baptized', *WE* 143 (Jun 10, 1916), p. 14; August Feick, 'Mrs. Etter In Petosky, Mich.', *WE* 150 (Jul 29, 1916), p. 15; R.H. Young, 'Reports From The Field', *CE* 258 & 259 (Oct 19, 1918), p. 14; L.A. Coote, 'Yokohama, Japan', *CE* 294 & 295 (Jun 28, 1919), p. 11.

[597] Will Trotter, 'Portland, Ore.', *CE* 73 (Jan 9, 1915), p. 3; Mrs. J.C. Miller, 'A Ten O'Clock Prayer Meeting', *CE* 76 (Jan 30, 1915), p. 1.

[598] Here are just the references from January 1915: M.D. Carelock, 'Tubal, Ark', *CE* 73 (Jan 9, 1915), p. 3. 'To Be baptized in the Holy Ghost as in Acts 2:4', Z.W. Bulloch and wife, 'Bellwood, Alabama', *CE* 73 (Jan 9, 1915), p. 3; W.R Carmichael and Winnie Clements, 'Enterprise, Alabama', *CE* 75 (Jan 23, 1915), p. 1; J.H. Dolby, 'Pentecostal Home in Lebanon', *CE* 75 (Jan 23, 1915), p. 1; D.K. Morris, 'Maryville, LA', *CE* 75 (Jan 23, 1915), p. 1; Van and Bob Merrill, 'Thirty-Five Baptized', *CE* 75 (Jan 23, 1915), p. 3; J.E. Langdoe, 'Hoopston, ILL', *CE* 75 (Jan 23, 1915), p. 3; H.E. Jackson, 'The First in Two Years', *CE* 75 (Jan 23, 1915), p. 4; W.H. Amiot, 'Collinsville, Okla.', *CE* 76 (Jan 30, 1915), p. 1

10:44-46',[599] 'received the Holy Ghost according to Acts 19:6',[600] and 'with other tongues as they did on the day of Pentecost'.[601]

G. An Historical 'Ground of Expectation'

In a series of articles, Lawrence notes that because the Pentecostal movement did not want to become 'slaves of customs and precedent ... [it] leaps the intervening years crying, *"Back to Pentecost"*; thereby, being 'indifferent' to church history.[602] To counter such thinking, Lawrence solicited historical accounts of Pentecostal outpourings from the readers of the *PE*, which he then contributed to the *PE*.[603] The existence of Lawrence's work is significant for two reasons: 1) tongues-speech was clearly the defining mark of Pentecostalism in all these articles, and 2) this was a significant attempt to use church history to normalize glossolalia. These articles sought to provide an historical 'ground of expectation that such a work (SB & tongues) was permanent in the church' because of God's unchanging 'attitude toward the church and the world'.[604] Lawrence reasoned that the absence of such activity was either because God lost 'all affection for us' or he is a 'weakening, failing

---

[599] Wm. A. Summers, 'Sinners Deeply Convicted', *WE* 86 (Apr 17, 1915), p. 1; L.W. Clark and Wife, 'Gipsey And Vinson, MO', *WE* 102 (Aug 7, 1915), p. 1; W.T. Robinson, 'Prayers Answered', *WE* 102 (Aug 7, 1915), p. 3.

[600] John T. Wilson, *WE* 143 (Jun 10, 1916), p. 14.

[601] F.P. Poole, 'God Is Love', *CE* 80 (Mar 6, 1915), p. 2; Dave Fisher, 'Pentecost In Rasutoland', *CE* 258 & 259 (Oct 19, 1918), pp. 8-9 (8). 'As they did at the beginning', C.A. Lasater, 'Ft. Smith, Ark.', *CE* 276 & 277 (Feb 22, 1919), p. 14.

[602] Lawrence, 'Article I', p. 4 (emphasis original). Lawrence admires the richness of church tradition, calling it a 'guide' and an 'inheritance', but notes that we desire 'a return to New Testament power and custom ... (when) healing for the body, expulsion of demons, speaking in tongues, were in early times the result of an activity of the Holy Spirit'.

[603] The first thirteen articles titled 'Apostolic Faith Restored' are published in a booklet: Lawrence, *The Apostolic Faith Restored*. A second series of articles had the same purpose. They were titled 'The Works of God', and ran regularly between Apr 22, 1916 and Oct 14, 1916 (roughly 25 issues), whereupon it morphed into reporting significant testimonies.

[604] Note the nuancing of his purpose: 'we shall present a few reports of the work of God down through the ages, more for the purposes of *providing a ground of expectation* that such a work was permanent in the church than in an effort to trace any historical connection with the primitive believers', Lawrence, 'Article I', p. 4 (emphasis added). 'We shall endeavor to trace, where possible, the conditions that allowed the activity of the Spirit ... (and) the characteristics and methods prevalent', p. 5. Cf. W.H. Turner, 'Pentecost in History', *PE* 358 & 359 (Sep 18, 1920), pp. 8-9.

God', or because 'believers may not allow God to do these things'.⁶⁰⁵ The content of these articles has been incorporated into the summary above.

---

⁶⁰⁵ Lawrence, 'Article I', p. 5.

5

THE ONENESS PENTECOSTAL PERIODICALS

I. Pre-Oneness – *The Good Report*

A. Robert E. McAlister and Frank J. Ewart

Robert E. McAlister[1] was at the ASM revival in 1906 and experienced SB whereupon he returned to Canada to establish churches and publish the periodical, *The Good Report* (TGR).[2] McAlister provided the impetus for Oneness thought at a camp meeting in Arroyo Seco, CA, in April 1913. He

> proposed that the reason the apostles baptized in the name of the Lord Jesus Christ (variations in Acts) instead of the triune name commanded by Jesus (Matt. 28:19) was that they understood 'Lord-Jesus-Christ' to be the Christological equivalent of 'Father-Son-Holy Spirit'.[3]

Frank J. Ewart received the Holy Spirit in 1908 and was dismissed by his Baptist organization. 'In 1911 he became the assistant

---

[1] In 1919, after hearing McPherson, McAlister returned to the Trinitarian camp but remained sympathetic to Oneness, Robin Johnston, 'Howard Goss: A Pentecostal Life' (PhD Dissertation, Regent University School of Divinity, 2010), p. 141. That same year, 'he joined with several other ministers to charter the Pentecostal Assemblies of God of Canada … (and) served as secretary-treasurer of the new organization (1919-32)', Everett A. Wilson, 'Robert Edward McAlister', in Stanley Burgess (ed.), *NIDPCM* (Grand Rapids, MI: Zondervan, rev. and expanded edn, 2002), p. 852. Reed believes that McAlister was rebaptized in Jesus' name, Reed, *'In Jesus' Name'*, p. 146.

[2] Wilson, 'Robert Edward McAlister', p. 852. McAlister had a Presbyterian background.

[3] Reed, 'Oneness Pentecostalism', p. 937; Reed, *'In Jesus' Name'*, p. 146.

pastor to William H. Durham in Los Angeles.'⁴ Ewart's anticipation of 'further revelation and a greater outpouring ... to bring about the close of the age' was fulfilled when he heard McAlister preach at Arroyo Seco.⁵ Ewart was one of the first to preach the message of Oneness⁶ and became one of its leading voices.⁷ McAlister moved *TGR* to Los Angeles in June or July, 1913⁸ and added Ewart as its co-editor.⁹

Two diverging streams of theology are seen in *TGR*.¹⁰ The first stream promoted the traditional Pentecostal theology of

---

⁴ J.L. Hall, 'Frank J. Ewart', in Stanley Burgess (ed.), *NIDPCM* (Grand Rapids, MI: Zondervan, rev. and expanded edn, 2002), pp. 623-24 (623).

⁵ Faupel, *The Everlasting Gospel*, p. 272; cf. pp. 275-81.

⁶ Historians record that Ewart preached his first Oneness message on Acts 2.38 at Belvedere, CA in April 15, 1914, Reed, 'Oneness Pentecostalism', p. 937. This examination reveals that Ewart was quickly moving towards Oneness positions on baptism, glossolalia, and salvation as early as August 1913, F.J. Ewart, 'False Teaching Regarding The Baptism in the Holy Ghost', *TGR* 2.3 (Aug 1, 1913), p. 4. Haywood can be seen moving towards Oneness positions by December 1913, Eld. G.T. Haywood, 'Baptised Into One Body', *TGR* 1.7 (Dec 1, 1913), p. 3.

⁷ Hall, 'Frank J. Ewart', p. 624. The fighting spirit of Durham lived on in Ewart who envisioned theology as constantly under construction. Two examples: 1) Luther's salvation by faith devolved into 'the heresy of consubstantiation', Calvin's reforms were reduced to 'infant sprinkling', and Wesley's 'crumbling unscriptural plank of a "second, definite work of grace"' has gratefully been dealt a death blow, F.J. Ewart, 'Defending Heresies', *TGR* 1.3 (1912), p. 12. 2) 'History again repeats itself ... God has graciously perpetuated His work by reconstructing "The Pentecostal platform" ... in conformity with the name ... the time will come ... when the system of theology that has been built around what is called "the finished work of Calvary," will have to go just the same as the theology of the second work of grace went', F.J. Ewart, 'The Unity of the Faith', *TGR* 1.10 (Mar 1, 1914), p. 4.

⁸ 'It is now six months since the "Good Report and The Apostolic Faith" were amalgamated and sent forth under the first name', Ewart & McAlister, 'Letter To Our Readers and Correspondents (#1)', p. 1.

⁹ McAlister embraced Oneness thought because of a revelation: 'dear Brother Ewart: Greetings in the name of Jesus! Well, we are coming along the line somewhere. I have had a revelation to my soul of *the one God in threefold manifestation*. How my heart melted in His presence. I could only weep and cry. Greet all the saints for me and tell them I am coming. Love to all the family, *in Jesus' name*.' R.E. McAlister, 'From Bro. McAlister', *MDS* 1.9 (Dec 1915), p. 2 (emphasis added).

¹⁰ *TGR* 'was indicative of the gradual transition occurring in the theological thought of its editors and their closest associates ... many of those involved with Ewart and The Good Report were among the first to embrace the Oneness position and champion its message', French, *Our God Is One*, p. 58.

glossolalia, including: evidential glossolalia;[11] a distinction between tongues as the Spirit gives utterance and the gift of the Spirit;[12] the standard purposes for tongues-speech;[13] the distinction between genuine and counterfeit tongues;[14] testimonies of xenolalia;[15] teaching and testimonies of spiritual gifts;[16] the nature of glossolalia consistent with other Pentecostal periodicals;[17] and a broad view of sanctification.[18] This stream fits comfortably with what

---

[11] R.E. McAlister, 'Have Ye Received The Holy Ghost Since Ye Believed', *TGR* 1 (May 1911), p. 2; 'Confession of Faith', *TGR* 1.3 (1912), pp. 3-5 (5); W.E. Moody, 'Preach The Word', *TGR* 1.3 (1912), pp. 7-8; A.H. Argue, 'At Evening Time It Shall Be Light', *TGR* 1.3 (1912), pp 6-7 (7); L.V. Roberts, 'Report of God's Working in Indianapolis', *TGR* 1.7 (Dec 1, 1913), p. 2; Harvey McAlister, 'The Church – Spiritual Gifts – Other Tongues', *TGR* 2.3 (Aug 1, 1913), p. 3; F.J. Ewart, 'Our Answer To Dr. Torrey', *TGR* 1.8 (Jan 1, 1913), p. 3.

[12] R.E. McA., 'Difference Between Speaking in Tongues, and the Gift of Tongues (TGR)', *TGR* 1 (May 1911), p. 4; McAlister, 'The Church – Spiritual Gifts – Other Tongues', p. 3; F.J.E., *TGR* 2.3 (Aug 1, 1913), p. 3; Ewart, 'Our Answer To Dr. Torrey', p. 3; E.A. Paul, 'The Difference Between the Gift of Tongues and The Speaking in Tongues As The Spirit Giveth Utterance', *TGR* 1.10 (Mar 1, 1914), p. 2.

[13] Eld. G.T. Haywood, 'Mid-Summer Convention At Indianapolis, Ind.', *TGR* 2.4 (Sep 1, 1913), p. 3; Harvey McAlister, 'Toronto Convention', *TGR* 1.7 (Dec 1, 1913), p. 2.

[14] Andrew D. Urshan, '"Come" And "Go"', *TGR* 2.4 (Sep 1, 1913), p. 3.

[15] 'Seven Phases of the Revival in India', *TGR* 1.6 (Nov 1, 1913), p. 3, Reprint; *The Latter Rain Evangel*.

[16] H.E. Randall, 'Report From Egypt', *TGR* 2.4 (Sep 1, 1913), p. 1. (reprinted *TGR* 1.6 (Nov 1, 1913), p. 1; Albert Norton, 'Dhond, Poona District, India', *TGR* 1.7 (Dec 1, 1913), p. 1.

[17] McA., 'Difference Between', p. 3; Albert V. Peever, *TGR* 1 (May 1911), p. 2; Clara Hammerton, 'Church of England Girl Finds Jesus', *TGR* 1 (May 1911), p. 3; Mrs. J.A. Murphy, 'Testimonies', *TGR* 1 (May 1911), p. 4; Mrs. A.V. Peever, 'Testimonies', *TGR* 1 (May 1911), p. 4. H.E. Randall testified that he whistled along with tongues: 'I spoke and sang in tongues, and whistled sweet heavenly music', H.E. Randall, 'The Comforter Has Come To Hebert E. Randall', 'Testimonies', *TGR* 1 (May 1911), p. 7. There is even a testimony of deathbed glossolalia, 'Winnie Olde Thurmond Gone On Before', *TGR* 2.1 (Jun 1, 1913), p. 4.

[18] At times sounding WH: 'Jesus is our Savior, *sanctifier*, healer, baptizer, "glorious Lord and coming King." "Everything in Jesus, and Jesus everything."' R.E. McA., 'Apostolic Faith Movement', *TGR* 1 (May 1911), p. 3 (emphasis added). Cf. Hammerton, 'Church of England Girl', p. 3; Mabel Baker, 'Testimonies', *TGR* 1 (May 1911), p. 4; James E. Small, 'Testimonies', *TGR* 1 (May 1911), p. 4. At other times sounding FW: 'it follows that if at conversion a soul received pardon ONLY, and does not get deliverance from the principle within that … the old man, or the Adamic nature, stands as a criminal condemned to death by the law of God', 'Confession of Faith', p. 3. Cf. 'A Good Report', *TGR* 1.3 (1912), p. 1; 'Sanctification Not A Second Work of Grace', *TGR* 1.3 (1912),

preceded it and adds little to this study. The diverging second stream is what will be examined. This stream revealed an emerging Oneness theology culminating in a significant revision of its theology of tongues. Hereafter, only the development of Oneness thought as it is related to the development of glossolalia will be addressed.

B. The Development of Oneness Glossolalia

In *TGR*, noteworthy articles and several testimonies point toward a significant change in the perception of glossolalia in what would become Oneness theology. First, just two months after the Arroyo Seco camp, Ewart wrote, 'the church of Christ was formed by the Holy Spirit on the day of Pentecost ... there never was a church until after Pentecost'.[19] This reinterpreted the Day of Pentecost outpouring to be salvific rather than empowering. Three defences were offered in *TGR*: 1) Ewart reasoned that not all of the 120 on the Day of Pentecost 'were called to preach or minister in a public way. *But they were baptized into the body*.'[20] 2) To support this claim, a distinction was made between being 'born into the kingdom, and baptized into the church';[21] he reasoned that on the Day of Pentecost, the disciples were baptized into the church. 3) A few months later, Garfield. T. Haywood,[22] a highly respected and influential African American pastor, explained that the disciples were like a Jewish baby fully born, but not recognized before his circumcision on the eighth day.[23]

---

p. 2; Moody, 'Preach The Word', pp. 7-8; 'Gentile Pentecost', *TGR* 1.3 (1912), pp. 3, 11; F.J. Ewart, 'The Work On The Coast', *TGR* 1.3 (1912), p. 6; Ewart, 'Defending Heresies', p. 12.

[19] F.J.E., 'The Church – What is It?', *TGR* 2.1 (Jun 1, 1913), p. 3; cf. Ewart, 'False Teaching', p. 4; Haywood, 'Baptised Into One Body', p. 3.

[20] Ewart, 'False Teaching', p. 4 (emphasis added).

[21] Ewart, 'False Teaching', p. 4. A few months later, Haywood concurred: 'now if we are brought into the body by the new birth, then we conclude that the new birth and the baptism of the Holy Ghost are synonymous', Haywood, 'Baptised Into One Body', p. 3.

[22] Haywood was a gifted songwriter, artist, and pastor in Indianapolis, IN who in January 1915 was rebaptized in Jesus' after hearing a message by Cook, Cecil M. Robeck, Jr, 'Garfield Thomas Haywood', in Stanley Burgess (ed.), *NIDPCM* (Grand Rapids, MI: Zondervan, rev. and expanded edn, 2002), pp. 693-94 (694). Haywood was highly respected by Flower and many in the AG. He served as bishop of PAW, a major Oneness denomination, and was known for his 'balanced, visionary, and progressive' leadership.

[23] Haywood, 'Baptised Into One Body', p. 3.

Second, though defending their SB experience from the book of Acts,[24] these developers of Oneness thinking reinterpreted it through the Pauline conversion texts.[25] For example, Paul's use of 'baptized by one Spirit into one body (1 Cor. 12.13)' was given more hermeneutical importance than Luke's power for ministry:[26] 'we believe that the baptism in the Spirit is designed by God to be vastly more than an enduement of power ... they were baptized into the body', wrote Ewart.[27] Haywood reasoned that it had to be conversion otherwise, 'this would be a direct contradiction of the word of God which says there is one baptism (Eph. 4:4)'.[28]

Third, rich word-pictures were employed to nuance their message.[29] SB as a metaphor emphasized being overwhelmed or bathed in the Spirit, but Ewart nuanced it to mean incorporation. For example, crossing the Jordan became a type for salvation and the Day of Pentecost its 'anti-type':

> if we divest our minds of traditional teaching and study the anti-type in the book of Acts we will find that the thing is perfect. On the great day of Pentecost, the two baptisms (water and Spirit) are connected by the conjunction AND in Peter's instructions.[30]

Significantly, two sign-value metaphors nuanced glossolalia away from SB as a sign of empowerment or intimacy to Oneness' sign of salvation: 1) using the seal of circumcision, Haywood wrote:

---

[24] Ewart, 'False Teaching', p. 4; F.J. Ewart, 'Union of Two Largest Pentecostal Missions In Los Angeles', *TGR* 1.6 (Nov 1, 1913), p. 4; Haywood, 'Baptised Into One Body', p. 3; F.J. Ewart, 'A Beautiful Type of Redemption', *TGR* 1.10 (Mar 1, 1914), p. 3.

[25] Ewart, 'False Teaching', p. 4; Haywood, 'Baptised Into One Body', p. 3.

[26] Ewart, 'False Teaching', p. 4.

[27] Ewart, 'False Teaching', p. 4.

[28] Haywood, 'Baptised Into One Body', p. 3.

[29] Even the concept of 'Oneness' was in flux. In a fascinating pre-Oneness article, Kerr wrote extensively about the believers' oneness with each other and with God. However, Kerr never embraced the doctrine of Oneness as it later developed, D.W. Kerr, 'The Oneness of Believers', *TGR* 1.7 (Dec 1, 1913), p. 4.

[30] Ewart, 'A Beautiful Type', p. 3. 'These two births, or baptisms, were always in evidence in the early church where God's normal plan was carried out', F.J. Ewart, 'The Gospel of the Kingdom', *TGR* 1.10 (Mar 1, 1914), p. 2.

circumcision was given as a seal of righteousness ... this being true we find it to correspond with the baptism of the Holy Spirit which is also spoken of as a 'seal' after believing. Eph. 1:13 ... See Col 3:11; Rom. 2:29. So the subject is not 'circumcision' but the 'baptism in the Holy Ghost' ... Now if the 'type' was entered into by the birth in the 'flesh' and the 'seal of circumcision,' why not the 'antitype' by the 'birth of the Spirit' and the 'seal of the Holy Spirit of promise?' John 3:3-7; Eph. 1:13.[31]

2) Sister King gave a poignant example of glossolalia being the sign of a full spiritual birth: 'until [a baby] gives the essential cry, and we say, "it is born and has life and brain, because it has cried?" ... [similarly], the *full-born spiritual babe, babbles its infantile notes else we are not satisfied*'.[32] Although evidentiary language was used in *TGR*,[33] the traditional Pentecostal purposes for the sign were minimized.[34] Additionally, one can see the elevation of water baptism as an objective sign. For example:

we die with him by faith, the 'old man' is buried in a watery grave, and we now are fully and eternally saved to the uttermost, being a new creature, quickened by the Holy Ghost, which is freely given to us. This new creation should now speak in new tongues and do the other things Jesus said he would do.[35]

Finally, at this Pre-Oneness stage, there are two further observations on Oneness' development. First, the testimonies in *TGR* revealed that the ground-breaking ideas of Oneness would take a

---

[31] Haywood, 'Baptised Into One Body', p. 3.
[32] Sister King, 'Abnormality', *TGR* 1.10 (Mar 1, 1914), p. 4 (emphasis added).
[33] The preferred nomenclature was 'Bible evidence', or simply 'the evidence', cf. McA., 'Difference Between (TGR)', p. 4, 'Confession of Faith', p. 5.
[34] Ewart specifically states that 'the baptism in the Spirit is designed by God to be vastly more than an endurement of power', Ewart, 'False Teaching Regarding The Baptism in the Holy Ghost', p. 4. Rather, it is a sign of baptism into the body: 'the baptism of the Holy Spirit is called in the word "a seal unto the day of redemption." ... the Scriptures plainly declare "that in one spirit we are all baptized into this body." (1 Cor. 12:13)'.
[35] Glenn A. Cook, 'Standards of Justification', *TGR* 2.4 (Sep 1, 1913), p. 2; cf. Ewart, 'The Gospel of the Kingdom', p. 2; Ewart, 'A Beautiful Type', p. 3.

few more years to reach the average person.³⁶ Even Andrew D. Urshan, who would become a staunch supporter of Oneness, thanked God for 'the blessed evidence of the baptism, "speaking in other tongues"'.³⁷ Second, though Ewart's trajectory of thought would collapse the distinction between SB and salvation into one work, at this time he was reluctant to let go of his roots:

> there are people who profess to believe in the 'Finished work of Calvary,' and yet are preaching the very thing this great truth destroys, namely, *that one is not saved until they are baptized in the Spirit*. No one can have the revelation of the Pauline gospel in their souls who hold to this theory.³⁸

II. Oneness Periodicals – Meat in Due Season and the Blessed Truth³⁹

A. History of the Oneness Movement⁴⁰

Oneness thought developed within the FW stream of Pentecostalism,⁴¹ especially the AG, until it overflowed the banks of the AG and developed its own unique theology. D. William Faupel sug-

---

³⁶ Randall, 'Report From Egypt', p. 1.
³⁷ Andrew D. Urshan, 'A Call For Prayer And Intercession For Chicago', *TGR* 2.1 (Jun 1, 1913), p. 2. Cf. 'The Lord's Doings At KinBurn', *TGR* 1 (May 1911), pp. 1, 6 (emphasis added). Cf. Harvey McAlister, 'Testimonies', *TGR* 1 (May 1911), p. 4; Mrs. T.H. Lewis, 'Testimonies', *TGR* 1 (May 1911), p. 4; Randall, 'The Comforter Has Come To Hebert E. Randall', p. 7; Mrs. Lillian Garr, 'Pentecost in India', *TGR* 2.1 (Jun 1, 1913), p. 4; Harvey McAlister, 'Philadelphia Revival', *TGR* 2.4 (Sep 1, 1913), p. 4.
³⁸ Ewart, 'False Teaching', p. 4 (emphasis added).
³⁹ *MDS* was the new name for *TGR*. The first two extant issues of *MDS* occur between the 3rd and 4th General Councils and provide a snapshot of the theology and raw emotions just prior to the formal schism. Consider Ewart's note to a friend: 'we published the above letter to do away with all misunderstanding ... we desire love and cherish the fellowship and co-operation of all the ministerial brethren and respect all their convictions *that are derived from the word of God*', Editorial note to, Faulkner, 'From Brother Faulkner', p. 2 (emphasis added).
⁴⁰ For the earliest stage, please see *TGR* above.
⁴¹ Some historians believe that 'many key Pentecostal leaders were simply being consistent with their previous Reformed and Keswick backgrounds', French, *Our God Is One*, p. 51; cf. Reed, 'Oneness Pentecostalism', p. 936. Others see 'a fast and furious evangelization' of the FW message among the WH people, Alexander, *Pentecostal Healing*, p. 182.

gests three latent tributaries were especially significant for its development:[42] 1) 'a concern to harmonize the two (Mt. 28.19 and Acts 2.38) baptismal formulae';[43] 2) a devotional emphasis on the name of Jesus;[44] and 3), a 'reappraisal of the divine nature'.[45] The movement began to separate from classic Pentecostalism when it was observed by McAlister at the World-Wide Apostolic Camp Meeting at Arroyo Seco, CA, in April 1913, that 'the words Father, Son, and Holy Ghost were never used in Christian baptism'.[46] Reflection upon these items led to a soteriological reformulation of SB, which, when fully developed, became the distinctive position of Oneness – that 'God's standard of full salvation' includes glossolalia:[47]

> the basic and fundamental doctrine of this organization shall be the *Bible standard of full salvation*, which is repentance, baptism in water by immersion in the name of the Lord Jesus Christ for the remission of sins, and the baptism of the Holy Ghost *with*

---

[42] Oneness has many theological roots. David K. Bernard notes, 'the groundwork was laid in the teaching and terminology of John Wesley and other early Methodists and then by the earliest Pentecostals, including Charles Parham, William Seymour, and especially William Durham', David K. Bernard, *A History of Christian Doctrine, Vol. 1: The Twentieth Century* (Weldon Spring, MO: Word Aflame, 1999), pp. 111-12. French believes that an eschatological impetus re-ignited Pentecostal's early 'restorationist fervor, with the incendiary elements of pietistic experiential perfectionism, dispensational fundamentalism, and Christocentric "name" theology', French, *Our God Is One*, p. 53; cf. James L. Tyson, *The Early Pentecostal Revival* (Hazelwood, MO: Word Aflame Press, 1992), p. 170.

[43] Faupel, *The Everlasting Gospel*, p. 281. Faupel adds, as 'proponents of the Scottish Realism ... they all accepted the principle that the Scripture could not be self-contradictory', pp. 281-82. Dayton believes that 'the emphasis on the baptismal formula lifted the importance of baptism in this wing of Pentecostalism in such a way as to lead to a very high-powered initiatory experience that included not only conversion but also "water baptism" and "Spirit baptism" with speaking in tongues as essential elements', Dayton, *Seven 'Jesus Only' Tracts*, pp. vii-viii. Reed notes that Durham raised awareness of Acts 2.38, Reed, '*In Jesus' Name*', p. 92, 121-28, 144.

[44] Reed, 'Oneness Pentecostalism', p. 936. Cf. Reed, '*In Jesus' Name*', pp. 44-73, 98; Faupel, *The Everlasting Gospel*, pp. 282-85.

[45] Faupel, *The Everlasting Gospel*, pp. 285-88.

[46] French, *Our God Is One*, p. 58. French reports that there was an 'audible shudder' when he said this and a missionary '"mounted the platform in one bound" to censor McAlister. But, all too late'. Cf. Reed, 'Oneness Pentecostalism', p. 937.

[47] Bernard, *A History of Christian Doctrine*, p. 111; cf. Reed, 'Oneness Pentecostalism', p. 943.

the initial sign of speaking with other tongues as the Spirit gives utterance.[48]

For a short time, the emerging Oneness scheme fit uncomfortably within the AG.[49] At the 3rd General Council, the AG formally sought to 'appease the entire body',[50] but one year later, in October of 1916, it adopted what Oneness proponents believed to be an 'ultra-Trinitarian "Statement of Fundamental Truths"'.[51] As a result, one hundred and fifty six ministers resigned the AG and became the pioneers of Oneness organizations.[52] Though the theology of Oneness emerged rather quickly, it would take several years before stable organizations developed.[53]

B. The Glossolalic Witness to 'God's Standard of Salvation'[54]

In the early Oneness writings, glossolalia as an evidence of SB was affirmed. For example, she 'received her baptism *because we heard her speak* with tongues and magnify God'.[55] Urshan wrote that

---

[48] 'Fundamental Doctrine', *Articles of Faith of the United Pentecostal Church International*, p. 31 (emphasis added). Bernard wrote there is 'some debate' on this issue within Oneness and there are some 'differences between groups ... on the proper characterization of these three steps of faith', these groups are minority voices within the tradition, Bernard, *A History of Christian Doctrine*, pp. 111-12. For contemporary survey of glossolalia in the Oneness tradition, see: David K. Bernard, *The New Birth* (Hazelwood, MO: Word Aflame Press, 1989), pp. 220-56.

[49] French notes that it was just 3 days after the AG's founding council, on April 15, 1914, and one year to the date of the Arroyo Seco camp meeting, that Ewart and Cook rebaptized each other in Jesus' name, French, *Our God Is One*, p. 62. Faupel, *The Everlasting Gospel*, pp. 291-94.

[50] Tyson, *The Early Pentecostal Revival*, p. 174. Cf. Reed, '*In Jesus' Name*', pp. 158-61; Reed, 'Oneness Pentecostalism', p. 938; Faupel, *The Everlasting Gospel*, pp. 294-98.

[51] French, *Our God Is One*, p. 71. Cf. Reed, '*In Jesus' Name*', pp. 161-66; Reed, 'Oneness Pentecostalism', p. 938; Faupel, *The Everlasting Gospel*, pp. 298-99.

[52] Reed, 'Oneness Pentecostalism', p. 938; French, *Our God Is One*, p. 71.

[53] Reed, 'Oneness Pentecostalism', pp. 938-40; Tyson, *The Early Pentecostal Revival*, pp. 181-208; French, *Our God Is One*, pp. 77-83; Faupel, *The Everlasting Gospel*, pp. 299-300.

[54] Ewart wrote, 'repentance, water baptism in the name of Jesus Christ and the reception of the Holy Ghost are the three great acts of faith, by which a sinner is identified with Jesus Christ', Ewart, 'To Our Friends', p. 4. Reed believes that Haywood and Urshan were important for this component of Oneness thought, Reed, '*In Jesus' Name*', pp. 198; cf. pp. 78, 197-206.

[55] E.J. Douglas, 'Mt. Tabor, Tenn.', *TBT* 4.11 (Jun 1, 1919), p. 6 (emphasis added).

these anti-Holy-Ghost-Tongues people are misrepresenting and misinterpreting many Scriptures which plainly prove that *the baptism of the Holy Ghost must be accompanied by the speaking in tongues as the Spirit gives utterance* (see, please, Mark 16:17-18; 1 Cor. 14:22; Isa. 28:11-12; Acts 2:4, 10:45-46, 19:6, etc.).[56]

However, there was a modification of what was meant by SB. Urshan meant 'oneness with Christ', or a 'full salvation',[57] which was the final component of the *ordo salutis* and not empowerment or any other traditional Pentecostal purpose for SB:

> you may get angry if someone tells you that unless you speak in other tongues as the Spirit gives utterance you lack the heavenly sign of youra [sic] oneness with Christ or the Spiritual Christ's presence within you, but ... our Lord said to His Disciples, in the day they receive the Holy Spirit Baptism they will know then that He was in the father and they were in Him ... 'the Spirit of God bears witness with our Spirit that *we are children of God*'.[58]

William E. Booth-Clibborn called for a single salvific event and argued that breaking up the *ordo salutis* into theological categories was divisive and inefficient:

> we have named, labeled, stamped, designated and numbered a series of different blessings that should arrive on the individual at different stages of his salvation in numerical sequence. It's foolish, ridiculous in the extreme ... what if God would wrap up in one bundle repentance, salvation, justification, sanctification, healing, cleansing, baptism in the Spirit and unknown

---

[56] Andrew Urshan, 'The Almighty God in the Lord Jesus Christ', in Donald W. Dayton, *Seven 'Jesus Only' Tracts* (New York: Garland Publishing, reprint; U.P.C. of Portland, 1919), p. 67 (emphasis added).

[57] This phrase is found only once in the early extant literature, G.T. Haywood, 'The Birth of the Spirit in the Days of the Apostles', in Donald W. Dayton, *Seven 'Jesus Only' Tracts* (New York: Garland Publishing, reprint; Indianapolis, IN: Christ Temple Book Store, n.d.), pp. 2-3. It is the official phraseology for the doctrine, 'Fundamental Doctrine', *Articles of Faith of the United Pentecostal Church International*, p. 31. Cf. Bernard, *A History of Christian Doctrine*, pp. 111-12.

[58] Andrew Urshan, 'The Doctrine of the New Birth of the Perfect Way to Eternal Life', in Donald W. Dayton, *Seven 'Jesus Only' Tracts* (New York: Garland Publishing, reprint; Cochrane, WI: Witness of God, Publishers, 1921), pp. 46-47 (emphasis added).

tongues and any other favorite blessing?[59]

Booth-Clibborn wrote: 'I have seen very many cases in the early days of this outpouring when one could not distinguish between salvation and Pentecost they were one. They are one and the same thing.'[60] Haywood, simply stated that 'to be born of the Spirit is to be baptized with the Holy Ghost, is the conclusion drawn from the word of God',[61] and that 'the birth of the Spirit and the baptism of the Spirit are synonymous'.[62] Tongues always accompanied a completed salvation: 'every man "speaks as the Spirit gives utterance" when he receives the "gift" of the Holy Ghost'.[63]

C. Understanding the Oneness Interpretation of Glossolalia

Oneness' glossolalic sign of a completed salvation applied the same polemics of an appeal to Scripture, experience, and history that the early Pentecostals used to defend the Bible sign of empowerment. First, in line with their Pentecostal heritage, Oneness' defence followed the pattern from the book of Acts.[64] The best example was Winifred Westfield, who wrote that Peter recounted, 'that he (God) had "granted repentance unto life" to the Gentiles. (Acts 11:18) We notice they did not call it the baptism of the Holy Ghost or power for service, but simply REPENTANCE UNTO LIFE.'[65] She continued with the pattern from Acts,

> the Ephesians ... were baptized in the NAME of the LORD JESUS, and when Paul laid his hands on them the Holy Ghost

---

[59] Booth-Clibborn, 'Suddenly', p. 4. He writes, 'I had moreover to get rid of the idea of two Spirits entering at two different times causing two different experiences which occurred after two tarryings and heart searching's preceded by two repentings', Booth-Clibborn, 'A Preacher's Testimony', p. 4.

[60] Booth-Clibborn, 'A Preacher's Testimony', p. 4 (emphasis added).

[61] Haywood, 'The Birth of the Spirit', p. 14.

[62] Haywood, 'The Birth of the Spirit', p. 16.

[63] Haywood, 'The Birth of the Spirit', p. 19. Haywood believes the *gift* of the Spirit with tongues is distinct from *gifts* of the Spirit, the former is 'the life of Christ himself' while the latter are gifts 'given for edifying the Church', p. 18; cf. p. 20

[64] Urshan, 'The Doctrine of the New Birth', p. 24; Urshan, 'The Almighty God in the Lord Jesus Christ', p. 67; Haywood, 'The Birth of the Spirit', p. 18; H.E. Reed, 'The Birth of Water and Spirit', *TBT* 3.11 (Aug 15, 1918), pp. 1-2 (1).

[65] Westfield, 'What is Truth', p 2.

came upon them and they spoke with tongues and prophesied. (Acts 19:5-6) DO YOU KNOW that the BAPTISM of the Holy Ghost (Acts 2:4), the GIFT of the Holy Ghost (Acts 10:45), and RECEIVING the Holy Ghost (Acts 19:2), *are one and the same thing*, and accompanied with speaking in TONGUES?[66]

Winfield concluded that,

> the Scriptures thus record that the disciples *came into the church* (the body or into Christ) SPEAKING IN TONGUES; likewise the Ephesians; also the Gentiles; and the Samaritans too *came into the church* 'baptized by one Spirit into the BODY.' This is God's scriptural way of adding to his church.[67]

Ewart pleaded from the lack of Scripture: 'will someone please find us a single Scripture where the reception of the Holy Ghost is called the baptism of the Holy Ghost this side of Pentecost?'[68] In addition to Acts, Haywood connected the stammering lips of Isa. 28.11-12 to salvation using this logic: the 'rest' of Isa. 11.12 was the salvation Jesus promised in Mt. 11.28, which was then given on the Day of Pentecost. Therefore, 'it can be plainly seen that the "rest" and the baptism of the Holy Ghost are one and the same thing'.[69]

The Oneness paradigm required a particular hermeneutic of Scripture and theology. For example, though Jesus' teaching on salvation was carefully expounded upon, his promises of an equipping power for ministry (Lk. 24.49, Acts 1.8) were not addressed. Theologically, what about those who were 'very near the blessing' of tongues?[70] Was an incomplete state of salvation possible? Westfield believed so and construed two levels of salvation: 'DO YOU KNOW that the disciples had their names written in heaven before Pentecost? (Lk. 10:20.) But it does not signify that they were BORN AGAIN.'[71] However, most just accepted this in-between

---

[66] Westfield, 'What is Truth', p 2 (Upper case original and italics added).
[67] Westfield, 'What is Truth', p 2 (Upper case original and italics added).
[68] Ewart, 'To Our Friends', p. 4; cf. John Schaepe, *MDS* 1.21 (Aug 1917), p. 3.
[69] Haywood, 'The Birth of the Spirit ', pp. 2-3.
[70] Douglas, 'Mt. Tabor, Tenn.', p. 6.
[71] Westfield, 'What is Truth', p 2 (upper case original).

state as a fact. For example, *'ten* were granted repentance and *five* were filled with the Holy Ghost as in Acts 2:4', or *'two* have been converted and *one* filled with the Holy Ghost'.[72] Seekers were encouraged to get up to 'the standard, (and) down with our theories'.[73]

Second, Oneness proponents appealed to their personal experience and likened water baptism in Jesus' name to their prior glossolalic SB.[74] For example, Bartleman wrote that

> the experience *was an exact parallel* of my speaking in 'tongues' nine years ago ... (When) I experienced this baptism in the name of Jesus in my spirit I seemed to get a connection of what water baptism meant that I had never had before ... I was melted with liquid love of God ... (later) the old anointing came upon me and the heavenly song flowed from my lips.[75]

Third, just as Pentecostals utilized occurrences of glossolalia in church history to prove its ongoing nature in the face of cessationism,[76] church history recorded changes in the baptismal formula

> from the name of Jesus to Father, Son and Holy Spirit. It saw the light of its earliest form between the years of 150 and 160 A.D., and as it offered a means of defense extremely easy and

---

[72] Lawrence McFarland, 'Monteagle, Tenn', *TBT* 4.2 (Jan 15, 1919), p. 4; H.E. Jackson, 'Aquilla, Texas', *TBT* 4.11 (Jun 1, 1919), p. 7 (emphasis added). Cf. William E. Booth-Clibborn, 'Great Victory At Lodi Cal.', *MDS* 1.21 (Aug 1917), p. 1; 'Victory With Much Opposition At San Antonio, Tex.', *MDS* 1.21 (Aug 1917), p. 1.

[73] Reed, 'The Birth of Water and Spirit', p. 1.

[74] Reed argues that 'like other Pentecostals ... the truth of a doctrine lay primarily in the spiritual effect it registered rather than in intellectual argumentation ... the deciding vote on a doctrine must be the manifestation of apostolic blessing and power', Reed, '*In Jesus' Name*', p. 143.

[75] F. Bartleman, 'Why I Was Re-Baptized In The Name of Jesus Christ', *MDS* 1.9 (Dec 1915), p. 1 (emphasis added). Cf. Booth-Clibborn, 'A Preacher's Testimony', p. 4.

[76] Ewart also defended against cessationism with an appeal to experience: 'the haired critics are too late in their endeavor to cut the last part of Mark's gospel out of the Bible; for God has experimentally (sic.) written on his people's hearts ... All your efforts to make a man believe that the "gift of tongues" was only for a bygone age will be futile, if that man has the gift of tongues ... For they have the author of the Scriptures dwelling within them', F.J. Ewart, 'The Last Great Crisis', *MDS* 1.13 (Jun 1916), p. 2.

sure, it passed rapidly from the Roman Church to the other Churches.[77]

Ewart's vision was to restore the apostolic norm to when 'they baptized their converts in that one name invariably'.[78] For Haywood, the historical record revealed that 'the doctrine of Sabellius was more scripturally based than that of the Athanasian Creed'.[79] History gave Bartleman a pragmatic missiological defence: 'the christians of the second, and even of the third century, were far from having a clearly understood and recognized doctrine of the subject of the Trinity ... (even) the Jews and the Moslems [sic] think the Christians worship three Gods'.[80]

D. The Purpose and Nature of Glossolalia

First, the clearest purpose of initial glossolalia in these early Oneness writings, was to bear witness of one's salvation:

> one must have the Holy Spirit to have New Testament *salvation* ... It is a blessed thing to know without a doubt that you are *in this one body*, the Spirit itself also bearing witness with our spirit that we are the *children of God* – Rom. 8:16. 'He shall TESTIFY and ye shall bear WITNESS. – John 15:26-27. This was the way it was on the day of Pentecost ... they all began to speak in tongues.[81]

Several hymns highlighted this assurance for the believer: Jesus 'gives me His Spirit a witness within, Whisp'ring of pardon, and saving from sin'.[82] The only mention of an equipping from SB was by Thoro Harris who noted in a hymn that it 'equips the weak with

---

[77] F.J. Ewart, 'The Mark of the Beast', *MDS* 1.21 (Aug 1917), p. 3 (Org. cite: Augusta Sabatier, *Religion of Authority* [unknown], p. 37).

[78] Ewart, 'The Mark of the Beast', p. 3.

[79] G.T. Haywood, 'The Victim of the Flaming Sword', in Donald W. Dayton, *Seven 'Jesus Only' Tracts* (New York: Garland Publishing, reprint; Indianapolis, IN: Christ Temple Book Store, n.d.), p. 65.

[80] F. Bartleman, 'The One True God', *TBT* 4.2 (Jan 15, 1919), pp. 1, 4

[81] Reed, 'The Birth of Water and Spirit', pp. 1-2 (emphasis added). Cf. J.B. Price, 'Hollywood, MO.', *TBT* 3.11 (Aug 15, 1918), p. 3.

[82] Wm. J. Kirkpatrick, 'Saved to the Uttermost', Mattie Crawford (ed.), *The Pentecostal Flame* (Los Angeles, CA: 1926) #205; Cf. Thoro Harris, 'The Pentecostal Presence', Mattie Crawford (ed.), *The Pentecostal Flame* (Los Angeles, CA: 1926) #22; G.T. Haywood, 'These Signs Shall Follow Them', Mattie Crawford (ed.), *The Pentecostal Flame* (Los Angeles, CA: 1926) #88.

pow'r, Giving boldness to deliver Heaven's message for the hour'.[83] A few testified of glossolalic praise, for example, 'let praise your tungs [sic] employ'.[84] After tongues as a sign of salvation and this single reference to equipping power, personal testimonies added little to a theology of glossolalia. Most simply stated they 'received the Holy Spirit',[85] or reported that 'fourteen have been baptized in Jesus Name, and ten received the Holy Ghost. They all spake in other tongues.'[86]

Second, the nature of glossolalia was identical to what was written in other Pentecostal periodicals. It was the Holy Spirit who spoke through the individual: 'I am praising God for baptising [sic] me with the Holy Ghost, speaking through me in other tongues'.[87] Tongues were either an 'unknown tongue'[88] or xenolalia.[89] For example, John Schaepe wrote, 'God baptized me with the Holy Spirit, and the Spirit spoke through me in Chinese, Korean and Japanese languages of which the Japanese was understood'.[90] Because glossolalia was not ecstatic or gibberish, 'a clear definite language' was desired.[91] The HA was mentioned both by Bartleman[92] and in a hymn by Harris: 'our lips repeat the word (Jesus), Glad to tell the strains that ne'er shall cease ... O my soul *would join the seraph choir, Chanting* His unchanging love'.[93]

---

[83] Harris, 'The Pentecostal Presence' #22.

[84] Thoro Harris, 'The Awakening', Mattie Crawford (ed.), *The Pentecostal Flame* (Los Angeles, CA: 1926) #28; cf. James Rowe, 'Mine At Last', Mattie Crawford (ed.), *The Pentecostal Flame* (Los Angeles, CA: 1926) #119; D.R. Aikenhead, 'Great Outpouring At Trossachs', *MDS* 1.21 (Aug 1917), p. 1

[85] Arthur S. Davis, *TBT* 3.11 (Aug 15, 1918), p. 3; Mike Sullivan, *TBT* 4.2 (Jan 15, 1919), p. 4.

[86] S.R. Burrow, 'Troy City, Tenn', *TBT* 3.11 (Aug 15, 1918), p. 3.

[87] Crissie Phillips, 'A Happy Family', *TBT* 3.11 (Aug 15, 1918), p. 3.

[88] Haywood, 'The Birth of the Spirit', p. 20; Booth-Clibborn, 'Suddenly', p. 4; Booth-Clibborn, 'Great Victory At Lodi Cal.', p. 1.

[89] Booth-Clibborn, 'A Preacher's Testimony', p. 4; McFarland, 'Monteagle, Tenn', p. 4. Missionaries received language training and there was no evidence of 'missionary tongues', Sarah A. Kugler, 'News From the Mission Field', *TBT* 4.2 (Jan 15, 1919), pp. 1, 3 (3).

[90] John Schaepe, 'A Remarkable Testimony', *MDS* 1.21 (Aug 1917), p. 3.

[91] 'From Winnipeg', *MDS* 1.13 (June 1916), p. 2.

[92] Bartleman, 'Why I Was Re-Baptized', p. 1.

[93] Thoro Harris, 'His Name', Mattie Crawford (ed.), *The Pentecostal Flame* (Los Angeles, CA: 1926) #133 (emphasis added). The verse of a song by James Rowe included, 'sweet is the song that my spirit sings', as another possible reference to the HA, Rowe, 'Mine At Last' #119.

E. Testimonies

These early Oneness periodicals included far fewer testimonies than other Pentecostal periodicals because the bulk of the space was used apologetically for baptism in The Name or the Oneness of God.[94] Also, testimonies from clergy greatly outnumbered those from the people, so the *voca populi* was somewhat muted.[95] As expected, many testimonies conformed to the Oneness polemic. For example, 'nine have been baptized in Jesus' name, and three have received the Holy Ghost as in Acts 2:4',[96] and 'about forty-five have been *added to the body of the Lord* through receiving the baptism in the Spirit according to Acts 2:4'.[97] However, two elements emerged in Oneness testimonies that were unique from prior Pentecostal testimonies. First, though tongues indicated when an individual was baptized with the Holy Spirit, slightly different terminology emerged. There were only two references to tongues as an 'evidence'.[98] Overall, 'sign' was the preferred term: 'we cannot believe that a man has received the Holy Ghost until we see *the signs* as were manifested in Apostolic days, therefore tongues were *for a sign*'.[99]

---

[94] Alexander, *Pentecostal Healing*, p. 185.

[95] Of the testimonies that include glossolalia or SB in *MDS*, eleven are by ministers or those reporting on a revival and two are by lay people. There is only one first person testimony, Bartleman, 'Why I Was Re-Baptiszed', p. 1. Of the testimonies that include glossolalia or SB in *TBT*, thirty-three are by ministers or those reporting on a revival and two are by lay people. There is only one first person testimony, Phillips, 'A Happy Family', p. 3.

[96] G.B. Rowe and Wife, 'South Bend, Ind.', *TBT* 4.11 (Jun 1, 1919), p. 6. 'As in Acts 2.4' was the most common way of delineating SB. Westfield, 'What is Truth', p 2; Joe Barnett, 'Carrollton, IL', *TBT* 4.2 (Jan 15, 1919), p. 4; J.S. Jones, 'Reeds Springs, MO', *TBT* 4.11 (Jun 1, 1919), p. 6; G.J. Finley, 'Royalton, ILL', *TBT* 4.11 (Jun 1, 1919), p. 7; Aikenhead, 'Great Outpouring At Trossachs', p. 1; Schaepe, p. 3.

[97] Finley, 'Royalton, ILL', p. 7 (emphasis added). 'Pastor Frank Small Baptized', *MDS* 1.9 (December 1915), p 2; 'From Winnipeg', p. 2; E.J. Douglas, 'Beacon, Tenn.', *TBT* 4.11 (Jun 1, 1919), p. 6.

[98] Aikenhead, 'Great Outpouring At Trossachs', p. 1; J.R. Beeler, 'Joplin, MO', *TBT* 4.11 (June 1, 1919), p. 6. Twice 'witness of the Holy Ghost' was used, Price, 'Hollywood, MO.', p. 3. Cf. Reed, 'The Birth of Water and Spirit', pp. 1-2.

[99] Haywood, 'The Birth of the Spirit', p. 21; cf. Anthony Pelliccotti, 'Refreshing Showers Falling At Kelso', *MDS* 1.21 (Aug 1917), p. 1; Urshan, 'The Doctrine of the New Birth', pp. 46-47; R.E. Winsett, 'Evening Light', Mattie Crawford (ed.), *The Pentecostal Flame* (Los Angeles, CA: 1926) #52; Haywood, 'These Signs Shall Follow Them' #88.

Second, whereas other Pentecostal periodicals highlighted glossolalia as the effect or culmination of the SB experience, Oneness testimonies included tongues but emphasized water baptism. Note T.B. Walker's report: 'some are being baptized with the Holy Ghost (but) ... fourteen have been baptized in water in Jesus' name and more to be baptized [sic]'.[100] In fact, one can see an idealized connection between tongues and waters of baptism: Gertrude Randol wrote that 'eight in one week have received the baptism of the Holy Ghost, and eight have been baptized in Jesus Name [sic]. *Only one received the Holy Spirit in the water*, but as they press on they do get it.'[101] Several testimonies affirmed this connection between water baptism and SB.[102] For example, they 'received the Holy Ghost. I baptized six in Jesus Name. One came out of the water filled with the Spirit and speaking in tongues.'[103] Tongues were a sign, but water baptism was the objective, 'divinely appointed means of identifying the sinner with his Savior'.[104]

---

[100] T.B. Walker, 'Truman, Ark.', *TBT* 4.2 (Jan 15, 1919), p. 2; cf. Floyd I. Douglass, 'Louisville, KY', *TBT* 3.11 (Aug 15, 1918), pp. 3-4 (3); Price, 'Hollywood, MO.', p. 3; Cora Huffington, *TBT* 3.11 (Aug 15, 1918), p. 3.

[101] Gertrude Randol, 'St. Louis, MO', *TBT* 3.11 (Aug 15, 1918), p. 3 (emphasis added). Bartleman, 'Why I Was Re-Baptized', p. 1.

[102] 'Pastor Frank Small Baptized', p 2; *MDS* 1.13 (June 1916), p. 2; Barnett, 'Carrollton, IL', p. 4; Beeler, 'Joplin, MO', p. 6.

[103] Davis, *TBT* 3.11, p. 3

[104] F.J. Ewart, 'Baptism – Is It For The Remission of Sins', *MDS* 1.21 (Aug 1917), p. 2.

Categories that Emerged from the Periodicals

	Evidences		Language?		Sanctification	Heavenly Anthem	Eschatology	Nature	Unique Nuances
	Sign Terminology	Divine Love	Missionary Tongues	Xenolalia					
AF	Bible evidence	X	X		X	X		Passive	
BGM	Bible evidence	X	X		X		X	Passive & Ecstatic	
TWT	Bible evidence					X			
COGE	As the Spirit gives utterance		X	X	X	X		Passive	Signs & Wonders
THA / PHA	Initial evidence		X	X		X	X	Passive	
TOF	The evidence	X	X	X	X	X	X	Ecstatic & Mystery	Affect: Joy
TP	Full consummation		X					Inspired Speech	
PT	The evidence								Finished Work
WW	The evidence			X		X			
PE	The sign & the evidence	X		X		X	X	Human & Divine	Sacramental & Historical
TGR*	Sign of a completed salvation								
MDS / TBT	Standard of salvation							Divine	Water Baptism

* Emerging Oneness was the only topic examined.

Categories that Emerged from the Periodicals

	Purpose						Response to Critics			
	Power	Prayer	Praise	Revelation	Gift	Edify	Signs & Wonders	Cessation	Counterfeits	New Issue
AF	X	X	X	X	X					
BGM	X	X	X	X	X					
TWT										
COGE	X	X	X	X	X	X				
THA/PHA	X	X	X	X	X		X			
TOF	X	X	X	X						
TP	X	X	X							
PT										
WW								X	X	
PE	X	X	X	X	X			X	X	X
TGR*									X	X
MDS/TBT										

* Emerging Oneness was the only topic examined.

6

REVISIONING[1] A PENTECOSTAL THEOLOGY OF GLOSSOLALIA

I. Metaphor as a Means of Revisioning

This study of glossolalia carefully examined the reception history of the earliest Pentecostals. Pentecostal theology 'is not first and foremost a doctrinal or intellectual tradition; it is an affective constellation of practices and embodied "rituals"';[2] therefore, it is best expressed in its spirituality[3] whereby – 'if reduced to concepts and propositions – it loses its very essence'.[4] To give expression to their

---

[1] Land, *Pentecostal Spirituality*, pp. 190-92. Chan observes 'a community that seeks consciously to preserve its own values and way of life is more likely to be open to change as it faces new challenges than one that has no *explicit* tradition ... traditioning by nature is a communal affair', Chan, *Pentecostal Theology*, p. 17 (emphasis original).

[2] James K.A. Smith, *Thinking in Tongues: Pentecostal Contributions to Christian Philosophy* (Grand Rapids, MI: Eerdmans, 2010), p. xv, cf. p. 110. Luke T. Johnson observes that the altar area of most churches represents 'institutional power' because religion is 'concerned with correctness: of doctrine, morality, authority, procedure'; whereas the bulletin/prayer boards in the foyer of most churches reveals the lived-faith that is 'much more about the experience of transforming power', Luke Timothy Johnson, *Religious Experience in Earliest Christianity: A Missing Dimension in New Testament Studies* (Minneapolis, MN: Fortress Press, 1998), pp. 1-2.

[3] Christianity 'did not begin as a book religion but as a lived religion', Walter J. Hollenweger, 'The Ecumenical Significance of Oral Christianity', *Ecumenical Review* 41.2 (1989), pp. 259-65 (262). Gunkel, *The Influence of the Holy Spirit*, pp. 10, 13-14; Hollenweger, 'After Twenty Years', pp. 10-11; Land, *Pentecostal Spirituality*, p. 33; Cox, *Fire From Heaven*, p. 15; Hollenweger, *Pentecostalism*, pp. 2, 35.

[4] Hollenweger, 'Pentecostals and the Charismatic Movement', p. 553.

experience, the early Pentecostals co-opted the theological categories and explanations of the modern worldview. Nevertheless, it is clear that they struggled to put the totality of their experience into words.[5] Their testimonies and articles were ill-fit within many theological categories because 'glossolalia is *irrational by design* ... **It's not logical, was not meant to be and only suffers damage to its essence in trying to force it through Aristotelian linear Euclidian constructs**'.[6] Thus, the very task of this constructive chapter is at risk because glossolalia is a symbol that points to the very limitation of theological and linguistic categories. It 'resists even the most exalted human language'.[7]

Therefore, rather than working within limiting and Modernistic theological categories, this chapter will use metaphor as a constructive tool for revisioning a Pentecostal theology of glossolalia. It is believed that a symbol can express what theological proposition cannot. As homage to the wonderful theological work done by these Pentecostal pioneers, this chapter will carefully analyse their testimonies, which liberally used biblically inspired images to describe their experiences, and it will engage contemporary scholarship using the metaphor's intended point of correspondence

---

[5] For example, Blumhofer writes,

> the 'Pentecostal experience' referred ... to an intense religious experience known as the baptism in the Holy Spirit that was marked by tongues speech ... (which) became known as the 'uniform initial evidence' ... *This dogmatic description, however, fails to capture* (1) the process many early Pentecostals typically believed Spirit baptism was a part of, (2) the results they insisted authenticated such baptism, or (3) the dispensational significance they assigned it, which developed a climate of anticipation and intensity, Edith L. Blumhofer, *'Pentecost in My Soul': Explorations in the Meaning of the Pentecostal Experience of the Early Assemblies of God* (Springfield, MO: Gospel Publishing House, 1989), p. 17 (emphasis added).

Cf. Rybarczyk, 'Reframing Tongues', p. 90. C.S. Lewis observed that when a higher medium is reproduced in a lower medium, the lower medium cannot fully grasp or contain the higher medium. For example, a pencil sketch of a landscape is quite limited compared to seeing a real landscape, Lewis, 'Transposition', pp. 109-10.

[6] Tarr, *The Foolishness of God*, pp. 6, 165 (emphasis original).

[7] Baker, 'Pentecostal Experience', p. 263; cf. Lewis, 'Transposition', p. 99; Mills, *Understanding*, p. 38; Mills, *Theological/Exegetical*, pp. 69-70; Hollenweger, 'Pentecostals and the Charismatic Movement', p. 553; Cox, *Fire From Heaven*, pp. 163, 96; Rybarczyk, 'Reframing Tongues', p. 84; Smith, *Thinking in Tongues*, p. 123; Brandon Kertson, 'Spirit Baptism in the Pentecostal Evangel', *Pneuma* 37.5 (2015), pp. 244-61 (250), and Castelo, *Christian Mystical Tradition*, pp. 128, 176.

with glossolalia. In so doing, it is hoped that this modest methodology will provide an overture for today's Pentecostals to give comprehension to what cannot be fully put into words. The motivation for revisioning is the challenge that Pentecostalism is in jeopardy of losing its most distinctive element – glossolalia:[8]

> Pentecostalism is fast developing into an evangelical middle-class religion. Many of the elements that were vital for its rise and expansion into the Third World are disappearing. They are being replaced by efficient fund-raising structures, a streamlined ecclesiastical bureaucracy, and a Pentecostal conceptual theology ... (that) follows the evangelical traditions, to which is added the belief in the baptism of the Spirit.[9]

Hollenweger's point is well made here: Pentecostalism must 're-oralize' its theology away from modernistic or 'literary theology'.[10] Therefore, this attempt to construct a thoroughly revisioned Pentecostal view of glossolalia will not be bound to traditional theological categories.[11]

---

[8] Margaret M. Poloma, *The Assemblies of God at the Crossroads: Charisma and Institutional Dilemmas* (Knoxville, TN: The University of TN Press, 1989), pp. 83, 191; Blaine Charette, 'Presidential Address – Reflective Speech: Glossolalia and the Image of God', *Pneuma* 28.2 (Fall, 2006), pp. 189-201 (189-90); Paul Alexander, *Signs & Wonders: Why Pentecostalism is the World's Fastest Growing Faith* (San Francisco, CA: Jossey-Bass, 2009), p. 39; Margaret M. Poloma, 'Glossolalia, Liminality and Empowered Kingdom Building: A Sociological Perspective', in Mark J. Cartledge (ed.), *Speaking in Tongues: Multi-Disciplinary Perspectives* (Studies in Pentecostal and Charismatic Issues; Bletchley, Milton Keynes, England: Paternoster Press, 2006), pp. 147-73 (158); Margaret M. Poloma, in 'North American Pentecostalism', in Adam Stewart (ed.) *Handbook of Pentecostal Christianity* (DeKalb, IL: Northern Illinois University Press, 2012), p. 157. Alexander believes decline is due to 'accommodation to dominant cultural norms regarding race, ethnicity, gender, class, and age: a move toward more individualism; and a hermeneutic incongruent with Pentecostal spirituality', Kimberly Ervin Alexander, 'Heavenly Choirs in Earthly Spaces: The Significance of Corporate Singing in Early Pentecostal Experience', *JPT* 25 (2016), pp. 254-68 (268).

[9] Hollenweger, *Pentecostalism*, p. 19.

[10] Hollenweger, *Pentecostalism*, p. 39.

[11] The most notable theological discussion excluded is whether SB is a CI or a subsequent experience. If one extrapolates the point of correspondence between the biblical metaphor and its intended tenant, it reveals two completely separate tenants. Being born again (CI) corresponds to an either/or tenant: one is either born again (or adopted) or one is not. Whereas the SB metaphors correspondence to levels of intensity or fullness tenants. The Pentecostal pioneers did not confuse the natural tenants: 'water baptism is generally admitted to be the door into the church militant ... (but) Holy Ghost baptism is an entering

Some guidelines for the use of symbols and metaphors are in order before theological construction: 1) metaphor is a legitimate means of theological construction: 'religious metaphors do permit theological inferences ... the better the metaphor is, the more pregnant it will be with possible implications'.[12] Images 'help us approach the incomprehensible mystery ... and mediate the sacred'.[13] 2) Both sides of the symbol need to be understood to be meaningful – 'the subject which the metaphor is about and the metaphorical description'.[14] Meaning is therefore derived from an analogous correspondence or 'an interconnection'[15] in one of four ways: 'perceptual, synaesthetic, affective and pragmatic'.[16] 3) 'A

---

into the *very closest relations and fellowship* with God', Webb, 'Baptized Into One Body', p. 2 (emphasis added). Cf. Southern, 'The Baptism of the Holy Ghost, p. 3.

[12] George D. Chryssides, 'Meaning, Metaphor and Meta-Theology', *Scottish Journal of Theology* 38 (1985), pp. 145-53 (149). Metaphor enables 'the believer to filter out appropriate sets of connotations ... (by which they are) at least partially able to understand the meaning of concepts which defy definition at a literal level', p. 153. There are some things that can only be expressed in a non-literal fashion, because some things 'are momentarily beyond our grasp', p. 146. George B. Caird believes that metaphor comprises 'almost all the language of theology', George Bradford Caird, *The Language and Imagery of the Bible* (Philadelphia, PA: Westminster Press, 1980), p. 144. Amos Yong believes that some 'truth(s) can be accessed and communicated only via symbols which contrast the finite and the infinite', Amos Yong, '"Tongues of Fire" in the Pentecostal Imagination: The Truth of Glossolalia in Light of R.C. Neville's Theory of Religious Symbolism', *JPT* 12 (1998), pp. 39-65 (48).

[13] Clark Pinnock, *Flame of Love: A Theology of the Holy Spirit* (Downers Grove, IL: Intervarsity Press, 1996), p. 120.

[14] Chryssides, 'Meaning, Metaphor and Meta-Theology', p. 151; cf. Lewis, 'Transposition', p. 100. Gordon T. Smith adds, 'the whole point of a symbol is that it is a symbol ... (take Holy Communion for example) if it looks too much like every other meal, it loses its capacity as a symbol to link heaven and earth', Gordon T. Smith, *Evangelical, Sacramental & Pentecostals: Why the Church Should be All of These* (Downers Grove, IL: IVP Academic, 2017), p. 76. These two sides are called the vehicle and tenant: 'vehicle being the thing to which the word normally and naturally applies, the thing from which it is transferred, and tenant (is) the thing to which it is transferred', Caird, *The Language and Imagery of the Bible*, p. 152.

[15] Boulos, 'In Defense of the Truth', pp. 10-11 (11); cf. Stanton, 'The Effect of the Divine Indwelling', pp. 160-61 (160); Irwin, 'My Pentecostal Baptism – A Christmas Gift', p. 114.

[16] Caird, *The Language and Imagery of the Bible*, p. 145; cf. pp. 145-48. Perceptual comparisons appeal to the five senses, pp. 145-46. Synaesthetic is an artifi-

metaphor is seldom wholly descriptive: a metaphor is capable of adding *expressive* dimensions to purely descriptive ones.'[17] 'We have to distinguish those respects in which analogy holds from those in which it does not',[18] because it may have either a low or high degree of correspondence with the element symbolized.[19] 4) Metaphor expands our imagination. It allows the interpreter to break from old boundaries and create new possibilities. Such imagination is 'the peculiarly distinguishing mark of the *imago Dei* ... it is worldmaking (or world-view-making)'.[20] Finally, 5) a metaphor 'is not identical with the reality to which it points'.[21]

The following theological construction will be organized thus: encounter metaphors, public metaphors, and personal metaphors, followed by a look at a metaphor for the nature of tongues and a poignant Oneness metaphor.

II. Encounter Metaphors

A. Introduction
The Pentecostal doctrine of IE has used up more printer's ink than any other aspect of glossolalia. Before revisioning, several introductory points need to be made. First, though the term 'initial evidence' was once a great apologetic and polemic, it has become an example of musty Modernistic thinking, akin to Darwin's 'fossil proof'.[22]

---

cial and ridiculous comparison, like colour in music, p. 147. Affective comparisons are those in which feelings and emotions are valued, p. 147. Pragmatic comparisons are those that compare an 'activity or result', pp. 147-48.

[17] Chryssides, 'Meaning, Metaphor and Meta-Theology', p. 147 (emphasis original). The author notes the role of experience as a means to 'check' the metaphor with reality, pp. 150-51.

[18] Baker, 'Pentecostal Experience', p. 265.

[19] For example a low degree of correspondence would be between the oil running down Aaron's beard. It is 'restricted to the fragrance', Caird, *The Language and Imagery of the Bible*, p. 153. A high degree of correspondence would be between the church and the human body in which 'the variety of function in the members contribute to the organic unity of the whole', p. 153.

[20] Yong, 'Tongues of Fire', p. 45; cf. p. 46.

[21] J. Rodman Williams, *Renewal Theology, Vol. Two: Systematic Theology from a Charismatic Perspective* (Grand Rapids, MI: Zondervan 1996), p. 234; cf. S.H.F., 'From The Pentecostal Viewpoint', p. 8.

[22] Spittler, 'Suggested Areas for Further Research in Pentecostal Studies', p. 48; Walters, 'Why Tongues?', pp. 85-86. In a similar fashion, Evangelicals fell into the modernistic terminology trap with the terms 'inerrant and infallible' to

Nearly all theological explanations of IE have tried to squeeze it through these scientific and Modernistic categories.[23] Second, the theological and exegetical arguments within these categories have been fought to a standstill, and one's position largely depends on personal experience and presuppositions.[24] Third, despite these difficulties, the biblical sign-value of one's first glossolalic experience simply cannot be ignored[25] or downplayed in favour of a more ecumenically acceptable 'prayer language'.[26] Finally, Pentecostalism's IE

---

describe the Bible as a result of Darwin's influence, McDonald, *Theories of Revelation*, pp. 196-217; cf. Cox, *Fire From Heaven*, p. 303.

[23] For example, Lederle notes that glossolalia cannot be proved as the 'first effect' of SB, Lederle, 'An Ecumenical Appraisal', p. 132. Consider Montgomery's quote of Evan Roberts: 'prayer force is a scientific force as truly as electricity, steam or any other force known to science, and has its laws embodied in God's word', Sisson, 'A Call To Prayer', p. 60.

[24] For example, Castelo deconstructs IE with: 1) 'the waning of revivalist culture on the American scene impacts this way of reflecting on religious experience', Castelo, *Christian Mystical Tradition*, p. 146. 2) Exegetical issues: a) challenges to the pattern from the book of Acts, b) Paul's theology of glossolalia, and c) 'it is always a challenge to draw a normative pattern from historical occurrences', p. 147. 3) It commodifies Christian spirituality into the haves and the have nots.

[25] Here are two examples that ignore any sign-value: 1) '*it is essentially a prayer gift*', Suenens, 'Malines Document', p. 30; cf. pp. 24-25, 30-31 (emphasis added). 2) Cox devotes only two sentences to IE. His point is that Pentecostals have changed from tongues as the IE to it is 'one gift among many', Cox, *Fire From Heaven*, p. 88. For the exegetical arguments surrounding Paul's statement that tongues are a sign (1 Cor. 14.20-22), see: J.P.M. Sweet, 'A Sign for Unbelievers: Paul's Attitude to Glossolalia', in Watson E. Mills (ed.), *Speaking in Tongues: A Guide to Research on Glossolalia* (Grand Rapids, MI: Eerdmans, 1986 [org. pub. 1967]), pp. 141-64; Fee, *The First Epistle to the Corinthians*, pp. 677-83; David Lim, *Spiritual Gifts: A Fresh Look* (Springfield, MO: Gospel Publishing House, 1999), pp. 155-62; Anthony C. Thiselton, *New International Greek Commentary: The First Epistle to the Corinthians* (Grand Rapids, MI: Eerdmans, 2000), pp. 1120-26; Roy E. Ciampa and Brian S. Rosner, '1 Corinthians', in G.K. Beale and D.A. Carson (eds.), *Commentary on the New Testament Use of the Old Testament* (Grand Rapids, MI: Baker Academic, 2007), pp. 740-42; Dunn, *Jesus and the Spirit*, p. 231; Menzies, *Speaking in Tongues*, pp. 107-23. Some Charismatic scholars who hold a classical Pentecostal view of IE are: Howard M. Ervin, *Conversion-Initiation and the Baptism in the Holy Spirit: An engaging critique of James D.G. Dunn's 'Baptism in the Holy Spirit'* (Peabody, MA: Hendrickson, 1984); Howard M. Ervin, *Spirit Baptism: A Biblical Investigation* (Peabody, MA: Hendrickson, 1987); and Williams, *Renewal Theology, Vol. Two*, pp. 209-12.

[26] Baker, 'Pentecostal Experience', pp. 152-82, 200, 227, 236. Baker's position is 'that the infilling ... need not be attested to by glossolalia', and one's 'personal Pentecost is only an expectation and a commencement of the conclusive theophany of God that will come in the Parousia for all believers', pp. 234, 292. Cf. Hayford, *Beauty*, pp. 93, 98.

is an outflow of what John the Baptist, Jesus, and the disciples all described with the metaphor of 'Spirit Baptism'.[27] The point of correspondence between SB and the metaphor is that 'the term baptism implies to be *immersed in, plunged under and even drenched or soaked*, suggesting that the whole being of a person is imbued with or enveloped in the Holy Spirit'.[28] Therefore, all descriptions of the glossolalic outflow of SB are, in a sense, secondary descriptions of this overarching image of being overwhelmed with the Spirit. The pioneers were careful to make the distinction between secondary and primary word pictures. For example, evidential glossolalia was compared to a stamp on an envelope and not the meaningful letter inside, or to an inedible restaurant sign that points to a nourishing meal inside.[29] Consequently, the following attempt at theological engagement with secondary metaphors should, in some way, define and support the primary metaphor of being overwhelmed in order for it to have integrity.

B. A Crucifixion of Self – Hunger, Tarrying, and Yieldedness

For the early Pentecostals, the crucifixion of self was an important metaphor of the evidence, comparable to Jesus' *kenosis*:[30] 'as we yield through death and deep interior crucifixion of our fine parts to the indwelling of the Holy Ghost', the Spirit 'communicate(s) to us the fullness of the life of the glorified Christ'.[31] Emptying and yielding oneself is still the common means to SB. Cashwell's quote is well-known: 'as soon as I reached Azusa Mission, a new

---

[27] Ivan Satyavrata points out that six of the seven references contrast John the Baptist's baptism with Jesus'(Mt. 3.11; Mk 1.8; Lk. 3.16; Jn 1.33; Acts 1.4-5; 11.16), Ivan Satyavrata, *The Holy Spirit: Lord and Live-Giver* (Downers Grove, IL: IVP Academic, 2009), p. 127. Significantly, Acts 1.4-5 records Jesus' command to wait in Jerusalem and prophesies that the disciples will be baptized in Jerusalem in a few days. In Acts 11.16, Peter identifies the outpouring of the Holy Spirit on Cornelius' household as the same one he had received, because of glossolalia (10.46). Paul's single use in 1 Cor. 12.13 is an outlier, rotating the metaphor's meaning to unity rather than encounter, Roger Stronstad, *The Charismatic Theology of St. Luke* (Peabody, MA: Hendrickson, 1984), p. 10; Fee, *First Corinthians*, p. 605.

[28] Satyavrata, *The Holy Spirit: Lord and Live-Giver*, p. 127 (emphasis added).

[29] S.H.F., 'From The Pentecostal Viewpoint', p. 8; McPherson, 'What is the Evidence of the Baptism of the Holy Ghost', p. 7; cf. Boulos, 'In Defense of the Truth', p. 11.

[30] Romans 6.6; Gal. 2.19-20; 5.23; Phil. 2.7.

[31] Ward, 'Soul Food For Hungry Saints', p. 8.

crucifiction [sic] began in my life and I had to die to many things'.[32] The periodicals are replete with testimonies describing a hunger for more of God, tarrying for the Spirit, and ultimately, yielding one's tongue to the Spirit. For example, 'when we got to the place that we gave up everything and everybody, unloaded everything ... then we received the blessed baptism of the Holy Ghost and spoke in tongues as the Spirit gave utterance'.[33]

Hungering, tarrying, and yielding were modest sacramental actions,[34] like the action of receiving Holy Communion:[35] these seeker-initiated activities placed the individual in a position to apprehend the immanent presence of the Holy Spirit; nevertheless, this revelation was dependent upon divine initiative.[36] An individual could receive immediately or continue seeking for years. Further, this sacramental action of seeking God was not for incorporation into the body of Christ,[37] but was analogous to the disciples

---

[32] Cashwell, 'Came 3,000 Miles', p. 3.

[33] Hayes, 'Slack up in Pentecostal Saints', p. 3; cf. Ward, 'Soul Food For Hungry Saints', p. 8. This process often merges with sanctification because 'when a seeker is tarrying for the power, the Spirit frequently convicts of many things that would hinder his incoming. This is "the way of holiness"', S.H.F., 'Our Distinctive Testimony', p. 8.

[34] Kilian McDonnell, 'The Function of Tongues in Pentecostalism', *One in Christ* 19.4 (1984), pp. 332-54; Hollenweger, 'After Twenty Years' Research', p. 7; Macchia, 'Tongues as a Sign', pp. 61-76; Macchia, 'Initial Evidence', pp. 122, 125; Macchia, 'Towards a Theology of Initial Evidence', p. 155; Chan, 'Evidential Glossolalia', p. 211; Taves, *Fits, Trances & Visions*, p. 332; Chan, *Pentecostal Theology*, p. 78; Hovenden, *Speaking in Tongues*, pp. 167-68; Augustine, *Pentecost, Hospitality, and Transfiguration*, p. 37; and Randal Ackland, 'Towards a Sacramental View of Glossolalia', unpublished paper presented at the Society for Vineyard Studies (New Haven: Yale Divinity School, 2017).

[35] 'It is as much of a command to receive the Holy Ghost and talk in other tongues as it is to be baptized with water or take the bread and wine to commemorate the Lord's death till he comes again', Tomlinson, 'We Would Not Know', p. 1. Cf. Polman, 'Speaking in Tongues (*TBM*)', pp. 236-37; Montgomery, 'The Promise of the Father (#2)', pp. 4-5.

[36] Macchia, 'Tongues as a Sign', p. 70; Chan, 'Evidential Glossolalia', p. 211.

[36] Macchia, 'Sighs Too Deep for Words', pp. 63, 69-70, 74; Macchia, 'Tongues as a Sign', pp. 61-76; Chan, *Pentecostal Theology*, p. 50.

[37] Contra Bruner in Frederick Dale Bruner, *A Theology of the Holy Spirit: The Pentecostal Experience and the New Testament Witness* (Grand Rapids, MI: Eerdmans, 1970). Cf. Ervin, *Conversion-Initiation*; Randal H. Ackland, 'Spirit Baptism: An Appraisal of Frederick Dale Bruner's Book, A Theology of the Holy Spirit: The Pentecostal Experience and the New Testament Witness, and an Examination of Possible Pentecostal Responses to Bruner's Criticisms' (MA Thesis, Wheaton College, Wheaton, IL, 1988), pp. 165-69.

staying in Jerusalem for the promised power from on high.[38] Though one did not seek tongues, it was significant to the image of crucifixion that the yielding of one's tongue was yielding the most 'unruly member' of the body:[39]

> glossolalia serves as a sign of submission to God. Anyone who yields his speech to the Spirit's linguistic control will find it possible to be available to the Spirit's control ... for the operation of other gifts of the Spirit ... it is an indication that the person has crossed the first hurdle of strangeness.[40]

Tongues 'became a sign of responsiveness and surrender to God'.[41] There is an analogous correspondence between this crucifixion of self and Jesus' *kenosis*: the 'practice of glossolalic prayer may be understood as emptying out of the self before God (*kenosis*) so that one might become full of the Holy Spirit and thereby participate in Christ's nature (*theosis*)'.[42]

C. Bride and Groom or Mother and Child – Intimacy

Two biblical metaphors used by the early Pentecostals highlight aspects of intimacy between the seeker and the Holy Spirit. The first image is that of a bride and groom who have a special idiolect between them, sometimes called 'pillow-talk' or 'sweet-nothings'. Despite the lack of a linear word/symbol connection, an 'impres-

---

[38] Luke 24.49.

[39] James 3.8; cf. Burk, 'Cliff View, Va.', p. 2; Throop, 'A Partial Experience', p. 131.

[40] William G. MacDonald, 'The Place of Glossolalia in Neo-Pentecostalism', in Watson E. Mills (ed.) *Speaking in Tongues: A Guide to Research on Glossolalia* (Grand Rapids, MI: W. B. Eerdmans Pub. Co., 1986), pp. 221-34 (227).

[41] Alexander, *Pentecostal Healing*, pp. 81-82; cf. Gordon Fee, 'Toward a Pauline Theology of Glossolalia', in Wonsuk Ma and Robert P. Menzies (eds.), *Pentecostalism in Context: Essays in Honor of William W. Menzies* (JPTSup 11; Sheffield: Sheffield Academic Press, 1997), pp. 24-37 (25, 36). 'Pentecostal ascetics thus will sometimes speak in tongues quite deliberately as a means of cultivating intimacy with God through an act of *anamesis* ... they simply pray and in the course of praying they will find themselves moving from activity to passivity', Chan, *Pentecostal Theology*, p. 81.

[42] Baker, 'Pentecostal Experience', p. 253. Others use different terminology: Costelo prefers the term 'purgation', Castelo, *Christian Mystical Tradition*, pp. 77-79. Augustine prefers the term *askesis*, Augustine, *Pentecost, Hospitality, and Transfiguration*, p. 20.

sion' is communicated between lovers.⁴³ In the same way,

> the baptism in the Holy Spirit is to prepare the real, true, Spiritual church as a bride for Jesus, the bridegroom ... (Just as) lovers have a language that strangers do not understand ... Jesus understands and he is able to make us understand also ... he tells me I am his and my heart responds in whispers of love, 'he is mine'.⁴⁴

As the bride of Christ,⁴⁵ we, like the Shulamite bride who gave herself to Solomon, share an intimacy with the Spirit.⁴⁶

> When your body gets full of the oil of the Holy Spirit your lips and tongue get filled also, and the new tongues drop off your lips like honey; you will be distinctly conscious that it is the Heavenly Dove who is speaking through you in other tongues ... Do not be satisfied until you have the indwelling spirit HIMSELF.⁴⁷

Chan is correct in noting that relationship is an excellent category for IE;⁴⁸ yet he still chooses to 'ground' evidential tongues 'in the doctrine of conversion-initiation'.⁴⁹ That is like saying all intimacy or romance ends with the wedding ceremony, or merely looks back to the signing of the wedding license as its highpoint.⁵⁰ Rather, the metaphor's strength is that there are

---

⁴³ For a fascinating discussion from the perspective of a missionary linguist, cf. Tarr's work on 'drum-talk', Tarr, *The Foolishness of God*, pp. 157-59; cf. Tarr, *Double Image*, pp. 151-55.

⁴⁴ Collins, 'Three More Points', p. 4; cf. Eckman, 'Speaking in Tongues', p. 4. Welch believes that glossolalia is coded for their own protection: 'God has given the bride a new tongue to utter it, yea to whisper it, so the world shall not hear it, and the enemy cannot understand it', Welch, 'Just A Word From The General Office', pp. 9-10 (9); cf. 'They Shall Speak with New Tongues', *PE* 320 & 321 (Dec 27, 1919), p. 3; Frodsham, 'What is the Use of Speaking in Tongues', p. 59.

⁴⁵ 2 Corinthians 11.2; Rev. 19.7; cf. Polman, 'Speaking in Tongues (*TOF*)', pp. 236-37; Caddell, 'Kimberly, Ala.', p. 2.

⁴⁶ CJM, 'The Promise of the Father (#2)', pp. 1-6 (3). She references SOS 1.3; 4.11. It is so intimate 'that even your lips and tongue are not your own anymore; and your tongue is made "glad"'.

⁴⁷ CJM, 'The Promise of the Father (#2)', pp. 1-6 (4).

⁴⁸ Chan, 'The Language Game of Glossolalia', pp. 84-85.

⁴⁹ Chan, 'Evidential Glossolalia', p. 210; cf. 206.

⁵⁰ Contra Pinnock: 'it may be best to speak of spiritual breakthroughs as actualizations of our initiation', Pinnock, *Flame of Love*, p. 169.

non-formal,[51] completely spontaneous[52] moments of intimacy that are of such pure delight that one desires to 'express oneself and, concomitantly, the less one is able to find adequate expression'.[53] As emotional as the salvation experience may be, SB is not like the forensic prayer of repentance nor the public confession at water baptism; rather, it is the 'certitude' that God has made direct contact.[54] The Bible sign is analogous to a spontaneous kiss between married lovers, a symbol of intimate relationship.[55] Glossolalia is intimate 'love talk';[56] it is an 'insider's language' shared only between two hearts;[57] it is a 'natural cry'[58] whose purpose is to adore the other. In other words, it is the selfless, whispered 'true worship' of the other.[59]

As the beloved adores their lover, self-awareness disappears and they are concurrently filled with the Holy Spirit; there is 'a participation in the divine nature';[60] a liminal overlap of the *a priori* / real world and the unseen / eternal worlds.[61] Perhaps repurposing the concept of *'theosis'* is the best theological explanation of this mingling of the divine with *imago Dei* in humankind:

---

[51] Macchia, 'Initial Evidence', pp. 119-20.

[52] Macchia, 'Sighs Too Deep for Words', p. 48. Randall Holm proposes that tongues are a verbal 'blush in the presence of God when ... we are left chasing words', Holm, 'New Frontiers in Tongues Research: A Symposium', p. 129.

[53] Macchia, 'Sighs Too Deep for Words', p. 62.

[54] Wacker, *Heaven Below*, p. 12; Grant Wacker, 'The Functions of Faith in Primitive Pentecostalism', *Harvard Theological Review* 77 (Jul 1, 1984), pp. 353-75 (360); cf. Morton T. Kelsey, *Tongue Speaking: An Experiment in Spiritual Experience* (Garden City, NY: Doubleday and Company, 1964), p. 229.

[55] Land, 'Be Filled With The Spirit', p. 116.

[56] MacDonald, 'The Place of Glossolalia in Neo-Pentecostalism', p. 225.

[57] Vessie D. Hargrave, 'Reformation to the Twentieth Century', in Wade H. Horton (ed.) *The Glossolalia Phenomenon* (Cleveland, TN: Pathway Press, 1986), pp. 97-139 (119).

[58] Chan, 'The Language Game of Glossolalia', p. 90.

[59] Kimberly Ervin Alexander, 'Boundless Love Divine: A Re-evaluation of Early Understandings of the Experience of Spirit Baptism', in Steven Jack Land, Rickie D. Moore, and John Christopher Thomas (eds.), *Passover, Pentecost and Parousia: Studies in Celebration of the Life and Ministry of R. Hollis Gause* (JPTSup 35; Blandford Forum: Deo Publishing, 2006), pp. 145-70 (168).

[60] Baker, 'Pentecostal Experience', p. 258. '*The filling of the Spirit is primarily an experience of the Spirit Himself for inhabitation and empowerment*', Joseph R. Flower, 'Holiness, the Spirit's Infilling, and Speaking with Tongues', *Paraclete* 2.2 (Summer 1968), pp. 7-9 (8) (emphasis original).

[61] Richard A. Hutch, 'The Personal Ritual of Glossolalia', in Watson E. Mills (ed.), *Speaking in Tongues: A Guide to Research on Glossolalia* (Grand Rapids, MI: W.

the Eastern Orthodox understanding of deification (*theosis*) as attaining the likeness of God in Christ-likeness is affirmed as the ultimate calling and purpose of all humanity ... it takes one will to create humanity, but two to sanctify it ... the synergistic collaboration between the divine and human will.[62]

Therefore, the glossolalic response 'is not to inform, but to participate in the divine nature':[63] 'what appealed to my spirit more than the miraculous gift of tongues was this sense of God's presence; this intimacy and fellowship with the Infinite'.[64]

The second image for intimacy that was used by the early Pentecostals is that of a mother and child. Just as at salvation, there is a revelation that causes the human heart to cry 'Abba'.[65] There is at SB a revelation that causes the human heart to cry out beyond its understanding:

> just as the baby's cooing is perfectly intelligible to the mother so the unintelligible, Spirit-given, utterances of the believer are intelligible to His Father, and the child, unimpeded by the limits of human language, fully and freely communes with its God.[66]

Noteworthy in this word picture is the gap between the human and the divine.[67] It is precisely this understanding / not understanding that is the strength of the metaphor:

> tongues helps to restore awareness of supernatural mystery to Christian worship ... the two go together: revelation to the human spirit leads to praise from the human spirit. As revelation received goes deeper, so the praise in tongues become richer.[68]

When an infant plays with its parent, it is in fact learning about its

---

B. Eerdmans Pub. Co., 1986), pp. 381-95 (392); Poloma, 'Glossolalia, Liminality', pp. 147-73.

[62] Augustine, *Pentecost, Hospitality, and Transfiguration*, p. 22, cf. p. 21; Timothy Ware, *The Orthodox Church* (New York, NY: Penguin Putnam 1997, reprint, 1963), pp. 231-33.

[63] Baker, 'Pentecostal Experience', pp. 279-80.

[64] Lange, 'The Glory That Excelleth', pp. 250-55.

[65] Romans 8.15; 1 Cor. 14.2.

[66] Lawrence, 'Article VII(a)', p. 6. Here Lawrence refers to 1 Cor. 14.2.

[67] 1 John 3.2. 'The reality of God utterly transcends our puny capacity to describe it', Cox, *Fire From Heaven*, p. 96.

[68] Peter D. Hocken, 'Jesus Christ and the Gifts of the Spirit', *Pneuma* 5.1 (Spring 1983), pp. 1-16 (12-13).

potential adult world.⁶⁹ In the same way, glossolalia is a playful 'means which enables the speaker to open up to a new spiritual dimension'.⁷⁰ It is the 'restoration of the divine image' within humankind.⁷¹ It is when the badly scarred *imago Dei* within receives 'mysteries' of what will be, because:⁷²

> human beings were created with the capacity to be mystically encountered by God ... an 'organ of vision' in our souls ... something in us that experientially-ontologically corresponds to God himself. This something is not simply our moral capacity, our rationale, or our aesthetic sense ... there is a spiritual *something* constitutive of mankind that was created in order to apprehend God.⁷³

There is an apophatic component here, an understanding that one will not fully understand.⁷⁴ 'God, for his own loving and mysterious reasons, re-creates us to be vehicles for unintelligible and non-rational modes of communication'.⁷⁵ Glossolalia then 'becomes the language of divine mystery'.⁷⁶ This mystery is not a puzzle to

---

⁶⁹ Tarr, *The Foolishness of God*, pp. 139-40, 277. In 1 Cor. 13.11, 'Paul's point in context has to do not with "childishness" and "growing up," but with the difference between the present and the future', Gordon Fee, *God's Empowering Presence: The Holy Spirit in the Letters of Paul* (Peabody, MA: Hendrickson, 1994), p. 209. Wolf believes that glossolalia is a 'prototype' or 'marginal' language, Holm, 'New Frontiers in Tongues Research: A Symposium', pp. 133-34, 138.

⁷⁰ Chan, *Pentecostal Theology*, p. 56.

⁷¹ Charette, 'Glossolalia and the Image of God', pp. 189-201 (198); cf. Castelo, *Christian Mystical Tradition*, p. 48; cf. p. 153.

⁷² Charette, 'Glossolalia and the Image of God', p. 198.

⁷³ Rybarczyk, 'Reframing Tongues', p. 89.

⁷⁴ Apophatic theology is knowing by 'the way of unknowing, or the *via negativa*', that is, even though our human minds are limited to knowable categories, there is an understanding beyond what we know, Rybarczyk, 'Reframing Tongues', p. 89. For example, 'just as the senses can neither grasp nor perceive the things of the mind ... the inscrutable One is out of the reach of every rational process. Nor can any words come up to the inexpressible Good, this One, this Source of all unity, this supra-existent Being', Castelo, *Christian Mystical Tradition*, p. 173.

⁷⁵ Rybarczyk, 'Reframing Tongues', p. 92; cf. Castelo, *Christian Mystical Tradition*, p. 48; cf. 138.

⁷⁶ Baker, 'Pentecostal Experience', pp. 260-61. This 'subject could only be approached by means of the language of metaphor – the use of symbolism – and the context of prayer and wonder' because 'it is clear that the God of Orthodoxy and Pentecostalism is a living God, both transcendent and willingly immanent. He will not, therefore, fit into pre-possessed philosophical categories. The apophatic characteristic of the theological tradition of the East may

be solved, but something that 'remains a mystery even after it (God) has been revealed'.[77] And the 'mystical sounds are "as sonorous forms of the divinity, as icons composed as sounds"'.[78]

D. Bells and Trumpets – A Signal

The early Pentecostals compared the Bible sign to alarm bells or a signal trumpet.[79] This metaphor is the closest to what Pentecostals understand as IE and exists because 'as long as man is subject to earthly frailties he is in need of at least a few outward symbols of truth'.[80] Such as, Peter's observation on the Day of Pentecost that tongues were the sign 'spoken by the prophet Joel'.[81] Glossolalia is a symbol of God's immediate presence: 'the tongues are like a bell, ringing the people up. They are waking up to the fact that God is in the land.'[82] Like the joyous bells of a wedding day, God's

---

also help us to perceive in some way the ongoing experience and practice of glossolalic prayer', pp. 261, 260.

[77] Castelo, *Christian Mystical Tradition*, p. 48; cf. pp. 48-51.

[78] Baker, 'Pentecostal Experience', p. 274 (Org. cite: Carmen Blacker, in J. Bowman [ed.] *Comparative Religion* [Leiden: Brill, 1972], p. 89); cf. Williams, *Tongues of the Spirit*, p. 201.

[79] Lawrence, *A.F. Restored*, p. 31.

[80] Brumback, *'What Meaneth This?'*, p. 236. Dunn's work reveals the mixed exegetical opinions on IE: 'in favor of the Pentecostalist thesis it must be said at once that their answer is more soundly rooted within the NT than is often recognized ... the fact is that *in every case* where Luke describes the giving of the Spirit it is accompanied and "evidenced" by glossolalia. The corollary is then not without force that Luke *intended* to portray "speaking in tongues" as "the initial physical evidence" of the outpouring of the Spirit', Dunn, *Jesus and the Spirit*, pp. 189-90. However, while 'Luke certainly believes that the glossolalia was *a* manifestation of the Spirit's coming ... he had no intention of presenting glossolalia as *the* manifestation of the Spirit', p. 191 (emphasis original).

[81] Acts 2.16-21, especially when coupled with the stated sign value at Caesarea in Acts 10.44-46 and its retelling in Jerusalem, Acts 11.15-17. Cf. Mk 16.16-18; Acts 8.14-18; 19.1-6. Dunn writes that if Mark 16:9-20 is a second century addition, that means that 'speaking in tongues was regarded as a typical sign of the gospel's expansion in the first century and perhaps also in the second', Dunn, *Jesus and the Spirit*, p. 246; cf. 242-48; Brumback, *'What Meaneth This?'*, p. 62; Martin, 'Glossolalia in the Apostolic Church', p. 126.

[82] 'Notice', p. 4; cf. Nina White, 'A Song of the "Tongues"', *Confidence* 4.7 (Jul 1911), p. 147; cf. Brumback, *'What Meaneth This?'*, p. 231; James L. Slay, 'Glossolalia: Its Value to the Individual', in Wade H. Horton (ed.), *The Glossolalia Phenomenon* (Cleveland, TN: Pathway Press, 1986), pp. 217-43 (226); Mills, 'Counterculture', p. 950; Williams, *Tongues of the Spirit*, p. 197; Chan, *Pentecostal Theology*, p. 55; Smith, *Thinking in Tongues*, p. 133.

presence brings great joy.⁸³ The emphasis of the image was not on the bells, but their significance – 'The Comforter Has Come'!⁸⁴ The trumpets at the dedication of Solomon's Temple offered another simile: 'He will fill the room and you shall be baptized with the Holy Ghost and with fire, and God will give you a new tongue as a trumpet in singing or speaking'.⁸⁵ This connection with bells continues in the Orthodox Christian tradition: 'in the Russian Orthodox faith, bells are widely considered to be "aural icons," … "an icon of the voice of God"'.⁸⁶

Also, glossolalia signals for Pentecostals that 'the last days (Acts 2.17)' are here.⁸⁷ Tongues are like the bells on the high priest's (Jesus') robes. They are 'peeling forth the sound of His out coming, for He is nearing the door' of heaven.⁸⁸ It was believed that glossolalia would 'increase in volume' (become more widespread) as the second coming approaches.⁸⁹ Some even envisioned that tongues might possibly have some function at 'the sounding of the trumpet, when the dead in Christ shall be brought forth from their graves singing' in tongues with some purpose 'scarcely thought of before'.⁹⁰ It is an eschatological sign of 'the ultimate destiny of heaven and earth … being called together in one holy

---

⁸³ Brott, 'Testimonies', p. 15; Mason, 'TN Evangelist Witnesses', p. 7.

⁸⁴ The most popular chorus at the ASM revival, Robeck, *Azusa Street*, pp. 145-46; Josh P.S. Samuel, *The Holy Spirit in Worship Music, Preaching, and the Altar* (Cleveland, TN: CPT Press, 2018), p. 34.

⁸⁵ 'Type of Pentecost', *AF* 1.7 (Apr 1907), p. 3; cf. 'Work of the Holy Ghost in Switzerland', *TBM* 1.15 (Jun 1, 1908), p. 1.

⁸⁶ 'Just as painted icons are not intended to be mimetic representations of a spiritual object, but magical windows into the world of the spiritual' a Russian bell 'must never be tuned to either a major or minor chord … (it) is prized for its individual, untuned voice, produced by an overlay of numerous partial frequencies', Elif Batuman, 'The Bells: Onward and Upward with the Arts', *The New Yorker* 85.11 (Apr 27, 2009), p. 22.

⁸⁷ Glossolalic encounters 'only make sense with … (an) eschatological framework', Cartledge, *Encountering the Spirit*, p. 114. Cf. Fee, 'Paul's Glossolalia', p. 35.

⁸⁸ Chambers, 'Wherefore The Tongues', p. 5. Sutphin's word picture is of us entering into the holy place with bells on our robes, signalling purity, Sutphin, 'Our Weekly Sermon: The Holy of Holies', p. 3.

⁸⁹ Lawrence, *A.F. Restored*, p. 31.

⁹⁰ Tomlinson, 'Tongues, Tithes, Knowledge', p. 1; cf. Tomlinson, 'Translation Power', p. 1.

koinonia.⁹¹ Tongues are 'a reminder that they (glossolalists) still *await* the final glory';⁹² it is 'broken speech for the broken body of Christ until perfection arrives'.⁹³

A telephone metaphor is similar to bells, but nuances the human / divine roles in IE: 'He baptized us with the Holy Ghost and fire from heaven with the Bible evidence of speaking in other tongues ... I began to prophesy through the Royal Telephone the mysteries of God's eternal kingdom.'⁹⁴ Though some used Balaam's donkey⁹⁵ to highlight this Spirit speaking through the individual, a donkey can still bray and is well-known for its stubbornness; whereas a telephone is an inanimate and passive device through which others speak. On the one hand, divine speech passes through the individual and is a 'manifestation of possession by the Spirit'.⁹⁶ The most popular phrases describing the initial encounter are 'the Spirit spoke through me' and 'the Spirit spoke for himself', both highlight this inner correspondence.⁹⁷ The Spirit announces his presence through the yielded tongue.⁹⁸ 'Tongues are *not constitutive* of the gift of the Holy Spirit, that is comprising the gift, *but declarative*, namely, that the gift has been received.'⁹⁹ On the other hand, there is an inner connection between tongues as a symbol and the thing it signifies – relationship. Speech 'lies on the

---

⁹¹ Augustine, *Pentecost, Hospitality, and Transfiguration*, p. 36.
⁹² Fee, *God's Empowering Presence*, pp. 89, 199, 206.
⁹³ Tarr, *The Foolishness of God*, p. 381.
⁹⁴ Mrs. W.G. Fainter, 'Testimonies', *PHA* 3.27 (Oct 30, 1919), p. 12.
⁹⁵ 'The Love of Jesus', *AF* 1.10 (Sep 1907), p. 1; Bell, 'Questions and Answers #648', p. 5. 'If Balaam's mule could stop in the middle of the road and give the first preacher that went out for money a "Bawling out" in Arabic than anybody today ought to be able to preach in the language of the world if they had horse sense enough to let God use their tongue and throat', Sarah E. Parham, 'The Life of Charles F. Parham: Founder of the Apostolic Movement', in *'The Higher Life Christian Life' Sources For The Study of the Holiness, Pentecostal, And Keswick Movements* (New York: Garland Publishing, 1985), pp. 51-52.
⁹⁶ Martin, 'Glossolalia in the Apostolic Church', pp. 126-27; cf. MacDonald, *Glossolalia*, p. 5.
⁹⁷ John 15.26; 16.13. Though it sounds overly simplistic today, the point of the early Pentecostals is still valid: just how is the Holy Spirit going to 'testify' or 'speak' if not through the voice of God's people, Taylor, *The Spirit and the Bride*, pp. 38-39?
⁹⁸ Varley, 'Fullness of the Holy Ghost', pp. 160-62 (160); Aaron A. Smith, 'Wimauma Camp Meeting Continued', *COGE* 5.24 (Jun 13, 1914), p. 4.
⁹⁹ Williams, *Renewal Theology, Vol. Two*, p. 223, n. 65 (emphasis original).

borderline between oneself and the other' and it is a sign of 'accepting the other'.[100]

E. Reversal of Babel – Unity and Mission

Another metaphor adopted[101] by the early Pentecostals to define the Bible sign was the reversal[102] of Babel's curse at Pentecost:[103]

> skeptics might think this (ASM revival) was Babel let loose; but it was the very opposite of Babel. Then the people ceased to understand each other … When God touches wicked tongues, they can't understand each other … At Pentecost saintly tongues were touched by the Holy Spirit, all understand each other in their 'own tongue'.[104]

The primary points of correspondence with the image are unity and mission:[105]

> God recognized a mighty principle. This principle is *the power of united action* … Unity of spirit was absolutely necessary in the realization of Pentecost, and it is absolutely necessary in the

---

[100] Augustine, *Pentecost, Hospitality, and Transfiguration*, p. 34; cf. Miroslav Volf, *Exclusion & Embrace* (Nashville, TN: Abingdon Press, 1996), p. 228.

[101] This idea was not original to the early Pentecostals, Shumway believes it originated with Gregory of Nyssa and was picked up by Chrysostom, Cyril, and Augustine, Shumway, 'The Gift of Tongues', p. 35.

[102] Macchia's 'positive reading' stresses that these two narratives point towards God's gracious *fulfilment* rather than a simple *reversal*, Macchia, 'Babel and the Tongues of Pentecost', p. 44.

[103] Genesis 11.1-9; Acts 2.1-13. Textually, Davies makes a strong case in favour of connecting the two accounts. He believes that Luke had the LXX's account of Gen. 11.1-9 in mind when he wrote his account of Pentecost, Davies, 'Pentecost and Glossolalia', p. 228; cf. Mills, *Theological/Exegetical*, p. 51. Gundry believes Davies position 'gives too much weight' to the argument, Gundry, 'Ecstatic Utterance', p. 299 n. 2. Hovenden mildly disagrees with Davies, stating that at best Babel was a 'backcloth', Hovenden, *Speaking in Tongues*, p. 88.

[104] Simmons, 'Tongues', p. 1.

[105] Secondary correspondence with the metaphor include: 1) support for MTs, 'Chinese Want The Gospel of the Bible', *AF* 1.2 (Oct 1906), p. 3; Taylor, *The Spirit and the Bride*, pp. 33, 34; 2) the understanding of languages at Pentecost assures us of a universal heavenly language in the eschaton, Barth, 'The Things of the Kingdom', p. 4; J.R.F., 'Wiser Than Children of Light', p. 1; and 3) both Babel and Pentecost were God's design to 'baffle the Devil', Reid, 'Concerning The Tongues', p. 3.

continuation of Pentecost. *No unity – no Pentecost. Unity – Pentecost.*[106]

First, an overwhelming encounter with the Holy Spirit unifies the tongues-speaker with others of similar experience. The strength of this aspect of the metaphor is divine involvement with speech: God acted to divide the languages and then united them through glossolalia.[107] Though the glossolalia of an encounter with the Holy Spirit is 'babbling' in an unknown language, the connection point is that they *all babel* – each experiences a 'personal Pentecost'.[108] This babbling is '*over*comprehensible', meaning that there was 'a common understanding that floods over cultural boundaries to include everyone',[109] making it 'the first ecumenical language of the church' because 'no single language or voice in the dialogue can unambiguously hold the truth'.[110] In this way, glossolalia is the mark of a new community.[111] The Mt. Sinai story could be added to this metaphor because there, at Sinai, 'God's voice was heard in every language' and the message of Pentecost went from incoherence to understanding for all nations.[112]

Second, 'logically connected to the purpose of baptism in the Spirit was power to testify cross-culturally; what better sign to evidence this particular empowerment of the Spirit than inspiration to speak in the language of other cultures?'[113] Note again that there is an internal connection between the symbol, Babel's reversal, and

---

[106] J.R.F., 'Wiser Than Children of Light', p. 1 (emphasis added). Cf. Reid, 'Concerning The Tongues', p. 3.

[107] Brumback, *What Meaneth This?'*, pp. 40-41, 44; Mills, *Understanding*, p. 36; Mills, *Theological/Exegetical*, p. 66.

[108] Personal Pentecost was a common synonym for SB, e.g. Seymour, 'The Baptism with the Holy Ghost (2)', p. 3; Atterberry, 'They Shall Speak with New Tongues', p. 2. Cf. Conn, *Pillars of Pentecost*, p. 53.

[109] Macchia, 'Babel and the Tongues of Pentecost', p. 44.

[110] Macchia, 'Babel and the Tongues of Pentecost', p. 49. Unity obtained through human means would be idolatrous, p. 44. Cf. Suenens, 'Malines Document 1', p. 20; Baker, 'Pentecostal Experience', p. 216.

[111] Powers, 'Missionary Tongues?', p. 51.

[112] Mills, *Theological/Exegetical*, pp. 51-52.

[113] Craig S. Keener, 'Why Does Luke Use Tongues as a sign of the Spirit's Empowerment?', *JPT* 15-2 (April 1, 2007), p. 178. Cf. Taylor, *'The Spirit and the Bride'*, pp. 62-64; Culbreth, 'Pentecost Foreshadowed', p. 2; J. Rodman Williams, *The Pentecostal Reality* (Plainfield, NJ: Logos International, 1972), p. 2; Robeck, *Azusa Street*, p. 186.

what it signifies, Spirit-inspired proclamation.[114] Though humanity's plan at Babel was a rebellious 'shortcut' to heaven, God's plan through Pentecost is accomplished through submissive obedience.[115] Submission to God's plan is what connects the individual with power:

> at Pentecost they were connected to the Great Power Plant ... cloven tongues (came) upon them like as a fire ... At Babel God sent tongues which scattered the people over the face of the earth. After Pentecost, God also sent them abroad, and 'they went everywhere preaching the word, the Lord working with them and confirming the Word with signs following'.[116]

Tongues are not power in itself but is a symbol that God can use people to carry his message in a new and powerful way.[117] Perhaps revelation is a more accurate and broader category than power:[118] 'the real wonder is the *new world of realities in which we live*, the new forces, the new possibilities that arise from our spirit being restored to its proper place under the guidance of the Holy Spirit'.[119] Babel focused on the singular goal of building a tower through brute force, but Pentecost is God's anointed people going out with diverse languages into varied cultures to fulfil the mission of Jesus to heal, release, preach, and create 'a new heaven and a new earth where justice and compassion would reign' under the daily revelation of the Holy Spirit.[120] This new 'capacity' or vision of spiritual

---

[114] Hovenden, *Speaking in Tongues*, pp. 93-94.

[115] Both the Garden of Eden and the tower of Babel were 'short-cuts' to humanity's ultimate calling of 'deification (*theosis*)', Augustine, *Pentecost, Hospitality, and Transfiguration*, p. 22, cf. p. 21.

[116] Hudson, 'The Personality of the Holy Spirit and Other Observations', p. 3.

[117] Abrams, *Holy Ghost & Fire*, p. 38; Berkhof, *The Doctrine of the Holy Spirit*, p. 89.

[118] '*Revelation* is a more basic category than *power*. There is no power from the Spirit of God where there is no revelation from the Spirit of God. Power in the Spirit is a consequence of revelation', Hocken, 'The Meaning and Purpose of "Baptism in the Spirit"', p. 128; cf. Hovenden, *Speaking in Tongues*, p. 91, cf. pp. 89-93.

[119] A.E. Street, 'To Our Readers', *Intercessory Missionary* 1.4 (Jan 1908), pp. 49-50 (50) (emphasis original). 'All human activities have their origin in the spiritual world, and *Pentecost merely introduces us to a new region of the heavenlies*', A.E. Street, 'Pentecost Cannot Satisfy', *Intercessory Missionary* 1.4 (Jan 1908), pp. 60-61 (60) (emphasis original).

[120] Cox, *Fire From Heaven*, p. 316.

possibilities, is naturally joined with an eschatological passion to reach the lost, like two sides of the same coin.[121]

F. The Latter Rain – God's Metanarrative

An important metaphor highlighting the sign-value of glossolalia is the latter rain.[122] This study has shown that the concept of a latter rain revival was popular and predates the ASM revival.[123] Because Peter connected SB and its accompanying glossolalia on the Day of Pentecost to the fulfilment of Joel's latter rain prophecy,[124] Pentecostals interpreted Peter's context as the 'former' or first rains of the prophecy and their current revival as its complete fulfilment:

> He is pouring out his Spirit upon all flesh, all over the wide world, *causing the prophecy of Joel to be fulfilled* ... The glad news of this outpouring is sounded all over the world, amongst all kindred, tongues and nations, singing in natural and heavenly languages ... the sound of the latter rain upon us has been heard all over the world.[125]

But it was also a metaphor with three points of correspondence with tongues. First the latter rain gave logic to glossolalia's reappearance in history. Second, and as Peter himself observed, SB and its glossolalia signalled 'the last days'. Third, it connected glossolalists with the apostolic church: they 'read the book of Acts as a model for their life'.[126]

First, the latter rain's logic: the fact of an eighteen hundred year drought of glossolalia in church history with only occasional

---

[121] Menzies, 'Evidential Tongues', p. 232.

[122] A parallel is drawn from the rainfall in Palestine: the early spring rains which accompanies the planting of the crops are compared to the Day of Pentecost and the latter fall rains which helps to ripen the crop for harvest are compared to the Pentecostal revival, Myland, 'The Latter Rain', p. 94.

[123] For example, E. Sission's article expounding on the principle of the latter rain calls Christians to prayer for a revival greater than the Day of Pentecost or the Welsh revival two months before the ASM revival, Sisson, 'A Call To Prayer', pp. 57-60; cf. McGee, 'Shortcut to Language Preparation', p. 122.

[124] Acts 2.16-21; cf. Joel 2.23, 28-29; Zech. 10.1; Jas 5.7.

[125] Andrew Urshan, 'The Sound of the Latter Rain', *TOF* 33.8 (Aug 1913), pp. 185-86 (emphasis added). Cf. 'Rivers of Living Water', *TOF* 28.11 (Nov 1908), pp. 248-49.

[126] Menzies, *This Story Is Our Story*, p. 17.

'showers' fits perfectly with the latter rain metaphor.[127] As for the showers, many attempted to trace a single stream of glossolalia through church history[128] to counter cessationism[129] and to reclaim history:[130] 'many wonder why ... Pentecost all but disappeared from the Church for upwards of 1800 years, and that only an occasional shower fell ... (but) through these nineteen centuries Pentecost has fallen here and there'.[131] Despite the strengths[132] and weaknesses[133] of the continuation theory, restorationism was a far

---

[127] Restoration and continuance were not seen in conflict with each other. For example, Taylor simply says, 'during the long drought of the Middle Ages a few saints received the baptism of the Holy Spirit, and spake with other tongues', Taylor, *The Spirit and the Bride*, p. 92. 'To me there is only one Tongues movement: the one that had its beginning at the Upper Room', Boulos, 'In Defense of the Truth', p. 10.

[128] See Appendix 2.

[129] Jon Ruthven believes that this method ultimately had limited success because cessationism collapsed due to 'internal inconsistencies with respect to its concept of miracle and its biblical hermeneutics ... (which were) far more dogmatically than scripturally based', Jon Ruthven, *On the Cessation of the Charismata: The Protestant Polemic on Postbiblical Miracles* (JPTSup 3; Sheffield: Sheffield Academic Press, 1993), pp. 189-90; cf. Mills, 'Counterculture', p. 950. Denying the possibility of tongues today 'cannot be defended exegetically or theologically', Suenens, 'Malines Document', p. 24.

[130] For example, 'the golden chain of truth that links together time; which has been smoked and cankered by the darkness of age, is being washed and garnished by the environment of the Holy Spirit till it is almost as bright as it was when Jesus was on earth', Marion T. Whidden, 'The Latter Rain Revival', *COGE* 1.1 (Mar 1, 1910), p. 3.

[131] Turner, *Pentecost and Tongues*, pp. 126, 128; cf. Appendix 2.

[132] This historical hermeneutic proved that during a spiritual revival, glossolalia was a natural occurrence. There was a 'direct correlation, throughout history, between spirituality and the reappearance of spiritual gifts ... (that) when spiritual life ran high, the Holy Spirit has been received just as at Pentecost', Edith Waldvogel, 'The "Overcoming Life": A Study In The Reformed Evangelical Origins of Pentecostalism' (PhD Dissertation, Harvard University, 1977), pp. 9, 10; cf. Frodsham, *With Signs Following*, p. 253.

[133] Weaknesses include: 1) historical interpretations 'readily betray the perspectives (or should I say biases) of their authors', E. Glenn Hinson, 'The Significance of Glossolalia in the History of Christianity', in Watson E. Mills (ed.), *Speaking in Tongues: A Guide to Research on Glossolalia* (Grand Rapids, MI: Eerdmans, 1986), pp. 181-203 (181); 2) tracing a continuous stream back may account for the phenomena of glossolalia, but it does not answer why it occurs or what theological claims support it, Dayton, *Theological Roots*, p. 17; 3) to be credible historically, the definition of glossolalia must be broadened to include ecstatic speech and spiritual gifts, Russell P. Spittler, 'Glossolalia', in Stanley Burgess (ed.), *NIDPCM* (Grand Rapids, MI: Zondervan, rev. and expanded edn,

more important image because 'in Pentecostalism, every generation is the first generation'.[134]

The primary correspondence between glossolalia and the latter rain image is the restoration of God's activity for an end-time revival after a spiritual drought.[135] God responded to the prayers of those living in a spiritual desert:

> God heard the cry of His children and began to pour out His rain upon the earth ... Pentecostal gifts are being restored and the sign or seal of Pentecost – Mark 16:17 – power to speak with other tongues, is coming upon those thus baptized by the Spirit.[136]

The outpouring's 'scope is worldwide and not limited to (one) location'.[137] The latter rain was even used as a synonym for SB:[138]

> it would be most natural to expect *the same Sign to accompany the out-pouring of the Latter Rain,* and thus it has been ... There has been the same wonderful Sign that accompanied Pentecost in early days, viz., the speaking with other tongues.[139]

The restoration meant that God was again equipping his Church with all the necessary spiritual gifts of Pentecost to prepare 'for

---

2002), pp. 670-76 (673); and 4) there is no way to know for sure if the phenomena is the same as the apostles, Currie, 'Speaking in Tongues', pp. 274-94; cf. Shumway, 'The Gift of Tongues', pp. 64, 65.

[134] Everett Wilson, 'Pentecostal Historiography and Global Christianity: Rethinking the Questions of Origins', *Pneuma* 27.1 (Spring, 2005), pp. 35-50 (45). Wilson notes that 'the logic of the Pentecostal message ... led to an immediate globalization, and to the immediate localization ... rapid adoption and adaption of Pentecostal spirituality and practice', p. 45.

[135] 'The Promised Latter Rain Now Being Poured out on God's Humble People', p. 2; 'Everything is Pointing Toward the Coming of the Lord', p. 1. An early monograph on the subject is, Myland, 'The Latter Rain'.

[136] Duncan, 'What The Movement Is', p. 4; Land, *Pentecostal Spirituality*, p. 61.

[137] E.A. Sexton, 'Editorial, Some Interesting Facts', p. 1.

[138] Montgomery, 'Letter From Mrs. Montgomery (#2)', p. 124; A.B. Simpson, 'Rivers of Living Water', *TOF* 29.8 (Aug 1909), pp 174-75; Kathleen Miller, 'A Testimony From Cuttack, India', *TOF* 30.6 (Jun 1910), p. 128; A.L.H., 'How Are We To Know God?' (Omega), *TOF* 30.7 (Jul 1910), p. 161; Taylor, 'Question Box #1335', p. 6.

[139] Carrie Judd Montgomery, 'The Latter Rain', *TOF* 34.1 (Jan 1914), pp. 1-4 (2).

the imminent harvest and the return of Christ the king':[140]

> they enjoyed the outpouring of the 'former rain' and we are enjoying the outpouring of the 'latter rain.' The former rain was given to start the grain growing. The latter was to ripen the grain for harvesting ... Now we are in the end of the world and people are receiving the same experience that they did at the beginning. This is the time for the ripening of the grain (people) for the great harvest time.[141]

Second, the restoration of glossolalia signalled that the last 'and perilous days' were here,[142] that the coming of Jesus was imminent.[143] It was 'a sign or token of a new era', a dispensation in God's dealings with humankind,[144] and many prophesied that 'Jesus is coming soon'.[145] The return of glossolalia to the church meant that all the spiritual gifts were again restored, if not doubled.[146] The Spirit-baptized believer sensed an urgency, as if a storm were coming and a harvest of souls could be lost. Therefore 'apocalyptic affections' became the 'integrating core' of Pentecostalism's spirituality.[147]

Third, the prophetic link between the former rain and a latter rain opened up an historical thread to connect contemporary glossolalia with its past on the Day of Pentecost: 'we have the same evidence as the Disciples received on the Day of Pentecost (Acts

---

[140] Cartledge, *Encountering the Spirit*, p. 113.
[141] Tomlinson, 'The Holy Ghost And Fire', p. 1.
[142] Hayes, 'Perilous Times', p. 1; cf. Craig, 'Woodworth-Etter Meeting, Sidney, Iowa', p. 15.
[143] 'The all absorbing theme of Pentecost and its significance regarding the early appearing of our Lord ... keep(s) us in a hopeful and expectant attitude, waiting our Lord's appearing', E.A. Sexton, 'Editorials, Signs of the Times', *TBM* 3.53 (Jan 1, 1910), p. 1; cf. Boddy, 'Pentecostal Outpouring', pp. 234-35; Argue, 'An Essential Sign?', p. 2.
[144] Howell, 'Windsor, Fla.', p. 6; S.H.F., 'The Latter Rain', pp. 8-9; 'When Shall We Rise To Meet The Lord?', p. 2; McCafferty, 'The Time of the Latter Rain', p. 5.
[145] Bowen, 'Akron Visited With Pentecost', p. 1; Sexton, 'Editorials, Jesus Is Coming', p. 1; Sisson, 'A Sign People', p. 3; Studd, 'My Convictions', p. 6.
[146] The 'gifts of healing; gifts of prophecy; gifts of tongues, etc. were "former rain *moderately.*" What, then, shall the doubled ... latter rain be', Sisson, 'A Call To Prayer', p. 59? (emphasis original).
[147] Land, *Pentecostal Spirituality*, pp. 23, 58-121.

2:3, 4), in speaking in new tongues'.[148] 'Tongues serve as a sign that "their experience" is "our experience" and that all the gifts of the Spirit (including the "sign gifts") are valid for the church today'.[149] This linkage enabled Pentecostals 'to experience life as part of the biblical drama of participation in God's history',[150] or God's 'metanarrative':[151] 'the ages overlap like links in a chain ... Pentecost itself really belongs to the next dispensation ... every sign is a foretaste of that coming age ... (let's) live in advance of our time'.[152] The historical gap between the apostolic church then and today disappears and is morphed into a single, ongoing story in which Pentecostals sees themselves as active participants. As such, there was confidence that God would act with power through the believer because it was a divine continuing drama. The Pentecostal claim is that an encounter with the Holy Spirit changes everything. That there is a 'Pentecostal reality'[153] or cosmology, 'to experience life as part of a biblical drama of participation in God's history'.[154]

Of the metaphors parsed above, rekindling the latter rain is critical for revitalizing the apostolic and early Pentecostal passion

---

[148] 'The Apostolic Faith Movement', p. 2; cf. Tomlinson, 'The Holy Ghost And Fire', p. 1; Poole, 'God Is Love', p. 2; Fisher, 'Pentecost In Rasutoland', p. 8. A similar phrase was: 'as they did at the beginning', Sutphin, 'Coming of the Son of Man', p. 2; Lasater, 'Ft. Smith, Ark.', p. 14; Polhill, 'The Pentecostal Movement In The Foreign Mission Field', p. 81. Myland encouraged Pentecostals to get their 'experiences and lives to harmonize' with the apostles, Myland, 'The Latter Rain', p. 17.

[149] R. Menzies, *This is Our Story*, p. 68. Menzies believes that Luke intended Luke-Acts to be a model for mission and ministry for his readers, and that a thorough examination reveals a model to be emulated today, p. 144, cf. pp. 21-39; cf. Hollenweger, *The Pentecostals*, p. 339.

[150] Land, *Pentecostal Spirituality*, pp. 74, 75; Wacker, *Heaven Below*, p. 71.

[151] Cartledge writes that this connection 'is a form of contextualized hermeneutics whereby the communal story of the Church is understood in the light of the overarching story of Scripture', Cartledge, *Encountering the Spirit*, p. 129.

[152] Barth, 'The Things of the Kingdom', p. 4. Cf. also, Alexander, *Pentecostal Healing*, pp. 91-93; McQueen, *Toward a Pentecostal Eschatology*, pp. 91-92.

[153] By Pentecostal reality, Williams means Pentecostals claim to have 'experienced a coming of the Holy Spirit wherein God's presence and power has pervaded their lives ... they know what it means to be "filled with the Holy Spirit." There has been a breakthrough of God's Spirit into their total existence – body, soul, and spirit – reaching into the conscious and subconscious depths, and setting loose powers hitherto unknown', Williams, *The Pentecostal Reality*, p. 2; cf. Chan, *Pentecostal Theology*, p. 53.

[154] Land, *Pentecostal Spirituality*, pp. 74-75.

that flowed out of SB for post-modern Pentecostals. When the logic of SB is lost, it is likely that the restoration of equipping power and the urgent motivation to spread the gospel is lost as well.[155]

G. A Way Forward

Just as a land-surveyor will establish two points on a line and then flip the transit over to extend that line, our two fixed points are the biblical accounts and the testimonies of the early Pentecostals. Before we 'flip over' to look at the future, a brief look back will complete the picture of the doctrine of evidential glossolalia for the early Pentecostals. While it is clear that tongues were the undisputed evidence of SB for the early Pentecostals, this investigation revealed considerable variety and theological space surrounding the evidence doctrine, even in Durham's strongly worded *PT*.[156] In a sense, these outliers or variables functioned like a pressure release valve on the Modernistic worldview. There were three variables that revealed the 'outer boundaries' and 'framed' the accepted evidence doctrine: 1) many testimonies indicated a delay between SB and the Bible sign:

> the baptism of the Spirit is a gift of power on the sanctified life, and when people receive it, *sooner or later* they will speak in tongues as the Spirit gives utterance. A person *may not speak in tongues for a week after the baptism*, but as soon as he gets to praying or praising God *in the liberty of the Spirit*, the tongues will follow.[157]

A lot of periodicals published testimonies of a delayed sign.[158] 2) Numerous individuals testified to pre-glossolalic experiences which they defined as 'stammering lips',[159] a 'pre-Pentecostal

---

[155] Cox, *Fire From Heaven*, pp. 87, 317; Menzies, 'Evidential Tongues', p. 231.

[156] For example, Durham's own testimony noted multiple experiences before the evidence, Durham, 'Personal Testimony of Pastor Durham', p. 7. Even subsequent Oneness papers noted that a delay between water baptism and evidential glossolalia was not unusual, e.g. Randol, 'St. Louis, MO', p. 3.

[157] 'Questions Answered (AF)', p. 2 (emphasis added).

[158] E.g. Harvey, 'Key West, Fla', p. 4; Montgomery, '"The Promise of the Father (#1)"', pp. 145-49; Lindley, 'The Beginning of Days for Me', p. 3. Passim.

[159] Standley, 'Worth Tarrying For', p. 3; Benefield, 'Midland City, Ala.', p. 8; Sackett, 'Words From Johannesburg', p. 8; 'The Latter Rain In Atlantic City, N.J.', p. 14.

fullness',[160] 'whispering words',[161] 'not fully satisfied',[162] or 'gracious anointings'.[163] While any pre-glossolalic state was an 'incomplete baptism' and somewhat 'abnormal', it was just a part of the process.[164] With pastoral compassion, seekers were encouraged to come up to the 'Azusa standard'[165] or the 'New Testament standard'.[166] Thus, despite the strong statements on the evidence, scores testified that glossolalia was not a mechanical-like cause and effect – one can say that God, in his sovereignty, interacts individually with the seeker's yieldedness and heart.[167] Further, and despite criticism,[168] some claimed their SB 'by faith' and then pressed on until they spoke in tongues.[169] The fully nuanced formal AG position of 1918 emphasized this concept with the terminology of 'full consummation'.[170] 3) Significantly, Flower reprioritized the evidence by pointing to what sequentially followed. He wrote that evidential tongues are just the 'top layer *of the foundation* of such experiences'[171] because there is 'always more

---

[160] Copley, 'The Threefold Standard', p. 8; Sackett, 'Words From Johannesburg', p. 8.
[161] Gray, 'His Wedding Garments', p. 3.
[162] Simpson, 'W.W. Simpson', p. 6.
[163] Schoonmaker, 'Missionary Gleanings', p. 12.
[164] Bell, 'Questions and Answers #647', p. 5.
[165] Seymour, 'The Baptism of the Holy Ghost (2)', p. 3.
[166] Bell, 'Questions and Answers #647', p. 5
[167] *TP* 2.5 (Apr 1, 1910), p. 4; Flower, 'God Honors Faith', p. 1.
[168] Gaston, 'The Baptism According to Acts 2:4', p. 3.
[169] Throop, 'A Partial Experience', pp. 129-31; Flower, 'God Honors Faith', p. 1.
[170] 'A Statement of Fundamental Truths Approved By The General Council of the Assemblies of God, October 2-7, 1916 (#2)', p. 8.
[171] Flower, 'The Apostolic Question Box', p. 9 (emphasis added). The earliest conceptualization is found in A.E.S., 'Pentecost is Not an Advanced Step in the Christian Life – A Warning', *Intercessory Missionary* 1.3 (Jun 1907), pp. 39-42 (40). Flower seems to follow Durham's phraseology of five months prior, Durham, 'A Word To Ministers, From A Minister', p. 11; cf. Consider: 'we do not teach that all who have been baptized in the Holy Ghost, even if they should speak in in tongues, have already received the fullness of the blessings of Christ implied in this Baptism. There may be, and in most cases will be, a progressive entering in of the believer into this fullness, according to the measure of faith, obedience, and knowledge of the recipient', 'International Declaration', p. 1. '**It is the first** of the gifts … it is the steppingstone … to higher things', Fraser, 'A Contrast in Values', p. 3. Taylor observed that tongues were not 'the **greatest** phase of the Baptism' and that '*other* Bible evidences, or rather results' should

to follow'.¹⁷² In other words, 'an encounter with God should serve as the *gateway* to life in the Spirit, rather than as the *goal* which can always be formally verified *once* it has been reached!'¹⁷³ There is always more, for example, 'there are times when even tongues cease, when His presence is so all-pervading in the atmosphere so heavenly that I cannot talk at all in any language'.¹⁷⁴ This perspective on the backside of SB softened the hardness of the doctrine away from a 'have and have not' category to a continuum of yieldedness and multiple fillings that would never be fully satisfied. These three variables expose a certain fuzziness to the doctrine and opens up theological space regarding the Bible sign.

Two further observations about evidential tongues from the early thinkers that need attention: first, these pioneers recognized the impossibility of theologically classifying glossolalia because it occurs 'when no longer words in our vocabulary can do justice' to explain the encounter with God.¹⁷⁵ Even AG leader Bell openly criticized evidence terminology as 'woefully at fault' for opening the door for 'every devil possessed ... person in the world to claim the baptism'.¹⁷⁶ He recommended that 'we advocates of this truth must hedge about more carefully our statements'.¹⁷⁷ Second, much of this monograph's construction interacts with concepts from Eastern Orthodox theology to explain Pentecostal glossolalia.¹⁷⁸ It was exciting to see the Eastern worldview represented in the early periodicals with an article by Boulos, who noted that there is a

---

follow the believer, Taylor, 'Editorial: Speaking in Tongues', p. 8 (emphasis original). 'It is only the beginning', wrote Tomlinson, Tomlinson, 'Converted, Sanctified, and Baptized with the Holy Ghost', p. 1.

¹⁷² Boulos, 'In Defense of the Truth', p. 11; cf. Simpson, 'A Methodist Minister's Personal Testimony', p. 7.

¹⁷³ Lederle, 'An Ecumenical Appraisal', p. 136.

¹⁷⁴ Montgomery, 'The Life on Wings', pp. 175-76.

¹⁷⁵ Gaston, 'The Ministry of the Spirit', p. 6.

¹⁷⁶ E.N.B., 'What is the Evidence of the Baptism In The Spirit', p. 7. Flower wrote, 'too much stress on speaking in tongues as the Bible evidence weakens that argument' because some glossolalia is of human origin and some Satanic, TP 2.11 & 12 (Nov/Dec 1910), p. 9.

¹⁷⁷ E.N.B., 'What is the Evidence of the Baptism In The Spirit', p. 7.

¹⁷⁸ These authors contributed to an eastern voice to this construction: Chan, *Pentecostal Theology*; Rybarczyk, 'Reframing Tongues'; Augustine, *Pentecost, Hospitality, and Transfiguration*; Castelo, *Christian Mystical Tradition*. A well-known work in German is, Johannes Reimer, 'Mission Des Frühen Mönchtums In Rubland' (DTh Thesis, University of South Africa, 1994).

natural 'interconnection' between glossolalia as speech and the metaphor of SB.[179]

Now a look forward. In the light of the above, a Pentecostal theology of glossolalia would be well served to note the following: first, that one's first encounter with the Holy Spirit that results in glossolalia will never be mechanical-like nor an 'empirical proof' to anyone other than the glossolalist. Evidentiary language should be replaced with clear terms from the historic and broader church, such as sign, symbol, and sacrament. Second, because tongues are symbolic of the liminal and unclassifiable encounter with God, simplified concepts of *kenosis*, apophaticism and mystery should be employed into any definition of what was IE. Such language will help point not only to what tongues are, but what they are not. Third, because a wide variety of experiences with the Holy Spirit are possible before and after one's first glossolalic encounter, emphasis should be given to a lifelong journey of *kenosis* / *theosis* rather than tongues. Then the Church as Jesus' body on earth might become the eschatological, Spirit-directed and empowered community that it was intended to be.[180] A simplified sample doctrinal statement could read:

> The passionate seeker of God, when completely surrendered and within God's sovereignty, will receive a revelation of God's glorious presence. That portion of the human soul created for relationship with God will at once cry out expressions of worship in an unknown language and, at the same time, recognize its inability to comprehend fully the Divine; this is called SB. Because the seeker has encountered God and has been filled with the same, they are forever changed, knowing God's power through personal yieldedness. Thereafter, the individual longs for more of the Holy Spirit and lives a life of daily sacrifice and obedience to the whispers of Spirit in bringing the lost to salvation in God's grand story before it is too late.

---

[179] Boulos, 'In Defense of the Truth', p. 11; cf. Hayes, *Gift of Tongues*, p. 96.

[180] 'One gives up control … so as to put one's whole self … at God's disposal', Fee, 'Paul's Glossolalia', p. 36.

III. Public Metaphors

After the initial encounter in the above discussion, there are further stages or uses for glossolalia, some public and some private.[181] Encounter symbolism implies a public use for tongues, someone to witness the sign. Here are two additional metaphors for public glossolalia to be explored: singing in the Spirit and the gift of tongues.

A. The Heavenly Anthem – Singing in the Spirit

The word-picture of HA was rooted in several scriptures for the early Pentecostals.[182] 'It is difficult to overstate the significance of the heavenly choir'[183] in the early Pentecostal revival and thankfully, there is a growing body of theological reflection.[184] This study has shown that singing in the Spirit is an essential component of Pentecostal spirituality because it: 1) is widely accepted by outsiders,[185] 2) creates a hunger and an environment for future

---

[181] Yong proposes three successive stages, each with accompanying metaphors: 1) 'innocence' is his first stage when 'glossolalia functions primarily as a sign denoting the experience of the liberating Holy Spirit', Yong, 'Tongues of Fire', p. 52. 2) 'Growth stage': 'the dominant metaphor during *growth* shifts from the performative "*speaking* as the Spirit gives utterance" to that of "receiving power after the spirit comes upon you"', the purpose of which is 'Christian *witness* ... a symbol of the divine message and power', pp. 54, 56. 'Metaphors are less useful' at Yong's third stage: 3) 'adept ... an embodiment of the divine unity ... participation in the divine life through the divine language ... (bringing) his or her will into conformity with the divine's ... the reverse of Babel ... the re-gathering of the people of God', pp. 57-58, 60.

[182] 1 Corinthians 14.15, Eph. 5.19, Col. 3.16, and Revelation 4 & 5.

[183] Alexander, 'Heavenly Choirs', p. 256. The phrase 'heavenly choir' was a 'household phrase' among the Pentecostals, p. 263.

[184] Brumback, 'What Meaneth This?', pp. 294-95; William J. Samarin, *Tongues of Men and Angels* (New York, NY: Macmillan Company, 1972), pp. 174-82; Eddie Ensley, *Sounds of Wonder: A Popular History of Speaking in Tongues in the Catholic Tradition* (Ramsey: Paulist, 1977), pp. 72-104; Francis A. Sullivan, *Charisms and Charismatic Renewal: A Biblical and Theological Study* (Ann Arbor, MI: Servant Books, 1982), pp 144-48; Jon Michael Spencer, 'The Heavenly Anthem: Holy Ghost Singing in the Primal Pentecostal Revival', *The Journal of Black Sacred Music* 1.1 (Spring 1987) pp. 1-33; Robeck, *Azusa Street*, pp 149-53; Steven Dove, 'Hymnody and Liturgy in the Azusa Street Revival', *Pneuma* 31 (2009) pp. 242-63; Joel Hinck, 'Heavenly Harmony: An Audio Analysis of Corporate Singing in Tongues', *Pneuma* 40.1-2 (2018), pp. 167-91; Samuel, *The Holy Spirit in Worship Music*, pp. 31-37.

[185] 'Perhaps nothing so greatly impressed people as the singing; at once inspiring a holy awe, or a feeling of indescribable wonder', Lawrence, 'Article X',

glossolalists,[186] and 3) is often someone's first experience with glossolalia.[187] The metaphor of joining with the angels in singing praise is, in itself, theologically rich. Consider:

> Pentecost is a baptism of praise coming over the balconies of heaven from the glorified presence of our Savior ... striking up cords of praise we never dreamed existed ... finding adequate expression only in the tongues, which come with it from the scenes of heavenly praise and adoration ... the preliminary notes of that 'new song'.[188]

There are three degrees of correspondence with the metaphor. First, there is a new depth of worship. Recognition of God's immanent presence demands a response, like a hometown hero passing by in a parade – one just has to clap and shout.[189] The HA was 'one of the most indisputable evidences of the presence of God'.[190] Because God is outside of time, participants join with heavenly beings[191] and those in history who sang with their 'spirits' instead of their 'minds', those who voiced 'spiritual songs',[192] such as St. Augustine's congregation 'jubilating', or St. Hildegard of Bingen's 'concerts in the Spirit', or Ignatius of Loyola singing his 'loquela',[193] and the

---

p. 4. Robeck notes that it was the singing in the Spirit that was recognized by Russian Molokans when passing by the ASM, Robeck, *Azusa Street*, p. 153.

[186] H.L. Blake, 'A Minnesota Preacher's Testimony', *AF* 1.6 (Feb/Mar 1907), p. 5; Sexton, 'Set Thine Heart To Understand', p. 1; Bartleman, *Azusa Street*, p. 63. Alexander writes, 'the fact that Sexton uses the heavenly choir manifestation as the pivotal event in turning the heart of the cynic is significant', Alexander, 'Heavenly Choirs', p. 258.

[187] Poloma writes that it 'creates an atmosphere where non-glossolalics may come to have this experience', Poloma, *The Assemblies of God at the Crossroads*, p. 191.

[188] Carothers, 'The Speaking in Tongues', p. 24.

[189] 'The participants are aware of such close presence of God's Spirit and nearness', Tarr, *The Foolishness of God*, p. 204.

[190] Lawrence, 'Article X', p. 4.

[191] Alexander, 'Heavenly Choirs', p. 257.

[192] 1 Corinthians 14.15; Eph. 5.19; Col. 3.16; cf. Dunn, *Jesus and the Spirit*, pp. 238-39; Hayford, *Beauty*, pp. 193-95.

[193] Cf. Appendix 2; Augustine, 'Expositions of the Psalms: 99-120', in Boniface Ramsey (ed.), *The Works of Saint Augustine: A Translation for the 21st Century*, 3.19 (trans. Maria Boulding; Hyde Park, NY: New City Press, 2003), Psalm 99, p. 14. For Hildegard: George H. Williams and Edith Waldvogel, 'A History of Speaking in Tongues and Related Gifts', in Michael P. Hamilton (ed.) *The Char-*

ASM revival participants.[194] Proleptically, choir members added their voices to the yet-future heavenly scene with the four-living creatures, the twenty-four elders and innumerable people in singing a 'new song'.[195] It is a revelation of God's presence corporately that changes everything:

> Pentecostals believe that they encounter deeply and transformatively the God of their confession and adoration. This theme is central to Pentecostal identity ... God presents Godself (or quaintly put, 'God shows up'), and God goes on to establish a different kind of order, one in which God's glory and holiness alter and renarrate all else that is.[196]

Singers of the HA sense an overlap of the unseen phenomenal world with the earthly nominal world, because it is 'the singing by the lips of the Holy Ghost through human lips as he played upon the vocal cords'.[197]

Second, there is a new, creative means of corporate worship. The former rules of language and music seem dull and limiting.[198] It is as if the worshippers are accompanying a melody beyond the audible hearing range of others.[199] For this reason, many scholars have noted a parallel between glossolalia and jazz music.[200] Classic art forms adhere to rules and a strict realism, but like jazz,

---

ismatic Movement (Grand Rapids, MI: Eerdmans, 1975), p. 70. For Ignatius: Harvey D. Egan, *Ignatius of Loyola* (Wilmington, DE: Michael Glazier, 1987), pp. 193-94.

[194] 'The Heavenly Anthem', p. 3.

[195] Cf. Revelation 4 & 5; Archer, *'I Was in the Spirit on the Lord's Day'*, pp. 173-91.

[196] Castelo, *Christian Mystical Tradition*, pp. 180-81.

[197] Tomlinson, 'Supernatural Occurrences', p. 1.

[198] Stephen J. Casmier and Donale H. Matthews, 'Why Scatting is like Speaking in Tongues: Post-Modern Reflections On Jazz, Pentecostalism and "Africomysticism"', *Literature & Theology* 13.2 (Jun 1999), pp. 166-76 (169); cf. McGee, 'The New World of Realities', pp. 119-20.

[199] This is roughly the point Lewis makes with 'transposition', Lewis, 'Transposition', pp. 91-115; cf. Williams, *Renewal Theology, Vol. Two*, p. 227.

[200] Land, *Pentecostal Spirituality*, p. 166; Cox, *Fire from Heaven*, pp. 139–157; Hollenweger, *Pentecostalism*, p. 32; Cartledge, *Encountering the Spirit*, p. 61; Alexander, *Signs & Wonders*, pp. 35-39. Casmier and Matthews note that the following jazz pioneers were exposed to Pentecostalism: Louis Armstrong, Edward 'Kid' Ory, John Coltrane, Albert Ayler, and Charles Mingus in Casmier and Matthews, 'Why Scatting is like Speaking in Tongues', pp. 167, 174-75. Paul Alexander

glossolalia breaks out of limiting forms to express the inexpressible and therefore is truly 'creative' rather than merely imitating reality, as with a photograph.[201] Further, there is a spontaneity to jazz, that 'once you write it down, it is no longer jazz; it has to be improvised *on the spot*'.[202] The HA reveals 'an attitude that nothing is inexpressible or unspeakable … [singers] delight in their ability to lend their voice to the holy spirit … at the very moment of utterance'.[203] In this way, jazz helps explain why a new, creative, and spontaneous song occurs in response to God-encounters.[204] The heavenly choir sings more vividly and creatively than a 'fixed liturgy', if liturgy is defined as an inflexible ritual. The HA 'was the quintessential expression of the *free* liturgy of Azusa Street'.[205]

Third, there is an audience. Clearly, God Almighty is the 'Audience of One',[206] for whom the praise is intended. However, the HA is a communal activity and there is an earth-bound audience as well. Seymour wrote, 'no one but those who are baptized with the Holy Ghost are able to join in – or better, the Holy Ghost only

---

notes that Elvis Presley also had Pentecostal roots, Alexander, *Signs & Wonders*, p. 35.

[201] Casmier and Matthews, 'Why Scatting is like Speaking in Tongues', pp. 168-69.

[202] Alexander, *Signs & Wonders*, p. 38 (emphasis original).

[203] Casmier and Matthews, 'Why Scatting is like Speaking in Tongues', p. 175-76. 'Non-mimetic discourse usurps the power of creativity. It escapes the clutches of the known, dips its fingers into the unknown and molds into existence that which has never been before', p. 170.

[204] Twice Casmier and Matthews note a connection between non-mimetic art and spirituality: 'the non-mimetic (non-realistic) brings God closer' and it is 'profoundly spiritual', Casmier and Matthews, 'Why Scatting is like Speaking in Tongues', pp. 168, 172.

[205] Dove, 'Hymnody and Liturgy', pp. 249, 252 (emphasis added). Dove infers that we can trust the Holy Spirit to convey depth of meaning. He highlights that once, when the HA was interpreted, the Holy Spirit revealed both an OT and NT text in a perfect liturgical manner even though there was 'no intentionally directed structure', p. 251; cf. Seymour, 'The Heavenly Anthem', p. 3. Hollenweger calls the HA an 'oral liturgy for which the whole congregation is responsible', Land, *Pentecostal Spirituality*, p. 112. Hollenweger believes that 'when a whole congregation sings in tongues in many harmonies (without following a set piece of music), Pentecostals are building a "cathedral of sounds," a "socio-acoustic sanctuary," which is particularly important for Pentecostals who do not have cathedrals', Hollenweger, 'After Twenty Years', p. 7.

[206] Os Guinness, *The Call: Finding and Fulfilling the Central Purpose of Your Life* (Nashville, TN: Word Publishing, 1998), pp. 73-87.

sings through such in that manner'.²⁰⁷ There is a public exposing of one's private faith, 'a literal crossing of the bridge from the private to the public'. ²⁰⁸ A sociologist or psychologist could view the HA as a 'bridge-burning' or as an 'initiation-rite'.²⁰⁹ The HA breaks out of 'dominant cultural constructs based on race, gender, ethnicity, and age'; anyone could lead the choir if the Spirit moved them.²¹⁰ The noteworthy point of correspondence is not the joining of a choir because one needs something to do on a Thursday night, but the impulse to worship. Internally, something deep within the affections calls for one to join the song of praise. Perhaps, the badly scarred *imago Dei* within humankind longs for its created purpose to be restored.²¹¹ Listeners evaluate at a spiritually-affective level and conclude that God is near.²¹² 'People are melted to tears in hearing this singing. It is the harmony of heaven and the Holy Ghost (that) puts music in the voices that are untrained'.²¹³ Significantly, these spiritual affections 'exist in a *reciprocally conditioning mode* with the beliefs and practices'.²¹⁴ Belief *and practice* naturally reinforce each other. Therefore, because the HA was widely accepted, because it created a spiritual hunger, and because it was often someone's first glossolalic experience, it is essential that Pentecostal leaders open up space for singing in the

---

²⁰⁷ 'The Heavenly Anthem', p. 3.
²⁰⁸ Augustine, *Pentecost, Hospitality, and Transfiguration*, p. 25.
²⁰⁹ McDonnell believes this bridge-burning cements an individual's commitment to the group's 'goals, ideology and organization', McDonnell, 'Function of Tongues', p. 338, cf. pp. 337-39; cf. Sullivan, *Charisms and Charismatic Renewal*, p. 142. Williams believes it does three things: 1) 'strengthen a believer's confidence in the authority of the group', 2) reorients an 'individual's image of himself', and 3) 'commits him to certain changes in attitudinal or behavioral patterns', Williams, *Tongues of the Spirit*, pp. 159, 164.
²¹⁰ Alexander, 'Heavenly Choirs', pp. 264-67.
²¹¹ Charette, 'Glossolalia and the Image of God', pp. 189-201.
²¹² Chan observes that 'among second-generation Pentecostals Spirit-baptism is received first as a doctrine before it is actualized in personal experience', Chan, *Pentecostal Theology*, p. 10.
²¹³ 'The Heavenly Anthem', p. 3; cf. Williams, *Renewal Theology, Vol. Two*, p. 400 n. 246.
²¹⁴ Land, *Pentecostal Spirituality*, p. 56 (emphasis added). 'It is the belief *and practice* which shapes and evokes the affections, and is essential to discernment and every other gift', p. 164. 'Worship must precede service' wrote Myland in Alexander, 'Boundless Love Divine', p. 157; cf. p. 163.

Spirit so that another generation can be exposed and experience a new level of worship.[215]

B. Good Gifts – The Gift of Tongues

The gift of tongues in 1 Corinthians 12-14 is itself a biblical metaphor that needed no further symbolization for the early Pentecostals.[216] The reception of the Holy Spirit at SB is the 'promise of the Father',[217] and subsequent glossolalia is a 'good gift'.[218] The high level of correspondence between the metaphor of a gift and the gift of tongues highlights three facets of public tongues. First, the image reveals a loving father who desires to help his Church by 'restoring all the gifts to His church'.[219] Contrary to this is the cessationists position, which implies a father taking back his gift:

> the gifts *cannot have ceased or been entirely withdrawn*, although they have been suspended and temporarily withdrawn as a mark of displeasure for the apostasizing of the church from her first love ... *these gifts are perpetually there*, for they are inseparable from the presence of the Holy Spirit.[220]

In other words, the gift is an irrevocable gift. Second, it is not decorative but is practical. It 'builds up'[221] the whole church through a prophetic voice:

> we have before us not praise, not prayer and unanimous worship by the whole church at once, but a case where two or three are anointed by the Holy Ghost to speak messages for the Lord

---

[215] Opening up space for the humble and spontaneous HA is not easy today. Up-to-date music requires playing by the rules of popular culture, which presently depends heavily on electronics. Also, Pentecostal churches have grown and now require amplification and have multiple services. These put pressure on the length of services. Yet, the very point of singing in Spirit is that it breaks out of the rules that culture creates, even Pentecostal cultures.

[216] 1 Corinthians 12.10, 28; 14.2, 5, 13.

[217] Luke 24.49; Acts 1.4; 2.33.

[218] Luke 11.13; cf. Mt. 7.11.

[219] *AF* 1.2 (Oct 1906), p. 4; Rickard, 'Days of Revelation', p. 3.

[220] Kahrs, 'The Nine Gifts', p. 4; Tomlinson, 'The Opposition Weakening', p. 1; Webb, 'Spiritual Gifts', p. 7; Bushnell, 'Reflected Light', p. 243; Divine, 'Spiritual Manifestations and the Churches', p. 5; Durham, 'Manifestations Number II', pp. 7-8; Editor, 'Editorials: Tongues Cease', p. 2; Bell, 'Questions and Answers #11', p. 8; Ewart, 'The Last Great Crisis', p. 2.

[221] 1 Corinthians 12.7; 14.12; cf. Montgomery, 'Edifying The Body of Christ', p. 121; Wigglesworth, 'Spiritual Gifts', pp. 249-50.

to the church and one, the interpreter, is to interpret the message spoken in tongues so the church and congregation can understand.[222]

It also can edify through vertical communication, such as gratitude, intercession, or worship.[223] In this sense, the gift's utility is emphasized over one's possession of the gift.[224] As a supernatural gift[225] it is used only as the 'Spirit wills'.[226] Third, it is for everyone.[227]

The Pentecostal periodicals elaborated about the gift of tongues. First, the initial euphoria over the restoration of glossolalia, along with a lack of understanding, resulted in the phrase 'gift of tongues' having multiple meanings.[228] Because there was no prior example to follow in the actual practice of public tongues, they were largely pioneering what is now standard Pentecostal praxis from their reading of Scripture and experience.[229] Second, these pioneers quickly discerned that the gift of tongues was distinct from the glossolalia of IE:

> the baptism with the Holy Spirit, with the speaking in tongues, is for all (Acts 2:39). But the gift of tongues is for those only to whom God give it, just as the other gifts are, with this distinction that the gift of tongues only follows and never precedes Pentecost'.[230]

---

[222] Bell, 'Question and Answers #80', p. 8.
[223] Taylor, 'Editorial: 1 Corinthians 14', p. 9; Taylor, 'Question Box #458', p. 10.
[224] 'Field Notes', p. 7.
[225] Cashwell, 'Speaking in Other Tongues', p. 2; Taylor 'Question Box #41', p. 15.
[226] Cress, 'Abilene, Kan.', p. 6.
[227] Seymour, 'Gifts of the Spirit', p. 2; J.T.B. 'Do All Speak with Tongues', p. 4; Gaston, 'The Baptism According to Acts 2:4', p. 3.
[228] Gift of tongues could refer to: 1) the tongues of IE, 'The Promised Latter Rain Now Being Poured out on God's Humble People', p. 1; 2) missionary tongues, or 3) the Holy Spirit, *AF* 1.1 (Sep 1906), p. 1; or 4), Paul's gift in 1 Corinthians 12-14, 'Came From Alaska', p. 2.
[229] Seymour, 'Gifts of the Spirit', p. 2.
[230] Carothers, 'The Speaking in Tongues', p. 20; cf. Cashwell, 'Speaking in Other Tongues', p. 2; Barrett, *Works*, p. 21; Tomlinson, 'The Gift of Tongues', p. 1; Taylor, 'Question Box #32', p. 15. Goff notes that Parham did not waver from missionary tongues but did add the gift of interpretation, Goff, *Fields White unto Harvest*, p. 78.

Third, Paul offered specific guidance for the use[231] and evaluation[232] of public tongues in 1 Corinthians 12-14, and his view was complementary with Luke's glossolalia.[233] As early as 1907, these pioneers discerned that reading Luke solely through a Pauline lens would lessen the richness of what they had experienced.[234] Their theology of glossolalia was at stake. Fourth, SB was the doorway to all the spiritual gifts.[235] Finally, the early Pentecostals also elaborated on 1) the uniqueness of tongues,[236] 2) the gift of interpretation,[237] and 3) tongues as the least important gift.[238]

Though this investigation is broader than just the gift of tongues and because it is a significant field of study in itself,[239] the following theological observations are offered as a starting point for further investigation. When there is a high degree of 'correspondence' between a metaphor and what it symbolizes, it is likely that the image will become a 'stock or faded metaphor'.[240] It is like an adult who knows the contents of all the gifts under the Christmas tree and then loses the childlike wonder of Christmas. Perhaps this has happened with Pentecostal's public 'gifts of tongues'. There are a couple of related issues: first, does the gift have any value in today's worship service? Many

---

[231] 'The True Pentecost', p. 2; Cashwell, 'Speaking in Other Tongues', p. 2; Taylor, 'Question Box #732', p. 10; Kerr, 'Paul's Interpretation of the Baptism', p. 6; Polman, 'As The Spirit Gave Them Utterance', pp. 5-6.

[232] Pinson, 'Prove All Things', p. 2.

[233] Cashwell, 'Speaking in Other Tongues', p. 2; Stark, 'Paul's Doctrine', p. 3.

[234] Cashwell, 'Speaking in Other Tongues', p. 2.

[235] Taylor, 'Editorial: 1 Corinthians 14', p. 8; Webb, 'Baptized Into One Body', p. 2; Bell, 'Questions and Answers #723', p. 5; 'Mistaken Message in Tongues', p. 4.

[236] 'Tongues as a Sign', p. 2; Jacobs, 'The Spirit Before Pentecost', pp. 213-14.

[237] Sexton, 'Editorials – Interpretation of Tongues', p. 1; Tomlinson, 'Hold Steady Now', p. 1.

[238] Tomlinson 'Covet The Best Gifts', p. 1.

[239] E.g. Nils Ivar Johan Engelsen, 'Glossolalia and Other Forms of Inspired Speech According to 1 Corinthians 12-14' (PhD Dissertation, Yale University, 1970); Harold Horton, *The Gifts of the Spirit* (Springfield, MO: Gospel Publishing House, 1975); Yongnan Jeon Ahn, *Interpretation of Tongues and Prophecy in 1 Corinthians 12-14* (JPTSup 41; Blandford Forum: Deo Publishing, 2013).

[240] Caird, *The Language and Imagery of the Bible*, p. 155. In the same way, a low degree of correspondence adds freshness and shock.

Pentecostals see the gift of tongues today as embarrassing or as a hindrance to the gospel, because it is 'noisy, unintelligible, and has pagan counterparts'.[241] It runs counter to popular 'missional' or attractional approaches to ministry. Second, there has been a reaction to excessive public tongues,[242] going so far as to say there is 'little Pauline evidence for the traditional Pentecostal phrase "a message in tongues"'.[243] However, Paul's mention of a 'gift of interpretation' seems to refute this position.[244] Finally, there are some Pentecostals who believe that all public glossolalia should be vertical, directed to God as praise, intercession, or mysterious speech.[245] This interpretation 'misses the larger context'[246] and then elevates it to an ironclad hermeneutic for all glossolalia beyond what Luke,[247]

---

[241] R. Menzies, *This is Our Story*, p. 95.

[242] 'I have often (wrongly) heard both clergy and laity bemoan the absence of such "messages" in the assembly ... as an absence of a lack of spiritual vigor in the church', Fee, 'Toward a Pauline Theology of Glossolalia', p. 24 n. 3. Cf. William Graham MacDonald, 'Biblical Glossolalia: Thesis Seven', *Paraclete* 28.2 (Spring 1994), pp. 1-12 (7-8).

[243] Fee, 'Toward a Pauline Theology of Glossolalia', p. 33; cf. Fee, *First Corinthians*, p. 656; Fee, *God's Empowering Presence*, p. 218.

[244] Williams, *Renewal Theology, Vol. Two*, pp. 404-406; Menzies, *Speaking in Tongues*, pp. 125-51.

[245] 1 Corinthians 14.2. First proposed by Walker, *The Gift of Tongues*, pp. 30-31, 36; cf. Fee, 'Toward a Pauline Theology of Glossolalia', p. 33; Fee, *First Corinthians*, p. 656; Fee, *God's Empowering Presence*, p. 218. There are two proponents: 1) MacDonald, who limits all glossolalia, both personal and public to vertical communication in 'praise or petition, thanksgiving or intercession', MacDonald, 'Thesis Seven', p. 1. 2) Even though Fee notes that Paul's answer is intended to be corrective, not instructional or informative', he holds to this position, Fee, *God's Empowering Presence*, p. 148. Which makes Fee's statement confusing: 'Paul will *not forbid* interpreted glossolalia in the assembly ... (as) evident by his explicit preference for prophecy ... (and) by the clear implication in 1 Cor. 14.18-19 ... and v. 28', Fee, 'Toward a Pauline Theology of Glossolalia', p. 34 (emphasis added). Further, the existence of a 'gift of interpretation' seems to imply horizontal speech similar to prophecy and not just interpretation of vertical praise or intercession. Fee's mere three sentence description of 'interpretation of tongues' seems rather thin, Fee, *First Corinthians*, pp. 598-99; Fee, *God's Empowering Presence*, p. 173.

[246] Menzies, *Speaking in Tongues*, p. 149; cf. pp. 148-50. That is, it 'serves to highlight their unintelligibility (only God understands them) rather than define the specific nature of their content'.

[247] See Acts 2.4-13 and 19.6. 'Luke's account of Acts 2 highlights the missiological significance of the Pentecostal gift ... the result of this divine enabling

John,[248] and even Paul reveal.[249]

The suburbanization/homogenization of Pentecostalism through Evangelical theology and missional methods lessens the heart and soul of what it means to be Pentecostal.[250] The voice of the people is muted. Hollenweger's call for Pentecostals to return to their black-oral-inclusive root as the very key to Pentecostalism should be heeded.[251] Yes, the public gift of tongues can be messy, embarrassing, and at times abused; however, it 'liberate(s) the people of God and free(s) them from dehumanizing cultural, economic and social forces', even from a tightly-controlled, platform-driven liturgy.[252] The gift of tongues closely resembles the inclusive voices of Pentecost with imperfect sentences and a 'broken speech for a broken world' declaring the wonders of God until perfection comes.[253] Such speech is not intended to inform linguistically but spiritually and mystically to 'transform' and 'inspire celebration'.[254] Finally, when yielded to the Holy Spirit, not only can the most common of persons become a boundary-breaking prophetic voice,[255] he or she can become visionary and call 'things that are not as though they were'.[256] Therefore, the existence of an irrevocable gift from God for all of God's people calls for reflection and useful incorporation, rather than neglect or prohibition.

---

should not be understood simply as praise directed to God. It is above all, proclamation', Menzies, *Speaking in Tongues*, p. 149; cf. pp. 149-50.

[248] See Jn 16.13.

[249] Paul used a vertical ecstatic experience ('inexpressible things' [2 Cor. 12.4]) during his vision as a means to convey truth in a horizontal fashion, cf. Dunn, *Jesus and the Spirit*, p. 215. 'Col. 3.16 … refers to singing in tongues, the singing of "spiritual songs" is pictured as one way that the Colossians might "*teach and admonish* one another"', Menzies, *Speaking in Tongues*, p. 150 (emphasis added).

[250] Menzies, 'Evidential Tongues: An Essay on Theological Method'.

[251] Hollenweger, *Pentecostalism*, p. 18, cf. Hollenweger, 'After Twenty Years', p. 6.

[252] Hollenweger, 'Pentecostals and the Charismatic Movement', p. 553.

[253] Tarr, *The Foolishness of God*, p. 381

[254] Hollenweger, 'Significance of Oral Christianity', p. 262. Cf. James Gorden King, 'The Pentecostal View of the Gift of Tongues' (MA Thesis, Wheaton College, Wheaton, IL, 1974), p. 122.

[255] Menzies, *Speaking in Tongues*, pp. 146-51.

[256] Romans 4.14; cf. Yong, 'Tongues of Fire', pp. 64-65.

IV. Personal Metaphors

The early Pentecostals were quite taken with public glossolalia and some argued that public tongues overshadowed personal uses.[257] Yet personal or devotional glossolalia was greatly appreciated. Most were delighted by the discovery that they could speak in tongues 'at will'.[258] Today, personal glossolalia is emphasized over public glossolalia by many[259] and draws little criticism other than from the most extreme quarters.[260] The early Pentecostal periodicals offer a rich supply of metaphors for personal glossolalia and is worth exploring. There are four word-pictures for personal tongues that somehow edify or build up[261] the believer and advance God's purposes in the world.[262]

---

[257] An overemphasis on IE detracted 'from the broader significance of glossolalic prayer', Baker, 'Pentecostal Experience', p. 182. 'Tongues-speech as a missio-linguistic tool drove the notoriety of the new movement, the concomitant role of prayer and worship was obscured', McGee, 'The New World of Realities', pp. 113-14.

[258] E.g. Boddy, 'Personal Testimonies', p. 8; McA., 'Difference Between (*TGR* & *TBM*)', p. 4.

[259] Cox, *Fire From Heaven*, p. 87; Hayford, *Beauty*; Cartledge, 'Future of Glossolalia', p. 239.

[260] John MacArthur, *Strange Fire: The Danger of Offending the Holy Spirit with Counterfeit Worship* (Nashville, TN: Thomas Nelson, 2013).

[261] 1 Corinthians 14.4. Theories of just how tongues build up the believer include: 1) a reintegration of a fractured psyche, Kelsey, *Speaking in Tongues*, p. 199. 2) It 'permit(s) the analytical mind to rest ... thus freeing other dimensions of the person ... (to) a deeper reality', Richard A. Baer, 'Quaker Silence, Catholic Liturgy, and Pentecostal Glossolalia – Some Functional Similarities', in Russell P. Spitter (ed.), *Perspectives on the New Pentecostalism* (Grand Rapids, MI: Eerdmans, 1976), pp. 150-64 (152). 3) Edification is drawn from the belief system, Williams, *Tongues of the Spirit*, pp. 152-53, 230. 4) It 'results in added faith', Gordon L. Anderson, 'Baptism in the Holy Spirit, Initial Evidence, and a New Model', *Enrichment Journal* 10.1 (Winter, 2005), pp. 70-78 (76). 5) There is a restoration of the *imago Dei*, Charette, 'Glossolalia and the Image of God', p. 200. 6) Through the continual process of searching, encountering, transforming, Cartledge, *Encountering the Spirit*, pp. 25-32.

[262] The heretofore unaddressed works on psychology and glossolalia, perhaps might be helpful in explaining how tongues-speech builds up the glossolalist. Cf. Kelsey, *Tongue Speaking*; Arnold Bittlinger, *Gift and Graces: A Commentary of 1 Corinthians 12-14* (Grand Rapids, MI: Eerdmans, 1967), pp. 100-103; Samarin, *Tongues of Men and Angels*; Lewis J. Willis, 'Glossolalia in Perspective', in Wade H. Horton (ed.) *The Glossolalia Phenomenon* (Cleveland, TN: Pathway Press, 1986), pp. 247-84; Williams, *Tongues of the Spirit*; Hutch, 'The Personal Ritual of Glossolalia', pp. 381-95.

A. Secret Prayer – Praying in Tongues

Praying in tongues is thought by many to be 'the foremost reason for tongues',[263] and is rooted in the biblical metaphor of 'groaning'[264] or praying in a 'prayer closet'.[265] The early Pentecostals metaphor of 'secret prayer' implies several points of correspondence with glossolalic prayer.[266] First, the secret aspect implies intimate and coded communication between the Holy Spirit and God through a human intercessor.[267] Human participation with the divine is synergistically needed and welcomed.[268] It is 'God in the earth pleading with God in the heavens on behalf of God and man'.[269] It is prayer 'according to the will of God'.[270] It is 'prayer as you never experienced it before';[271] it is 'inarticulate (ness) on the very verge of eloquence'.[272] It is prayer unvarnished by human agenda. Simply stated, it is 'superlative intercession'.[273] It was even speculated that glossolalia was God's design to 'baffle the Devil'.[274]

Second, through glossolalic prayer, one admits their weakness and reliance on God's strength. Imagine a child who, because of fear, suddenly cries out for their parent's rescue: 'fluency in speaking (is not) essential to prayer. When words fail and we can only groan out our hearts to God, perhaps our prayer is most big with meaning and will prove most efficacious.'[275] It occurs when 'the intensity of the prayer (is) so great that it is impossible to express it with the understanding, and then is when [sic] the Spirit prays.

---

[263] Taylor, 'Question Box #595', p. 10. Cf. Suenens, 'Malines Document 1', p. 30; Baker, 'Pentecostal Experience', pp. ii; cf. pp. 208-33.

[264] Romans 8.26; 1 Cor. 14.14.

[265] Matthew 6.6; 'Praying For The Holy Ghost', *AF* 1.2 (Oct 1906), p. 3; Mrs. Anna Hall, 'The Polishing Process', *AF* 1.2 (Oct 1906), p. 3; 'Questions Answered (*AF*)', p. 2; T.W. Weaver, 'My Experience', *TBM* 1.14 (May 15, 1908), p. 3.

[266] Murrah, 'Macon, GA., April 27, 1908', p. 4; cf. 'Arrested for Jesus' Sake', p. 3; 'Prayer', p. 3; Flower, 'Prayer', p. 12.

[267] Doering, 'A Missionary's Testimony', p. 126; Copley, 'The Prayer of the Righteous', p. 2.

[268] Mills, 'Counterculture', p. 950.

[269] Copley, 'The Prayer of the Righteous', p. 2.

[270] Hesson, 'Seeking The Baptism', p. 5.

[271] Hesson, 'Seeking The Baptism', p. 5.

[272] Harold Horton in Brumback, *What Meaneth This?*, p. 293.

[273] Copley, 'Pentecost in Type', p. 7.

[274] Reid, 'Concerning The Tongues', p. 3; cf. 'Unlocked Prayer', p. 3.

[275] Flower, 'Rightly Dividing The Word of Truth', p. 10.

(Rom. 8:26).'[276] Overall, 'the purpose of this form of prayer is not to inform, but to participate in the divine nature', through *kenosis* and *theosis*.[277] Third, such prayer reaches beyond known boundaries and is new 'world-view-making';[278] it is Spirit-directed imagination. An established world-view would be like a daughter knowing that her earthly father is not in a position to lend her a $1,000. She does not even need to ask. But a child playing make-believe can imagine a spaceship in a faraway galaxy or a ball at a grand palace. In the same way, the Holy Spirit in glossolalic prayer sparks this daughter to dream beyond her perceived boundaries, to 'call into being that which does not exist':[279] 'glossolalic (prayer) is ... the human prototype of the divine word ... disclosure of the Spirit who speaks and empowers'.[280] Such creating and imaginary prayer originates with the Holy Spirit; it is selfless and missional. At times it is pleading for lost humanity and was called 'soul travail' by the Pentecostal pioneers.[281] It is prayer that 'looks outward and ministry to the church and world ... (and is) a catalyst or trigger which opens the soul up to new dimensions of life in Christ'.[282] It is God in heaven using his church on earth to 'vanquish all the forces of hell and possess the land';[283] 'you are conscious of having a force within you'.[284]

B. Satisfied Praise – Worship

'A new medium' of worship is another personal function of glossolalia.[285] A metaphor that described this aspect is 'satisfied' praise: 'praise and worship swelled up within and sought expression, but

---

[276] Taylor, 'Editorial: 1 Corinthians 14', p. 9.
[277] Baker, 'Pentecostal Experience', pp. 279-80. The 'practice of glossolalic prayer may be understood as emptying out of the self before God (kenosis) so that one might become full of the Holy Spirit and thereby participate in Christ's nature (theosis)', p. 253.
[278] Yong, 'Tongues of Fire', p. 45.
[279] Romans 4.17 NASB.
[280] Yong, 'Tongues of Fire', p. 54.
[281] Wilkes, 'Healed And Baptized In The Spirit', pp. 6-7; Tomlinson, 'Soul Travail', p. 1. Urshan, 'The Baptism of the Holy Ghost', p. 6; Editor, 'Pentecostal Outpouring And Beulah', p. 195.
[282] Suenens, 'Malines Document', pp. 25, 30.
[283] Gaston, 'Onward, Yet Tested', p. 6.
[284] 'The Imperative Mood', p. 70.
[285] Acts 2.11; 10.46. Montgomery, 'A Year With The Comforter', p. 147.

words cannot be found which satisfied until the Holy Spirit Himself gave utterance through other tongues'.[286] The word picture has two perspectives: on the one hand, like a meal that does not nourish, human categories of thought and speech are insufficient for worship and, only through glossolalic praise is there 'sweetness',[287] or an 'adequacy'.[288] On the other hand,

> as the soul of a loving mother grows hungry and longs to hear an expression of love from the thoughtless child who is ever receiving but never giving ... so our Father in Heaven loves to have wafted to Him ... a real note of praise and thanksgiving ... from lips of clay praises that are wholly acceptable.[289]

Second, glossolalic praise is not just a consequence of God's presence. Sacramentally, it is something that facilitates entrance into God's presence,[290] comparable to the singers and trumpeters at the dedication of Solomon's Temple who ushered in God's presence and then worshiped.[291] Third, the glossolalic perceives when they are worshipping and when they are praying.[292] Many early Pentecostals saw this as one of the purposes for glossolalia.[293]

C. Mysteries – Revelation

The early Pentecostals did not consider their glossolalia as monologues to God.[294] Rather, the Holy Spirit could teach, reveal, and

---

[286] Dempster, 'That I May Know Him', p. 31. My praise was 'beyond all expression, *finding vent* only in another "tongue"', Boddy, 'Reports from England', p. 1 (emphasis added).

[287] A.E.L., 'Physical Manifestations of the Spirit', pp. 2-3.

[288] S.H.F., 'Our Distinctive Testimony', p. 8. 'An increased spirit of praise ... in the new tongues', Montgomery, 'A Year With The Comforter', p. 146.

[289] Atterberry, 'They Shall Speak with New Tongues', p. 3.

[290] Powers, 'A Wonderful Experience', p. 8; Chan, *Pentecostal Theology*, pp. 77-81.

[291] 2 Chronicles 5.13; 'Type of Pentecost. II Chron. 5', p. 3.

[292] Sisson, 'Much Incense', p. 6.

[293] Carothers, 'The Speaking in Tongues', pp. 21, 24; Barratt, *Works*, pp. 6, 45, 82, 149; Myland, 'The Latter Rain', p. 148.

[294] Contra MacDonald, William Graham MacDonald, 'Biblical Glossolalia: Thesis Four', *Paraclete* 27.3 (Summer 1993), pp. 32-43 (32); cf. MacDonald, 'Thesis Seven', pp. 1, 3, 6.

even grant visions during the mysterious conversation.[295] Mystery was a common metaphor for personal tongues: 'these are the mysteries the Holy Spirit speaks to us in tongues'.[296] At times, the content was 'things that we need to know',[297] such as 'a deeper sense of the realness of God, of the life of the Word, of the love of the Spirit and the supremacy of Christ',[298] a greater understanding of the Bible,[299] or 'love, mercy, and power'.[300] However, comprehensible content was not essential to the revelation, even though 'the secrets have taken on sound … the sense is concealed'.[301] Apophatically, what is revealed is untranslatable into mortal categories of thought or language.[302] Glossolalia is 'a symbol to the world of the possibility and fact of a divine access to the soul, and a divine operation in it',[303] meaning that the 'realities of Christianity are sometimes better simply beheld, simply encountered … (because) words sometimes damage the mystery':[304] 'I beheld His majesty and beauty',[305] or 'I was alone with Christ in spirit. I spoke

---

[295] John 14.26. God's people were the recipients of God's mysteries, 1 Cor. 4.1 (cf. Eph. 1.9; 3.3; Col. 1.6); 2 Cor. 12.1; prophecy in Acts 19.6. Tomlinson compared it one time to the Urim and Thummim, Tomlinson, 'More About the Gifts', pp. 2, 3.

[296] 'Bengali Lady's Pentecost', *TBM* 3.56 (Feb 15, 1910), p. 3. E.g. 'the Pentecostal outpouring of the Spirit, in these days of the Latter Rain is revealing the mysteries of the real Kingdom of God as never before', J.E. Sawders, 'The Mystery of the Kingdom', *TBM* 5.107 (Apr 1, 1912), p. 4.

[297] Anderson, 'Baptized with the Holy Ghost', p. 3.

[298] Myland, 'A Personal Word', p. 2.

[299] Chi, 'Testimony of Mok Lai Chi', p. 4.

[300] Evans, 'Report', p. 3. McDonnell limits such knowledge to 'memory retrieval … in which is brought forth that which is antecedent, which had already been bestowed', McDonnell, 'Function of Tongues', p. 344. MacDonald is most comfortable with revelations of Christ, MacDonald, 'Theses One and Two', p. 6.

[301] Rev. John S. Mercer, 'Speaking In An Unknown Tongue', *WE* 136 (Apr 22, 1916), p. 6. 'When an individual speaks in tongues, he and God alone are communing. They deal in secrets (mysteries) … its beauty stems from the intimacy of the love talk in the glory of God in transcending man's intellectually limited inventory of languages as a communicator', MacDonald 'The Place of Glossolalia in Neo-Pentecostalism', p. 225; Macchia, 'Towards a Theology of Initial Evidence', p. 163.

[302] Rybarczyk, 'Reframing Tongues', p. 88; Tarr, *The Foolishness of God*, pp. 102-21; Castelo, *Christian Mystical Tradition*, p. 129; cf. pp. 22-23, 173.

[303] Bushnell, 'Supernatural Manifestations', p. 37.

[304] Rybarczyk, 'Reframing Tongues', p. 103.

[305] Freeman, 'Lithia, Fla.', p. 6.

in other tongues as the Spirit gave utterance'.[306] A restoration of the *imago Dei* through glossolalia is possible.[307]

D. The Jordon River – Power

There is a built-in correspondence between the Spirit that descended upon Jesus at his baptism and the equipping power of Pentecostal SB, hence Spirit 'baptism'. All believers should 'receive the baptism that Christ received on the banks of Jordan. He had the fullness of the Godhead, but He had to be baptized for His great work. Jesus was anointed with the Holy Ghost and power and went about doing good.'[308] Further, just as the Father spoke from heaven,[309] so now the Holy Spirit speaks through fully empowered believers about Jesus.[310] Devotional glossolalia provides no power, per se, but is symbolic of God's equipping power,[311] of God's 'empire' within.[312] As the entryway into power, if one was not fully immersed in the Holy Spirit, there was a lack of power: the participants of the Keswick meeting 'returned to their respective spheres *without having received the gift of tongues, or the power to work miracles*, or the gift of prophecy, or the gift of healing, or *the power to cast out devils*'.[313] Spirit baptism is a power for all the spiritual gifts;[314] it is 'power to meet the triune evil, the world, the flesh and the devil, as well as power for service'.[315] Significantly, glossolalia facilitates an anointing for spiritual speech, whether it be

---

[306] Barnett, 'Unicoi, Tenn.', p. 4.

[307] Charette, 'Glossolalia and the Image of God', p. 200.

[308] 'Pentecostal Notes', p. 3; cf. Noble, 'Sunday School Lesson: Baptism and Temptation of Jesus', p. 4; 'In The House of God', p. 7.

[309] Cf. Mt. 3.16-4.1; Mk 1.11-12; Lk. 3.22, 4.1-2; Jn 1.32-34.

[310] Menzies, *This is Our Story*, pp. 29-39.

[311] 'I praise Him for the power in the sign He gave me of speaking in tongues', Jeffries, 'Another Witness', p. 1; cf. Foster, 'Modern Pentecostal Missionary Work', p. 14; Slay, 'Glossolalia: Its Value to the Individual', p. 222.

[312] Seymour, 'The Baptism of the Holy Ghost (2)', p. 3.

[313] Barratt noted of a 1905 a Keswick meeting, Barratt, *Works*, p. 209.

[314] 'Pentecost With Signs Following', p. 1; Street, 'What is Pentecost', p. 6.

[315] Sexton, 'Editorial, Entering The Fifth Year of Service', p. 1; cf. Ingham, 'Glorious Convention at Pretoria, South Africa', p. 9. It is power for 'every emergency', Wigglesworth, 'Spiritual Gifts', pp. 249-50. 'Is it possible that speaking in tongues is a sign of God's radical invasion of countless lives in preparation for the final outreach of the gospel ... to war against the powers of the darkness that increasingly are pressing upon us', Williams, *Renewal Theology, Vol. Two*, p. 235.

preaching, testimony, prophecy, or encouragement.[316] In this sense, glossolalia is intimately connected to 'the missionary spirit'.[317] 'We have the promise of the same power today' that the disciples received on the Day of Pentecost.[318] Conversely, that power is unlocked through humility and obedience; it is 'power in weakness'.[319]

> He does not give us power. We are still as weak as ever. He has the power, and it is He that continues to exercise it, but He gives us 'authority' to claim the exercise of His power, and as we do this in our helplessness, His strength is made perfect in our weaknesses. We have the faith and He has the power.[320]

Just as one puts on clothes each day, the believer is to be clothed with the Spirit each day.[321] Power as a theological category[322] moves beyond an introspective, and at times, selfish focus on whether I am a child of God or not, and focuses in on an actual life in the Spirit, one's missional purpose.[323] Tongues serves as a sign and somehow facilitates God's empowerment for living an obedient and yielded Spirit-filled life.[324]

---

[316] Epps, 'Another Witness', p. 3; Hesson, 'Seeking The Baptism', p. 5.

[317] Flower, 'Editorial', p. 4. Cf. Macchia, 'Sighs Too Deep for Words', p. 68; Cox, *Fire From Heaven*, p. 316; Keener, 'Why Does Luke', p. 178; Menzies, 'Evidential Tongues', p. 230.

[318] 'The Promise Still Good', p. 3.

[319] Durham, 'A Chicago Evangelist's Pentecost', p. 4.

[320] 'Christ Has The Power', p. 1.

[321] Luke 24.49; Acts 1.8.

[322] Largely found in Luke's writings; cf. Mills, *Understanding*, p. 70; Hovenden, *Speaking in Tongues*, pp. 89-93; Keener, 'Why Does Luke', p. 180.

[323] Land, *Pentecostal Spirituality*, p. 111; Macchia, 'Tongues as a Sign', p. 70; Alexander, 'Boundless Love Divine', p. 156. Chan's criticism, that power is only a result of SB and not its theological essence, is only a problem because he places SB into a CI category and thus arrives at a 'normal' but not the 'norm' dead-end, Chan, 'Evidential Glossolalia and the Doctrine of Subsequence', p. 197; cf. pp. 202, 208, 210. In other words, there is no borderless category that resembles an actual life lived in the Spirit; cf. Menzies, 'Evidential Tongues', p. 228.

[324] Abrams, *Holy Ghost & Fire*, p. 38. Barratt links SB with power, but also connects it with the entire being, talents, being 'energized in His service', implying a greater sanctification as well, Barratt, *Works*, pp. 39, 44, 196, 198.

V. Two Final Metaphors

Two final metaphors from the early Pentecostals address the nature of tongues and Oneness' unique salvific-glossolalia.

A. MENE, MENE, TEKEL, PARSIN – The Nature of Glossolalia

'Mysterious' is the best way to describe the nature of tongues. A fitting metaphor for this mysterious nature of glossolalia would be the handwriting on the Babylonian banquet hall, which Daniel understood though revelation.[325] However, among the early Pentecostals, the nature of tongues was fluid. At times it was MT, xenolalia, passive, and/or ecstatic,[326] and a mystery.

According to the earliest periodicals, glossolalia was a real, spoken language given for the purpose of cross-cultural evangelism, that is, MT:[327] 'God is solving the missionary problem, sending out new-tongued missionaries'.[328] Initially called 'the gift of language',[329] it was believed that missionaries could speak in any language using glossolalia.[330] Yieldedness[331] was the key to speaking fluently in any known language because the Holy Spirit spoke 'all the languages of the world'.[332] As early as fall of 1906 and as late as 1909,[333] three things made it clear they were wrong about

---

[325] Daniel 5.25-26; cf. Noble, 'Questions Answered', p. 3.

[326] Barrett is comfortable with the term ecstatic and holds that MT are theoretically possible if the Holy Spirit gets 'perfect control over them' but such a possibility does not 'usurp the ordinary study of languages', Barrett, *Works*, pp. 44, 170-71. There is a cooperation between the human and divine, cf. pp. 90-93.

[327] *TBM* wrestled openly with the issue before stating, that tongues 'do not seem to be an enabling … a continuous use of foreign language without study or practice', The Value of Speaking in Tongues', p. 4. *TOF* morphed from MTs to an 'ecstatic and worshipping voice', Polhill, 'This is That', pp. 101-102. *TP* was at first excited about MTs and then ceased publishing testimonies of MTs in Oct 1909.

[328] *AF* 1.3 (Nov 1906), p. 2.

[329] Only in the first two issues of *AF*: *AF* 1.1 (Sep 1906), p. 1; 'Missionaries To Jerusalem', *AF* 1.1 (Sep 1906), p. 4; 'Notice (*AF*)', p. 4.

[330] *TBM*, Cashwell distinguished between the 'gift of tongues' as 'divers kinds of tongues of many languages', from 'speaking in tongues' or the 'manifestation' of tongues, Cashwell, 'Speaking in Other Tongues', p. 2.

[331] Standley 'Worth Tarrying For', p. 3; 'A Testimony', p. 3.

[332] Seymour, 'The Precious Atonement', p. 2.

[333] McGee, 'Shortcut to Language Preparation', p. 122.

these understandings:[334] 1) Spirit-filled missionaries were reporting that they needed to learn the local language[335] and 2) that they needed local interpreters.[336] Finally, 3) a careful investigation by the respected CMA concluded that tongues 'does not seem to be intended as a means of communication'.[337] Though they were wrong about MT they did not discredit what is now called xenolalia: the anecdotes containing, at times, parts of a known language were too numerous.[338] In later periodicals, xenolalia was reported simply because of its rarity[339] and is still reported today.[340]

A growing understanding of Paul's 'tongues of men *and of angels*' slowly opened up theological room for an ecstatic understanding of glossolalia.[341] For some periodicals, this led them to nuance human passivity with glossolalia:[342] 'there was at least a short period in which there was no consciousness of what was going on ... talking in tongues is not possible for man to do, it is God who talks'.[343] Other periodicals nuanced a synergistic human / divine

---

[334] Sexton, 'Editorials, Raised Us Up Together', p. 1; Pike, 'A Plea For Charity And Forbearance', p. 2; Perry, 'What is the Use of Speaking in Tongues #2', p. 3.

[335] Garr, 'From Distant Lands', p. 1; Garr, 'News from China', p. 1; Editor, 'A Word to Foreign Missionaries', p. 3; Kelly, 'Days of Blessing', p. 4.

[336] Kelly, 'Work in a Chinese Village', p. 1.

[337] 'The Promise of the Father and Speaking with Tongues in Chicago', p. 3; cf. 'Pentecost in England', p. 1.

[338] McGee, 'Shortcut to Language Preparation', p. 122.

[339] Scott, 'What The Pentecost Did For One Family', p. 7; Agar, 'Life More Abundant', p. 28; Carlson, 'Language Recognized', p. 1; 'A Visitation of God In The Great Prisons', p. 11.

[340] Ralph W. Harris, *Spoken by the Spirit: Documented Accounts of 'Other Tongues' From Arabic to Zulu* (Springfield, MO: Gospel Publishing House, 1973).

[341] 1 Corinthians 13.1. 'Paul offers the first evidence of a separation of intelligible and unintelligible speech by his separation of prophecy and speaking in tongues', Engelsen, 'Glossolalia and Other Forms of Inspired Speech', p. ii; cf. p. 95.

[342] Published accounts of MT were somewhat rare in the *COGE* and the *PHA*. *COGE*: Brawner, 'Maitland, Fla (2)', p. 6; Wilcox, 'Mater, Ky.', p. 2. *PHA*: Sawgalsky, 'Testimony and Experience of Lewis Sawgalsky', p. 5; Noble, 'Questions Answered', p. 3; Anderson, 'The Witness Stand', p. 2. For passive accounts in *COGE*: Wood, 'Nassau, N.P., Bahama Islands', p. 6; Pirkle, 'Chickamauga, Ga', p. 7; Bowker, 'Charlotte, Tenn.', p. 3. Though at times it was viewed synergistically, both human and divine, Tomlinson, 'Holy Ghost and Us', p. 1. For passive accounts in *PHA*: Taylor, 'Question Box #1108', p. 10; Taylor, 'Question Box #839', p. 5; Branch, 'The Baptism of the Holy Ghost', p. 4.

[343] Anderson, 'Baptized with the Holy Ghost', p. 3.

role in glossolalia[344] and were comfortable using the term 'ecstatic' in a qualified manner.[345] Though both human and divine cooperated to produce glossolalia, many pioneers looked to mystery as the best way to describe this cooperation. For example,

> the language of which the apostle is here speaking (1Co 14:2) seems to have been of a very peculiar sort – an unintelligible vocal utterance ... in my younger days I have heard such untranslatable sounds under the mighty sermons of grand old Welch [sic] preachers ... (these) *mysteries* are 'things hidden from the hearers, and sometimes from the speaker himself' ... The secrets have taken on sound, but the sense is concealed.[346]

The correspondence between the image of Daniel's MENE, MENE, TEKEL, PARSIN and glossolalia is twofold. First, God's words are now revealed to human recipients. The Holy Spirit now speaks through ordinary human tongues individually and through Christ's world-wide body on earth, the church, collectively: 'they (the apostles) were filled with the glorified Word. This glorified Word began to manifest itself through the vocal organ.'[347] Furthermore, glossolalia is 'ecstatic only in the technical sense of being automatic speech in which the conscious mind played no part, but not ecstatic in the more common sense of "produced or accompanied by exalted states of feeling, rapture, or frenzy"'.[348] Spirit-induced glossolalia[349] is an unclassifiable, free speech in response to an unclassifiable, free God. It is the language of the *imago Dei* ... language as rational communication cannot follow one into the depths of the encounter between *the mystery of God and the mystery*

---

[344] Specifically, the *TOF* and *WW* periodicals: Brinkman, p. 1; Bosworth, 'Power in the Holy Ghost' (*TOF*), pp. 246-47; Berg, 'My Pentecostal Baptism' (*TOF*), pp. 251-53 (pp 252-53); cf. MacDonald, 'Thesis Four', p. 36.

[345] Conybeare and Howson, 'The Gift of Tongues', p. 168; Fraser, 'A Contrast in Values', p. 3. Dunn, *Jesus and the Spirit*, p. 243; Powers, 'Missionary Tongues?', p. 51.

[346] Mercer, 'Speaking in An Unknown Tongue', p. 6 (emphasis added).

[347] Taylor, 'Sunday School Lesson: The Holy Spirit Our Helper', pp. 2, 3; cf. Beall, 'The Holy Spirit Is a Person', p. 2.

[348] Dunn, *Jesus and the Spirit*, p. 243.

[349] The Christian glossolalist believes that the spirit comes upon from without; whereas the mystic 'realizes the beyond *within*', Williams, *Tongues of the Spirit*, p. 197.

of self before God.³⁵⁰ Therefore, the real significance is not that 'God can manipulate' one's tongue, but that 'God can use the whole person for His divine purpose'.³⁵¹

Second, the mysterious content of the message can only be understood through revelation. Daniel was able to give an interpretation only because 'there is a God ... who reveals mysteries'.³⁵² The logic is that 'language can emanate only from an intelligence, and since the language does not exist in the mind of persons thus speaking, it must come from a superior mind'.³⁵³ The argument that Pentecostal glossolalia cannot be proven to be the same as apostolic glossolalia³⁵⁴ cuts both ways – for neither can it be disproved;³⁵⁵ furthermore, there is the testimony of tens of millions who speak of its effect in their life.³⁵⁶ Simply put, this mysterious nature is best understood by those who have experienced it.³⁵⁷ Finally, though it 'resist(s) all categories currently on hand in the philosophy of language',³⁵⁸ 'glossolalia may still communicate

---

³⁵⁰ Macchia, 'Sighs Too Deep for Words', p. 61 (emphasis added). Poloma believes glossolalia begins as a learned behavior, but that one 'moves into a mystical state of prayer where the divine is personally encountered', Poloma, 'Glossolalia, Liminality', p. 155.

³⁵¹ Williams, *Tongues of the Spirit*, p. 164; cf. McDonnell, 'Function of Tongues', p. 346.

³⁵² Daniel 5.16; 2.28.

³⁵³ Piper, 'The Sovereignty of God', p. 4.

³⁵⁴ Willis, 'Glossolalia in Perspective', pp. 253-54.

³⁵⁵ Williams notes that there would be serious exegetical 'inconsistency if all the phenomenon was not the same', Williams, *Renewal Theology, Vol. Two*, pp. 212-13, 215; cf. MacDonald, 'Thesis Four', p. 32.

³⁵⁶ Pentecostalism is 'a revolution comparable to ... the original apostolic church', Ray H., Hughes, 'Glossolalia in Contemporary Times', in Wade H. Horton (ed.), *The Glossolalia Phenomenon* (Cleveland, TN: Pathway Press, 1986), pp. 143-77 (153). 'We must therefore not ignore the interpretation of those who experienced the phenomena', Dunn, *Jesus and the Spirit*, p. 152. Synan, 'The Role of Tongues as Initial Evidence', pp. 67-82.

³⁵⁷ 'Music can only be interpreted by one who has a feeling for music, and as the inarticulate language of tears, or sighs, or groans can be comprehended by a sympathetic soul, so tongues could be interpreted by those whose spiritual state corresponded to that of the gifted person', W. Robertson Nicoll in Hargrave, 'Reformation to the Twentieth Century', p. 119; cf. MacDonald 'The Place of Glossolalia in Neo-Pentecostalism', p. 221; 'Popular Expositions', p. 129. McGee wrote, 'a person that has eaten an apple ... is better qualified to speak on the question of the kind and quality of the apple', McGee, 'Popular Expositions', p. 129.

³⁵⁸ Smith, *Thinking in Tongues*, p. 123.

effectively, despite being ideationally deficient', because the community of faith can infer meaning.[359]

B. A 'Full-Born' Baby's Cry – Oneness Pentecostalism

Perhaps the most affective metaphor of this entire study is located in Oneness Pentecostalism. Sister King witnessed 'half-born' babies in an incubator at the St. Louis fair and she perceived these babies to be stuck and not yet 'fully born'.[360] We are not satisfied, she wrote, that one is a 'full-born spiritual babe' until we hear the tongues.[361] Such a view seems to take Durham's FW theology of justification to its logical conclusion and make SB all about the start of life.[362] Such reasoning is akin to the Evangelical hermeneutic that sees SB only as CI[363] but with the addition of tongues as the finale – a cry of the new birth.[364] However, the very point of correspondence in King's metaphor with its theological

---

[359] David Hilborn, 'Glossolalia as Communication', in Mark J. Cartledge (ed.), *Speaking in Tongues: Multi-Disciplinary Perspectives* (Studies in Pentecostal and Charismatic Issues; Bletchley, Milton Keynes, England: Paternoster Press, 2006), pp. 111–46 (139, 141).

[360] Haywood had another striking metaphor: until the child was circumcised on the eighth day, a Jewish child was born but not fully recognized as being alive, Haywood, 'Baptized Into One Body', p. 3.

[361] King, 'Abnormality', p. 4. The full quote reads:

all over the world are imperfectly born spiritual babes ... If a human baby is born into this world without a cry, is there not an alarm as to its (im)perfect state, and is it not gently shaped and padded until he gives the essential cry, and we say, 'it is born and has life and brain, because it has cried?' So the full-born spiritual babe, babbles its infantile notes else we are not satisfied ... So let us get settled in the fact of what constitutes the being born again of the Spirit, and that the new-born spiritual babes are more quickly born and of faster growth than those of our previous experiences. And, understand, that an imperfectly born spiritual baby is not according to the pattern, and will not be able to stand before the King of Kings and the Lord of Lords, no more surely, than those who neglect the midnight oil though they be perfectly born into the spirit-life.

[362] Ewart, 'False Teaching', p. 4; French, *Our God Is One*, p. 51; Bernard, *A History of Christian Doctrine*, pp. 111-12. We ultimately do not know what Durham thought as 'the Finished Work doctrine remained underdeveloped' at the time of Durham's death, Reed, *'In Jesus' Name'*, p. 106.

[363] Anthony A. Hoekema, *What About Tongue-Speaking?* (Grand Rapids, MI: Eerdman's Publishing Company, 1966), pp. 57-81, 119-20; *Report of the Special Committee on the Work of the Holy Spirit to the 182nd General Assembly*, pp. 43-47; Dunn, *The Baptism in the Holy Spirit*; Bruner, *A Theology of the Holy Spirit*.

[364] 'Fundamental Doctrine', *Articles of Faith of the United Pentecostal Church International*, p. 31.

inference reveals the problem with traditional *ordo salutis* categories. Exactly when is someone born-again? Upon justification (conception?), upon water baptism (out of the birth cannel?), or when they speak in tongues (baby's first cry?)? Indeed, Paul's purpose for using the metaphor 'baptized by one Spirit into one body'[365] is his desire for unity based upon a common salvation, and not to parse out the *ordo salutis*. A parallel metaphor from a Oneness perspective is Jesus' baptism. The early Oneness periodicals consistently interpret Jesus' baptism at the Jordan River as paradigmatic of 'the manner in which we should come to be sons of God'.[366] However, 1) when did Jesus became God's son? After all, the Holy Spirit filled Elizabeth to recognize her 'Lord' while Jesus was still in Mary's womb.[367] 2) Did Jesus' Jordan River experience bring sonship or was it an anointing of the Holy Spirit that launched his ministry?[368] 3) What are we to make of Luke's explicit purpose for the Holy Spirit's coming on the Day of Pentecost?[369] Oneness Pentecostalism has much in common with its Pentecostal family and there appears to be a mixing of two metaphors: new birth and SB. As wonderful as spiritual birth is, there is a delight in the ongoing relationship with God that is signified in SB. Perhaps the metaphors of SB should be re-examined and emphasised for their points of correspondence over against the Modernistic categories of dogmatic theology.[370]

---

[365] 1 Corinthians 12.13.
[366] Haywood, 'The One True God', *MDS* 1.9 (Dec 15, 1915), pp. 3-4 (3); cf. Ewart, 'A Beautiful Type of Redemption', p. 3. Cf. Mt. 3.13-17; Mk 1.9-12; Lk. 3.21-22.
[367] Luke 1.39-45.
[368] Matthew 4.1; Mk 1.12-13; Lk. 4.1.
[369] Acts 1.8.
[370] Stronstad points out that Paul used the metaphor one time and Luke three times, and Paul used a similar image of 'filled with the Spirit' one time compared with Luke's nine occurrences, Stronstad, *The Charismatic Theology of St. Luke*, p. 10; cf. Johns, 'New Directions in the Hermeneutics', p. 147.

7

Conclusion

This investigation makes several contributions to the study of glossolalia. First, it reviews the major works on glossolalia. Though not every piece was able to be included in the survey, those surveyed: 1) chronologically reveal the main issues of glossolalia, 2) provide an understanding of the language and theology for reading the early Pentecostal periodicals, and 3) form a database of ideas for the constructive section. Finally, it shows the need for this study.

Second, this is the most significant reading and compilation of the theology of glossolalia by the early Pentecostals to date. It has carefully listened to the earliest Pentecostal voices (1906 to ca. 1920) about their distinctive doctrine. This reading has revealed that there are no major differences between the WH and the FW branches of Pentecostalism regarding glossolalia. Neither the WH experience of sanctification as a second experience after justification nor the FW understanding of sanctification happening at justification affected their outlook of SB with the accompanying sign of tongues as a unique third or second experience. However, even though Oneness Pentecostalism embraces the experience and terminology of SB, glossolalia is connected to the theological category of justification. One is not fully saved until one speaks in tongues according to the record of these early pioneers. This bundling of Paul's soteriology (1 Cor. 12.13) with Luke's glossolalic sign is unique and is a natural outflow of reading Luke through Paul's lens. Evangelicals might be shocked at the logical conclusion of their CI theory of SB.

Third, and one of the more notable discoveries, is that the best and brightest theological reflections of today echo these pioneers! Every great theological nuance or concept from the numerous books and journal articles that were read for this monograph can be found in these periodicals; at times humbly stated but occasionally equally nuanced as today's best theological understanding. Also, the collective voice of the Pentecostal pioneers is quite remarkable. These men and women guided the theological discussions about glossolalia through three theological controversies: 1) the FW, 2) the new issue (Oneness), and 3) evidential tongues.[1]

Fourth, though evidential glossolalia is thought to be an ironclad universal doctrine, this investigation has revealed three items that should trigger a reexamination of the IE doctrine. First, the terminology itself is quite late. 'Initial evidence' occurs eleven years after the ASM revival and 'initial physical evidence' occurs a year after that. In other words, these phrases are not organic to the 'heart of pentecostal spirituality', but are the offspring of a 'Pentecostal church bureaucracy (that) soon tamed the revival'.[2] This study reveals that it is possible to revision out the Modernistic terminology of 'initial evidence' without losing the essence of the encounter and resulting glossolalia. Initial evidence terminology appears to be too mechanical and scientific for today's post-modern world to describe sufficiently the rich relational dynamic of an encounter with God. Homogenizing a rich and personal encounter with the Holy Spirit into a 'one-size-fits-all' description is ill-fitting today. Second, there was tolerance for theological variety. There was compassionate discussion when someone had a SB-like experience, but glossolalia was delayed. Also, there was allowance for a variety of pre-glossolalic experiences before a full glossolalic SB.[3] Third, statements like the full consummation of SB 'is not the end, but the beginning of a blessed life. There is always more to follow',[4] put the emphasis on life in the Spirit instead of glossolalia as a sign. It also replaces the have / have not categories of IE with

---

[1] Synan, *The Holiness-Pentecostal Tradition*, pp. 143-66.
[2] Hollenweger, 'Pentecostals and the Charismatic Movement', p. 551.
[3] Phrases like 'stammering lips', 'gracious anointings', 'stutterings', 'pre-Pentecostal fulness', 'whispering words', and 'not fully satisfied' were used to describe pre-glossolalic experiences.
[4] Boulos, 'In Defense of the Truth', pp. 10-11.

a continuum of spiritual experiences. As in any relationship, the ongoing life together is more important than its beginning. Further, the process of seeking, emptying, and being filled and refilled should be emphasized. The resulting glossolalia of an encounter will naturally occur, but the ongoing relationship of a life in the Spirit is far more important than its inexpressible start.

Fifth, glossolalia is a symbol of the unclassifiable speech of the mystery of God and the mystery of humankind before God. However, attempts to quantify this mystery dogmatically have reached their end, the theological discussion has become stale. Proponents and doubters have well-worn arguments and counter arguments. It is believed that these pioneers' first expressions help point us towards a more organic Pentecostal construction of glossolalia rather than a dogmatic Evangelicalism with tongues. Using metaphor for theological construction grew naturally out of the soil of these early Pentecostal periodicals themselves. Their attention to biblical metaphors and their subsequent homespun metaphors may help reorient and guide the theological conversation for a new post-modern generation. Perhaps theological metaphors can explain what words cannot.

Sixth, this monograph provides a rare look at the early Oneness materials at a scholarly level. Forgotten issues of *TGR*, *MDS*, and *TBT* were found to be extant and are now online through the *Consortium of Pentecostal Archives* as a result of this research. *TGR* is an especially rich find, as it reveals the development of Oneness thought as it diverged from Trinitarian Pentecostalism, and extended Durham's FW to its logical conclusion. It is hoped that Oneness scholars will pick up the challenge to revision their theology in light of this study, even as Trinitarian Pentecostalism must revision its theology of glossolalia away from Modernistic categories.

Seventh, philosophically, this work envisions glossolalia as a symbol of the liminal overlap between the unseen and seen realities. On the one hand, tongues are so thoroughly common to this earth that infants can babble without cognizance; but on the other hand, it symbolizes a deep mystery: the *imago Dei* within the human heart crying out in glossolalic awareness of its Creator's presence. This is why Pentecostalism is not dismissible through intellectual or exegetical argumentation alone. The experience of tongues is symbolic of a new worldview.⁵ Old boundaries of reality are pushed aside, and a Spirit-inspired imagination opens up a 'new world of realities'.⁶ Further, this worldview then 'suffices as truth until it is demonstrated otherwise'.⁷ In other words, if a worldview does not fit with the real-world lived realities it will be abandoned or replaced. However, the experience of Pentecostals worldwide informs and supports a worldview that is tested daily against the real world and so far has proved to be accurate.⁸

Eighth, though it was not the subject of this investigation, it is clear that 'there are still certain ways of thinking and writing that are … gender-specific'.⁹ In the periodicals women tended to express themselves with 'emotive, descriptive, and visionary language'.¹⁰ In the first issue of *AF*, Jennie Moore's testified that she was a vessel that surged like a torrent, such beautiful and poetic expressions of glossolalia continued throughout the literature, while male testimonies tended to be 'concise and accurate'.¹¹ Also, females seemed to be more likely either to have or express their experiences in mystical or ecstatic terms. For example, Myrtle K. Schideler spoke of being glued to the floor.¹² A reading of the periodicals that specifically examines the language of gender would be a fascinating study. Finally, females were strong theologians and very well represented in these periodicals. Three period-

---

⁵ Pentecostals have 'experienced a coming of the Holy Spirit wherein God's presence and power has pervaded their lives … they know what it means to be "filled with the Holy Spirit." There has been a breakthrough of God's Spirit into their total existence – body, soul, and spirit – reaching into the conscious and subconscious depths, and setting loose powers hitherto unknown', Williams, *The Pentecostal Reality*, p. 2.

⁶ Yong, 'Tongues of Fire', pp. 45-46; cf. Street, 'To Our Readers', p. 50; McGee, 'The New World of Realities', p. 108.

⁷ Yong, 'Tongues of Fire', pp. 64-65.

⁸ Appeals to Pentecostalism's growth seem quaint or braggadocios, until one realizes this is also a guardrail: people will abandon what does not fit with their lived reality and experience; cf. Hughes, 'Contemporary Times', pp. 153-76; Synan, 'The Role of Tongues', p. 79.

⁹ Kimberly Ervin Alexander, 'Girl Talk: A Feminist Re-Imagination of Pentecostal Theological Discourse and Experience', in Jon Huntzinger and David Moore (eds.), *The Pastor and the Kingdom: Essays Honoring Jack W. Hayford* (Southlake, TX: Gateway Academic, 2017), pp. 135-56 (139).

¹⁰ Alexander, 'Girl Talk', p. 145.

¹¹ Alexander, 'Girl Talk', p. 146.

¹² Schideler, 'Received Her Pentecost', p. 3.

icals were edited by women and some of the more significant theological insights were from women: Mrs. Polman's sacramental glossolalia, Hattie Barth's liminal eschatology, Elizabeth Sexton's global vision, Carrie Montgomery's divine love and steadfast refusal to disavow xenolalia, the rich metaphors of Aimee Semple McPherson and Sister King, and many others. We are richer for their writing, editing, and constructing theology.

Ninth, there is a practical outflow from this study. Because fewer Pentecostals identify as glossolalists, pastors and leaders are encouraged to: 1) give space in the worship service for singing in tongues and the gift of tongues. Though Pentecostal-like worship music has become popular, platform-driven worship and time constraints limit the opportunities for the next generation. The HA and the gift of tongues can introduce a new world of realities for a new generation, but it requires timely and thoughtful explanation. Hopefully this study will provide a foundation for such explanations. 2) The revitalization of a vibrant, unhurried, altar ministry is also necessary for providing opportunity for seeking and yielding. Though we now have multiple services, streaming services, and segments of television to fill, courting the Holy Spirit requires a sacrifice of time and distractions. The corporate altar, like the upper room, seems the logical place for such courting.

To sum up this investigation,

> human attempts to explain glossolalia (mine included) will fall short of the majesty, the mystery, the power available to witness the gospel, and the self-edification properties – all which accompany this gift of the Holy Spirit that God has clothed with the aura of that which seems foolish and undesirable for the uninitiated.[13]

---

[13] Tarr, *The Foolishness of God*, p. 121.

APPENDIX 1

WALTER J. HOLLENWEGER'S BLACK-ORAL-INCLUSIVE ROOT

Even though 'tongues remain for most Pentecostalists the decisive experience of the spirit centered life',[1] Hollenweger defined Pentecostalism as having a black-oral and inclusive root of which glossolalia is an integral component.[2] He calls Pentecostalism to return to this root, a 're-oralization', if Pentecostalism is to survive.[3]

I. Black Oral Root

Hollenweger believes Pentecostalism's black oral root is a separate root from the holiness root of Wesley, and can be traced back through an Afro-American slave religion to a traditional African religion.[4] He believes that the key to Pentecostalism's growth 'lies in its black root' and not with its 'inconsistent doctrine':[5] 'there is hardly a Pentecostal movement in the world that is not built on

---

[1] Hollenweger, *The Pentecostals*, p. 336.

[2] Hollenweger, 'After Twenty Years', p. 6; Cf. Leonard Lovett, 'Perspective on the Black Origins of the Contemporary Pentecostal Movement', *The Journal of the Interdenominational Theological Center* 1.1 (Fall, 1973), pp. 36-49; Marne L. Campbell, '"The Newest Religious Sect Has Started In Los Angeles": Race, Class, Ethnicity, and the Origins of the Pentecostal Movement, 1906-1913', *The Journal of African American History* 95.1 (2010), pp. 1-25.

[3] He calls for 're-oralization' of Christianity: 'our theological specialization has a future only if we can re-oralize our insights, translate critical findings into parables, stories, songs and dramas ... learn again from the Bible – and in fact from a number of Third World theologians – to do real, critical and helpful theology in the oral language of our own people', Hollenweger, 'The Ecumenical Significance of Oral Christianity', p. 264.

[4] Wesley's Methodism included catholic, evangelical, critical, and ecumenical stems. See chart, Hollenweger, *Pentecostalism*, p. 2; cf. Lovett, 'Black Origins', pp. 123-41.

[5] Hollenweger, *Pentecostalism*, p. 18, cf. Hollenweger, 'After Twenty Years', p. 6.

Seymour's black oral modes of communication'.[6]

This black root adds both dynamic and inclusive components to Pentecostalism. The ASM revival was

> an outburst of enthusiastic religion of a kind well-known and frequent in the history of Negro churches in America which derived its specifically Pentecostal features from Parham's theory that speaking with tongues is a necessary concomitant of the baptism of the Spirit.[7]

However, it was also 'love in the face of hate'.[8] Seymour was an ecumenist who sought a theology which would 'provide a basis for mutual process of learning and recognition'.[9] Though the inclusiveness of Azusa Street quickly re-segregated,[10] Hollenweger believes that Pentecostalism 'offers the key to overcoming racism in the world today'.[11]

II. Definition of Oral Theology

Biographer, Lynne Price calculates that, 'all Hollenweger's knowledge, professional and personal experience pointed cumulatively in the direction of oral and narrative categories'.[12] At times writing about Pentecostalism and other times a broader Third World oral Christianity, Hollenweger officially defined oral theology as:

---

[6] Hollenweger, *Pentecostalism*, p. 23.
[7] Hollenweger, *The Pentecostals*, p. 24.
[8] Hollenweger, 'After Twenty Years', p. 5, cf. Hollenweger, 'Pentecostals and the Charismatic Movement', p. 550.
[9] Lynne Price, *Theology Out of Place: A Theological Biography of Walter J. Hollenweger* (JPTSup 23; Sheffield: Sheffield Academic Press, 2002), p. 82.
[10] However, Hollenweger contends that it would 'be unfair to blame the white Pentecostals alone for this development' because 1) the mainline churches tried to discredit Pentecostals by pointing to their lowly beginnings in a Negro church, and 2) there were the laws in the southern states which prohibited mixed meetings, Hollenweger, *Pentecostalism*, p. 31, cf. p. 30.
[11] Hollenweger, *Pentecostalism*, p. 23. He finds it significant that '"this interracial accord took place among the very groups that had traditionally been most at odds, the poor whites and the poor blacks." Even more astonishing, white Pentecostals received their ordination from the hands of black Pentecostal Bishops', p. 30.
[12] Price, *Theology out of Place*, p. 78.

1. an emphasis on the oral aspect of liturgy; 2. theology and witness cast in narrative form; 3. maximum participation at the levels of reflection, prayer and decision-making ... ; 4. inclusion of dream and vision [sic] in personal and public forms of spirituality ... ; 5. an understanding of the body/mind relationship which is informed by experiences of correspondence between the body and mind.[13]

Additionally, 1) oral theology has a world view that includes 'kind and malignant spirits';[14] 2) the medium is the message whether celebrating at a banquet[15] or singing a song;[16] 3) it arises from experience and

> is not based on books imprinted liturgies or on the personal study of the Bible, but on the experience of the presence of God in worship and everyday life. These experiences are expressed and described in songs, proverbs, stories, parables and dances.[17]

That does not mean, however, that it is simplistic or primitive. It is 'a prime and highly complex mode of communication ... function(ing) as a logistic system for passing on theological and social values and information in oral societies in a way that can be likened to a modern computer'.[18] In contrast to literary theology, oral theology is, 1. Easy to memorize. 2. Is not based on proposition but parables. 3. Can be put to music and song, as compared to literary forms which must be discussed. 4. It does not lead to clear con

---

[13] Hollenweger, 'Pentecostals and the Charismatic Movement', pp. 551-52, cf.. Hollenweger, *Pentecostalism*, pp. 2, 18-24; Price, *Theology out of Place*, pp. 79-89.

[14] Hollenweger, 'Significance of Oral Christianity', p. 260.

[15] 'The medium of communication is, just as in biblical times, not the definition but the description, not the statement but the story, not the doctrine but the testimony, not the book but the parable, not a systematic theology but a song, not the treatise but the television programme, not the articulation of concepts but the celebration of banquets', Hollenweger, 'After Twenty Years', p. 10.

[16] The 'Pentecostal movement began in the same milieu in which the spiritual, jazz, and blues emerged', and in a way can be compared with jazz, Hollenweger, *Pentecostalism*, p. 30, cf. p. 32.

[17] Hollenweger, 'Significance of Oral Christianity', p. 259.

[18] Hollenweger, 'After Twenty Years', pp. 10, 11.

cepts, 'but inspires ... celebration'.¹⁹ In short, 'oral literature *transforms*, literary literature *informs*'.²⁰

III. The Case for Oral Theology

Hollenweger gives two significant reasons for a re-oralization of theology. First, he believes that the contemporary historical-critical method is 'bankrupt':

> Biblical studies increasingly fell prey to a form of technology which regards as legitimate only those questions which its methods can answer ... it has become a highly specialized academic discipline which no longer serves the community for which it was once intended.[21]

The second reason to re-oralize theology follows what he saw in Seymour, unity and ecumenism: 'the ecumenical problem of the immediate future is not the relationship between Catholic and Protestant', he wrote, 'but between "oral" and "literary" theology'.[22] The Church is at conflict between the authority of 'speech, narrative and communication,' and 'the authority which is based on status, education, money and juridical power.'[23] He calls Pentecostals to 'a new appraisal of pre-Christian cultures and their own Third World sister churches, for ecumenical openness and dialogue'.[24] He admires[25] the ecumenical potential within Pentecostalism as

---

[19] Hollenweger, 'Significance of Oral Christianity', p. 262.
[20] Hollenweger, 'Significance of Oral Christianity', p. 262. Cf. King, 'The Pentecostal View', p. 122.
[21] Hollenweger, 'Significance of Oral Christianity', p. 263, cf. p. 262.
[22] Hollenweger, *Pentecostalism*, p. 39. The dividing lines are 'racism (or European/American superiority complex) versus an intercultural and inter-racial understanding of Christianity; literacy versus orality; abstract concepts versus narrativity; the anonymity of bureaucratic organizations versus family and personal relationships; medical technology versus a holistic understanding of health and sickness; Western psycho-analytical techniques versus a group and family therapy that centers on the human touch, prayer and a daily in formal education in dreams and visions', Hollenweger, 'After Twenty Years', p. 10.
[23] Hollenweger, 'Pentecostals and the Charismatic Movement', p. 552.
[24] Hollenweger, *Pentecostalism*, p. 1.
[25] He also worries about Pentecostalism because of neo-Pentecostalism, 'it will become harder and harder to make a clear-cut distinction between American Pentecostals and American non-Pentecostals in the future, now that the

revolutionary because it offers alternatives to 'literary' theology and thus defrosts the 'frozen thinking' within literary forms of worship and committee-debate and gives the same chances to all – including the 'oral' people. It allows for a process of democratization of language through a dismantling of the privileges of abstract, rational and propositional systems.[26]

Pentecostal spirituality, he believes, is well positioned to bridge the literary and oral 'cultural divide'[27] if Pentecostals take up the challenge.[28]

---

experience and message of the baptism of the Spirit have found a way into all American denominations', Hollenweger, *The Pentecostals*, p. 15.

[26] Hollenweger, *Pentecostalism*, p. 35. Price, *Theology out of Place*, p. 79, observes, 'Oral categories were important, according to his (Hollenweger's) understanding, because "the church of Jesus Christ is the place where cultural, academic, political and theological conflicts become organized in such a way that new insights emerge for all participants, and narrative forms enable the 'ruling language' to be brought into intercultural dialogue as one possible language next to other possible languages"'.

[27] Hollenweger, *Pentecostalism*, p. 38.

[28] However, he sees Pentecostalism going the other way. It is, 'fast developing into an evangelical middle class religion. Many of the elements that were vital for its rise and expansion into the third world are disappearing. They are being replaced by efficient fund-raising structures, a streamlined ecclesiastical bureaucracy, and a Pentecostal conceptual theology', Hollenweger, *Pentecostalism*, p. 19; cf. Hollenweger, 'After Twenty Years', p. 6.

APPENDIX 2

GLOSSOLALIC OUTPOURINGS IN CHURCH HISTORY

I. Introduction

As a backdrop to the examination of early Pentecostal discussions of glossolalia, the following appendix is devoted to a brief survey of glossolalic occurrences in church history.[1] Its function at this point in this monograph is to provide a bit of historical and theological context for the practice as described in the early Pentecostal periodical literature. These Pentecostals soon looked to history for

---

[1] There is a wealth of scholarly literature available on this subject. Significant early examinations are: J.J. Görres, *Die Christliche Mystik*, 5 vols. (Regensburg: G.J. Manz, 1836-41); Philip Schaff, *History of the Christian Church, Volume 1: Apostolic Christianity, From the Birth of Christ to the Death of St. John, A.D. 1-100* (Peabody, MA: Hendrickson, 2011, reprint; 1890), pp. 234-42; Heinrich Weinel, *Die Wirkungen des Geistes und der Geister im nachapostolischen Zeitalter bis auf Irenaus* (Freiburg: J.C.B. Mohr, 1899); Clemen, 'The Speaking with Tongues'; Federick C. Conybeare, 'The Gift of Tongues', *Encyclopedia Britannica* 11th edition (New York, Cambridge University Press, 1911, vol. 27), pp. 9-10. Recent significant works are: Harold D. Hunter, 'Tongues Speech: A Patristic Analysis', *JETS* 23.2 (June 1980), pp. 125-37; Williams and Waldvogel, 'A History of Speaking in Tongues and Related Gifts'; Harold D. Hunter, *Spirit-Baptism: A Pentecostal Alternative* (Lanham, MD: University Press of America, 1983), pp. 117-93; Ronald Alfred Narfi Kydd, 'Charismata to 320 A.D.: A Study of the Overt Pneumatic Experience of the Early Church' (PhD Thesis, University of St. Andrews, 1972), revised and published as Ronald Kydd, *Charismatic Gifts in the Early Church* (Peabody, MA: Hendrickson, 1984); Stanley Burgess, *The Holy Spirit: Ancient Christian Traditions* (Peabody, MA: Hendrickson, 1994); Kilian McDonnell, *Christian Initiation and Baptism in the Holy Spirit: Evidence from the First Eight Centuries* (Collegeville, MN: Liturgical Press, 1991); Stanley Burgess, *The Holy Spirit: Medieval Roman Catholic and Reformation Traditions (sixth-sixteenth centuries)* (Peabody, MA: Hendrickson, 1997); Stanley Burgess, *The Holy Spirit: Eastern Christian Traditions* (Peabody, MA: Hendrickson, 1989). Written and notable at a popular-level are: Jeff Oliver, *Pentecost to the Present: Early Prophetic And Spiritual Gifts Movement* (Newberry, FL: Bridge Logos, 2017); Jeff Oliver, *Pentecost to the Present: Reformations and Awakenings* (Newberry, FL: Bridge Logos, 2017); Jeff Oliver, *Pentecost to the Present: Worldwide Revivals and Renewal* (Newberry, FL: Bridge Logos, 2017).

antecedents.[2] Hopefully, this survey will assist the reader in seeing similarities and differences between the cases here cited and the early Pentecostal theological reflection upon the phenomenon they experienced. No claim will be made for direct influence except in cases where the early Pentecostals themselves explicitly drew upon such antecedents. These texts will be examined in a limited manner, sufficient to understand the material, and not examined in their broader contexts.[3] There will be an attempt to get as close to the primary source as possible.

II. The Didache through Augustine

In the period from the Apostolic Fathers through Augustine, there were many who wrote on topics relevant to glossolalia,[4] and some

---

[2] Parham, 'The Baptism with the Holy Ghost', p. 6; 'The Promise Still Good', p. 3; Taylor, *The Spirit and the Bride* (Dunn, NC, 1907); Simmons, 'History of Tongues', p. 2; Simmons, 'History of Tongues – Additional Testimony', p. 2; Tomlinson, 'The Opposition Weakening', pp. 1-2; Turner, 'Pentecost in History', pp. 6-7; 'Pentecost in the year 1830', pp. 41-42; 'A Wonderful Work', pp. 128-29; Divine, 'Spiritual Manifestations and the Churches', p. 5; Durham, 'Manifestations Number II', pp. 7-9 (7); Lawrence, 'Article III(a)', pp. 4-5; Wm. G. Schell, 'Manifestations of the Holy Spirit In Post-Apostolic Times', *WE* 126 (Feb 12, 1915), pp. 5, 7; 'What Meaneth This?', *CE* 300 & 301 (Aug 9, 1919), pp. 1-2; Turner, *Pentecost and Tongues*, pp. 99-124; Dalton, *Tongues Like as of Fire*; Frodsham, *With Signs Following*; Brumback, *'What Meaneth This?'*, pp. 89-96; Lenonard R. Carroll, 'Glossolalia: Apostles to The Reformation', in Wade H. Horton (ed.), *The Glossolalia Phenomenon* (Cleveland, TN: Pathway Press, 1986), pp. 69-94; Menzies, *Anointed to Serve*, pp. 29-33; Hargrave, 'Reformation to the Twentieth Century', pp. 97-139; *Menzies, Anointed to Serve*, pp. 29-33.

[3] For works that address the broader pagan, Hebrew, or Greco-Roman contexts see, Williams, *Tongues of the Spirit*; Mills, *Theological/Exegetical*; Christopher Forbes, *Prophecy and Inspired Speech in Early Christianity and its Hellenistic Environment* (Peabody, MA: Hendrickson, 1997); Hovenden, *Speaking in Tongues*.

[4] For example, neither Clement of Rome nor Ignatius of Antioch are included in this survey though they 'claimed to be inspired' and 'recognize(d) the operation of spiritual gifts among average Christians', Stanley M. Burgess, 'Holy Spirit, Doctrine of: The Ancient Fathers', in Stanley Burgess (ed.), *NIDPCM* (Grand Rapids, MI: Zondervan, rev. and expanded edn, 2002), pp. 730-46 (731); cf. Clement, 'The First Epistle of Clement', in Robert M. Grant and Holt H. Graham (eds.), *First and Second Clement: The Apostolic Fathers: A New Translation* (New York: Thomas Nelson & Sons, 1965), vol. 2, pp. 64-65 n. 37:1-5; Ignatius of Antioch, 'Polycarp', in Robert M. Grant (ed.) *Ignatius of Antioch: The Apostolic Fathers: A New Translation* (Camden, NJ: Thomas Nelson & Sons, 1966), pp. 130-31 n. 2:1-3. Ignatius also told of a time he spoke prophetically via the Holy Spirit in a loud voice, Ignatius 'Epistle of Ignatius to the Philadelphians', p. 7; cf. Kydd, *Charismatic Gifts*, p. 16.

whose account of ecstatic prophecy or glossolalia was straightforward.[5] Given the quantity of writing during this period and the infrequency of glossolalia, scholars have drawn two conclusions: Pentecostal academics argued that glossolalia was so commonplace that it deserved little discussion, while non-Pentecostal scholars claimed that the gift ceased.[6] However, 'an argument from silence has as much support for the continuance of the gift as for the cessation of the gift'.[7] Simmons offered a third position, that perhaps the scant picture from the early church is to be expected due to the *Sitz im Leben* of persecution, martyrdom, theological controversy, and a fervent missionary endeavour. These pressures 'crowded out much pertaining to spiritual devotion and spiritual exercise', especially glossolalia.[8]

A. The Didache[9]

The Didache was a church manual from the second century which

---

[5] This is a broad definition of glossolalia that includes ecstatic speech and prophecy, because the early terminology 'glossolalia' or 'tongues speech' is not universal and glossolalia is inclusive of both ecstatic speech and prophecy (Spirit-inspired speech); cf. Kelsey, *Tongues Speaking*, p. 34. 'Irenaeus has substituted the word "prophecy" for the glossolalia', p. 35. Engelson noted that 'the term γλώσσιας γλώσση λαλεῖν ... does not occur in any of the (ancient Greek) texts ... outside of the New Testament. The obvious reason is that inarticulate or unintelligible speech is looked upon only as a feature of ecstatic speech', Engelson, 'Glossolalia', p. 20. Further, Ash notes that ecstatic prophecy implies 'that Christian prophecy arose from something more than the prophet's rationally derived conviction ... (in fact) "nonecstatic" prophecy would have been a contradiction in terms', James L. Ash, 'The Decline of Ecstatic Prophecy in the Early Church', *Theological Studies* 37.2 (June 1976), pp. 227-52 (230-32, 239).

[6] 'The wide geographical (and doctrinal) coverage of the Apostolic Fathers makes their silence significant', wrote Rogers, 'if the gift of tongues were widespread and in abundance, it surely would have been alluded to or mentioned in some way', Cleon L. Rogers, 'The Gift of Tongues in the Post Apostolic Church', *Bibliotheca Sacra* 122.486 (April-June 1965), pp. 134-43 (135). Schaff represents a moderate position, that tongues were 'more ornamental than useful, and vanished away with the bridal season of the church ... (however, there was) analogous phenomena, of an inferior kind, and not miraculous, yet serving as illustrations, either by approximation or as counterfeits, (that) reappeared from time to time in seasons of special religious excitement', Schaff, *Apostolic Christianity*, pp. 236-37.

[7] Rogers, 'Tongues in the Post Apostolic Church', p. 134.

[8] Simmons, 'History of Tongues', p. 2; cf. Kelsey, *Tongues Speaking*, p. 33.

[9] The Didache is an anonymous document that 'represents the preserved oral tradition whereby mid-first-century house churches detailed the step-by-step transformation by which gentile converts were to be prepared for active

made clear that itinerant 'teachers, prophets, and apostles' were still common and had 'equal importance to the ordained, resident ministry'.[10] Two references to glossolalia occurred in the context of how the local assembly was to deal with these ecstatic prophets: 'while a prophet is uttering words in the spirit, you are on no account to subject him to any tests or verifications ... nevertheless, not all who speak in the spirit are prophets'.[11] Stanley Burgess believed the phrase 'speak in the Spirit'[12] referred to 'a similar kind of vocal ecstasy that characterized Paul's time'.[13] Because of its Syrian origin, Ronald Kydd noted that prophecy played a strong role in Antioch.[14] A third possible reference to glossolalia noted that prophets were 'free to give thanks as they please', even outside the prescribed Eucharistic pattern.[15]

---

participation in their assemblies', Aaron Milavec, *The Didache: Text, Translation, Analysis and Commentary* (Collegeville, MN: Liturgical Press, 2003), p. ix.

[10] Burgess, *Ancient Christian Traditions*, p. 21. These elected officials were expected to minister charismatically: 'you must choose for yourselves bishops and deacons who are worthy of the Lord ... for they are carrying out the ministry of the prophets and teachers for you', Maxwell Staniforth (trans.), 'The Didache', in *The Apostolic Fathers: Early Christian Writings* (London: Penguin Books, 1987), pp. 191-99 (197); cf. Kydd, *Charismatic Gifts*, pp. 10, 11.

[11] Staniforth, 'The Didache', p. 196 (emphasis added). Respectful boundaries were given as were guidelines on how to identify a true prophet, specifically: 1) the content of the message, p. 195; 2) a godly lifestyle, p. 196; 3) and a few practical guidelines, pp. 195-96, cf. Kydd, *Charismatic Gifts*, pp. 8-9; Ash, 'Decline of Ecstatic Prophecy', pp. 232-33.

[12] (λαλοῦντα ἐν πνεύματι)' cf. Milavec, *The Didache*, p. 28. Cyril Richardson translates the phrase, 'ecstatic utterances', Cyril Richardson (ed.), 'The Didache', *Early Christian Fathers* (New York: Macmillian Publishing Co., 1970), p. 176.

[13] Burgess, *Ancient Christian Traditions*, p. 21; cf. Milavec, *The Didache*, p. 70. However, the phrase occurred a few lines later, where ecstatic speech was not implied: 'if any prophet, *speaking in the spirit*, says, "Give me money (or anything else)", do not listen to him', Staniforth, 'The Didache', p. 196.

[14] Kydd, *Charismatic Gifts*, p. 7. He notes that in Antioch 'things had not changed much', cf. Acts 13.1, 2; 15.32.

[15] Staniforth, 'The Didache', p. 195. Milavec notes that these prophets may have spoken during 'natural breaks' in the Eucharist, but he believed they generally spoke to bring 'a dramatic close' to the Eucharist, Milavec, *The Didache*, pp. 70-71. These prophecies could be lengthy considering Polycarp spoke for two hours, p. 70.

B. Justin Martyr (100-165 CE)[16]

'But my spirit was immediately set on fire, and an affection for the prophets ... took hold of me' wrote Justin Martyr of the gifts of the Spirit that were active in his time.[17] In his apologetic to a Jew named Trypho, Justin argued that 'the charisms of prophecy (which) exist down to the present day' which had been on the Jewish prophets 'have now been transferred to us (Christians)'.[18] Even though Justin does not list tongues,[19] his argument is clear: 'if you look around, you can see among us Christians both male and female endowed with charisms from the Spirit of God'.[20]

C. Irenaeus of Lyons (130-202 CE)[21]

Irenaeus, the bishop of Lyons, recognized 'the continuous operation of charismatic gifts, including prophecy, among the brethren in his own church'.[22] Much of his writing sought to protect the

---

[16] He was raised as a 'Samaritan' and he did not worship the God of Israel, Dennis Minns and Paul Parvis, *Justin, Philosopher and Martyr: Apologies* (New York: Oxford University Press, 2009), p. 32. As a young man he studied philosophy extensively and opened a school in Rome where 'he taught Christianity to all comers, presenting it as the only safe and profitable system', Kydd, *Charismatic Gifts*, p. 25. He became a strong apologist for Christianity and wrote a tract for the Emperor where 'he pleaded for fair treatment for Christians'. He died as a Christian martyr sometime between 162-168, Minns and Parvis, *Philosopher and Martyr*, p. 32.

[17] Justin Martyr, *Dialogue with Trypho* (trans. Thomas B. Falls; Washington, DC: The Catholic University Press of America, 2003), p. 15.

[18] Justin Martyr, *Dialogue with Trypho*, p. 128, §82.1 (Παρὰ γὰρ ἡμῖν καὶ μέχρι νῦν προφητικὰ χαρίσματά ἐστιν).

[19] Justin lists the 'spirit of wisdom, another of counsel, another of fortitude, another of healing, another of foreknowledge, another of teaching, and another of the fear of God', Justin Martyr, *Dialogue with Trypho*, p. 60. Rogers believes the absence of glossolalia is suspicious; however, Justin Martyr had been accused of talking like a madman and needs to make a cogent response to Trypho and somewhat distance himself from ecstatic speech, Rogers, 'Tongues in the Post Apostolic Church', p. 137; cf. Justin Martyr, 'Second Apology', in Philip Schaff (ed.), *ANF, First Series: The Apostolic Fathers with Justin Martyr and Ireneaus* (Peabody, MA: Hendrickson 1995), VI, p. 190.

[20] Justin Martyr, *Dialogue with Trypho*, p. 137, §88.1 (Καὶ παρ' παρ' ἐμοῦ ἡμῖν ἔστιν ἰδεῖν καὶ θελείας καὶ ἄρσενας, χαρίσματα ἀπὸ τοῦ πνεύματος τοῦ θεοῦ ἔχοντας).

[21] Irenaeus 'was a disciple of Polycarp of Smyrna, who had been a follower of the Apostle John' defended Christianity against Gnosticism with scientific expressions of belief and 'the first systematic exposition of the young Church's belief', Burgess, *Ancient Christian Fathers*, p. 58.

[22] Burgess, *Ancient Christian Fathers*, p. 61. Clemen believed Irenaeus was only speculating because he 'himself had certainly not heard ... (and had) absolutely

church from false prophets.²³ His comments on 1 Cor. 2.6 affirmed the ongoing nature of genuine glossolalia in the Church:

> in like manner we do also hear many brethren in the Church who possess prophetic gifts, and who through the Spirit speak *all kinds of languages,* and bring to light for the general benefit the hidden things of men, and declare the mysteries of God.²⁴

William Green called this text 'the one notable exception'; otherwise, 'there is an almost complete silence about tongues' in the second century.²⁵ In other words, 'Irenaeus went on record, saying the church he knew was charismatic' and that he was an eyewitness.²⁶ However, Irenaeus also 'played a powerful role' in teaching that the gifts of the Spirit were 'located in the office of the bishop' rather than with spontaneous prophets.²⁷

D. Montanus

Montanus and his followers were a growing Christian movement²⁸

---

no personal observation', Clemen, 'The Speaking with Tongues', p. 346. William Green was not so quick to dismiss Irenaeus' testimony because a few of the disciples of the Apostle John might still be alive, William M. Green 'Glossolalia in the Second Century', *RQ* 16.3-4 (1973), pp. 231-39 (239).

²³ Irenaeus, in Dominic J. Unger (trans.), *St. Irenaeus of Lyons Against the Heresies*, Vol. 1, Book 1 (New York, NY: Paulist Press, 1992), pp. 55-57.

²⁴ 'παντοδαπαῖς γλώσσιας', Irenaeus, 'Against Heresies', in Alexander Roberts and James Donaldson (eds.), *ANF, First Series: Translations of the Writings of the Fathers Down to A.D. 325* (Peabody, MA: Hendrickson, 1995), v.6.1, p. 531.

²⁵ Green, 'Glossolalia in the Second Century', p. 238, cf. Schaff, *Apostolic Christianity*, p. 236; Kydd, *Charismatic Gifts,* pp. 44-46; Forbes, *Prophecy and Inspired Speech,* pp. 78, 79, 157.

²⁶ Kydd, *Charismatic Gifts,* p. 45.

²⁷ Burgess, *Ancient Christian Fathers,* p. 62. 'In his fear of abuse and his intense desire to structure the movement of the Holy Spirit within the proper doctrine of the bishopric, he may have set the stage for a reduction in the Church's vitality. The Spirit ... was becoming institutionalized.' Cf. Irenaeus, *Against Heresies,* iii.24.1, 1.458.

²⁸ William Tabbernee describes Montanism as 'a diverse prophetic movement intent on bringing Christianity into line with what it believed to be the ultimate revelation of the Holy Spirit given to the church via its prophets and prophetesses', Cecil M. Robeck, Jr, 'Montanism and Present Day "Prophets"', *Pneuma* 32 (2010), pp. 413-29 (424). Green notes that it was originally called the 'Phrygian heresy', after its place of origin, or was also known as the 'New Prophecy', Green, 'Glossolalia in the Second Century', p. 231; cf. Kydd, *Charismatic Gifts,* p. 41. Rogers claims that Montanism 'was neither widespread nor the normal Christian experience', Rogers, 'Tongues in the Post Apostolic Church', p. 143; cf. p. 141. However, that claim is now widely disputed by others, such as

that experienced glossolalia[29] into the late second and early third centuries; however, they were not welcomed by the established Church and everything known of them is through the writings of their opponents.[30] Ecstatic tongues-speech was at the centre of the Montanist controversy. Eusebius recorded three Montanist sayings that referenced glossolalia. First, Montanus

> laid himself open to the adversary, was filled with spiritual excitement and suddenly fell into a kind of trance and unnatural ecstasy. He raved, and began to chatter and talk nonsense, prophesying in a way that conflicted with the practice of the Church.[31]

Second, two Montanist prophetesses 'chattered crazily, inopportunely, and wildly, like Montanus himself'.[32] The third reference was a fragment: 'they called us "prophet-killers" because we would not receive their garrulous prophets'.[33] Kydd believed it was

---

Tabbernee, who has chronicled the rapid spread 'throughout the empire', Robeck, 'Present Day "Prophets"', pp. 421-23 (23); cf. Shumway, 'The Gift of Tongues', p. 79; Green, 'Glossolalia in the Second Century', p. 231.

[29] For example, Tabbernee *imagined* a scene where Montanus has 'fallen into a trance, throwing his arms and legs around wildly … it stops … (then) strange sounds are coming from his mouth. He begins to babble incomprehensibly.' Then, a *genuine* quote by Montanus: 'behold! A human being is like a lyre, and I hover like a plectrum. The human being sleeps, but I remain awake. Behold! The Lord who stirs up the hearts of human beings and the one who strikes the heart in human beings', William Tabbernee, *Prophets and Gravestones: An Imaginative History of Montanists and Other Early Christians* (Peabody, MA: Hendrickson, 2009), p. 11., cf. Green, 'Glossolalia in the Second Century', p. 232.

[30] 'In the sixth century, the Emperor (Justinian) issued instructions to put an end to Montanism once and for all and to destroy all the known Montanist documents', Robeck, 'Montanism and Present Day "Prophets"', p. 419; cf. Kydd, *Charismatic Gifts*, p. 31. However, 'around thirty inscriptions and an equal number of fragments of the *logia*, or sayings … have survived because they are quoted in extant anti-Montanist works', Tabbernee, *Prophets and Gravestones*, p. 2.

[31] Eusebius, in *Eusebius: The History of the Church from Christ to Constantine* (trans. G.A. Williamson; Minneapolis, MN: Augsburg Publishing House, 1965), p. 218 (ἐνθουσιᾶν ἄρξασθαί τε λαλεῖν καὶ ξενοφωνεῖν). Eusebius, *Ecclesiastical History*, Volume 1: Books 1-5 (trans. Kirsopp Lake; Loeb Classical Library; Cambridge, MA: Harvard University Press, 1926), 5.16.7, p. 474.

[32] Eusebius, *The History of the Church*, p. 219 (ὡς καὶ λαλεῖν ἐκφρόνως καὶ ἀκαίρως καὶ ἀλλοτριοτρόπως ὁμοίως τῷ προειρημένῳ). Eusebius, *Ecclesiastical History*, 5.16.9, p. 476.

[33] Eusebius, *The History of the Church*, p. 219 (ὅτι μὴ τοὺς ἀμετροφώνους αὐτῶν προφήτας ἐδεξάμεθα), Eusebius, *Ecclesiastical History*, 5.16.12, p. 478.

'probable' these are references to glossolalia.³⁴ Despite the claim that 'there is no unambiguous evidence'³⁵ that this was glossolalia, Nils Engelsen noted that such 'strong expressions' to describe this ecstatic speech made it difficult to deny glossolalia.³⁶ The orthodox had three criticisms of Montanism: first, that the Montanists believed they were fully 'possessed by God', which was 'a departure from the Pauline pattern in 1 Cor. 14:28-31, where the prophets were able to control themselves'.³⁷ Second, Montanus 'believed and taught ... that it was open to continuing revelation through prophecies, dreams, and visions'.³⁸ Third, Montanism highlighted the struggle between 'nonepiscopal voices through the power of spontaneous prophetic utterances and the voices of legitimate, episcopal authorities'.³⁹ In the end, the institutional church triumphed over the spontaneous prophets and the 'Montanists suffered acute persecution by the orthodox faithful, until at last they were exterminated in the 6th century under Justinian'.⁴⁰ Some

---

'This is the only place in Greek literature where the word *ametrophonous* appears ... I suggest that we translate the phrase so that it means prophets "who speak in an indefinite number of what sounds like languages"', Kydd, *Charismatic Gifts*, p. 35.

³⁴ Kydd, *Charismatic Gifts*, p. 35. Even Rogers, who believed that 'the miraculous gifts of the first century died out', writes that 'the experience of Montanus "showed all the manifestations of glossolalia"', Rogers, 'Tongues in the Post Apostolic Church', pp. 141, 143. Green calls it 'some kind of glossolaly ... if we allow a certain elasticity in our definition', Green, 'Glossolalia in the Second Century', p. 235.

³⁵ Forbes, *Prophecy and Inspired Speech*, p. 160.

³⁶ Engelsen is quoted in Forbes, *Prophecy and Inspired Speech*, p. 161. Engelsen translates ξενοφωεῖν as 'to speak like a foreigner'.

³⁷ Kydd, *Charismatic Gifts*, pp. 33, 35; cf. Ash, 'Decline of Ecstatic Prophecy', pp. 237, 239; Green, 'Glossolalia in the Second Century', p. 232.

³⁸ Robeck, 'Present Day "Prophets"', p. 427. Burgess believes these 'new prophecies' were not so much the problem as the fact that the Montanists saw them 'superseding even the teachings of Jesus and the apostles', Burgess, *Ancient Christian Fathers*, p. 51. Montanus even 'identified himself with the Paraclete promised in John 14, and claimed to be God', Burgess, *Ancient Christian Traditions*, p. 49; cf. p. 52.

³⁹ Robeck, 'Present Day "Prophets"', p. 417, cf. Burgess, *Ancient Christian Fathers*, pp. 52, 53; Ash, 'Decline of Ecstatic Prophecy', pp. 239-41, 249-50.

⁴⁰ Burgess, 'Holy Spirit, Doctrine of: The Ancient Fathers', p. 732. Emperors sought peace and unity in the church by seeking uniformity of belief, Robeck, 'Present Day "Prophets"', p. 424.

believed that after Montanism, glossolalia solely occurred in the 'minor traditions' of the Church.[41]

E. Tertullian (150-220 CE)[42]

'The gifts of the Spirit were not passing fancies with Tertullian ... he knew them throughout his literary career and his high regard for them never slipped'.[43] In fact, he is called 'the first important "Pentecostal" theologian'.[44] His final apologetic against Marcion's theory of dual-gods presumed the ongoing revelation though the spiritual gifts.[45] Tertullian challenged Marcion to

> exhibit, as gifts of his god, some prophets, such as have not spoken by human sense, but with the Spirit of God ... let him produce a psalm, a vision, a prayer – only let it be by the Spirit, *in an ecstasy,*[46] *that is, in a rapture, whenever an interpretation of tongues has occurred to him* ... Now all these signs (of spiritual gifts) are forthcoming from my side without any difficulty'.[47]

---

[41] 'In all subsequent periods of Church history, the prophetic voices within the minor tradition continued to be heard', Burgess, *Ancient Christian Traditions*, p. 53. Hinson believed that as the gospel extended beyond the lower classes, the 'phenomenal displays' no longer convinced the educated, so the church relied on the Holy Spirit to work through more orderly institutions and liturgy, Hinson, 'The Significance of Glossolalia', p. 198.

[42] Born around 150 CE as the son of a Roman centurion, he was trained as a lawyer and converted to Christianity in his midlife and became a leading apologist, Burgess, *Ancient Christian Fathers*, pp. 62-63.

[43] Kydd, *Charismatic Gifts*, p. 70.

[44] Kydd, *Charismatic Gifts*, p. 66; Burgess, 'Ancient Fathers', p. 734, cf. Shumway, 'The Gift of Tongues', p. 10. Tertullian cast a large shadow over orthodox theology. His 'work also sparkles with doctrinal brilliance (it took the rest of the Church a century or more to catch up with his thinking)', Kydd, *Charismatic Gifts*, p. 66. Specifically, 'the church's understanding of the person and work of the Holy Spirit. He gave to Christianity its language of the "Trinity" and of "Persons" in the Trinity,' Burgess, 'Ancient Fathers', p. 734. He also, 'authored the first treatise on water baptism', Hunter, *Spirit Baptism*, p. 120, cf. pp. 120-23.

[45] Marcion's theory was that 'there are two gods; the good supreme god ... and the evil creator god, who is revealed in the Old Testament', Kydd, *Charismatic Gifts*, p. 67.

[46] Tertullian wrote six books on ecstasy, *De ectasi*, of which only one sentence is extant, and it revealed little, Tabbernee, *Prophets and Gravestones*, p. 136.

[47] Tertullian, 'Against Marcion', in Alexander Roberts and James Donaldson (eds.), *ANF, First Series: Latin Christianity: Its Founder, Tertullian I. Apologetic; II.*

Here, the present and ongoing spiritual gifts and glossolalia proved his point.[48] Despite Tertullian's clarity on tongues, critics have downplayed its significance in history[49] due to his later attachment to Montanism.[50] However, Kydd cautioned against reading too much into this Montanist connection because 'maybe these two groups were not as far apart as we normally think'.[51]

F. Origen (born 185 CE)[52]

Origen was asked to respond to Celsus' arguments against Christianity.[53] His response quoted often from Celsus' book *True Discourse* which then preserved a snapshot of glossolalia.[54] From that

---

Anti-Marcion; III. Ethical, Vol. 3 (Peabody, MA: Hendrickson, 1995), 5.8, pp. 446-447 (in ecstasi, id est amentia, si qua linguae interpretatio accessit.).

[48] Kydd, *Charismatic Gifts*, pp. 66-70; Forbes, *Prophecy and Inspired Speech*, pp. 78-80; Burgess, *Ancient Christian Traditions*, pp. 52-68.

[49] For example, 'it is only a later montanistic idea of speaking in tongues, from which inferences as to the first Christian form of the phenomenon ought not to be drawn', Clemen, 'The Speaking with Tongues', p. 346, cf. Schaff, *Apostolic Christianity*, p. 236.

[50] Forbes believes Tertullian's 'conversion to Montanism' occurred approximately in 212 CE, making this a pre-Montanist passage, Forbes, *Prophecy and Inspired Speech*, p. 160. Whereas Tabbernee cautions against dividing Tertullian 'artificially' into a pre and post Montanist period, 'much of what Tertullian believed and practiced before 208 CE he continued to believe and practice after that year', Tabbernee, *Prophets and Gravestones*, p. 2.

[51] Kydd, *Charismatic Gifts*, p. 70. Montanism was officially accepted at one time. Tertullian wrote, 'the Bishop of Rome had acknowledged the prophetic gifs of Montanus, Prisca, and Maximillan', Burgess, *Ancient Christian Traditions*, p. 67, cf. 62; Burgess, 'Ancient Fathers', p. 734; Ash, 'Decline of Ecstatic Prophecy', p. 241; Lloyd D. Franklin, 'The Spiritual Gifts in Tertullian' (PhD Dissertation, Saint Louis University, 1989), p. 99. Augustine (De Haeresibus § 6) reports that Tertullian left the Montanists and founded a new sect which was later reconciled to the Catholic congregation at Carthage, Philip Schaff, *History of the Christian Church, Volume 2: Ante-Nicene Christianity, From the Death of John the Apostle to Constantine the Great, A.D. 100-325* (Peabody, MA: Hendrickson, 2011, reprint; 1890), pp. 420-21.

[52] He succeeded his mentor, Clement of Alexandria as the head of a catechetical school and was a philosopher as well as a theologian, Burgess, *Ancient Christian Traditions*, pp. 72-73. He became the first to set forth a systematic theology – a balanced treatment of the whole of Christian doctrine, p. 73.

[53] Celsus was a Platonist philosopher and his work was entitled *The True Word*, Kydd, *Charismatic Gifts*, p. 36.

[54] Celsus wrote roughly seventy years prior, or around 177 CE; cf. Eusebius, *Eusebius Pamphilius Ecclesiastical History, Books 6-10*, in Roy J. Deferrari (trans.) *The Fathers of the Church: A New Translation* (New York: Fathers of the Church, 1955), 6.36, p. 61.

response, we learn that Celsus witnessed prophets who 'become enraptured and prophesy', and then enumerated:

> to these things which were held up before men were added *unheard of raving* and *entirely unknown speech, the meaning of which no rational man was able to determine*; for being obscure and meaningless they allow any irrational person or cheat to make of the words whatever he wishes.[55]

This 'case was obviously an example of the familiar glossolalia with subsequent interpretation', wrote Hans Lietzmann.[56] Kydd believes that Celsus' testimony stands as a credible witness to glossolalia 'in Palestine in the second half of the second century'.[57]

Origin himself 'was no wide-eyed charismatic', wrote Kydd. He held an 'even more conservative (view) than the moderate view which Paul held'.[58] On the one hand, he frequently spoke of 'traces' of the spiritual gifts, but these are diminishing.[59] For example, regarding prophecy:

> moreover, the Holy Spirit gave signs of His presence at the beginning of Christ's ministry, and after His ascension He gave still more; but since that time these signs have diminished,

---

[55] Kydd, *Charismatic Gifts*, p. 36 (his own translation); cf. Origen, 'Against Celsus' in Philip Schaff (ed.), ANF, First Series: *Fathers of the Third Century: Tertullian, Part Fourth; Minucius Felix; Commodian; Origen,* Parts First and Second, Vol. IV (Peabody, MA: Hendrickson, 1995, reprinting; 1885), Book VII, Chapter IX, p. 614. See also, George W. Dollar, 'Church History and the Tongues Movement', *BibSac* 120.480 (October-December 1963), pp. 316-21 (317); Rogers, 'Tongues in the Post Apostolic Church', p 142.

[56] Hans Lietzmann, *The Founding of the Church Universal: A History of the Early Church* (trans. B.L. Woolf; London: Lutterworth Press, 1961), p. 55; cf. Weinel, *Die Wirkungen des Geistes*, p. 76; Kydd, *Charismatic Gifts*, p. 38.

[57] Kydd notes that while Celsus was able to distinguish between the Marcionites and the Gnostics and knew that they were outside of mainstream Christianity, both he and Origen were confused as to who these prophets were, Kydd, *Charismatic Gifts*, pp. 38-39; cf. Origen, 'Against Celsus', Book VII, Chapter VIII, p. 614.

[58] Kydd, *Charismatic Gifts*, p. 81.

[59] For Origen himself, following his philosophical education, he believed that the spiritual gifts were largely academic, because 'he saw the Christian life as a pursuit of true knowledge', Kydd, *Charismatic Gifts*, p. 77. Kydd notes that the most frequently mentioned gifts are 'word of wisdom' and 'word of knowledge' for which one should pray in order to 'bring personal benefit ... (and) strengthen individuals' intellectual grasp on Christianity', pp. 76-77. Origen, 'Against Celsus', Book I, Chapter II, pp. 397-98. Cf. Rogers, 'Tongues in the Post Apostolic Church', p 142 n. 48.

although *there are still traces* of His presence in a few who have had their souls purified by the Gospel, and their actions regulated by its influence.[60]

On the other hand, they are '*still preserved* among the Christians', and are 'to be found *to a considerable extent* among the Christians ... and these *we ourselves have witnessed*'.[61]

G. Novatian (200-258 CE)[62]

Novatian's *Concerning the Trinity* was a significant theological work in Latin and his arguments regarding the Holy Spirit indicated an awareness of glossolalia.[63] The spiritual gifts given to 'the apostles, that He might abide in them forever ... wholly poured out ... (and) lavishly bestowed'.[64] The present tense of Novatian's argument is significant.[65] The Spirit 'places prophets in the Church, instructs teachers, bestows the gift of tongues ... and sets in order and arranges whatever charismatic gifts there are'.[66] His subsequent soliloquy noted that the Holy Spirit 'importunes the divine ears "on our behalf with ineffable groanings"'.[67]

H. Cyprian (d. 258 CE)[68]

Cyprian was a 'strongly charismatic' bishop who believed 'that the bishop has the sole claim to prophetic gifts'.[69] For example, the

---

[60] Origen, 'Against Celsus', Book VII, Chapter VIII, p. 614 (emphasis added).

[61] Origen, 'Against Celsus', Book I, Chapter XLVI (46), p. 415; Book II, Chapter VIII, p. 433 (emphasis added).

[62] Novatian was a prominent elder in Rome who vigorously denied the right to be reinstated if one had apostatized in the face of persecution or sinned in the flesh, Burgess, 'Holy Spirit, Doctrine of: The Ancient Fathers', p. 735; cf. Kydd, *Charismatic Gifts*, p. 60; Burgess, *Ancient Christian Fathers*, p. 78.

[63] Burgess, 'Holy Spirit, Doctrine of: The Ancient Fathers', p. 735.

[64] Novatian, 'The Trinity', in Russell J. DeSimone (trans.), *Novatian: The Trinity, The Spectacles, Jewish Foods, In Praise of Purity, Letters* (Washington, DC: The Catholic University of America, 1972), p. 100.

[65] Kydd, *Charismatic Gifts*, pp. 62-3.

[66] Novatian, 'The Trinity', p. 101.

[67] Novatian, 'The Trininy', p. 103.

[68] Cyprian rose to become the bishop of Carthage and was beheaded for his faith in 258 CE, he 'laid the doctrinal foundation for the conception of the Church in the post-Nicene age and for the development of the Roman hierarchy ... Cyprian believes that the Church is the indispensable ark of salvation', Burgess, *Ancient Christian Fathers*, p. 84; cf. Kydd, *Charismatic Gifts*, pp. 70-71.

[69] Burgess, *Ancient Christian Fathers*, p. 85. He 'personally reports having numerous revelations though visions'. Even his contemporaries saw him as a

people were to follow his instruction and not let those who compromised their faith in order to avoid persecution receive the Eucharist. To support his position, he noted he had received visions: 'besides the nightly visions, by the days also, the innocent age of children among us is filled with the Holy Spirit, which in ecstasy sees with eyes and hears and speaks those things by which the Lord condemns speak to warn and instruct us'.[70] These boys were filled with ecstasy, implying that they recognized him as a true prophet.[71] 'With Cyprian, the process of institutionalization of the prophetic element was complete', wrote Burgess. 'Office and charismata were now one.'[72]

I. St. Gregory the Illuminator (240-325 CE)[73]

Gregory the Illuminator was called the 'apostle of Armenian Christianity' and even won the Armenian king Trdat (Tiridates) to Christ.[74] For Gregory, the tongues of Pentecost were seventy-two real languages through which the apostles went out and preached

---

prophet, Kydd, *Charismatic Gifts*, p. 71. Ash believes this institutionalization of the gifts began as early as 110 CE with Ignatius, Ash, 'Decline of Ecstatic Prophecy', pp. 234-35.

[70] Cyprian, '16. Cyprian to the Priests and Deacons', in *Saint Cyprian Letters (1-81)* (trans. Rose Bernarg Donna; Washington, DC: The Catholic University of America Press, 1964), pp. 48-49. Here Cyprian might be referring to Mt. 21.14, 15, where the children recognized Jesus as the son of David when the Pharisees did not. Kydd believes that these children were speaking prophetically, Kydd, *Charismatic Gifts*, p. 74.

[71] Cyprian received a letter from Firmilian, Bishop of Caesarea about a false prophetess who in ecstasy 'announced herself as a prophetess filled with the Holy Spirit', who backed up her claims by walking barefoot in the snow without harm, and by foretelling earthquakes, Tabbernee, *Prophets and Gravestones*, p. 154, cf. p. 156 n. 5; Kydd, *Charismatic Gifts*, pp. 83-84.

[72] Burgess 'Ancient Fathers', p. 736. Ash writes that it was the 'enhanced authority of the monarchial bishop' that 'forced the exit of the prophets' and not the 'conception of a closed canon', Ash, 'Decline of Ecstatic Prophecy', pp. 227-28; cf. Burgess, *Ancient Christian Fathers*, p. 52.

[73] According to tradition, Gregory was the only one that survived a family massacre and was raised by his Christian nurse in Cappadocia. He, along with king Trdat 'spread the Christian faith throughout the country ... so that Armenia justifiably claims to be the first Christian nation', Burgess, *Eastern Christian Traditions*, p. 119.

[74] Burgess describes him as 'the fourth century apostle of Armenian Christianity' because there were Christians in Armenia before Gregory, as a result of the ministry of Thaddeus and Bartholomew, Burgess, *Eastern Christian Traditions*, p. 111. Gregory won the king Trdat to Christ even though he was tortured 'in various horrible ways' by the king.

the gospel with a prophetic power.[75] In his *Teaching*, there is one sentence that speaks of tongues as ongoing:

> and [the Spirit] was revealed as (tongues of) fire, that the reprobate might burn and the elect be filled with the cups of joy of the Spirit, with *the gifts of the inexhaustible treasure which passes not away*; and that filled with the unfailing torrents of the Spirit, they might at the same time be illuminated by the power of the fiery Spirit.[76]

There is no other indication that Gregory had first-hand knowledge of glossolalia.

J. Eusebius of Caesarea (260-339 CE)[77]

In addition to recording most of the Montanist sayings above, Eusebius offered a significant personal opinion about Montanism:

> *it was at that very time,* in Phrygia, that Montanus, Alcibiades, Theodotus, and their followers began to acquire a widespread reputation for prophecy; for numerous other manifestations of the miraculous gift of God, still occurring in various churches, led many to believe that these men too were prophets.[78]

In other words, Montanism spread rapidly because 'at that time many churches were still familiar with spiritual gifts'; glossolalia

---

[75] First, tongues were a reversal of Babel's punishment. 'God scattered them into seventy-two mutually unintelligible tongues ... the gathering together again of these seventy-two tribes to the worship of the only God is the task of the church, begun by the seventy-two apostles who travelled to the farthest ends of the earth', Gregory, *The Teaching of Saint Gregory* (Robert W. Thomson, trans.; New Rochelle, NY: St Nersess Armenian Seminary, 2001), p. 7; cf. pp. 196, 202, 155-56. Second, Gregory described the Holy Spirit as prophetic inspiration that fills and 'attest(s) to them truly about the completed deeds which had been done through Christ', p. 156; cf. 154-57.

[76] Thomson, *The Teaching of Saint Gregory,* pp. 156-57 (emphasis added).

[77] He was a student of the learned priest, Pamphilus of Caesarea, and rose to become the bishop of Caesarea in Palestine. He became the official court theologian for the Emperor Constantine, and wielded considerable influence at the First Ecumenical Council of Nicaea in 325 CE, cf. Burgess, *Ancient Christian Traditions*, p. 101.

[78] Eusebius, *The History of the Church*, pp. 205-206 (emphasis added). πλεῖσται γὰρ οὖν καὶ ἄλλαι παραδοξοποιίαι τοῦ θείου χαρίσματος εἰσέτι τότε κατὰ διαφόρους ἐκκλησίας ἐκτελούμεναι πίστιν παρὰ πολλοῖς τοῦ κἀκείνους προφητεύειν παρεῖχον, Eusebius, *Ecclesiastical History,* 5.3.4, p. 442.

was a familiar phenomenon.[79]

K. St. Pachomius (d. 348 CE)[80]

A vivid account of speaking in foreign languages[81] occurred when Pachomius, an Egyptian monk, went to counsel a Roman monk under his care who only spoke Latin. This man wanted Pachomius to hear all his faults directly and not through an interpreter. Pachomius

> ordered the interpreter to withdraw and he made a sign with his hand to the Roman to wait until he came back to him ... He prayed for three hours, entreating God earnestly for this. Suddenly something like a letter written on a piece of papyrus was sent from heaven into his right hand. Reading it, he learned the speech of all the languages ... he came back to that brother with great joy, and began *to converse with him faultlessly in Greek and Latin*.[82]

On the surface,[83] this account was a case of xenolalia similar to

---

[79] Kydd, *Charismatic Gifts*, pp. 47-48. Eusebius recalled Quadratus and Philip's daughters who did 'a great many wonderful works', Burgess, *Ancient Christian Traditions*, p. 103.

[80] He was an Egyptian soldier and converted when he was shown kindness by some Christians. He founded several large monastic communities in Tabennisi, near the Nile River. He is considered to be the founder of cenobitic monasticism (communal), and was famous for his visions, his asceticism, and his leadership. See, Philip Schaff, *History of the Christian Church, Volume 3: Nicene and Post-Nicene Christianity, From Constantine the Great to Gregory the Great, A.D. 311-590* (Peabody, MA: Hendrickson, 2011, reprint; 1890), pp. 170-71; Terrence G. Kardong, *Pillars of Community: Four Rules of Pre-Benedictine Monastic Life* (Collegeville, MN: Liturgical Press, 2010), pp. 61-77.

[81] There is at least one reference to him falling into 'ecstasy' and that 'great lights would come out of his words', Arnand Veilleux (trans.), *Pachomian Koinonia. Cistercian Studies* 46.1 (Kalamazoo, MI: Cistercian Publications), p. 112. For an extensive bibliography of primary sources for xenolalia, see Stanley M. Burgess, 'Medieval Examples of Charismatic Piety in the Roman Catholic Church', in Russell P. Spitter (ed.), *Perspectives on the New Pentecostalism* (Grand Rapids, MI: Eerdmans, 1976), pp. 15-26 (20 n. 10).

[82] Veilleux, *Pachomian Koinonia*, pp. 51-52 (καὶ ἤρξατο αὐτῷ διαλέγεσθαι καὶ ἑλληνιστὶ καὶ ῥωμαϊστὶ ἀπταίστως, ὥστε τὸν ἀδελφὸν ἀκούσαντα λέγειν περὶ τοῦ μεγάλου ὅτι πάντας ὑπερβάλλει τοὺς σχολαστικοὺς εἰς τὴν διάλεκτον). Cf. *Acta Sanctorum* (Antwerp: apud Ioannem Meursium, 1643-1931), (hereafter *AASS*) May III, pp. 319-42.

[83] Some believe that what is written about Pachomius is just zealous hagiography. For example, 'tradition ascribes to him all sorts of miracles, even the gift of tongues and perfect dominion over nature so that he trod without harm on

Acts two.[84]

L. St. Hilary of Potiers (d. 367 CE)[85]

Kilian McDonnell found it strange that Hilary wrote from near the centre of Montanism and yet 'showed almost no interest in the threat'[86] but worked in Paul's full list of spiritual charisms, including tongues, four times in a formal treatise on the Trinity![87] McDonnell concluded that 'the repetitive listing of charisms signals a determination to protect and foster charisms in the church'.[88] Hilary wrote,

> speaking in tongues may be bestowed as a sign of the gift of the Holy Spirit; or by the interpretation of tongues ... clearly *these are* the churches agents of ministry and work of whom the body of Christ consists; and God has ordained them.[89]

---

serpents and scorpions and crossed the Nile on the backs of crocodiles', Schaff, *History of the Christian Church, Volume 3*, p. 171; cf. Robert Glenn Gromacki, *The Modern Tongues Movement* (Philadelphia, PA: Presbyterian and Reformed Publishing Company, 1967), p. 16.

[84] Alban Butler, *Butler's Lives of the Saints*, Vol. IV (Westminster, MD: Christian Classics, 1990), p. 327.

[85] Hilary was bishop of Poitiers in Gaul and was actively involved in the theological arguments of the Trinity of his day. His thought revealed an Eastern influence, that the Holy Spirit 'is beyond defining, for he is incomprehensible', Burgess, 'Holy Spirit, Doctrine of: The Ancient Fathers', p. 744.

[86] McDonnell, *Christian Initiation*, p. 135. He speculates that 'Montanists were not numerous in the great cities because of the presence of monarchical bishops', p. 137. He found only two 'very brief allusions' to Montanism, cf. pp. 134-35.

[87] McDonnell, *Christian Initiation*, pp. 144, 147 (emphasis added).

[88] McDonnell, *Christian Initiation*, p. 147. Further, McDonnell stated: 'no enthusiastic group at enmity with their bishops is going to drive out the charisms', p. 148. 'Although he made no direct claim to firsthand knowledge (to spiritual gifts) ... he implied acceptance of their place in ordinary Christian life', Williams, 'A History of Speaking in Tongues', p. 67; cf. Stanley Burgess, 'Evidence of the Spirit: The Ancient and Eastern Churches', in Gary B. McGee (ed.) *Initial Evidence: Historical and Biblical Perspectives on the Pentecostal Doctrine of Spirit Baptism* (Eugene, OR: Wipf & Stock, 2007, reprint: Hendrickson Publishers, 1991), pp. 3-15 (5).

[89] Hilary, 'On The Trinity', in Philip Schaff (ed.), *NPF, First Series: Homilies on the Gospel of John; Homilies on the First Epistle of John; Soliloquies*, Vol. 9, 30-33 (Peabody, MA: Hendrickson, 1995, reprint; 1887), pp. 146-47. Hilary was 'more open and affirming of the range of charisms' wrote McDonnell, along with Tertullian and Cyril, McDonnell, *Christian Initiation*, p. 323. Hilary 'distinguishes between "the sacraments of baptism and of the Spirit"', Burgess, 'Ancient and Eastern Churches', p. 5; cf. Hunter, *Spirit Baptism*, p. 128.

Burgess concluded, 'it is quite apparent that these (gifts) were functioning in the church of his day'.[90]

M. St. Augustine (354-430 CE) and the Complexities of the Age[91]

Augustine is a good representative of the complexities that studies of glossolalia face at this juncture in church history. He is included here not because of a specific occurrence of glossolalia, but to reveal the different undercurrents that emerged around this period. The prevailing scholarship holds that Augustine's view is that occurrences of glossolalia diminished and then ceased.[92] For example, Augustine wrote that the Spirit

> was given *in former days* to be the credentials of a rudimentary faith, and for the extension of the first beginnings of the Church. *For who expects* in these days that those on whom hands are laid that they may receive the Holy Spirit should forthwith begin to speak with tongues.[93]

In other words, the actual phenomenon had diminished so much that there was virtually no expectation of glossolalia.[94] Tongues on

---

[90] Burgess, 'Holy Spirit, Doctrine of: The Ancient Fathers', p. 745.

[91] Though not from a Christian family, his conversion and strong intellect compelled him to study under Ambrose. He became the premier theologian of this period (354-430 CE) and was the bishop of Hippo for 34 years, Burgess, *Ancient Christian Traditions*, p. 179. Burgess notes that 'his genius combined the mystical warmth and intellectual depth of the East with the pragmatism of the Latin mind ... above all, Augustine gave definitive shape to Western theology', p. 180.

[92] Sullivan wrote, 'The cessationist doctrine of tongues was dominant and powerful during the fourth and fifth centuries, but it was not universal', Charles A. Sullivan, 'Chrysostom on the Dogma of Tongues', http://charlesasullivan.com/5347/chrysostom-on-the-dogma-of-tongues/ accessed 31-3-2016. For support, Sullivan noted that the earliest cessationists were not uniform: for Augustine, tongues continued in the corporate voice of the Church while Cyril of Alexandria held that 'the miraculous endowment of languages was a temporary sign for the Jews'.

[93] Augustine, 'On Baptism, Against the Donatists', in Philip Schaff (ed.), *NPF, First Series: Augustin: Writings Against The Manicheans, And Against The Donatists*, Vol. 4 iii.16-21 (trans. J.R. King; New York: Charles Scribner and Sons, 1901), p. 443 (emphasis added).

[94] Augustine notes the cessation of tongues on several occasions. For example, he writes,

> in the first days ... they spoke in tongues that they hadn't learned, as the Spirit gave them to speak. These signs were appropriate for the time. For it

the Day of Pentecost,[95] according to Augustine, were a sign of the Church's future unity and breadth, reversed Babel's curse,[96] and continued on through the various languages where the Church is established.[97]

However, there were four additional undercurrents in Augustine's theology of tongues that challenge the above prevailing view. First, Augustine would not agree that *all miracles* had ceased.[98] He wrote on the contrary, 'he (the Holy Spirit) is manifest today in all

---

was necessary that the Holy Spirit be signified thus in all tongues, because the gospel of God was going to traverse all tongues throughout the earth. That was the sign that was given, and it passed. Is it expected now of those upon whom a hand is imposed, so that they may receive the Holy Spirit, that they speak in tongues? Or, when we imposed our hands upon those infants, was any one of you paying attention to see if they would speak in tongues? Augustine, 'Homilies on the First Epistle of John', in Boniface Ramsey (ed. and trans.), *The Works of Saint Augustine: A Translation for the 21st Century*, 1.14 (Hyde Park, NY: New City Press, 2008), Homily 6.10, p. 97.

Cf. Augustine, in Philip Schaff (ed.), *NPF, First Series: The Answer to the Letters of Petilian, the Donatist*, ii.32.74 & 4.548 (Peabody, MA: Hendrickson, 1995); cf. Augustine, 'On Baptism, Against the Donatists', iii.16.21, 4.443; Augustine, *St. Augustine: Tractates on the Gospel of John, 28-54*, in John W. Rettig (trans.), *The Fathers of the Church: A New Translation* (Washington, DC: The Catholic University Press of America, 1993), Tractate 32.7, pp. 46-47.

[95] Augustine believed that 'each person ... was speaking in the tongues of all nations', Augustine, 'Sermons', in John E. Rotelle (ed.) and Edmund Hill (trans.), *The Works of Saint Augustine: A Translation for the 21st Century*, 3.7, Sermon 266 (Hyde Park, NY: New City Press, 1993), p. 267; cf. Sermons 267-271, pp. 274-99. Edmund Hill calls this 'his own idiosyncratic interpretation', p. 281 n. 2.

[96] Augustine, 'Expositions of the Psalms: 51-72', John E. Rotelle (ed.), *The Works of Saint Augustine: A Translation for the 21st Century*, 3.17 (trans. Maria Boulding; Hyde Park, NY: New City Press, 2001), Psalm 54, p. 267; cf. Augustine, 'Sermons', Sermon 271, pp. 298-99.

[97] Augustine wrote that 'tongues ... was the sign of unity', Augustine, 'Sermons', Sermon 266, pp. 64-65; cf. Augustine, 'Sermons', Sermon 267, p. 275. Also, 'whoever has the Holy Spirit is in the Church, which speaks the languages of all people. Whoever is outside the Church, hasn't got the Holy Spirit', Augustine, 'Sermons', Sermon 268, p. 278.

[98] Augustine wrote 'I cannot record all the miracles I know', Augustine, in Marcus Dods (trans.), *City of God* 22.8 (New York: The Modern Library, 1993), p. 828. He entitled this chapter: 'Of Miracles Which Were Wrought that the World Might Believe in Christ, and Which Have Not Ceased Since the World Believed', pp. 819-31. A variation on this view is that, 'Augustine later repudiated this (early) position (of cessation)' because he later acknowledged that miracles continued ... contemporary miracles are relatively unknown not because they no longer occur, but simply because of bad communication', Ruthven, *On the Cessation of the Charismata*, p. 192.

tongues',[99] and 'why does no one speak in the languages of all nations? Because now the Church herself *speaks* in the languages of all nations.'[100] In other words, 'the gift (of tongues) being expressed through individuals has died, and now has been incorporated and operated by the corporate church'.[101] However, to arrive at this position Augustine limited glossolalia to foreign languages[102] and ignored any analysis of ecstatic glossolalia.[103] Further, he freely wrote about speech-miracles[104] such as the story of a man who spoke 'Christ, receive my spirit' involuntarily his whole life after being healed.[105] The response of his church when a young woman was healed in front of them was: 'they now rejoiced (jubilated) ... they shouted God's *praises without words*, but with such noise that our ears could scarcely bear it'.[106]

Second, historically, glossolalia may have continued among groups outside of the Latin Church. Charles A. Sullivan 'postulates' that Augustine's theology of tongues was largely in response to the Donatists,[107] who were popular in his

---

[99] Augustine, 'Expositions of the Psalms: 121-150', Boniface Ramsey (ed.), *The Works of Saint Augustine: A Translation for the 21ˢᵗ Century*, 3.20 (trans. Maria Boulding; Hyde Park, NY: New City Press, 2004), Psalm 147, p. 464.

[100] Augustine, *Tractates on the Gospel of John*, Tractate 32.7, pp. 46-47; cf. Tractate 52.8, p. 286.

[100] Burgess, 'Medieval Examples', p. 19; cf. p. 22.

[101] Charles A. Sullivan, 'Augustine on the Tongues of Pentecost: Intro', http://charlesasullivan.com/3668/augustine-on-the-tongues-of-pentecost-intro, accessed 3/21/2016, 8 a.m.

[102] Sullivan wrote, 'practically everyone who wrote on this until quite recently, understood the gift of tongues to be the miraculous ability to preach the gospel in foreign languages'; it was a 'mistaken notion', Sullivan, *Charisms and Charismatic Renewal*, p. 148; cf. Burgess, 'Medieval Examples', p. 19.

[103] Sullivan, 'Augustine on the Tongues of Pentecost: Intro'. Augustine interpreted all glossolalic occurrences in the Bible as foreign languages. For example, 'and then there was enacted this sign; whoever received the Holy Spirit, suddenly, filled with the Spirit, started speaking with the tongues of all', Augustine, 'Sermons', Sermon 267, pp. 274-75.

[104] Augustine, 'Homilies on the First Epistle of John', Homily 6.10, p. 97. Augustine himself was so overwhelmed with the Spirit one time that he could not pray out loud, Augustine, *City of God*, p. 822.

[105] Augustine, *City of God*, p. 827; cf. p. 826.

[106] Augustine, *City of God*, p. 831 (emphasis added), see 'jubilate' below.

[107] The Donatists were a protest movement in North Africa that believed it was the true church for not comprising during persecution. It viewed Augustine's church as compromised, political (secularly), and apostate. Despite persecution, it survived until North Africa was 'submerged by the invading moors in

region.[108] Sullivan wrote,

> because they personally spoke in tongues and the Catholic Church did not ... Augustine's polemic against their use of Christian tongues was a perceived weakness that he could exploit ... (when) it may not have been central to the Donatist movement at all ... tongues were supposed to be a sign of unity, not dissension.[109]

In other words, Augustine's cessationist view of glossolalia may have been only a rhetorical device, 'a way to demonstrate the Catholic Church's superiority over what was perceived as a populist heresy'.[110]

Third, although Augustine said little about ecstatic glossolalia, Eddie Ensley argued that Augustine encouraged its functional equivalent, called 'jubilation'.[111] Jubilation was a 'form of praying and singing aloud without words' that could be at times ecstatic[112] and mystical.[113] For example, in his commentary on the Psalms, Augustine wrote:

---

the seventh century', David F. Wright, 'The Donatists in North Africa', in *Eerdman's Handbook to the History of Christianity* (Grand Rapids, MI: Eerdmans, 1977), pp. 202-203 (203).

[108] Charles A. Sullivan, 'An Analysis of Augustine on Tongues and the Donatists', http://charlesasullivan.com/3662/an-analysis-of-augustine-on-tongues-and-the-donatists/, accessed 3/21/2016. Burgess wrote, 'one can *only speculate* that, in specifically denying the "evidence" of tongues (multiple times), he might have been reacting against contemporary enthusiasts of whom we have no historic record', Burgess, 'Ancient and Eastern Churches', p. 9.

[109] Sullivan, 'Augustine and the Donatists'. Sullivan understands this position to be 'a postulation'; however, also believes his position would be clearer if all of Augustine's works were available in English. Some of Augustine's writing is only accessible in Latin, Sullivan, 'Augustine on the Tongues of Pentecost: Intro'.

[110] Sullivan 'Augustine and the Donatists'.

[111] Jubilation (or jubilus) was a 'form of spontaneous prayer ... a form of prayer without words, closely resembling the "tongues" of present-day charismatic renewal', Ensley, *Sounds of Wonder*, pp. 2, 3.

[112] Ensley quoted music historian Albert Seay: 'it was "an overpowering expression of ecstasy of the spirit, a joy that could not be restricted to words"', Ensley, *Sounds of Wonder*, p. 7.

[113] Jubilation 'is the expression of the soul in a higher sense ... the (human) spirit's yearning for the inner things of God ... not only in a Christian, but in a

a person who is shouting with gladness does not bother to articulate words. The shout is a wordless shout of joy; it is the cry of the mind expanded with gladness, expressing its feelings as best it can rather than comprehending the sense. When someone is exulting and happy *he passes beyond words that can be spoken and understood, and bursts forth into a wordless cry of exultation.* Such a person is clearly rejoicing vocally, but is so full of intense joy that he is unable to explain what makes him happy.[114]

Though the nomenclature is extra-biblical, it may well be that Augustine was describing ecstatic glossolalia. Ensley's thesis merits further academic investigation.[115]

Fourth, Church politics played a role in Augustine's thought as well. James L. Ash credited the phenomena's decline to the rise of a 'monarchical' bishopric. Montanism, 'became a major threat to establishmentarians, whose spokesmen were the emerging monarchial bishops ... (who) simply captured it (ecstatic prophecy) and used it for their own ends'.[116] And Morton T. Kelsey suggested

---

distinctively mystical way', G.B. Chambers, *Folksong – Plainsong: A Study in Origins and Musical Relationships* (London: The Merlin Press, 1972), p. 5.

[114] Augustine, 'Expositions of the Psalms 99-120', Psalm 99, p. 14 (emphasis added). Consider these two descriptive sentences by Augustine: 1) to shout with joy 'means to give voice to a wondering happiness that cannot be adequately expressed in words', Augustine, 'Expositions of the Psalms: 33-50', John E. Rotelle (ed.), *The Works of Saint Augustine: A Translation for the 21st Century*, 3.16 (trans. Maria Boulding; Hyde Park, NY: New City Press, 2000), Psalm 46, p. 329. 2) 'Jubilation is wordless praise that proceeds from the soul', Augustine, 'Expositions of the Psalms: 121-150', Psalm 150, p. 514. Cf. Augustine, 'Expositions of the Psalms: 1-32', in John E. Rotelle (ed.), *The Works of Saint Augustine: A Translation for the 21st Century*, 3.15 (trans. Maria Boulding; Hyde Park, NY: New City Press, 2000), Psalm 32, pp. 400-401; Augustine, 'Expositions of the Psalms: 51-72', Psalm 65, p. 286; Augustine, 'Expositions of the Psalms: 73-98', John E. Rotelle (ed.), *The Works of Saint Augustine: A Translation for the 21st Century*, 3.18 (trans. Maria Boulding; Hyde Park, NY: New City Press, 2002), Psalm 80, p. 155; Psalm 94, p. 411; Psalm 97, p. 461. Here, Ensley's work refers back to the Latin, Ensley, *Sounds of Wonder*, p. 131; cf. Chambers, *Folksong – Plainsong*, pp. 110-11.

[115] Sullivan concurs and notes that eventually jubilation moved from corporate to individual wordless singing and that there is a 'close analogy between what St. Paul called "singing with the Spirit" and what Christian tradition has called "jubilation"', Sullivan, *Charisms and Charismatic Renewal*, p. 148.

[116] Ash, 'Decline of Ecstatic Prophecy', pp. 249-50. For support he cites: 1) the bishop's 'embarrassment that the charisma has become less active among them'; 2) the bishops claimed that their glossolalia was genuine simply because it was 'tested by the Holy Spirit in the holy Church'; 3) and that after 'prophecy

that the RCC's 'ban on speaking in and interpreting an unknown language' was because ecstatic glossolalia became a sign of demonic possession.[117]

Clearly the great theologian Augustine lived at a complex time for the theology of glossolalia. Perhaps he was limited by the theological undercurrents of the institution he served, but regardless, he allowed charismatic expressions he knew to be genuine in his own parish.

III. The Middle Ages through the Reformation

Contrary to the claims of cessationists[118] and some Pentecostals,[119] an argument could be made that there was no gap in historical accounts of tongues speech between the fifth and seventeenth centuries.[120] This brief survey will show that glossolalia did occur in the Western Church even though the reports were hagiographic[121] and occurred among the monastics or

---

began to wane within Montanism ... (the Bishops claimed that) "the prophetic gift must continue in the whole Church until the final coming, as the apostle (Paul) insists"', pp. 239, 240, 241.

[117] Kelsey, *Tongue Speaking*, p. 47. 'The official position of the Roman church ... is found expressed in the official Catholic book of public services, the *Rituale Romanum*, which came to a large extent to its present form around 1000 A.D.', p. 46; cf. Stanley M. Burgess, *Christian Peoples of the Spirit: A Documentary History of Pentecostal Spirituality from the Early Church to the Present* (New York: New York University Press, 2011), p. 98. Even praying in one's own mother tongue was 'frowned upon' given the Latin Church's severity, Williams, 'A History of Speaking in Tongues', p. 71; cf. Burgess, 'Medieval Examples', p. 19.

[118] Hinson, 'Significance of Glossolalia', pp. 188-89.

[119] Pentecostal scholars were slow to examine glossolalia in the medieval church 'because the absence of information fits their thesis', Burgess, 'Medieval Examples', p. 15 n. 2. For example, F.J. Lee dovetails Jer. 5.25 with Hos. 6.3, when he writes that God gives 'the former and latter rain in HIS season, but (Jeremiah) further tells them their iniquities have turned away these things', but if we will return (Hosea) 'He will come unto us as the rain', Lee, '"Is the Present Tongue Movement of God?"', p. 1.

[120] Michael J. McClymond, 'Charismatic Gifts: Healing, Tongue-Speaking, Prophecy, and Exorcism', in Lamin Sanneh and Michael McClymond (ed.), *The Wiley Blackwell Companion to World Christianity* (Boston, MA: John Wiley & Sons, 2016), p. 402.

[121] Sullivan argues that even though these hagiographic 'accounts cannot be taken as factual historical documents' and are a 'special genre', they do 'reflect the theological, mystical and intellectual perceptions of the late-Medieval period', Sullivan, http://charlesasullivan.com/6166/late-medieval-peaking-in-tongues, accessed 18/4/2016; cf. Burgess, 'Medieval Examples', p. 17. The most

mystics.[122] In fact, Christine F. Cooper-Rompato, argued that these popular hagiographic accounts revealed that 'the gift of tongues (xenolalia) was *almost expected* in the vitae of famous preachers',[123] and that 'xenoglossia is intimately linked with perceptions of holiness and inspiration'.[124] Ensley argued that 'one can still see large groups of ordinary people improvising expressive jubilations well into the Middle Ages and mystically oriented small groups entering into heartfelt jubilations at least into the seventeenth'.[125] The conflicted Latin Church's understanding[126] was best described by Burgess:

> the medieval Roman Church developed a dual standard in the treatment of tongue-speaking. While condemning the ability to speak in an unknown language and to interpret the utterance as an evidence of demon possession, the church also honored a few of its more illustrious number for their tongues-speaking … including the phenomenon … on their behalf in the canonization process.[127]

---

readily available hagiographic works in English are: *Acta Sanctorum* (AASS), *Bulter's Lives of the Saints*, and Jacobus de Voragine, *The Golden Legend: Readings on the Saints* (trans. William Granger Ryan; Princeton: Princeton University Press, 1993).

[122] 'The one aspect of medieval pneumatology that has been ignored is also that which is of most interest – namely, that of the Holy Spirit and spiritual gifts', Burgess, *Medieval Traditions*, p. 8; cf. p. 6. Dollar called these tendencies 'superstitious, mystical, unexplainable, awesome, weird, and monastic', Dollar, 'Church History and the Tongues Movement', p. 317.

[123] Christine F. Cooper-Rompato, *The Gift of Tongues: Women's Xenoglossia in the Latter Middle Ages* (University Park, PA: Pennsylvania State University, 2010), p. 14 (emphasis added). 'Xenoglossia forms a vital part of later medieval religious culture', p. 2.

[124] Cooper-Rompato, *Women's Xenoglossia in the Latter Middle Ages*, p. 12.

[125] Ensley, *Sounds of Wonder*, p. 15. Ensley notes that 'during the ninth century … improvisation of the jubilus ceased to be an expected part of the liturgy' due to a lack of 'spiritual sensitivity' from the large number of new converts and 'the constant disruption … caused by the successive influx of the barbarians', pp. 14, 15.

[126] Williams, 'A History of Speaking in Tongues', p. 67. 'Given their mistaken notion of what the gift of tongues really was, it was understandable that they would not identify the wordless singing of jubilation with the NT charism', Sullivan, *Charisms and Charismatic Renewal: A Biblical and Theological Study*, p. 148; cf. Burgess, 'Medieval Examples', p. 23.

[127] Burgess, 'Medieval Examples', p. 25. Burgess notes three canonizations where glossolalia was noted: Vincent Ferrer by Pope Pius II in 1445; Francis Xavier by Pope Gregory XV in 1623; and Louis Bertrand by Clement X in 1671,

Two trajectories diverged here between the Western and the Eastern Churches. Kelsey noted that due to the barbarian invasions in the fifth century the Latin west and Orthodox east 'developed different attitudes towards the gifts of the Spirit in general and speaking in tongues in particular'.[128] In the west, because of the fall of civic government,

> the church remained as virtually the only organization of civilized life and was forced to take upon it many of the functions of secular authority ... it became intensely practical and this-worldly ... individual experience of the gifts of the Spirit was soft-pedaled.[129]

The following accounts are representative of this conflicted period in the history of glossolalia.[130]

A. St. Hildegard of Bingen (1098-1179 CE)[131]

St. Hildegard was called a 'great seeress and prophetess, the Sibyl of the Rhine',[132] and was known for her voluminous prophetic and musical writings, her healings, and miracles.[133] Hildegard was revered and yet so misunderstood that some contemporaries 'denounced her as demon-possessed,[134] and she has not officially

---

pp. 24-25. The rationale was spelled out by Pope Benedict XIV; cf. http://charlesasullivan.com/6199/pope-benedict-xiv-on-the-gift-of-tongues/ accessed 25/4/2016.

[128] Kelsey, *Tongue Speaking*, p. 41; cf. Ensley, *Sounds of Wonder*, p. 1.

[129] Kelsey, *Tongues Speaking*, p. 42.

[130] Cooper-Rompato, discovered fifteen episodes of xenolalia beyond the twelve that Burgess and Cutten chronicled, Cooper-Rompato, *Women's Xenoglossia in the Latter Middle Ages*, pp. 11, 12.

[131] 'She was given when eight years old into the keeping of ... the Benedictine monastery at Disibodenberg ... (in time) she became the manager of the convent at Disibodenberg ... (and) the founder of two other convents', Sarah L. Higley, *Hildegard of Bingen's Unknown Language: An Edition, Translation, and Discussion* (New York, NY: Palgrave MacMillan, 2007), p. 13.

[132] Gromacki, *The Modern Tongues Movement*, p. 18.

[133] Because she had only rudimentary reading and writing skills a 'monk was ordered to put into writing whatever she related', Francis Mershman, 'St. Hildegard', *The Catholic Encyclopedia VII* (NY: The Encyclopedia Press, 1913), p. 352. Her works include three volumes of visions similar to 'Ezekiel and the Apocalypse'; musical compositions; a musical drama; nearly 400 letters; sermons; and notes on natural medicine and cures, Hildegard, *Riesencodex*.

[134] Cooper-Rompato's thesis is that accounts of women's xenolalia are 'more narrow in scope for the purpose of semiprivate spiritual conversation and counseling' so as not to challenge the authority of their male counterparts, Cooper-

been beatified'.[135] She

> sang in unknown words with such facility and winsomeness that her utterances were called 'concerts in the Spirit.' Although the strange language of her songs seemed to be a peculiar combination of local German dialect and Latin, both of which languages she of course knew well, she herself felt so strongly that the words ... were of such inspirited and revealing significance that she prepared a glossary codex providing the translation.[136]

This codex, the *Lingua Ignota*,[137] contains one thousand and twelve words and is considered by some to be a 'made up' language';[138] however, Jeffery Schnapp considers it 'typical of glossolalia' and an early attempt to codify glossolalia.[139]

Rompato, *Women's Xenoglossia in the Latter Middle Ages*, p. 16; cf. pp. 72, 73. To go beyond the cultural and institutional boundaries would 'indicate devilish possession', p. 84.

[135] Williams, 'A History of Speaking in Tongues', p. 70. 'No formal canonization has ever taken place, but her name is in the Roman Martyrology and her feast is celebrated', Mershman, 'St. Hildegard', p. 352.

[136] Williams, 'A History of Speaking in Tongues', p. 70.

[137] Literally, 'unknown language'. Hildegard describes it as, 'an unknown language brought forth by the simple human Hildegard (Ignota lingua per simplicem hominem Hildegardem prolata)', *Riesencodex*, f. 461v.

[138] Higley compared it to the fictional languages of J.R.R. Tolkien or Lewis Carol, Higley, *Hildegard of Bingen*, pp. 10-11. Nevertheless, she notes that at times Hildegard seems to hear a language 'separate from the published lists', p. 21. 'I have no doubt', writes Higley, 'that Hildegard was familiar with the xenoglossia of Acts and considered what she was exercising a charisma, offering a "new" language, in fact an "unknown language" inspired in her by God, which she then translated in the list ... (and that) there is something of the "ecstatic" that is suggested in Hildegard's antiphon "O Orzchis Ecclesia"', p. 41.

[139] Linguistically, Jeffery Schnapp, believed that it 'repeats a pattern typical of glossolalia ... (in) its somewhat limited phonetic "palette"', because it is on the 'expressive' rather than 'analytical' end of the linguistic spectrum, Jeffery T. Schnapp, 'Virgin Word: Hildegard of Bingen's *Lingua Ignota* and the Development of Imaginary Languages Ancient to Modern', *Exemplaria* 3.2 (Fall, 1991), pp. 267-98 (290; cf. pp. 271, 273). Schnapp believes that the *Lingua Ignota* 'represents an effort to begin language anew ... an effort to recover the purity and innocence of Adam's act of naming', p. 287. He also observes that Hildegard herself notes its connection to music, specifically her 'liturgical *Symphonia*', p. 291; cf. n. 40. Burgess writes that 'she is remembered for her unknown language (*Lingua Ignota*) or glossolalia, her "concerts" or singing in the Spirit', Burgess, *Christian Peoples of the Spirit*, p. 99.

B. St. Anthonius of Padua (1195-1231 CE)

A short hagiographic account of Saint Antonius of Padua stated that

> St. Anthony of Padua ... was preaching before the Pope and Cardinals in a consistory where there were men from different countries ... And being inflamed by the Holy Spirit and inspired with apostolic eloquence, he preached and explained the word of God so effectively ... that all ... heard and understood every one of his words as if he had spoken in each of their languages ... it seemed to them that the former miracle of the Apostles at the time of Pentecost had been renewed.[140]

Padua's account revealed that 'people during this period perceived the miracle of tongues to be' foreign languages.[141]

C. St. Vincent Ferrer (1350-1419 CE)[142]

St. Vincent Ferrer was a natural and powerful preacher[143] who had 'the gift of tongues'.[144] Though he was limited to his native language of Valencian or Latin,[145] he was understood by people of many countries on his missionary journeys through Europe.[146] On

---

[140] Cooper-Rompato, *Women's Xenoglossia in the Latter Middle Ages*, p. 28; cf. AASS, June 2.13.

[141] Sullivan, http://charlesasullivan.com/6274/st-anthony-of-paduas-miraculous-speech, accessed 18/4/2016.

[142] Born in Valentia, Spain, he excelled in his studies and forsaking family wealth became a monk in the Order of St. Dominic. Declining both the position of bishop and cardinal by Pope Benedict XIII, he 'earnestly entreated to be appointed (an) apostolic missionary', Butler, *Butler's Lives of the Saints, Vol. IV*, p. 31; cf. p 29. He was canonized by Pope Pius II in 1458, p. 36. Burgess writes, 'this is one of the most extreme cases of hagiography in Christian history', Burgess, *Christian Peoples of the Spirit*, p. 126.

[143] The content of his peaching was the 'ordinary subjects' but 'he delivered his discourses with so much energy that he filled the most insensible with terror ... his who auditory was seized with trembling ... he was frequently obliged to stop to give leisure for the sobs and sighs of the congregation', Butler, *The Lives of the Saints, Vol. IV*, p. 32; cf. p. 35; Eddie Hyatt, *2000 Years of Charismatic Christianity* (Lake Mary, FL: Charisma House, 2002), p. 61.

[144] Nicholas Clemangis, a medical doctor at the University of Paris, heard him preach and believed that 'he was endowed with the gift of tongues', Albert Reinhart, 'St. Vincent Ferrer', *The Catholic Encyclopedia* (NY: The Encyclopedia Press, 1913), XV, p. 438.

[145] Butler, *The Lives of the Saints*, IV, p. 33.

[146] His evangelized in England, Scotland, Ireland, Aragon, Castile, France, Switzerland, and Italy, even converting 'a prodigious number of Jews and Mohometans [sic]' people to Catholicism, Butler, *The Lives of the Saints*, IV, p. 31.

one occasion, everyone could understand him despite their being present people who spoke several different languages:

> the gift of languages ... had been granted to him ... each person ... comprehending his speech every single word of them perfectly. Just as if he was born in the country of every single one of them and had been speaking their language ... they distinctly understood the man of God speaking his own native language.[147]

Like Padua, emphasis was on the hearing to validate the piety of the speaker.[148] Williams noted that miracles 'accompanied the ministries of those who spoke in tongues', and Ferrer was no exception.[149]

D. St. Ignatius of Loyola (1491-1556 CE)[150]

In writing about his mystical experiences with the Holy Spirt,[151] Ignatius included an ongoing experience that sounded very similar to singing in glossolalia. He called it *loquela*.[152] In *Spiritual Diary* Ignatius wrote that

> during the interior and exterior *loquela* everything moves me to divine love and to the gift of *loquela* divinely bestowed. I felt so much harmony in the inner *loquela* that I cannot explain it ...

---

[147] Sullivan, http://charlesasullivan.com, accessed 2/5/2016; cf. Butler, *The Lives of the Saints*, IV, p. 33.

[148] Sullivan, http://charlesasullivan.com, accessed 2/5/2016. 'This is the closest parallel, in fact or imagination, to the experience of Acts 2 that we find recorded', Kelsey, *Tongues Speaking*, p. 50.

[149] Williams, 'A History of Speaking in Tongues', p. 71; cf. Butler, *The Lives of the Saints, Vol. IV*, pp. 31-33.

[150] He founded the Society of Jesus (the Jesuits) and attempted to reform the Roman church from within 'principally by education, more frequent use of the sacraments, and preaching the gospel to the newly discovered pagan world', Burgess, 'Holy Spirit, Doctrine of: The Ancient Fathers', p. 765.

[151] Ignatius discerned the Holy Spirit as the source for *loquela* and clearly distinguished between the influences of Holy Spirit and the devil, Egan, *Ignatius of Loyola*, p. 195; cf. Burgess, *Medieval Traditions*, p. 181. 'For Ignatius, tears signified the presence of the Holy Spirit', Burgess, 'Holy Spirit, Doctrine of: The Ancient Fathers', p. 766.

[152] Which means '"voices," "speech," "language," or "discourse" ... moreover, (he) always mentions them in conjunction with the presence or absence of tears', Egan, *Ignatius of Loyola*, p. 193. Burgess notes that Ignatius carefully parsed his writings to avoid any connection with a persecuted religious movement (the Alumbrados) which claimed 'direct and constant inspiration of the Holy Spirit', Burgess, 'Holy Spirit, Doctrine of: The Ancient Fathers', p. 765.

(perhaps) I took too much delight in the tone of the *loquela,* attending to the sound, without paying so much attention to the meaning (*significación*) of the words (*palabras*) and of the *loquela*.'[153]

Harvey Egan explained that '*loquela* seem to be mystical music, unusually lovely in tonality, pregnant with meaning and often accompanied by significant words', words that were 'the language of the mystic's psychosomatic structure' and 'they took place *ineffably*, beyond understanding'.[154] Egan says 'perhaps one can even connect (it) … with today's charismatic phenomenon of sung glossolalia'.[155]

E. St. Francis Xavier (1506 – 1552 CE)[156]

Biographer, Dominique Bouhours, noted that St. Francis Xavier was frustrated with his inability to speak in the languages of the people to whom he ministered, but believed that Xavier was occasionally given the gift of tongues:[157]

> then it was that, for the first time, God communicated to Xavier the gift of tongues … Xavier spoke the language of the barbarous people, and instructed them in it, without the aid of an interpreter, although he had never learned it.[158]

Later in his missionary journey, his 'Portuguese was understood by

---

[153] Egan, *Ignatius of Loyola*, pp. 193-94. Original citation in *Spiritual Diary*, 'May 11' and 'May 22', translated into English in Antonio T. de Nicholas, *Powers of Imagining* (Albany: S.U.N.Y., 1986).

[154] Egan, *Ignatius of Loyola*, pp. 194, 197, 198.

[155] Egan, *Ignatius of Loyola*, p. 196.

[156] He was a Jesuit missionary from Spain to India, Indonesia, Japan and China. He was a co-founder of the Society of Jesus along with Ignatius of Loyola. He was canonized 12-3-1622 by Pope Gregory XV.

[157] Dominique Bouhours, *The Life of St. Francis Xavier, of the Society of Jesus, Apostle of India* (trans. James Dryden; Philadelphia: Eugene Cummiskey, 1841), originally published in French in 1688, pp. 90, 448; cf. *Monumenta Xaveriana et Autographis vel ex Antiquioribus Exemplis Collecta* (Madrid: Typis Gabrielis Lopez del Horno, 1912), II, pp. 224, 546, 555, 689, 694, 698. Bouhours noted that 'none of the biographers … have ascribed to him a constant or habitual gift of tongues', just 'at Travancor, – and afterwards at Amanguchi; – and on some other occasions', p. 448; Burgess, *Christian Peoples of the Spirit*, pp. 152-56.

[158] Bouhours, *The Life of St. Francis Xavier,* p. 93. Burgess believed this to be Tamil and the language of the Molucca Islands, Burgess, 'Medieval Examples', p. 20.

both the Japanese and Chinese'.[159] 'At the beatification, Pope Gregory XIII remarked that his gift of tongues had been the means of attracting widespread interest in Christianity'.[160] Bouhours noted that the Church's careful investigation of the above events included interviews of eyewitnesses.[161]

F. The Anabaptists (1525 CE)[162]

The Anabaptist movement began in Switzerland in house meetings, called conventicles, and it spread rapidly.[163] Anabaptists were committed to restoring the church 'to the vigour and faithfulness of its earliest centuries'.[164] In the early years of the movement, it

---

[159] Burgess, 'Medieval Examples', p. 21; cf. n. 15; Benedictus XIV, *Opera Omnia in Unum Corpus Collecta et Nunc Primum in Quindecim Tomos Distributa* (Venice: Sumptibus J. Remondini, 1787-88), III, p. 250. This claim was also made by his first biographer: Horatius Tursellini, *De vita Francisci Saverii* (Rome, 1594). An episode at Amanguchi, Japan was not as clear as the others because Xavier was acquainted with three levels of Japanese speech, but miraculously was able to answer multiple questions on a wide variety of subjects with just a few Japanese words simultaneously, Bouhours, *The Life of St. Francis Xavier*, pp. 249-250, 274-275.

[160] Williams, 'A History of Speaking in Tongues', p. 74.

[161] Bouhours, *The Life of St. Francis Xavier*, p. 275.

[162] 'The Anabaptists made the most radical attempt of the Reformation era to renew the church. They did not consist of a single, coherent organization, but (was) a loose grouping of movements', John H. Yoder and Alan Kreider, 'The Anabaptists', in *Eerdman's Handbook to the History of Christianity* (Grand Rapids, MI: Eerdmans, 1977), pp. 399-403 (399). Despised by both the Catholics and the Protestants, they were persecuted so much, that 'the principles of British dissent originated' as a reaction to their suffering, Roland Bainton, *The Reformation of the Sixteenth Century* (Boston, MA: Beacon Press, 1952), p. 107; cf. Yoder and Kreider, 'The Anabaptists', p. 402. 'Only three groups were able to survive beyond the sixteenth century ... the 'brethren' in Switzerland and south Germany; the Mennonites in the Netherlands and north Germany; and the Hutterites in Moravia', p. 403. Walter Klaassen dates the Anabaptism movement from 21-1-1525, when in Zurich, a half a dozen men 'baptized one another' and 'commissioned each other to build Christ's church on earth', Walter Klaassen, *Anabaptism: Neither Catholic nor Protestant* (Waterloo, ON: Conrad Press, 1973), p. 4.

[163] Franklin Hamlin Littell, *The Origins of Sectarian Protestantism: A Study of the Anabaptist View of the Church* (New York: Macmillan, 1964), pp. 18-9. Conventicles were 'outside the control of the local church', Charles H. Byrd II, 'Pentecostalism's Anabaptist Heritage: The Zofingen Disputation of 1532', *JEPTA* 28.1 (2008), pp. 49-61 (53-54).

[164] Yoder and Kreider, 'The Anabaptists', p. 401. They embraced a literal reading of the Bible, George Hunston Williams, *The Radical Reformation* (Philadelphia: The Westminster Press, 1962), pp. 828-32. Walter Rauschenbusch called the Anabaptists the 'root and branch' of the Reformation because the Reformers only went 'half-way' to a biblical faith, Littell, *Anabaptist View of the*

was not unusual for there to be charismatic phenomenon including tongues.[165] In 1525, Johannes Kessler became an influential leader in the St. Gallen conventicle and chronicled the events.[166] Kessler witnessed Margaret Hottinger of Zollikon speak in languages no one could understand.[167] In Appenzell, adults 'became as little children, *babbling* and playing in the dirt'.[168] In his anti-Anabaptist[169] polemic Zwingli's successor, Heinrich Bullinger, preserved an entire early Anabaptist tract[170] which stated nine reasons why the Anabaptists did not worship in Lutheran and Zwinglian

---

Church, p. 2 (Org. cite: Walter Rauschenbusch, 'The Zurich Anabaptists and Thomas Muntzer', *American Journal of Theology* 9 [1905], pp. 91-106 [92]); cf. Klaassen, *Anabaptism*, pp. 9, 79-80. They also embraced a 'mysticism ... a direct experience of God in the soul ... a cultivation of certain disciplines that would lead to the direct vision of God', Klaassen, *Anabaptism*, p. 67.

[165] 'Revivalist symptoms showed on occasion, with dancing, acting like children, and speaking in tongues', Littell, *Anabaptist View of the Church*, p. 19; cf. Yoder and Kreider, 'The Anabaptists', pp. 400-401; Klaassen, *Anabaptism*, p. 2.

[166] Byrd, 'Pentecostalism's Anabaptist Heritage', p. 54.

[167] Johannes Kessler, *Sabata: St. Galler Reformationschronik 1523-1539* (ed. Traugott Schiess; Leipzig: Im Kommissionsverlag von Rudolf Haupt, 1911), pp. 51-52.

[168] Heinold Fast, *Quellen Zur Geschichte der Täufer in der Schweiz, 2 Band, Ostschweis* (Zurich: Theologiischer Verlag, 1973), in C.A. Snyder and Linda A.H. Hecht (eds.), *Profiles of Anabaptist Women* (Waterloo, ON: Wilfrid Laurier University Press, 1996), p. 19 (emphasis added).

[169] Most of what is known of these early Anabaptists, came from her critics; cf. Williams, *The Radical Reformation,* p. 443; Conrad Grebel, 'Grebel to Müntzer, Zurich, 9/5/1524', in Leland Harder (ed.), *The Sources of Swiss Anabaptism: The Grebel Letters and Related Documents* (Scottsdale, PA: Herald Press, 1985), p. 286.

[170] Heinrich Bullinger, Der Widertoufferen Vrsprung, fürgang, secten, wäsen, fürnemme vnd gemeine jrer leer artickel, ouch jre gründ und warumb sy sich absünderind, vnnd ein eigne kirchen anrichtind, mit widerlegung vnd antwort vff alle und yede jre gründ und artickel, sampt Christenlichem bericht vnd vermanen, dass sy jres irrthumbs und absünderens abstandind, und sich mit der kirchen Christi vereinigind, abgeteilt in VI Bücher, und beschriben durch Heynrichen Bullingern. ['The Anabaptists' origin, development, sects, nature, the clarification and appreciation of their doctrines, and also of their reasons and why they separate themselves and establish their own church. Including a rebuttal and response to each and every one of their fundamental beliefs and articles, and including a Christian report and admonition of their fallacy, their distinct separation, and their uniting of themselves with the Church of Christ. Provided in six volumes and described by Heinrich Bullinger.'] (Zurich: Christoph Frochauer, 1560), in 'Answer of Some Who Are Called (Ana) Baptists, Why They Do Not Attend The Churches: A Swiss Brethren Tract', Shem Peachey and Paul Peachey (ed. & trans.), Paul Peachey, *Mennonite Quarterly Review* 45.1 (Jan 1971), pp. 5-32.

churches.[171] 'The congregation is deprived and robbed' when only one professional was allowed to speak, because 'Paul ... commands that they not forbid to speak in tongues, which ... serves to the edification of the congregation'.[172] Though the tract's argument was broader than glossolalia alone, it was clear that they 'insisted that the manifestation of the gifts of the Holy Spirit defined a true Christian church':[173]

> Anabaptists' understanding of Paul was that the conventicle attendees were bound by love to speak out and to edify the church using Psalms, doctrine, *tongues, interpretation*, revelation and prophesies ... the presence of the Holy Spirit ... through the working of His gifts within the congregation was the mark of any true Christian church.[174]

G. St. Louis Bertrand (1526-1581 CE)[175]

Burgess wrote that 'Luis Bertrand spoke in the language of the Moors under the inspiration of the Holy Spirit'[176] and that the miraculous gift of tongues facilitated his canonization.[177] However, he is better known as the 'Apostle of South America', because during his seven years as a missionary, his Spanish 'was understood by the Indian natives in the Western Hemisphere' and 'was reported to have converted tens of thousands of American inhabitants'.[178]

IV. The Eastern Church

Kelsey noted that in the East 'the door was never closed to the

---

[171] Byrd noted that all nine reasons argued that the Reformers were not following the Bible closely, Byrd, 'Pentecostalism's Anabaptist Heritage', pp. 58-61.

[172] Peachey, 'Swiss Brethren Tract', pp. 13, 11.

[173] Byrd, 'Pentecostalism's Anabaptist Heritage', p. 61.

[174] Byrd, 'Pentecostalism's Anabaptist Heritage', p. 58.

[175] He was a Spanish Dominican who served in Valencia, Spain and also served as a missionary to Latin America. He was a spiritual counsellor to St. Teresa of Alvia, Butler, *Butler's Lives of the Saints, Vol. IV*, pp. 72-74.

[176] Burgess, 'Medieval Examples', p. 20; cf. *AASS*, October V, 322-23, 382, 483.

[177] Bertrand was canonized by pope Clement X in 1671, Burgess, 'Medieval Examples', p. 25; cf. *AASS*, October V, p. 481.

[178] Burgess, 'Medieval Examples', p. 21; Cooper-Rompato, *Women's Xenoglossia in the Latter Middle Ages*, p. 31; cf. *AASS*, October V, 322-23, 382, 481, 483.

experiences of tongues',[179] and some scholars even called the Eastern Church 'pneumocentric'.[180] However, its historical context and theological trajectory differed from its Latin sister. In contrast to the Western Church, historically, there was a strong central government that

> provided the base for a brilliant and colorful civilization which never passed through the throes of the Dark Ages ... its capital remained secure against pagan invasion until 1451 ... the Greek church remained far more other-worldly and mystical ... (continuing) the Greek bent of introspection and individuality ... the individual gifts of the Spirit flourished.[181]

Although glossolalia occurred throughout the history of the Eastern Church, there are several theological differences with the Western Church. They are: 1) audible manifestations[182] of the Holy Spirit were downplayed in favor of Spirit-inspired visions;[183] 2) soteriology was re-creative and not judicial,[184] therefore, the

---

[179] Kelsey, *Tongues Speaking*, p. 42. Kelsey writes,

the Patriarch of Constantinople ... had always recognized and controlled the practice of tongues. While historical evidence of tongues within the Greek tradition has not been compiled, it is a fair inference that tongues speaking, being no more bizarre than other Eastern monastic practices, has simply continued within the traditional Greek monasticism without attracting much notice ... There is a sympathetic understanding of the practice of tongues ... It is known, and has been known through the centuries, in the monasteries, p. 43.

Cf. Valentine Zander, in Gabriel Anne (trans.), *St Seraphim of Sarov* (Crestwood, NY: St. Valdimir's Seminary Press, 1975), p. x; McClymond, 'Charismatic Gifts', pp. 399-418.

[180] Church, Burgess, *Eastern Christian Traditions*, p. 1.

[181] Kelsey, *Tongues Speaking*, p. 42.

[182] The notable exception here is the Jesus Prayer, Williams, 'A History of Speaking in Tongues', p. 69, Burgess, *Eastern Christian Traditions*, p. 15.

[183] 'In the East, Byzantine Hesychasm, with its preoccupation with the manifestations of the Uncreated Light, concentrated on mystical vision rather than mystical audition', Williams, 'A History of Speaking in Tongues', p. 69. For example, an acolyte of St. Seraphim of Sarov asked 'how is it possible to be absolutely sure of living in God's Spirit. How can it be proved?"' The Seraphim then asked the student to look at him because, in a fashion similar to Moses after Mount Sinai, his face had a brilliant 'charismatic shining' to it, Zander, *St Seraphim of Sarov*, pp. 90, xi; cf. 83-96; Burgess, *Eastern Christian Traditions*, pp. 79-83. 'The closer one gets to God, fewer are the words', Burgess, 'Evidence of the Spirit: the Ancient and Eastern Churches', p. 9.

[184] Aulén, *Christus Victor*.

Holy Spirit's work was the perfecting of the saints in a process called *theosis*;[185] 3) experiences of the spirit were widely discussed. This discussion produced 'divisions' in the Eastern church over how the spirit could be known.[186]

A. St. Symeon the New Theologian (949-1022 CE)[187]

Symeon presented a 'prophetic challenge to the institutional order'[188] of his day and called for leadership based on 'a personal experience of the Spirit rather than on ecclesiastical position'.[189]

---

[185] Burgess, 'Evidence of the Spirit: the Ancient and Eastern Churches', p. 20. 'The eastern Orthodox understanding of deification (*theosis*) as attaining the likeness of God in Christ-likeness is affirmed as the ultimate calling and purpose of all humanity ... it takes one will to create humanity, but two to sanctify it ... the synergistic collaboration between the divine and human will', Augustine, *Pentecost, Hospitality, and Transfiguration*, p. 22, cf. p. 21.

[186] There are roughly three positions. First, and 'most prominent' is that the 'Spirit provides both the unction (*chrism*) and the seal (*sphragis*), so that the Christian's senses ... (are) made alive to realities previously unexperienced', Burgess, *Eastern Christian Traditions*, p. 3. The second position is that 'true knowledge of God must ... transcend any created thing', p. 4. The final position is the apophatic position: 'only in utter darkness of unknowing ... there is a mystical union of the mind with God', p. 4; cf. Burgess, 'Evidence of the Spirit: the Ancient and Eastern Churches', pp. 3-19.

[187] At an early age he moved to Constantinople to be mentored by Symeon the Studite (Symeon the Venerable), and it was here that his love for the interior life flourished. He was promoted to lead a neighbouring monastery, St. Mamas, which he led for twenty-five years. He was exiled and then exonerated by the Patriarch and Emperor, 'probably as a result of jealousy over Symeon's spiritual influence ... and because of his (Stepheon's, the archbishop of Nicomedia) fear of Symenon's "enthusiasm" or charismatic approach', Burgess, *Eastern Christian Traditions*, p. 55.

[188] This is the struggle between institution and charisma. Stephen, the archbishop of Nicomedia and the chief advisor and theologian (called the syncellus) to the Patriarch in Constantinople, represented the institution and ruthlessly attacked Symeon. George Maloney wrote, 'there were also at stake two opposing views of theology: Stephen's type of rational speculation about the mysteries of faith, using man's reason, philosophy and rhetoric against Symeon's more charismatic and apophatic theology', Symeon the New Theologian, in George A. Maloney (trans.), *Hymns of Divine Love by Symeon The New Theologian* (Denville, NJ: Dimension Books, 1976), p. 7.

[189] Burgess, *Eastern Christian Traditions*, p. 62. Note his experience of theosis: 'and when I am united to Him I ascend higher than the heavens ... where my body remains then I know not ... He Who stands far off from every creature, receives me into Himself and enfolds me in His embrace and that then I rest outside the world', S. Bulgakov, 'From a World of Religious Contemplation', *Sobornost* 2 (June 1935), pp. 4-7 (5).

Noteworthy was his claim to 'speak with new tongues'.[190] He specifically prayed for the vocal gifts of the Spirit:

> O Christ, furnish me with words of wisdom, words of knowledge and divine intelligence! ... give me a direct language, give me strength, give me power to speak to all those dedicated to Your service, and worshipping You, King of all.[191]

Though some might question the biblical foundation for his gift of tears[192] or mystical experience of the Eucharist,[193] his prayer for prophecy was very Pauline.[194]

B. St. Gregory Palamas (1296-1359 CE)[195]

In response to his critic, Barlaam the Calabrian, Gregory defended the hesychast's position that one could 'directly experience God' by distinguishing between the energies of God and the essence of

---

[190] He prayed that all may see God's glory and wisdom 'since I, even I am now heard to speak with new tongues by thy grace', Symeon the New Theologian in Patrick Thompson (trans.), 'A Prayer to God of St. Simon the New Theologian', *Sobornost* 6 (June 1936), pp. 19-21 (20). Bulgakov noted Symeon's attempt to express the inexpressible: 'can any tongue describe what I know ... can words express it?', p. 5, cf. p. 6.

[191] Symeon, *Hymns of Divine Love*, Hymn 58, p. 288. Further, genuine spiritual fathers must pass on an inheritance: 'all who have received a spiritual gift from God are under an obligation to impart it without grudging ... to their spiritual son, and then to friends and acquaintances ... to slaves and to rich and poor alike', Symeon the New Theologian, 'Epistle 3', in H.J.M. Turner (ed. and trans.), *The Epistles of St. Symeon the New Theologian* (Oxford: Oxford University Press, 2009), p. 89.

[192] Burgess warns that 'Symeon has no expectation that a miraculous gift of tongues will accompany the infilling of the Spirit ... (rather) the Spirit's reception is accompanied by the gift of tears', Burgess, *Eastern Christian Traditions*, p. 60; cf. Burgess, *Christian Peoples of the Spirit*, p. 87.

[193] 'When I feed on thy flesh then am I joined to thy nature, Thereby indeed do I come of thine own life to partake', Symeon, 'A Prayer to God', p. 20.

[194] Symeon, *Hymns of Divine Love*, Hymn 40, pp. 205-207.

[195] The Emperor, Andronicus II, saw to it that Gregory was well educated after his father's early death in the hopes that he would go into government service. Instead, Gregory withdrew to Mount Athos for a life of monastic asceticism. Despite his desire to live a quiet life, he was drawn into theological controversy, was imprisoned for his political friendships, and was kidnapped by the Turks; nevertheless, he would eventually become the archbishop of Thessaloniki and become known as a preeminent theologian of Hesychasm, St. Gregory Palamas, in John Meyendorff (ed.), *Gregory Palamas: The Triads* (trans. Nicholas Gendle; NewYork: Paulist Press, 1983), pp. 5-8; cf. Burgess, *Eastern Christian Traditions*, p. 69.

God.[196] To prove his point Gregory wrote,

> most of the charisms of the Spirit are granted to those worthy of them at the time of prayer ... this applies not only to being ravished 'even to the third heaven', but to all the gifts of the Spirit. The *diversity of tongues and their interpretation* ... In the case of the gifts of instruction and of *tongues and their interpretation*, even though these are acquired by prayer, yet it is possible that they may operate even when prayer is absent from the soul.[197]

It is significant that Gregory wrote of tongues in the present-tense to defend prophetic, pneumatic inspiration.[198] Even though he made no claim of glossolalia he regularly practiced the *Jesus Prayer*,[199] which Williams sees as a 'kind of' glossolalia.[200]

V. Post-Reformation to 1900

After the Reformation, historical accounts of glossolalia among individuals and groups of people are more readily available and give the impression of increasing activity. This survey is merely a sample and will end roughly around 1900.[201]

---

[196] Burgess, *Eastern Christian Traditions*, p. 69, cf. p. 70. Barlaam denied that true divinity could be known through experience.

[197] Palamas, *Gregory Palamas: The Triads*, pp. 52-53 (emphasis added).

[198] Later he writes, 'for when the Spirit has come to dwell in him, a man receives the dignity of a prophet, of an apostle, of an angel of God, whereas hitherto he was only earth and dust ... the mouth of the prophets is the mouth of God ... for it is not you who will speak, but the Spirit of your Father who speaks in you'", Palamas, *Gregory Palamas: The Triads*, pp. 91-92.

[199] The concept of the 'Jesus Prayer' is based on 1 Thess. 5.17, to 'pray continually'. The prayer is: 'Lord Jesus Christ, Son of God, have mercy on me, a sinner'.

[200] 'The famous "Jesus Prayer," which, when mastered ... (is) a continuous ejaculation of certain formulas even during sleep and during conversations – thus *a kind of* subliminal speaking in a familiar tongue in the midst of other tongues', Williams, 'A History of Speaking in Tongues', p. 69; cf. Palamas, *Gregory Palamas: The Triads*, p. 5; cf. Chan, *Pentecostal Theology*, pp. 80-82.

[201] For example: 1) a revival in rural India, 1860-65, G.H. Lang, *The History and Diaries of an Indian Christian* (Suffolk: Walsham-Le-Willows, 1939), pp. 144-45, 158, 194-98, 201-203; 2) Pandita Ramabai Sarasvati reported tongues at her mission/farm, Mukti Sada (salvation) in Khedgaon, India, Burgess, *Christian Peoples of the Spirit*, p. 243-48.

A. Society of Friends (1650 CE)[202]

Founder George Fox 'was weary' of formal religion that was locked up by either the government, the Mass, or the Bible until he had a vision that launched his ministry.[203] He believed 'that the "Inner Light" was in every man ... (and we) sat in silence ... until God revealed Himself directly to someone'.[204] This experiential emphasis,[205] along with Fox's goal to 'promote the revival of primitive Christianity',[206] naturally led to glossolalic occurrences among the early Friends: 'we spoke with new tongues, as the Lord gave us utterance, and as his spirit led us ... things unutterable were known and made manifest', wrote eyewitness Edward Burrough.[207] 'Fox eventually discouraged such ecstatic utterances.'[208]

---

[202] The Society of Friends, also called the Quakers, was founded around 1650 by George Fox, Arthur O. Roberts, 'George Fox and the Quakers', in *Eerdman's Handbook to the History of Christianity* (Grand Rapids, MI: Eerdmans, 1977), pp. 480-83 (480). The movement has grown and experienced persecution, including three Quakers who 'were hanged on Boston common (1660-61)' which caused an outcry which 'helped pave the way for religious liberty', p. 483.

[203] Roberts, 'The Quakers', pp. 480-81. Fox says, 'Christ has been too long locked up in the Mass or in the Book ... let him be your prophet, priest and king', p. 481.

[204] Gromacki, *The Modern Tongues Movement*, p. 21. 'True and acceptable worship of God stems from the inward and unmediated moving and drawing of his own Spirit ... it is the Spirit of God which should be the direct activator, mover, persuader, and influencer', Robert Barclay, in Dean Freiday (ed.), *Barclay's Apology in Modern English* (Philadelphia, PA: Religious Society of Friends, 1967), pp. 237, 244.

[205] Baer notes that 'quaking' was similar to tongues speech: although rare, 'the phenomenon of quaking or shaking is still found among some Friends and would seem to be religiously and psychologically similar to glossolalia', Baer, 'Quaker Silence', pp. 155. He writes that because, 'the process ... involves a resting of the analytical mind, a refusal to let deliberative, objective thinking dominate ... one tries to ... become open to the 'inner light' within himself ... to the "leading of the Spirit"', p. 154.

[206] Gromacki, *The Modern Tongues Movement*, p. 21. They sought to follow the pattern of the primitive church, specifically 1 Cor. 14.30-31, where all are to keep silent, 'unless they are given a revelation for the edification of others', Barclay, *Barclay's Apology*, pp. 284-85.

[207] Edward Burrough, 'Epistle to the Reader', in *The Great Mystery of the Great Whore Unfolded; and Antichrist's Kingdom Revealed Unto Destruction. The Works of George Fox* (New York: Isaac T. Hooper, 1831, reprint; 1659), III, p. 13. This was Spirit-inspired speech: 'as truth becomes victorious and dominant in their souls, they receive an utterance and speak unfaltering for the edification of their brethren', Barclay, Barclay's Apology, p. 252.

[208] Stanley M. Burgess, 'Evidence of the Spirit: The Medieval and Modern Western Churches', in Gary B. McGee (ed.), *Initial Evidence: Historical and Biblical*

B. The Huguenots (1685-1715 CE)[209]

The Huguenots were Protestants who suffered severe reprisals for an armed rebellion against the French state in the rugged region of Cevennes.[210] It was widely reported that as many as sixty children and some adults spoke in tongues, prophesied, and had convulsive movements at once.[211] It 'consisted very often of inarticulate sounds or newly created words, which ... were supposed to belong to unknown languages, or were explained artificially from foreign sources'.[212] At other times, it was xenolalia: for example, one illiterate shepherdess, Isabeau Vincent, composed prayers and poems in a state of ecstasy in proper French or Latin and not in her native language of Jamaican Patois.[213] Others would speak

---

Perspectives on the Pentecostal Doctrine of Spirit Baptism (Eugene, OR: Wipf & Stock, 2007 reprint; Hendrickson, 1991), pp. 20-40 (29).

[209] In the southeastern part of France, they are also known as the Camisards, the French Prophets, the French Calvinists or even the Little Prophets of Cevennes. The name Camisard supposedly comes from a type of indigenous linen from which a smock-like uniform was fashioned, Cutten, *Speaking with Tongues*, p. 64. Cf. Shumway, 'The Gift of Tongues', pp. 90-101.

[210] There was twenty years of severe persecution before they rebelled, Clemen, 'The Speaking with Tongues', p. 350; Taylor, *The Spirit and the Bride*, p. 92; Cartledge, *Encountering the Spirit*, p. 50; Hinson, 'Significance of Glossolalia', p. 186. The response of the state was so vicious that many of these fled to other countries and it is estimated that ten thousand were executed, Cutten, *Speaking with Tongues*, p. 48. The countries of flight include Holland, England, Ireland, Germany, Switzerland, and America, Hargrave, 'Reformation to the Twentieth Century', p. 101.

[211] Estimates of up to one thousand were common and Shumway attempted to connect the ASM historically with the Camisards, Shumway, 'The Gift of Tongues', p. 98. Cutten believed it to be 'psychic contagion', Cutten, *Speaking with Tongues*, p. 54.

[212] Clemen, 'The Speaking with Tongues', p. 350.

[213] Cutten, *Speaking with Tongues*, pp. 61, 52-55. Kelsey wrote that it began with 10 year old 'Isabeau Vincent, who had fled from the mistreatment of her father and had seen the king's soldiers bayonet women and children worshipping together in their own church. In an ecstatic experience she called for repentance, speaking in the patois which was all the language she knew' and later spoke in 'perfect French' and 'parts of the Latin Mass', Kelsey, *Tongues Speaking*, pp. 52-53. 'Soon children all over the Cevennes were seized by the spirit and prophesied ... (speaking in) eloquent, well-chosen French (which) was completely foreign to them', p. 53. The messages turned political and became a foretaste of the French Revolution. This ecstatic speech seems to be 'in languages to which they had been exposed', Wamble, 'Glossolalia in Christian History', p. 36.

Hebrew or Latin.[214] Harold D. Hunter noted that they 'believed their actions to be in response to the Spirit'.[215] The case of the Camisards was so well known that no less than John Wesley refuted Dr. Middleton's theory of cessation using them as an example of the continuing gifts of the Spirit.[216]

C. The Moravian Revival (1727 CE)[217]

In the summer of 1727 the Holy Spirit fell on religious refugees who had established a small church on the estate of Count Nikolaus Ludwig von Zinzendorf.[218] The ensuing revival was characterized by fervent prayer,[219] singing, intercession, and missionary zeal. Critic and eyewitness John Roche noted a similarity to the Montanists, in that they 'broke into some form of disconnected jargon ... "evacuations of the Spirit"'.[220] Burgess found it interesting that 'Zinzendorf believed ... that the gift of tongues had originally

---

[214] Cutten, *Speaking with Tongues*, p. 56; Shumway, 'The Gift of Tongues', p. 98; Ronald A. Knox, *Enthusiasm: A Chapter in the History of Religion* (Oxford: Oxford University Press, 1950), p. 366.

[215] Hunter, *Spirit Baptism*, p. 167. For example, my words were 'formed by the spirit or the angel of God himself, who at this time made use of my organs of speech. To him alone I surrender during my ecstasy the guidance of my tongue, while I strive only to turn myself towards God ... I know that then a higher and another Power speaks through me', Clemen, 'The Speaking with Tongues', p. 350.

[216] Cutten, *Speaking with Tongues*, p. 56; cf. Williams, 'A History of Speaking in Tongues', pp. 77-79. Original citation is John Wesley, *Wesley's Works* (New York: Harper, 1826-1827), V, p. 744.

[217] The Moravian Church, also called the *United Brethren* in Moravia, trace their roots back to John Hus who preached justification by faith one hundred years before Luther, eventually being burned at the stake as a heretic in 1415. Despite persecution, especially during the Counter Reformation in the Roman Church, they effectively propagated their beliefs through small home churches, Hyatt, *2000 Years of Charismatic Christianity*, pp. 94-97.

[218] There was a growing hunger and a series of experiences that led to a Pentecost-like 'baptism with the Holy Ghost' on 13-8-1727, John Greenfield, *When the Spirit Came: The Story of the Moravian Revival of 1727* (Minneapolis, MN: Bethany Fellowship, 1967), p. 13. For example, on 10-8-1727, the Spirit fell on Pastor Rothe: 'he felt himself overwhelmed by a wonderful and irresistible power of the Lord, and sunk down into the dust before God, and with him sunk down the whole assembled congregation, in ecstasy of feeling', p. 24.

[219] Just like 'the sacred fire (that) was never permitted to go out on the altar (Lev. 6:13 and 14)' a 24 hour prayer watch was established and continued for one hundred years, Greenfield, *When the Spirit Came*, p. 24; cf. pp. 22-26.

[220] John Roche, *The Moravian Heresy* (Dublin, 1751), p. 44. The similarity is specifically, 'the frequent behavior, speeches and affection of those deluded and deluding people ... to the public Voice [sic]', p. 44.

been given in order to facilitate the missionary enterprise'.[221] John Wesley and early Methodists were greatly impacted by their close relationship with Moravian missionaries and evangelists.[222]

D. Convulsionnaires of Saint-Médard (1731 CE)[223]

The Convulsionnaires were 'known for their spiritual dancing, for healings, and for prophetic utterances. When seized by convulsions, some spoke in an unknown tongue and understood languages in which they were addressed.'[224] For example, Pierre Mathieu quoted an anti-Jansenist pamphlet whose author 'heard more than a hundred times a convulsionary talking in an unknown tongue, and understanding any language that was spoken to her'.[225]

---

[221] Burgess, 'Evidence of the Spirit: The Medieval and Modern Western Churches', p. 32.

[222] 'Both (John and Charles Wesley) were influenced by ... Moravian, Peter Böhler. Within three days each had a vital Christian experience – Charles on Whitsunday, and John on 24 May 1738, when his heart was 'strangely warmed'', A. Skevington Wood, 'John and Charles Wesley', in Tim Dowley (ed.), *Eerdman's Handbook to the History of Christianity* (Grand Rapids, MI: Eerdmans, 1977), p. 447. At a revival in London on 1 January 1739, 'the Wesleys were present, along with Whitefield and Benjamin Ingham, who was to become an outstanding evangelist among the Moravians', Wood, 'Awakening', p. 448. John Wesley 'knew that the gift of tongues was frequently dispensed in his day; and ... that it had had authentic existence on other post-Apostolic centuries', Williams, 'A History of Speaking in Tongues', p. 80. John Wesley wrote that he received 'a tongue of fire' that enabled him to preach with 'eloquence' and 'zeal'. Tongues probably occurred among Wesley's early followers. For example, Thomas Walsh wrote 'this morning the Lord gave me a language I knew not of, raising my soul to Him in a wonderful manner', Hyatt, *2000 Years of Charismatic Christianity*, p. 104.

[223] A segment within Jansenism. They were a reform movement that tried to call the Roman Church back to a form of Augustinian theology, even though this theology had already been condemned in 1653 by Pope Innocent X. They were named after the bishop of Ypres, Cornelius Jansen, Burgess, 'Evidence of the Spirit: The Medieval and Modern Western Churches', p. 30; cf. Gromacki, *The Modern Tongues Movement*, p. 21; Knox, *Enthusiasm*, pp. 372-88.

[224] Burgess, 'Evidence of the Spirit: The Medieval and Modern Western Churches', p. 30. Burgess warns that 'most of their primary sources have never been studied critically' and therefore 'it is impossible to judge fully their understanding of the Holy Spirit', p. 31. Historian Brian Strayer categorized them into six broad groupings, one of which he called the 'Prophetess' group, who 'delivered ecstatic speeches', Brian E. Strayer, *Suffering Saints: Jansenists and Convulsionnaires in France, 1640-1799* (Portland: Sussex Academic Press, 2008), p. 247; cf. p. 267.

[225] Knox, *Enthusiasm*, p. 380 (orig. citation: Pierre François Mathieu, *Histoire des Miraculés et Convulsionnaires de Saint-Médard* [Paris: Librairie Academique, 1864], p. 226).

An eyewitness noted that at vespers, Chevalier Folard 'used to talk in monosyllables: it was "complete gibberish, of which nobody understands one word. Some declare that at these moments he is talking Slavonic, but I do not believe that anyone can follow him".'[226] Another said, 'the words she pronounced (the widow Thévenet) were rapid and unintelligible – they do not belong to any known language'.[227] The Convulsionnaires believed 'that their organs of speech were controlled by another power'.[228]

E. Shakers (1747 CE)

Founder 'Mother' Ann Lee[229] was directly influenced by the 'Huguenot refugees formerly connected with the "Little Prophets"'.[230] 'In Shaker practice, glossolalia was only one of several gifts ... signifying divine anointing.'[231] William Haskett, an eyewitness and former Shaker noted that the Shakers 'profess to receive all the divine gifts given to the apostles on the day of Pentecost, besides others given in the "gospel of Mother"'.[232] He described a 'quick meeting'[233] where every member was encouraged to display their spiritual gifts. The leading elder shouted and stamped his feet, whereupon, 'the *spirit* seized all the members ... (and) the sisters

---

[226] Knox, *Enthusiasm*, p. 380.

[227] Knox, *Enthusiasm*, p. 380 (translation mine). ('Les mots qu'elle pronounce avec rapidité sont inintelligibles et n'appartienent à aucune langue connue').

[228] 'The nature of their ecstasy varied: 'they were not conscious of the words until they heard themselves utter them. At times they retained their full consciousness ... remembered exactly all they had done and spoken, so that they could correct and complete their speeches which were written down by the hearers', Clemen, 'The Speaking with Tongues', p. 350.

[229] Ann Lee (1706-1783), 'claimed that she could discourse in seventy-two languages', Dollar, 'Church History and the Tongues Movement', p. 320; cf. Edward Deming Andrews, *The People Called Shakers: A Search for the Perfect Society* (NY: Oxford University Press, 1953), pp. 9, 12.

[230] Williams, 'A History of Speaking in Tongues', pp. 81-82; Wamble, 'Glossolalia in Christian History', p. 37.

[231] Wamble, 'Glossolalia in Christian History', p. 37.

[232] William Haskett, *Shakerism Unmasked, or the History of the Shakers* (Pittsfield: N.H. Walkley, Printer, 1828), p. 189. In a short section on their doctrine Haskett enumerates that there was a 'fanaticism' with the 'pretentions of Apostolic Gifts. They profess to be divinely inspired at times, and they say, that the Holy Ghost takes up its abode in them; and that it causes them to shake, speak in unknown and divers tongues', p. 212.

[233] Quick meetings were announced just a few hours before their occurrence and generally were 'held preceding and after Christmas', and were 'not, with a few exceptions, held in the presence of spectators', Haskett, *Shakerism Unmasked*, p. 189.

began to talk in "unknown tongues" … (then) the whole room began to shake, jump, turn, and talk in "unknown tongues"'.²³⁴ However, their official history is silent on glossolalia and 'quick meetings'.²³⁵

F. Finish Revivals (1796 CE)

Jouko Ruohomäki noted a series of revivals in Finland that experienced charismatic phenomenon from 1756 until it merged with Pentecostalism in 1911.²³⁶ Tongues first occurred in 1796 at Savojärvi, a small village in the north;²³⁷ however, glossolalia was more common from 1809 to 1850.²³⁸ Ruohomäki wrote that 'whenever new revivals took place falling, speaking in tongues, prophesying, visions and revelations were included'.²³⁹ A history of that revival described glossolalia negatively: 'they spoke continuously, incomprehensible for most people, speech like foreign language or disconnected incomprehensible words, which little by little changed into syllables presented like sentences'.²⁴⁰ Despite opposition,²⁴¹ Ruohomäki believed that an 1845 revival

---

²³⁴ Haskett, *Shakerism Unmasked*, p. 190 (emphasis original). He describes it as an 'awful riot' that for 45 minutes alternated between loud shouts of the entire group and 'the soft, but hurried note of the sisters, whose "gifts" were the apostolic gifts of tongues'.

²³⁵ See, *A Summary View of the Millennial Church of United Society of Believers (Commonly Called Shakers)* (Albany: Packard & VanBenthuysen, 1823); cf. John Dunlavy, *The Manifesto, or Declaration of the Doctrine and Practice of the Church of Christ* (NY: Edward O. Jenkins, 1847).

²³⁶ Jouko Ruohomäki, 'The Call of Charisma: Charismatic Phenomena during the 18th and 19th Centuries in Finland', in *JEPTA* 29.1 (2009), pp. 25-40 (29). The 1756 revival experienced 'ecstasy, eschatological expectations … visions and revelations', but there was no mention of glossolalia, p. 26. Significantly, 'ecstatic phenomena were considered a sign of the Holy Spirit's immediate presence'. Cf. L. Ahonen, 'Awakened', in Stanley Burgess (ed.), *NIDPCM* (Grand Rapids, MI: Zondervan, rev. and expanded edn, 2002), p. 343.

²³⁷ Ruohomäki, 'Charismatic Phenomena in Finland', p. 29.

²³⁸ Ruohomäki, 'Charismatic Phenomena in Finland', p. 31. One church member even had 'tongue-speaker' written beside her name on the church register.

²³⁹ Ruohomäki, 'Charismatic Phenomena in Finland', p. 30.

²⁴⁰ Ruohomäki, 'Charismatic Phenomena in Finland', p. 30 [Orig. cite. Mauno Rosendal, *Suomen herännäisyyden historia XIX:llä uvosisdalla I* (Oulu: Herättäjä, 1902), p. 59].

²⁴¹ 'Two "trance preachers" were taken to Stockhom and put into a mental hospital … (and) both the minister Grape and his assistant pastor Wiklund were prosecuted', Ruohomäki, 'Charismatic Phenomena in Finland', p. 28; cf. p. 33.

continued on until it unofficially merged with the 'modern Pentecostal movement in Finland'.[242]

G. The Frontier Revivals (1800 CE)[243]

In June of 1800, a revival broke out in rural Kentucky under the ministry of James McGready and spread rapidly as a part of the Second Great Awakening.[244] Though the physical 'exercise'[245] of being 'slain' in the spirit came to characterize these localized revivals, there were also accounts of glossolalia.[246] At Cane Ridge, Kentucky,[247] an eyewitness wrote that 'the present revival exceeds anything of the kind I have ever heard of', there were two young boys who spoke in a 'rapturous language'.[248] Others believed it was the 'full and perfect accomplishment' of Joel's prophecy, the restoration of Spiritual gifts to the church.[249] A witness in North

---

[242] Ruohomäki, 'Charismatic Phenomena in Finland', p. 37; cf. p. 40. This occurred when, in 1911, they invited T.B. Barratt from Norway to preach.

[243] Also known as the Cane Ridge or Logan County, Kentucky revival. It impacted the Presbyterians, Baptists, Methodists, Shakers, and Cumberland Presbyterians, and attracted leaders such as Barton Stone, Francis Asbury, and Peter Cartwright, Paul Conkin, *Cane Ridge: America's Pentecost* (Madison, WI: The University of Wisconsin Press, 1990), pp. 64-114. People camped onsite during the 'Scottish sacrament season' and listened to speakers, sang, and prayed in preparation for Holy Communion, which was the finale of the gathering, pp. 16-19, 60-62. This revival popularized camp meetings and was reminiscent of services during the Great Awakening, pp. 85-87.

[244] Williams, 'A History of Speaking in Tongues', p. 84.

[245] Other physical exercises included barking like dogs, laughter, jerking, jumping, and running, Conkin, *'America's Pentecost'*, passim.

[246] John McGee's personal testimony is a possible account: 'I went through the house shouting, and exhorting with *all possible ecstasy* and energy … amongst these were many small home-bred boys, who spoke with the tongue … a new song in their mouths', John McGee, 'Letter to the Rev. T.L. Douglass (1821)', in *The Methodist Magazine* IV (N. Bangs and T. Mason, for the Methodist Episcopal Church, 1821), pp. 189-91 (190, 191). Cf. Adam Rankin, *A Review of the Noted Revival in Kentucky* (Lexington, KY: Bradford, 1802); David Rice, *Sermon on the Present Revival of Religion* (Lexington, KY: Chapless, 1803); John Cree, *Evils of the Work Now Prevailing in the United States of America, Under the Name of a Revival of Religion* (Washington: n.p., 1804); Samuel M. Wilson, *John Lyle's Diary* (Kentucky Historical Society, 1922).

[247] This was the largest and most well-known of the revival sites, some accounts state that an astonishing 20,000 attended, though Conkin believes the largest number to be 10,000, Conkin, *'America's Pentecost'*, p. 88.

[248] W. & R. Dickson, 'Letter Published in Lancaster', in *Increase of Piety, or the Revival of Religion in the United States of America* (Newburyport, CT: Angier March 1802), p. 82.

[249] Richard M'Nemar, *The Kentucky Revival* (Cincinnati, 1808), p. 68. 'Supernatural and extraordinary gifts of the Spirit that were visible … the restitution

Carolina noted that,

> a wave of emotion swept over the congregation like an electric shock ... sobs, moans, and cries arose from every part of the church ... many were struck down, or thrown into a state of helplessness if not of insensibility ... (and there were) miraculous attestations from Heaven, *such as cloven tongues like fire and the power of speaking different languages, it was like the day of Pentecost.*[250]

Historian Paul Conkin stated that accounts of 'holy laughter or singing, coming from deep within the body ... (were) suggestive of glossolalia'.[251]

H. Edward Irving (1792-1834 CE) and the Catholic Apostolic Church[252]

'Sometime between March 23, 1830 and the end of that month, on the evening of the Lord's day, the gift of the Spirit with tongues was restored to the Church', wrote Edward Irving.[253] Then, after approximately three months of use in private prayer meetings, Irving allowed it publicly in his church.[254] He wrote 'the baptism with the Holy Ghost, whose standing sign, if we err not, is the

---

of that sacred panoply, which, together with the apostolic faith, had been trodden underfoot for many hundred years by the power of the antichrist', p. 32.

[250] Guion Griffis Johnson, 'Revival Movements in Ante-Bellum North Carolina', *North Carolina Historical Review* 10.1 (Jan 1933), pp. 21-44 (30). This episode occurred in 'the summer of 1801 ... in Orange County', N.C. when 'a man, by the name of Hodge, happened to be there who had seen something of the work in the west and he, rising slowly from his seat, said in a calm but earnest voice, *Stand still and see the salvation of God*', p. 29.

[251] Conkin, 'America's Pentecost', p. 113.

[252] See, D.W. Dorries, 'Catholic Apostolic Church', in Stanley Burgess (ed.), *NIDPCM* (Grand Rapids, MI: Zondervan, rev. and expanded edn, 2002), pp. 459-60.

[253] Shumway, 'The Gift of Tongues', p. 133; cf. Burgess, *Christian Peoples of the Spirit*, p. 191. There are extensive extant works by Irving himself. Shumway, 'The Gift of Tongues', pp. 118-43; Larry Christenson, 'Pentecostalism's Forgotten Forerunner', in Vinson Synan (ed.), *Aspects of Pentecostal – Charismatic Origins* (Plainfield, NJ: Logos International, 1975), pp. 15-37; Hunter, *Spirit Baptism*, pp. 174-78; D.D. Bundy, 'Edward Irving', in Stanley Burgess (ed.), *NIDPCM* (Grand Rapids, MI: Zondervan, rev. and expanded edn, 2002), pp. 803-804.

[254] On October 16, 1831, D.W. Dorries, 'Edward Irving and the "Standing Sign" of Spirit Baptism', in Gary B. McGee (ed.), *Initial Evidence: Historical and Biblical Perspectives on the Pentecostal Doctrine of Spirit Baptism* (Eugene, OR: Wipf & Stock, 2007 reprint; Hendrickson Publishers, 1991), pp. 41-56 (42-44).

speaking with tongues'.²⁵⁵ Every believer was to seek this 'standing sign' subsequent to salvation as a new level of communication with the Spirit that would lead to a heightened availability to other spiritual gifts such as prophecy.²⁵⁶ Initial glossolalia

> is the root and stem of them all, out of which they all grow, and by which they are all nourished ... (it) is a chief means of God for training up the children of the Spirit into the capacity of prophesying and speaking in the Church for the edification of all whether 'by revelation, or knowledge, or by prophesying, or by doctrine'.²⁵⁷

Though ridiculed²⁵⁸ and persecuted, this movement was a forerunner of modern Pentecostalism.

I. The Latter-Day Saints (LDS) or Mormons (1830 CE)

Ecstatic glossolalia²⁵⁹ and xenolalia²⁶⁰ occurred among the early

---

²⁵⁵ Dorries, 'Standing Sign', p. 49. The sign value is to believers and nonbelievers alike. In the case of the nonbeliever, it will move the humble person to repentance and move the proud to reject God's message. In the case of the believer 'it is a means of grace, for the end of edifying himself, that he may edify the whole body of the saints', p. 50. Gromacki noted that 'the Irvingites distinguished between Pentecostal glossolalia in foreign languages and Corinthian glossolalia in ecstatic, unknown languages', Gromacki, *The Modern Tongues Movement*, p. 22 (Org. cite: J Barton Payne, *The Imminent Appearing of Christ* [Grand Rapids, MI: Eerdmans, 1962], p. 32.).

²⁵⁶ Dorries, 'Standing Sign', p. 49.

²⁵⁷ Dorries, 'Standing Sign', pp. 49, 51. 'It is evident from early periodical articles that the Irving phenomenon became an interpretive grid by which Pentecostal theologians came to understand and evaluate their own experience', Dorries, 'Edward Irving', p. 804, specifically, subsequence and spiritual gifts, Dorries, 'Apostolic Catholic Church', p. 459.

²⁵⁸ 'It was Carlyle's eye-witness report that his views were accepted by the "fanatical." In another letter the essayist added that evidently "God was working miracles by hysterics." The London Times sent reporters to watch the services and to look out for "ravings, screaming`s, bawling`s." of course, Irving was ousted for his part in this by the Presbyterian Church', Dollar, 'Church History and the Tongues Movement', p. 319.

²⁵⁹ One critical eyewitness described the phenomena as 'a rapid succession of articulate and connected sounds, not understood by the speaker, but which are explained by some one [sic] having the "interpretation of tongues." ... [It is] more naturally accounted for either by imposture of the effects of a wild fanaticism ... a cognate branch of that "dog-Latin" which belongs to the erudition of school-boys days,' J.H. Beadle, *Life in Utah; or, The Mysteries and Crimes of Mormonism* (Philadelphia, PA: National Publishing Co., 1870), pp. 322-23.

²⁶⁰ Clark, 'We believe in the gift of tongues', p. 76.

Mormons[261] and was noted at pivotal times in their history.[262] A glossolalist himself, Joseph Smith wrote, 'we believe in the gift of tongues'.[263] The idea was that through 'the Holy Ghost, all the "gifts" of the first Church were to be restored; prophecy, healing, miracles, speaking in tongues'.[264] Brigham Young said, 'the Spirit came on me, and I spoke in tongues, and we thought only of the day of Pentecost'.[265] Glossolalia was readily acknowledged in the *Book of Mormon*[266] but there was 'neither

---

[261] This church was founded by Joseph Smith in western New York after receiving a revelation from the Angel Moroni who revealed to him where some golden plates were buried. These plates explained the history of native Americans. Alan J. Clark reports that Mormons spoke in tongues in 1831, and he was instrumental in the conversion of LDS stalwart Herbert C. Kimball, Alan J. Clark, '"We believe in the gift of tongues": The 1906 Pentecostal Revolution and Its Effects on the LDS Use of the Gift of Tongues in the Twentieth Century', *Mormon Historical Studies* 14.1 (Spring 2013), pp. 67-80 (70).

[262] They 'preceded a "revelation" that polygamy is an abomination', aided in the selection of a presiding officer in 1853, and they accompanied times of spiritual renewal in 1836 and 1861, Wamble, 'Glossolalia in Christian History', p. 40.

[263] 'We believe in the gift of tongues, prophesy, revelation, visions, healing, interpretation of tongues & c.', Joseph Smith, 'The Wentworth Letter', in *Times and Seasons* 3.9 (March 1, 1842); cf. Williams, 'A History of Speaking in Tongues', p. 87. For Joseph Smith, 'tongues would accompany the reception of the Holy Spirit and would open the door for visionary understandings and Revelation. After all, this is the way the book of Mormon had come to him', Dollar, 'Church History and the Tongues Movement', p. 320. For an account of Smith's glossolalia, see, Joseph Smith, *History of Joseph Smith, the Prophet* (Salt Lake City, 1902), I, p. 296. Burgess writes that Smith 'struggled' with tongues, at first embracing it and then distancing himself from it, Burgess, *Christian Peoples of the Spirit*, p. 198.

[264] Beadle, *Life in Utah*, p. 321.

[265] Brigham Young, 'The History of Brigham Young,' *The Latter-Day Saints Millennial Star*, XXV (11 July 1863), p. 439. He was praying with a friend, Alpheus Gifford. 'Gifford commenced speaking in tongues … the spirit came on me like an electric shock to speak in an unknown tongue, and though I was kneeling looking in an opposite direction, the same moment I turned round on my knees toward him and spoke in tongues also', John G. Turner, *Brigham Young: Pioneer Prophet* (Cambridge, MA: Harvard University Press, 2012), p. 30.

[266] Joseph Smith, *The Book of Mormon* (Salt Lake City, UT: The Church of Jesus Christ of Latter-day Saints, 1950) Omni 25, p. 131; Alma 9.21, p. 217; 3 Nephi 29.6, p. 455; Mormon 9.7, p. 476. For the ongoing nature of spiritual gifts, see Moroni 10.8-19, pp. 520-21. For an allusion to the tower of Babel, see Mosiah 28.11-20, pp. 190-91; cf. John Christopher Thomas, *A Pentecostal Reads The Book of Mormon: A Literary and Theological Introduction* (Cleveland, TN: CPT Press, 2016), pp. 215-20.

fixed theory nor uniform practice regarding glossolalia'.²⁶⁷ Glossolalia was once so common that whole days were devoted to 'speaking meetings', but by 1870 the practice had become rare.²⁶⁸ Matthew Davies noted the ASM revival of 1906 when combined with rising institutionalism, was instrumental in turning glossolalia from 'one of the heralding signs of the restored gospel' to the LDS church turning its back on this 'historic practice'.²⁶⁹

J. The Molokan-Jumpers (Russian Pryguny), 1833 CE – ASM Revival

In 1833 a revival broke out in Russia among the Molokans²⁷⁰ that 'manifested the activity of the gifts of the Spirit of revelation and various tongues'.²⁷¹ This caused a spilt among the Molokans, and 'those who accepted the experience were called the Pryguny (Jumpers) by their antagonists, signifying their common response to the Spirit'.²⁷² In 1853 there was another mighty outpouring that

---

²⁶⁷ Wamble, 'Glossolalia in Christian History', p. 40. 'In 1833, the Presidency said that Mormons received "the gift of tongues … as the ancient did" but failed to explain how the ancients received it', p. 39.

²⁶⁸ Beadle, *Life in Utah*, p. 323. Some within the Kirtland, OH community in 1830 felt that the presence of 'false tongues' would discredit Mormonism, Wamble, 'Glossolalia in Christian History', p. 39. 'The gift of tongues has now been replaced by the belief that Mormon missionaries are blessed by the Holy Spirit to learn foreign languages', Burgess, *Christian Peoples of the Spirit*, p. 199.

²⁶⁹ Clark, 'We believe in the gift of tongues', p. 76 (Org. cite: Matthew R. Davies, 'The Tongues of the Saints: A Historical Inquiry into the LDS Perception of the Azusa Street Revival and the Changing definition of Tongues', [paper presented at the BYU Church History Symposium, March 3, 2012]).

²⁷⁰ 'The Molokans (milk-drinkers) were a religious sect among Russian peasants who broke away from the Russian Orthodox church in the 1550's', Burgess, *Christian Peoples of the Spirit*, p. 213. In addition to rejecting icons, the tsar's rule, the Nicaean definition of the Trinity, military service, and water baptism, they did not honour Orthodox fasts and in protest drank milk. They were punished by exile into the Caucasus area (Armenia, Azerbaijan, Ukraine, central Asia, and Siberia).

²⁷¹ Maxim Gavrilovich Rudometkin, 'Discourses', 5.4.3-4, in Ivan Gureivich Shubin and Daniel H. Shubin (eds.), *Spirit and Life – Book of the Sun: Divine Discourses of the Preceptors and the Martyrs for the Word of God, the Faith of Jesus, and the Holy Spirit, of the Religion of the Spiritual Christian Molokan-Jumpers* (trans. John Wm. Volkov; USA: Daniel H. Shubin, 1983 reprint, 1928), pp. 48-49; cf. Herschel Odell Bryant, *Spirit Christology in the Christian Tradition: From the Patristic Period to the Rise of Pentecostalism in the Twentieth Century* (Cleveland, TN: CPT Press, 2014), pp. 379-91.

²⁷² Bryant, Spirit *Christology*, p. 380; cf. Burgess, *Christian Peoples of the Spirit*, p. 213.

included 'various tongues'.[273] Their most prominent leader, Maxim Gavrilovich Rudometkin, prayed for wisdom and 'the Spirit of wisdom descended upon me under the sign of the indescribable gift of my God, that is, in the new fiery tongues; in them I then sang a new song'.[274] Thereafter, he 'was endowed personally ... (with) the word of wisdom, and of various tongues as well as discernment of tongues'.[275] The Pryguny envisioned themselves as 'the true church of pneumatic believers, standing under the sign of glossolalia'[276] which was given at SB:[277] 'this baptism must ... have the spiritual sign upon him, *which is speech of the Spirit in new, fiery tongues*'.[278] H. Odell Bryant wrote, their beliefs had 'remarkable similarities with early classical Pentecostals'.[279] Twelve year old Pryguny, Efim Gerasimovich Klubnikin, wrote 'the Holy Spirit enveloped me. I was in the state of ecstasy ... I wrote songs, prayers, prophecies, stories, and drew plans.'[280] Shortly afterwards, 2,000 Pryguny followed his plan and immigrated to the USA.[281] Some of

---

[273] *Spirit and Life*, pp. 50-52; cf. Bryant, *Spirit Christology*, p. 383 n. 13.
[274] Rudometkin, 'Discourses', pp. 296-97.
[275] *Spirit and Life*, pp. 50-51.
[276] Bryant, *Spirit Christology*, p. 388.
[277] Bryant, *Spirit Christology*, p. 389.
[278] Rudometkin, 'Discourses', p. 222. Rudometkin's subsequent description does not help us to understand the purpose or nature of these tongues. He wrote that glossolalia represented judgment from the Lord on the final day but he gave no hint as to their present role – other than as 'the spiritual sign'.
[279] Bryant, *Spirit Christology*, p. 390.
[280] Efim Gerasimovich Klubnikin, 'Articles and Plans', 1.4, in Ivan Gureivich Shubin and Daniel H. Shubin (eds.), John Wm. Volkov (trans.), *Spirit and Life – Book of the Sun: Divine Discourses of the Preceptors and the Martyrs for the Word of God, the Faith of Jesus, and the Holy Spirit, of the Religion of the Spiritual Christian Molokan-Jumpers* (USA: Daniel H. Shubin, 1928 [1983 reprint]), p. 636.
[281] The vision encouraged them to 'go on a long journey over the great and deep waters', 5.7, p. 638. The purpose was to seek 'refuge in order to survive the coming war', Bryant, *Spirit Christology*, p. 391 n. 47; cf. Klubnikin, 'Articles and Plans', pp. 635-39; Ivan Gureivich Shubin and Daniel H. Shubin, 'The Journey to Refuge', in Ivan Gureivich Shubin and Daniel H. Shubin (eds.), *Spirit and Life – Book of the Sun: Divine Discourses of the Preceptors and the Martyrs for the Word of God, the Faith of Jesus, and the Holy Spirit, of the Religion of the Spiritual Christian Molokan-Jumpers* (trans. John Wm. Volkov; 1983 repr; USA: Daniel H. Shubin, 1928), pp. 747-58. According to Demos Shakarian there was 'unimaginable horror' for Armenia and their home village of Kara Kala was completely exterminated in 1914 during WWI, Demos Shakarian, John L. Sherrill, and Elizabeth Sherrill, *The Happiest People on Earth: The Long-Awaited Personal Story of Demos Shakarian* (Old Tappan, NJ: Spire Books: Distributed by Flemin H. Revell Company, 1975), pp. 13-30 (21).

these Pryguny participated in the ASM revival because when passing by they recognized 'the unmistakable sounds of people praising God in tongues'.[282] A mention in the *Los Angeles Times* verified their participation in the revival: 'before the meeting closed the picturesque "Priguni" out rivaled the wildest orgies of the Azusa Street revelers'.[283]

K. The 'Gift People' of New England (1844 CE)[284]

Pastor R.B. Swan of Providence, RI, was the most prominent voice of the small but widespread 'Gift People'.[285] He wrote in 1875, that

> my wife and I, with a few others, began to utter a few words in the 'unknown tongue.' A sister ... did not want this gift and kept her lips closed. We labored with her to yield to the Spirit, and when she did, she broke forth in a volume of words in an unknown tongue which continued for quite a time.[286]

Simmons, witnessed a revival in Rhode Island in 1873 where there was 'the talking in tongues'.[287] Several historians of early Pentecostalism contacted Pastor Swan directly to verify the glossolalia.[288]

---

[282] Shakarian, *The Happiest People on Earth*, p. 24; cf. Bryant, *Spirit Christology*, p. 391; Burgess, *Christian Peoples of the Spirit*, p. 214.

[283] *Los Angeles Times*, October 9, 1906, p. 17. Cf. Bryant, *Spirit Christology*, p. 391 n. 48.

[284] Also known as the 'Second Adventists', Simmons, 'By V.P. Simmons', p. 2; cf. Lawrence, *Apostolic Faith Restored*, pp. 38-43; Shumway, 'The Gift of Tongues', pp. 153-54; Simmons, 'Bro. V.P. Simmons, of Frostproof, Florida', p. 2; Simmons, 'The Speaking in Tongues in A.D. 1884', p. 1.

[285] Lawrence notes people from the six New England states (RI, MA, VT, NH, ME, CT) and NY, Lawrence, *Apostolic Faith Restored*, pp. 39-43. Cf. Frodsham, *With Signs Following*, p. 10; Shumway, 'The Gift of Tongues', p. 154; Simmons, 'By V.P. Simmons', p. 2. The leader before him (over him?) was Pastor John Starkweather of Boston, MA who came to believe in a 'second work of grace in the human heart, which ... must be accompanied by physical manifestations'. Shumway, 'The Gift of Tongues', pp. 153-54. John Starkweather was seminary-educated and pastored a church that broke away from the 'Miller' branch of Second Adventism over baptism.

[286] Lawrence, *Apostolic Faith Restored*, pp. 38, 39; cf. Frodsham, *With Signs Following*, p. 10.

[287] Frodsham, *With Signs Following*, p. 9; cf. Simmons, *History of Tongues*, p. 7.

[288] In 1909, Simmons, 'By V.P. Simmons', p. 2; in 1914, Lawrence, *Apostolic Faith Restored*, p. 38; in 1914, Shumway, 'The Gift of Tongues', p. 154.

L.W. Jethro Walthall in Arkansas (1879 CE)[289]

W. Jethro Walthall wrote that in 1879 'I was blessedly filled with the Holy Spirit, but knew no name or theory to attach to it ... I never heard of the baptism of the Spirit as such. I only knew that I had an experience that corresponded with the records given in the Acts of the Apostles'.[290] His experience with glossolalia was later mirrored in multiple congregations before there was any awareness of the ASM revival.[291] These congregations eventually affiliated with the AG.[292]

M. Early Holiness (1885 CE) and the Fire-Baptized Holiness Revivals

There was a series of revivals among the early WH people in which glossolalia occurred. The earliest claim was Fanny White who 'was baptized with the Spirit and spoke in tongues at Barney Creek sometime between 1885 and 1886'.[293] More well-known was the Shearer Schoolhouse revival[294] of 1895 in Camp Creek, NC, led by FBHA evangelists.[295] Also, 'more than 100 persons were said to have been Spirit-baptized during the Camp Creek revival in 1899-1900[296] with the manifestation of

---

[289] W. Jethro Walthall was a Baptist minister in Camden, AR, who was ejected from his denomination for his holiness preaching. He formed the Holiness Baptist Association (HBA) which later was enfolded into the Assemblies of God.

[290] Walthall, 'Letter From A Brother Minister', p. 8.

[291] 'Soon after the Spirit's outpour [sic], accompanied with tongues, our people (HBA) began to speak in other tongues, without ever having come in contact with others who spoke, or with a minister who taught it definitely', Walthall, 'Letter From A Brother Minister', p. 8.

[292] Walthall, 'Letter From A Brother Minister', p. 9. At the time of this testimony he was in the process of enfolding his organization, the HBA, with the AG, p. 9.

[293] Phillips, *Quest*, p. 107 n. 4; cf. p. 78; Frodsham, *With Signs Following*, pp. 16-17.

[294] It is also known by Cherokee County, Synan, *The Holiness-Pentecostal Tradition*, p. 72.

[295] Phillips writes that '"Speaking in tongues" was not at first recognized as a significant and distinct manifestation ... (though) eyewitnesses later recalled occurrences of tongues speech in their meetings', Phillips, *Quest*, p. 107, cf. Conn, *Like a Mighty Army*, pp. 22-24. There were testimonies of glossolalia as early as 1886 in the CU, p. 107 n. 4.

[296] Phillips, *Quest*, p. 140. 'Billy Martin came back to Camp Creek teaching the baptism with the Holy Ghost and speaking in tongues ... at least by 1899 and possibly as early as 1898', p. 139.

glossolalia'.²⁹⁷ Philips was hesitant about the larger numbers reported but was confident of the occurrences themselves.²⁹⁸ Though these people did not fully know what was happening to them,²⁹⁹ and despite a lull between their experience and the ASM revival,³⁰⁰ Philips argued that these early WH Pentecostals should be considered the first modern Pentecostals.³⁰¹

N. Carl M. Hanson of Dalton, MN (1895 CE)

Minnesota evangelist Carl M. Hanson wrote of an individual who was baptized in the Holy Spirit and 'came clear through and spoke

---

²⁹⁷ For example, Sarah A. Smith at nearby Cooker Creek, 'claimed that she was baptized with the Holy Spirit ... and spoke in other tongues with about forty others in 1900', Phillips, *Quest*, p. 140; cf. p. 141; Frodsham, *With Signs Following*, p. 17.

²⁹⁸ On the one hand, 'a close scrutiny of the records, however, indicates that the number of those who had been Spirit-baptized may have been inflated; for the distinction of speaking in tongues seems not to have been carefully considered in the estimates', Phillips, *Quest*, p. 271 n. 252. On the other hand, 'several second-generation members of Christian Union congregations ... testified that their fathers and mothers told them the outpouring of the Spirit in 1895-1900 including [sic] manifestations of speaking in tongues', 107 n. 4. Also, the sheer volume of 'the testimonies ... leaves no doubt that a great many in the revival at Camp Creek and in Monroe, Polk, and Bradley counties actually spoke in tongues in 1899-1900'.

²⁹⁹ Phillips, *Quest*, p. 139. '"Speaking in tongues" was not yet recognized as a significant and distinct manifestation ... they failed to see the significance of tongues-speech ... (its) significance ... still lay under the darkness of the Dark Ages', pp. 107, 108; cf. Conn, *Like a Mighty Army*, p. 12.

³⁰⁰ After Irwin's fall 'interest in the manifestation of tongues-speech faded, particularly in regard to connecting tongues-speech with Spirit-baptism. Then too, the understanding of tongues-speech in the FBHA in 1989-1900 never evolved into the "initial evidence" formula. Glossolalia was considered to be only one manifestation of the dynamic continuum' Phillips, *Quest*, p. 233.

³⁰¹ Specifically, that Irwin was the father of modern Pentecostalism because: 1) 'Irwin had distinguished as early as April 1899 the manifestation of "tongues of fire" on the day of Pentecost in Acts 2.3 from the manifestation of the various dialects in verse four', Phillips, *Quest*, p. 138. 2) 'Irwin's reference to "ecstatic speech" as a result of the baptism of *lyddite* predates by eight months Charles Fox Parham's introduction of SB with its connection to speaking in tongues at Topeka, Kansas in January 1901', p. 136. 3) Parham may have seen tongues between 1895 and 1900 in a FBHA meeting. 4) 'Irwin's theology of tongues-speech ... was superior to Parham's in that it was more consistent with Scripture ... (in that it) distinguished between the "gift of tongues" and the "witness of tongues"', p. 137. This sounds like what would develop later with Seymour. 5) Irwin distinguishes between the '"manifestation of fire" on the Day of Pentecost in Acts 2.3 from the manifestation of the various dialects in verse four' with the prior being subsequent to sanctification, p. 138.

in tongues' in 1895 under his ministry.³⁰² Another women 'shouted, praised God, sang and prophesied and spoke in other tongues' in 1897, while he experienced his own SB in 1899.³⁰³ His testimony and a local newspaper article³⁰⁴ highlighted not only the phenomena of glossolalia, but just how prevalent the theology of evidential tongues and restorationism were pre-ASM revival.³⁰⁵

O. The Welsh Revival (1904-1905 CE)

The Welsh Revival is included in this survey even though it occurred after 1900 for two reasons. First, there was a 'cross-pollination' of leadership between it and the emerging ASM revival. Williams noted that the Welsh Revival 'prepared the way for Pentecostalism in Britain'³⁰⁶ because there was a 'constant interflow back and forth across the Ocean'.³⁰⁷ Second, the references to glossolalia reflected both the curiosity and reservation that existed prior to

---

³⁰² C.M. Hanson, *My Personal Experiences of the Graces of Salvation, Healing and Baptism in the Holy Spirit* (Dalton, MN: self-published tract, 1905), p. 3. Not much is known of Carl M. Hanson other than he ministered in and around Fergus Falls and Minneapolis, MN. He may have been of Swedish descent because he published a tract on the rapture in Swedish (*Skola De Heliga bortryckas i Skyar till Herens Möte i Luften?*). He was ordained on 25-9-1909 and affiliated with the Assemblies of God on 11-9-1817, and died on 28-6-1954

³⁰³ Hanson, *My Personal Experiences*, p. 4. He wrote, 'I knelt down to pray ... (and) the Holy Spirit then, as a person, took possession of His Temple, speaking in other tongues, while I realized myself as a listener and an instrument in the hands of the Almighty'.

³⁰⁴ The article reported that Hanson said, that 'converts are frequently given the gift of tongues, as they were of old, and that they talk in whatever language the spirit directs', 'Fined $35', *Fergus Falls Daily Journal* (Mar 11, 1905), p. 3. The interview publishes the story of a woman was able to speak in German. Finally, 'the converts know exactly what they are doing at all times', meaning that they do not lose consciousness as he reported he did in his personal testimony.

³⁰⁵ Regarding IE, he clearly distinguished between his SB, which was known to him by glossolalia, from an earlier experience where he testified: 'became unconscious of a single word spoken' even though it too was a dramatic encounter', Hanson, *My Personal Experiences*, pp. 3, 4. He stated clearly that 'when the Holy Spirit came in He spoke in other tongues magnifying God', p. 5. He also noted a fifteen-century gap in the Church's Spiritual power that is now being restored, p. 5.

³⁰⁶ Williams, *Tongues of the Spirit*, p. 51.

³⁰⁷ Though a causal relationship does not exist, 'certain links between the Welsh Revival and the Los Angeles awakening can be established', Williams, *Tongues of the Spirit*, p. 53. The following leaders had significant connection with the Welsh Revival: Boddy, Smale, and Bartleman. Edwin J. Orr writes that 'there was no glossolalia during the first two years of the Welsh Revival, but the visit of a pastor from Los Angeles (Smale?) carried the fire to that metropolis where

the ASM revival. For example, on the one hand, Williams wrote, 'I have found no explicit reference to glossolalia in any first hand report'.[308] On the other hand, wrote Williams, the 'Revivalist Evan Roberts ... discouraged speaking with tongues', and then questioned, why would Roberts 'discourage it unless there had been some eruption of tongues?'[309] In Seth Johnson's diary there was a veiled reference to glossolalia:

> Sept. 22nd. – SEVERAL SOULS. We held another remarkable meeting to-night. Group after group came out to the front seeking "Ilawn sicrwydd ffydd" – full assurance of salvation. What was wonderful to me was the fact that every person engaged in prayer without one exception. The *tongue of fire came upon each*. We lost all sense of time in this service.[310]

Most accounts about tongues in the writings surrounding the Welsh Revival focused on counterfeit tongues;[311] however, there were a significant number of biblical references to glossolalia that were used to justify the revival's 'enthusiasm'.[312] Also, there were testimonies of 'new tongues' which were defined as a 'change in their manner and speech'.[313]

---

the zealots of the movement experienced glossolalia', Edwin J. Orr, 'The Welsh Revival Goes Worldwide', *Western Mail* (Dec. 9, 1974), in Tony Cauchi (ed.), *Welsh Revival Library* (Bishop's Waltham, UK: Revival Library, 2004), p. 7; cf. 'New Scandinavian Revival', *AF* 1.6 (Feb & Mar 1907), p. 1; W.J. Tomlinson, 'In Wales', *AF* 1.11 (Oct to Jan 1908), p. 1; Evans, 'Pentecost in Wales', p. 1.

[308] Williams, *Tongues of the Spirit*, p. 55. Williams believes there were episodes of cryptomnesia, where English speakers recalled 'impressions from childhood' of idiomatic Welsh and reverted to this unconscious tongue under the excitement of the Holy Spirit, p. 54.

[309] Williams, *Tongues of the Spirit*, pp. 53, 55.

[310] J. Vyrnwy Morgan, *The Welsh Religious Revival, 1904-05*, in Tony Cauchi (ed.), *Welsh Revival Library* (Bishop's Waltham, UK: Revival Library, 2004 reprint; 1909), p. 107. Morgan, who addressed the lack of propriety with the physical 'exercises', wrote that there were 'many outward signs. Forked flames, likened by the bewildered assemblage to tongues of fire', p. 200.

[311] Jessie Penn-Lewis, 'Revival Dawn and the Baptism in the Holy Spirit': Chapter 12 of 'War on the Saints', in Tony Cauchi (ed.), *Welsh Revival Library* (Bishop's Waltham, UK: Revival Library, 2004), pp. 17-18.

[312] Mrs. Jessie Penn-Lewis, *The Awakening in Wales, And Some of the Hidden Springs* (1904) (PDF from *The Revival Library*, King's Christian Centre, High Street, Bishop's Waltham, Hants, SO32 1AA, UK), pp. 11, 12, 15, 53.

[313] David Matthews, *I Saw The Welsh Revival*, in Tony Cauchi (ed.), *Welsh Revival Library* (Bishop's Waltham, UK: Revival Library, 2004 reprint), p. 43. This was distinguished from a reverence for the 'melody of speech' and the Welsh

VI. Conclusion to Appendix 2

This brief historical survey has revealed the following: first, though accounts of glossolalia were intermittent, there are enough historical accounts to affirm that tongues likely occurred throughout church history. Second, biblical terminology was probably replaced with colloquial equivalents as the church expanded to various language groups and passed through the centuries. Third, the rise of the institutional Latin Church in the fourth century reshaped the 'who' and 'what' of glossolalia. Glossolalia was redefined to be symbolic of the Church's presence in the world and no longer resided with individuals but resided solely in the office of bishop; however, allowance was made for xenolalia amongst the most pious of saints. Ecstatic glossolalia evolved to become a sign of the demonic, while at the same time personal and public jubilation, which sounds very much like ecstatic glossolalia, was encouraged by the Latin Church. Fourth, the Eastern Church retained glossolalia but deemed it less significant than visual revelations. Fifth, following the Reformation, glossolalia often spontaneously erupted in restorationist movements and revivals in diverse places.

'hwyl', Howell Elvet Lewis, *With Christ Among The Miners: Incidents and Impressions of the Welsh Revival*, in Tony Cauchi (ed.), *Welsh Revival Library* (Bishop's Waltham, UK: Revival Library, 2004 reprint, 1906), p. 12; cf. Williams, *Tongues of the Spirit*, pp. 172-73.

Bibliography

Early Pentecostal Periodicals
The Apostolic Faith (Azusa Street Mission, Los Angeles, CA).
The Blessed Truth (Daniel C.O. Opperman, Eureka Springs, AR).
The Bridegroom's Messenger (The Pentecostal Mission, Atlanta, GA).
The Christian Evangel (Assemblies of God, Plainfield, NJ; Findley, OH).
The Church of God Evangel (Church of God, Cleveland, TN).
The Good Report (R.E. McAlister, Ottawa, Canada & Los Angeles, CA).
Meat in Due Season (Frank J. Ewart, Los Angeles, CA).
The Pentecost (J. Roswell Flower, Indianapolis, IN).
The Pentecostal Evangel (Assemblies of God, Springfield, MO).
The Pentecostal Holiness Advocate (The Pentecostal Holiness Church, Falcon, NC; Franklin Springs, GA).
Pentecostal Testimony (William H. Durham, Chicago, IL; Los Angeles, CA).
Triumphs of Faith (Carrie Judd Montgomery, Oakland, CA).
The Weekly Evangel (Assemblies of God, St. Louis, MO; Springfield, MO).
The Whole Truth (Argenta, AR).
Word and Witness (E.N. Bell, Malvern, AR; Findley, OH; St. Louis, MO).

Other Works Cited
A Summary View of the Millennial Church of United Society of Believers (Commonly Called Shakers) (Albany: Packard & VanBenthuysen, 1823).
Abrams, Minnie, *The Baptism of the Holy Ghost and Fire* (Kedgaon: Mukti Mission Press, 2nd edn, 1906).
Ackland, Randal H., 'Spirit Baptism: An Appraisal of Frederick Dale Bruner's Book, *A Theology of the Holy Spirit: The Pentecostal Experience and the New Testament Witness*, and an Examination of Possible Pentecostal Responses to Bruner's Criticisms' (MA Thesis, Wheaton College, Wheaton, IL, 1988).
—'Towards a Sacramental View of Glossolalia', unpublished paper presented at the Society for Vineyard Studies (New Haven: Yale Divinity School, 2017).
Acta Sanctorum (Paris: V. Palme, 1863-1940).
Acta Sanctorum (Antwerp: apud Ioannem Meursium, 1643-1931).
Ahonen, L., 'Awakened', in Stanley Burgess (ed.), *NIDPCM* (Grand Rapids, MI: Zondervan, rev. and expanded edn, 2002), p. 343.
Albrecht, Daniel, 'Carrie Judd Montgomery: Pioneering Contributor to Three Religious Movements', *Pneuma* 8.1 (1986), pp. 101-19.
Alexander, Estrelda Y., *Black Fire: One Hundred Years of African American Pentecostalism* (Downers Grove, IL: IVP Academic, 2011).
Alexander, Kimberly Ervin, *Pentecostal Healing: Models in Theology and Practice* (JPTSup, 29; Blandford Forum: Deo Publishing, 2006).

—'Boundless Love Divine: A Re-evaluation of Early Understandings of the Experience of Spirit Baptism', in Steven Jack Land, Rickie D. Moore, and John Christopher Thomas (eds.), *Passover, Pentecost, and Parousia: Studies in Celebration of the Life and Ministry of R. Hollis Gause* (JPTSup 35; Blandford Forum: Deo Publishing, 2006), pp. 145-70.

—'Heavenly Choirs in Earthly Spaces: The Significance of Corporate Singing in Early Pentecostal Experience', *JPT* 25 (2016), pp. 254-68.

—'Girl Talk: A Feminist Re-Imagination of Pentecostal Theological Discourse and Experience', in Jon Huntzinger and David Moore (eds.), *The Pastor and the Kingdom: Essays Honoring Jack W. Hayford* (Southlake, TX: Gateway Academic, 2017), pp. 135-56.

Alexander, Paul, *Signs & Wonders: Why Pentecostalism is the World's Fastest Growing Faith* (San Francisco, CA: Jossey-Bass, 2009).

Anderson, Allan, *An Introduction to Pentecostalism* (Cambridge, UK: Cambridge University Press, 2004).

—*Spreading Fires: The Missionary Nature of Early Pentecostalism* (Maryknoll, NY: Orbis Books, 2007).

—'The Vision of the Apostolic Faith: Early Pentecostalism and World Mission', *Swedish Missiological Themes* 97.3 (2009), pp. 295-314.

Anderson, Gordon L., 'Baptism in the Holy Spirit, Initial Evidence, and a New Model', *Enrichment Journal* 10.1 (Winter, 2005), pp. 70-78.

Anderson, Robert Mapes, *Vision of the Disinherited* (New York: Oxford University Press, 1979).

Andrews, Edward Deming, *The People Called Shakers: A Search for the Perfect Society* (NY: Oxford University Press, 1953).

Archer, Kenneth J., *A Pentecostal Hermeneutic: Spirit, Scripture, and Community* (Cleveland, TN: CPT Press, 2009).

—*The Gospel Revisited* (Eugene, OR: Pickwick Publications, 2011).

Archer, Melissa, *'I Was in the Spirit on the Lord's Day': A Pentecostal Engagement with Worship in the Apocalypse* (Cleveland, TN: CPT Press, 2015).

Ash, James, L., 'The Decline of Ecstatic Prophecy in the Early Church', *Theological Studies* 37.2 (June, 1976), pp. 227-52.

Augustine, in *City of God* (trans. Marcus Dods; New York: The Modern Library, 1993).

—Augustine, 'Sermons', in John E. Rotelle (ed.), *The Works of Saint Augustine: A Translation for the 21st Century*, 3.7, Sermon 266 (trans. Edmund Hill; Hyde Park, NY: New City Press, 1993)

—'On Baptism, Against the Donatists', in Philip Schaff (ed.), *NPF, First Series: Augustin: Writings Against The Manicheans, And Against The Donatists*, Vol. 4 (trans. J.R. King; New York: Charles Scribner and Sons, 1901).

—*St. Augustine: Tractates on the Gospel of John, 28-54*, in John W. Rettig (trans.) *The Fathers of the Church: A New Translation* (Washington, DC: The Catholic University Press of America, 1993).

—'Expositions of the Psalms: 1-32', in John E. Rotelle (ed.), *The Works of Saint Augustine: A Translation for the 21st Century*, 3.15 (trans. Maria Boulding; Hyde Park, NY: New City Press, 2000).

—'Expositions of the Psalms: 33-50', John E. Rotelle (ed.), *The Works of Saint Augustine: A Translation for the 21st Century*, 3.16 (trans. Maria Boulding; Hyde Park, NY: New City Press, 2000).
—'Expositions of the Psalms: 51-72', John E. Rotelle (ed.), *The Works of Saint Augustine: A Translation for the 21st Century*, 3.17 (trans. Maria Boulding; Hyde Park, NY: New City Press, 2001).
—'Expositions of the Psalms: 73-98', John E. Rotelle (ed.), *The Works of Saint Augustine: A Translation for the 21st Century*, 3.18 (trans. Maria Boulding; Hyde Park, NY: New City Press, 2002).
—'Expositions of the Psalms: 99-120', Boniface Ramsey (ed.), *The Works of Saint Augustine: A Translation for the 21st Century*, 3.19 (trans. Maria Boulding; Hyde Park, NY: New City Press, 2003).
—'Expositions of the Psalms: 121-150', Boniface Ramsey (ed.), *The Works of Saint Augustine: A Translation for the 21st Century*, 3.20 (trans. Maria Boulding; Hyde Park, NY: New City Press, 2004).
—'Homilies on the First Epistle of John', in Boniface Ramsey (ed. and trans.) *The Works of Saint Augustine: A Translation for the 21st Century*, 1.14 (Hyde Park, NY: New City Press, 2008).
—*The Answer to the Letters of Petilian, the Donatist*, in Philip Schaff (ed.), *NPF, First Series* (Peabody, MA: Hendrickson, 1995).
—*On the Gospel of St. John*, in Philip Schaff (ed.), NPF, First Series.
Augustine, Daniela C., *Pentecost, Hospitality, and Transfiguration* (Cleveland, TN: CPT Press, 2012).
Aulén, Gustaf, *Christus Victor: An Historical Study of the Three Main Types of the Idea of the Atonement* (New York: Macmillan Publishing Co., 1969).
Baer, Richard A., 'Quaker Silence, Catholic Liturgy, and Pentecostal Glossolalia – Some Functional Similarities', in Russell P. Spittler (ed.), *Perspectives on the New Pentecostalism* (Grand Rapids, MI: Eerdmans, 1976), pp. 150-64.
Bainton, Roland, *The Reformation of the Sixteenth Century* (Boston, MA: Beacon Press, 1952).
Baker, Heidi G., 'Pentecostal Experience: Towards a Reconstructive Theology of Glossolalia' (PhD Thesis, King's College, London, England, 1995).
Barclay, Robert, in Dean Freiday (ed.), *Barclay's Apology in Modern English* (Philadelphia, PA: Religious Society of Friends, 1967).
Barratt, Thomas Ball, *The Works of T.B. Barratt* (New York: Garland Publishing, 1985 reprint; London: Elim Publishing Company, 1928).
Bartleman, Frank, *Azusa Street: An Eyewitness Account, The Centennial Edition, 1906-2006* (Gainesville, FL: Bridge-Logos, 2006 reprint; 1925).
Basham, Don, *A Handbook on Holy Spirit Baptism* (Pittsburgh, PA: Whitaker House, 1969).
Batuman, Elif, 'The Bells: Onward and Upward with the Arts', *The New Yorker* 85.11 (Apr 27, 2009), p. 22.
Beadle, J.H., *Life in Utah; or, The Mysteries and Crimes of Mormonism* (Philadelphia, PA: National Publishing Co., 1870).
Beare, Frank W., 'Speaking with Tongues: A Critical Survey of the New Testament Evidence', *JBL* 83 (September 1964), pp. 229-46.

Bellshaw, William G., 'The Confusion of Tongues', *BibSac* 120.478 (April 1963), pp. 145-53.
Bennett, Dennis J., *Nine O'clock in the Morning* (Plainfield, NJ: Logos International, 1970).
Berkhof, Hendrikus, *The Doctrine of the Holy Spirit* (Richmond, VA: John Knox Press, 1964).
Bernard, David K., *The New Birth* (Hazelwood, MO: Word Aflame, 1989).
—*A History of Christian Doctrine, Vol. 1: The Twentieth Century* (Weldon Spring, MO: Word Aflame, 1999).
Bittlinger, Arnold, *Gift and Graces: A Commentary of 1 Corinthians 12-14* (Grand Rapids, MI: Eerdmans, 1967).
Blumhofer, Edith L., *'Pentecost in My Soul': Explorations in the Meaning of the Pentecostal Experience of the Early Assemblies of God* (Springfield, MO: Gospel Publishing House, 1989).
—*The Assemblies of God: A Chapter in the Story of American Pentecostalism* (Springfield, MO: Gospel Publishing House, 1989).
Bosworth, Fred F. *'Do All Speak with Tongues?'* (New York, NY: The Christian Alliance Publishing Company, n.d.).
Bouhours, Dominique, *The Life of St. Francis Xavier, of the Society of Jesus, Apostle of India* (trans. James Dryden; Philadelphia: Eugene Cummiskey, 1841).
Brathwaite, Renea, 'Tongues and Ethics: William J. Seymour and the "Bible Evidence": A Response to Cecil M. Robeck, Jr', *Pneuma* 32.2 (2010), pp. 203-22.
Brumback, Carl, *What Meaneth This? – A Pentecostal Answer to a Pentecostal Question* (Springfield, MO: Gospel Publishing House, 1947).
—*Suddenly ... From Heaven: A History of the Assemblies of God* (Springfield, MO: Gospel Publishing House, 1961).
—*A Sound from Heaven: The Dramatic Beginning of the 20th Century Pentecostal Revival* (Springfield, MO: Gospel Publishing House, 1961).
Bruner, Frederick Dale, *A Theology of the Holy Spirit: The Pentecostal Experience and the New Testament Witness* (Grand Rapids, MI: Eerdmans, 1970).
Bryant, Herschel Odell, *Spirit Christology in the Christian Tradition: From the Patristic Period to the Rise of Pentecostalism in the Twentieth Century* (Cleveland, TN: CPT Press, 2014).
Bulgakov, S., 'From a World of Religious Contemplation', *Sobornost* 2 (June, 1935), pp. 4-7.
Bullinger, Heinrich, Der Widertoufferen Vrsprung, fürgang, secten, wäsen, fürnemme vnd gemeine jrer leer artickel, ouch jre gründ und warumb sy sich absünderind, vnnd ein eigne kirchen anrichtind, mit widerlegung vnd antwort vff alle und yede jre gründ und artickel, sampt Christenlichem bericht vnd vermanen, dass sy jres irrthumbs und absünderens abstandind, und sich mit der kirchen Christi vereinigind, abgeteilt in VI Bücher, und beschriben durch Heynrichen Bullingern (Zurich: Christoph Frochauer, 1560), in 'Answer of Some Who Are Called (Ana) Baptists Why They Do Not Attend The Churches: A Swiss Brethren Tract', Shem Peachey and Paul Peachey (ed. & trans. Paul Peachey) *Mennonite Quarterly Review* 45.1 (Jan 1971), pp. 5-32.

Bullock, Warren D., *When the Spirit Speaks: Making Sense of Tongues, Interpretation & Prophecy* (Springfield, MO: Gospel Publishing House, 2009).
Bundy, D.D., 'Thomas Ball Barratt', in Stanley Burgess (ed.), *NIDPCM* (Grand Rapids, MI: Zondervan, rev. and expanded edn, 2002), pp. 365-66.
—'Keswick Higher Life Movement,' in Stanley Burgess (ed.), *NIDPCM* (Grand Rapids, MI: Zondervan, rev. and expanded edn, 2002), pp. 820-21.
—'Edward Irving' in Stanley Burgess (ed.), *NIDPCM* (Grand Rapids, MI: Zondervan, rev. and expanded edn, 2002), pp. 803-804.
Burgess, Stanley M., 'Medieval Examples of Charismatic Piety in the Roman Catholic Church', in Russell P. Spittler (ed.), *Perspectives on the New Pentecostalism* (Grand Rapids, MI: Eerdmans, 1976), pp. 15-26.
—*The Holy Spirit: Eastern Christian Traditions* (Peabody, MA: Hendrickson, 1989).
—*The Holy Spirit: Ancient Christian Traditions* (Peabody, MA: Hendrickson, 2002 reprint; *The Spirit and the Church: Antiquity*, 1984).
—*The Holy Spirit: Medieval Roman Catholic and Reformation Traditions* (sixth-sixteenth centuries) (Peabody, MA: Hendrickson, 1997).
—'Holy Spirit, Doctrine of: The Ancient Fathers' in Stanley Burgess (ed.), *NIDPCM* (Grand Rapids, MI: Zondervan, rev. and expanded edn, 2002), pp. 730-746.
—'Evidence of the Spirit: The Ancient and Eastern Churches', in Gary B. McGee (ed.), *Initial Evidence: Historical and Biblical Perspectives on the Pentecostal Doctrine of Spirit Baptism* (Eugene, OR: Wipf & Stock, 2007 reprint; Hendrickson, 1991), pp. 3-19.
—'Evidence of the Spirit: The Medieval and Modern Western Churches', in Gary B. McGee (ed.), *Initial Evidence: Historical and Biblical Perspectives on the Pentecostal Doctrine of Spirit Baptism* (Eugene, OR: Wipf & Stock, 2007 reprint; Hendrickson, 1991), pp. 20-40.
—*Christian Peoples of the Spirit: A Documentary History of Pentecostal Spirituality from the Early Church to the Present* (New York: New York University Press, 2011).
Burrough, Edward, 'Epistle to the Reader', in *The Great Mystery of the Great Whore Unfolded; and Antichrist's Kingdom Revealed Unto Destruction. The Works of George Fox*, Vol. 3 (New York: Isaac T. Hooper, 1831, reprint; 1659).
Butler, Alban, *Butler's Lives of the Saints*, Vol. IV (Westminster, MD: Christian Classics, 1990).
Byrd II, Charles H., 'Pentecostalism's Anabaptist Heritage: The Zofingen Disputation of 1532', *JEPTA* 28.1 (2008), pp. 49-61.
Caird, George Bradford, *The Language and Imagery of the Bible* (Philadelphia, PA: Westminster Press, 1980).
Campbell, Marne L., '"The Newest Religious Sect Has Started In Los Angeles": Race, Class, Ethnicity, and the Origins of the Pentecostal Movement, 1906-1913', *The Journal of African American History* 95.1 (2010), pp. 1-25.
Cantalamessa, Raniero, *Sober Intoxication of the Spirit: Filled with the Fullness of God* (Cincinnati, OH: Servant Books, 2005).
Carothers, W.F., 'Notes and Paragraphs' in *The Baptism With the Holy Ghost and the Speaking in Tongues* (Zion City, IL: Carothers, 1906).

Carroll, R. Leonard., 'Glossolalia: Apostles to The Reformation', in Wade H. Horton (ed.) *The Glossolalia Phenomenon* (Cleveland, TN: Pathway Press, 1986), pp. 69-94.

Carson, D.A., *Showing the Spirit: A Theological Exposition of 1 Corinthians 12-14* (Grand Rapids, MI: Baker Book House, 1989).

Cartledge, Mark J., 'The Future of Glossolalia: Fundamentalist or Experientialist?', *Religion* 28 (1998), pp. 233-44.

—'The Nature and Function of New Testament Glossolalia', *The Evangelical Quarterly* 72.2 (2000), pp. 135–50.

—*Encountering the Spirit: The Charismatic Tradition* (Maryknoll, NY: Orbis Books, 2007).

Casmier, Stephen J. and Donale H. Matthews, 'Why Scatting is like Speaking in Tongues: Post-Modern Reflections On Jazz, Pentecostalism and "Africomysticism"', *Literature & Theology* 13.2 (Jun 1999), pp. 166-76.

Castelo, Daniel, *Pentecostalism as a Christian Mystical Tradition* (Grand Rapids, MI: Eerdmans, 2017).

Chambers, George B., *Folksong – Plainsong: A Study in Origins and Musical Relationships* (London: The Merlin Press, LTD, 1972).

Chan, Simon, 'The Language Game of Glossolalia, or Making Sense of the "Initial Evidence"', in Wonsuk Ma and Robert P. Menzies (eds.), *Pentecostalism in Context: Essays in Honor of William W. Menzies* (JPTSup 11; Sheffield: Sheffield Academic Press, 1997), pp. 80-95.

—*Pentecostal Theology and the Christian Spiritual Tradition* (JPTSup 21; Sheffield: Sheffield Academic Press, 2000).

—'Evidential Glossolalia and the Doctrine of Subsequence', *AJPS* 2.2 (Jl 1999), pp. 195–211.

Charette, Blaine, 'Presidential Address – Reflective Speech: Glossolalia and the Image of God', *Pneuma* 28.2 (Fall, 2006), pp. 189-201.

Christenson, Larry, 'Pentecostalism's Forgotten Forerunner', in Vinson Synan (ed.), *Aspects of Pentecostal – Charismatic Origins* (Plainfield, NJ: Logos International, 1975), pp. 15-37.

Chryssides, George D., 'Meaning, Metaphor and Meta-Theology', *Scottish Journal of Theology* 38 (1985), pp. 145-53.

Ciampa, Roy E. and Brian S. Rosner, '1 Corinthians', in G.K. Beale and D.A. Carson (eds.), *Commentary on the New Testament Use of the Old Testament* (Grand Rapids, MI: Baker Academic, 2007), pp. 740-42.

Clark, Alan J., '"We believe in the gift of tongues": The 1906 Pentecostal Revolution and Its Effects on the LDS Use of the Gift of Tongues in the Twentieth Century', *Mormon Historical Studies* 14.1 (Spring 2013), pp. 67-80.

Clark, Steve, *Baptized in the Spirit and Spiritual Gifts* (Pecos, NM: Dove Publications, 1976).

Clemen, Carl, 'The Speaking with Tongues of the Early Christians', *The Expository Times* 10.344 (1899), pp. 344-52.

Clement, 'The First Epistle of Clement', in Robert M. Grant and Holt H. Graham (eds.), *First and Second Clement: The Apostolic Fathers: A New Translation* (New York: Thomas Nelson & Sons, 1965), vol. 2.

Clemmons, J.C., 'Charles Harrison Mason', in Stanley Burgess (ed.), *NIDPCM* (Grand Rapids, MI: Zondervan, rev. and expanded edn, 2002), pp. 865-67.

Conkin, Paul, *Cane Ridge: America's Pentecost* (Madison, WI: The University of Wisconsin Press, 1990).

Conn, Charles W., *Pillars of Pentecost* (Cleveland, TN: The Pathway Press, 1956).

—'Glossolalia and the Scriptures', in Wade H. Horton (ed.), *The Glossolalia Phenomenon* (Cleveland, TN: Pathway Press, 1986), pp. 23-65.

—*Like a Mighty Army: A History of the Church of God* (Cleveland, TN: Pathway Press, 1977).

—'Church of God (Cleveland, TN)', in Stanley Burgess (ed.), *NIDPCM* (Grand Rapids, MI: Zondervan, rev. and expanded edn, 2002), pp. 530-34

Conybeare, Federick C., 'The Gift of Tongues', *Encyclopedia Britannica* 11th edition (New York, Cambridge University Press, 1911, vol. 27), pp. 9-10.

Conzelmann, Hans, *The Theology of St Luke* (trans. Geoffrey Buswell; London: Faber and Faber, 1960).

Cooper-Rompato, Christine F., *The Gift of Tongues: Women's Xenoglossia in the Latter Middle Ages* (University Park, PA: Pennsylvania State University, 2010).

Cox, Harvey Gallagher, *Fire from Heaven: The Rise of Pentecostal Spirituality and the Reshaping of Religion in the Twenty-First Century* (Reading, MA: Addison-Wesley Pub, 1995).

Crawford, Mattie (ed.), *The Pentecostal Flame* (Los Angeles, CA: 1926).

Cree, John *et al.*, *Evils of the Work Now Prevailing in the United States of America, Under the Name of a Revival of Religion* (Washington: n.p., 1804).

Currie, Stuart D., 'Speaking in Tongues, Early Evidence Outside the New Testament Bearing on "Glossais Lalein"', *Interpretation* 19 (1965), pp. 274-94.

Cutten, George Barton, *Speaking with Tongues, Historically and Psychologically Considered* (New Haven, London: Yale University Press; Humphrey Milford, Oxford University Press, 1927).

Cyprian, 'The Epistles of Cyprian', *ANF: Hippolytus, Cyprian, Caius, Novatian, Appendix* (ed. Alexander Roberts and James Donaldson; Vol. 5; Peabody, MA: Hendrickson, 1995).

Dalton, Robert Chandler, *Tongues like as of Fire* (Springfield, MO: Gospel Publishing House, 1945).

Davies, John G., 'Pentecost and Glossolalia', *JTS* 3.2 (O 1952), pp. 228-31.

Dayton, Donald W., *Theological Roots of Pentecostalism* (Peabody, MA: Hendrickson Pub, 1987).

—*Seven 'Jesus Only' Tracts* (New York: Garland Publishing, 1985).

de Voragine, Jacobus, *The Golden Legend: Readings on the Saints* (trans. William Granger Ryan; Princeton: Princeton University Press, 1993).

Dempster, Murray W., 'The Church's Moral Witness: A Study of Glossolalia in Luke's Theology of Acts', *Paraclete* 23.1 (1989), pp. 1-7.

Dickson, W. & R., 'Letter Published in Lancaster' in *Increase of Piety, or the Revival of Religion in the United States of America* (Newburyport, CT: Angier March, 1802).

Dollar, George W., 'Church History and the Tongues Movement', *BibSac* 120.480 (October-December, 1963), pp. 316-21.

Dorries, David W., 'Edward Irving and the "Standing Sign" of Spirit Baptism', in Gary B. McGee (ed.), *Initial Evidence: Historical and Biblical Perspectives on the Pentecostal Doctrine of Spirit Baptism* (Eugene, OR: Wipf & Stock, 2007 reprint; Hendrickson, 1991), pp. 41-56.

—'Catholic Apostolic Church', in Stanley Burgess (ed.), *NIDPCM* (Grand Rapids, MI: Zondervan, rev. and expanded edn, 2002), pp. 459-60.

Dove, Stephen, 'Hymnody and Liturgy in the Azusa Street Revival, 1906-1908', *Pneuma* 31.2 (2009), pp. 242-63.

Dunlavy, John, *The Manifesto, or Declaration of the Doctrine and Practice of the Church of Christ* (NY: Edward O. Jenkins, 1847).

Dunn, James D.G., *The Baptism in the Holy Spirit* (Philadelphia, PA: The Westminster Press, 1970).

—*Jesus and the Spirit* (Philadelphia: The Westminster Press, 1975).

DuPlessis, David J., *The Spirit Bade Me Go* (Plainfield, NJ: Logos International, 1970).

Egan, Harvey D., *Ignatius Loyola the Mystic* (Wilmington, DE: Michael Glazier, 1987).

Engelsen, Nils Ivar Johan, 'Glossolalia and Other Forms of Inspired Speech According to 1 Corinthians 12-14' (PhD Dissertation, Yale University, 1970).

Ensley, Eddie, *Sounds of Wonder: A Popular History of Speaking in Tongues in the Catholic Tradition* (Ramsey: Paulist, 1977).

Ervin, Howard M., *Conversion-Initiation and the Baptism in the Holy Spirit: An Engaging Critique of James D.G. Dunn's 'Baptism in the Holy Spirit'* (Peabody, MA: Hendrickson, 1984).

—*Spirit Baptism: A Biblical Investigation* (Peabody, MA: Hendrickson, 1987).

Eusebius, in G.A. Williamson (trans.), *Eusebius: The History of the Church from Christ to Constantine* (Minneapolis, MN: Augsburg Publishing House, 1965).

—Eusebius Pamphilius, *Ecclesiastical History*, Books 6-10, in Roy J. Deferrari (trans.), *The Fathers of the Church: A New Translation* (New York: Fathers of the Church, 1955).

—*Ecclesiastical History*, Volume 1: Books 1-5 (trans. Kirsopp Lake; Loeb Classical Library; Cambridge, MA: Harvard University Press, 1926).

Everts, Jenny, 'Tongues or Languages? Contextual Consistency in the Translation of Acts 2', *JPT* 4 (1994), pp. 71-80.

Fast, Heinold, *Quellen Zur Geschichte der Täufer in der Schweiz, 2 Band, Ostschweis* (Zurich: Theologiischer Verlag, 1973), in C.A. Snyder and Linda A.H. Hecht (eds.), *Profiles of Anabaptist Women* (Waterloo, Ontario: Wilfrid Laurier University Press, 1996).

Faupel, William D., *The Everlasting Gospel: The Significance of Eschatology in the Development of Pentecostal Thought* (JPTSup 10; Sheffield: Sheffield Academic Press, 1996).

Fee, Gordon, 'Tongues – Least of the Gifts? Some Exegetical Observations on 1 Corinthians 12-14', *Pneuma* 2 (1980), pp. 3-14.

—*The First Epistle to the Corinthians* (Grand Rapids, MI: Eerdmans, 1987).

—*God's Empowering Presence: The Holy Spirit in the Letters of Paul* (Peabody, MA: Hendrickson, 1994).

—'Toward a Pauline Theology of Glossolalia', in Wonsuk Ma and Robert P. Menzies (eds.), *Pentecostalism in Context: Essays in Honor of William W. Menzies* (JPTSup 11; Sheffield: Sheffield Academic Press, 1997), pp. 24-37.
Fettke, Steven M., & Robby Waddell (eds.), *Pentecostals in the Academy: Testimonies of Call* (Cleveland, TN: CPT Press, 2012).
Flower, Joseph R., *'Is it Necessary to Speak In An Unknown Tongue'* (Toronto, Canada: Full Gospel Publishing House, 1954).
—'Speaking with Tongues – Sign or Stumbling Block', *Paraclete* 2.2 (Spring 1968), pp. 16-19.
—'Holiness, the Spirit's Infilling, and Speaking with Tongues', *Paraclete* 2.3 (Summer 1968), pp. 7-9.
—'The Evangel's Roots', *PE* 4132 (Jul 18, 1993), pp. 7, 22.
Forbes, Christopher, *Prophecy and Inspired Speech in Early Christianity and its Hellenistic Environment* (Peabody, MA: Hendrickson, 1997).
Franklin, Lloyd D., 'The Spiritual Gifts in Tertullian' (PhD Thesis, Saint Louis University, 1989).
French, Talmadge L., *Our God Is One* (Indianapolis, IN: Voice & Vision Publications, 1999).
Frodsham, Arthur W., 'What is the Use of Speaking in Tongues?', in *Filled With the Fulness of God* (Springfield, MO: Gospel Publishing House, 1930), pp. 56-62.
Frodsham, Stanley H., *With Signs Following* (Springfield, MO: Gospel Publishing House, 1946).
Gee, Donald, 'Immersed in the Fulness of God', in *Filled With the Fulness of God* (Springfield, MO: Gospel Publishing House, 1930), pp. 35-43.
Goff, James R., *Fields White unto Harvest: Charles F. Parham and the Missionary Origins of Pentecostalism* (Fayetteville: University of Arkansas Press, 1988).
—'Charles Fox Parham', in Stanley Burgess (ed.), *NIDPCM* (Grand Rapids, MI: Zondervan, rev. and expanded edn, 2002), pp. 955-57.
Goodman, Felicitas D., *Speaking in Tongues: A Cross-Cultural Study of Glossolalia* (Chicago, IL: University of Chicago, 1972).
Görres, J.J., *Die Christliche Mystik* (5 vols.; Regensburg: G.J. Manz, 1836-41).
Gortner, J. Narver, 'How to Receive the Baptism', in *Filled With the Fulness of God* (Springfield, MO: Gospel Publishing House, 1930), pp. 44-6.
Goss, Ethel, *The Winds of God: The Story of the Early Pentecostal Movement (1901-1914) in the Life of Howard A. Goss* (Hazelwood, MO: Word Aflame Press, 1977).
Grebel, Conrad, 'Grebel to Müntzer, Zurich, 9/5/1524', in Leland Harder (ed.), *The Sources of Swiss Anabaptism: The Grebel Letters and Related Documents* (Scottsdale, PA: Herald Press, 1985).
Green, Chris, E.W., *Toward a Pentecostal Theology of the Lord's Supper: Foretasting the Kingdom* (Cleveland, TN: CPT Press, 2012).
Green, William M., 'Glossolalia in the Second Century', *RQ* 16.3-4 (1973), pp. 231-39.
Greenfield, John, *When the Spirit Came: The Story of the Moravian Revival of 1727* (Minneapolis, MN: Bethany Fellowship, 1967).

Gregory, *The Teaching of Saint Gregory* (trans. Robert W. Thomson; New Rochelle, NY: St Nersess Armenian Seminary, 2001).
Gromacki, Robert Glenn, *The Modern Tongues Movement* (Philadelphia, PA: Presbyterian and Reformed Publishing House, 1967).
Gundry, Robert H., 'Ecstatic Utterance (NEB)', *JTS* 17.2 (O 1966), pp. 299-307.
Guinness, Os, *The Call: Finding and Fulfilling the Central Purpose of Your Life* (Nashville, TN: Word Publishing, 1998).
Gunkel, Hermann, *The Influence of the Holy Spirit: The Popular View of the Apostolic Age and the Teaching of the Apostle Paul* (Roy A. Harrisville and Philip A Quanbeck II, trans.: Philadelphia, PA: Fortress Press, 1970).
Hanson, C.M., *My Personal Experiences of the Graces of Salvation, Healing and Baptism in the Holy Spirit* (Dalton, MN: self-published tract, 1905).
Hargrave, Vessie D., 'Glossolalia: Reformation to the Twentieth Century', in Wade H. Horton (ed.), *The Glossolalia Phenomenon* (Cleveland, TN: Pathway Press, 1966), pp. 97-139.
Harris, Ralph W., *Spoken by the Spirit: Documented Accounts of 'Other Tongues' From Arabic to Zulu* (Springfield, MO: Gospel Publishing House, 1973).
Haskett, William, *Shakerism Unmasked, or the History of the Shakers* (Pittsfield: N.H. Walkley, Printer, 1828).
Hayes, D.A., *The Gift of Tongues* (New York: The Methodist Book Concern, 1914).
Hayford, Jack W., *The Beauty of Spiritual Language* (Nashville, TN: Thomas Nelson, 1996).
Haywood, G.T., 'The Birth of the Spirit in the Days of the Apostles', in Donald W. Dayton, *Seven 'Jesus Only' Tracts* (New York: Garland Publishing, reprint; Indianapolis, IN: Christ Temple Book Store, n.d.).
—'The Victim of the Flaming Sword', in Donald W. Dayton, *Seven 'Jesus Only' Tracts* (New York: Garland Publishing, reprint; Indianapolis, IN: Christ Temple Book Store, n.d.).
Higley, Sarah L., *Hildegard of Bingen's Unknown Language: An Edition, Translation, and Discussion* (New York, NY: Palgrave MacMillian, 2007).
Hilary, 'On the Trinity', in Philip Schaff (ed.), *NPF, First Series: Homilies on the Gospel of John; Homilies on the First Epistle of John; Soliloquies*, Vol. 9 (Peabody, MA: Hendrickson, 1995, reprint; 1887).
Hilborn, David, 'Glossolalia as Communication', in Mark J. Cartledge (ed.), *Speaking in Tongues: Multi-Disciplinary Perspectives* (Studies in Pentecostal and Charismatic Issues; Bletchley, Milton Keynes, England: Paternoster Press, 2006), pp. 111-46.
Hinck, Joel, 'Heavenly Harmony: An Audio Analysis of Corporate Singing in Tongues', *Pneuma* 40 (2018), pp. 167-91.
Hinson, E. Glenn, 'The Significance of Glossolalia in the History of Christianity', in Watson E. Mills (ed.), *Speaking in Tongues: A Guide to Research on Glossolalia* (Grand Rapids, MI: Eerdmans, 1986), pp. 181-203.
Henke, Frederick G., 'The Gift of Tongues and Related Phenomena at the Present Day', *The American Journal of Theology* 13.2 (April 1909), pp. 193-206.

Ho, Melvin, 'A Comparison of Glossolalia in Acts and Corinthians', *Paraclete* (Spring, 1987), pp. 15-19.
Hocken, Peter D., 'Jesus Christ and the Gifts of the Spirit', *Pneuma* 5.1 (Spring 1983), pp. 1-16.
—'The Meaning and Purpose of "Baptism in the Spirit"', *Pneuma* 7.2 (Fall 1985), pp. 125-33
—'Charismatic Movement', in Stanley Burgess (ed.), *NIDPCM* (Grand Rapids, MI: Zondervan, rev. and expanded edn, 2002), pp. 477-519.
Hoekema, Anthony A., *What About Tongue-Speaking?* (Grand Rapids, MI: Eerdmans, 1966).
Holdcroft, L. Thomas, *The Holy Spirit: A Pentecostal Interpretation* (Springfield, MO: Gospel Publishing House, 1979).
Hollenweger, Walter J., 'Handbuch der Pfingstbewegung' (PhD dissertation, University of Zurich, 1965).
—'Pentecostals and the Charismatic Movement', in Cheslyn Jones, Geoffrey Wainwright, and Edward Yarnold (eds.), *The Study of Spirituality* (London: SPCK, 1986), pp. 549-54.
—'After Twenty Years' Research on Pentecostalism', *International Review of Mission* 75.297 (1986), pp. 3-12.
—*The Pentecostals* (Peabody, MA: Hendrickson, 1988).
—'The Ecumenical Significance of Oral Christianity', *Ecumenical Review* 41.2 (1989), pp. 259-65.
—*Pentecostalism: Origins and Developments Worldwide* (Peabody, MA: Hendrickson, 1997).
Holm, Randall, Matthew Wolf, and James K.A. Smith, 'New Frontiers in Tongues Research: A Symposium', *JPT* 20 (2011), pp. 122-54.
Horton, Harold, *The Gifts of the Spirit* (Springfield, MO: Gospel Publishing House, 1975).
—*What the Bible Says About the Holy Spirit* (Springfield, MO: Gospel Publishing House, 1976).
—*The Book of Acts* (Springfield, MO: Gospel Publishing House, 1981).
Horton, Wade H., *The Glossolalia Phenomenon* (Cleveland, TN: Pathway Press, 1986).
Hovenden, Gerald, *Speaking in Tongues: The New Testament Evidence in Context* (JPTSup, 22; Sheffield: Sheffield Academic Press, 2002).
Hudson, Neil, 'Strange Words and Their Impact on Early Pentecostals – A Historical Perspective,' in Mark J. Cartledge (ed.), *Speaking in Tongues: Multi-Disciplinary Perspectives* (Studies in Pentecostal and Charismatic Issues; Bletchley, Milton Keynes, England: Paternoster Press, 2006), pp. 52-80.
Hughes, Ray H., 'Glossolalia in Contemporary Times', in Wade H. Horton (ed.), *The Glossolalia Phenomenon* (Cleveland, TN: Pathway Press, 1986), pp. 143-177.
Hunter, Harold D., 'Tongues Speech: A Patristic Analysis', *JETS* 23.2 (June, 1980), pp. 125-37.
—*Spirit-Baptism: A Pentecostal Alternative* (Lanham, MD: University Press of America, 1983).

—'Ambrose Jessup Tomlinson', in Stanley Burgess (ed.), *NIDPCM* (Grand Rapids, MI: Zondervan, rev. and expanded edn, 2002), pp. 1143-45.

—'Church of God of Prophecy', in Stanley Burgess (ed.), *NIDPCM* (Grand Rapids, MI: Zondervan, rev. and expanded edn, 2002), pp. 539-42.

Hurtado, Larry W., 'Normal, but not a Norm: "Initial Evidence" and the New Testament', in Gary B. McGee (ed.) *Initial Evidence: Historical and Biblical Perspectives on the Pentecostal Doctrine of Spirit Baptism* (Eugene, OR: Wipf & Stock, 2007 reprint; Hendrickson, 1991), pp. 189-201.

Hurst, Dom David (trans.), *Gregory the Great Forty Gospel Homilies, Cistercian Series Studies: One-Hundred-Twenty-Three* (Kalamazoo, MI: Cistercian Publications, 1990).

Hutch, Richard A., 'The Personal Ritual of Glossolalia', in Watson E. Mills (ed.), *Speaking in Tongues: A Guide to Research on Glossolalia* (Grand Rapids, MI: Eerdmans, 1986), pp. 381-95.

Ignatius, 'Polycarp', in Robert M. Grant (ed.), *Ignatius of Antioch: The Apostolic Fathers: A New Translation* (Camden, NJ: Thomas Nelson & Sons, 1966).

Inch, Morris A., *Saga of the Spirit: A Biblical, Systematic, and Historical Theology of the Holy Spirit* (Grand Rapids, MI: Baker Book House, 1985).

Irenaeus, in Dominic J. Unger (trans.), *St. Irenaeus of Lyons Against the Heresies*, Vol. 1, Book 1 (New York, NY: Paulist Press, 1992).

—'Against Heresies', in Alexander Roberts and James Donaldson (eds.), *ANF, First Series: Translations of the Writings of the Fathers Down to A.D. 325* (Peabody, MA: Hendrickson, 1995).

Irvin, Dale, 'Pentecostal Historiography and Global Christianity: Rethinking the Questions of Origins' *Pneuma* 27.1 (Spring, 2005), pp. 35-50.

Jacobsen, Douglas, *Thinking in the Spirit: Theologies of the Early Pentecostal Movement* (Indianapolis, IN: Indiana University Press, 2003).

Johns, Donald A., 'Some New Directions in the Hermeneutics of Classic Pentecostalism's Doctrine of Initial Evidence', in Gary B. McGee (ed.), *Initial Evidence: Historical and Biblical Perspectives on the Pentecostal Doctrine of Spirit Baptism* (Eugene, OR: Wipf & Stock, 2007 reprint; Hendrickson, 1991), pp. 145-67.

Johnson, David R., *Pneumatic Discernment in the Apocalypse: An Intertextual and Pentecostal Exploration* (Cleveland, TN: CPT Press, 2018).

Johnson, Guion Griffis, 'Revival Movements in Ante-Bellum North Carolina', *North Carolina Historical Review* 10.1 (Jan, 1933), pp. 21-44.

Johnson, Luke Timothy, *Religious Experience in Earliest Christianity: A Missing Dimension in New Testament Studies* (Minneapolis, MN: Fortress Press, 1998).

Johnston, Robin, 'Howard Goss: A Pentecostal Life' (PhD Dissertation, Regent University School of Divinity, 2010).

Kardong, Terrence G., *Pillars of Community: Four Rules of Pre-Benedictine Monastic Life* (Collegeville, MN: Liturgical Press, 2010).

Kay, William K., 'The Mind, Behaviour and Glossolalia: A Psychological Perspective', in Mark J. Cartledge (ed.), *Speaking in Tongues: Multi-Disciplinary Perspectives* (Studies in Pentecostal and Charismatic Issues; Bletchley, Milton Keynes, England: Paternoster Press, 2006), pp. 174-205.

—*Pentecostalism: A Very Short Introduction* (New York: Oxford University Press, 2011).
Keener, Craig S., 'Why Does Luke Use Tongues as a sign of the Spirit's Empowerment?', *JPT* 15.2 (April 1, 2007), pp. 177-84.
Kelsey, Morton T., *Tongue Speaking: An Experiment In Spiritual Experience* (Garden City, NY: Doubleday & Company, 1964).
Kenyon, Howard N., 'Black Ministers in the Assemblies of God', *AG Heritage* (Spring, 1987), pp. 10-13, 20.
Kertson, Brandon, 'Spirit Baptism in the Pentecostal Evangel', *Pneuma* 37.5 (2015), pp. 244-61.
Kessler, Johannes, *Sabata: St. Galler Reformationschronik 1523-1539* (Traugott Schiess, ed.: Leipzig: Im Kommissionsverlag von Rudolf Haupt, 1911), pp. 51-52.
King, James Gorden, 'The Pentecostal View of the Gift of Tongues' (MA Thesis, Wheaton College, Wheaton, IL, 1974).
Klaassen, Walter, *Anabaptism: Neither Catholic nor Protestant* (Waterloo, On: Conrad Press, 1973).
Klubnikin, Efim Gerasimovich, 'Articles and Plans', 1.4, in Ivan Gureivich Shubin and Daniel H. Shubin (eds.) and John Wm. Volkov (trans.), *Spirit and Life – Book of the Sun: Divine Discourses of the Preceptors and the Martyrs for the Word of God, the Faith of Jesus, and the Holy Spirit, of the Religion of the Spiritual Christian Molokan-Jumpers* (1983 repr; USA: Daniel H. Shubin, 1928).
Knox, Ronald A., *Enthusiasm: A Chapter in the History of Religion* (Oxford: Oxford University Press, 1950).
Kydd, Ronald Alfred Narfi, 'Charismata to 320 A.D. A Study of the Overt Pneumatic Experience of the Early Church' (PhD Thesis, University of St. Andrews, 1972).
—*Charismatic Gifts in the Early Church* (Peabody, MA: Hendrickson, 1984).
Land, Steven Jack, *Pentecostal Spirituality: A Passion for the Kingdom* (JPTSup 1; Sheffield: Sheffield Academic Press, 1993).
—'Be Filled with the Spirit: The Nature and Evidence of Spiritual Fullness', *Ex Auditu* 12 (January 1, 1996), pp. 108-20.
Lang, G.H., *The History and Diaries of an Indian Christian* (Suffolk: Walsham-Le-Willows, 1939).
Lawrence, Bennett Freeman, *The Apostolic Faith Restored: A History of the Present Latter Rain Outpouring of the Holy Spirit Known as the Apostolic Pentecostal Movement* (St. Louis, MO: Gospel Publishing House, 1916).
Lederle, Henry I., 'Initial Evidence and the Charismatic Movement: An Ecumenical Appraisal', in Gary B. McGee (ed.), *Initial Evidence: Historical and Biblical Perspectives on the Pentecostal Doctrine of Spirit Baptism* (Eugene, OR: Wipf & Stock, 2007 reprint; Hendrickson, 1991), pp. 131-41.
Lewis, Clives Staples, 'Transposition' in *The Weight of Glory and Other Addresses* (San Francisco: HarperCollins Publishers, 2001), pp. 91-115.
Lewis, Howell Elvet, *With Christ Among The Miners: Incidents and Impressions of the Welsh Revival*, in Tony Cauchi (ed.), *Welsh Revival Library* (Bishop's Waltham, UK: Revival Library, 2004 reprint; 1906).

Lietzmann, Hans, *The Founding of the Church Universal: A History of the Early Church* (trans. B.L. Woolf II; London: Lutterworth Press, 1961).
Lim, David, *Spiritual Gifts: A Fresh Look* (Springfield, MO: Gospel Publishing House, 1999).
Littell, Franklin Hamlin, *The Origins of Sectarian Protestantism: A Study of the Anabaptist View of the Church* (New York: Macmillian, 1964).
Lovett, Leonard, 'Black Origins of the Pentecostal Movement', in Vinson Synan (ed.) *Aspects of Pentecostal – Charismatic Origins* (Plainfield, NJ: Logos International, 1975), pp. 123-41.
MacArthur, John, *Strange Fire: The Danger of Offending the Holy Spirit with Counterfeit Worship* (Nashville, TN: Thomas Nelson, 2013).
Macchia, Frank D., 'Sighs Too Deep for Words: Toward a Theology of Glossolalia', *JPT* 1 (October 1992), pp. 47-73.
—'Tongues as a Sign: Towards a Sacramental Understanding of Pentecostal Experience', *Pneuma* 15.1 (March 1, 1993), pp. 61-76.
—'The Question of Tongues as Initial Evidence: A Review of Initial Evidence', Edited by Gary B. McGee', *JPT* 2 (1993), pp. 117-27.
—'Groans Too Deep for Words: Towards a Theology of Tongues as Initial Evidence', *AJPS* 1.2 (1998), pp. 149-73.
—'Babel and the Tongues of Pentecost: Reversal or Fulfillment? – A Theological Perspective', in Mark J. Cartledge (ed.), *Speaking in Tongues: Multi-Disciplinary Perspectives* (Studies in Pentecostal and Charismatic Issues; Bletchley, Milton Keynes, England: Paternoster Press, 2006), pp. 34-51.
—*Baptized in the Spirit: A Global Pentecostal Theology* (Grand Rapids, MI: Zondervan, 2006).
—'Blessed Beyond Measure: An Autobiographical Reflection', in Steven Fettke and Robby Waddell (eds.), *Pentecostals in the Academy* (Cleveland, TN: CPT press, 2012), pp. 129-47.
MacDonald, William G., *Glossolalia in the New Testament* (Springfield, MO: Gospel Publishing House, 1964).
—'The Place of Glossolalia in Neo-Pentecostalism', in Watson E. Mills (ed.), *Speaking in Tongues: A Guide to Research on Glossolalia* (Grand Rapids, MI: Eerdmans, 1986), pp. 221-34.
—'Biblical Glossolalia: Theses One and Two', *Paraclete* 27.1 (Winter 1993), pp. 1-7.
—'Biblical Glossolalia: Thesis Three', *Paraclete* 27.2 (Spring 1993), pp. 7-14.
—'Biblical Glossolalia: Thesis Four', *Paraclete* 27.3 (Summer 1993), pp. 32-43.
—'Biblical Glossolalia: Thesis Five', *Paraclete* 27.4 (Fall 1993), pp. 15-21.
—'Biblical Glossolalia: Thesis Six', *Paraclete* 28.1 (Winter 1994), pp. 23-26.
—'Biblical Glossolalia: Thesis Seven', *Paraclete* 28.2 (Spring 1994), pp. 1-12.
Mackie, Alexander, *The Gift of Tongues: A Study in Pathological Aspects of Christianity* (New York: George H. Doran Company, 1921).
Martin III, Ira Jay, 'Glossolalia in the Apostolic Church', *JBL* 63.2 (June 1944), pp. 123-30.

Martyr, Justin, 'Second Apology', in Philip Schaff (ed.), *ANF, First Series: The Apostolic Fathers with Justin Martyr and Ireneaus* (Peabody, MA: Hendrickson 1995).
—*Dialogue with Trypho* (trans. Thomas B. Falls; Washington, DC: The Catholic University Press of America, 2003).
Mathieu, Pierre François, *Histoire des Miraculés et Convulsionnaires de Saint-Médard* (Paris: Librairie Academique, 1864).
Matthews, David, *I Saw The Welsh Revival*, in Tony Cauchi (ed.), *Welsh Revival Library* (Bishop's Waltham, UK: Revival Library, 2004 reprint).
Mauchline, John, 'Ecstasy', *ExpT*, 49 (1938), pp. 295-99.
McClymond, Michael J., 'Charismatic Gifts: Healing, Tongue-Speaking, Prophecy, and Exorcism', in Lamin Sanneh and Michael McClymond (ed.), *The Wiley Blackwell Companion to World Christianity* (Boston, MA: John Wiley & Sons, 2016), pp. 399-418.
McDonald, H.D., *Theories of Revelation: An Historical Study 1700-1960* (Grand Rapids, MI: Baker Book House, 1970).
McDonnell, Kilian, 'The Function of Tongues in Pentecostalism', *One in Christ* 19.4 (1984), pp. 332-54.
—*Christian Initiation and Baptism in the Holy Spirit: Evidence from the First Eight Centuries* (Collegeville MN: Liturgical Press, 1991).
McGee, Gary B., 'Joseph James Roswell Flower and Alice Reynolds', in Stanley Burgess (ed.), *NIDPCM* (Grand Rapids, MI: Zondervan, rev. and expanded edn, 2002), pp. 642-44.
—'Early Pentecostal Hermeneutics: Tongues as Evidence in the Book of Acts', in Gary B. McGee (ed.), *Initial Evidence: Historical and Biblical Perspectives on the Pentecostal Doctrine of Spirit Baptism* (Eugene, OR: Wipf & Stock, 2007 reprint; Hendrickson, 1991), pp. 96-188.
—'Popular Expositions of Initial Evidence', in Gary B. McGee (ed.), *Initial Evidence: Historical and Biblical Perspectives on the Pentecostal Doctrine of Spirit Baptism* (Eugene, OR: Wipf & Stock, 2007 reprint; Hendrickson, 1991), pp. 119-130.
—'Shortcut to Language Preparation? Radical Evangelicals, Missions, and the Gift of Tongues', *International Bulletin of Missionary Research* 25.3 (July 1, 2001), pp. 118-23.
—*People of the Spirit: The Assemblies of God* (Springfield, MO: Gospel Publishing House, 2004).
—'"Brought into the Sphere of the Supernatural": How Speaking in Tongues Empowered Early Pentecostals', *Encounter: Journal for Pentecostal Ministry* 4.1 (Fall 2007), pp. 1–17.
—'"The New World of Realities in Which We Live": How Speaking in Tongues Empowered Early Pentecostals', *Pneuma* 30.1 (January 1, 2008), pp. 108-35.
McGee, John, 'Letter to the Rev. T.L. Douglass (1821)', in *The Methodist Magazine* 4 (N. Bangs and T. Mason, for the Methodist Episcopal Church, 1821), pp. 189-91.
M'Nemar, Richard, *The Kentucky Revival* (Cincinnati, 1808).

McQueen, Larry R., *Toward a Pentecostal Eschatology: Discerning the Way Forward* (JPTSup 39; Dorset, UK: Deo Publishing, 2012).
McVicar, Michael J., 'Take Away the Serpents from Us: The Sign of Serpent Handling and the Development of Southern Pentecostalism', *The Journal of Southern Religion* 15 (2013): http://jsr.fsu.edu/issues/vol15/mcvi car.html.
Menzies, Glen W., 'Tongues as 'The Initial Physical Sign' of Spirit Baptism in the Thought of D.W. Kerr', *Pneuma* 20.2 (1998), pp. 175–89.
Menzies, Robert P., *Empowered for Witness: The Spirit in Luke-Acts* (JPTSup 6; Sheffield: Sheffield Academic Press, 1991).
—'Evidential Tongues: An Essay on Theological Method', *AJPT* 1 (1998), pp. 111-23.
—'Evidential Tongues: An Essay on Theological Method', in Gary B. McGee (ed.), *Initial Evidence: Historical and Biblical Perspectives on the Pentecostal Doctrine of Spirit Baptism* (Eugene, OR: Wipf & Stock, 2007), pp. 220-33.
—'The Role of Glossolalia in Luke-Acts', *AJPT* 15.1 (2012), pp. 47-72.
—*Pentecost: This Story is Our Story* (Springfield, MO: Gospel Publishing House, 2013).
—*Speaking in Tongues: Jesus and the Apostolic Church as Models for the Church Today* (Cleveland, TN: CPT Press, 2016).
Menzies, William, 'Editorial', *Pneuma* 1.1 (Spring 1979), pp. 3-5.
—*Anointed to Serve: The Story of the Assemblies of God* (Springfield, MO: Gospel Publishing House, 1971).
—'The Initial Evidence Issue: A Pentecostal Response', *AJPS* 2/2 (1999), pp. 261-78.
Menzies, William & Robert Menzies, *Spirit and Power: Foundations of Pentecostal Experience* (Grand Rapids, MI: Zondervan, 2000).
Milavec, Aaron, *The Didache: Text, Translation, Analysis, and Commentary* (Collegeville, MN: Liturgical Press, 2003), p. 25.
Miller, B.C., 'The Baptism in the HolySpirit – What? When? Where?', in *Filled With the Fulness of God* (Springfield, MO: Gospel Publishing House, 1930), pp. 15-34.
Mills, Watson E., 'A Theological Interpretation of Tongues in Acts and 1 Corinthians' (PhD dissertation, Southern Baptist Seminary, 1968).
—*Understanding Speaking in Tongues* (Grand Rapids: Eerdmans, 1972).
—'Glossolalia: Christianity's "Counterculture" Amidst a Silent Majority', *The Christian Century* (Sep 27, 1972), pp. 949-51.
—*A Theological/Exegetical Approach to Glossolalia* (Lanham: University Press of America, 1985).
—*The Holy Spirit: A Bibliography* (Peabody, MA: Hendrickson, 1988).
Millsaps, Willie T., 'Willie T. Millsaps Remembers C.H. Mason at Hot Springs', *AG Heritage* 4.2 (Summer 1984), p. 8.
Minns, Dennis and Paul Parvis, *Justin, Philosopher and Martyr: Apologies* (New York: Oxford University Press, 2009).
Miskov, Jennifer A., *Life on Wings: The Forgotten Life and Theology of Carrie Judd Montgomery (1858-1946)* (Cleveland, TN: CPT Press, 2012).

Molenaar, William J., 'Christian Unity: A Founding Principle of the Assemblies of God', *Heritage* 34 (2014), pp. 57-65.

Montgomery, Carrie Judd, *Speaking in Tongues* (Framingham, MA: Christian Workers Union, n.d.).

Morgan, J. Vyrnwy, *The Welsh Religious Revival, 1904-05,* in Tony Cauchi (ed.), *Welsh Revival Library* (Bishop's Waltham, UK: Revival Library, 2004 reprint, 1909).

Myland, D. Wesley, 'The Latter Rain Covenant and Pentecostal Power: With Testimony of Healings and Baptism,' in Donald W. Dayton (ed.) *Three Early Pentecostal Tracts* (New York: Garland Publishing, 1985 reprint; Chicago: Evangel Publishing House, 1910).

Nelson, P.C., 'My Baptism in the Holy Spirit', in *Filled with the Fulness of God* (Springfield, MO: Gospel Publishing House, 1930), pp. 47-55.

Novatian, 'The Trinity', in Russell J. DeSimone (trans.), *Novatian: The Trinity, The Spectacles, Jewish Foods, In Praise of Purity, Letters* (Washington, DC: The Catholic University of America, 1972).

Origen, 'Against Celsus' in Philip Schaff (ed.), *ANF, First Series: Fathers of the Third Century: Tertullian, Part Fourth; Minucius Felix; Commodian; Origen, Parts First and Second,* Vol IV (Peabody, MA: Hendrickson, 1995, reprinting; 1885).

Oliver, Jeff, *Pentecost to the Present: Early Prophetic and Spiritual Gifts Movement* (Newbury, FL: Bridge Logos, 2017).

—*Pentecost to the Present: Reformations and Awakenings* (Newbury, FL: Bridge Logos, 2017).

—*Pentecost to the Present: Worldwide Revivals and Renewal* (Newbury, FL: Bridge Logos, 2017).

Orr, J. Edwin, 'The Welsh Revival Goes Worldwide', *Western Mail* (Dec. 9, 1974), in Tony Cauchi (ed.), *Welsh Revival Library* (Bishop's Waltham, UK: Revival Library, 2004).

Palamas, Gregory, in Nicholas Gendle (trans.) & John Meyendorff (ed.), *Gregory Palamas: The Triads* (NewYork: Paulist Press, 1983).

Parham, Charles F., 'The Baptism with the Holy Ghost', in W.F. Carothers, *The Baptism with the Holy Ghost and the Speaking in Tongues* (Zion City, IL: Carothers, 1906 reprint; January 1902).

—*Kol Kare Bomidbar: A Voice Crying in the Wilderness* (Reprint, Joplin, MO: The Joplin Printing Co., 1944).

Parham, Sarah E., 'The Life of Charles F. Parham: Founder of the Apostolic Movement', in *'The Higher Life Christian Life' Sources for the Study of the Holiness, Pentecostal, and Keswick Movements* (New York: Garland Publishing, 1985).

Penn-Lewis, Jessie, 'Revival Dawn and the Baptism in the Holy Spirit': Chapter 12 of 'War on the Saints', in Tony Cauchi (ed.), *Welsh Revival Library* (Bishop's Waltham, UK: Revival Library, 2004).

Phillips, Wade H., *Quest to Restore God's House: A Theological History of the Church of God* (Cleveland, TN), Volume I, 1886-1923 (Cleveland, TN: CPT Press, 2014).

Pinnock, Clark, *Flame of Love: A Theology of the Holy Spirit* (Downers Grove, IL: Intervarsity Press, 1996).
Poloma, Margaret M., *The Assemblies of God at the Crossroads: Charisma and Institutional Dilemmas* (Knoxville, TN: The University of TN Press, 1989).
—*Main Street Mystic: The Toronto Blessing & Reviving Pentecostalism* (Walnut Creek, CA: Altamira Press, 2003).
—'Glossolalia, Liminality and Empowered Kingdom Building: A Sociological Perspective', in Mark J. Cartledge (ed.), *Speaking in Tongues: Multi-Disciplinary Perspectives* (Studies in Pentecostal and Charismatic Issues; Bletchley, Milton Keynes, England: Paternoster Press, 2006), pp. 147-73.
—'North American Pentecostalism', in Adam Stewart (ed.), *Handbook of Pentecostal Christianity* (DeKalb, IL: Northern Illinois University Press, 2012).
Powers, Janet Everts, 'Missionary Tongues?', *JPT* 17 (October 1, 2000), pp. 39-55.
Price, Lynne, *Theology Out of Place: A Theological Biography of Walter J. Hollenweger* (JPTSup 23; Sheffield: Sheffield Academic Press, 2002).
Rankin, Adam, *A Review of the Noted Revival in Kentucky* (Lexington, KY: Bradford, 1802).
Reed, David A., 'Oneness Pentecostalism', in Stanley Burgess (ed.), *NIDPCM* (Grand Rapids, MI: Zondervan, rev. and expanded edn, 2002), pp. 936-44.
—*'In Jesus' Name', The History and Beliefs of Oneness Pentecostals* (JPTSup 31; Blandford Forum: Deo Publishing, 2009).
Reimer Johannes, 'Mission Des Frühen Mönchtums In Rubland' (DTh Thesis, University of South Africa, 1994).
Reinhart, Albert, 'St. Vincent Ferrer', *The Catholic Encyclopedia* XV (NY: The Encyclopedia Press, 1913).
Rice, David, *Sermon on the Present Revival of Religion* (Lexington, KY: Chapless, 1803).
Richardson, Cyril (ed.), *Early Christian Fathers* (New York: Macmillan Publishing Co., 1970).
Riss, Richard M., 'Finished Work Conrtoversy', in Stanley Burgess (ed.), *NIDPCM* (Grand Rapids, MI: Zondervan, rev. and expanded edn, 2002), pp. 638-39.
—'Fred Francis Bosworth', in Stanley Burgess (ed.), *NIDPCM* (Grand Rapids, MI: Zondervan, rev. and expanded edn, 2002), pp. 439-40.
—'William H. Durham', in Stanley Burgess (ed.), *NIDPCM* (Grand Rapids, MI: Zondervan, rev. and expanded edn, 2002), pp. 594-95.
—'The Latter Rain Movement', in Stanley Burgess (ed.), *NIDPCM* (Grand Rapids, MI: Zondervan, rev. and expanded edn, 2002), pp. 830-33.
Robeck, Cecil M., Jr, 'Azusa Street Revival', in Stanley Burgess (ed.), *NIDPCM* (Grand Rapids, MI: Zondervan, rev. and expanded edn, 2002), pp. 344-50.
—'Garfield Thomas Haywood', in Stanley Burgess (ed.), *NIDPCM* (Grand Rapids, MI: Zondervan, rev. and expanded edn, 2002), pp. 693-94.
—'William Joseph Seymour', in Stanley Burgess (ed.), *NIDPCM* (Grand Rapids, MI: Zondervan, rev. and expanded edn, 2002), pp. 1053-58.

—'An Emerging Magisterium? The Case of the Assemblies of God', *Pneuma* 25.2 (Fall 2003), pp. 164-215.

—*The Azusa Street Mission and Revival: The Birth of the Global Pentecostal Movement* (Nashville, TN: Thomas Nelson, 2006).

—'William J. Seymour and 'The Bible Evidence'", in Gary B. McGee (ed.), *Initial Evidence: Historical and Biblical Perspectives on the Pentecostal Doctrine of Spirit Baptism* (Eugene, OR: Wipf & Stock, 2007 reprint; Hendrickson, 1991), pp. 72–95.

—'Montanism and Present Day "Prophets"', *Pneuma* 32 (2010), pp. 413-29.

Roberts, Alexander and James Donaldson (eds.), *'Irenaeus', ANF: Translations of the Writings of the Fathers Down to A.D. 325*, Vol. I, Book III, Chapter XVI (Grand Rapids: W.B. Eerdmans Pub. Co., 1956).

Roberts, Arthur O., 'George Fox and the Quakers', in Tim Dowley (ed.), *Eerdman's Handbook to the History of Christianity* (Grand Rapids, MI: Eerdmans, 1977), pp. 480-83.

Roberts, P., 'A Sign – Christian or Pagan', *ExpT* 90.7 (April 1979), pp. 199-203.

Roche, John, *The Moravian Heresy* (Dublin, 1751).

Rogers, Cleon L. Jr., 'The Gift of Tongues in the Post Apostolic Church (A.D. 100-400)', *BibSac* 122.486 (April-June 1965), pp. 134-43.

Report of the Special Committee on the Work of the Holy Spirit to the 182nd General Assembly (Philadelphia, PA: The United Presbyterian Church in the United States of America, 1970).

Rudometkin, Maxim Gavrilovich, 'Discourses', 5.4.3-4, in Ivan Gureivich Shubin and Daniel H. Shubin (eds.) and John Wm. Volkov (trans.), *Spirit and Life – Book of the Sun: Divine Discourses of the Preceptors and the Martyrs for the Word of God, the Faith of Jesus, and the Holy Spirit, of the Religion of the Spiritual Christian Molokan-Jumpers* (1983 repr; USA: Daniel H. Shubin, 1928), pp. 296-97.

Ruohomäki, Jouko, 'The Call of Charisma: Charismatic Phenomena during the 18th and 19th Centuries in Finland', *JEPTA* 29.1 (2009), pp. 25-40.

Ruthven, Jon, *On the Cessation of the Charismata: The Protestant Polemic on Postbiblical Miracles* (JPTSup 3; Sheffield: Sheffield Academic Press, 1993).

Rybarczyk, Edmund J., 'Reframing Tongues: Apophaticism and Postmodernism', *Pneuma* 27.1 (Spring, 2005), pp. 83-104.

Samarin, William J., *Tongues of Men and Angels* (New York, NY: The Macmillan Co., 1970).

Samuel, Josh P.S., *The Holy Spirit in Worship Music, Preaching, and the Altar* (Cleveland, TN: CPT Press, 2018).

Satyavrata, Ivan, *The Holy Spirit: Lord and Life-Giver* (Downers Grove, IL: IVP Academic, 2009).

Schaff, Philip, *History of the Christian Church, Volume 1: Apostolic Christianity, from the Birth of Christ to the Death of St. John, A.D. 1-100* (Peabody, MA: Hendrickson, 2011, reprint; 1890).

—*History of the Christian Church, Volume 2: Ante-Nicene Christianity, from the Death of John the Apostle to Constantine the Great, A.D. 100-325* (Peabody, MA: Hendrickson, 2011, reprint; 1890).

—*History of the Christian Church, Volume 3: Nicene and Post-Nicene Christianity, from Constantine the Great to Gregory the Great, A.D. 311–590* (Peabody, MA: Hendrickson, 2011, reprint; 1890).

—*The Ante-Nicene Fathers: The Apostolic Fathers with Justin Martyr and Ireneaus*, Vol I (Peabody, MA: Hendrickson, 1995, reprint; 1885).

Schnapp, Jeffery T., 'Virgin Word: Hildegard of Bingen's Lingua Ignota and the Development of Imaginary Languages Ancient to Modern', *Exemplaria* 3.2 (Fall, 1991), pp. 267-69.

Shakarian, Demos, and John and Elizabeth Sherril, *The Happiest People on Earth* (Old Tappan, NJ: Fleming H. Revell Co., 1975).

Shults, F. LeRon & Andrea Hollingsworth, *Guides to Theology: The Holy Spirit* (Grand Rapids, MI: Eerdmans, 2008).

Shubin, Ivan Gureivich and Daniel H. Shubin (eds.), and John Wm. Volkov (trans.), *Spirit and Life – Book of the Sun: Divine Discourses of the Preceptors and the Martyrs for the Word of God, the Faith of Jesus, and the Holy Spirit, of the Religion of the Spiritual Christian Molokan-Jumpers* (1983 repr; USA: Daniel H. Shubin, 1928)

—'The Journey to Refuge', in Ivan Gureivich Shubin and Daniel H. Shubin (eds.) and John Wm. Volkov (trans.), *Spirit and Life – Book of the Sun: Divine Discourses of the Preceptors and the Martyrs for the Word of God, the Faith of Jesus, and the Holy Spirit, of the Religion of the Spiritual Christian Molokan-Jumpers* (1983 repr; USA: Daniel H. Shubin, 1928), pp. 747-58

Shumway, Charles, 'A Study of "The Gift of Tongues"' (AB Thesis, University of Southern California, 1914).

—'A Critical History of Glossolalia' (PhD Dissertation, Boston University, 1919).

Simmons, V.P., *History of Tongues* (n.d.).

Slay, James L., 'Glossolalia: Its Value to the Individual', in Wade H. Horton (ed.), *The Glossolalia Phenomenon* (Cleveland, TN: Pathway Press, 1986), pp. 217-43.

Smith, Gordon T., *Evangelical, Sacramental & Pentecostal: Why the Church Should be All Three* (Downers Grove, IL: IVP Academic, 2017).

Smith, James K.A., *Thinking in Tongues: Pentecostal Contributions to Christian Philosophy* (Grand Rapids, MI: Eerdmans, 2010).

Smith, Joseph, *History of Joseph Smith, the Prophet*, Vol. 1 (Salt Lake City, 1902).

—'The Wentworth Letter', *Times and Seasons* 3.9 (March 1, 1842).

—*The Book of Mormon* (Salt Lake City, UT: The Church of Jesus Christ of Latter-day Saints, 1950).

Spencer, Jon Michael, 'The Heavenly Anthem: Holy Ghost Singing in the Primal Pentecostal Revival', *The Journal of Black Sacred Music* 1.1 (Spring 1987) pp. 1-33.

Spittler, Russell P., 'Suggested Areas for Further Research in Pentecostal Studies', *Pneuma* 5.2 (Fall 1983), pp. 39-57.

—'Are Pentecostals and Charismatics Fundamentalists? A Review of American Uses of These Categories', in Karla Poewe (ed.), *Charismatic Christianity as a*

Global Culture (Colombia, SC: University of South Carolina Press, 1994), pp. 103-18.
—'Glossolalia', in Stanley Burgess (ed.), *NIDPCM* (Grand Rapids, MI: Zondervan, rev. and expanded edn, 2002), pp. 670-76.
Staniforth (trans.), Maxwell, 'The Didache', in *The Apostolic Fathers: Early Christian Writings* (London: Penguin Books, 1987).
Stephens, Randall J., *The Fire Spreads: Holiness and Pentecostalism in the American South* (Cambridge, MA; London: Harvard University Press, 2008).
Strayer, Brian E., *Suffering Saints: Jansenists and Convulsionnaires in France, 1640-1799* (Portland: Sussex Academic Press, 2008).
Stronstad, Roger, *The Charismatic Theology of St. Luke* (Peabody, MA: Hendrickson, 1984).
Suenens, Leo Joseph, 'Malines Document 1, Theological and Pastoral Orientations on the Catholic Charismatic Renewal', in *The Holy Spirit, Life-Breath of the Church Book II*, 1st part (Belgium: FIAT Association, 1974), pp. 3-35.
Sullivan, Charles A., 'The Gift of Tongues Project', https://charlesasullivan.com/gift-tongues-project/
—'Chrysostom on the Dogma of Tongues', http://charlesasullivan.com/5347/chrysostom-on-the-dogma-of-tongues.
—'Augustine on the Tongues of Pentecost: Intro', http://charlesasullivan.com/3668/augustine-on-the-tongues-of-pentecost-intro.
—http://charlesasullivan.com/6166/late-medieval-peaking-in-tongues.
—'An Analysis of Augustine on Tongues and the Donatists', http://charlesasullivan.com/3662/an-analysis-of-augustine-on-tongues-and-the-donatists.
—http://charlesasullivan.com/6274/st-anthony-of-paduas-miraculous-speech.
—http://charlesasullivan.com/6199/pope-benedict-xiv-on-the-gift-of-tongues.
Sullivan, Francis A., *Charisms and Charismatic Renewal: A Biblical and Theological Study* (Ann Arbor, MI: Servant Books, 1982).
Sweet, J.P.M., 'A Sign for Unbelievers: Paul's Attitude to Glossolalia', in Watson E. Mills (ed.), *Speaking in Tongues: A Guide to Research on Glossolalia* (Grand Rapids, MI: Eerdmans, 1986), pp. 141-64.
Symeon the New Theologian – in Patrick Thompson (trans.), 'A Prayer to God of St. Simon the New Theologian', *Sobornost* 6 (June 1936), pp. 19-21.
—*Hymns of Divine Love by Symeon The New Theologian* (trans. George A. Maloney; Denville, NJ: Dimension Books, 1976).
—'Epistle 3', in H.J.M. Turner (ed. and trans.), *The Epistles of St. Symeon the New Theologian* (Oxford: Oxford University Press, 2009).
Synan, H. Vinson, *The Holiness-Pentecostal Tradition: Charismatic Movements in the Twentieth Century* (Grand Rapids, MI: Eerdmans, 2nd edn, 1997).
—'The Role of Tongues as Initial Evidence', in Mark W. Wilson (ed.), *Spirit and Renewal* (JPTSup 5; Sheffield: Sheffield Academic Press, 1994), pp. 67-82.
—*Old Time Power – A Centennial History of the International Pentecostal Holiness Church* (Franklin Springs, GA: LifeSprings Resources, 1998).

—*The Century of the Holy Spirit: 100 Years of Pentecostal and Charismatic Renewal* (Nashville, TN: Thomas Nelson Publishers, 2001).

—'Gaston Barnabas Cashwell', in Stanley Burgess (ed.), *NIDPCM* (Grand Rapids, MI: Zondervan, rev. and expanded edn, 2002), pp. 457-58.

—'International Pentecostal Holiness Church' in Stanley Burgess (ed.), *NIDPCM* (Grand Rapids, MI: Zondervan, rev. and expanded edn, 2002), pp. 798-801.

—'Fire-Baptized Holiness Church' in Stanley Burgess (ed.), *NIDPCM* (Grand Rapids, MI: Zondervan, rev. and expanded edn, 2002), p. 640.

—'Joseph Hillery King' in Stanley Burgess (ed.), *NIDPCM* (Grand Rapids, MI: Zondervan, rev. and expanded edn, 2002), pp. 822-23.

—'George Floyd Taylor', in Stanley Burgess (ed.), *NIDPCM* (Grand Rapids, MI: Zondervan, rev. and expanded edn, 2002), pp. 1115-16.

—'Ambrose Blackman Crumpler', in Stanley Burgess (ed.), *NIDPCM* (Grand Rapids, MI: Zondervan, rev. and expanded edn, 2002), p. 566.

—'Nickels John Holmes' in Stanley Burgess (ed.), *NIDPCM* (Grand Rapids, MI: Zondervan, rev. and expanded edn, 2002), p. 730.

Tabbernee, William, *Prophets and Gravestones: An Imaginative History of Montanists and Other Early Christians* (Peabody, MA: Hendrickson, 2009).

Tarr, Del, *Double Image: Biblical Insights from African Parables* (New York: Paulist Press, 1994).

—*The Foolishness of God: A Linguist Looks at the Mystery of Tongues* (Springfield, MO: Access Group, 2010).

Taves, Ann, *Fits, Trances, & Visions: Experiencing Religion and Explaining Experience from Wesley to James* (Princeton, NJ: Princeton University Press, 1999).

Taylor, G.F., *The Spirit and the Bride* (Dunn, NC, 1907).

Taylor, Malcolm John, 'Publish and Be Blessed: A Case Study in Early Pentecostal Publishing History' (PhD Thesis, Birmingham, UK: University of Birmingham, 1994).

Tertullian, 'Against Marcion', in Alexander Roberts and James Donaldson (eds.) *ANF, First Series: Latin Christianity: Its Founder, Tertullian I. Apologetic; II. Anti-Marcion; III. Ethical, Vol. 3* (Peabody, MA: Hendrickson, 1995).

Thiselton, Anthony C., *The First Epistle to the Corinthians* (NIGC; Grand Rapids, MI: Eerdmans, 2000).

Thomas, John Christopher, *Footwashing in John 13 and the Johannine Community* (JSNTS 61; New York, NY: T & T Clark, 2004).

—*A Pentecostal Reads the Book of Mormon: A Literary and Theological Introduction* (Cleveland, TN: CPT Press, 2016).

Thomas, John Christopher and Alexander, Kimberly, '"And The Signs Are Following": Mark 16.9-20', *JPT* 11-2 (April 2003), pp. 147-70.

Turner, John G., *Brigham Young: Pioneer Prophet* (Cambridge, MA: Harvard University Press, 2012).

Turner, Max, *Power from on High: The Spirit in Israel's Restoration and Witness in Luke-Acts* (JPTSup 9; Sheffield: Sheffield Academic Press, 1996).

—*The Holy Spirit and Spiritual Gifts* (Peabody, MA: Hendrickson, 1996).

—'Tongues: An Experience for All in the Pauline Churches?', *AJPS* 1.2 (1998), pp. 231-53.
—'A Response to the Responses of Menzies and Chan', *AJPS* 2.2 (1999), pp. 297-308.
—'Early Christian Experience and Theology of "Tongues" – A New Testament Perspective', in Mark J. Cartledge (ed.), *Speaking in Tongues: Multi-Disciplinary Perspectives* (Studies in Pentecostal and Charismatic Issues; Bletchley, Milton Keynes, England: Paternoster Press, 2006), pp. 1-33.
Turner, W.H., *Pentecost and Tongues* (Shanghai: Shanghai Modern Publishing House, 1939).
Tyson, James L., *The Early Pentecostal Revival* (Hazelwood, MO: Word Aflame Press, 1992).
Unger, Merrill F., *New Testament Teaching on Tongues* (Grand Rapids, MI: Kregel Publications, 1972).
Urshan, Andrew, 'The Almighty God in the Lord Jesus Christ', in Donald W. Dayton, *Seven 'Jesus Only' Tracts* (New York: Garland Publishing, reprint; U.P.C. of Portland, 1919).
—'The Doctrine of the New Birth of the Perfect Way to Eternal Life', in Donald W. Dayton, *Seven 'Jesus Only' Tracts* (New York: Garland Publishing, reprint; Cochrane, WI: Witness of God, Publishers, 1921).
Veilleux, Arnand (trans.), *Pachomian Koinonia. Cistercian Studies: Number 46*, Vol. 1 (Kalamazoo, Michigan. Cistercian Publications Inc.).
Volf, Miroslav, *Exclusion & Embrace* (Nashville, TN: Abingdon Press, 1996).
Waddell, Robby, 'Whence Pentecostal Scholarship? The Coming of Age of the Pentecostal Critical Tradition and a Forecast for its Future', in Steven M. Fettke and Robby Waddell (eds.), *Pentecostals in the Academy: Testimonies of Call* (Cleveland, TN: CPT Press, 2012), pp. 243-59.
Wacker, Grant, 'The Functions of Faith in Primitive Pentecostalism', *Harvard Theological Review* 77.3-4 (July 1, 1984), pp. 353-75.
—*Heaven Below: Early Pentecostals and American Culture* (Cambridge, MA: Harvard University Press, 2001).
Waldvogel, Edith, 'The "Overcoming Life" A Study in the Reformed Evangelical Origins of Pentecostalism' (PhD Dissertation, Harvard University, 1977).
Walker, Dawson A., *The Gift of Tongues and Other Essays* (Edinburgh: T & T Clark, 1906).
Walters, Jr., Kenneth Richard, 'Why Tongues? The History and Philosophy Behind the Initial Evidence Doctrine in North American Pentecostal Churches' (PhD Dissertation; Fuller Theological Seminary, 2010).
—*Why Tongues? The Initial Evidence Doctrine in North American Pentecostal Churches* (JPTSup 42; Blandford Forum: Deo Publishing, 2016).
Wamble, Hugh, 'Glossolalia in Christian History', Luther B. Dyer (ed.), *Tongues* (Orlando, FL: Daniels Publisher, 1972), pp. 24-59.
Ware, Timothy, *The Orthodox Church* (New York, NY: Penguin Putnam 1997, reprint, 1963).

Warfield, Benjamin B., *Counterfeit Miracles* (Carlisle, PA: The Banner of Truth Trust, 1976).

Warner, Wayne E., 'Eudorus N. Bell', in Stanley Burgess (ed.), *NIDPCM* (Grand Rapids, MI: Zondervan, rev. and expanded edn, 2002), p. 369.

—'International Pentecostal Church of Christ', in Stanley Burgess (ed.), *NIDPCM* (Grand Rapids, MI: Zondervan, rev. and expanded edn, 2002), pp. 797-98.

—'Carrie Judd Montgomery', in Stanley Burgess (ed.), *NIDPCM* (Grand Rapids, MI: Zondervan, rev. and expanded edn, 2002), pp. 904-906.

—'Periodicals', in Stanley Burgess (ed.), *NIDPCM* (Grand Rapids, MI: Zondervan, rev. and expanded edn, 2002), pp. 974-82.

Weinel, Heinrich, *Die Wirkungen des Geistes und der Geister im nachapostolischen Zeitalter bis auf Irenaus* (Freiburg: J.C.B. Mohr, 1899).

Welchel, Tom, *Azusa Street: They Told Me Their Stories* (Mustang, OK: Dare2Dream Books, 2008).

Wesley, John. *Wesley's Works* (Vol. V; New York: Harper, 1826-1827).

Wigglesworth, Smith, 'A Transformation', in *Filled with the Fulness of God* (Springfield, MO: Gospel Publishing House, 1930), pp. 3-14.

Williams, Cyril Glyndwr, *Tongues of the Spirit: A Study of Pentecostal Glossolalia and Related Phenomena* (Cardiff: University of Wales Press, 1981).

Williams, George Hunston, *The Radical Reformation* (Philadelphia: The Westminster Press, 1962).

Williams, George Hunston and Edith Waldvogel, 'A History of Speaking in Tongues and Related Gifts' in Michael P. Hamilton (ed.), *The Charismatic Movement* (Grand Rapids, MI: Eerdmans, 1975).

Williams, J.D., 'The Modern Pentecostal Movement in America: A Brief Sketch of Its History and Thought', *Lexington Theological Quarterly*, 9.2 (1974), pp. 50-59.

Williams, J. Rodman, *The Pentecostal Reality* (Plainfield, NJ: Logos International, 1972)

—*Renewal Theology: Systematic Theology from a Charismatic Perspective* (Grand Rapids, MI: Zondervan, 1996).

Willis, Lewis J., 'Glossolalia in Perspective', in Wade H. Horton (ed.), *The Glossolalia Phenomenon* (Cleveland, TN: Pathway Press, 1986), pp. 247-84.

Wilson, Everett A., 'Robert Edward McAlister', in Stanley Burgess (ed.), *NIDPCM* (Grand Rapids, MI: Zondervan, rev. and expanded edn, 2002), p. 852.

—'Pentecostal Historiography and Global Christianity: Rethinking the Questions of Origins' *Pneuma* 27.1 (Spring, 2005), pp. 35-50.

Wilson, Samuel M., *John Lyle's Diary* (Kentucky Historical Society, 1922).

Wood, A. Skevington, 'John and Charles Wesley', in Tim Dowley (ed.), Eerdmans *Handbook to the History of Christianity* (Grand Rapids, MI: Eerdmans, 1977), p. 447.

Wright, David F., 'The Donatists in North Africa', in Eerdmans *Handbook to the History of Christianity* (Grand Rapids, MI: Eerdmans, 1977), pp. 202-203.

Yoder, John H. and Alan Kreider, 'The Anabaptists', in Eerdmans *Handbook to the History of Christianity* (Grand Rapids, MI: Eerdmans, 1977), pp. 399-403.

Yong, Amos, '"Tongues of Fire" in 'The Pentecostal Imagination: The Truth of Glossolalia in Light of R.C. Neville's Theory of Religious Symbolism', *JPT* 12 (1998), pp. 39-65.

Young, Brigham, 'The History of Brigham Young', *The Latter-Day Saints Millennial Star* 25 (11 July 1863).

Zander, Valentine, in Gabriel Anne (trans.), *St Seraphim of Sarov* (Crestwood, NY: St. Valdimir's Seminary Press, 1975).

INDEX OF BIBLICAL (AND OTHER ANCIENT) REFERENCES

Genesis
11   73
11.1-9   42, 365

Exodus
28.30   203

Leviticus
6.13-14   447

Numbers
11.29   58

Deuteronomy
17.6   283
19.15   283
28.49   43

1 Samuel
10.5-13   87
19.20-24   87

2 Chronicles
5   136, 390
5.13   390

Job
20.13-16   61
20.16   61

Psalm
16   57, 59, 60
16.9   60
19   60
32   430
46   430
54   427
65   430
80   430

94   430
97   430
99   378, 430
126.2   263
147   428
150   430

Isaiah
6.6-7   195
11.12   341
28.9-13   87, 235
28.11   123, 285
28.11-12   26, 43, 62,
            302, 303, 316,
            339, 341
28.11-13   169
33.19   43

Jeremiah
5.15   43
5.25   431

Daniel
2.28   397
3   195
5.16   397
5.25-26   394, 396

Hosea
6.3   431

Joel
2.23   259, 368
2.28-29   368
2.28-31   173
2.28-32   658

Amos
4.4   167

Zechariah
4.6   132
10.1   260

Matthew
3.11   189, 355
3.13-17   399
3.16-4.1   392
4.1   399
6.6   388
6.7   46
7.11   382
10.39   92
11.28   341
12.39   194
18.16   283
24.7   172
24.7-8   172
24.14   115, 172, 175
24.29   322
25.5-6   174
28.19   314, 330, 337
28.19-20   189

Mark
1.8   355
1.9-12   399
1.11-12   392, 399
16.9-20   121, 221, 224,
            362
16.15   168, 314
16.15-18   309
16.15-20   304
16.16-17   117, 303
16.16-18   293, 362
16.17   19, 29, 31, 31,
            38, 40, 54, 61,
            62, 105, 121,
            151, 172, 178,

Index of Biblical (and Other Ancient) References   489

	181, 188, 220, 233, 285, 297, 322, 370	1.33	355		293, 299, 304, 306, 327, 339, 341, 342, 345
		3.3-7	335		
		3.30	102		
16.17-18	26, 105, 116, 193, 205, 221, 223, 248, 252, 291, 339	4.10	302	2.4-11	123
		4.18	290	2.4-13	386
		7.39	223	2.6-11	43
		7.37-39	37, 302	2.9-11	123
16.17-20	189	14	417	2.11	60, 389
16.18	193	14.18	288	2.12-17	117
16.19-20	221	14.26	391	2.13	44
		15.16	197	2.16-20	173
Luke		15.26	188, 189, 220, 237, 283	2.16-21	362, 368
1.39-45	399, 403			2.17	172, 363
1.41-42	58	15.26-27	26, 37, 297, 343	2.17-20	23
1. 42-45	58			2.19	62
1.46-55	58	16.13	37, 188, 386	2.25-28	59
1.47	60	20	314	2.26	60, 71
1.64	60	20.21-23	313, 314	2.33	60, 382
1.67	58	20.22	23, 25, 48	2.38	281, 287, 331, 337
1.67-79	58	20.22-23	182		
2.13-14	58			2.39	23, 189, 383
2.29-32	58	*Acts*		3	46
3.16	355	1.4	382	4	46
3.21-22	399	1.4-5	355	4.8	59
3.22	58, 392	1.4-8	117, 189	4.31	38, 59, 63, 307
3.32	59	1.5	120, 219		
4.1	399	1.8	88, 120, 132, 163, 317, 341, 393, 399	6.9	25
4.1-2	392			8	34, 39, 64, 219, 220
4.14	58				
4.18-19	58	1.15	54	8.4-39	219, 220
10.1-16	58	2	19, 21, 31, 33, 42-44, 48, 54, 57, 64, 114, 120, 169, 204, 385, 425, 436	8.14-18	362
10.20	341			8.14-19	64
10.21	60			8.15	58
10.21-24	58			8.17	219
11.9-13	59			8.18	58
11.13	219, 302, 382	2.1-4	63, 119, 128, 219	8.26-39	25
19.39-40	58			9	39
24.49	37, 120, 132, 189, 317, 341, 357, 382, 393	2.1-6	48	9.1-7	63
		2.1-12	65	9.17	58, 59
		2.1-13	30, 58, 365	9.20	58
		2.3	184, 459	10	21, 39, 46, 74, 154, 169, 277
24.49-53	189	2.3-4	115, 371		
24.50	25	2.4	48, 58-60, 120, 189, 197, 218, 222, 227, 230, 232, 277, 282, 283, 285,	10.45	282, 341
				10.44-46	115, 189, 219, 282, 306, 327, 339, 362
John					
1.1	223				
1.14	223				
1.32-34	392			10.44-47	63, 283

10.44-48	64	15.18-19	189	14.14	22, 206, 232, 388
10.45-46	285, 389				
10.46	58, 60, 117, 136, 152, 266, 293	*1 Corinthians*		14.14-15	98
		2.6	415	14.14-19	44
		4.1	391	14.15	143, 377, 378
10.47	54, 278	12	21, 222	14.18	39, 64
11	39, 154, 220, 277	12-14	43, 62, 72, 146, 147, 157, 168, 204, 282- 84	14.18-19	98, 385
				14.19	44
11.1-18	63			14.20-22	354
11.14-16	306			14.21	115, 285, 302, 316
11.15	54, 278	12.1-11	189		
11.15-17	362	12.2	98	14.21-22	169
11.16	355	12.7	382	14.22	22, 62, 153, 233, 339
11.18	340	12.7-31	222		
12.5	226	12.8-11	293	14.23	44
13.1-2	413	12.10	382	14.27	44, 222, 234
13.9	59	12.11	222	14.28	83, 385
15.9	154	12.13	334, 335, 355, 399, 400	14.28-31	417
15.8-9	306			14.29	44
15.32	413	12.14-30	49	14.30-31	445
17.27	74	12.28	382	14.34-35	44
19	21, 34, 39, 46, 64, 169, 222, 277, 298	12.28-31	189	14.39	49
		12.29-30	88		
		12.30	49, 192, 304	*2 Corinthians*	
19.1-6	117, 362	13	46	11.2	358
19.1-7	64, 189	13.1	32, 123, 395	12.1	391
19.2	283, 341	13.2-3	44	12.4	386
19.5-6	341	13.8	49, 225, 285	13.1	283
19.6	54, 58, 60, 115, 219, 226, 282, 285, 293, 328, 339, 391	13.9	45		
		13.8-10	27	*Galatians*	
		13.8-12	285	1.19-20	355
		13.10	27, 309	5.22-23	156
19.12	291	13.11	361		
		13.13	205	*Ephesians*	
Romans		14	31, 42, 127, 169, 171, 219, 258, 320	1.9	391
2.29	335			1.13	335
4.14	386			3.3	391
4.17	389	14.1	189	4.4	334
6.6	355	14.2	29, 44, 106, 162, 232, 360, 385	5.19	377, 378
8.15	360				
8.16	343			*Philippians*	
8.26	72, 106, 135, 165, 166, 202, 235, 269, 388, 389	14.4	232, 387	2.7	355
		14.5	49		
		14.9	49	*Colossians*	
		14.10-11	45	1.6	391
8.26-27	98	14.12	382	3.11	335
12	52	14.13	49, 168	3.16	377, 378, 386

1 Thessalonians
4.16-17   172
5.17   444

2 Timothy
3.1   172
4.1-2   170

Hebrews
2.4   189

James
3.8   357
5.7   368

1 John
3.2   360

Revelation
4 & 5   377, 379
19.7   358

Didache   412, 413

Dionysus Literature 87

Mari Documents   87

Oracle of Delphi   87

Index of Names

Abrams, M. 22, 23, 241, 246, 247, 255, 256, 261, 367, 393
Ackerman, F. 233, 237
Ackland, R.H. 356
Adams, A.S. 322
Agar, G.C. 261, 263, 395
Ahn, Y.J. 384
Ahonen, L. 450
Aikenhead, D.R. 344, 345
Akers, W.O. 224
Alady, G.T. 222
Albrecht, D. 240-42, 244
Alcibiades 423
Alexander of Abunoteichos 88
Alexander, E.Y. 1, 292
Alexander, K.E. 2-4, 6, 121, 149, 154, 174, 179-81, 184, 185, 192, 194, 195, 239, 240, 243, 273, 291, 292, 336, 345, 351, 357, 359, 372, 377, 378, 381, 393, 403
Alexander, P. 351, 379, 380
Alfred, D. 220
Allen, H.M. 146, 264, 267
Ambose 426
Amiot, W.H. 327
Anderson, A. 1, 163
Anderson, F. 236, 238, 395
Anderson, F.R. 282
Anderson, G.L. 387
Anderson, R.M. 1, 4
Anderson, T. 136, 290, 325
Anderson, T.O. 320
Anderson, W.G. 188, 204, 211, 391, 395
Andrews, E.D. 449
Andronicus II 443
Angstead, R. 265, 270
Anthonius of Padua 435
Archer, M. 2, 240, 379
Argue, A.H. 129, 172, 272, 289, 300-302, 322, 332, 371
Argue, Z. 241
Armstrong, C.R. 291, 292, 294, 296

Armstrong, E. 318, 325
Armstrong, L. 379
Asberry, R. 112
Asbury, F. 451
Ash, J.L. 93, 412, 413, 417, 419, 422, 430
Aston, A. 289, 290, 325
Atchison, R. 163
Atnipp, R.D. 194, 201
Atterberry, T. 303, 309, 310, 316, 320, 322, 366, 390
Augustine of Hippo 309, 326, 365, 378, 411, 419, 426-31
Augustine, D.C. 99, 100, 356, 357, 360, 364, 365, 367, 375, 281, 442
Aune, D.E. 87
Ayler, A. 379

Baer, R.A. 387, 445
Bailey, C. 282
Bailly, G. 253
Bainton, R. 438
Baker, H.G. 75-77, 97, 350, 353, 354, 357, 359-62, 366, 387-89
Baker, M. 332
Baldree, D.F. 192, 195, 209
Banister, L. 232
Bants, E.L. 326
Barclay, R. 445
Barnes, A.H. 227
Barnett, C. 227
Barnett, J. 344, 346
Barnett, J.F. 232
Barnett, L. 203, 392
Barr, E.S. 205
Barratt, T.B. 27, 28, 152, 156, 161, 163, 165, 169, 170, 318, 383, 390, 392-94, 451
Barth, H.M. 9, 153, 154, 156, 174, 365, 372, 404
Barth, P. 9
Bartleman, F. 2, 145, 167, 177, 241, 244, 245, 272, 293, 342-46, 378,

460
Bartlett, R.   227
Bass   290
Batman, G.W.   124, 125
Batuman, E.   363
Bau, Y.C.   161
Baxter, E.   241
Baxter, M.   251
Beadle, J.H.   453-55
Beall, R.B.   221, 226, 231-33, 238, 396
Beare, F.W.   44, 46, 47
Beeler, J.R.   345, 346
Bell, E.N. (E.N.B.)   3, 13-15, 180, 272, 277-81, 283-95, 299-305, 307-17, 320-24, 364, 374, 375, 382-84
Bell, J.W.   187
Bellshaw, W.G.   45
Benedict XIII   435
Benedict XIV   433, 438
Benefield, W.P.   197, 283, 373
Berg, D.   272, 327
Berg, G.E.   122, 127, 128, 260, 396
Berhard, W.   252, 253, 259, 262
Berkhof, H.   47, 367
Bernard, D.K.   337-39, 398
Bernauer, B.   325
Bernsten, B.   152, 163
Bertrand, L.   432, 440
Bishop, C.   211
Bittlinger, A.   387
Bizzell, T.M.   228
Blackburn, A.   290, 320
Blacker, C.   362
Blake, E.H.   229
Blake, H.L.   378
Blumhofer, E.L. (Waldvogel)   14, 16, 263, 291-97, 350, 369, 378, 410
Boardman, W.E.   213, 241, 243
Boddy, A.A.   118, 132, 136, 152, 154, 156, 241, 245, 248, 252, 259, 299, 310, 313, 314, 317, 371, 387, 390, 460
Boddy, J.T. (J.T.B.)   141, 143, 144, 303
Boddy, M.   131, 250

Boehmer, E.J.   200
Böhler, P.   448
Bolen, E.C.   229
Booker, M.   269
Booth, C.   241
Booth-Clibborn, W.E.   339, 340, 342, 344
Bosworth, F.F.   39, 165, 249, 260, 263, 290, 297, 306, 325, 396
Bott, L.F.   176
Boucher, P.C.   303
Bouhours, D.   437, 438
Boulos, S.   299-301, 306, 309, 352, 355, 369, 375, 376, 401
Bourman, J.G.   133
Bowe, J.   10, 182
Bowen, F.   236
Bowen, P.   125, 371
Bower, F.E.   205
Bowker, J.   188, 211, 395
Bradley, A.   162, 163
Brady, H.J.   196
Bramwell, W.   245, 254
Branch, W.M.   220, 237, 395
Brann, O.P.   281, 282, 284
Brathwaite, R.   8, 107, 108
Brawner, C.   175
Brawner, E.   187, 209, 395
Break, S.R.   249, 256, 259
Brenzinger, A.W.   264, 269
Bright, C.F.   188
Brinkman, G.C.   281, 289, 396
Brinson-Rushire   198, 283
Britton, F.M.   158, 172, 175, 219, 220, 225, 228, 230, 235, 236
Brooks, H.S.   226
Brott, A.   228, 363
Brouayer, G.T.   196, 211
Broughton, G.   199
Brown, L.E.   320
Brown, M.C.D.   228
Bruce, F.F.   89
Brumback, C.   2, 13, 39-41, 154, 240, 263, 264, 272, 280, 281, 285, 287, 292, 294-96, 304, 362, 366, 377, 388, 411
Bruner, F.D.   51, 356, 398

Bryant, H.O.   255, 456, 457
Bryant, W.F.   186, 206, 210
Buckalew, J.W.   195, 209
Buffum, H.   282
Bulgakov, S.   442, 443
Bullin, E.   220, 233
Bullinger, H.   439
Bullock, Z.W.   289
Bundy, D.D.   27, 452
Burgess, S.M.   410, 411, 413-15, 417-19, 421-26, 428, 429, 431-38, 440-45, 447, 448, 452, 454, 455, 457
Burk, J.   200, 357
Burrough, E.   445
Burrow, S.R.   344
Burton, W.F.P.   314, 326
Bush, F.   290
Bush, H.   176
Bushnell, H.   178, 179, 249, 252, 253, 258, 260, 261, 382
Butler, A.H.   8, 153, 229, 230, 233
Butler, A.   425, 435, 436, 440
Byerler, W.   197
Byrd, C.H.   438-40

Caddell, E.C.   207, 358
Cadwalder, H.   289
Cagle, J.   195
Cain, F.J.   226
Caird, G.B.   352, 353, 384
Campbell, K.   325
Campbell, M.L.   405
Canada, A.G.   296
Carelock, M.D.   327
Carelock, W.B.   323
Carlson, C.   289, 395
Carlyle, T.   453
Carmichael, W.R.   327
Carol, L.   434
Carothers, W.F.   19, 21, 22, 70, 109, 292, 317, 378, 383, 390
Carroll, L.   411
Carter, B.A.   212
Cartledge, M.J.   17, 82-86, 364, 371, 372, 379, 387, 398, 446
Cartwright, P.   451
Cary, C.C.   242

Cashwell, G.B.   8, 11, 121, 122, 123, 135, 136, 140, 147-49, 151, 155, 157, 159, 160, 168, 169, 172, 173, 176, 184-86, 213, 215-18, 273, 355, 356, 383, 384, 394
Casmier, S.J.   379, 380
Cassandra of Troy   87
Castelo, D.   102-104, 350, 354, 357, 361, 362, 375, 379, 391
Causey, D.B.   228
Celsus   419-21
Chambers, G.B.   430
Chambers, L.M.   196
Chambers, R.B.   316, 321, 322, 363
Chan, S.   77-82, 97, 102, 349, 356-59, 361, 362, 372, 375, 381, 390, 393, 444
Chapman, Mary   314, 319, 324
Charette, B.   351, 361, 381, 387, 392
Childers, E.C.   176, 198
Childers, W.W.   324
Christenson, L.   452
Chrysostom, J.   173, 309, 365, 426
Chryssides, G.D.   352, 353
Ciampa, R.E.   354
Clark, A.   243
Clark, A.J.   453-55
Clark, E.W.   299
Clark, L.W.   328
Clark, L.   197
Clarke, A.   220
Clemangis, Nicholas   435
Clement of Alexander   419
Clement of Rome   411
Clement X   431, 440
Clements, W.   327
Clemen, C.   19, 24, 410, 414, 415, 419, 446, 447, 449
Clemmons, J.C.   10, 179-81
Clevenger, L.   200
Cline, J.   197
Cobb, D.   236
Cody, S.   259
Coleman, W.M.   206, 282
Collier, P.T.   200
Collins, A.P.   286, 293, 299, 301, 303, 305, 324, 358

Index of Names   495

Collins, W.D. 195
Coltrane, J. 379
Conkin, P. 451, 452
Conley, J.C. 237
Conn, C.W. 2, 10, 35, 111, 183-86, 366, 458, 459
Constantine 423
Costellow, Etta 252, 257
Conybeare, F.C. 260, 396, 410
Cook, E. 232
Cook, G.A. 125, 133, 134, 180, 263, 293, 294, 333, 335, 338
Cooper-Rompato, C.F. 432, 433, 435, 440
Coote, L.A. 327
Coote, L.W. 319
Copley, A.S. 12, 132, 165, 264, 265, 269, 270, 374, 388
Cotnam, R.L. 194
Cotton, L. 170, 209
Couch, F.M. 282
Courtney, Mary 170
Cox, H.G. 1, 3, 4, 83, 85, 93, 349, 350, 354, 360, 367, 373, 379, 383, 393
Cragin, C. 324
Craig, R.J. 303, 307, 321, 371
Cramer, W.A. 233
Crawford, F. 8, 129, 133, 147, 292
Crawford, Mattie 16, 343-45
Cree, John 451
Crowder, M. 194
Crumpler, A.B. 11, 216, 217, 221, 224, 228, 233, 235, 236
Culbreth, J.A. 8, 152, 158, 220, 221, 366
Cullis, C. 115, 241
Cunningham, E.F. 282
Currie, S.D. 49, 370
Curtis, C.R. 204, 209
Cutten, G.B. 19, 433, 446, 447
Cuyler, T.L. 242, 252
Cyprian 421, 422
Cyril of Alexandria 365, 425, 426

Dailey, D.G. 290
Dalton, R.C. 36, 114, 411

Darwin, C. 95, 353, 354
Davies, J.G. 42, 43, 365
Davies, M.R. 455
Davis, A.S. 344, 346
Davis, E. 323
Davis, F.H. 229
Davis, L.J. 202, 229
Davis, R.H. 323
Dawson, N. 232
Dayton, D.W. 1, 4, 5, 16, 213, 242, 337, 339, 343, 369
Delany, M.M. 290
Dempster, G. 257, 390
Dempster, M.W. 68
DeNicholas, A. 437
Dennis, D.M. 226, 227
Denton, F.A. 326
DeVoragine, J 432
Deweese, M. 282
Dickson, W. 451
Divine, J.M. 197, 268, 382, 411
Dixon, A.C. 278-80
Dixon, B.P. 253
Dobbins, E. 227
Doering, A.E. 256, 262, 388
Doering, B.C. 238
Dolby, J.H. 327
Dollar, G.W. 420, 432, 449, 453, 454
Doney, C.W. 281, 320
Dorries, D.W. 452, 453
Doucette, C. 261
Douglass, F.I. 346
Douglass, J.W. 196
Dove, S. 378, 380
Dowie, J.A. 263, 292, 297
Draper, M.T. 307
Driver, T. 69
Dudley, N.E. 228
Duncan, A.M. 200
Duncan, B.F. 152
Duncan, S.A. 175, 370
Dunlap, W.G. 322
Dunlavy, J. 450
Dunn, J.D.G. 19, 50, 51, 81, 89, 90, 230, 354, 362, 378, 386, 396-98
Durham, W.H. 2, 13, 15 117, 118, 131, 134, 138, 140, 143, 154, 237,

272, 280, 287, 292, 294, 298-301, 305, 307, 312, 313, 331, 337, 273, 374, 382, 393, 398, 402, 411
Dyer, C. 282
Dyke, H. 261

Earle, A.B. 213
Eckert, C. 143
Eckman, C. 151, 174, 358
Edwards, J. 107
Egan, H.D. 379, 436, 437
Ellis, J.B. 194, 198
Ellis, W.T. 161
Engelsen, N.I.J. 384, 395, 417
Ensley, E. 377, 429, 430, 432, 433
Epps, T.B. 164, 393
Ervin, H.M. 354, 356
Eusebius of Caesarea 416, 419, 423, 424
Evans, D.E. 150, 461
Evans, M. 263
Evans, R.M. 153, 186, 188, 192
Evans, W.E. 204, 210, 391
Everts, J. 57
Ewart, F.J. (F.J.E.) 15, 16, 195, 293, 294, 330-36, 338, 341-43, 346, 382, 398, 399

Fainter, W.G. 364
Farrow, L. 130
Fast, H. 439
Faulkner, H. 16, 336
Faupel, W.D. 293, 331, 336-38
Favacuia, F. 315
Fee, G.D. 72, 88, 89, 90, 98, 354, 355, 357, 361, 363, 364, 376, 385
Feick, A. 315, 327
Ferrer, V. 432, 435, 436
Finely, Minnie 229
Finley, G.J. 345
Finney, C.G. 213, 242
Firmilian of Caesarea 422
Fisher, D. 328, 372
Fisher, E.K. 107, 153
Fitzgerald, E.R. 323
Fletcher, J. 213, 233
Flower, A.R. 290

Flower, A.M. (Reynolds) 268, 271, 290, 302, 306, 309, 310, 314, 318, 388
Flower, G.L. 263
Flower, J. Roswell (J.R.F.) 12, 172, 109, 263-69, 280, 281, 283, 286, 293, 295, 298, 302, 307, 309, 317, 323, 324, 333, 374, 375, 393
Flower, Joseph R. 14, 15, 359
Folard, C. 449
Forbes, C. 83, 89, 411, 415, 417, 419
Foster, P.S 231, 392
Foulston, W.W. 242, 253
Fox, G. 445
Francescon, L. 272
Franklin, L.D. 419
Fraser, A.L. 282, 283, 287, 289, 374, 396
Frazer, L. 152, 159, 261
Freeman, C.A. 203, 391
Freeman, H.V. 197, 199
French, T.L. 16, 331, 336-38, 398
Fricks, M. 198
Frodsham, A.W. 36, 241, 321, 358
Frodsham, S. (S.H.F. 301) 2, 36, 112, 299, 301, 314, 319, 320, 369, 411, 457-59

Gamble, A. 236
Gardner, E. 151, 152, 177
Garner, S.G. 289
Garr, A.G. 129, 134, 136, 158, 159, 162, 395
Garr, L. 162, 163, 165, 336
Gaston. W.T. 284, 285, 288, 289, 298, 300-305, 308, 313, 323, 374, 375, 383, 389
Gatlin, E.D. 151
Geddis, M. 146
Gee, D. 36, 109
Gifford, A. 454
Gillespie, R. 321
Gillet, H.L. 212
Godbey, W 106
Godet, F.L. 178
Goff, H.H. 8, 152

Index of Names 497

Goff, J.R. 1, 13, 20, 21, 106, 111, 112, 184, 213, 214, 383
Goins, J. 175, 176
Goodrich, D. 318
Görres, J.J. 410
Goss, E. 2, 272, 296
Goss, H.A. 272, 290, 292, 293
Graham, L.R. 229
Gray, F.H. 290, 299, 325
Gray, J.G. 283, 374
Gray, J.H. 319
Grebel, C. 439
Green, A. 282
Green, C.E.W. 2, 240
Green, G.M. 194
Green, J.C. 322
Green, W.M. 415-17
Greenfield, John 447
Greenwood, N.E. 228
Greer, J.F. 326
Gregory of Nyssa 365
Gregory of Palamas 77, 443
Gregory the Illuminator 422, 423
Gregory XIII 448
Gregory XV 432, 437
Griffin, D.W. 178
Gromacki, R.G. 425, 433, 445, 448, 453
Guinness, O. 380
Gundry, R.H. 42-45, 365
Gunkel, H. 2, 18, 19, 73, 349

Hackney, G. 200
Hale, F.A. 323
Hall, A. 388
Hall, G.W. 152
Hall, J.L. 331
Hall, L.C. 281, 298
Hall, M. 202
Hamburg, E. 156
Hamilton, B. 161
Hammerton, C. 332
Hammond, E.B. 289
Hammond, E.L. 188
Hansen, C. 258
Hansen, G. 158, 161, 270, 326, 327
Hansen, H.E. 323

Hanson, C.M. 459, 460
Harden, W. 197
Hargrave, V.D. 359, 397, 411, 446
Harnack, A. 38, 46
Harris, H.O. 229
Harris, H.S. 202
Harris, R.W. 395
Harris, T. 343, 344
Harrison, W.M. 289, 314, 324
Harvey, W.J. 152, 373
Haskett, W. 449, 450
Hayes, D.A. 29, 30, 376
Hayes, E. 195
Hayes, R.B. 8, 153, 155, 172, 176, 356, 371
Hayes, S. 195
Hayes, V. 227
Hayford, J.W. 76, 354, 378, 387
Haynes, C. 193
Haywood, G.T. 16, 318, 319, 331-35, 338-341, 343-45, 398, 399
Head, B.P 253, 257
Heath, S.J. 188
Hebden, J. 132, 144, 146
Hendricks, B. 205
Henke, F. G. 19
Henry, C. 323
Hesson, W.F. 201, 388, 393
Hettiaratchy, C.T. 257, 263
Hezmalhalch, T. 125, 130
Hicks, B.L. 197, 283
Hicks, G.H. 290, 325
Higgins, W.J. 324
Higley, S.L. 433, 434
Hilary of Potiers 425
Hilborn, D. 398
Hilbun, B. 198
Hildegard of Bingen 378, 433, 434
Hill, F.E. 121
Hill, P.A. 315
Hinck, J. 377
Hines, R.P. 325
Hinson, E.G. 369, 418, 431, 446
Hocken, P.D. 51, 78, 360, 367
Hodges, F. 299, 311
Hoekema, A.A. 398
Holcomb, D.R. 197

Hollenweger, W.J.   1, 4-6, 50, 54, 55, 85, 102, 114, 349-51, 356, 372, 379, 380, 386, 401, 405-409
Hollingsworth, A.   50
Holme, R.   41
Holmes, N.J.   8, 164, 165, 213, 217
Holmes, R.L.   289
Holmquist, A.   269
Hopper, M.E   211
Horton, H.   384, 388
Horton, J.B.   230
Hottinger, M.   439
Hough, A.J.   151
Hovenden, G.   86-90, 356, 365, 367, 393, 411
Howell, E.N.   206, 207, 371
Howell, M.   193
Hudson, R.W.   301, 367
Huffington, C.   346
Hughes, R.H.   397, 403
Hume, D.   94
Hunter, H.D.   184, 185, 410, 418, 425, 447, 452
Hurtado, L.W.   63, 64
Hus, J.   447
Hutch, R.A.   359, 387
Hyatt, E.   435, 447, 448

Ignatius of Antioch   411
Ignatius of Loyola   378, 379, 422, 436, 437
Ingham, B.   448
Ingham, J.W.   317, 392
Ingram, G.   203
Innocent X   458
Irenaeus of Lyons   412, 414, 415
Irving, E.   5, 30, 70, 111, 452, 453
Irwin, B.H.   111, 121, 183, 184, 213-15, 249, 261, 352, 459
Ivens, Minnie   206

Jackson, H.E.   327, 342
Jacobs, S.P.   259, 384
Jacobson, D.   6
James, H.A.   155
James, J.H.   291
Jamieson, S.A.   282

Jansen, C.   448
Jarrett, E.J.   237
Jeffreys, T.M.   248
Jeffries, G.   133, 392
Jennison, E.V.   307, 327
Jeter, J.   127
Johns, D.A.   64, 65, 399
Johns, H.J.   324
Johnson, A.   122
Johnson, A.G.   116, 124
Johnson, C.P.   291
Johnson, D.R.   2
Johnson, G.G.   452
Johnson, L.T.   349
Johnson, Seth   461
Johnston, Robin   330
Jones, Byron A.   227
Jones, C.P.   9, 179, 180
Jones, E.   205
Jones, H.H.   271
Jones, J.S.   344
Jones, L.L.   206
Joyner, P.M.   314, 323
Juillerat, L.H.   196
Junk, T.   124, 150, 151, 155
Jurgensen, M.   325
Justinian   416

Kahrs, B.B.   173, 382
Kardong, T.G.   424
Käsemann, E.   90
Kay, W.K.   90, 91, 239
Keener, C.S.   366, 393
Kellner, J.   300, 301
Kelly, G.M.   162, 322, 324, 395
Kelly, M.   324, 395
Kelsey, M.T.   359, 387, 412, 430, 431, 433, 436, 440, 441, 446
Kennedy, V.W.   168, 176, 195
Kent, C.E.   151, 175, 176
Kenyon, H.N.   292
Kerr, D.W.   95, 108, 109, 295, 304-306, 313, 315, 320, 323, 334, 384
Kertson, B.   350
Kessler, J.   439
Kies, F.   260-62
Kilgore, J.B.   176

Index of Names 499

Kimball, H.C. 454
Kimrey, J.G. 220
King, J.G. 386, 408
King, J.H. 148, 153, 214, 215, 237
King, S. 335, 398, 404
Kinne, S.D. 287
Kinney, N.M. 195
Kinsey, H. 194
Kirke, G. 307
Kirkpatrick, W.J. 343
Klaassen, W. 438, 439
Klubnikin, E.G. 456
Knight, A.C. 227
Knox, R.A. 447-49
Krater, E. 256
Kreider, A. 438, 439
Kugler, S.A. 324, 344
Kydd, R.A.N. 410, 411-22, 424
Kyper, A. 248

LaBaw, E.B. 176
Lacy, J. 188
Lacy, P. 196
Ladd, C.F. 255
Ladd, E.C. 146
Lake, J.G. 66, 241
Lake, W.S. 179
Lance, J.H. 208
Land, S.J. 4, 5, 102, 349, 370-72, 379-81, 393
Landis, E.F. 157, 176
Landon, B.D. 319
Lane, J.H. 319
Lang, G.H. 444
Langdoe, J.E. 327
Lange, A.T. 245, 246, 257, 360
Lanier, L.H 197
Lasater, C.A. 328, 372
Lawrence, B.F. 34-36, 299-301, 303, 305-307, 309, 311, 317, 318, 323, 324, 326, 328, 329, 360, 362, 363, 377, 378, 411, 457
Lawson, c. 220
Leatherman, L. 136, 150
Lederle, H.I. 65, 66, 354, 375
Lee, A. 449
Lee, E. 112, 113

Lee, F. 153
Lee, F.J. 188, 189, 191, 192, 431
Lee, M. 112, 113
Lee, S.O. 158, 195
Lehman, J.O. 161, 228, 253, 261, 266-69
Lemons, M.S. 189, 195-97, 207
Lester, G.H. 143
Letsinger, M.W. 196
Lewis, B. 230
Lewis, C.S. 41, 42, 350, 352, 379, 434
Lewis, H.E. 462
Lewis, M.J. 371
Lewis, T.H. 336
Lietzman, H. 420
Lim, D. 354
Lind, E. 143
Lindblad, F. 323
Lindley, M. 265, 373
Littell, F.H. 438, 439
Llewellyn, J.S. 10
Lockard, C.E. 207
Long, F. 198
Long, H. 198
Longdon, J.E. 283
Lord, W.E. 205
Love, W.A. 120
Lovett, L. 405
Lowman, W.M. 196
Lucas, J.B. 199
Luce, A.E. (A.E.L.) 310, 315, 324, 390
Lum, C. 7, 8, 180
Lupton, L. 147
Lupton, R.L. 117
Luther, M. 115, 331, 447
Luther, S.C. 195
Lynn, D. 320

M'nemar, R. 451
Macchia, F.D. 5, 66-76, 79, 90, 92, 102, 103, 264, 265, 356, 359, 365, 366, 391, 397
MacDonald, W.G. 47, 50, 357, 359, 364, 385, 390, 391, 396, 397
Mackie, A. 19

Maloney, G. 442
Marks, I.H. 203
Marrisett, M. 197
Marshall, B. 249, 263
Martin, B. 458
Martin, I.J. 38, 39, 362, 364
Martin, M. 120
Martin, W.J. 224, 233
Martyr, J. 414
Mason, C.H. 9, 10, 116, 143, 148, 179-82, 292, 363
Massey, J.P 176
Massey, M.E. 176
Massey, R.E. 162, 163, 168, 176
Mathieu, P.F. 448
Matthews, D. 461
Matthews, D.H. 379, 380
Mauchline, J. 37
May, R. 322
Mayo, M.F. 125
McAlister, H. 332, 336
McAlister, R.E. 15, 294, 330-32, 337
McArthur, J. 387
McCafferty, B. 302, 321, 371
McClymond, M.J. 431, 441
McCurley, W.H. 219, 229
McDaniel, L. 226
McDonald, H.D. 226, 354
McDonnell, D.H. 299
McDonnell, K. 73, 356, 381, 391, 397, 410, 425
McFail, A. 190
McFarland, L. 342
McGee, G.B. 2, 24, 104-107, 110, 123, 261, 263, 316, 368, 379, 387, 394, 395, 397, 403
McGee, J. 451
McGready, J. 451
McIntosh, T.J. 8, 158
McIntyre, J.W. 304
McKinney, S. 209
McLain, T.L. 210
McPhail, J.A. 314
McPherson, A.S. 104, 241, 272, 298, 299, 302, 307-309, 330, 355, 404
McQueen, Larry R. 2, 21, 115, 171, 174, 175, 240, 372

McVicar, M.J. 194
Mead, A. 126, 131, 140
Mead, L.J. 154
Mead, S.J. 126, 135
Menzies, G.W. 108, 109
Menzies, R.P. 51, 56-62, 71, 78, 79, 81, 87, 88, 354, 368, 372, 373, 385, 386, 392, 393
Menzies, W. 13, 14, 50, 239, 264, 272, 273, 280, 281, 285, 292-97, 411
Mercer, J.S. 391, 396
Merrill, B. 327
Merrill, V. 327
Merrin, W.H. 282, 290, 322
Mershman, F. 433
Milavec, Aaron 413
Miller, B.C. 36
Miller, J.C. 327
Miller, K. 370
Miller, L. 227, 236
Miller, R.O. 321
Mills, W.E. 50-53, 86, 87, 350, 362, 365, 366, 369, 388, 393, 411
Millsap, O.M. 236
Millsaps, W.T. 292
Mingus, C. 379
Minns, D. 414
Miskov, J.A. 240-43, 249, 250, 252, 254, 255, 257, 259, 262
Mitchel, G.G. 271
Mitchel, M. 195
Mix, S. 240
Mok, L.C. 168, 391
Molenaar, W.J. 181
Montague G. 73
Montanus 415-17, 419, 423
Montgomery, C.J. (C.J.M.) 12, 158, 176, 177, 185, 240-45, 249-52, 254-59, 261, 262, 265, 354, 356, 370, 373, 375, 382, 389, 390, 404
Montgomery, G.H. 227
Moody, D.L. 213, 217
Moody, J.B. 323
Moody, W.E. 332, 333
Moomau, A. 114, 145, 270
Moore, B.S. 327

Moore, J. 112, 113, 142, 403
Moorhead, M.W. 174, 257
Morgan, H.H. 230
Morgan, H.S. 257
Morgan, J.V. 461
Morris, D.K. 327
Mullen, M.B. 261, 262
Murphy, J.A. 332
Murphy, N. 212
Murrah, E.G. 153, 166, 176, 178, 388
Murrah, E.L. 172
Murray, A. 243
Murray, G.A. 245, 247
Myland, D.W. 28, 29, 167, 368, 370, 372, 381, 390, 391

Nelson, C. 203
Nelson, E.A. 211
Nelson, P.C. 36
New, E. 207
Newton, M.L 199
Nicoll, W.R. 397
Niswander, D. 229
Noble, C.F. 20, 221, 223, 224, 226, 238, 394, 395
Noble, W.J. 223, 232, 392
Norton, A. 124, 150, 162, 261, 262, 332, 448
Norton, E.D. 226
Norton, M. K. 165, 173
Novatian 421
Noyes, J.H. 213
Nuzum, C. 261

O'Neal, B.S. 172, 178
Oatrandor, H.M. 324
Oden, M.E. 228, 237
Offiler, W.H. 322
Ogle, I.W. 157
Oliver, J.L. 228
Oliver, J. 400
Olzábal, F. 241
Opie, E.L. 249, 252, 263
Opperman, D.C.O. (D.C.O.O.) 16, 282, 288, 291, 293
Origen 419-21

Orr, J.E. 460
Orwig, A.W. 290
Ory, E. 379
Osborn, J.E. 324
Osment, M. 197
Osterberg, L. 131
Oxendine, H.E. 230
Ozman, A. (LaBerge) 112

Pachomius 424
Padget, M. 206
Page, S.D. 228
Palmas, G. 77, 443, 444
Palmer, P. 254
Pamphilus of Caesarea 423
Parham, C.F. 13, 18, 19-22, 33, 95, 105-107, 111-113, 115, 122, 131, 145, 184, 214, 241, 292, 293, 297, 337, 383, 406, 411, 459
Parham, S.E. 364
Parker, K. 228, 236
Parks, W.W. 304.
Parvis, P. 414
Pate, J.H. 219, 221
Patterson, S.W. 194
Paul, E.A. 332
Paul, J.A.A. 156
Payne, J.B. 453
Payne, S.H. 326, 327
Payne, T.S. 187, 188
Peace, E. 327
Peachey, P. 439, 440
Pearson, C. 198
Pearson, E.H. 198
Peeples, G.W. 196
Peever, A.V. 332
Pelliccotti, A. 345
Pennington, N. 170
Penn-Lewis, J. 461
Perry, M. 157
Perry, S.C. 191-93, 200-203, 206, 207, 209, 276, 395
Pesch R. 73
Phillips, C. 344, 345
Phillips, W.H. 183-86, 188, 189, 192, 194, 199, 214, 270, 458, 459
Pike, J.M. 159, 160, 162, 253, 395

Pinnock, C. 102, 352, 358
Pinson, M.M. 8, 149, 154-56, 168, 170, 175, 281, 282, 286, 293, 384
Piper, W.H. 114, 177, 272, 292, 397
Pirkle, A. 211, 395
Pius II 432
Planter, J. 290
Plummer, J.M. 259
Plummer, M. 252
Poe, I. 195
Polhill, C. 156, 248, 260, 273, 394
Polman, G. 156, 301, 302, 321, 384
Polman, W. 166, 251, 258, 356, 358, 404
Poloma, M.M. 107, 108, 351, 360, 378, 397
Polycarp 413, 414
Poole, F.P. 328, 372
Pope, W.H. 298, 300-305, 307, 309
Post, A.H. 132, 146, 147, 167
Poteat, H.W. 196
Powers, I.V. 203, 390
Powers, J.E. 366, 396
Poythress, V.S. 89
Prather, H. 327
Presley, E. 380
Preston, J.A. 290
Price, J.B. 343, 345, 346
Price, L. 406, 407, 409
Pride, C. 323

Quadratus 424
Quinn, Minnie 268

Ramabai, P. 165, 242, 256, 444
Ramlie, R.M. 224
Ramsey, J.F. 227
Randall, H.E. 332, 336
Randol, G. 346, 373
Rankin, A. 451
Ranming, R.E. 198
Rauschenbusch, W. 438
Rawlings, J.C. 177
Ray, L.A. 205
Reed, D.A. 2, 272, 280, 285, 287, 330, 331, 336-38, 342, 398
Reed, H.E. 340, 342, 343, 345

Reeves, E.D. 228, 229, 237
Reid, J. 158, 163, 365, 366, 388
Reid, T. 94
Reimer, J. 375
Reneker, J.D. 211
Reuss, A.B. 156
Reynolds, W.L. 211
Rice, D. 451
Richardson, C. 413
Riss, R.M. 154, 239, 272, 292, 297
Ritchie, C.E. 166
Robbins, W.T. 282
Robeck, C.M. 1, 5, 7, 8, 16, 21-24, 106-109, 111-114, 145, 148, 149, 180, 181, 186, 217, 218, 265, 292, 333, 363, 366, 377, 378, 415-17
Roberts, A.O. 445
Roberts, E. 166, 167, 354, 461
Roberts, H.F. 171
Roberts, L.V. 291, 332
Robinson, A.B. 290
Robinson, A.E. 121
Robinson, C.G. 316
Robinson, W.P. 322
Robinson, W.T. 328
Roche, J. 447
Rogers, C.L. 412, 414, 415, 417, 420
Rogers, H.G. 149, 295
Rogers, W.H. 193
Rose, W.W. 200
Rosendal, M. 450
Rosner, B. 354
Ross, J. 304
Rosselli, J. 322
Rowe, G.B. 345
Rowe, J. 344
Rowe, M. 226
Rowland, C.A. 212
Rudometkin, M.G. 455, 456
Rue, A. 203
Rumler, W.M. 195
Ruohomäki, J. 450, 451
Rushin, P.R. 209
Russum, W.J.A. 228
Ruthven, J. 369, 427
Ryan, M.L. 128
Rybarczyk, E.J. 92, 97-99, 350, 361,

Index of Names   503

375, 391

Sackett, I.   264, 266, 373, 374
Salmon, J.   249
Samarin, W.J.   55, 88, 377
Samuel, J.P.S.   363, 377
Sandgren, F.A.   272
Sanford, F.   111
Sapp, C.   195
Satyavrata, I.   355
Savage, H.M.   286
Sawders, J.E.   164, 391
Sawgalsky, L.   158, 219, 237, 238, 395
Scarce, N.   236, 237
Schaepe, J.   341, 344, 345
Schaff, P.   178, 410, 412, 415, 419, 424, 425
Schell, W.G.   324, 411
Scheppe, John G.   297
Schnapp, J.T.   434
Schoonmaker, V.   305, 374
Scoggins, Belle   199, 207
Scott, K.   143
Scott, M.C.   260
Scott, R.J.   144, 395
Seay, A.   429
Sellers, B.C.   227
Sellers, M.D.   159
Seraphim of Sarov   441
Sexton, E. (E.A.S.)   8, 149-52, 154-57, 159-62, 164, 165, 167-69, 171-75, 177-79, 254, 370, 371, 378, 384, 392, 395, 404
Seymour, W.J.   7, 8, 20, 22, 93, 96, 107, 108, 112-14, 116-20, 123, 125-34, 138-42, 146-49, 180, 181, 184, 241, 272, 337, 366, 374, 380, 383, 392, 394, 406, 408, 459
Shakarian, D.   456, 457
Sharron, J.O.   321
Shelton, J.   210
Shepherd, A.B.   133, 146
Sherrill, A.B.   202
Sherrill, E.   456
Sherrill, J.L.   456
Shideler, M.   137

Shimer, H.M.T.   262
Shirlaw, A.   326
Short, L.   321
Shults F.L.   50
Shumway, C.   19, 30-35, 111, 113, 365, 370, 416, 418, 446, 447, 452, 457
Shurron, J.O.   320
Silver, C.L.   199
Simmons, E.   196, 199
Simmons, E.L.   192
Simmons, E.R.   198
Simmons, J.E.   289
Simmons, M.B.   173
Simmons, V.P.   158, 170, 171, 173-75,178, 179, 253, 365, 411, 412, 457
Simpson, A.B.   96, 106, 241, 242, 259, 370
Simpson, C.E.   307, 324, 375
Simpson, W.W.   263, 283, 300-302, 306, 312, 313, 374
Simpson, Z.D.   201
Sims, L.A.   145
Sisler, A.L.   225
Sisson, E.   241-43, 253, 256, 276, 298, 309, 312, 313, 319, 321, 324, 326, 354, 368, 371, 390
Slay, J.L.   362, 392
Slaybaugh, E.L.   177
Slaybaugh, E.T.   248, 252
Sly, L.B.   271
Smale, J.   107, 460
Small, J.E.   332
Smith, A.   271
Smith, A.A.   195, 364
Smith, B.   200
Smith, C.   195
Smith, G.T.   352
Smith, J.   454
Smith, J.E.   120
Smith, J.K.A.   41, 349, 350, 362, 397
Smith, J.X.   197
Smith, S.A.   271, 290, 459
Smith, W.D.   326
Snyder, J.W.   321
Southern, D.B.   230, 231, 352

Spain, J.P. 228
Spears, W.W. 204
Spencer, J.M. 377
Spittler, R.P. 21, 55, 94, 239, 276, 353, 369
Sproull, O.E. 228
Spurling, R. 183, 188
Staley, E. 151
Standlee, L. 322
Standley, W.H. 124, 129, 131, 269, 283, 373, 394
Staniforth, M. 413
Stanley, G.W. 230
Stanton, E.M. 245, 248, 249, 258, 352
Stargel, G.T. 195
Stark, S.E. 234, 384
Starkweather, J. 457
Stephens, R.J. 1, 3, 9, 11, 147-49, 179, 185, 213, 214
Steven of Nicomedia 442
Stewart, M.C. 167
Stewart, R.L. 233
Stokely, P.M. 283
Stone, B. 451
Storey, S. 323
Story, W.F.E. 176
Stover, D.R. 322
Strayer, B.E. 448
Street, A.E. (A.E.S.) 106, 187, 189, 201, 367, 374, 392, 403
Strickland, V. 324
Stronstad, R. 51, 355, 399
Stroud, C.A. 228
Studd, C.J. 322
Studd, G.B. 247, 249, 252, 311, 321, 371
Sublet, S.W. 223
Suenens, L.J. 53, 54, 354, 366, 369, 388, 389
Sullivan, C.A. 426, 428-31, 435, 436
Sullivan, F.A. 377, 381, 428, 432
Sullivan, M. 344
Summers, W.A. 282, 328
Surglon, A. 230
Sutphin, Z.A. 224, 228, 236, 363, 372

Swan, R.B. 457
Swann, L. 229
Sweet, J.P.M. 90, 354
Symeon the New Theologian 77, 442, 443
Symeon the Venerable 442
Synan, H.V. 1, 2, 4, 5, 11, 24, 111, 121, 147-49, 154, 179-81, 183-86, 212-18, 296, 397, 401, 403
Synan, J.A. 229, 230

Tabbernee, W. 415, 416, 418, 419
Tallent, W.M. 165
Tarpley, A.L. 199
Tarr, D. 91-94, 350, 358, 361, 364, 378, 386, 391, 404
Taves, A. 113, 356
Taylor, G.H. 8, 11, 24-27, 118, 216-26, 229-35, 237, 238, 308, 364-66, 369, 370, 374, 375, 383, 384, 388, 389, 395, 396, 411, 446
Taylor, M. 3
Taylor, W.J. 317
Teresa of Alvia 81, 82, 440
Tertullian 418, 419, 425
Theodotus 423
Thigpen, C.L. 202
Thiselton, A.C. 354
Thomas, G.R. 228
Thomas, J.C. 16, 121, 454
Thomas, L. 209
Thomas, Z.R. 193
Thompson, M. 220
Thorp, S.A. 323
Throop, I.M. 246, 357, 374
Tilghman, L. 195
Tillich, P. 69
Tolkien, J.R.R. 434
Tomlinson, A.J. 8, 10, 95, 148, 184-97, 199, 200, 202-208, 210-12, 356, 363, 371, 372, 375, 379, 382-84, 389, 391, 395, 411
Tomlinson, W.J. 46
Torrey, R.A. 196
Tower, H. 176
Townsend, F.R. 124
Trdat (Tirdates) 422

Index of Names   505

Trim, H.L.   197
Trotter, W.C.   289, 290, 308, 314, 315, 319, 326, 327
Tubbs, M.   197
Tunmore, J.   301
Turlington, S.   227, 228
Turner, J.G.   454
Turner, L.L.   195
Turner, Max   50, 78, 79, 81, 87, 88, 90
Turner, Molet   176
Turner, W.H.   37, 238, 328, 369, 411
Turney, H.M.   124, 131, 152
Tursellini, H.   438
Tutter, H.   210
Tyson, J.L.   337, 338

Ulyate, S.M.   316
Underwood, J.C.   196
Urshan, A.D.   272, 302, 309, 318, 319, 332, 336, 338-40, 345, 368, 389

VanLoon, H.   158
Varley, H.   256, 364
Vincent, I.   446
Voget, C.O.   156
Volf, M.   365

Wacker, G.   1, 17, 24, 359, 372
Waddell, R.   18, 50, 51
Walker, A.J.   324
Walker, C.C.   198
Walker, D.A.   23, 24, 385
Walker, T.B.   346
Walker, W.A.   195
Walsh, T.   448
Walters, K.R.   94-97, 353
Walthall, W.J.   303-306, 324, 458
Ward, A.G.   310, 355, 356
Ware, T.   360
Warfield, B.B.   27
Warner, D.   96
Warner, W.E.   3, 7-9, 12, 13, 240, 241, 280, 281
Watts, H.   187
Way, N.   207

Weaver, T.W.   388
Webb, H.C.   224, 225, 230, 231, 234, 352, 382, 384
Weigle, A.   177
Weinel, H.   410, 420
Welch, J.W.   322, 358
Welchel, T.   2
Wells, J.D.   325
Wengler, J.   324
Wesley, C.   448
Wesley, J.   107, 115, 331, 337, 447, 448
Westfield, W.   340, 341, 345
Westman, J.   327
Wheeler, R.   203
Whidden, M.T.   369
Whitcomb, E.L.   305
White, C.E.   235
White, F.   458
White, J.   168
White, K.   251
White, N.   362
White, S.D.   229
Whitefield, G.   448
Wigglesworth, S.   36, 255, 258, 259, 382, 392
Wightman, S.   151
Wilcox, N.   125
Wilcox, W.A.   209, 395
Wiley, O.   146
Wilkes, P.   318, 326, 389
Wilkins, O.C.   219
Wilkinson, A.G.   324
Williams, B.C.   327
Williams, C.G.   19, 55, 73, 87, 362, 381, 387, 396, 397, 411, 460, 462
Williams, G.H.   378, 410, 425, 431, 432, 434, 436, 438, 439, 441, 444, 447-49, 451, 454
Williams, J.A.   195
Williams, J.D.   198
Williams, J.R.   353, 354, 364, 366, 372, 379, 381, 385, 392, 397, 403
Williamson, C.   314
Willis, L.J.   387, 397
Wilson, A.E.   320
Wilson, A.R.   303, 309

Wilson, E.A. 330, 370
Wilson, H. 128
Wilson, H.G. 319
Wilson, J.T. 328
Wilson, S.M. 451
Winn, F. 152, 162, 163
Winsett, R.E. 345
Winter, E.M. 245, 251
Wolf, M. 41, 361
Wood, A.S. 448
Wood, M. 211, 395
Wood, W.L. 290, 326
Woodruff, J. 129
Woods, S. 321
Woodworth-Etter, M.B. 241
Wooten, S. 165
Worrell, A.S. 165, 168, 190, 244-47, 253, 254, 283

Wright, D.F. 429

Xavier, F. 432, 437, 438

Yeomans, L.B. (L.B.Y.) 256
Yoakum, F.E. 269
Yoder, J.H. 438, 439
Yong, A. 352, 353, 377, 386, 389, 403
Young, B. 454
Young, D.J. 10, 181
Young, R.H. 327
Young, V. 182

Zander, V. 441
Ziegler, G. 128
Zinzendorf, N.L. 447
Zwingli, H. 4

www.ingramcontent.com/pod-product-compliance
Lightning Source LLC
Chambersburg PA
CBHW050511170426
43201CB00013B/1917